Chapter-wise **Topical** Objective Study Package *for*

CBSE 2022 Class 12 Term I

Chemistry

Corporate Office

DISHA PUBLICATION

45, 2nd Floor, Maharishi Dayanand Marg,
Corner Market, Malviya Nagar, New Delhi - 110017
Tel : 49842349 / 49842350

Typeset by Disha DTP Team

www.dishapublication.com
Books & ebooks for School & Competitive Exams

www.mylearninggraph.com
Etests for Competitive Exams

Write to us at **feedback_disha@aiets.co.in**

Contents

1 The Solid State

SOLIDS

Structure of solids

- **Unit cell: Smallest repeating pattern**
  - **Primitive Unit Cell** — No. of atoms per unit cell = 1
  - **Body Centered** — No. of atoms per unit cell = 2
  - **Face Centered** — No. of atoms per unit cell = 4
- **Close packed structure**
  - **Close packing in one dimension :** Lattice point arranged in a row C.N. = 2
  - **Close packing in two dimensions :**
    - (a) Square close paking : C.N. = 4
    - (b) Hexagonal close packing: C.N. = 6
  - **Close packing in three dimensions :**
    - (a) Primitive cubic unit cell: AAA...type arrangement, CN = 6, P.F. = 52%
    - (b) *hcp* : ABAB...type pattern, C.N. = 12, PF = 74 %
    - (c) *ccp* or *fcc* ABCABC... type pattern, CN = 12, PF = 74%

Imperfection in solids

- **Point Defects**
  - **Stoichiometric Defects**
    - In Non Ionic Solids
      - Vacancy Defect
      - Interstitial Defect
    - In Ionic Solids
      - **Schottky Defect:** Cations and anions are missing equally
      - **Frenkel Defect:** Ions missing from their lattice site occupy interstitial sites
  - **Non-Stoichiometric Defects**
    - Metal Excess Defects
    - Metal Deficiency Defects
  - **Impurity Defects**
- **Line Defects**

Type of Solids

- **Crystalline Solids**
  - Definite characteristic geometrical shape
  - Long range order
  - Anisotropic in nature
  - e.g., NaCl, KNO_3, LiF etc.
  - **Ionic Solids** (NaCl, CaF_2 etc.)
  - **Metallic Solids** (Fe, Cu etc.)
  - **Molecular Solids** (Iodine, Phosphorus etc.)
  - **Covalent Solids** (Diamond, Graphite etc.)
- **Amorphous Solids**
  - Irregular in shape
  - Short range order
  - Isotropic in nature
  - e.g. plastic, glass etc.

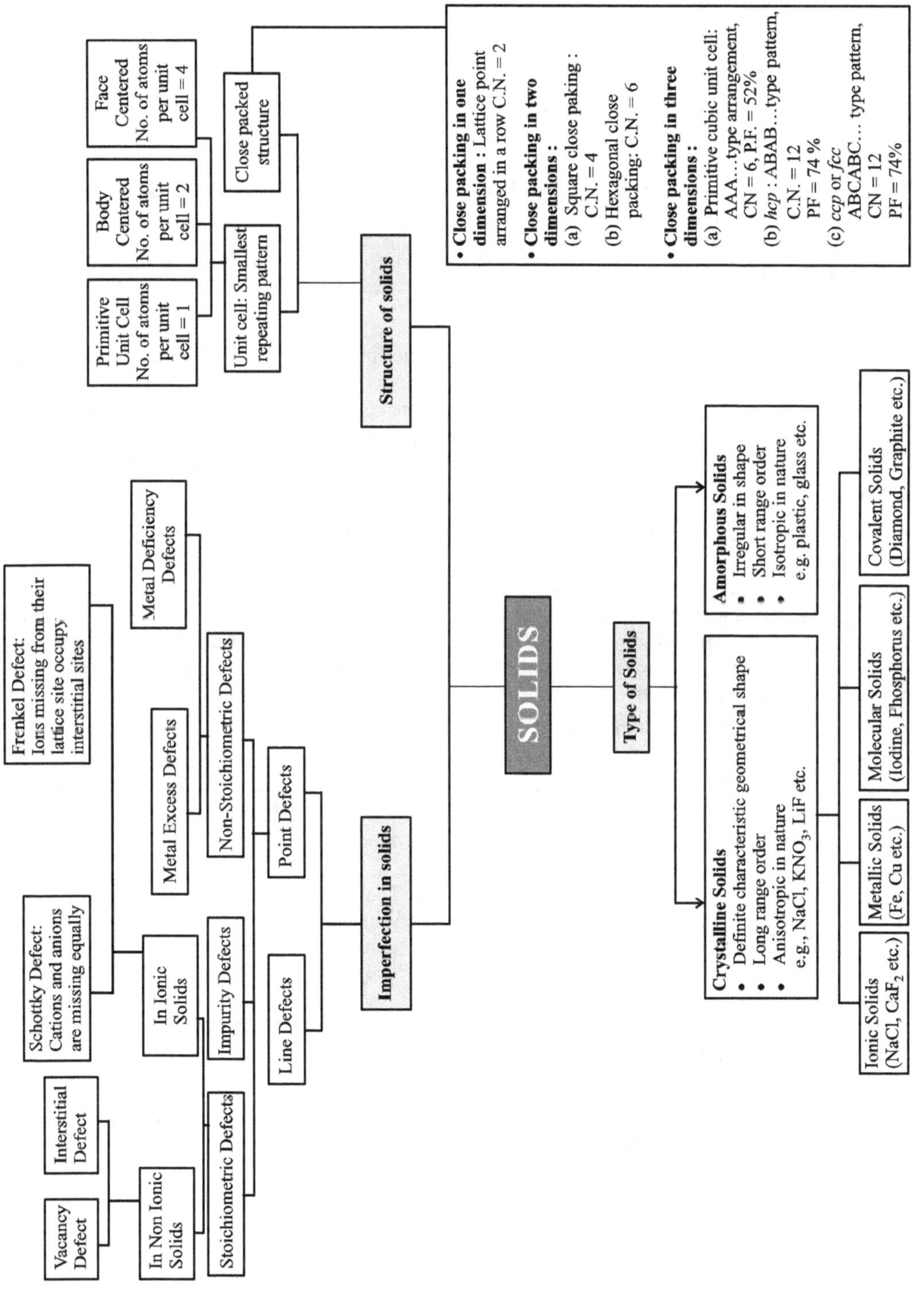

Topic 1   Classification of Solids, Crystal Lattice and Unit Cells 

INTRODUCTION

Matter exists in three different states solid, liquid and gas. The stability of a state depends upon the net effect of two opposing factors which are listed below:

(a) **Intermolecular force** that tends to keep the constituent particles i.e., atoms, molecules or ions together

(b) **Thermal energy** that tends to move them apart

At low temperature thermal energy is low and intermolecular forces bring the constituent particles so close that they cling to one another and occupy fixed position and substance exists in solid state. A solid substance has melting point above room temperature under atmospheric pressure. We are all surrounded by a vast variety of solid objects which differ in size, shape and also in mass.

CHARACTERISTIC PROPERTIES OF SOLIDS

(a) In solid state, the particles are not able to move randomly.

(b) They have definite shape and volume.

(c) Solids have high density.

(d) Solids have high and sharp melting point which depends on the strength or value of binding energy.

(e) They are very less compressible.

(f) They show very slow rate of diffusion.

CLASSIFICATION OF SOLIDS

Crystalline Solids

A crystalline solid usually consists of a large number of small crystals, each of them having a definite characteristic geometrical shape. In a crystal the arrangement of constituent particles i.e., atoms, molecules or ions is in an ordered pattern. It has a long range order which means there is a regular pattern of arrangement of particles which repeats itself periodically over the entire crystal. Crystalline solids are anisotropic in nature which means some of the physical properties like refractive index, electrical resistance etc. have different values along different directions in the same crystal. Examples of crystalline solids : $NaCl$, KNO_3, LiF and $CuSO_4 \cdot 5H_2O$.

Amorphous Solids

A solid is said to be amorphous if the various constituent particles are not arranged in any regular fashion. Amorphous solid has short range order i.e. no periodically repeating pattern. Amorphous solids have no precise melting point but when heated, become increasingly pliable until they assume the properties usually associated with liquids; they are supercooled liquids in which the force of attraction holding the molecules together is so great that the material is rigid but there is no regularity of structure. *e.g.,* glass and rubber. These are isotropic solids i.e. the value of same physical property is same along all directions.

Amorphous solids on heating become crystalline at some temperature. That's why some glass objects from ancient civilisation found to become milky in appearance due to crystallisation.

Differences Between Crystalline and Amorphous Solids:

Crystalline solids	Amorphous solids
(a) They have a definite geometrical shape due to the definite and orderly arrangement of particles in the three dimensional space.	(a) They do not have an orderly arrangement of particles and therefore, do not possess a definite geometrical shape.
(b) They have sharp melting point.	(b) They do not have sharp melting point.
(c) When cut with a sharp edged tool, they split into two pieces and the newly generated surfaces are plain and smooth.	(c) When they are cut, they split into two pieces and the newly generated surfaces are irregular in shape.
(d) They have crystal symmetry.	(d) They do not have crystal symmetry.
(e) They possess anisotropic properties.	(e) They have isotropic properties.

Classification of Crystalline Solids

The crystalline solids are further classified as:

(a) Metallic solids:

(i) Their constituent particles are atoms which are packed together as closely as possible.

(ii) In a metallic lattice, the positive ions are embedded in a sea of electrons.

(iii) They are generally good conductors of heat and electricity.

(iv) They have moderate to high melting point.

(v) They are highly malleable and ductile

(vi) Examples are Cu, Ag, Mg, Al, etc.

(b) Ionic solids:
(i)   Their constituent particles are positive and negative ions, which are held together by strong electrostatic (coulombic) attractions.
(ii) The crystal structure depends largely upon the relative sizes of the concerned cations and anions.
(iii) They have high melting points and are insulators in the solid state, and conducting in molten state.
(iv) Examples are NaCl, MgO, KCl, $BaCl_2$, etc.

(c) Covalent solids:
(i)   Their constituent particles are atoms.
(ii) The bonding is covalent and directional in nature.
(iii) They have high melting points and are insulators and do not conduct electricity.
(iv) Examples are diamond, silica (SiO_2), silicon carbide (SiC), etc.

(d) Molecular solids:
(i)   Their constituent particles are molecules.
(ii) The molecules are held together by weak van der Waals forces and hydrogen bonding.
(iii) They have low melting points.
(iv) They are electrical insulators and poor thermal conductors.
(v) Examples are iodine, ice, solid CO_2, etc.

Types of molecular solids:
Non-polar molecular solids: In these solids, atoms are held together by weak dispersion forces or London forces.
Polar molecular solids: In these solids, molecules are held together by relatively stronger dipole-dipole interactions.
Hydrogen bonded molecular solids: The molecules are held together by hydrogen bonds.

Illustration 1 :

Which of the following are example(s) of molecular crystals?
Noble gas, Ice, Iodine crystals, Diamond and Graphite
Sol. Noble gas, ice and iodine crystals are example(s) of molecular crystals.

Illustration 2 :

What kind of attractive forces are present in the molecular solids?
Sol. Dipole-dipole interactions, London dispersion forces and hydrogen bonding.

Illustration 3 :

What is anisotropy?
Sol. The phenomenon due to which in crystalline solids same physical properties have different values in different directions is called anisotropy.

Illustration 4 :

Which property of glass enables it to be moulded and blown into various shapes?
Sol. Amorphous solids soften over a range of temperature. This enables the glass to be moulded and blown into various shapes.

CRYSTAL LATTICE AND UNIT CELLS

Crystal

A crystal is a homogeneous portion of a solid substance made by regular pattern of structural units bonded by plane surface making definite angles with each other.

Space Lattice

A regular three dimensional arrangement of points in space is called a **space lattice** or **crystal lattice**.

Unit Cell

A unit cell is the smallest unit of the crystal which when repeated again and again gives the crystal of the given substance.
Unit cell has characteristic dimensions along the three edges a, b and c and interfacial angle α (between 'b' and 'c'), β (between 'a' and 'c') and γ (between 'a' and 'b').

Types of unit cells based on the cube. These are:
(a) Primitive or **simple cube** which has one constituent at each corner.
(b) Centered unit cell : These are of three types:
    (i)   **Body-centred cube** in which one constituent at the centre of the cube as well as one at each corner.
    (ii) **Face-centred cube** in which there is one constituent at the centre of each face as well as one at each corner.
    (iii) End centered in which there is one constituent at centre of opposite face as well as at each corner.

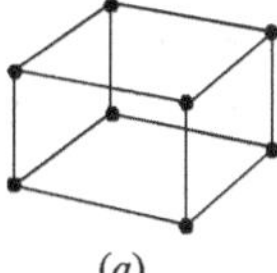 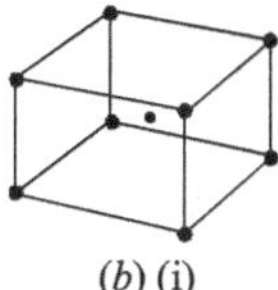 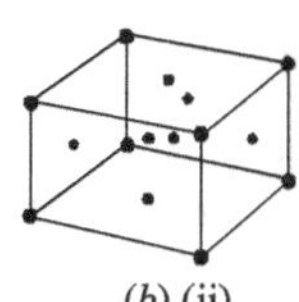

(a)   (b) (i)   (b) (ii)

Types of unit cells based on dimensions and angles

There are seven types of primitive unit cells.

(a) Cubic (b) Tetragonal (c) Orthorhombic (d) Rhombohedral (e) Hexagonal (f) Monoclinic (g) Triclinic

Bravais Lattice : On the basis of position of lattice point there are 14 three dimensional arrangement of lattice known as Bravais lattice.

Seven primitive unit cells and their possible variations as centered unit cell.

S.No.	Crystal system	Possible Variations	Axis and Angles Symmetry	Examples
1.	Cubic	Primitive, face centered, body centered	$a = b = c$ $\alpha = \beta = \gamma = 90°$	Pb, Hg, Ag, Au, Cu, Diamond, NaCl, KCl, ZnS, Cu_2O, CaF_2 and Alums.
2.	Tetragonal	Primitive, body centered	$a = b \neq c$ $\alpha = \beta = \gamma = 90°$	SnO_2, ZnO_2, TiO_2, $NiSO_4$, $ZrSiO_4$, $PbWO_4$, White Sn.
3.	Hexagonal	Primitive, face centered, body centered, end centered	$a = b \neq c$ $\alpha = \beta = 90°, \gamma = 120°$	ZnO, Pbl_2, CdS, HgS, Graphite, Ice, Beryl, Mg, Zn, Cd.
4.	Trigonal or Rhombohedral	Primitive, end centered	$a = b = c$ $\alpha = \beta = \gamma \neq 90°$	$NaNO_3$, $CaSO_4$, Calcite, ICl, Quartz, As, Sb, Bi.
5.	Orthorhombic	Primitive	$a \neq b \neq c$ $\alpha = \beta = \gamma = 90°$	KNO_3, K_2SO_4, $PbCO_3$, $BaSO_4$, Rhombic sulphur, $MgSO_4$, $7H_2O$.
6.	Monoclinic	Primitive	$a \neq b \neq c$ $\alpha = \gamma = 90°; \beta \neq 90°$	$Na_2SO_4 \cdot 10H_2O$, $Na_2B_4O_7 \cdot 10\,H_2O$, $CaSO_4 \cdot 2H_2O$, Monoclinic sulphur
7.	Triclinic	Primitive	$a \neq b \neq c$ $\alpha \neq \beta \neq \gamma \neq 90°$	$CaSO_4 \cdot 5H_2O$, $K_2Cr_2O_7$, H_3BO_3.

(i) A point that lies at the corner of unit cell is shared among eight unit cells and thus, it contributes for 1/8 of each such point to unit cell.

(ii) A point along an edge is shared by four unit cells and thus contribute for 1/4 of each such point to unit cell.

(iii) A face-centred point is shared by two unit cells and thus contributes for 1/2 of each such point to unit.

(iv) A body-centred point lies entirely within the unit cell and thus contributes for one each such point to unit cell.

Type of cell	No. of constituent at corners	No. of constituent on faces	No. of constituent in the centre of cube	Total no. of constituents in the unit cell
Primitive or simple cube	$8 \times \dfrac{1}{8} = 1$	0	0	1
Body-centred cube	$8 \times \dfrac{1}{8} = 1$	0	1	2
Face-centred cube	$8 \times \dfrac{1}{8} = 1$	$6 \times \dfrac{1}{2} = 3$	0	4

Practice Exercise-1

Multiple Choice Questions

1. Schottky defect defines imperfection in the lattice structure of
(a) solid   (b) gas
(c) liquid   (d) plasma

2. The crystal system of a compound with unit cell dimensions "$a = 0.387, b = 0.387$ and $c = 0.504$nm and $\alpha = \beta = 90°$ and $\gamma = 120°$ " is :
(a) cubic   (b) hexagonal
(c) orthorhombic   (d) rhombohedral

3. The space lattice of graphite is
(a) cubic   (b) tetragonal
(c) rhombic   (d) hexagonal

4. The existence of a substance in more than one solid modifications is known as
(a) Isomorphism
(b) Polymorphism
(c) Amorphism
(d) Allotropy

5. Example of molecular solid is :
(a) $SO_2(s)$ (b) SiC
(c) C (graphite)   (d) NaCl

6. A crystalline solid
(a) changes abruptly from solid to liquid when heated
(b) has no definite melting point
(c) undergoes deformation of its geometry easily
(d) has an irregular 3-dimensional arrangements

7. Which of the following is not a crystalline solid?
(a) KCl   (b) CsCl
(c) Glass   (d) Rhombic S

Assertion & Reason Questions

DIRECTIONS (Qs. 8-10) : *Each of these questions contains an assertion followed by reason. Read them carefully and answer the question on the basis of following options. You have to select the one that best describes the two statements.*

(a) If both Assertion and Reason are correct and the Reason is a correct explanation of the Assertion.

(b) If both Assertion and Reason are correct but Reason is not a correct explanation of the Assertion.

(c) If the Assertion is correct but Reason is incorrect.

(d) If the Assertion is incorrect but the Reason is correct.

8. **Assertion :** Graphite is an example hexagonal crystal system.
   Reason : For a hexagonal system, $a = b \neq c$, $\alpha = \beta = 90°$, $\gamma = 120°$.

9. **Assertion :** Stability of a crystal is reflected in the magnitude of its melting point.
   Reason : The stability of a crystal depends upon the strength of the interparticle attractive force.

10. **Assertion :** Crystalline solids are isotropic in nature.
    Reason : Crystalline solids are long range order solids.

Case/Passage Based Questions

DIRECTIONS (Qs. 11-15) : *Following are the case/passage based questions. Attempt any 4 out of 5 questions.*

Solids can be classified as crystalline or amorphous on the basis of the nature of order present in the arrangement of their constituent particles. Amorphous solids behave like super cool liquids as the arrangement of constituent particles has short-range order, isotropic in nature and no sharp melting point. Crystalline solids have a characteristic shape, with the arrangement of constituent particles of long-range order, anisotropic in nature and a sharp melting point. The classification of crystalline solids is based on their property. The crystalline property depends on the nature of interactions between the constituent particles, and therefore these solids are divided into four different categories:

• Ionic solids
• Covalent or Network solids
• Molecular solids
• Metallic solids

11. Which of the following statement(s) is/are correct?
    (i) Crystalline solids have definite characteristic geometrical shape.
    (ii) Crystalline solids have long range order.
    (iii) Sodium chloride and quartz glass are examples of crystalline solids.
    (iv) Crystalline solids are isotropic in nature.
    (a) (i), (ii) and (iii)   (b) (i), (ii) and (iv)
    (c) (i) and (ii)   (d) (i) only

12. Crystalline solids are anisotropic in nature. What is the meaning of anisotropic in the given statement?
    (a) A regular pattern of arrangement of particles which repeats itself periodically over the entire crystal.
    (b) Different values of some of physical properties are shown when measured along different directions in the same crystals.
    (c) An irregular arrangement of particles over the entire crystal.
    (d) Same values of some of physical properties are shown when measured along different directions in the same crystals.

13. Which of the following statements about amorphous solids is incorrect ?
    (a) They melt over a range of temperature
    (b) They are anisotropic
    (c) There is no orderly arrangement of particles
    (d) They can be compressible

DIRECTIONS (Qs. 14-15) : *Each of these questions contains an assertion followed by reason. Read them carefully and answer the question on the basis of following options. You have to select the one that best describes the two statements.*

(a) If both Assertion and Reason are correct and the Reason is a correct explanation of the Assertion.

(b) If both Assertion and Reason are correct but Reason is not a correct explanation of the Assertion.

(c) If the Assertion is correct but Reason is incorrect.

(d) If the Assertion is incorrect but the Reason is correct.

14. **Assertion :** Amorphous solids are also known as pseudo solids or super cooled liquids.
    Reason : Like liquids, amorphous solids have a tendency to flow, though very slowly.

15. **Assertion :** Refractive index shows different values when measured along different directions in the same crystal.
    Reason : Crystalline solids are anisotropic in nature, so the arrangement of particles is different along different directions.

Very Short Answer Questions

16. How many atoms are there in a unit cell of a metal crystallising in *fcc* structure?

17. Name the three types of crystalline structures generally found in ionic solids of the type AB.

18. How can you convert NaCl structure into CsCl structure and vice versa?

19. Which positions are occupied by Na^+ and O^{2-} in Na_2O structure?

20. Give three examples of amorphous solids.

21. What is a body centred cubic?

22. The unit cell of substances has cation A^+ at the corners of the unit cell and the anions B^- in the centre. What is the simplest formula of the substance?

23. What is the name of unit cell in which atoms are placed at the corners of all 12 edges of a cubic unit cell?

Short Answer Questions

24. How does amorphous silica differ from quartz?

25. A cubic unit cell has one atom on its each corner and two atoms on its each diagonal. Find the number of atoms in the unit cell.

26. In a face centred cubic arrangement of A and B atoms, A atoms are present at corners and B atoms at face-centres; one of A atoms is missing from one corner in each unit cell. What is the simplest formula of compound?

27. (a) What are molecular crystals?
     (b) Give one example of hydrogen bonded crystals.
     (c) Give one example of metallic crystal with low melting point of about 100 °C.

28. Classify the following as amorphous or crystalline solids: Polyurethane, naphthalene, benzoic acid, teflon, potassium nitrate, cellophane, polyvinyl chloride, fibre glass, copper.

29. Why are amorphous solids to be considered as supercooled liquids ?

> ### Topic 2   Close Packed Structure, Density of Solid, Imperfection in Solids 

CLOSE PACKED STRUCTURE

Close Packing in One Dimension

Lattice points are arranged in a row touching each other. Each sphere is in contact with two neighbouring spheres. Coordination number is 2 in this arrangement.

Close Packing in Two Dimensions

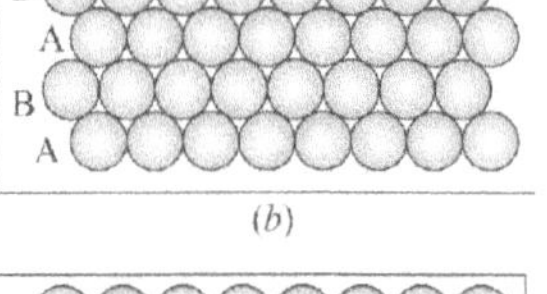

(a) **Square close packing :** Spheres of second row are exactly above the spheres of first row and spheres of third row are just above the second row and so on. Coordination number is 4 in this type of arrangment.

(b) **For the third layer, there are two possibilities:**

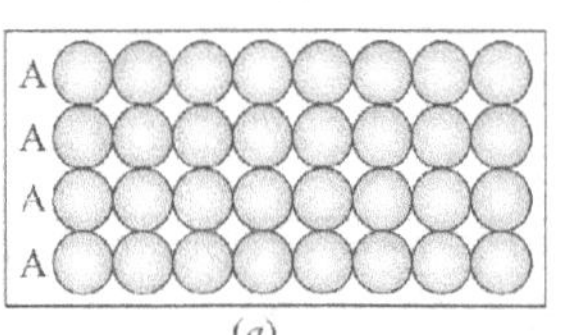

  (i)   The spheres can be placed in the depressions of the second layer in such a way so that they are directly above the first layer. Here the third layer is directly above the first, the fourth directly above the second and so on. This leads to the arrangement ABABAB...... This type of arrangement is known as **hexagonal close-packing (hcp)** structure, e.g., Zn and Mg. There are 6 spheres per unit cell in such arrangement. Therefore coordination number is 6 in this type of arrangment.

  (ii) **Cubic closed Packing structure :** In this type of arrangement the spheres can be placed in those depressions of the second layer, that do not lie directly above the atoms of the first layer. It follows that all the spheres in the third layer are not exactly above the spheres in the first layer. In this type of arrangement, the pattern repeats every fourth layer, i.e., the spheres in the fourth layer lie exactly above the first, the fifth above the second, the sixth above the third and so on. If the three layers are represented by A, B and C then the resulting structure has on ABCABCABC....... arrangement. This is known as **cubic- closed packing (ccp) structure or face-centred cubic (fcc)** arrangement, e.g., Cu, Ag and Au.

The co-ordination number of the atom is 12 as the central atom of a layer is surrounded by six atoms in its own layer and by three atoms each from the layers at the top and at the bottom. The *ccp* arrangement of atoms occupy 74% of the available space and thus has 26% vacant space.

Note: Close packing in three dimension can be done by placing layer one over the other.

Coordination Number :

The number of nearest neighbours of an atom, ion or a molecule is called its **coordination number**. In ionic crystals, the coordination number may be defined as the number of oppositely charged ions surrounding a particular ion.

Metallic elements	Lattice types	Coordination numbers
Be, Mg, Cd, Zn, Ti	hcp	12
Cu, Ca, Si, Ag, Au	ccp or fcc	12
Li, Na, K, Rb, Cs	bcc	8

Packing Fraction (P.F.) :

It is defined as ratio of the volume of the unit cell that is occupied by spheres of the unit cell to the total volume of the unit cell.

(a) **Simple cubic unit cell :**

$$\text{P.F.} = \frac{\frac{4}{3}\pi r^3}{(2r)^3} = \frac{\pi}{6} = 0.52, \text{ % P.F.} = 52\%,$$

void fraction $= 100 - $ packing fraction $= 100 - 52 = 48\%$

(b) **Body centered cubic unit cell :**

$$\text{P.F.} = \frac{2 \times \frac{4}{3}\pi r^3}{(4r/\sqrt{3})^3} = \frac{\sqrt{3}\pi}{8} = 0.68$$

% P.F. $= 68\%$; % of void $= 100 - 68 = 32\%$

(c) **Face centered cubic unit cell :**

$$\text{P.F.} = \frac{4 \times \frac{4}{3}\pi r^3}{(4r/\sqrt{2})^3} = \frac{\sqrt{2}\pi}{6} = 0.74$$

% P.F. $= 74\%$ % of void $= 100 - 74 = 26\%$

Interstitials or Voids

When the spheres are stacked together in different layers, there is always a **void** or **hole** (or **interstices**) between the touching spheres. Two types of voids or holes are created among the spheres in close-packed arrangement of spheres:

(a) **Tetrahedral void:** It is created by four spheres in contact with each other. Its coordination number is four. The number of tetrahedral voids = 2N (Where, N is number of points per unit cell)

(b) **Octahedral void:** It is created when six spheres are in contact with each other. Its coordination number is 6. Number of octahedral voids = N

In a closed packed arrangement, the octahedral voids are present at edge centres and at body centres. As each edge is shared between four unit cells, so $\frac{1}{4}$ th of the void belongs to each unit cell. The void at body centre is not shared. So in f.c.c. the no.

of octahedral voids will be $\frac{1}{4} \times 12$ (there are 12 edges in an unit cell) + 1 i.e. 4.

DENSITY OF SOLID

The density of the unit cell, $d = \dfrac{ZM}{a^3 N_A}$ $\Rightarrow$ where a^3 = volume of the unit cell ; Z = Number of lattice points per unit cell ; N_A = Avogadro constant ; M = Molar mass of lattice point.

Illustration 5 :

What is the number of octahedral and tetrahedral voids per unit cell of cubic close packing (fcc)?

Sol. Number of tetrahedral voids = 8, number of octahedral voids = 4.

Illustration 6 :

In a face centred cubic arrangement of A and B atoms where A are present at the corner and B at the face centres, A atoms are missing from 4 corners in each unit cell ? What is the simplest formula of the compound ?

Sol. Number of cations = $4 \times \dfrac{1}{8} = \dfrac{1}{2}$;   Number of anions = $6 \times \dfrac{1}{2} = 3$

Formula = $A_{1/2}B_3 = AB_6$

Illustration 7 :

The intermetallic compound LiAg crystallizes in a cubic lattice in which both lithium and silver atoms have coordination number of eight. What will be the crystal class of the unit cell?

Sol. A body-centred cubic system consists of all eight corners plus one atom at the centre of cube.

IMPERFECTIONS IN SOLIDS

Any departure from perfectly ordered arrangement of atoms or ions in crystals is called **imperfection** or **defects**. These are of two types:

(a) **Point defects:** When there exists irregularities (from the ideal arrangement) around a point or an atom in a crystalline substance, it is called point defect.

(b) **Line defects:** When there exists irregularities (from the ideal arrangement) along the entire row of lattice points, it is called line defect.

Note: Detailed discussion of line defect in crystalline solids is beyond the scope of the syllabus.

Types of Point Defects

(a) **Stoichiometric defect :** The compounds in which the number of positive and negative ions are exactly in the ratio indicated by their chemical formula are called stoichiometric compounds. e.g. NaCl (1 : 1)

Stoichiometric defects in non-ionic solids are of two types:

(i) Vacancy defects   (ii) Interstitial defects

Vacancy defect : In this type of defect some of the lattice sites of a crystal are vacant. This defect lowers the density of the solid.

Interstitial defect : In this defect atoms or ions occupy the interstitial sites in a crystal . It results in increase in density of crystal.

Stoichiometric defects in ionic-solids are of following two types.

(i) **Schottky defects** occurs when a pair of ions of opposite charge, *i.e.*, cations and anions are missing from the ideal lattice. The presence of a large number of schottky defects lowers the density of a crystal, *e.g.*, AgBr.

(ii) **Frenkel defects** is a combination of schottky defects and interstitials. It occurs when an ion leaves its position in the lattice and occupies an interstitial site leaving a gap in the crystal. For example, AgX, the Ag^+ ions are considerably smaller than the X^- ions and thus, can get into the interstitial sites. It does not change the density of the crystal.

(b) **Impurity defect :** In impurity defects some other atoms (foreign atoms) are present at the lattice sites in place of original atoms (host atoms) or at the vacant interstitial sites. For example, if molten NaCl containing a little amount of $SrCl_2$ is crystallised, some of the sites of Na^+ ions are occupied by Sr^{2+}. Each Sr^{2+} replaces two Na^+ ions. It occupies the site of one ion and other site remains vacant.

(c) **Non-stoichiometric defects :** There are a large number of inorganic solids in which the ratio of the number of atoms of one kind to the number of atoms of the other kind does not correspond to the ideal whole number ratio. Such compounds are called **non-stoichiometric compounds**. These compounds do not obey the laws of chemical combination, *e.g.,* oxides and sulphides of transition elements.

The ratio of Fe : O in FeO is not exactly 1 : 1. It is $Fe_{0.98}O$. There can be either an excess of metal ions or a deficiency of metal ions in the crystal.

When there is an excess of metal ions in non-stoichiometric compounds, the crystal lattice has vacant anion sites. These sites are occupied by electrons. The anion sites occupied by electrons are called **F-centres**. F centres are associated with the colour of compounds. For example, excess of K in KCl makes the crystal of KCl violet and excess of Li in LiCl makes it pink. In the metal deficiency defect, a metal ion of lower oxidation state is replaced by metal ion of higher oxidation state. For example in the example sited above of $Fe_{0.98}O$, some of Fe^{+2} are replaced by Fe^{+3}, that is why amount of iron is less than its stoichiometric requirement.

Illustration 8 :

Which of the following possess Frenkel defect? AgBr, ZnS, AgI and AlI

Sol. Frenkel defect is shown by aℓI. It arises when the cations are missing from their lattice sites and occupy interstitial sites. As a result of Frenkel defect, density remains unchanged but dielectric constant increases.

Practice Exercise-2

Multiple Choice Questions

1. An element (atomic mass 100 g/mol) having *bcc* structure has unit cell edge 400 pm. The density of element is
   (a) $2.144 \, g/cm^3$ (b) $7.289 \, g/cm^3$
   (c) $5.188 \, g/cm^3$ (d) $10.376 \, g/cm^3$

2. What is the coordination number of sodium in Na_2O?
   (a) 6   (b) 4   (c) 8   (d) 2

3. If *z* is the number of atoms in the unit cell that represents the closest packing sequence ..... ABC ABC ......, the number of tetrahedral voids in the unit cell is equal to :
   (a) z (b) $2z$ (c) $z/2$ (d) $z/4$

4. The Ca^{2+} and F^- are located in CaF_2 crystal, respectively at face centred cubic lattice points and in
   (a) tetrahedral voids   (b) half of tetrahedral voids
   (c) octahedral voids   (d) half of octahedral voids

5. The coordination number in *hcp* is
   (a) 6   (b) 12   (c) 18   (d) 24

6. Coordination numbers of Zn^{2+} and S^{2-} in the crystal structure of wurtzite are
   (a) 4, 4   (b) 6, 6   (c) 8, 4   (d) 8, 8

7. If AgI crystallises in zinc blende structure with $\overline{I}$ ions at lattice points. What fraction of tetrahedral voids is occupied by Ag^+ ions?
   (a) 25%   (b) 50%   (c) 100%   (d) 75%

8. Sodium metal crystallizes in a body centred cubic lattice with a unit cell edge of 4.29Å. The radius of sodium atom is approximately:
   (a) 5.72Å   (b) 0.93Å   (c) 1.86Å   (d) 3.22Å

Assertion & Reason Questions

DIRECTIONS (Qs. 9-11) : *Each of these questions contains an assertion followed by reason. Read them carefully and answer the question on the basis of following options. You have to select the one that best describes the two statements.*

(a) If both Assertion and Reason are correct and the Reason is a correct explanation of the Assertion.

(b) If both Assertion and Reason are correct but Reason is not a correct explanation of the Assertion.

(c) If the Assertion is correct but Reason is incorrect.

(d) If the Assertion is incorrect but the Reason is correct.

9. **Assertion :** No compound has both Schottky and Frenkel defects.
   Reason : Only Schottky defect change the density of the solid.

10. **Assertion :** Due to Frenkel defect, there is no effect on the density of the crystalline solid.
    Reason : In Frenkel defect, no cation or anion leaves the crystal.

11. **Assertion :** In close packing of spheres, a tetrahedral void is surrounded by four spheres whereas an octahedral void is surrounded by six spheres.
    Reason : A tetrahedral void has a tetrahedral shape whereas an octahedral void has an octahedral shape.

Very Short Answer Questions

12. What is meant by 'point defects' in crystals?

13. In a rock-salt structure, how many Na^+ ions occupy second nearest neighbour locations of Na^+?

14. What is the cause of electrical conductivity in (*a*) metals (*b*) ionic solids (*c*) semiconductors?

15. Why common salt is sometimes yellow instead of being pure white?

16. Which of these two $CdCl_2$ and NaCl will produce schottky defect, if added to a AgCl crystal?

17. Name a solid substance in which the cation occupies all of the tetrahedral voids.

18. Which type of crystals exhibits piezoelectricity?

19. What is schottky defect relating to crystals?

20. What is frenkel defect?

21. What is the coordination number of an octahedral void?

22. What is the effect of mechanical stress on a piezoelectric crystal?

23. What are coordination number of each ion present in the cubic close packed structure of Na_2O at ordinary temperature and pressure?

24. Why is frenkel defect found in AgCl?

25. What are stoichiometric defects or intrinsic defects in ionic crystals?

26. Which transition metal oxide has appearance and conductivity like that of copper?

Short Answer Questions

27. MgO has the structure of NaCl and TlCl has the structure of CsCl. What are the coordination numbers of the ions in MgO and TlCl?

28. Why glass panes fixed to windows or doors of old buildings are found to be thicker at the bottom?

29. Give two reasons of crystal imperfections.

30. What is the coordination number of each sphere in the following types of closed packed structure of uniform hard spheres:
    (*a*) Simple cubic lattice (*b*) *bcc* lattice
    (*c*) *fcc* lattice   (*d*) *hcp* lattice

31. Find the edge length of a unit cell of an element having *fcc* structure and radius of atom is 100 pm.

32. A metallic element has *bcc* structure and atoms has radius of 250 pm. Calculate the edge of unit cell.

33. The radius of anion in an ionic solid is 100 pm. Find the radius of cation, which just fits in its
    (*a*) cubic hole, (*b*) octahedral hole, and (*c*) tetrahedral hole.

34. In a compound AX, the radius of A^+ ion is 95 pm and that of X^- ion is 181 pm. Predict the crystal structure of AX and write the coordination numbers of each of the ions.

35. A solid A^+B^- has NaCl type closed packed structure. If the anion has a radius of 241.5 pm, what should be the minimum radius of cation? Can a cation C^+, having a radius of 50 pm be fitted into tetrahedral hole of crystal A^+B^-?

36. Copper crystallises in *fcc* lattice and has density of 8.930 g cm^{-3} at 293 K. Calculate the radius of copper atom. Atomic mass of Cu = 63.55 amu, Avogadro's constant, $N_A = 6.02 \times 10^{23}$.

Important Tips & Formulae

▶ **Non Stoichiometric Point Defects**
   (i)   **Metal excess (due to anion vacancy)**
         F-Centres
         NaCl is yellow
         KCl is violet
   (ii) **Metal excess due to interstitial cations**
         e.g., ZnO
   (iii) **Metal deficiency due to cation vacancy**
         FeO

▶ All noble gases have *ccp* structure except He which has *hcp* structure.

▶ The space occupied by hard spheres in *fcc* and *hcp* is 74%, in *bcc* it is 68%, in simple cubic it is 52% and in diamond it is 34%. Thus only *fcc* and *hcp* are close packed structures.

▶ *hcp* is present in Be, Mg, Ca, Cr, Mo, V, Zn.

▶ Lead zirconate (PbZrO$_3$) is an example of anti-ferroelectric crystal.

▶ *ccp* is present in Fe, Cu, Ag, Au, Pt, Al and Ni.

▶ TiO$_2$, NaCl and benzene are diamagnetic, Fe, Ni, Co, CrO$_2$ are ferromagnetic, MnO is anti ferromagnetic, ferrites are ferrimagnetic, Barium titanate (BaTiO$_3$), sodium potassium tartarate (Rochelle salt) and potassium dihydrogen phosphate (KH$_2$PO$_4$) are ferroelectric solids.

▶ Radius of Tetrahedral Void = $0.225r$
   Radius of Octahedral Void = $0.414r$
   where r is the radius of ions (mostly cations) in the packing.

▶ Number of TVs = $2 \times$ OVs = $2 \times$ Number of atoms in a close packed structure = 8/unit cell

▶ Number of TVs = $2 \times$ Number of occupied voids

▶ **Radius ratio rule**
   $$\text{Radius ratio} = \frac{\text{Radius of cation}}{\text{Radius of anion}} = \frac{r_+}{r_-} \text{ or } \frac{r_c}{r_a}$$

▶ **Structure of ionic crystals**
   (i)   **AB type**: Rock salt (NaCl) type, CsCl-type zinc blend (ZnS) or sphalerite-type structure.
   (ii) **AB$_2$ type**: Fluorite type, e.g., CaF$_2$, BaF$_2$
   (iii) **A$_2$B type**: Antifluorite type, e.g., Na$_2$O

▶ **Types of Ionic Crystal :**

Crystal structure type	Location of particle
AB or Rock Salt (NaCl)	Cl$^-$: *fcc* lattice, Na$^+$: octahedral voids
Zinc blende or Zns	S^{2-} : *fcc* lattice Zn^{2+} : alternate tetrahedral voids
AB$_2$ or Fluorite type (CaF$_2$)	Ca^{2+} : *fcc* lattice, F$-$: all tetrahedral voids
A$_2$B or anti-fluorite type (Na$_2$O)	O^{2-} : *fcc* lattice, Na$^+$: all tetrahedral voids
Caesium chloride (CsCl)	Cl$^-$: corners of cube Cs$^+$: body centre of cube

▶ **Effect of temperature and pressure on the crystal Structures:**
   On the application of high pressure, NaCl-type structures (6 : 6 coordination) transform to CsCl-type structures (8 : 8 coordination), while on heating reverse occurs.

   $$\text{NaCl-type structures} \underset{760 \text{ K}}{\overset{\text{Pressure}}{\rightleftharpoons}} \text{CsCl-type structures}$$
   (6:6 coordination)   (8:8 coordination)

NCERT Questions

1. Define the term 'amorphous'. Give a few examples of amorphous solids.

Sol. Amorphous solids are those substances, in which there is no regular arrangement of its constituent particles, (*i.e.,* ions, atoms or molecules). The arrangement of the constituting particles has only short range order, *i.e.,* a regular and periodically repeating pattern is observed over short distances only, *e.g.,* glass, rubber and plastics.

2. What makes a glass different from a solid such as quartz? Under what conditions could quartz be converted into glass?

Sol. Glass is made up of SiO_4 tetrahedral units. These constituent particles have short range order only. Quartz is also made up of SiO_4 tretrahedral units. On heating it softens and melts over a wide range of temperature. It is a crystalline solid having long range ordered structure. It has a sharp melting point.

Quartz can be converted into glass by first melting and then rapidly cooling it.

3. Classify each of the following solids as ionic, metallic, molecular, network (covalent) or amorphous:

    (*i*) Tetra phosphorus decoxide (P_4O_{10})

    (*ii*) Ammonium phosphate, $(NH_4)_3PO_4$

    (*iii*) SiC   (*iv*) I_2 (*v*) P_4

    (*vi*) Plastics (*vii*) Graphite (*viii*) Brass

    (*ix*) Rb   (*x*) LiBr   (*xi*) Si

Sol.

Ionic	Metallic	Molecular	Network	Amorphous
$(NH_4)_3PO_4$	Brass	P_4O_{10}	Graphite	Plastics
LiBr	Rb	I_2	SiC	
		P_4	Si	

4. (*i*) What is meant by the term 'coordination number'?

    (*ii*) What is the coordination number of atom

      (*a*) in a cubic close packed structure?

      (*b*) in a body centred cubic structure?

Sol. (*i*) The number of nearest neighbours of a particle are called its coordination number.

(*ii*) (*a*) 12   (*b*) 8

5. How can you determine the atomic mass of an unknown metal if you know its density and the dimensions of its unit cell? Explain.

Sol. Let the edge length of a unit cell = a

Density = d

Molar mass = M

Volume of the unit cell = a^3

Mass of the unit cell

= No. of atoms in unit cell × Mass of each atom = $Z \times m$

Mass of an atom present in the unit cell = $m = \dfrac{M}{N_a}$

$$\therefore\quad d = \frac{\text{Mass of unit cell}}{\text{Volume of unit cell}} = \frac{Z \cdot m}{a^3} = \frac{Z \cdot M}{a^3 N_a}$$

$$\therefore\quad \text{Atomic mass, } M = \frac{d \cdot a^3 \cdot N_a}{Z}$$

6. 'Stability of a crystal is reflected in the magnitude of its melting points'. Comment.

Collect melting points of solid water, ethyl alcohol, diethyl ether and methane from a data book. What can you say about the intermolecular forces between these molecules?

Sol. Higher the melting point, greater are the forces holding the constituent particles together and thus greater is the stability of a crystal. Melting points of given substances are following.

Water = 273 K, Ethyl alcohol = 155.7 K, Diethylether = 156.8 K, Methane = 90.5 K.

The intermolecular forces present in case of water and ethyl alcohol are mainly due to the hydrogen bonding which is responsible for their high melting points. Hydrogen bonding is stronger in case of water than ethyl alcohol and hence water has higher melting point then ethyl alcohol.

Dipole-dipole interactions are present in case of diethylether. The only forces present in case of methane is the weak van der Waal's forces (or London dispersion forces).

7. How will you distinguish between the following pairs of terms:

    (*i*) Cubic close packing and hexagonal close packing?

    (*ii*) Crystal lattice and unit cell?

    (*iii*) Tetrahedral void and octahedral void?

Sol. (*i*) **Cubic close packing:** When the third layer is placed over the second layer in such a way that the spheres cover the octahedral voids, a layer different from first (*A*) and second (*B*) is produced. If we continue packing in this manner, then a packing is obtained where the spheres in every fourth layer will vertically aligned. This pattern of packing spheres is called $ABCABC.....$ pattern or cubic close packing.

Hexagonal close packing: When a third layer is placed over the second layer in such a manner that the spheres cover the tetrahedral void, a three dimensional close packing is obtained where the spheres in every third or alternate layers are vertically aligned. If we continue packing in this manner, then the packing obtained would be called $ABAB.......$ pattern or hexagonal close packing.

(*ii*) **Crystal lattice:** It is a regular arrangement of the constituent particles (*i.e.,* ions, atoms or molecules) of a crystal in three dimensional space.

Unit cell: The smallest three dimensional portion of a complete space lattice which when repeated over and over again in different directions produces the complete crystal lattice is called the unit cell.

(*iii*) **Tetrahedral void:** A simple triangular void is a crystal is surrounded by four spheres and is called a tetrahedral void.

Octahedral void: A double triangular void is surrounded by six spheres and is called a octahedral void.

8. How many lattice points are there is one unit cell of each of the following lattices?
(*i*) Face centred cubic (*ii*) Face centred tetragonal
(*iii*) Body centred cubic

Sol. Lattice points in face centred cubic and face centred tetragonal
$= 8$ (at corners) $+ 6$ (at face centres) $= 14$

Particle per unit cell $= 8 \times \dfrac{1}{8} + 6 \times \dfrac{1}{2} = 4$

Lattice points in body centred cubic
$= 8$ (at corners) $+ 1$ (at body centre) $= 9$

Particles per unit cell $= 8 \times \dfrac{1}{2} + \dfrac{1}{8} \times 1 = 2.$

9. Explain:
(*i*) **The basis of similarities and differences between metallic and ionic crystals.**
(*ii*) **Ionic solids are hard and brittle.**

Sol. (*i*) Metallic and ionic crystals
Similarities:
(*a*) There is electrostatic force of attraction in both metallic and ionic crystals.
(*b*) Both have high melting points.
(*c*) Bonds are non-directional in both the cases.
Differences:
(*a*) Ionic crystals are bad conductors of electricity in solids state as ions are not free to move. They can conduct electricity only in the molten state or in aqueous solution. Metallic crystals are good conductors of electricity in solid state as electrons are free to move.
(*b*) Ionic bond is strong due to strong electrostatic forces of attraction.
Metallic bond may be strong or weak depending upon the number of valence electrons and the size of the kernels.
(*ii*) Ionic solids are hard and brittle. Ionic solids are hard due to the presence of strong electrostatic forces of attraction. The brittleness in ionic crystals is due to the non-directional bonds in them.

10. Calculate the efficiency of packing in case of a metal crystal for (*i*) simple cubic, (*ii*) body centred cubic, and (*iii*) face centred cubic (with the assumptions that atoms are touching each other).

Sol. **Packing efficiency:** It is the percentage of total space filled by the particles.
(*i*) **In simple cubic lattice:** Here $a = 2r$
No. of spheres per unit cell $= 1$
Volume of spheres $= \dfrac{4}{3}\pi r^3$
Volume of cube $= a^3 = (2r)^3 = 8r^3$

$\therefore$ Packing efficiency $= \dfrac{4/3\,\pi r^3}{8\,r^3} = 0.524,$ *i.e.,* $52.4\%.$

(*ii*) **In** *bcc* **:** $AD = 4r$

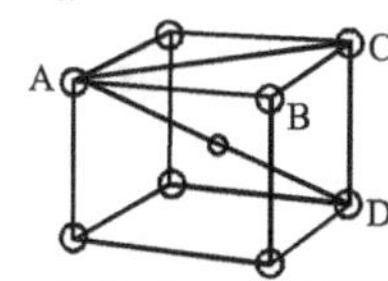

From right angled triangle ABC,
$AC = \sqrt{AB^2 + BC^2} = \sqrt{a^2 + a^2} = \sqrt{2}a$

Body diagonal, AD
$= \sqrt{AC^2 + CD^2} = \sqrt{2a^2 + a^2} = \sqrt{3a^2} = \sqrt{3}\,a$
$\therefore \quad \sqrt{3}\,a = 4r \quad a = 4r/\sqrt{3}$

$\therefore$ Volume of unit cell $= a^3 = \left(\dfrac{4r}{\sqrt{3}}\right)^3 = \dfrac{64r^3}{3\sqrt{3}}$

No. of spheres per unit cell $= 2$

$\therefore$ Volume of two spheres $= 2 \times \dfrac{4}{3}\pi r^3 = \dfrac{8}{3}\pi r^3$

$\therefore$ Packing efficiency $= \dfrac{8/3\,\pi r^3}{64r^3/3\sqrt{3}} = 0.68,$ *i.e.,* 68%

(*iii*) **In** *fcc*: Let the edge length of unit cell $= a$

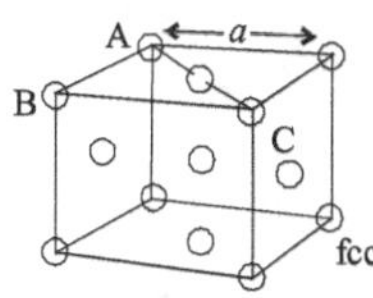

Let the radius of each sphere $= r$
$\therefore \qquad AC = 4r$
From right angled triangle ABC,
$AC = \sqrt{AB^2 + BC^2} = \sqrt{a^2 + a^2} = \sqrt{2a^2} = \sqrt{2}a$
$\therefore \qquad \sqrt{2}a = 4r$
$\therefore \qquad a = \dfrac{4r}{\sqrt{2}}$

$\therefore$ Volume of the unit cell
$= a^3 = \left(\dfrac{4}{\sqrt{2}}r\right)^3 = \dfrac{64r^3}{2\sqrt{2}} = \dfrac{32r^3}{\sqrt{2}}$

No. of unit cell in *fcc* $= 4$

$\therefore$ Volume of four spheres $= 4 \times \dfrac{4}{3}\pi r^3 = \dfrac{16}{3}\pi r^3$

$\therefore$ Packing efficiency $= \dfrac{16\pi r^3/3}{64r^3/3\sqrt{3}} = 0.74,$ *i.e.,* 74%

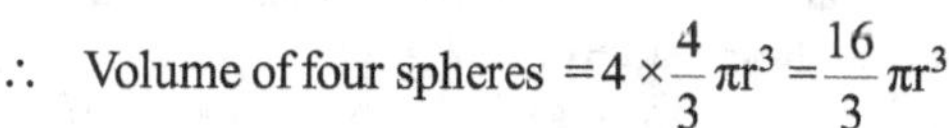

11. Silver crystallises in *fcc* lattice. If edge length of the cell is 4.07×10^{-8} cm and density is 10.5 g cm^{-3}, calculate the atomic mass of silver.

Sol. $M = \dfrac{d \cdot a^3 \cdot N_a}{Z} = \dfrac{10.5 \times (4.07 \times 10^{-8})^3 \times 6.023 \times 10^{23}}{4}$
$= 107.09$ g mol^{-1}.

12. A cubic solid is made up of two elements P and Q. Atoms of Q are at the corners of the cube and P at the body centre. What is the formula of the compound? What are the coordination numbers of P and Q?

Sol. As atoms Q are present at the eight corners of the cube, therefore, the contribution of atoms of Q in the unit cell
$= \dfrac{1}{8} \times 8 = 1.$

As atom P is present at the body centre, therefore, the contribution of atoms of P in the unit cell $= 1$.
$\therefore$ Ratio of atoms of P : Q $= 1 : 1$
Hence, the formula of the compound $=$ PQ
The coordination number of each P and Q $= 8$.

13. Niobium crystallises in a body centred cubic structure. If density is 8.55 g cm⁻³, calculate atomic radius of niobium, using its atomic mass 93u.

Sol.
$$a^3 = \frac{M \cdot Z}{d \cdot N_a} \times 10^{-30} = \frac{93 \times 2}{8.55 \times 6.02 \times 10^{23} \times 10^{-30}} = 3.61 \times 10^7$$

$$\therefore \quad a = (3.61 \times 10^7)^{1/3} = (36.1 \times 10^6)^{1/3}$$
$$= 3.304 \times 10^2 \, pm = 330.4 \, pm$$

14. If the radius of the octahedral void is *r* and radius of the atoms in close-packing is *R*, derive relation between *r* and *R*.

Sol. A sphere is fitted into the octahedral void as shown in the diagram.

$\triangle ABC$ is a right angled triangle.

$$\therefore \quad BC^2 = AB^2 + AC^2$$
$$(2R)^2 = (R+r)^2 + (R+r)^2$$
$$(2R)^2 = 2(R+r)^2$$

$$\Rightarrow \quad \frac{(2R)^2}{2} = (R+r)^2$$

$$\left(\sqrt{2}R\right)^2 = (R+r)^2$$

$$\Rightarrow \quad \sqrt{2} \, R = R + r$$

$$r = \sqrt{2} \, R - R \qquad\qquad r = R(\sqrt{2}-1)$$
$$r = R(1.414 - 1) \qquad\quad r = 0.414 \, R$$

15. Copper crystallises into a *fcc* lattice with edge length 3.61 × 10⁻⁸ cm. Show that the calculated density is in agreement with its measured value of 8.92 g cm⁻³.

Sol.
$$d = \frac{Z \times M}{a^3 \times N_a} = \frac{4 \times 63.5}{(3.61 \times 10^{-8})^3 \times 6.023 \times 10^{23}}$$
$$\{M = 63.5 \text{ for Cu}\}$$
$$= 8.96 \, g \, cm^{-3}.$$

This calculated value of density is closely in agreement with its measured value of 8.92 g cm³.

16. Analysis shows that nickel oxide has the formula $Ni_{0.98}O_{1.00}$. What fractions of nickel exist as Ni^{2+} and Ni^{3+} ions?

Sol. The formula $Ni_{0.98}O_{1.00}$ implies that 98 Ni atoms are associated with 100 O atoms.

Let out of 98 Ni atoms present, *x* atoms are present as Ni^{2+} ions and $(98 - x)$ are present as Ni^{3+} ions.

$\therefore$ Total charge on $x \, Ni^{2+}$ ions and $(100 - x) \, Ni^{3+}$ ions should balance the charge on $100 \, O^{2-}$ ions.

Hence, $x \times 2 + (98 - x) \times 3 = 100 \times 2$
$$2x + 294 - 3x = 200 \quad \therefore \quad x = 94.$$

$\therefore$ Fraction of Ni atoms present as

$$Ni^{2+} = \frac{94}{98} \times 100 = 95.91\%$$

and fraction of Ni atoms present as

$$Ni^{3+} = \frac{98 - 94}{98} \times 100 = \frac{4}{98} \times 100 = 4.081\%.$$

17. Ferric oxide crystallises in a hexagonal close packed array of oxide ions with two out of every three octahedral holes occupied by ferric ions. Derive the formula of the ferric oxide.

Sol. Let the number of oxide ions (O^{2-}) in the packing $= x$

$\therefore$ Number of octahedral voids $= x$

As out of every three octahedral holes, two are occupied by ferric ions, therefore, the number of ferric ions present

$$= \frac{2}{3} \times x = \frac{2x}{3}$$

$$\therefore \text{ Ratio of } Fe^{+3} : O^{2-} = \frac{2x}{3} : x \quad 2x : 3x = 2 : 3$$

Hence, the formula of ferric oxide is Fe_2O_3.

18. Gold (atomic radius = 0.144 nm) crystallises in a face centred unit cell. What is the length of a side of the cell?

Sol. In case of *fcc*, $a = 2\sqrt{2}r = 2 \times 1.414 \times 0.144 \, nm = 0.407 \, nm.$

19. Explain the following terms with suitable examples:
(i) Schottky defect   (ii) Frenkel defect
(iii) Interstitials and   (iv) F-centres

Sol. (i) Schottky defect occurs when a pair of ions of opposite charges, *i.e.*, cations and anions, are missing from the ideal lattice. Schottky defect is shown by ionic substances in which cation and anion are of almost similar sizes. For example, NaCl, KCl, CsCl and AgBr.

(ii) Frenkel defects is a combination of two basic types of point defects : Schottky and interstitial. It occurs when an ion leaves its position in the lattice and occupies an interstitial site leaving a gap in the crystal. It is shown by ionic substances having large difference in the size of oppositly charged ions, For example, ZnS, AgCl.

(iii) Interstitials are the atoms or ions which occupy the normally vacant interstitial sites in a crystal. Non ionic solids are examples of this defect.

(iv) When there is an excess of metal ions in non-stoichiometric compounds, the crystal lattice has vacant anion sites. These sites are occupied by electrons. The anion sites occupied by electrons are called F-centres. Alkali halides like NaCl, KCl and LiCl show this type of defect.

20. Aluminium crystallises in a cubic close–packed structure. Its metallic radius is 125 pm.
(i) What is the length of the side of the unit cell?
(ii) How many unit cells are there in 1.00 cm³ of aluminium?

Sol. Aluminium crystallises in *ccp* structure which is same as *fcc* structure.

(i) For fcc, $a = 2\sqrt{2}r = 2 \times 1.414 \times 125 \, pm = 354 \, pm$

(ii) Volume of one unit cell $= a^3 = (354 \times 10^{-12})^3$
$$= (354 \times 10^{-10} \, cm)^3 = 4.44 \times 10^{-23} \, cm^3$$

Number of unit cells in 1 cm³ $= \dfrac{1}{4.44 \times 10^{-23}}$

$$= 2.25 \times 10^{22}.$$

21. If NaCl is doped with 10⁻³ mol % $SrCl_2$, what is the concentration of cation vacancies?

Sol. Doping of NaCl with 10^{-3} mol % $SrCl_2$ means that 100 moles of NaCl are doped with 10^{-3} mol of $SrCl_2$.

$\therefore$ 1 mole of NaCl is doped with $SrCl_2 = \dfrac{10^{-3}}{100}$ mole $= 10^{-5}$ mole.

Each Sr^{2+} introduces one cation vacancy, therefore, concentration of cation vacancies

$$= 10^{-5} \times N_A = 10^{-5} \, mol \times 6.023 \times 10^{23} \, mol^{-1} = 6.023 \times 10^{18}.$$

Past year Exercise

Very Short Answer Questions

1. Analysis shows that FeO has a non-stoichiometric composition with formula $Fe_{0.95}O$. Give reason.

2. Which point defect in crystals of a solid does not change the density of the solid?

3. Write a distinguishing feature of metallic solids.

4. What type of interactions hold the molecules together in a polar molecular solid?

5. Give an example of an ionic compound which shows Frenkel defect.

6. 'Crystalline solids are anisotropic in nature'. What does this statement mean?

7. How do metallic and ionic substances differ in conducting electricity?

8. What type of stoichiometric defect is shown by AgCl ?

9. Calculate the number of atoms in a face centred unit cell.

10. Aluminium crystallizes in an *fcc* structure. Atomic radius of the metal is 125 pm. What is the length of the side of the unit cell of the metal?

Short Answer Questions

11. Chromium crystallises in bcc structure. If its edge length is 300 pm, find its density. Atomic mass of chromium is 52 u. [$N_A = 6 \cdot 022 \times 10^{23}$ mol^{-1}]

12. An element 'X' (At mass = 40 g mol^{-1}) having f.c.c. structure, has unit cell edge length of 400 pm. Calculate the density of 'X' and the number of unit cells in 4 g 'X'. ($N_A = 6.022 \times 10^{23}$ mol^{-1})

13. Calculate the number of unit cells in 8. 1 g of aluminium if it crystallizes in a face-centred cubic (f.c.c) structure. (Atomic mass of Al = 27 g mol^{-1})

14. The density of copper metal is 8.95 g cm^{-3}. If the radius of copper atom is 127.8 pm, is the copper unit cell a simple cubic, a body centred cubic or face centred cubic structure (Given atomic mass of Cu = 63.54 g mol^{-1} and $N_A = 6.02 \times 10^{23}$ mol^{-1})

15. How are the following properties of crystals affected by schottky and Frenkel defects?
    (i) Density   (ii) Electrical conductivity

16. Chromium metal crystallises in a body centred cubic lattice. The length of the unit cell edge is found to be 287 pm. Calculate the atomic radius of chromium.

17. A well known mineral fluorite is chemically calcium fluoride. It is known that in one unit cell of this mineral there are 4 Ca^{2+} ions and 8 F$^-$ ions and that Ca^{2+} ions are arranged in a *fcc* lattice. The F$^-$ ions fill all the tetrahedral holes in *fcc* lattice of Ca^{2+} ions. The edge of the unit cell is 5.46×10^{-8} cm in length. The density of the solid is 3.18 g cm^{-3}. Use this information to calculate Avogadro's number. (Molar mass of $CaF_2 = 78.08$ g mol^{-1})

18. An alloy of gold and cadmium crystallises with a cubic structure in which gold atoms occupy the corners and cadmium atoms fit into the face centres. Assign formula for this alloy.

19. Calculate the packing efficiency of a metal crystal for a simple cubic lattice.

20. Silver crystallizes in face centred cubic unit cell. Each side of this unit cell has a length of 400 pm. Calculate the radius of the silver atom. (Assume the atoms just touch each other on the diagonal across the face of the unit cell. That is each face atom is touching the four corner atoms).

21. Define the following terms in relation to crystalline solids.
    (i) Unit cell
    (ii) Coordination number
    Give one example in each case.

22. Explain how you can determine the atomic mass of an unknown metal if you know its mass density and the dimensions of unit cell of its crystal?

23. Silver crystallises with a face-centered cubic unit cell. Each side of unit cell has length of 409 pm. What is the radius of an atom of silver?

24. Aluminium crystallises in a cubic close packed structure. Radius of the atom in the metal is 125 pm.
    (i) What is the length of the side of the unit cell ?
    (ii) How many unit cells are there in 1 cm^3 of aluminium?

25. Copper crystallises with face centred cubic unit cell. If the radius of copper atom is 127.8 pm, calculate the density of copper metal. (Atomic mass of Cu = 63.55 u and Avogadro's number, $N_A = 6.02 \times 10^{23}$ mol^{-1})

26. Tungsten crystallises in a body centered cubic unit cell. If the edge of the unit cell is 316.5 pm, what is the radius of tungsten atom?

27. Iron has a body centered cubic unit cell with an edge length of 286.65 pm. The density of iron is 7.87 g cm^{-3}. Use this information to calculate Avogadro's number. (At. mass of Fe = 56 g mol^{-1})

28. Account for the following :
    (i) Schottky defects lower the density of related solids.
    (ii) Conductivity of silicon increases on doping it with phosphorus.

29. What is the formula of a compound in which the element Y forms *ccp* lattice and atoms of X occupy 1/3rd of tetrahedral voids?

30. (a) Why does presence of excess of lithium makes LiCl crystals pink?
    (b) A solid with cubic crystal is made of two elements P and Q. Atoms of Q are at the corners of the cube and P at the body-centre. What is the formula of the compound?

31. A compound forms *hcp* structure. What is the total number of voids in 0.5 mol of it? How many of these are tetrahedral voids?

32. An element occurs in *bcc* structure. It has a cell edge length of 250 pm. Calculate the molar mass if its density is 8.0 g cm^{-3}. Also calculate the radius of an atom of this element.

33. An element with density 2.8 g cm^{-3} forms of f.c.c. unit cell with edge length 4×10^{-8} cm. Calculate the molar mass of the element.
(Given: $N_A = 6.022 \times 10^{23}$ mol^{-1})

34. (i) What type of non-stoichiometric point defect is responsible for the pink colour of LiCl?
(ii) What type of stoichiometric defect is shown by NaCl ?

OR

How will you distinguish between the following pairs of terms:
(i) Tetrahedral and octahedral voids
(ii) Crystal lattice and unit cell

35. An element with density 11.2 g cm^{-3} forms a f.c.c. lattice with edge length of 4×10^{-8} cm. Calculate the atomic mass of the element.
(Given : $N_A = 6.022 \times 10^{23}$ mol^{-1})

36. Examine the given defective crystal

A$^+$	B$^-$	A$^+$	B$^-$	A$^+$
B$^-$	0	B$^-$	A$^+$	B$^-$
A$^+$	B$^-$	A$^+$	0	A$^+$
B$^-$	A$^+$	B$^-$	A$^+$	B$^-$

Answer the following questions :
(i) What type of stoichiometric defect is shown by the crystal ?
(ii) How is the density of the crystal affected by the defect ?
(iii) What type of ionic substances show such defect ?

37. Define the following terms.
(i) Primitive unit cells
(ii) Schottky defect

38. An element crystallizes in a *bcc* lattice with cell edge of 500 pm. The density of the element is 7.5 g cm^{-3}. How many atoms are present in 300 g of the element ?

NCERT Exemplar

1. Which of the following conditions favours the existence of a substance in the solid state?
(a) High temperature
(b) Low temperature
(c) High thermal energy
(d) Weak cohensive forces

2. Graphite cannot be classified as ....
(a) conducting solid
(b) network solid
(c) covalent solid
(d) ionic solid

3. Which of the following is a network solid?
(a) SO$_2$ (solid)   (b) I$_2$
(c) Diamond   (d) H$_2$O (ice)

4. Which of the following solids is not an electrical conductor?
1. Mg(*s*)   2. TiO(*s*)
3. I$_2$(*s*)   4. H$_2$O(*s*)
(a) Only 1   (b) Only 2
(c) 3 and 4   (d) 2, 3 and 4

5. Which of the following oxides shows electrical properties like metals?
(a) SiO$_2$ (b) MgO
(c) SO$_2$(*s*)   (d) CrO$_2$

DIRECTIONS (Qs. 6-8) : *Each of these questions contains an assertion followed by reason. Read them carefully and answer the question on the basis of following options. You have to select the one that best describes the two statements.*

(a) If both Assertion and Reason are correct and the Reason is a correct explanation of the Assertion.
(b) If both Assertion and Reason are correct but Reason is not a correct explanation of the Assertion.
(c) If the Assertion is correct but Reason is incorrect.
(d) If the Assertion is incorrect but the Reason is correct.

6. **Assertion :** Graphite is a good conductor of electricity however diamond belongs to the category of insulators.
Reason : Graphite is soft in nature on the other hand diamond is very hard and brittle.

7. **Assertion :** The packing efficiency is maximum for the *fcc* structure.
Reason : The coordination number is 12 in *fcc* structures.

8. **Assertion :** Semiconductors are solids with conductivities in the intermediate range from $10^{-6} - 10^4$ ohm^{-1}m^{-1}.
Reason : Intermediate conductivity in semiconductor is due to partially filled valence band.

9. Inspite of long range order in the arrangement of particles why are the crystals usually not perfect?

10. Why is FeO (s) not formed in stoichiometric composition?

11. Why does white ZnO(s) become yellow upon heating?

Objective Practice Exercise

Multiple Choice Questions

DIRECTIONS : *This section contains multiple choice questions. Each question has four choices (a), (b), (c) and (d) out of which only one is correct.*

1. Most crystals show good cleavage because their atoms, ions or molecules are
   (a) weakly bonded together
   (b) strongly bonded together
   (c) spherically symmetrical
   (d) arranged in planes

2. The sharp melting point of crystalline solids is due to
   (a) a regular arrangement of constituent particles observed over a short distance in the crystal lattice
   (b) a regular arrangement of constituent particles observed over a long distance in the crystal lattice
   (c) same arrangement of constituent particles in different directions
   (d) different arrangement of constituent particles in different directions.

3. An example of a covalent crystalline solid is:
   (a) Si   (b) Al   (c) NaF   (d) Ar

4. Which of the following compounds is a good conductor of electricity in solution state?
   (a) Covalent   (b) Molecular
   (c) Metallic   (d) Ionic

5. A solid with high electrical and thermal conductivity is
   (a) Si   (b) Li   (c) NaCl   (d) Ice

6. Solids which do not show the same physical properties in different directions are called
   (a) Pseudo solids   (b) Isotropic solids
   (c) Polymorphic solids   (d) Anisotropic solids

7. In h.c.p of A, $\frac{1}{3}$ of tetrahedral voids are occupied by B. What is the formula for compound:
   (a) A_2B_3 (b) A_3B_2 (c) AB_3 (d) A_2B

8. Which of the following statements is true for ionic solids ?
   (a) Ionic solids are soluble in CCl_4, C_6H_6, etc.
   (b) Under the electric field cations and anions acquire translatory motion in opposite directions
   (c) Structural units have strong electrostatic force of attraction
   (d) Structural units have dipole-dipole interactions

9. Crystals can be classified into basic crystal lattice, equal to
   (a) 7   (b) 4   (c) 14   (d) 2

10. The number of atoms present in a hexagonal close-packed unit cell is :
    (a) 4   (b) 6   (c) 8   (d) 12

11. If the radius of the anion in an ionic solid is 200 pm, what would be the radius of the cation that fits exactly into a cubic hole?
    (a) 146.4 pm   (b) 82.8 pm
    (c) 45 pm   (d) None of these

12. Which colour is observed when ZnO is heated?
    (a) Yellow   (b) Violet   (c) Green   (d) Blue

13. In which of the following pairs of structures, tetrahedral as well as octahedral holes are found?
    (a) bcc and fcc   (b) hcp and simple cubic
    (c) hcp and ccp   (d) bcc and hcp

14. Which of the following layering pattern will have a void fraction of 0.260?
    (a) ABCCBAABC   (b) ABBAABBA
    (c) ABCABCABC   (d) ABCAABCA

15. The most unsymmetrical and symmetrical systems are, respectively :
    (a) Tetragonal, Cubic
    (b) Triclinic, Cubic
    (c) Rhombohedral, Hexagonal
    (d) Orthorhombic, Cubic

16. In a hexagonal close packed (hcp) structure of spheres, the fraction of the volume occupied by the sphere is A. In a cubic close packed structure the fraction is B. The relation for A and B is:
    (a) $A = B$
    (b) $A < B$
    (c) $A > B$
    (d) A is equal to the fraction in a simple cubic lattice.

17. The radius of a calcium ion is 94 pm and of the oxide ion is 146 pm. The possible crystal structure of calcium oxide will be
    (a) tetrahedral   (b) trigonal
    (c) octahedral   (d) pyramidal

18. How many "nearest" and "next nearest" neighbours, respectively, does potassium have in bcc lattice ?
    (a) 8, 8   (b) 8, 6   (c) 6, 8   (d) 6, 6

19. In CsCl type structure, the co-ordination number of Cs^+ and Cl^- respectively are :
    (a) 6, 6   (b) 6, 8   (c) 8, 8   (d) 8, 6

20. In face centred cubic lattice, a unit cell is shared equally by how many unit cells
    (a) 2   (b) 4   (c) 6   (d) 8

21. The limiting radius ratio for tetrahedral shape is:
    (a) 0 to 0.155   (b) 0.225 to 0.414
    (c) 0.155 to 0.225   (d) 0.414 to 0.732

22. A solid AB crystallises as NaCl structure and the radius of the cation is 0.100 nm. The maximum radius of the anion can be:
    (a) 0.137 nm   (b) 0.241 nm
    (c) 0.274 nm   (d) 0.482 nm

23. In which of the following crystals alternate tetrahedral voids are occupied?
    (a) NaCl   (b) ZnS   (c) CaF_2 (d) Na_2O

24. In a solid 'AB' having the NaCl structure, 'A' atoms occupy the corners of the cubic unit cell. If all the face-centered atoms along one of the axes are removed, then the resultant stoichiometry of the solid is
(a) AB_2 (b) A_2B (c) A_4B_3 (d) A_3B_4

25. For orthorhombic system axial ratios are a ≠ b ≠ c and the axial angles are
(a) $\alpha = \beta = \gamma \neq 90°$ (b) $\alpha = \beta = \gamma = 90°$
(c) $\alpha = \beta = \gamma = 90°, \beta = 90°$ (d) $\alpha \neq \beta \neq \gamma = 90°$

26. In NaCl crystal each Cl^- ion is surrounded by
(a) $4\,Na^+$ ions   (b) $6\,Na^+$ ions
(c) $1\,Na^+$ ions   (d) $2\,Na^+$ ions

27. In face centred cubic arrangement of A and B atoms, whose A atoms are at the corners of the unit cell and B atoms at the face centres and A atoms are missing from two corners in each unit cell. What is the formula of the compound.
(a) AB_4 (b) AB_3 (c) A_2B (d) AB

28. In the unit cell of KCl (NaCl type), Cl^- ions constitute ccp and K^+ ions fall into the octahedral holes. These holes are:
(a) one at the centre and 6 at the centres of the faces
(b) one at the centre and 12 at the centres of the edges
(c) 8 at the centres of 8 small cubes forming the unit cell
(d) none of these

29. What would be the effective number of atoms per unit cell in end centered cubic unit cell, if this type of unit cell exist in nature?
(a) 1   (b) 2   (c) 3   (d) 4

30. The maximum proportion of available volume that can be filled by hard spheres in diamond is
(a) 0.52   (b) 0.34   (c) 0.32   (d) 0.68

31. The edge length of a face centered cubic cell of an ionic substance is 508 pm. If the radius of the cation is 110 pm, the radius of the anion is
(a) 288 pm   (b) 398 pm   (c) 618 pm   (d) 144 pm

32. An element (atomic mass = 100 g / mol) having bcc structure has unit cell edge 400 pm. Then, density of the element is
(a) $10.376\,g/cm^3$ (b) $5.188\,g/cm^3$
(c) $7.289\,g/cm^3$ (d) $2.144\,g/cm^{36}$

33. An element having an atomic radius of 0.14 nm crystallizes in an fcc unit cell. What is the length of a side of the cell ?
(a) 0.56 nm   (b) 0.24 nm
(c) 0.96 nm   (d) 0.4 nm

34. A solid has a 'bcc' structure. If the distance of nearest approach between two atoms is 1.73Å, the edge length of the cell is
(a) 314.20 pm   (b) 1.41 pm
(c) 200 pm   (d) 216 pm

35. Total volume of atoms present in a face-centred cubic unit cell of a metal is (r is atomic radius)
(a) $\dfrac{12}{3}\pi r^3$ (b) $\dfrac{16}{3}\pi r^3$
(c) $\dfrac{20}{3}\pi r^3$ (d) $\dfrac{24}{3}\pi r^3$

36. Potassium fluoride has NaCl type structure. What is the distance between K^+ and F^- ions if cell edge is 'a' cm.
(a) 2a cm   (b) a/2 cm
(c) 4a cm   (d) a/4 cm

37. The number of atoms in 100 g of an fcc crystal with density, $d = 10\,g/cm^3$ and cell edge equal to 100 pm, is equal to
(a) 1×10^{25} (b) 2×10^{25}
(c) 3×10^{25} (d) 4×10^{25}

38. The radii of Na^+ and Cl^- ions are 95 pm and 181 pm respectively. The edge length of NaCl unit cell is
(a) 276 pm   (b) 138 pm
(c) 552 pm   (d) 415 pm

39. Which of the following statements for crystals having Schottky defect is not correct?
(a) Schottky defect arises due to the absence of a cation and anion from the position which it is expected to occupy
(b) Schottky defect are more common in ionic compounds with high co-ordination numbers
(c) The density of the crystals having Schottky defect is larger than that of the perfect crystal
(d) The crystal having Schottky defect is electrically neutral as a whole

40. Which of the following defects does KBr show?
(a) Frenkel
(b) Schottky
(c) Metal excess
(d) Metal deficiency

41. Dopping of AgCl crystals with $CdCl_2$ results in:
(a) Schottky defect
(b) Frenkel defect
(c) Substitutional cation vacancy
(d) Formation of F-centres

42. Due to Frenkel defect, the density of the ionic solids
(a) Increases   (b) Decreases
(c) Does not change   (d) Changes

43. Which of the following is true about the value of refractive index of quartz glass?
(a) Same in all directions
(b) Different in different directions
(c) Cannot be measured
(d) Always zero

44. Iodine molecules are held in the crystals lattice by......... .
(a) London forces
(b) dipole – dipole interactions
(c) covalent bonds
(d) coulombic forces

45. Which of the following is not the characteristic of ionic solids?
(a) Very low value of electrical conductivity in the molten state
(b) Brittle nature
(c) Very strong forces of interactions
(d) Anisotropic nature

Chapter Test

Time : 30 min.   **Max. Marks : 15**

Direction :

- Questions number **1-15** carry **1 mark** each.

1. In *hcp* of A, $\frac{1}{3}$ of tetrahedral voids are occupied by B. What is the formula for compound:
   (a) A_2B_3 (b) A_3B_2 (c) AB_3 (d) A_2B

2. Which colour is observed when ZnO is heated?
   (a) Yellow   (b) Violet   (c) Green   (d) Blue

3. Gold has a face centred cubic lattice with an edge length of the unit cube of 407 pm. Assuming the closest packing, the diameter of the gold atom is
   (a) 576.6 pm   (b) 287.8 pm
   (c) 352.5 pm   (d) 704.9 pm

4. Which of the following is ferroelectric compound?
   (a) $BaTlO_3$ (b) $K_4[Fe(CN)_6]$
   (c) Pb_2O_3 (d) None of these

DIRECTIONS (Qs. 5-7) : *Each of these questions contains an assertion followed by reason. Read them carefully and answer the question on the basis of following options. You have to select the one that best describes the two statements.*

(a) If both Assertion and Reason are correct and the Reason is a correct explanation of the Assertion.

(b) If both Assertion and Reason are correct but Reason is not a correct explanation of the Assertion.

(c) If the Assertion is correct but Reason is incorrect.

(d) If the Assertion is incorrect but the Reason is correct.

5. **Assertion:** Coordination number of Zn in ZnS structure is 8.
   Reason: Coordination number is the number of nearest neighbour in a particle.

6. **Assertion :** Metal deficiency defect can be seen in FeO.
   Reason : Li compound (LiCl) have violet colour due to F-center.

7. **Assertion :** Vacancy defect results in decrease in density of the substance.
   Reason : Vacancy defect developed when a substance is heated.

Case/Passage Based Questions

DIRECTIONS (Qs. 8-11) : *Following are the case/passage based questions.*

Point defects explain about the imperfections of solids. Point defects are accounted when the crystallization process occurs at a very fast rate. These defects mainly happen due to deviation in the arrangement of constituting particles. The defects are of two types namely point defects and line defects.

Point defects can be further classified into types:
(i) Stoichiometric defect
(ii) Frenkel defect
(iii) Schottky defect

8. Schottky defect in crystals is observed when
   (a) an ion leaves its normal site and occupies an interstitial site
   (b) unequal number of cations and anions are missing from the lattice
   (c) density of the crystal increases
   (d) equal number of cations and anions are missing from the lattice

9. Which defect causes decrease in the density of crystal
   (a) Frenkel   (b) Schottky
   (c) Interstitia   (d) F – centre

OR

Frenkel and Schottky defects are :
(a) nucleus defects   (b) non-crystal defects
(c) crystal defects   (d) nuclear defects

DIRECTIONS (Qs. 10-11) : *Each of these questions contains an assertion followed by reason. Read them carefully and answer the question on the basis of following options. You have to select the one that best describes the two statements.*

(a) If both Assertion and Reason are correct and the Reason is a correct explanation of the Assertion.

(b) If both Assertion and Reason are correct but Reason is not a correct explanation of the Assertion.

(c) If the Assertion is correct but Reason is incorrect.

(d) If the Assertion is incorrect but the Reason is correct.

10. **Assertion :** Frenkel defect is found in ZnS.
    Reason : There is large difference in the size of Zn^{2+} and S^{2-} ions.

11. **Assertion :** Density of crystalline solid does not changes due to Frenkel defect.
    Reason : Equal number of cations and anions are absent from their lattice points in Frenkel defect.

Very Short Answer Questions

12. Doping of AgCl crystals with $CdCl_2$ results into which defect?

13. How many spheres are there in an *hcp* structure

14. AgI crystallises in cubic close packed ZnS structure. What fraction of tetrahedral sites are occupied by Ag^+ ions?

15. Define coordination number of a sphere in its own layer in *hcp*.

Solutions

Practice Exercise-1

1. **(a)** Schottky defect is found in ionic solids.

2. **(b)** As, $a = b \neq c$, $\alpha = \beta = 90°$ and $\gamma = 120°$ the given crystal system of a compound is a hexagonal system.

3. **(d)** In graphite, the carbon atoms are arranged in regular hexagons in flat parallel layers.

4. **(b)**   5. **(a)**

6. **(a)** In crystalline solid, there is perfect arrangement of the constituent particles only at 0 K. As the temperature increases the chance that a lattice site may be unoccupied by an ion increases. As the number of defects increases with temperature, solid changes into liquid.

7. **(c)** Glass is amorphous solid.

8. **(a)** Graphite is an example of hexagonal crystal system for which $\alpha = \beta = 90°$, $\gamma = 120°$ and $a = b \neq c$.

9. **(a)** The melting point of a solid depends on the strength of the interparticle attractive force acting between the constituent particles. Hence, the stability of a crystal gets reflected in its melting point and depends upon the strength of the interparticle attractive force.

10. **(d)** Crystalline solids are anisotropic in nature. Anisotropes have different physical properties when measured along different directions in the same crystals due to different arrangement of particles in different directions. Crystalline solids are long range order solid.

11. **(c)** Quartz glass is an example of amorphous solid and crystalline solids are anisotropic in nature.

12. **(b)** Crystalline solids are anisotropic in nature that is some of their physical properties like electrical resistance or refractive index show different values when measured along different directions in the same crystals.

13. **(b)** Amorphous solids are isotropic, because these substances show same properties in all directions.

14. **(a)** Inner layer of some solids can have fluidity, for example glass.

15. **(a)** Crystalline solids have different arrangement of particles along different axis.

16. Four.

17. Ionic solids of type AB may have generally any one of following types of crystalline structures:
    (a) Zinc sulphide type structure (ZnS type structure).
    (b) NaCl type structure (rock salt structure).
    (c) CsCl type structure.

18. NaCl structure (coordination number = 6 : 6) changes into CsCl structure (coordination number = 8 : 8) by applying high pressure. Similarly, CsCl structure changes to NaCl structure by heating to 760 K.

$$\text{NaCl structure} \underset{\text{Heat to 760K}}{\overset{\text{High Pressure}}{\rightleftharpoons}} \text{CsCl structure}$$
$$\text{(CN 6 : 6)} \qquad\qquad\qquad \text{(CN 8 : 8)}$$

19. In Na_2O structure (also called anti-fluorite structure), O^{2-} ions from ccp structure and Na^+ ions occupy all tetrahedral voids.

20. Glass, rubber and plastics.

21. Body centred cubic is an arrangement in which in addition to the particles at the corners, there is one particle present within the body of the unit cell.

22. AB.

23. Simple cubic (or primitive).

24. In amorphous silica, SiO_4 tetrahedra are randomly joined to each other. In quartz, SiO_4 tetrahedra are linked in a regular manner and thus, quartz is crystalline solid. Amorphous silica is obtained when molten silica is cooled rapidly and it lacks the long range order of repeating SiO_4 tetrahedra.
    Quartz has high degree of crystallinity in its structure.

25. In a cubic unit cell, there are eight corners and each corner atom contributes $\frac{1}{8}$th atom to unit cell. Similarly, there are four body diagonals and atoms on cross diagonal are entirely contributed to the unit cell.
    ∴ Total number of atoms in the unit cell
    $$= \left(8 \times \frac{1}{8}\right) + (4 \times 2) = 9 \text{ atoms}.$$

26. The atom A is present only on seven corners out of eight in each face-centred cubic unit cell.
    ∴ No. of atoms at corners per unit cell $= 7 \times \dfrac{1}{8} = \dfrac{7}{8}$ atoms of A.
    There are six faces so six face centres.
    Number of atoms of B at six face centres
    $$= 6 \times \frac{1}{2} = 3 \text{ atoms of B}.$$
    ∴ The compound has formula $A_{7/8}B_3$, i.e., A_7B_{24}.

27. (a) Crystals in which lattice points are occupied by molecules are known as molecular crystals.
    (b) Ice (solid form of H_2O) is an example of hydrogen bonded crystal.
    (c) Crystal of sodium metal (melting point 98 °C).

28. **Amorphous solids:** Polyurethane, teflon, cellophane, polyvinyl chloride, fibre glass.
    Crystalline solids: Benzoic acid, potassium nitrate, copper.

29. (i) Like liquids, amorphous solids are isotropic.
    (ii) Like liquids, they possess fluidity.

Practice Exercise-2

1. **(c)** Density $d = \dfrac{ZM}{a^3 N_A}$;
    where $a = 400$ pm $= 400 \times 10^{-10}$ cm
    $$= \frac{2 \times 100}{(400 \times 10^{-10})^3 \times 6.023 \times 10^{23}} = 5.188 \text{ g/cc}$$

2. **(b)** In Na_2O there is an antifluorite structure in which negative ions form the *ccp* arrangement so that each positive ion is surrounded by 4 negative ions and each negative ion is surrounded by 8 positive ions.

∴ coordination no. of Na^+ is 4.

3. **(b)** In a cubic closed packed system (*ccp*) ....ABC ABC....... type of arrangement of layers is found. In this system, there are atoms at the corners as well as centre of the unit cell.

∴ No. of atoms per unit cell $= 8 \times \dfrac{1}{8} + 1 = 2$.

Hence, the number of tetrahedral voids in the unit cell $= 2z$.

4. **(a)** Four atoms of Ca^{2+} and eight atoms of F^- are in the unit cell. Each F^- atom occupies 8 tetrahedral voids.

5. **(b)** In *hcp* type structure, each atom is surrounded by 12 nearest touching neighbours. Hence, coordination number in *hcp* is 12.

6. **(a)** Wurtzite has *fcc* structure in which each Zn^{2+} ion is attached to four S^{2-} ions and each S^{2-} ion remains in contact with four Zn^{2+} ions. Hence, coordination number of each ion (Zn^{2+} and S^{2-}) is 4.

7. **(b)** For each central atom there are two tetrahedral voids in AgI crystal. The number of Ag^+ ion is equal to number of I^- ion. It means only 50% of the void will be occupied by Ag^+ ion.

8. **(c)** In *bcc* the atoms touch along body diagonal

∴ $2r + 2r = \sqrt{3}a$

∴ $r = \dfrac{\sqrt{3}a}{4} = \dfrac{\sqrt{3} \times 4.29}{4} = 1.857 Å$

9. **(d)** Few ionic solids e.g., AgBr have both Schottky and Frenkel defects.

Only Schottky defects change the density of solids because anions or cations are missing, whereas Frenkel defects do not exhibit any change in density because overall the number of cations and anions are same, there is only a change in position of ions.

10. **(a)** In Frenkel defect an ion (cation or anion) only changes its position in the lattice and occupies vacant interstitial position and thus involves no effect on the density of the solid.

11. **(c)** In close packing spheres, a tetrahedral void is surrounded by four spheres *tetrahedrally* while octahedral void is surrounded by six spheres *octahedrally*.

12. Defects caused by missing or misplaced ions or atoms in the crystal lattice are known as point defects in the crystal.

13. Six.

14. (*a*) Due to flow of electrons.
(*b*) Due to flow of ions in solution or melt and defect in the solid state.
(*c*) Due to presence of impurities and defect in the crystal.

15. This is due to the presence of electrons in some lattice sites in place of anions. These sites act as F-centres.

16. $CdCl_2$, because each divalent Cd^{2+} ion will displace two Ag^+ from their sites and occupy only one site, thereby creating a cationic vacancy.

17. Sodium oxide (Na_2O). It has anti-fluorite structure.

18. Asymmetric crystals.

19. It occurs when there is vacancy of cation and anion sites in the lattice structure.

20. It occurs in an ionic crystal when an ion occupies an interstial position rather than normal site.

21. Six.

22. A stress applied to piezoelectric crystal will change the state of polarisation of dipoles and a small electrical signal is thus produced.

23. Na_2O has anti-fluorite structure. Oxide ion forms ccp lattice and Na^+ occupy all tetrahedral voids. Na^+ has coordination number four whereas O^{2-} has coordination number eight.

24. It is due to large differences in size of Ag^+ and Cl^-. Due to small size, Ag^+ can easily fit in a interstitial site.

25. Stoichiometric defects are those defects in which the ratio of cations to anions remains the same as represented by the molecular formula.

26. Rhenium oxide (ReO_3).

27. (*a*) Structure of NaCl is *fcc* and coordination numbers of Na^+ and Cl^- in its unit cell are 6 and 6 respectively. Therefore, coordination numbers of Mg^{2+} and O^{2-} ions in MgO are also 6 and 6 respectively.
(*b*) Structure of CsCl is *bcc* and coordination numbers of Cs^+ and Cl^- in its unit cell are 8 and 8 respectively. Therefore, coordination numbers of Tl^+ and Cl^- in TlCl are 8 and 8 respectively.

28. Glass panes fixed to windows or doors of old buildings are found to become thicker at the bottom because the glass flows down very slowly and makes the bottom portion thicker.

29. Two reasons of crystal defects are
(i) Improper growth of crystals at fast or moderate rate,
(ii) Presence of impurities.

30. The coordination number of a sphere in closed packed structure is the number of spheres with which it is in direct contact. The coordination number of each sphere on
(*a*) Simple cubic lattice is 6,
(*b*) *bcc* lattice is 8,
(*c*) *fcc* lattice is 12, and
(*d*) *hcp* lattice is 12.

31. In *fcc* structure, atoms touch each other along the face diagonal. If '*a*' is the edge of a unit cell and '*r*' is the radius of atom then

face diagonal, $a\sqrt{2} = 4r$

$a = 2\sqrt{2}r = 2 \times 1.414 \times 100 = 282.8\,pm.$

32. In *bcc* structure of a metallic element, atoms touch each other along the cross diagonal of cubic unit cell. If '*a*' is the edge length then length of cross diagonal is $a\sqrt{3}$.

∴ $a\sqrt{3} = 4r$

$a = \dfrac{4}{\sqrt{3}}r = \dfrac{4}{1.732} \times 250 \Rightarrow a = 577.37\,pm.$

33. (*a*) By radius ratio rule, $\dfrac{r_+}{r_-} = 0.732$ for a cubic hole.

∴ Radius of cation, $r_+ = 0.732 \times r_-$
$= 0.732 \times 100 = 73.2\,pm.$

(b) For octahedral hole,

$$\frac{r_+}{r_-} = 0.414 \Rightarrow r_+ = 0.414 \times 100 = 41.4\,pm.$$

(c) For tetrahedral hole, $\dfrac{r_+}{r_-} = 0.225\,r_+$

$$= 0.225 \times 100 = 22.5\,pm.$$

34. Radius ratio, $\dfrac{r_+}{r_-} = \dfrac{95}{181} = 0.525$.

As radius ratio lies between 0.414 and 0.732, it indicates that AX has NaCl type *fcc* structure. The coordination number of each ion is six.

35. For NaCl type structure, radius ratio, $\dfrac{r_+}{r_-} = 0 \cdot 414$

or $r_+ = 0.414\,r_-$

∴   The minimum radius of cation,

$r_+ = 0 \cdot 414 \times 241 \cdot 5\,pm = 99 \cdot 98\,pm.$

For the cation to be fitted into tetrahedral void, the minimum radius of cation is $0 \cdot 225 \times 241 \cdot 5 = 54 \cdot 34\,pm.$

As the cation C^+ (of radius 50 pm) is smaller than the minimum radius of cation, it can be slipped into tetrahedral void of the crystal.

36. For fcc lattice structure, $Z = 4$, $d = 8 \cdot 930\,g\,cm^{-3}$

$M = 63 \cdot 55, N_A = 6 \cdot 02 \times 10^{23}$

Let the edge length be 'a'.

Density, $d = \dfrac{ZM}{a^3 N_A}$ ∴ $a^3 = \dfrac{ZM}{d\,N_A}$

$$a^3 = \frac{4 \times 63 \cdot 55}{8.93 \times 6.02 \times 10^{23}} = 47.22 \times 10^{-24}$$

∴ $a = 3 \cdot 61 \times 10^{-8}\,cm = 361\,pm.$

For a fcc element, face diagonal, $a\sqrt{2} = 4r$

∴ Radius of copper atom $= \dfrac{a\sqrt{2}}{4} = \dfrac{a}{2\sqrt{2}} = \dfrac{361}{2 \times 1 \cdot 414} = 128\,pm.$

Past year Exercise

1. FeO has non-stoichiometric composition with formula $Fe_{0.95}O$. This is due to metal deficiency defect.

OR

This is because some Fe^{2+} ions are missing and in order to balance the charge of the lattice, the sites are filled by required number of Fe^{3+} ions.

2. Frenkel defect is due to dislocation of ion from its usual site to interstitial position. Density remains the same.

3. Metallic solids consist of positively charged kernels and valence electrons. Thus due to presence of valence electrons metallic solids are good conductors of electricity. Metallic solids are also malleable and ductile.

4. The molecules of a polar solid are held together by dipole-dipole interactions.

5. AgCl shows Frenkel defect.

6. Crystalline solids are anisotropic in nature. This means that some of their physical properties like resistance or refractive index show different values when measured along different directions.

7. Conductivity of metals is due to free electrons while that of ionic substances is due to ions which move in solution.

8. Frenkel defect.

9. Number of atoms in face centred cubic unit cell

$$= 8\,(\text{at corners}) \times \frac{1}{8} + 6\,(\text{at centres}) \times \frac{1}{2} = 1 + 3 = 4$$

10. For *fcc* edge length

$$a = 2\sqrt{2}r = 2 \times 1.414 \times 125 = 353.5\,pm$$

11. $d = \dfrac{ZM}{a^3\,N_A}$

Z = No. of lattice points per unit cell

M = Molar mass of metal

a^3 = Volume of the unit cell

N_A = Avagadro constant

For *bcc*   Z = 2

         M = 52

         a = 300 pm $= 300 \times 10^{-10}\,cm$

         N_A = 6.022×10^{23}

$$d = \frac{2 \times 52}{(300 \times 10^{-10})^3 \times 6.022 \times 10^{23}} = \frac{104}{16.259}$$

$$d = 6.396\,g\,cm^{-3}$$

12. Given : *fcc* structure, $Z = 4$

edge length, $a = 400\,pm = 400 \times 10^{-8}\,cm$

$N_A = 6.022 \times 10^{23}\,mol^{-1}$

$M = 40g\,mol^{-1}$

To find : density, $d = ?$

number of unit cells $= ?$

Solution: $d = \dfrac{Z.M}{a^3 N_A} = \dfrac{4 \times 40}{(400 \times 10^{-8})^3 \times 6.022 \times 10^{23}}$

$d = 4.15g\,cm^{-3}$

number of unit cells in 4g of element

$$= \frac{\dfrac{4}{40} \times 6.022 \times 10^{23}}{4} = 1.5055 \times 10^{22}$$

13. Number of Al atoms present in 27 g (1 mol) of Al

$= 6.023 \times 10^{23}$

Number of Al atoms present in 8.1 g (1 mol) of Al

$$= \frac{6.023 \times 10^{23}}{27} \times 8.1$$

Since, aluminium crystallizes in a face-centred cubic (f.c.c.) structure the number of atoms per unit cell is 4

Number of unit cells in 8.1 g of aluminimum

$$= \frac{1}{4} \times \frac{6.023 \times 10^{23}}{27} \times 8.1 = 4.5 \times 10^{22}$$

Hence, the number of unit cells in 8.1 g of aluminium if it crystallizes in a face-centred cubic (*f.c.c.*) structure is 4.5×10^{22}.

14. According to question

$d = 8.95\,g\,cm^{-3} = 8.95 \times 10^6\,g\,m^{-3}$

$r = 127.8\,pm = 127.8 \times 10^{-12}\,m$

$M = 63.54\,g\,mol^{-1}$

$N_A = 6.02 \times 10^{23}\,mol^{-1}$

by assuming that Cu crystallises in fcc unit cell

Edge length, $a = \dfrac{4r}{\sqrt{2}} \left(r = \dfrac{\sqrt{2} \cdot a}{4} \right) = \dfrac{4 \times 127.8 \times 10^{-12}}{\sqrt{2}}\,m$

$$a^3 = \left(\frac{4 \times 127.8 \times 10^{-12}}{\sqrt{2}} m\right)^3 = 4.725 \times 10^{-29} \, m^3$$

Rank of a unit cell

$$Z = \frac{d \cdot a^3 \cdot N_A}{M} = \frac{8.95 \times 10^6 \times 4.725 \times 10^{-29} \times 6.02 \times 10^{23}}{63.54}$$
$$= 4.006 \approx 4$$

Hence, copper unit cell is a face centred cubic structure.

15. (i) Schottky defect arises when some ions are missing from their normal sites thereby decreasing density of the substance while in Frenkel defect ions do not leave the lattice but occupy positions else where in the crystal lattice thus density of the substance remains the same.
(ii) Electrical conductivity of the crystal is increased in both Schottky and Frenkel defects.

16. For bcc, $r = \dfrac{\sqrt{3}a}{4}$

Given, edge length, $a = 287 \times 10^{-12}\,m$

$$r = \frac{\sqrt{3} \times 287}{4} \times 10^{-12}\,m = \frac{1.73 \times 287 \times 10^{-12}\,m}{4}$$

$$r = 124.12 \times 10^{-12}\,m$$

17. For *fcc*, $Z = 4$
$$M = 78.08 \text{ g mol}^{-1}$$
$$a = 5.46 \times 10^{-8} \text{ cm}$$
$$d = 3.18 \text{ g cm}^{-3}$$

Using formula, $d = \dfrac{Z.M}{a_3.N_A}$

$$\Rightarrow N_A = \frac{Z.M}{a^3.d} = \frac{4 \times 78.08}{(5.46 \times 10^{-8})^3 \times 3.18} = 6.022 \times 10^{23}$$

18. For face centred unit cell atoms are present at all the corners and at the centre of all the faces of the cube.
Gold atoms occupy all the corners of a unit cell. Contribution made by the atoms of gold present at all the eight corners of the cube.

$$= 8 \times \frac{1}{8} = 1$$

Contribution made by the atoms of cadmium present at the centre of all the six faces of the cube.

$$= 6 \times \frac{1}{2} = 6 \times \frac{1}{2} = 3$$

Formula for the given alloy $= AuCd_3$

19. Refer NCERT Question 10(i)
20. According to question
Edge length $a = 400 \times 10^{-12}\,m$
For fcc

$$r = \frac{\sqrt{2}a}{4} = \frac{1.414 \times 400 \times 10^{-12}\,m}{4} = 141.4 \times 10^{-12}\,m$$

21. Refer theory.
22. Density of a crystal can be given as

$$\rho = \frac{ZM}{a^3.N_A}$$

$$M = \frac{\rho.a^3.N_A}{Z}$$

where ρ, is the density in g cm^{-3}, Z is number of atoms in a unit cell, a^3 is the volume of a unit cell, N_A is Avogadro's number and M is molar atomic mass.

23. Edge length, $a = 409$ pm

Radius of *fcc* unit cell, $r = \dfrac{a}{2\sqrt{2}} = 0.3535\,a$

$$r = 0.3535 \times 409 = 144.58 \text{ pm}$$

24. Refer NCERT Question 20.
25. Given, $r = 127.8$ pm $= 127.8 \times 10^{-12}\,m$
$M = 63.55$ g mol^{-1}
$N_A = 6.02 \times 10^{23}$ mol^{-1}
For fcc,

$$a = \frac{4r}{\sqrt{2}} = \frac{4 \times 127.8 \times 10^{-12}}{1.414}\,m$$

$$a^3 = \left(\frac{4 \times 127.8 \times 10^{-12}}{1.414}\right)^3 = 4.725 \times 10^{-29}\,m^3$$

Density of a unit cell,

$$d = \frac{ZM}{a^3 N_A} = \frac{4 \times 63.55}{4.725 \times 10^{-29} \times 6.02 \times 10^{23}} = 8.936 \times 10^6 \text{ g cm}^{-3}$$

26. For *fcc*, $r = \dfrac{\sqrt{3}}{4} a = \dfrac{1.732 \times 316.5}{4} = 137.04$ pm

27. For *bcc*, $Z = 2$

Using the formula, $d = \dfrac{Z.M}{a^3.N_A} \Rightarrow N_A = \dfrac{Z.M}{a^3.d}$

$$\Rightarrow N_A = \frac{2 \times 56}{(286.65 \times 10^{-10})^3 \times 7.87} = \frac{112}{23.63 \times 7.87 \times 10^{-24}}$$
$$= 0.6022 \times 10^{24} \Rightarrow N_A = 6.022 \times 10^{23}$$

28. Refer theory.
29. Let the number of atoms of element Y present in *ccp* $= x$
Therefore, the number of tetrahedral voids $= 2x$
As 1/3rd of tetrahedral voids are occupied by atoms of element X, therefore, number of atoms of X present

$$= \frac{1}{3} \times 2x = \frac{2x}{3}.$$

$\therefore$ Ratio of Y : X $= x : \dfrac{2x}{3} = 3x : 2x = 3 : 2$

$\therefore$ The formula of the compound will be $= Y_3 X_2$ or $X_2 Y_3$.

30. (a) When crystals of LiCl is heated in presence of excess of lithium, Cl$^-$ ions from crystal diffuse on surface and combine with ionised Li to form LiCl. The released unpaired electrons occupy the anionic sites known as F-centres. The pink colour results by excitation of these electrons when they absorb energy from visible light falling on them.
(b) Given Q are present at the corner of the cube

$\therefore$ No. of atoms of Q in one unit cell $= 8 \times \dfrac{1}{8} = 1$

(at corners)
Also given that atoms of P are present at the body centre
$\therefore$ No. of atoms of P in one unit cell = 1 (at body centre)
i.e., P : Q = 1 : 1
$\therefore$ formula of the compound = PQ.

31. No. of atoms in the close packing = 0.5 mol
$$= 0.5 \times 6.022 \times 10^{23} = 3.011 \times 10^{23}$$
No. of octahedral voids = No. of atoms in the close packing
$\therefore$ No. of octahedral voids = 3.011×10^{23}
and, No. of tetrahedral voids = 2 × No. of octahedral voids
No. of tetrahedral voids
$$= 2 \times 3.011 \times 10^{23} = 6.022 \times 10^{23}$$
Total no. of voids = $6.022 \times 10^{23} + 3.011 \times 10^{23}$
$$= 9.033 \times 10^{23}$$

32. For cubic crystals,
$$\rho = \frac{Z \times M}{a^3 \times N_0} \implies M = \frac{\rho \times a^3 \times N_0}{Z}$$
For *bcc* structure Z = 2
On substituting these values,
$$M = \frac{8 \times (2.5 \times 10^{-4})^3 \times 6.022 \times 10^{23}}{2} = 37.6 \text{ g mol}^{-1}$$
For *bcc* structure, $a = \dfrac{4r}{\sqrt{3}}$
$$\therefore r = \frac{\sqrt{3}a}{4} = \frac{\sqrt{3} \times 250}{4} = \frac{1.732 \times 250}{4} = 108.25 \text{ pm}$$

33. $d = \dfrac{Z.M}{N_A . a^3}$
$$2.8 \text{ g cm}^{-3} = \frac{4 \times M}{6.022 \times 10^{23} \text{ mol}^{-1} \times (4 \times 10^{-8} \text{ cm})^3}$$
$$M = \frac{2.8 \text{ g cm}^{-3} \times 6.022 \times 10^{23} \text{ mol}^{-1} \times 64 \times 10^{-24} \text{ cm}^3}{4}$$
$M = 269.785 \times 10^{-1} = 26.97 \text{ gmol}^{-1}$
$\therefore$ molar mass = 26.97 g mol^{-1}

34. (i) Metal excess defect caused by anionic vacancies is responsible for pink colour of LiCl.
(ii) Schottky defect is the stoichiometric defect shown by NaCl.

OR

(i)

	Tetrahedral Voids	Octahedral Voids
1	It is a simple triangular void surrounded by four spheres.	It is a double triangular void surrounded by six spheres.

(ii)

	Crystal lattice		Unit cell
1	It is a regular arrangement of space lattice which when repeated over and again in different directions produces the space lattice.	1	It is the smallest 3D portion of a complete constituent particles in a 3D space.

35. We know, $d = \dfrac{ZM}{a^3 N_A}$
$$\implies M = \frac{d.a^3.N_A}{Z}$$

$$\implies M = \frac{11.2 \text{g cm}^{-3} \times (4 \times 10^{-8} \text{ cm})^3 \times 6.022 \times 10^{23} \text{ mol}}{4}$$
$\implies M = 1079.14 \times 10^{-24} \times 10^{23} \text{ g} = 107.9 \text{ g} \simeq 108 \text{ g}$

36. (i) The given crystal shows schottky defect.
(ii) The density of the crystal decreases.
(iii) Schottky defect is shown by ionic substances in which the cation and anion are of almost similar sizes for ex : NaCl, KCl, AgBr.

37. Refer theory.

38. Given : $a = 500 \text{ pm} = 500 \times 10^{-10} \text{ cm}$; $z = 2$; $m = 300 \text{ g}$
$$m = \frac{M}{N_A} \text{ (M is molar mass.)}$$
Density, $d = \dfrac{2 \times M}{a^3 N_A}$
$$7.5 = \frac{2 \times M}{(500)^3 \times 10^{-30} \times 6.02 \times 10^{23}}$$
$$M = \frac{7.5 \times (500)^3 \times 10^{-30} \times 6.02 \times 10^{23}}{2} = 282.1 \text{g / mol}$$
Molar mass, $M = \dfrac{\text{Mass of compound} \times N_A}{\text{Number of atoms}}$
$$282.1 = \frac{300 \times 6.02 \times 10^{23}}{\text{Number of atoms}}$$
Number of atoms = 6.4×10^{23}
Therefore, the number of atoms present in 300g of compound is 6.4×10^{23}.

NCERT Exemplar 

1. **(b)** At low temperature existence of a substance in solid state is due to
(a) slow molecular motion and
(b) strong cohesive forces
These two forces hold the constituent particles together thus causes existence of substance in solid state.

2. **(d)** Graphite can't be classified as ionic solid as graphite is not made up of ions. It is a covalent solid.

3. **(c)** Diamond is a giant molecule in which constituent atoms are held together by covalent bond. Hence, this is a network solid.

4. **(c)** Iodine is a non-polar molecular solid in which iodine molecules are held together by London force or dispersion force. This is soft and non-conductor of electricity.
Water is a hydrogen bonded molecular solid in which H and O are held together by polar covalent bond and each water molecule held together by hydrogen bonding. Due to non-ionic nature, pure water is insulator.

5. **(d)** CrO_2, TiO and ReO_3 are some typical metal oxides which show electrical conductivity similar to metal. While SiO_2, MgO and SO_2 are oxides of semimetal, metal and non-metal which do not show electrical properties.

6. **(b)** Graphite have layered structure with free electrons due to which it is a good conductor of electricity. On the other hand, diamond have tetrahedral arrangement with no unpaired electron. Therefore, diamond is hard and brittle but insulator.

7. **(b)** Packing efficiency is maximum for *fcc* structure because it consists of total four atoms per unit cell. Packing efficiency is maximum in *fcc* structure which is equal to 74%.

8. **(c)** Semiconductors are solids with conductivities in the intermediate range value from $10^{-6} - 10^{4}\ \Omega^{-1}m^{-1}$. Intermediate conductivity is due to small energy gap between valence band and conduction band.

9. Crystals have long range repeated pattern of arrangement of constitutent particles but in the process of crystallisation some deviations from the ideal arrangement (i.e. defects) may be introduced, therefore, crystals are usually not perfect.

10. In the crystals of FeO, some of the Fe^{2+} cations are replaced by Fe^{3+} ions. Three Fe^{2+} ions are replaced by two Fe^{3+} ions to make up for the loss of positive charge. Eventually there would be less amount of metal as compared to stoichiometric proportion.

11. On heating ZnO loses oxygen according to the following reaction.

$$ZnO \xrightarrow{\ heating\ } Zn^{2+} + \frac{1}{2}O_2 + 2e^{-}$$

Zn^{2+} ions and electrons move to interstitial sites and F-centres are created which impart yellow colour to ZnO(s).

Objective Practice Exercise

1. **(d)** Crystals show good cleavage because their constituent particles are arranged in planes.

2. **(b)** Crystalline solids has a regular arrangement of constituent particles observed over a long distance in the crystal lattice due to which they exhibit sharp melting point.

3. **(a)** Si is an example of covalent crystalline solid among the given choices. Si atoms are covalently linked in tetrahedral manner.

4. **(d)** Ionic compounds are dissociated in solution state and form ions. Ions are good carrier of charge which make solution conducting.

5. **(b)** Out of the given substances, only Li has high electrical and thermal conductivity as Li is a metallic solid.

6. **(d)** Anisotropy arises due to the difference in kinds or densities or both of the atoms in different directions.

7. **(b)** No. of atoms (A) = 6 (h.c.p.);

no. of B atoms $= \dfrac{1}{3} \times 12 = 4$

A_6B_4 or A_3B_2

8. **(c)**

9. **(a)** Seven crystal systems.

10. **(b)** $Z = 12 \times \dfrac{1}{6} + 2 \times \dfrac{1}{2} + 3 = 6$

11. **(a)** $\dfrac{r_c}{r_a} = 0.732 \Rightarrow r_c = 0.732 \times 200 = 146.4\ pm$

12. **(a)** Due to presence of F-centre yellow colour is observed.

13. **(c)** Tetrahedral & octahedral holes are present in hcp and ccp.

14. **(c)** F.C.C. unit cell ABCABCABC packing efficiency is 74 %. So, void fraction will be 0.260.

15. **(b)** Triclinic-unsymmetrical
$\alpha \neq \beta \neq \gamma \neq 90^\circ, a \neq b \neq c$
Cubic-symmetrical
$\alpha = \beta = \gamma = 90^\circ, a = b = c$

16. **(a)** Packing efficiency of HCP & CCP is same.

17. **(c)** As per formula,
$$\text{radius ratio} = \frac{\text{radius of cation}}{\text{radius of anion}} = \frac{94}{146} = 0.643$$
Since the value is between $0.414 - 0.732$ hence the coordination no. will be 6 and geometry will be octahedral.

18. **(b)** No. of nearest neighbour = 8 (All body centre atom w.r.t. corner atom).
No. of next nearest neighbour = 6 (No. of corner atoms along edge w.r.t. to any corner).

19. **(c)** The coordination number is 8 : 8 for Cs^+ and Cl^-.

20. **(c)**

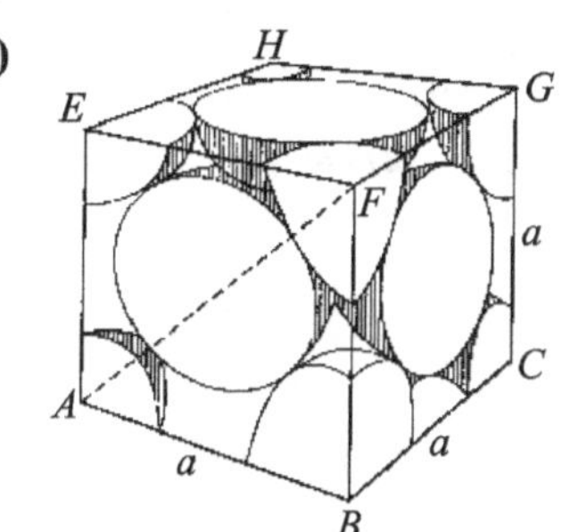

An isolated *fcc* cell is shown here. Each face of the cell is common to two adjacent cells. Therefore, each face centre atom contributes only half of its volume and mass to one cell. Arranging six cells each sharing the remaining half of the face centred atoms, constitutes fcc cubic lattice. e.g., Cu and Al.

21. **(b)** For tetrahedral shape radius ratio is $0.225 - 0.414$.

22. **(b)** Solid AB crystallizes as NaCl structure, so it has coordination number 6 and its r^+/r^- ranges from $0.414-0.732$. For maximum radius of anion, we have to take the lower limit of the range $0.414- 0.732$. So, $\dfrac{r^+}{r^-} = 0.414$

$\Rightarrow\ r^- = \dfrac{0.100}{0.414}\ nm = 0.241\ nm$

23. **(b)** In ZnS structure, sulphide ions occupy all *fcc* lattice points while Zn^{2+} ions are present in alternate tetrahedral voids.

24. **(d)** Effective number of 'A' atoms $= \left(8 \times \dfrac{1}{8}\right) + \left(4 \times \dfrac{1}{2}\right) = 3$

Effective number of 'B' atoms $= \left(12 \times \dfrac{1}{4}\right) + 1 = 4$

$\therefore$ Formula of the solid $= \mathbf{A_3B_4}$.

25. **(b)** For orthorhombic system, $\alpha = \beta = \gamma = 90^\circ$

26. **(b)** In NaCl crystal, each Cl^- ion is surrounded by 6 Na^+ ions. Similarly, each Na^+ is surrounded by 6 Cl^- ions.

27. **(a)** No. of Atoms per unit cell

$= 6(8 - 2 = 6)$ corners $\times \dfrac{1}{8}$ atom per unit cell $= \dfrac{6}{8} = \dfrac{3}{4}$

No. of atoms per unit cell = 6 faces $\times \dfrac{1}{2}$ atom per unit cell $= 3$

Hence, the formula of the compound $= A_{3/4}B_3$ or A_3B_{12} i.e., AB_4

28. **(b)** Octahedral sites in fcc are present at each edge centre as well as at body centre.

29. **(b)** Effective no. of atoms in end centred unit cell

$$= 8 \times \frac{1}{8} + 2 \times \frac{1}{2} = 2 \text{ atoms are present at corners as well as}$$

at end face's centre of unit cell.

30. **(b)** The volume to be filled by hard spheres in diamond is 0.34.

31. **(d)** For an Fcc crystal

$$r_{\text{cation}} + r_{\text{anion}} = \frac{\text{edge length}}{2}$$

$$110 + r_{\text{anion}} = \frac{508}{2} \Rightarrow r_{anion} = 254 - 110 = 144 \text{ pm}$$

32. **(b)** $\rho = \dfrac{Z \times M}{N_A \times a^3} = \dfrac{2 \times 100}{6.023 \times 10^{23} \times (400 \times 10^{-10})^3}$
$$= 5.188 \text{ g/cm}^3$$

33. **(d)** For a fcc unit cell

$$r = \frac{\sqrt{2}a}{4}$$

$$a = \frac{4r}{\sqrt{2}} = 2\sqrt{2} \times 0.14 = 0.39 \approx 0.4 \text{ nm}.$$

34. **(c)** For bcc structure

$$d = \frac{\sqrt{3}\, a}{2}$$

where d = distance between two atoms
a = edge length

$$1.73 = \frac{\sqrt{3}}{2} a$$

$$a = \frac{2 \times 1.73}{\sqrt{3}} = 2\text{Å} = 200\text{pm}$$

35. **(b)** The face centered cubic unit cell contains 4 atom

$$\therefore \text{ Total volume of atoms } = 4 \times \frac{4}{3}\pi r^3 = \frac{16}{3}\pi r^3$$

36. **(b)** Distance between K^+ and $F^- = \dfrac{1}{2} \times$ length of the edge

37. **(d)** $M = \dfrac{\rho \times a^3 \times N_A \times 10^{-30}}{Z}$

$$= \frac{10 \times (100)^3 \times 6.02 \times 10^{23} \times 10^{-30}}{4} = 15.05$$

$$\therefore \text{ Number of atoms in } 100\,\text{g} = \frac{6.02 \times 10^{23}}{15.05} \times 100 = 4 \times 10^{25}$$

38. **(c)** In a fcc lattice, the distance between the cation and anion is equal to the sum of their radii, which is equal to half of the edge length of unit cell,

i.e. $r^+ + r^- = \dfrac{a}{2}$ (where a = edge length)

$r^+ = 95$ pm, $r^- = 181$ pm
Edge length $= 2r^+ + 2r^- = (2 \times 95 + 2 \times 181)$ pm
$$= (190 + 362)\,\text{pm} = 552\,\text{pm}.$$

39. **(c)** Due to missing of ions. Density decreases in Schottky defect.

40. **(b)** Alkali metal halide shows schottky defect.

41. **(c)** Two Ag^+ ions will replaced by one Cd^{2+}, so there is one vacancy for each Cd^{2+}

42. **(c)** Due to Frenkel defects, density does not change.

43. **(a)** Since, quartz glass is an amorphous solid having short range order of constituents. Hence, value of refractive index is same in all directions, measurable and not to be equal to zero always.

44. **(a)** Iodine molecules belongs to a class of non – polar molecular solids in which constituents molecule are held together by London or dispersion forces.

45. **(a)** Ionic solids get easily dissociated into its ions in molten state and show high electrical conductivity.

Chapter Test

1. **(b)** No. of atoms (A) = 6 (hcp);

no. of B atoms $= \dfrac{1}{3} \times 12 = 4 \Rightarrow A_6B_4$ or A_3B_2

2. **(a)** Due to presence of F-centre yellow colour is observed.

3. **(b)** For a fcc lattice,

diagonal of the face $= a\sqrt{2} = 4r$;

$$r = \frac{a}{2\sqrt{2}} \Rightarrow 2r(\text{diameter}) = \frac{a\sqrt{2}}{2}$$

$$d = \frac{a\sqrt{2}}{2} = \frac{407 \times \sqrt{2}}{2} = 287.8 \text{ pm}$$

4. **(a)** $BaTlO_3$

5. **(d)** Coordination number of Zn in ZnS structure is 4.

6. **(b)** Both are true but reason is not the correct explanation.

7. **(b)** Since some of the lattice site are vacant, therefore it results into decrease in the density of the substance.

8. **(d)** If in an ionic crystal of the type $A^+ B^-$, equal number of cations and anions are missing from their lattice sites so that the electrical neutrality is maintained, the defect is called Schottky defect.

9. **(b)** More is the Schottky defect in crystal, more is the decrease in density of the crystal.

OR

(c) Frenkel and Schottky defects are crystal defects. It arises due to dislodgement of cation or anion from their places in the crystal lattice.

10. **(b)** Frenkel defect occurs in low coordination number compounds.

11. **(c)** Small size cations shift into the voids and density remains the same in Frenkel defect.

12. Substitutional cation vacancy.

13. In hcp structure total spheres $= \dfrac{1}{6} \times 12$ (corner) + 3

(between 2 layers) $+ \dfrac{1}{2} \times 2$ (at face centres) = 6

14. In AgI, the number of I^- ions and Ag^+ ions are equal. Let it be number n.
$\therefore$ No. of tetrahedral voids $= 2n$
Fraction of tetrahedral voids occupied by Ag^+ ions

$$= \frac{n}{2n} = \frac{1}{2} = 50\%$$

15. The coordination number of a constituent particle (atom, ion or molecule) in a crystal is the number of constituent particles which are the immediate neigbours of that particle in the crystal. In hcp, it is 6 in its own layer.

2 Solutions

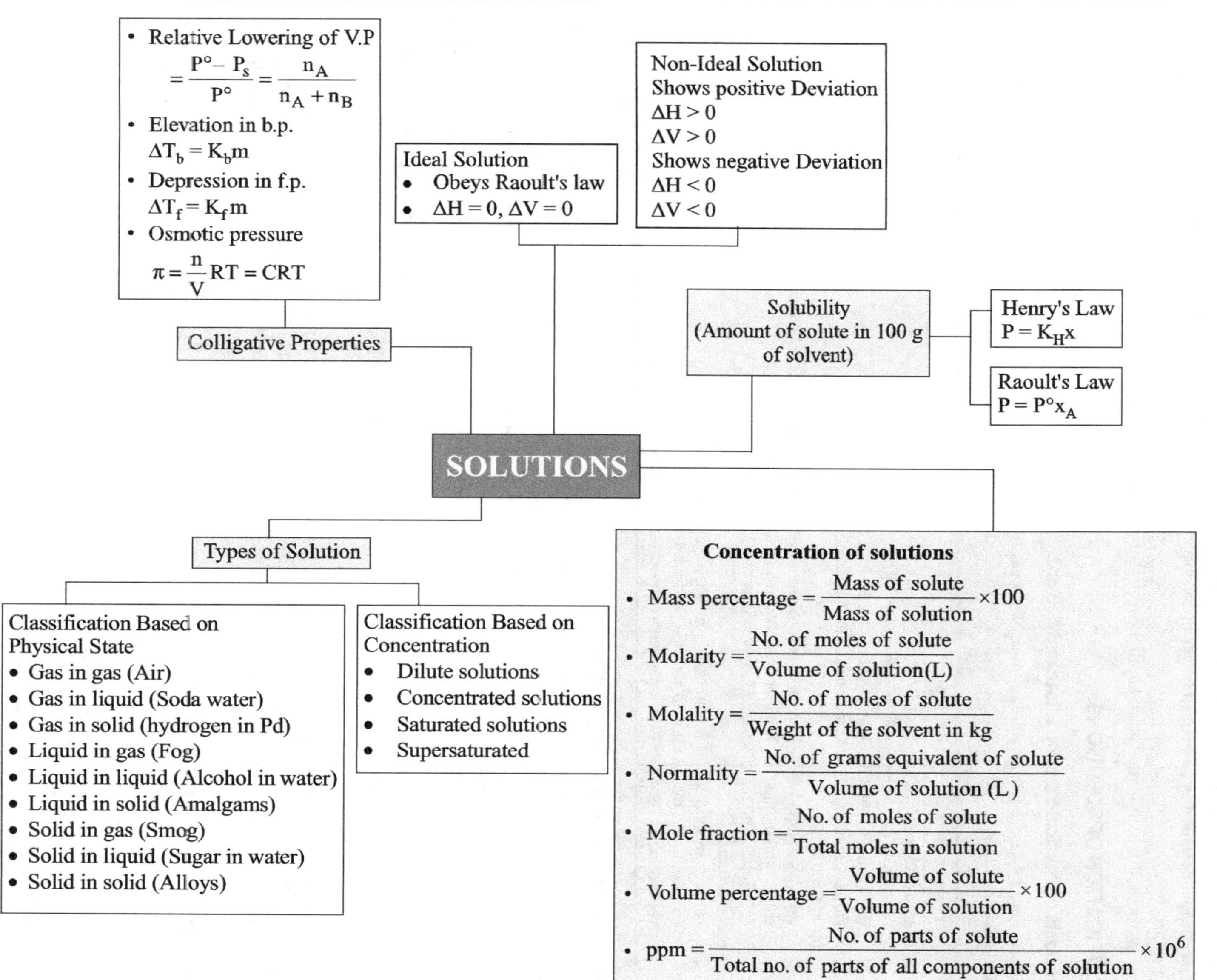

Relative Lowering of V.P
$$= \frac{P^\circ - P_s}{P^\circ} = \frac{n_A}{n_A + n_B}$$

Elevation in b.p. $\Delta T_b = K_b m$

Depression in f.p. $\Delta T_f = K_f m$

Osmotic pressure $\pi = \dfrac{n}{V} RT = CRT$

Ideal Solution: $\Delta H = 0, \Delta V = 0$

Non-Ideal Solution — Shows positive Deviation $\Delta H > 0$, $\Delta V > 0$; Shows negative Deviation $\Delta H < 0$, $\Delta V < 0$

Henry's Law $P = K_H x$

Raoult's Law $P = P^\circ x_A$

Concentration of solutions

- Mass percentage $= \dfrac{\text{Mass of solute}}{\text{Mass of solution}} \times 100$
- Molarity $= \dfrac{\text{No. of moles of solute}}{\text{Volume of solution(L)}}$
- Molality $= \dfrac{\text{No. of moles of solute}}{\text{Weight of the solvent in kg}}$
- Normality $= \dfrac{\text{No. of grams equivalent of solute}}{\text{Volume of solution (L)}}$
- Mole fraction $= \dfrac{\text{No. of moles of solute}}{\text{Total moles in solution}}$
- Volume percentage $= \dfrac{\text{Volume of solute}}{\text{Volume of solution}} \times 100$
- ppm $= \dfrac{\text{No. of parts of solute}}{\text{Total no. of parts of all components of solution}} \times 10^6$

Topic 1 — Classification of Solutions, Concentration of Solutions, Solubility 

INTRODUCTION

A **solution** is a homogeneous mixture of two or more chemically non-reacting substances. Its composition can be varied within certain limits. All particles in a solution are generally of molecular size, *i.e.,* 0.2 – 2nm. The components of a solution generally cannot be separated by filtration, settling or centrifuging.

A solution consists of two components: solute and solvent.

(a) The component which is present in larger proportion is termed as the **solvent**. It is usually in the same physical state as the solution.

(b) The component which is present in smaller proportion is called the **solute**.

CLASSIFICATION OF SOLUTIONS

On the Basis of Physical State of Solute and Solvent

A solution may be classified as solid, liquid or a gaseous solution. The different types of solutions along with examples are summarised below:

Types of Solution	Examples
Gaseous solution	
(a) Gas in gas	Air, mixture of oxygen and nitrogen, etc.
(b) Liquid in gas	Water vapour.
(c) Solid in gas	Camphor vapours in nitrogen gas.
Liquid solution	
(a) Gas in liquid	Carbon dioxide dissolved in water (aerated water) Oxygen dissolved in water, etc.
(b) Liquid in liquid	Ethanol dissolved in water, vinegar, formalin, etc.
(c) Solid in liquid	Sugar dissolved in water, saline water, etc.
Solid solutions	
(a) Gas in solid	Solution of hydrogen in palladium.
(b) Liquid in solid	Amalgams, e.g., sodium amalgam.
(c) Solid in solid	Gold ornaments (copper or silver dissolved in gold).

On the Basis of Concentration of Solution

(a) **Dilute solution :** A solution in which relatively a small amount of solute is dissolved in large amount of solvent is called a dilute solution.

(b) **Concentrated solution :** A solution in which relatively a large amount of solute is dissolved in small amount of solvent is called a concentrated solution.

(c) **Saturated solution :** A saturated solution is a solution containing the maximum concentration of a solute i.e. such a solution in which no more solute can be dissolved.

(d) **Supersaturated solution :** A solution containing more amount of solute than that required for saturation of a given amount of solvent at a particular temperature, is called a supersaturated solution. It is an unstable system.

Terms Used in Solution

(a) **Binary solution:** The solutions which contain two components are called binary solutions e.g., salt solution.

(b) **Aqueous solution:** When solute is dissolved in water it is known as aqueous solution e.g., ethanol in water.

(c) **Non-aqueous solution:** When solute is dissolved in solvent other than water, solution formed is called non-aqueous solution. e.g., Tincture of iodine.

CONCENTRATION OF SOLUTIONS

Methods of expressing concentration of solutions are listed below

Mass Percentage (w/w)

It is the amount of solute in grams present in 100g of solution.

$$\text{Mass percent of solute} = \frac{\text{Mass of solute}}{\text{Mass of solution}} \times 100$$

Illustration 1 :

What is the weight percentage of urea solution in which 10 gm of urea is dissolved in 90 gm of water?

Sol. Weight percentage of urea $= \dfrac{\text{Weight of urea}}{\text{Weight of solution}} \times 100 = \dfrac{10}{90+10} \times 100 = 10\%$ urea solution (w/W)

Volume Percentage (v/v)

It is the volume of the component per 100 parts by volume of the solution.

$$\text{Volume percent of component} = \frac{\text{Volume of component}}{\text{Volume of solution}} \times 100$$

Illustration 2 :

A solution is prepared by mixing of 10 mL ethanol with 190 mL of water. What is volume percentage of ethanol?

Sol. Volume percentage of ethanol $= \dfrac{\text{Volume of ethanol}}{\text{Volume of solution}} \times 100 = \dfrac{10}{10+190} \times 100 = 5\%$

Thus, 5% ethanol solution.

Mass Volume Percent (w/v)

It is the mass of solute dissolved in 100 mL of the solution. This unit is commonly used in medicine and pharmacy.

Strength

It is defined as amount of solute present in per litre of solution.

$$\text{Strength} = \frac{\text{Weight of solute (in grams)}}{\text{Volume of solution in litres}}$$

Molarity

It is defined as the number of moles of solute present in one litre of solution.

$$\text{Molarity (M)} = \frac{\text{Number of moles of solute}}{\text{Volume of Solution in litre}} = \frac{n}{V} \quad \text{where, } n = \frac{\text{Weight in grams}}{\text{Molecular weight of solute}}$$

$$\therefore \quad M = \frac{\text{Weight in grams}}{\text{Volume of solution in litres}} \times \frac{1}{\text{Molecular weight of solute}}$$

$$\therefore \quad \text{Molarity} = \frac{\text{Strength}}{\text{Molecular weight of solute}} \quad \text{or} \quad \text{Strength} = \text{Molarity} \times \text{Molecular weight}$$

Note: Molarity is the most common way of expressing concentration of a solution in laboratory. However, it has one disadvantage. It changes with temperature because volume of a solution alters due to expansion and contraction of the liquid with temperature.

Illustration 3 :

3.65 g of HCl gas is present in 100 ml of its aqueous solution. What is the molarity ?

Sol. Molarity $= \dfrac{w}{M} \times \dfrac{1000}{\text{volume(mL)}} = \dfrac{3.65}{36.5} \times \dfrac{1000}{100} = 1M$ $\therefore$ 1M solution of HCl.

Normality

The number of gram equivalents of the solute dissolved per litre of the solution. It is denoted by 'N' :

$$\text{Normality} = \frac{\text{Number of gram equivalents of solute}}{\text{Volume of solution (lit)}}$$

$$\text{As Gram equivalents of solute} = \frac{\text{Weight of solute (g)}}{\text{Equivalent weight of solute}}$$

$$\therefore \quad \text{Normality} = \frac{\text{Weight of solute (g)}}{\text{Equivalent weight of solute}} \times \frac{1}{\text{Volume of solution (lit)}}$$

Molality

It is defined as the number of moles of a solute present in 1000g (1kg) of a solvent.

$$\text{Molality (m)} = \frac{\text{Number of moles of solute}}{\text{Weight of solvent in kg}} = \frac{n}{W}$$

Note: Molality is considered better way of expressing concentration of solutions as compared to molarity because molality does not change with change in temperature since the mass of solvent does not vary with temperature.

Illustration 4 :

8 g NaOH is dissolved in 500 ml of its aqueous solution. If density of the solution is 1.2 g/mL, find the molality of the solution.

Sol. Weight of solute = 8 g, Volume of solution = 500 mL, Density of solution = 1.2 g/mL

$\therefore$ Weight of solution = vol × density = 500 × 1.2 = 600 g.

$\therefore$ Weight of solvent = weight of solution – weight of solute = 600 – 8 = 592 g

$\therefore$ $m = \dfrac{w}{M} \times \dfrac{1000}{W} = \dfrac{8}{40} \times \dfrac{1000}{592} = 0.34$

Parts Per Million

When a solute is present in trace quantities it is convenient to express concentration in parts per million (ppm).

$$\text{Parts per million (ppm)} = \frac{\text{Number of parts of solute}}{\text{Total number of parts of all components of the solution}} \times 10^6$$

The concentration of pollutants in water or atmosphere is often expressed in terms of ppm or mg mL^{-1}

Mole fraction

It is defined as the ratio of the number of moles of the solute to the total number of moles in the solution. If n_A is the number of moles of solute dissolved in n_B moles of solvent, then Mole fraction of solute

$$(x_A) = \frac{n_A}{n_A + n_B} \qquad \dots (1)$$

Mole fraction of solvent $\qquad (x_B) = \dfrac{n_B}{n_A + n_B} \qquad \dots (2)$

Adding the above two equations, we get

$$x_A + x_B = \frac{n_A}{n_A + n_B} + \frac{n_B}{n_A + n_B} = \frac{n_A + n_B}{n_A + n_B} = 1$$

i.e., $\qquad x_A + x_B = 1 \qquad \therefore \quad x_A = 1 - x_B \text{ or } x_B = 1 - x_A$

Note: Even if three components make a solution, then $x_A + x_B + x_C = 1$.

SOLUBILITY

It is defined as the amount of solute in a saturated solution per 100 g of a solvent.

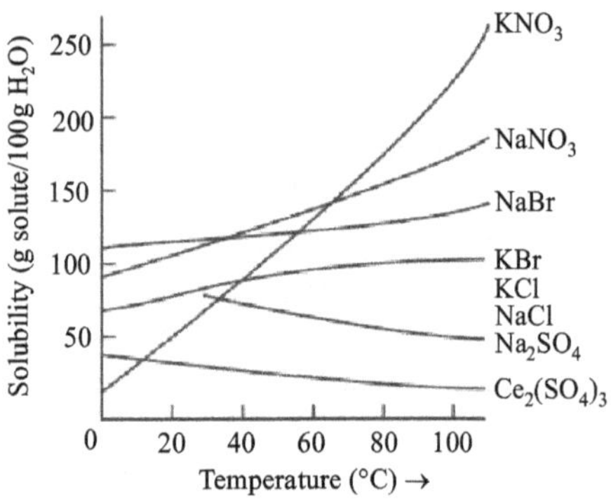

Solubility of Solid in Liquid

As the name suggests, solid invariably acts as the solute while liquid plays the role of solvent.

Solubility curves : The graphs which show the variation of solubility with temperature are called solubility curves. With the help of solubility curves solubility of any solute at a particular temperature can be find out.

Factors Aaffecting Solubility of Solid in Liquid

(a) **Effect of temperature :** According to Le-Chatelier's principle solubility of solid in liquid increases with increase in temperature if dissolution process is endothermic. i.e. ΔH = +ve Solubility decreases with rise in temperature if dissolution is exothermic i.e. ΔH = –ve

(b) **Effect of pressure :** Solids and liquids are highly incompressible and are generally not affected by change in pressure.

(c) **Nature of solute and solvent:** Solubility is guided by general principle of like dissolves like which means solute will dissolve particular solvent if both have the same nature.

Ionic and polar substances are generally soluble in polar solvents like water and are insoluble in non-polar solvents like benzene, chloroform, carbon disulphide, etc. Similarly, non-polar solutes like 'iodine', sulphur, phosphorus and organic substances are soluble in non-polar solvents like benzene, chloroform, etc., and are insoluble in polar solvents like water.

Solubility of Liquid in Liquid

When two liquids are mixed, their miscibility or solubility will depend upon the magnitude of the attractive forces between the particles / molecules of the two individual liquids as compared to the forces of attraction which arise in them. When they exist together.

Solubility of Gases in Liquids

Most of the gases are soluble in water as well as in some other solvents.

Factors affecting solubility of gases in liquids

(a) Nature of gas solvent: Generally, the gases which can be easily liquefied are more soluble in common solvents. For example, CO_2 is more soluble in water as compared to oxygen or nitrogen. The gases which are capable of forming ions in aqueous solution are much more soluble in water than in any other solvent. For example, HCl and NH_3 are highly soluble in water in which they form ions but not in benzene.

(b) Effect of temperature : The solubility of a gas in a liquid decreases with rise in temperature of the solution.

(c) Effect of Pressure : The effect of pressure on the solubility of a gas in a liquid is governed by Henry's Law. It states that the solubility of a gas in a liquid at a given temperature in directly proportional to the partial pressure of the gas Mathematically, $P = K_H x$ where P is the partial pressure of the gas; and x is the mole fraction of the gas in the solution and K_H is Henry's Law constant.

Applications of Henry's law

(*i*) To increase the solubility of CO_2 in soft drinks and soda water, the bottle is sealed under high pressure.

(*ii*) Scuba divers must cope with high concentrations of dissolved gases while breathing air at high pressure under water. Increased pressure increases the solubility of atmospheric gases in blood. When the divers come towards surface, the pressure gradually decreases. This releases the dissolved gases and leads to the formation of bubbles of nitrogen in the blood. This blocks capillaries and creates a medical condition known as bends, which are painful and dangerous to life. To avoid bends, as well as, the toxic effects of high concentrations of nitrogen in the blood, the tanks used by scuba divers are filled with air diluted with helium (11.7% helium, 56.2% nitrogen and 32.1% oxygen).

(*iii*) At high attitudes, the partial pressure of oxygen is less than that at the ground level. This leads to low concentrations of oxygen in the blood and tissues of people living at high altitudes or climbers. Low blood oxygen causes climbers to become weak and unable to think clearly, symptoms of a condition known as anoxia.

Limitations of Henry's Law: Henry's law is applicable only (a) when pressure of gas is not too high and temperature is not too low. (b) gas should not undergo any chemical change, association and dissociation in the solution.

Practice Exercise-1

Multiple Choice Questions

1. An X molal solution of a compound in benzene has mole fraction of solute equal to 0.2. The value of X is
   (a) 14   (b) 3.2   (c) 1.4   (d) 2

2. Molarity of H_2SO_4 is 18 M. Its density is 1.8 g/mL. Hence molality is
   (a) 36   (b) 200   (c) 500   (d) 18

3. What is the normality of a 1 M solution of H_3PO_4?
   (a) 0.5 N   (b) 1.0 N   (c) 2.0 N   (d) 3.0 N

4. How many grams of concentrated nitric acid solution should be used to prepare 250 mL of 2.0 M HNO_3 ? The concentrated acid is 70% HNO_3
   (a) 90.0 g conc. HNO_3
   (b) 70.0 g conc. HNO_3
   (c) 54.0 g conc. HNO_3
   (d) 45.0 g conc. HNO_3

5. A solution is prepared by dissolving 10 g NaOH in 1250 mL of a solvent of density 0.8 g/mL. The molality of the solution in mol kg^{-1} is
   (a) 0.25   (b) 0.2
   (c) 0.008   (d) 0.0064

6. 200 ml of water is added to 500 ml of 0.2 M solution. What is the molarity of this diluted solution ?
   (a) 0.5010 M   (b) 0.2897 M
   (c) 0.7093 M   (d) 0.1428 M

7. The volume of 4 N HCl and 10 N HCl required to make 1 litre of 6 N HCl are
   (a) 0.75 litre of 10 N HCl and 0.25 litre of 4 N HCl
   (b) 0.50 litre of 4 N HCl and 0.50 litre of 10 N HCl
   (c) 0.67 litre of 4 N HCl and 0.33 litre of 10 N HCl
   (d) 0.80 litre of 4 N HCl and 0.20 litre of 10 N HCl

8. Which of the following factor do not affect solubility of solid solute in liquid?
   (a) Temperature   (b) Pressure
   (c) Nature of solute   (d) All of these

9. Which of the following statements is incorrect?
    (a) A solution in which no more solute can be dissolved at the same temperature and pressure is called a saturated solution.
    (b) An unsaturated solution is one in which more solute can be dissolved at the same temperature.
    (c) The solution which is in dynamic equilibrium with undissolved solute is the saturated solution.
    (d) The minimum amount of solute dissolved in a given amount of solvent is its solubility.

10. Scuba divers may experience a condition called ______. To avoids this, the tanks used by scuba divers are filled with air diluted with ______ .
    (a) Migrains, Hydrogen
    (b) Cramps, Nitrogen
    (c) Nausea, Oxygen
    (d) Bends, Helium

Assertion & Reason Questions

DIRECTIONS (Qs. 11-13) : *Each of these questions contains an assertion followed by reason. Read them carefully and answer the question on the basis of following options. You have to select the one that best describes the two statements.*
(a) If both Assertion and Reason are correct and the Reason is a correct explanation of the Assertion.
(b) If both Assertion and Reason are correct but Reason is not a correct explanation of the Assertion.
(c) If the Assertion is correct but Reason is incorrect.
(d) If the Assertion is incorrect but the Reason is correct.

11. **Assertion :** Molarity of a solution in liquid state changes with temperature.
    Reason : The volume of a solution changes with change in temperature.

12. **Assertion :** One molal aqueous solution of glucose contains 180 g of glucose in 1 kg of water.
    Reason : Solution containing one mole of solute in 1000 g solvent is called one molal solution.

13. **Assertion :** Homogeneous mixture of two or more non-reacting substances is known as solution.
    Reason : State of solutions can be solid only.

Case/Passage Based Questions

DIRECTIONS (Qs. 14-18) : *Following are the case/passage based questions. Attempt any 4 out of 5 questions.*

Henry's law was formulated in the early 19th century by the English chemist William Henry. Henry's law is a gas law which states that at the amount of gas that is dissolved in a liquid is directly proportional to the partial pressure of that gas above the liquid when the temperature is kept constant. The constant of proportionality for this relationship is called Henry's law constant (usually denoted by 'k_H'). The mathematical formula of Henry's law is given by:

$P \propto C$ (or) $P = k_H.C$

14. Value of Henry's constant K_H ______.
    (a) increases with increase in temperature.
    (b) decreases with increase in temperature.
    (c) remains constant.
    (d) first increases then decreases.

15. Which is an application of Henry's law?
    (a) Spray paint
    (b) Bottled water
    (c) Filling up atire
    (d) Soft drinks (soda)

16. Which one of the following gases has the lowest value of Henry's law constant?
    (a) N_2
    (b) He
    (c) H_2
    (d) CO_2

17. Henry's law constant of oxygen is 1.4×10^{-3} mol. lit^{-1}. atm^{-1} at 298 K. How much of oxygen is dissolved in 100 ml at 298 K when the partial pressure of oxygen is 0.5 atm?
    (a) 1.4 g
    (b) 3.2 g
    (c) 22.4 mg
    (d) 2.24 mg

18. What is the ratio of no. of moles of oxygen to that of nitrogen in a container of 5 litre at atmospheric pressure? $[(K_H)_{O_2} = 34.86$ Kbar, $(K_H)_{N_2} = 76.48K$ bar
    (a) 1 : 1.71
    (b) 1 : 2
    (c) 2 : 1
    (d) 1 : 24

Very Short Answer Questions

19. Name two ways of measuring the concentration of a solution which are not temperature dependent.

20. When do we express the concentration of a solution in parts per million (ppm)?

21. Is smoke a solution?

22. Give an example of a solution that contains a gas dissolved in a liquid.

23. An old saying is that 'oil and water do not mix'. Why is this true?

24. Give an example of a solution containing a liquid solute in a solid solvent.

25. 10 cc of a liquid A were mixed with 10 cc of liquid B. The volume of the resulting solution was found to be 19·9 cc. What do you conclude ?

26. At the same temperature, hydrogen is more soluble in water than helium. Which of them will have a higher value of K_H and Why ? (K_H = Henry's constant).

27. What do you mean by 10% w/w aqueous solution of Na_2CO_3?

28. What is the relation between normality and molarity of a given solution of H_2SO_4?

Short Answer Questions

29. CCl_4 and H_2O are immiscible whereas C_2H_5OH and H_2O are miscible in all proportions. Correlate this behaviour with the molecular structures of the three compounds.

30. Differentiate between molarity and molality of a solution. When and why is molality is preferred over molarity in handling solutions in chemistry.

| Topic 2 | **Vapour Pressure, Ideal and Non-ideal Solutions Azeotropic Mixtures; Colligative Properties** |

VAPOUR PRESSURE

The **vapour pressure** of a liquid is the pressure exerted by its vapour when it is in dynamic equilibrium with its liquid, in a closed container.

When a non-volatile solute is added to a solvent to make a solution, the vapour pressure of the solutions will be the vapour pressure of the solvent as there is no contribution from the solute.

Vapour Pressure Depends Upon the Following Factors

(a) Nature of solvent: It depends upon the magnitude of the intermolecular forces present between liquid molecules.
(b) Temperature: Vapour pressure of liquid increases with rise in temperature.
(c) Percentage purity of liquid or surface area of liquid.

Raoult's Law

According to **Raoult's Law,** the vapour pressure of a solution containing a non-volatile solute is directly proportional to the mole fraction of the solvent (x_A). The proportionality constant being the vapour pressure of the pure solvent, i.e., $P \times x_A$ or $P = P° x_A$.
For liquid - liquid solution: If the solution consists of two volatile liquids, then Raoult's Law is applicable to each component of the solution, *i.e.,*

$$P_A = P_A° \ x_A \text{ and } P_B = P_A° \ x_B$$

The total vapour pressure of the solution is equal to the sum of the partial pressures of each component.

$$P_S = P_A + P_B = P_A° \ x_A + P_A° \ x_B$$

$$P_s = x_A P_A° + (1 - x_A) \ P_B° \qquad [\because x_A + x_B = 1]$$

$$P_s = x_A P_A° - x_A P_B° + P_B° \Rightarrow P_s = x_A[P_A° - P_B°] + P_B°$$

For solid - liquid solution

$$\frac{P° - P_s}{P°} = \frac{n_A}{n_A + n_B} = \frac{W_A . m_B}{m_A . W_B} \text{ or } \frac{w \ M}{m \ W}$$

where, w = wt. of solute dissolved in gram, W = wt. of solvent in gram, m = molecular mass of solute, M = molecular weight of solvent

Limitations of Raoult's Law
(a) As described earlier, Raoult's law is applicable only to very dilute solutions.
(b) Raoult's law is applicable to solutions containing non-volatile solute only.
(c) Raoult's law is not applicable to solutes which dissociates or associate in solution.

Illustration 5 :

The vapour pressure of pure benzene at a certain temperature is 640 mm Hg. A non-volatile solid weighing 2.175g is added to 39.0 g of benzene. The vapour pressure of the solution is 600 mm Hg. What is the molecular weight of the solid substance ?
Sol. According to Raoult's law

$$\frac{p° - p}{p°} = \frac{w / m}{w / m + W / M}$$

Here, $p° = 640$ mm Hg, $p = 600$ mm Hg, w = 2.175g, W = 39.0 g, M = 78, m = Molecular weight of solute

Substituting the various values in the above equation,

$$\frac{640 - 600}{640} = \frac{2.175 / m}{2.175 / m + 39 / 78} \Rightarrow m = 65.25$$

IDEAL AND NON-IDEAL SOLUTIONS

Ideal Solutions

A solution which obeys Raoult's Law at all concentrations and temperatures is known as an **ideal solution**.

Characteristics of an ideal solution:

(a) It obeys Raoults Law at all concentrations and temperatures.

(b) $\Delta_{sol} V = 0$, i.e., there is no change in volume when an ideal solution is formed.

(c) $\Delta_{sol} H = 0$; i.e., heat is neither evolved nor absorbed during the formation of an ideal solution.

(d) In ideal solutions intermolecular interactions A – B between its component are of same magnitude as the intermolecular interaction found in the pure components i.e. A–A interaction and B–B interactions.

Examples :

(a) Benzene and toluene   (b) n - Hexane and n - heptane   (c) Carbon tetrachloride and silicon tetrachloride

(d) Chlorobenzene + Bromobenzene   (e) Ethyl iodide + Ethyl bromide

Note: A dilute solution can be assumed to be an ideal solution.

Non-ideal Solutions

Solutions which do not obey Raoult's law are called non-ideal solutions.

(a) For such solutions $P_A \neq P_A^{\circ}.x_A$; $P_A \neq P_B^{\circ}.x_B$

(b) Non ideal solutions are formed when the components differ much in their structures and polarities.

(c) $\Delta H_{mixing} \neq$ zero

(d) $\Delta V_{mixing} \neq$ zero

(e) Non ideal solutions show either positive or negative deviation from Raoult's law.

Positive deviation from Raoult's Law

- This deviation is shown when the forces of attraction between A — B molecules are less than forces of attraction between A — A and B — B molecules in the two liquids forming the solution.

$P_A > P_A^{\circ}.x_A$, $P_B > P_B^{\circ}.x_B$

The total vapour pressure of the solution is greater than the corresponding vapour pressure expected in case of an ideal solution of same composition. i.e.,

$P_{total} > P_A^{\circ} .x_A + P_B^{\circ} .x_B$

- $\Delta H_{mix} > 0$, Endothermic dissolution ; heat is absorbed
- $\Delta V_{mix} > 0$, volume is increased after dissolution.
- 'A' and 'B' escape easily showing higher vapour pressure than the expected value.

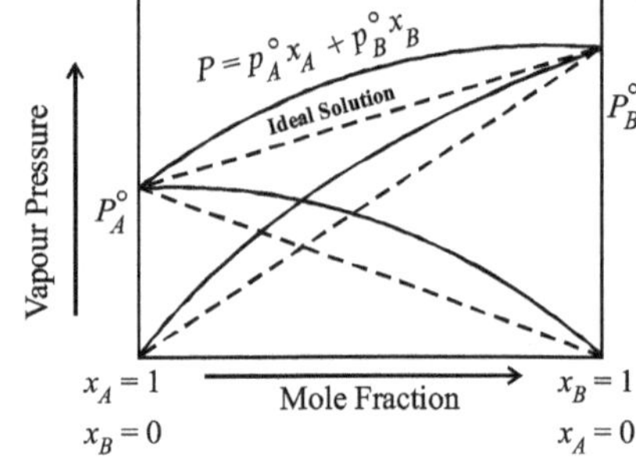

Examples :

(a) Acetone + ethyl alcohol   (b) Water + ethyl alcohol   (c) CCl_4 + $CHCl_3$ (d) CCl_4 + toluene

(e) Water and methyl alcohol   (f) Ethanol and cyclohexane   (g) Acetone and benzene   (h) Acetone + CS_2

Negative deviation from Raoult's Law :

In these solutions, the A—B interactions are stronger than the A—A and B—B molecular interactions present in the two liquids forming the solution.

$P_A < P_A^{\circ} . x_A$

$P_B < P_B^{\circ} . x_B$

$P_{total} < P_A^{\circ} . x_A + P_B^{\circ} . x_B$

$\Delta H_{mix} < 0$; exothermic dissolution heat is evolved.

$\Delta V_{mix} < 0$; volume is decreased during dissolution.

Escaping tendency of both components 'A' and 'B' is lowered showing lower vapour pressure than expected ideally.

Examples : (a) Water + HCl   (b) H_2O + HNO_3

            (c) Nitric acid and chloroform   (d) CH_3OH + CH_3COOH

            (e) Acetic acid + pyridine   (f) Chloroform + diethyl ether

            (g) Chloroform + benzene   (h) Acetone and chloroform

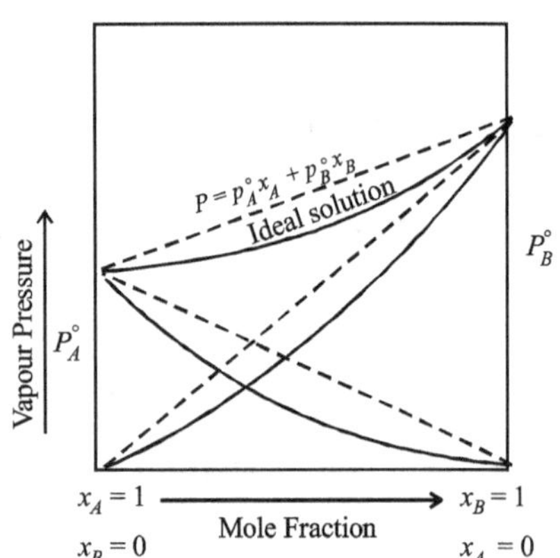

Relation Between Raoult's Law and Henry's Law

According to Raoult's Law, the vapour pressure of volatile component in a solution is given by expression,

$$P_A = P_A^o \, x_A \qquad \qquad ...(i)$$

According to Henry's Law, the solubility of a gas (volatile component) in a liquid is governed by the expression.

$$P = K_H \, x \qquad \qquad ...(ii)$$

(a) It can be seen from equations (i) and (ii) that the partial pressure of the volatile component or gas is directly proportional to its mole fraction in the solution. Only the proportionality constant K_H, in the Henry's Law equation, differs from P_A^o, the proportionality constant in Raoult's Law equation.

(b) If K_H becomes equal to P_A^o, the Raoult's Law becomes a special case of Henry's Law.

Note : In a very dilute solution of liquids, the solvent obeys Raoult's Law whereas the solute obeys Henry's Law.

AZEOTROPIC MIXTURES

They are binary mixtures of two liquids having same composition in liquid and vapour phase and boil at a constant temperature and can be distilled without any change in their composition. They are formed by non–ideal solutions. They are of two types.

(a) "**Minimum boiling azeotropes**" are the mixture of two liquids, whose boiling point is less than either of the two pure components. They are formed by non–ideal solutions showing positive deviation.
e.g., ethanol (95.5%) + water (4.5%) mixture boiling at 351.15K.

(b) "**Maximum boiling azeotropes**" are the mixtures of two liquids, whose boiling points are more than either of the two components. They are formed by non–ideal solutions showing negative deviation.
e.g., HNO_3 (68%) + water (32%) mixture boiling at 393.5 K.

COLLIGATIVE PROPERTIES

Colligative properties of solutions are those properties which depend only upon the number of solute particles in the solution and not on their nature. Such properties are

(a) Relative lowering in vapour pressure,
(b) Elevation of boiling point,
(c) Depression of freezing point and
(d) Osmotic pressure.

Relative Lowering of Vapour Pressure

According to Raoult's Law, the vapour pressure of a solution containing a non-volatile solute is given by

$$P = P_A = P_A^o \, x_A \quad \text{or} \quad \frac{P}{P_A^o} = x_A \quad \text{or} \quad 1 - \frac{P}{P_A^o} = 1 - x_A$$

Since for a binary mixture, $x_A + x_B = 1$

$$x_B = 1 - x_A \qquad \therefore \quad \frac{P_A^o - P}{P_A^o} = x_B$$

Relative lowering of vapour pressure $= \dfrac{P_A^o - P_A}{P_A^o} \Rightarrow \dfrac{P_A^o - P_A}{P_A^o} = x_B = \dfrac{n_B}{n_A + n_B}$

Thus, according to Raoult's Law, the relative lowering of vapour pressure of a solution is equal to the mole fraction of the solute.

For a very dilute solution, $\dfrac{n_B}{n_A + n_B} \simeq \dfrac{n_B}{n_A}$

$$\Rightarrow \quad \frac{P_A^o - P_A}{P_A^o} = \frac{n_B}{n_A} = \frac{W_B/M_B}{W_A/M_A} = \frac{W_B M_A}{M_B W_A}$$

Where, n_A = Moles of solvent, n_B = Moles of solute, W_B = Mass of solute, M_B = Molar mass of solute, W_A = Mass of solvent, M_A = Molar mass of solvent

In borderline cases it becomes difficult to decide whether the solution is dilute or not so it is better not to neglect n_A against n_B. Thus modified equation will be

$$\frac{P_A^o - P_A}{P_A} = \frac{n_B}{n_A} = \frac{W_B M_A}{M_B W_A} \left[\frac{P_A^o}{P_A^o - P_A} = \frac{n_A + n_B}{n_B} \quad \text{or} \quad \frac{P_A^o}{P_A^o - P_A} = \frac{n_A}{n_B} + 1 \right]$$

Elevation in Boiling Point

The **boiling point** of a liquid is the temperature at which the vapour pressure of the liquid becomes equal to the atmospheric pressure. When a non-volatile solute is dissolved in a solvent, its vapour pressure decreases as there is no contribution from the non-volatile solute. Therefore, the boiling point of the solution is always higher than the boiling point of the pure solvent. This is called elevation of boiling point.

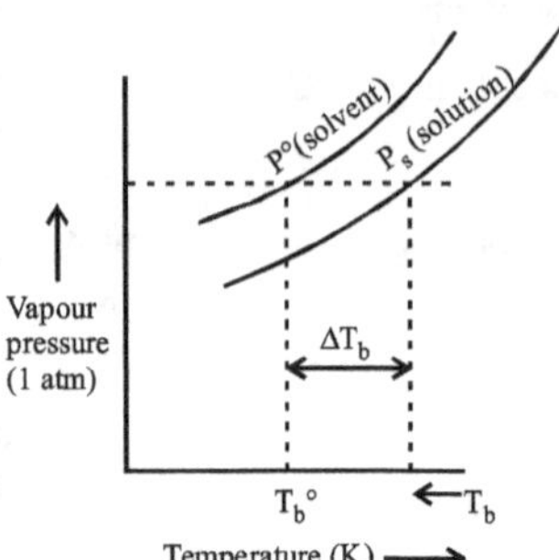

Elevation in boiling point, $\Delta T_b = T_s - T_b^\circ$

Where ΔT_b = Elevation in boiling point, T_b = Boiling point of solution, T_b° = Boiling point of solvent

For a dilute solution, the elevation in boiling point is found to be proportional to the molality of the solution, i.e., $\Delta T_b \propto m$ or $\Delta T_b = K_b\, m$

where ΔT_b is the elevation in boiling point, 'm' is the molality and K_b is the **Molal elevation constant** (boiling elevation constant) which is equal to the elevation in boiling point when one mole of the solute is dissolved in 1000 g of the solvent.

$$\Delta T_b = K_b\, \frac{n_B}{W_A\,(g)} \times 1000 \quad \Rightarrow \quad \Delta T_b = 1000\, \frac{K_b W_B}{M_B W_A}$$

where W_B = Mass of solute, W_A = Mass of solvent, M_B = Molar mass of solute.

Illustration 6 :

A solution of 0.450 g of urea (mol. wt 60) in 22.5 g of water showed 0.170°C of elevation in boiling point. Calculate the molal elevation constant of water.

Sol. Wt. of solute, w = 0.450 g

Wt. of solvent, W = 22.5 g

Mol. wt of solute (urea), m = 60

Molal elevation constant, K_b = ?

Boiling point elevation, $\Delta T_b = 0.170°C$

Substituting these values in the equation –

$$K_b = \frac{m \times W \times \Delta T_b}{1000 \times w} = \frac{60 \times 22.5 \times 0.170}{1000 \times 0.450} = 0.51°\,C$$

Depression in Freezing Point

Freezing point is the temperature at which the solid and the liquid state of the substance have the same vapour pressure. Since the presence of a non-volatile solute lowers the vapour pressure of the solvent, the freezing point of the solution is always less than that of the pure solvent.

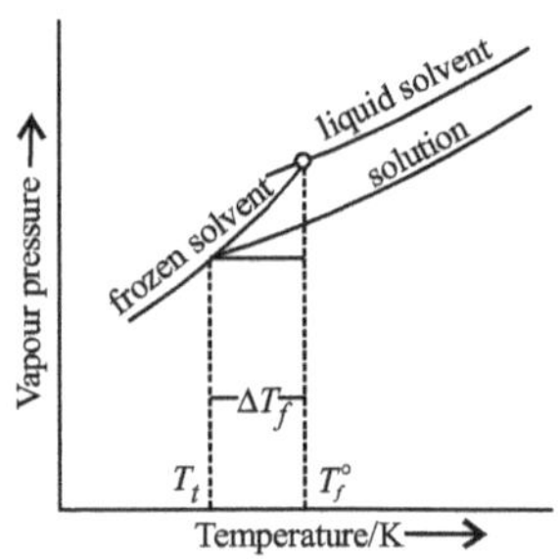

Depression in freezing point, $\Delta T_f = T_f^\circ - T_s$

Where, ΔT_f = Depressing in freezing point, T_f° = Freezing point of solvent, T_f = Freezing point of solution

The depression in freezing point (ΔT_f) is proportional to the molality of the solution.

$$\Delta T_f \propto m \quad \text{or} \quad \Delta T_f = K_f\, m$$

where K_f is **molal depression constant** (freezing point depression constant). It is the depression in freezing point when 1 mole of a solute is dissolved in 1000 g of the solvent

$$\Delta T_f = 1000\, K_f\, \frac{W_B}{W_A M_B}$$

where W_B = Mass of solute in g, W_A = Mass of solvent in g, M_B = Molar mass of solute

Antifreeze Solutions

In severe cold, the temperature usually falls below 0°C. As a result, water used in the radiators of cars and other automobiles is expected to freeze. This will cause expansion leading to the bursting of the radiator. In order to avoid this, **antifreeze solutions** are used. The most important solution is a mixture of water and ethylene glycol ($HO – CH_2 – CH_2 – OH$). It is popularly known as coolant. A mixture of ethylene glycol and water in equal proportion by volume freezes at –36°C.

Osmosis

The spontaneous flow of solvent molecules from a dilute solution into a concentrated solution when the two are separated by a perfect semipermeable membrane is called **osmosis.**

Osmotic pressure (π) is the pressure which must be applied to the solution side (more concentrated solution) to just prevent the passage of pure solvent into it through a semipermeable membrane.

Mathematically, $\pi = CRT = \dfrac{n_B}{V} RT \quad \left(\because C = \dfrac{n_B}{V} \right)$

$$n_B = \frac{W_B}{M_B} \qquad \therefore \pi = \frac{W_B RT}{V M_B}$$

where π is the osmotic pressure of the solution; C is the concentration of solution; n_B is the number of moles of solute; V is the volume of the solution in litres; R is the gas constant; and T is the temperature on the Kelvin scale; W_B is the weight of the solute and M_B is its molar mass.

While solving the problems, we have to take proper care of units. If π is in atm, then R should be taken as 0.083 lit atm mol^{-1}K^{-1}. Osmotic pressure can be determined at room temperature whereas other colligative properties such as elevation in boiling point and depression in freezing point cannot be evaluated at room temperature. It is particularly useful for biomolecules and polymers with high molecular masses such as proteins because in their dilute solutions both elevation in boiling point (ΔT_b) and depression in freezing point (ΔT_f) are too small to be measured accurately. Moreover, the polymers and biomolecules are generally not stable at higher temperature.

Classification of solutions on the basis of osmotic pressure.

Isotonic solutions are those solutions which have the same osmotic pressure. Also they have same molar concentration.

For isotonic solutions, $\pi_1 = \pi_2$

Also, $C_1 = C_2$ or $\dfrac{n_1}{V_1} = \dfrac{n_2}{V_2} \qquad \dfrac{W_1}{m_1 V_1} = \dfrac{W_2}{m_2 V_2}$

For example : 0.9% (W/V) NaCl solution is isotonic with the fluid inside the blood cells. This is called normal saline solution. Any solution of this concentration is safe for intravenous injection.

Hypotonic and hypertonic solutions :

When two solutions have different osmotic pressures, the solution with lesser osmotic pressure is called **hypotonic solution** and the solution with higher osmotic pressure is called **hypertonic solutions.**

Reverse osmosis

The movement of solvent particles from higher concentration to lower concentration through semipermeable membrane on applying pressure is known as **reverse osmosis.** If the external pressure greater than osmotic pressure is applied on more concentrated solution side, the solvent molecules start passing through semipermeable membrane from this solution to the solvent or less concentrated solution. This is known as reverse osmosis. It is used to purify the sea water.

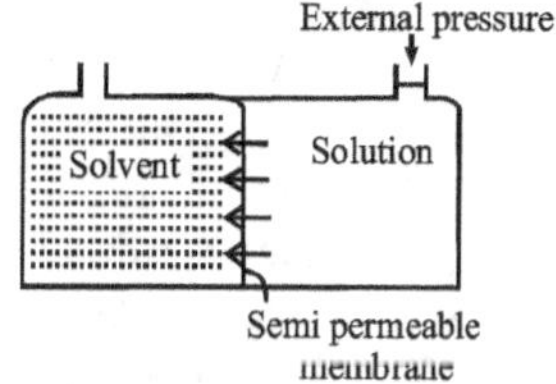

Illustration 7 :

The vapour pressure of CCl_4(density = 1.58 g cm^{-3}) at 30°C is 143 mm. 0.5 g of a non–volatile solute of molecular weight 65 is dissolved in 100 ml of CCl_4. Calculate the vapour pressure of the solution.

Sol. Here $w = 0.5$ g, $W = 100 \times 1.58 = 158$ g $(\because d = W/V)$, $m = 65$

Molar mass of $CCl_4 = 154$

$$\frac{P° - P}{P°} = \frac{wM}{mW} \text{ or } \frac{143 - P}{143} = \frac{0.5 \times 154}{65 \times 158} \text{ or } P = 141.93 \text{ mm}$$

Abnormal Colligative Properties

It has been observed that difference in the observed and calculated molecular masses of solute is due to association or dissociation of solute molecules in solution. It results in a change in the number of particles in solution.

Association of Solute Particles

The formation of a bigger molecule by the union of two, three or more solute molecules is called association.

As a result, the total number of particles in solution become less than the number of molecules initially dissolved in the solution and hence the colligative properties will have lower value.

Dissociation of Solute Molecules

Molecules of electrolytes undergo ionization or dissociation in ionizing solvents to give two or more particles in solution. This dissociation result in an increase in the total number of particles and therefore the value of colligative properties of such solution will be higher.

Practice Exercise-2

Multiple Choice Questions

1. The decrease in the vapour pressure of solvent depends on the
   (a) quantity of non-volatile solute present in the solution
   (b) nature of non-volatile solute present in the solution
   (c) molar mass of non-volatile solute present in the solution
   (d) physical state of non-volatile solute present in the solution

2. The vapour pressure of two liquids 'P' and 'Q' are 80 and 60 torr, respectively. The total vapour pressure of solution obtained by mixing 3 mole of P and 2 mole of Q would be
   (a) 72 torr (b) 140 torr (c) 68 torr (d) 20 torr

3. Which will form maximum boiling point azeotrope
   (a) $HNO_3 + H_2O$ solution
   (b) $C_2H_5OH + H_2O$ solution
   (c) $C_6H_6 + C_6H_5CH_3$ solution
   (d) None of these

4. Which one of the following is non-ideal solution
   (a) Benzene + toluene
   (b) n-hexane + n-heptane
   (c) Ethyl bromide + ethyl iodide
   (d) $CCl_4 + CHCl_3$

5. Which of the following liquid pairs shows a positive deviation from Raoult's law ?
   (a) Water - Nitric acid
   (b) Benzene - Methanol
   (c) Water - Hydrochloric acid
   (d) Acetone - Chloroform

6. Vapour pressure of benzene at 30°C is 121.8 mm Hg. When 15 g of a non volatile solute is dissolved in 250 g of benzene its vapour pressure decreased to 120.2 mm Hg. The molecular weight of the solute (Mo. wt. of solvent = 78)
   (a) 356.2 (b) 456.8 (c) 530.1 (d) 656.7

7. 12 g of a non-volatile solute dissolved in 108 g of water produces the relative lowering of vapour pressure of 0.1. The molecular mass of the solute is
   (a) 80 (b) 60 (c) 20 (d) 40

8. A solution of sucrose (molar mass = 342 g mol^{-1}) has been prepared by dissolving 68.5 g of sucrose in 1000 g of water. The freezing point of the solution obtained will be (K_f for water = 1.86 K kg mol^{-1}).
   (a) – 0.372°C   (b) – 0.520°C
   (d) + 0.372°C   (d) – 0.570°C

9. Which one of the following aqueous solutions will exihibit highest boiling point ?
   (a) 0.015 M urea   (b) 0.01 M KNO_3
   (c) 0.01 M Na_2SO_4 (d) 0.015 M glucose

10. An ideal solution is formed when its components
    (a) have no volume change on mixing
    (b) have no enthalpy change on mixing
    (c) have both the above characteristics
    (d) have high solubility.

Assertion & Reason Questions

DIRECTIONS (Qs. 11-13) : *Each of these questions contains an assertion followed by reason. Read them carefully and answer the question on the basis of following options. You have to select the one that best describes the two statements.*

(a) If both Assertion and Reason are correct and the Reason is a correct explanation of the Assertion.

(b) If both Assertion and Reason are correct but Reason is not a correct explanation of the Assertion.

(c) If the Assertion is correct but Reason is incorrect.

(d) If the Assertion is incorrect but the Reason is correct.

11. **Assertion :** A non volatile solute is added in liquid solvent then freezing point of mixture decreases.

    Reason : Vapour pressure decreases by addition of non volatile solute, so equilibrium point where V.P. of solid and V.P. of liquid are equal can reach at lower temp.

12. **Assertion:** When one solvent is mixed with other solvent, vapour pressure of one increases and other decreases.

    Reason: When any solute is added into solvent, vapour pressure of solvent decreases.

13. **Assertion :** If one component of a solution obeys Raoult's law over a certain range of composition, the other component will not obey Henry's law in that range.

    Reason : Raoult's law is a special case of Henry's law.

Very Short Answer Questions

14. Why semipermeable membrane of $Cu_2[Fe(CN)_6]$ is not used for osmosis in non-aqueous solution?

15. What types of membranes are used in reverse osmosis ? Name one such membrane.

16. Why is the osmotic pressure considered to be a colligative property?

17. Which is the most suitable method for determining the molecular weights of proteins?

18. Arrange the following aqueous solutions in order of increasing freezing points:
    (a) 0·10 M NH_2CONH_2 (b) 0·10 M KCl
    (c) 0·10 M CH_3COOH (d) 0·10 M Na_2SO_4.

19. Give one practical application of reverse osmosis.

20. What will happen if we place red blood cells in pure water ?

21. Explain why the melting point of a substance gives an indication of the purity of the substance.

22. What is an antifreeze?

23. If glycerine [$C_3H_5(OH)_3$] and ethylene glycol ($C_2H_6O_2$) are sold at same price per kg, which would be cheaper for preparing an antifreeze solution for the radiator of an automobile?

24. What does K_f stand for ?

25. Define freezing point of a solution.

26. When a solution freezes, name the substance that separates out first.

27. Define molal elevation constant.
28. Define colligative property of a solution.
29. Define normal boiling point of a liquid.
30. If the atmospheric pressure is decreased, what will happen to the boiling point of water?
31. Can we separate an azeotropic mixture by distillation?
32. What role does the molecular interaction play in solution of alcohol and water ?
33. How are the compositions of the vapour and the liquid phase related to each other in azeotropic mixtures?
34. What is the concentration of ethanol in an azeotropic mixture of ethanol and water?
35. What type of azeotrope is formed on mixing nitric acid with water?
36. Give one example of a
    (a) minimum boiling point azeotrope.
    (b) maximum boiling point azeotrope.
37. What is the enthalpy change and volume change when two liquids are mixed to form a non-ideal solution which shows negative deviation from Raoult's Law ?
38. Is the formation of a non-ideal solution showing positive deviation from Raoult's Law endothermic or exothermic?
39. Why is the vapour pressure of a liquid constant at constant temperature?
40. Cutting onions taken from the fridge is more comfortable than cutting onions lying at room temperature. Explain why.
41. Why is liquid ammonia bottle first cooled in ice before opening it?
42. Why does the use of a pressure cooker reduce cooking time?
43. Two liquids A and B on mixing produce a warm solution which type of deviation from Raoult's law does it show?
44. What happens of pressure greater than osmotic pressure is applied on the solution separated by a semi-permeable membrane from the solvent ?
45. What will happen to the elevation in boiling point of a solution if the weight of the solute dissolved is doubled but the weight of solvent taken is halved ?

Short Answer Questions

46. Why there is an increase in vapour pressure when HgI_2 is added to the aqueous solution of KI?
47. Will the elevation in boiling point be same if 0·1 mole of sodium chloride or 0·1 mole of sugar is dissolved in one litre of water?
48. When fruits and vegetables that have dried are placed in water, they slowly swell and return to original form why? Would a temperature increase accelerate the process? Explain.
49. (a) Name the factors which affect the solubility of a solute in a solvent.
    (b) Which one the following has the lowest freezing point?
    1 M urea solution, 1M Na_2SO_4 solution, 1 M NaCl
50. At 25 °C, the vapour pressure of pure water is 23·76 mm Hg and that of an aqueous dilute solution of urea is 22·98 mm Hg. Calculate the molality of this solution.
51. A solution containing 2·56g of sulphur in 100 g of CS_2 gave a freezing point of lowering of 0·383 K. Calculate molecular formula of sulphur (K_f for CS_2 = 3·83 K kg mol^{-1}, At. wt. of S = 32)
52. At 298 K, the vapour pressure of pure water is 23·75 mm Hg.
    (a) At same temperature calculate vapour pressure over 10% aqueous solution of an organic compound whose molecular weight is 60g mol^{-1}.
    (b) What will be the osmotic pressure of this solution at 298 K?
    (Given R = 0·082 L atm K^{-1} mol^{-1}].

Important Tips & Formulae

- **Ideal Solution :** Solutions which obey Raoult's Law (I) $\Delta H_{mix} = 0$, (II) $\Delta V_{mix} = 0$, the A–B intermolecular interactions are the same as A–A and B–B inter-molecular interactions.
  Examples:
  (a) benzene and toluene
  (b) ethyl bromide and ethyl chloride
  Non Ideal Solution: Solutions which do not obey Raoult's law, (I) $\Delta H_{mix} \neq 0$ (II) $\Delta V_{mix} \neq 0$.
  (i) Showing positive deviations : For such solutions (a) A–B inter-molecular interactions are weaker than A–A and B–B intermolecular interactions (b) ΔH_{mix} is +ve (c) ΔV_{mix} is +ve
  Examples: (a) Carbon tetrachloride + benzene
  (b) Carbon tetrachloride + chloroform
  (ii) Showing negative deviations : For such solutions (a) A–B intermolecular interactions are stronger than A–A and B–B intermolecular interactions (b) ΔH_{mix} is –ve (c) ΔV_{mix} is –ve.
  Examples: (a) Chloroform + Acetone (b) Chloroform + Benzene

- **Azeotropic Mixture with Minimum Boiling Point**
  It is formed by liquids showing positive deviation. An intermediate composition of liquids having highest vapour pressure, hence lowest boiling point gives this azeotrope. Such azeotropes have boiling points lower than either of the pure component e.g. Rectified spirit (ethanol 95.5% + H_2O 4.50%) bpt 351.5 K.

- **Azeotropic Mixture with Maximum Boiling Point :**
  It is formed by liquids showing negative deviation. An intermediate composition of liquids having minimum vapour pressure, hence highest boiling point gives this azeotrope. Such azeotropes have boiling points higher than either of the pure components e.g. Water and HNO_3 (HNO_3 68% + H_2O 32%) bpt 393.5K.

- Raoult's law

$$P_S = p_A + p_B = p_A^o x_A + p_B^o x_B$$
$$= (1 - x_B)\, p_A^o + p_B^o x_B = (p_B^o - p_A^o) x_B + p_A^o$$
$$\frac{P^o - P_S}{P^o} = \frac{n_A}{n_B} = \frac{w_A \times M_B}{M_A \times w_B}$$

  Here, P_S = Total pressure

  p_A^o or p_B^o = vapour pressure in pure state of component A or B, x_A or x_B = mole fraction of component A or B

- n_A and n_B = no. of moles of solute and solvent w_A and w_B are the masses and M_A and M_B are the molar masses of the solute and solvent respectively.

- Elevation in boiling point $\Delta T_b = K_b m$, where,
  m = Molality
  K_b = Boiling point elevation constant or Ebullioscopic constant

- Depression in freezing point, $\Delta T_f = K_f\, m$
$$\left(m = \text{Molality} = \frac{w_A\ (g)}{M_A\ (g/mol) \times w_B\ (g)} \times 1000 \right)$$

- The most frequently used semipermeable membrane in laboratory is that of copper ferrocyanide, $Cu_2[Fe(CN)_6]$ because it is very strong and can withstand very high pressure. Remember that semipermeable membrane of $Cu_2[Fe(CN)_6]$ does not work in non-aqueous solutions because it gets dissolved is non-aqueous solvents. Other synthetic semipermeable membrane is that of calcium phosphate. Natural semipermeable membranes are parchment paper, cell wall, pig's bladder etc.

- Colligative properties $\propto$ Number of particles $\propto$ Number of molecules (in case of non-electrolytes)
  $\propto$ Number of ions (in case of electrolytes)
  $\propto$ Number of moles of solute
  $\propto$ Mole fraction of solute

- Some liquids on mixing, form azeotropes which are binary mixtures having the same composition in liquid and vapour phase and boil at a constant temperature. It is not possible to separate the components by fractional distillation.

- The solutions which show a large positive deviation from Raoult's law, form minimum boiling azeotrope at a specific composition. *e.g.* ethanol-water mixture.

- The solutions which show a large negative deviation from Raoult's law, form maximum boiling azeotrape at a specific composition. *e.g.*, 68% nitric acid and 32% water by mass with a b.p. of 393.5K.

- Dissolution of gases in liquid is always exothermic because $\Delta S = $ –ve (movement of gas decreases in liquid) and ΔG to be –ve (spontaneous process), ΔH has to be negative.

- For ideal and non-ideal solutions, $\Delta S_{mix} > 0$.

- Modern R.O. (water purifiers) work on the principle of reverse osmosis (R.O.)

- NaCl or $CaCl_2$ (anhydrous) are used to clear snow on roads. It depresses the freezing point at which ice is expected to be formed.

NCERT Questions

1. Define the term solution. How many types of solutions are formed? Write briefly about each type with an example.

Sol. A solution is a homogeneous mixture of two or more chemically non-reacting substances.

Types of solutions: There are nine types of solutions.

Types of Solution   Examples

Gaseous solutions

(a) Gas in gas   Air, mixture of O_2 and N_2, etc.

(b) Liquid in gas   Water vapour

(c) Solid in gas   Camphor vapours in N_2 gas, smoke etc.

Liquid solutions

(a) Gas in liquid CO_2 dissolved in water (aerated water), and O_2 dissolved in water, etc.

(b) Liquid in liquid   Ethanol dissolved in water, etc.

(c) Solid in liquid   Sugar dissolved in water, saline water, etc.

Solid solutions

(a) Gas in solid   Solution of hydrogen in palladium

(b) Liquid in solid   Amalgams, e.g., Na-Hg

(c) Solid in solid   Gold ornaments (Cu/Ag with Au)

2. Give an example of a solid solution in which the solute is a gas.

Sol. Solution of hydrogen in palladium and dissolved gases in minerals.

3. Define the following terms:
(i) Mole fraction   (ii) Molality
(iii) Molarity   (iv) Mass percentage

Sol. **(i) Mole fraction:** It is defined as the ratio of the number of moles of the solute to the total number of moles in the solution. If n_A is the number of moles of solute dissolved in n_B moles of solvent, then mole fraction of solute

$$(X_A) = \frac{n_A}{n_A + n_B}$$

(ii) Molality: It is defined as the number of moles of a solute present in 1000g (1kg) of a solvent.

$$\text{Molality } (m) = \frac{\text{Number of moles of solute}}{\text{Weight of solvent in kg}} = \frac{n}{W}$$

(iii) Molarity: It is defined as the number of moles of solute present in one litre of solution.

$$\text{Molarity } (M) = \frac{\text{Number of moles of solute}}{\text{Volume of solution in litre}} = \frac{n}{V}$$

$$n = \frac{\text{Weight in grams}}{\text{Molecular weight of solute}}$$

$$\therefore \ M = \frac{\text{Weight in grams}}{\text{Volume of solution in litres}}$$
$$\times \frac{1}{\text{Molecular weight of solute}}$$

(iv) Mass percentage: It is the amount of solute in grams present in 100g of solution.

$$\text{Mass percent of solute} = \frac{\text{Mass of solute}}{\text{Mass of solution}} \times 100$$

4. Concentrated nitric acid used in laboratory work is 68% nitric acid by mass in aqueous solution. What should be the molarity of such a sample of the acid if the density of the solution is 1.504 g mL^{-1}?

Sol. 68% nitric acid by mass means that 68g mass of nitric acid is dissolved in 100g mass of solution.

Molar mass of $HNO_3 = 63$g mol^{-1}

$$\therefore \ 68\text{g of } HNO_3 = \frac{68}{63} = 1.079 \text{ mole.}$$

Density of solution $= 1.504$ g mL^{-1} (given)

$$\therefore \ \text{Volume of solution} = \frac{\text{Mass}}{\text{Density}} = \frac{100}{1.504} = 66.5 \text{ mL}$$

$\therefore$ Molarity of solution

$$= \frac{\text{Moles of solute} \times 1000}{\text{Volume of solution in mL}} = \frac{1.079 \times 1000}{66.5} = 16.23 \text{ M.}$$

5. A solution of glucose in water is labelled as 10% w/w, what would be the molality and mole fraction of each component in the solution? If the density of solution is 1.2 g mL^{-1}, then what shall be the molarity of the solution?

Sol. 10 percent w/w solution of glucose in water means 10g glucose and 90g of water.

Molar mass of glucose $= 180$g mol^{-1} and molar mass of water $= 18$g mol^{-1}

$$\therefore \ 10\text{g of glucose} = \frac{10}{180} = 0.0555 \text{ moles}$$

and $90\text{g of } H_2O = \dfrac{90}{18} = 5$ moles

$\therefore$ Molality of solution

$$= \frac{\text{Moles of solute} \times 1000}{\text{Mass of solution in grams}} = \frac{0.0555}{90} \times 1000 = 0.617 \text{ m}$$

Mole fraction of glucose

$$= X_g = \frac{\text{No. of moles of glucose}}{\text{No. of moles of glucose} + \text{No. of moles of water}} = \frac{0.0555}{5 + 0.0555} = 0.01$$

Mole fraction of water

$$= X_w = \frac{\text{No. of moles of water}}{\text{No. of moles of glucose} + \text{No. of moles of water}}$$

$$= \frac{5}{5 + 0.0555} = 0.99.$$

Volume of 100g of solution

$$= \frac{\text{Mass of solution}}{\text{Density}} = \frac{100}{1 \cdot 2} = 83 \cdot 33 \text{ mL}$$

$\therefore$ Molarity of solution $= \dfrac{0 \cdot 0555}{83 \cdot 33} \times 1000 = 0 \cdot 67$ M.

6. How many mL of $0 \cdot 1$ M HCl are required to react completely with 1g mixture of Na_2CO_3 and $NaHCO_3$ containing equimolar amounts of both?

Sol. Calculation of no. of moles of components in the mixture.

Let x g of Na_2CO_3 is present in the mixture.

$\therefore (1 - x)$ g of $NaHCO_3$ is present in the mixture.

Molar mass of $Na_2CO_3 = 2 \times 23 + 12 + 3 \times 16 = 106$ g mol^{-1} and molar mass of $NaHCO_3$

$= 23 \times 1 + 1 + 12 + 3 \times 16 = 84$ g mol^{-1}

No. of moles of Na_2CO_3 in x g $= \dfrac{x}{106}$

No. of moles of $NaHCO_3$ in $(1 - x)$ g $= (1 - x) / 84$

As given that the mixture contains equimolar amounts of Na_2CO_3 and $NaHCO_3$, therefore

$$\frac{x}{106} = \frac{1 - x}{84}$$

$106 - 106\, x = 84\, x$

$106 = 190\, x$

$\therefore \quad x = \dfrac{106}{190} = 0 \cdot 558$g

$\therefore$ No. of moles of Na_2CO_3 present

$$= \frac{0 \cdot 558}{106} = 0 \cdot 00526$$

and no. of moles of $NaHCO_3$ present

$$= \frac{1 - 0 \cdot 558}{84} = 0 \cdot 00526$$

Calculation of no. of moles of HCl required

$Na_2CO_3 + 2HCl \longrightarrow 2NaCl + H_2O + CO_2$

$NaHCO_3 + HCl \longrightarrow NaCl + H_2O + CO_2$

As can be seen, each mole of Na_2CO_3 needs 2 moles of HCl,

$\therefore 0 \cdot 00526$ mole of Na_2CO_3 needs

$= 0 \cdot 00526 \times 2 = 0 \cdot 01052$ mole

Each mole of $NaHCO_3$ needs 1 mole of HCl.

$\therefore 0 \cdot 00526$ mole of $NaHCO_3$ needs

$= 1 \times 0 \cdot 00526 = 0 \cdot 00526$ mole

Total amount of HCl needed will be

$= 0 \cdot 01052 + 0 \cdot 00526 = 0 \cdot 01578$ mole.

$0 \cdot 1$ mole of $0 \cdot 1$ M HCl are present in 1000 mL of HCl

$\therefore \quad 0 \cdot 01578$ mole of $0 \cdot 1$ M HCl will be present in

$$= \frac{1000}{0 \cdot 1} \times 0 \cdot 01578 = 157 \cdot 8 \text{ mL.}$$

7. A solution is obtained by mixing 300 g of 25% solution and 400 g of 40% solution by mass. Calculate the mass percentage of the resulting solution.

Sol. 300g of 25% solution will contain $= \dfrac{25 \times 300}{100}$

$= 75$ g of solute.

400g of 40% solution will contain

$$= \frac{40 \times 400}{100} = 160 \text{ g of solute.}$$

$\therefore$ Total mass of solute $= 160 + 75 = 235$g

Total mass of solution $= 300 + 400 = 700$g

Now, the percentage of solute in solution

$$= \frac{235}{700} \times 100 = 33 \cdot 5\%$$

and, the percentage of water in solution

$= 100 - 33 \cdot 5\% = 66 \cdot 5\%$

8. An antifreeze solution is prepared from 222·6 g of ethylene glycol, $(C_2H_6O_2)$ and 200 g of water. Calculate the molality of the solution. If the density of the solution is $1 \cdot 072$ g mL^{-1}, then what shall be the molarity of the solution?

Sol. Mass of solute $= 222 \cdot 6$g

Molar mass of solute, $C_2H_4(OH)_2$

$= 12 \times 2 + 4 + 2\,(12 + 1) = 62$ g mol^{-1}

$\therefore$ Moles of solute $= \dfrac{222 \cdot 6}{62} = 3 \cdot 59$

Mass of solvent $= 200$ g

$\therefore$ Molality $= \dfrac{3 \cdot 59}{200} \times 1000 = 17 \cdot 95$ mol kg^{-1}

Total mass of solution $= 422 \cdot 6$ g

Volume of solution $= \dfrac{422 \cdot 6}{1 \cdot 072} = 394 \cdot 21$ mL.

$\therefore$ Molarity $= \dfrac{3 \cdot 59}{394 \cdot 2} \times 1000 = 9 \cdot 1$ mol L^{-1}

9. A sample of drinking water was found to be severely contaminated with chloroform ($CHCl_3$), supposed to be a carcinogen. The level of contamination was 15 ppm (by mass).
(i) express this in percent by mass.
(ii) determine the molality of chloroform in the water sample.

Sol. 15 ppm means 15 parts in million (10^6) by mass in the solution.

$\therefore$ Percentage by mass $= \dfrac{15}{10^6} \times 100 = 15 \times 10^{-4}\%$

As only 15g of chloroform is present in 10^6g of the solution, mass of the solvent $= 10^6$ g

Molar mass of $CHCl_3 = 12 + 1 + 3 \times 35 \cdot 5 = 119 \cdot 5$ g mol^{-1}

Moles of $CHCl_3 = \dfrac{15}{119 \cdot 5}$

$\therefore$ Molality $= \dfrac{15/119 \cdot 5 \times 1000}{10^6} = 1 \cdot 25 \times 10^{-4}$ m

10. What role does the molecular interaction play in a solution of alcohol and water?

Sol. Alcohol and water both have strong tendency to form intermolecular hydrogen bonding. On mixing the two, a solution is formed as a result of formation of H-bonds between alcohol and H_2O molecules but these interactions are weaker and less extensive than those in pure H_2O. Thus they show a positive deviation from ideal behaviour. As a result of this, the solution of alcohol and water will have higher vapour pressure and lower boiling point than that of water and alcohol.

11. Why do gases always tend to be less soluble in liquids as the temperature is raised?

Sol. When gases are dissolved in water, it is accompanied by a release of heat energy, *i.e.,* process is exothermic. When the temperature is increased, according to Le-chatlier's Principle, the equilibrium shifts in backward direction, and thus gases becomes less soluble in liquids.

12. State Henry's law and mention some important applications.

Sol. The effect of pressure on the solubility of a gas in a liquid is governed by Henry's Law. It states that the solubility of a gas in a liquid at a given temperature is directly proportional to the partial pressure of the gas

Mathematically, $P = K_H X$

where P is the partial pressure of the gas; and X is the mole fraction of the gas in the solution and K_H is Henry's Law constant.

Applications of Henry's law

(i) In the production of carbonated beverages (as solubility of CO_2 increases at high pressure).

(ii) In the deep sea diving.

(iii) For climbers or people living at high altitudes. where low blood O_2 causes climbers to become weak and make them unable to think clearly

13. The partial pressure of ethane over a solution containing 6.56×10^{-3} g of ethane is 1 bar. If the solution contains 5.00×10^{-2} g of ethane, then what shall be the partial pressure of the gas?

Sol. We know that, $m = K_H \times P$

$\therefore$ 6.56×10^{-3} g $= K_H \times 1$ bar ...(i)

$\therefore$ 5.00×10^{-3} g $= K_H \times P$ ...(ii)

$K_H - 6.56 \times 10^{-3}/1$ bar (from i)

$K_H = 5.00 \times 10^{-2}/P$ bar (from ii),

$\therefore$ $\dfrac{6.56 \times 10^{-3}}{1} = \dfrac{5.00 \times 10^{-2}}{P}$

$\therefore$ $P = \dfrac{5.00 \times 10^{-2}}{6.56 \times 10^{-3}} = 7.62$ bar.

14. What is meant by positive and negative deviations from Raoult's law and how is the sign of $\Delta_{mix}H$ related to positive and negative deviations from Raoult's law?

Sol. Solutions having vapour pressures more than that expected from Raoult's law are said to exhibit positive deviation. In these solutions solvent - solute interactions are weaker and $\Delta_{sol}H$ is positive because stronger $A - A$ or $B - B$ interactions are replaced by weaker $A - B$ interactions. Breaking of the stronger interactions requires more energy & less energy is released on formation of weaker interactions. So overall $\Delta_{sol}H$ is positive. Similarly $\Delta_{sol}V$ is positive i.e. the volume of solution is some what more than sum of volumes of solvent and solute. So there is expansion in volume on solution formation.

Similarly in case of solutions exhibiting negative deviations, $A - B$ interactions are stronger than $A - A$ & $B - B$. So weaker interactions are replaced by stronger interactions so there is release of energy i.e. $\Delta_{sol.}H$ is negative.

15. An aqueous solution of 2% non-volatile solute exerts a pressure of 1.004 bar at the normal boiling point of the solvent. What is the molar mass of the solute?

Sol. Vapour pressure of pure water at the boiling point $(P°) = 1.013$ bar

Vapour pressure of solution $(P_s) = 1.004$ bar

Mass of solute $(w_2) = 2$g

Molar mass of solvent, water $(M_1) = 18$g

Mass of solvent $(w_1) = 98$g

Mass of solution $= 100$g

Applying Raoult's Law for dilute solutions,

$$\dfrac{P° - P_s}{P°} = \dfrac{n_2}{n_1 + n_2} \approx \dfrac{n_2}{n_1} \qquad \text{[Dilute solution being 2\%]}$$

$$\dfrac{P° - P_s}{P°} = \dfrac{n_2}{n_1} = \dfrac{W_2/M_2}{W_1/M_1}$$

$$\dfrac{(1.013 - (1.004)}{(1.013)} = \dfrac{2 \times 18}{M_2 \times 98}$$

$$\therefore M_2 = \dfrac{2 \times 18}{98 \times 0.009} \times 1.013 = 41.35 \text{ g mol}^{-1}.$$

16. Heptane and octane form an ideal solution. At 373 K, the vapour pressures of the two liquid components are 105.2 kPa and 46.8 kPa respectively. What will be the vapour pressure of a mixture of 26.0 g of heptane and 35.0 g of octane?

Sol. Molar mass of heptane $(C_7H_{16}) = 7 \times 12 + 16 = 100$ g mol^{-1}

Molar mass of octane $(C_8H_{18}) = 8 \times 12 + 18 = 114$ g mol^{-1}

Moles of heptane present in mixture $= \dfrac{26.0}{100} = 0.26$ mol

Moles of octane present in mixture $= \dfrac{35.0}{114} = 0.307$ mol

Mole fraction of heptane $x_H = \dfrac{0.26}{0.26 + 0.307} = 0.458$

Mole fraction of octane, $x_O = (1 - 0.458) = 0.542$

Vapour pressure of heptane $= x_H \times P°$

$= 0.458 \times 105.2$ kPa $= 48.18$ kPa

Vapour pressure of octane $= x_O \times P°$

$= 0.542 \times 46.8$ kPa $= 25.36$ kPa

Vapour pressure of mixture $= 48.18 + 25.36 = 73.54$ kPa.

17. The vapour pressure of water is 12.3 kPa at 300 K. Calculate vapour pressure of 1 molal solution of a non-volatile solute in it.

Sol. 1 molal solution of solute means 1 mole of solute in 1000g of the solvent.

Molar mass of water (solvent) $= 18$ g mol^{-1}

$\therefore$ Moles of water $= \dfrac{1000}{18} = 55.5$ moles.

$\therefore$ Mole fraction of solute $= \dfrac{1}{1 + 55.5} = 0.0177$

Now, $\dfrac{P^\circ - P_s}{P^\circ} = x_2$

$\dfrac{12{\cdot}3 - P_s}{12{\cdot}3} = 0{\cdot}0177 \Rightarrow P_s = 12{\cdot}08$ kPa

18. Calculate the mass of a non-volatile solute (molar mass 40 gmol^{-1}) which should be dissolved in 114 g octane to reduce its vapour pressure to 80%.

Sol. $P_s = 80\%$ of $P^\circ = \dfrac{80}{100}\, P^\circ = 0.8\, P^\circ$

Let Wg of solute is present in mixture.

Moles of solute present $= \dfrac{W}{40}$ moles

Molar mass of octane, C_8H_{18}
$= 8 \times 12 + 18 = 114$ g mol^{-1}

$\therefore$ Moles of octane $= \dfrac{114}{114} = 1$ mol

Now, $\dfrac{P^\circ - P_s}{P^\circ} = x_2 = \dfrac{W/40}{\dfrac{W}{40} + 1}$

$\dfrac{P^\circ - 0{\cdot}80\, P^\circ}{P^\circ} = \dfrac{W/40}{W/40 + 1}$

$1 - 0{\cdot}80 = \dfrac{W \times 40}{40\,(W + 40)} = \dfrac{W}{W + 40}$

$0{\cdot}20 = \dfrac{W}{W + 40}$

$0.2\,W + 8 = W$

$8 = W\,(1 - 0.2) = 0.8\,W$

$\therefore \qquad W = \dfrac{8}{0.8} = 10$g.

19. A solution containing 30g of non-volatile solute exactly in 90 g of water has a vapour pressure of 2·8 kPa at 298 K. Further, 18g of water is then added to the solution and the new of vapour pressure becomes 2·9 kPa at 298 K. Calculate
(i) molar mass of the solute.
(ii) vapour pressure of water at 298 K.

Sol. Let the molar mass of solute $=$ M g mol^{-1}
$\therefore$ Moles of solute present

$= \dfrac{30g}{\text{M g mol}^{-1}} = \dfrac{30}{M}$ mol

Moles of solvent present, $(n_1) = \dfrac{90}{18} = 5$ moles.

$\therefore \quad \dfrac{P^\circ - P_s}{P^\circ} = \dfrac{n_2}{n_1 + n_2} \Rightarrow \dfrac{P^\circ - 2{\cdot}8}{P^\circ} = \dfrac{30/M}{5 + 30/M}$

$1 - \dfrac{2{\cdot}8}{P^\circ} = \dfrac{30}{(5M + 30)} \Rightarrow 1 - \dfrac{30}{5M + 30} = \dfrac{2{\cdot}8}{P^\circ}$

$1 - \dfrac{6}{M + 6} = \dfrac{2.8}{P^\circ} \Rightarrow \dfrac{M + 6 - 6}{M + 6} = \dfrac{2.8}{P^\circ}$

$\dfrac{M}{M + 6} = \dfrac{2{\cdot}8}{P^\circ} \Rightarrow \dfrac{P^o}{2{\cdot}8} = 1 + \dfrac{6}{M}$ ...(i)

After adding 18 g of water,
Moles of water becomes

$= \dfrac{90 + 18}{18} = \dfrac{108}{18} = 6$ moles

$\therefore \quad \dfrac{P^\circ - P_s}{P^\circ} = \dfrac{30/M}{6 + 30/M}$

P_s New vapour pressure $= 2{\cdot}9$ kPa

$\dfrac{P^\circ - 2{\cdot}9}{P^\circ} = \dfrac{30\,M}{M\,(6M + 30)} = \dfrac{5}{M + 5}$

$1 - \dfrac{2{\cdot}9}{P^\circ} = \dfrac{5}{M + 5} \Rightarrow 1 - \dfrac{5}{M + 5} = \dfrac{2{\cdot}9}{P^\circ}$

$\dfrac{M + 5 - 5}{M + 5} = \dfrac{2{\cdot}9}{P^\circ}$

$\dfrac{P^\circ}{2{\cdot}9} = \dfrac{M + 5}{M} \Rightarrow = 1 + \dfrac{5}{M}$ ...(ii)

Dividing equation (i) by (ii), we get,

$\dfrac{2{\cdot}9}{2{\cdot}8} = \dfrac{1 + 6/M}{1 + 5/M}$

$2{\cdot}9\left(1 + \dfrac{5}{M}\right) = 2{\cdot}8\left(1 + \dfrac{6}{M}\right)$

$2{\cdot}9 + \dfrac{2{\cdot}9 \times 5}{M} = 2{\cdot}8 + \dfrac{2{\cdot}8 \times 6}{M}$

$2{\cdot}9 + \dfrac{14{\cdot}5}{M} = 2{\cdot}8 + \dfrac{16{\cdot}8}{M}$

$0{\cdot}1 = \dfrac{16{\cdot}8}{M} - \dfrac{14{\cdot}5}{M} = \dfrac{2{\cdot}3}{M}$

$M = \dfrac{2{\cdot}3}{0{\cdot}1} = 23$ g mol^{-1}

Putting M $= 23$, in equation (i), we get,

$\dfrac{P^\circ}{2{\cdot}8} = 1 + \dfrac{6}{23} = \dfrac{29}{23}$

$P^\circ = \dfrac{29}{23} \times 2{\cdot}8 = 3{\cdot}53$ kPa.

20. A 5% solution (by mass) of cane sugar in water has freezing point of 271 K. Calculate the freezing point of 5% glucose in water if freezing point of pure water is 273·15 K.

Sol. Mass of sugar in 5% (by mass) solution means 5g in 100g of solvent (water)
Molar mass of sugar $= 342$g mol^{-1}

Molality of sugar solution $= \dfrac{5 \times 1000}{342 \times 100} = 0{\cdot}146$

$\therefore \Delta T_f$ for sugar solution $= 273\cdot15 - 271 = 2\cdot15°$

$\Delta T_f = K_f \times m$

$\Delta T_f = K_f \times 0.146 \Rightarrow K_f = 2\cdot15/0\cdot146$

Molality of glucose solution $= \dfrac{5}{180} \times \dfrac{1000}{100} = 0.278$

(Molar mass of glucose $= 180$ g mol^{-1})

$\Delta T_f = K_f \times m = \dfrac{2\cdot15}{0\cdot146} \times 0\cdot278 = 4\cdot09$ K

$\therefore$ Freezing point of glucose solution

$$= 273\cdot15 - 4\cdot09 = 269\cdot06 \text{ K}.$$

21. Two elements A and B form compounds having formula AB$_2$ and AB$_4$. When dissolved in 20g of benzene (C$_6$H$_6$), 1g of AB$_2$ lowers the freezing point by 2·3 K whereas 1·0 g of AB$_4$ lowers it by 1·3 K. The molar depression constant for benzene is 5·1 K kg mol^{-1}. Calculate atomic masses of A and B.

Sol. Using the relation, $M_2 = \dfrac{1000 \times k_f \times w_2}{w_1 \times \Delta T_f}$

$\therefore \quad M_{AB_2} = \dfrac{1000 \times 5\cdot1 \times 1}{20 \times 2\cdot3} = 110\cdot87$ g mol^{-1}

$M_{AB_4} = \dfrac{1000 \times 5\cdot1 \times 1}{20 \times 1\cdot3} = 196\cdot15$ g mol^{-1}

Let the atomic masses of A and B are 'p' and 'q' respectively.

Then molar mass of

$AB_2 = p + 2q = 110\cdot87$ g mol^{-1} ...(i)

And molar mass of

$AB_4 = p + 4q = 196\cdot15$ g mol^{-1} ...(ii)

Substracting equation (ii) from equation (i), we get

$2q = 85.28 \Rightarrow q = 42.64$

Putting q = 42.64 in equ. (i), we get

$p = 110.87 - 85.28 = 25.59$

Thus, atomic mass of $A = 25.59$ g mol^{-1} and atomic mass of $B = 42.64$ g mol^{-1}

22. At 300 K, 36g of glucose present in a litre of its solution has an osmotic pressure of 4·98 bar. If the osmotic pressure of the solution is 1·52 bars at the same temperature, what would be its concentration?

Sol. $\pi = CRT$

$4\cdot98 = \dfrac{W_1}{M_1} \times R \times 300$

$4\cdot98 = \dfrac{36}{180} \times R \times 300$

$4\cdot98 = 60\,R$ ...(i)

In second case $1\cdot52 = C \times R \times 300$ ...(ii)

Diving equation (ii) by equation (i), we get

$$C = \dfrac{60 \times 1.52}{300 \times 4.98} = 0.06 \text{ M}$$

23. Suggest the most important type of intermolecular attractive interaction in the following pairs :

(i) *n*-hexane and *n*-octane

(ii) I$_2$ and CCl$_4$

(iii) NaClO$_4$ and water

(iv) methanol and acetone

(v) acetonitrile (CH$_3$CN) and acetone (C$_3$H$_6$O)

Sol. **(i)** Both *n*-hexane and *n*-octane are non-polar. Thus, the intermolecular interactions will be London dispersion forces.

(ii) Both I$_2$ and CCl$_4$ are non-polar. Thus, the intermolecular interactions will be London dispersion forces.

(iii) NaClO$_4$ is an ionic compound and gives Na$^+$ and ClO$_4^-$ ions in the solution. Water is a polar molecule. Thus, the intermolecular interactions will be ion-dipole interactions.

(iv) Both methanol and acetone are polar molecules. Thus, intermolecular interactions will be dipole-dipole interactions.

(v) Both CH$_3$CN and C$_3$H$_6$O are polar molecules. Thus, intermolecular interactions will be dipole-dipole interactions.

24. Based on solute-solvent interactions, arrange the following in order of increasing solubility in *n*-octane and explain.

Cyclohexane, KCl, CH$_3$OH, CH$_3$CN.

Sol. **(a)** Cyclohexane and *n*-octane both are non-polar. They mix completely in all proportions.

(b) KCl is an ionic compound, KCl will not dissolve in *n*-octane.

(c) CH$_3$OH is polar. CH$_3$OH will dissolve in *n*-octane.

(d) CH$_3$CN is polar but lesser than CH$_3$OH. Therefore, it will dissolve in *n*-octane but to a greater extent as compared to CH$_3$OH.

Hence, the order is

KCl < CH$_3$OH < CH$_3$CN < Cyclohexane.

25. Amongst the following compounds, identify which are insoluble, partially soluble and highly soluble in water?

(i) phenol   **(ii)** toluene

(iii) formic acid   **(iv)** ethylene glycol

(v) chloroform   **(vi)** pentanol

Sol. **(i)** Phenol (having polar – OH group) – Partially soluble.

(ii) Toluene (non-polar) – Insoluble.

(iii) Formic acid (form hydrogen bonds with water molecules) – Highly soluble.

(iv) Ethylene glycol (form hydrogen bonds with water molecules) – Highly soluble.

(v) Chloroform (non-polar) – Insoluble.

(vi) Pentanol (having polar –OH) – Partially soluble.

26. If the density of some lake water is 1·25 g mL^{-1} and contains 92g of Na$^+$ ions per kg of water, calculate the molality of Na$^+$ ions in the lake.

Sol. Molar mass of Na = 23 g mol^{-1}

$\therefore$ No. of moles of Na$^+$ ions present $= \dfrac{92}{23} = 4$ moles

$\therefore$ Molality $= \dfrac{4 \times 1000}{1000} = 4$ m.

27. **If the solubility product of CuS is 6×10^{-16}, calculate the maximum molarity of CuS in aqueous solution.**

Sol. $CuS \rightleftharpoons Cu^{2+} + S^{2-}$, $K_{sp} = 6 \times 10^{-16}$

Maximum molarity of CuS in aqueous solution means solubility of CuS.

Let the solubility of CuS be S mol L^{-1}

$\therefore$ $K_{sp} = [Cu^{2+}][S]^{2-}$

$6 \times 10^{-16} = S \times S = S^2$

$\therefore$ $S = \sqrt{6 \times 10^{-16}} = 2.45 \times 10^{-8}$ mol L^{-1}.

28. **Calculate the mass percentage of aspirin ($C_9H_8O_4$) in acetonitrile (CH_3CN) when 6·5g of $C_9H_8O_4$ is dissolved in 450 g of CH_3CN.**

Sol. Mass percentage of aspirin

$= \dfrac{\text{Mass of aspirin}}{\text{Mass of aspirin + Mass of acetonitrile}} \times 100$

$= \dfrac{6.5}{6.5 + 450} \times 100 = 1.424\%$

29. **Nalorphene ($C_{19}H_{21}NO_3$), similar to morphine, is used to combat withdrawal symptoms in narcotic users. Dose of nalorphene generally given is 1·5 mg. Calculate the mass of $1·5 \times 10^{-3}$ m aqueous solution required for the above dose.**

Sol. $1·5 \times 10^{-3}$ m aqueous solution of nalorphene means that $1·5 \times 10^{-3}$ mole of nalorphene is dissolved in 1 kg of water.

Molar mass of nalorphene, $C_{19}H_{21}NO_3$

$= 19 \times 12 + 21 + 14 + 3 \times 16 = 311$ g mol^{-1}

$\therefore$ $1·5 \times 10^{-3}$ mole of nalorphene

$= 1·5 \times 10^{-3} \times 311g = 0·467$ g

$\therefore$ Mass of solution $= 0·467 + 1000 = 1000·467$ g.

For 0·467g of nalorphene, mass of solution required $= 1000·467$g

For 1·5 mg ($1·5 \times 10^{-3}$g) of nalorphene,

mass of solution required

$= \dfrac{1000·467}{0·467} \times 1·5 \times 10^{-3} = 3·21g.$

30. **Calculate the amount of benzoic acid (C_6H_5COOH) required for preparing 250 mL of 0·15 M solution in methanol.**

Sol. 0·15 M solution means than 0·15 mole of benzoic acid is dissolved in 1L of solution.

Molar mass of C_6H_5COOH

$= 12 \times 6 + 5 + 12 + 2 \times 16 + 1 = 122g$ mol^{-1}

$\therefore$ 0·15 mol of $C_6H_5COOH = 0·15 \times 122 = 18·3g$

Thus, 1 L or 1000 mL of solution contain

$= 18·3g$ of C_6H_5COOH

$\therefore$ 250 mL of the solution will contain

$= \dfrac{18·3}{1000} \times 250 = 4·575g$ of C_6H_5COOH.

31. **The depression in freezing point of water observed for the same amount of acetic acid, trichloroacetic acid and trifluoroacetic acid increases in the order given above. Explain briefly.**

Sol. $CH_3COOH <$ $\underset{\underset{Cl}{|}}{\overset{Cl}{\diagup}} C-COOH <$ $\underset{\underset{F}{|}}{\overset{F}{\diagup}} C-COOH$

Fluorine being more electronegative than chlorine has the highest electron withdrawing inductive effect. Thus, triflouroacetic acid is the strongest trichloroacetic acid is second most and acetic acid is the weakest acid due to absence of any electron withdrawing group. Thus, F_3CCOOH ionizes to the largest extent while CH_3COOH ionizes to minimum extent in water. Greater the extent of ionization greater is the depression in freezing point. Hence, the order of depression in freezing point will be $CH_3COOH < Cl_3CCOOH < F_3CCOOH$.

32. **Vapour pressure of water at 293 K is 17·535 mm Hg. Calculate the vapour pressure of water at 293 K when 25g of glucose is dissolved in 450g of water.**

Sol. $P° = 17·535$ mm Hg

Molar mass of glucose = 180 g mol^{-1}

Molar mass of water = 18 g mol^{-1}

According to Raoult's law,

$$\dfrac{P° - P_s}{P°} = \dfrac{n_2}{n_1 + n_2} \simeq \dfrac{n_2}{n_1} = \dfrac{W_2/M_2}{W_1/M_1}$$

$$1 - \dfrac{P_s}{P°} = \dfrac{25/180}{450/18} = \dfrac{25 \times 18}{180 \times 450}$$

$$1 - \dfrac{P_s}{P°} = \dfrac{450}{81000}; \quad 1 - \dfrac{450}{81000} = \dfrac{P_s}{P°}$$

$$1 - 0.0055 = \dfrac{P_s}{17·535}$$

$$0.9945 = \dfrac{P_s}{17·535}$$

$\therefore$ $P_s = 0.9945 \times 17·535 = 17·44$ mm Hg.

33. **Henry's law constant for the molality of methane in benzene at 298 K is $4·27 \times 10^5$ mm Hg. Calculate the solubility of methane in benzene at 298 K under 760 mm Hg.**

Sol. Using relation, $P = K_H x$

$$\therefore \quad x = \dfrac{P}{K_H} = \dfrac{760 \text{ mm Hg}}{4·27 \times 10^5 \text{ mm Hg}} = 1·78 \times 10^{-3}$$

i.e., mole fraction of methane in benzene $= 1·78 \times 10^{-3}$.

34. **100g of liquid A (molar mass 140 g mol^{-1}) was dissolved in 1000g of liquid B (molar mass 180 g mol^{-1}). The vapour pressure of pure liquid B was found to be 500**

torr. Calculate the vapour pressure of pure liquid A and its vapour pressure in the solution if the total vapour pressure of the solution is 475 torr.

Sol. No. of moles of solute, $n_2 = \dfrac{100}{140} = \dfrac{5}{7}$ mole

No. of moles of solvent, $n_1 = \dfrac{1000}{180} = \dfrac{50}{9}$ mole

Mole fraction of solute,

$$x_2 = \dfrac{n_2}{n_1 + n_2} = \dfrac{5/7}{5/7 + 50/9} = 0.114$$

Mole fraction of solvent, $x_1 = (1 - x_2) = (1 - 0.114) = 0.886$

According to Raoult's law

$$P_A = x_A\, P_A^\circ = 0.114 \times P_A^\circ$$

$$P_B = x_B\, P_B^\circ = 0.886 \times 500 = 443 \text{ torr}$$

$$P_{\text{Total}} = P_A + P_B$$

$$475 = 0.114\, P_A^\circ + 443$$

$$P_A^\circ = \dfrac{475 - 443}{0.114} = 280.7 \text{ torr}$$

$$\therefore \quad P_A = 0.114 \times 280.7 = 32 \text{ torr.}$$

35. **Vapour pressures of pure acetone and chloroform at 328 K are 741.8 mm Hg and 632.8 mm Hg respectively. Assuming that they form ideal solution over the entire range of composition, plot P_{total}, $P_{\text{chloroform}}$ and P_{acetone} as a function of χ_{acetone}. The experimental data observed for different compositions of mixtures is:**

$100 \times \chi_{\text{acetone}}$	0	11.8	23.4	36.0	50.8	58.2	64.5	72.1
P_{acetone}/mm Hg	0	54.9	110.1	202.4	322.7	405.9	454.1	521.1
$P_{\text{chloroform}}$/mm Hg	632.8	548.1	469.4	359.7	257.7	193.6	161.2	120.7

Plot this data also on the same graph paper. Indicate whether it has positive deviation or negative deviation from the ideal solution.

Sol.

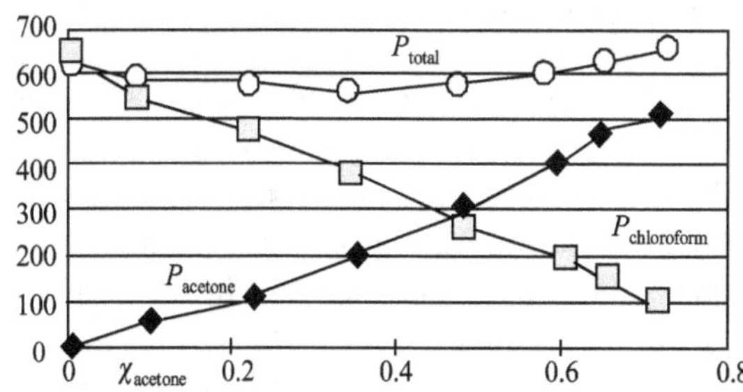

As the plot for P_{total} dips downwards, hence the solution shows negative deviation from the ideal behaviour.

36. **Benzene and toluene form ideal solution over the entire range of composition. The vapour pressure of pure benzene and toluene at 300 K are 50·71 mm Hg and 32·06 mm Hg respectively. Calculate the mole fraction of benzene in vapour phase if 80g of benzene is mixed with 100g of toluene.**

Sol. Molar mass of $C_6H_6 = 78$ g mol^{-1}
Molar mass of $C_6H_5CH_3 = 92$ g mol^{-1}

No. of moles of $C_6H_6 = \dfrac{80}{78} = 1.026$ mole

No. of moles of $C_6H_5CH_3 = \dfrac{100}{92} = 1.087$ mole

Mole fraction of C_6H_6, $x_B = \dfrac{1.026}{1.026 + 1.087} = 0.486$

Mole fraction of $C_6H_5CH_3$, $x_T = \dfrac{1.087}{1.026 + 1.087} = 0.514$

According to Raoult's Law,

$$P_B = x_B \times P_B^\circ = 0.486 \times 50.71 = 24.65 \text{mm}$$

$$P_T = x_T \times P_T^\circ = 0.514 \times 32.06 = 16.48 \text{ mm}$$

Mole fraction of C_6H_6 in vapour phase

$$= \dfrac{P_B}{P_B + P_T} = \dfrac{24.65}{24.65 + 16.48} = 0.599.$$

37. **The air is a mixture of a number of gases. The major components are oxygen and nitrogen with approximate proportion of 20% is to 79% by volume at 298 K. The water is in equilibrium with air at a pressure of 10 atm. At 298 K if the Henry's law constants for oxygen and nitrogen are 3.30×10^7 mm and 6.51×10^7 mm respectively, calculate the composition of these gases in water.**

Sol. Air containing 20% oxygen and 79% nitrogen by volume means

Partial pressure of $O_2\,(P_{O_2}) = \dfrac{20}{100} \times 10 = 2$ atm

$$= 2 \times 760 \text{ mm} = 1520 \text{ mm}$$

Partial pressure of $N_2\,(P_{N_2}) = \dfrac{79 \times 10}{100} = 7.9$ atm

$$= 7.9 \times 760 \text{ mm} = 6004 \text{ mm}$$

According to Henry's Law,

$$P_{O_2} = K_H\, x_{O_2}$$

$$x_{O_2} = \dfrac{P_{O_2}}{K_H} = \dfrac{1520}{3.30 \times 10^7} = 4.61 \times 10^{-5}$$

$$P_{N_2} = K_H\, x_{N_2}$$

$$x_{N_2} = \dfrac{P_{N_2}}{K_H} = \dfrac{6004}{6.51 \times 10^7} = 9.22 \times 10^{-5}.$$

Past year Exercise

Very Short Answer Questions

1. Identify which liquid will have a higher vapour pressure at 90°C if the boiling points of two liquids A and B are 140°C and 180°, respectively.
2. What is meant by reverse osmosis?
3. State Raoult's law.
4. Explain boiling point elevation constant for a solvent or Ebullioscopic constant.
5. Some liquids on mixing form 'azeotropes'. What are 'azeotropes'?
6. What type of intermolecular attractive interaction exists in the pair of methanol and acetone?
7. What are isotonic solutions ?

Short Answer Questions

8. For a 5% solution of urea (Molar mass = 60 g/mol), calculate the osmotic pressure at 300 K. [R = 0.0821 L atm K^{-1} mol^{-1}]

    OR

    Visha took two aqueous solutions – one containing 7.5 g of urea (Molar mass = 60 g/mol) and the other containing 42.75 g of substance Z in 100 g water, respectively. It was observed that both the solutions froze at the same temperature. Calculate the molar mass of Z.
9. Calculate the mass of ascorbic acid (Molar mass = 176 g mol^{-1}) to be dissolved in 75 g of acetic acid, to lower its freezing point by 1.5°C. (K_f = 3.9 K kg mol^{-1})
10. Give reasons for the following:
    (a) Aquatic species are more comfortable in cold water than warm water.
    (b) At higher altitudes, people suffer from anoxia resulting in inability to think.

    OR

    What type of azeotropic mixture will be formed by a solution of acetone and chloroform? Justify on the basis of strength of intermolecular interactions that develop in the solution.
11. At 300 K, 30 g of glucose present in a litre of its solution has an osmotic pressure of 4·98 bar. If the osmotic pressure of a glucose solution is 1·52 bar, at the same temperature what would be its concentration?
12. Calculate the freezing point of a solution containing 60 g glucose
    (Molar mass = 180 g mol^{-1}) in 250 g of water.
    (K_f of water = 1.86 K kg mol^{-1})

13. Given reasons for the following :
    (a) Measurement of osmotic pressure method is preferred for the determination of molar masses of macro-molecules such as proteins and polymers.
    (b) Aquatic animals are more comfortable in cold water than in warm water.
    (c) Elevation of boiling point of 1 M KCl solution is nearly double than of 1 M sugar solution.
14. Find the boiling point of a solution containing 0.520 g of glucose ($C_6H_{12}O_6$) dissolved in 80.2 g of water.
    (K_b = 0.52 K/m)
15. A solution prepared by dissolving 1.25 g of oil of winter green (methyl salicylate) in 99.0 g of benzene has a boiling point of 80.31°C. Determine the molar mass of this compound.
    (Given: B.Pt. of benzene = 80.10°C; K_b for benzene = 2.53°C kg mol^{-1})
16. Calculate the mass of ascorbic acid ($C_6H_8O_6$) to be dissolved in 75 g of acetic acid to lower its melting point by 1.5°C. (K_f for acetic acid = 3.9 K kg mol^{-1})
17. Explain why a solution of chloroform and acetone shows negative deviation from Raoult's law?
18. What would be the molar mass of a compound if 6.21g of it dissolved in 24.0 g of chloroform form a solution that has a boiling point of 68.04°C. The boiling point of pure chloroform is 61.7°C and the boiling point elevation constant, K_b for chloroform is 3.63°C/m.

    OR

    A solution prepared by dissolving 8.95 mg of a gene fragment in 35.0 mL of water has an osmotic pressure of 0.335 torr at 25° C. Assuming the gene fragment is non-electrolyte, determine its molar mass.
19. Differentiate between molarity and molality for a solution, How does a change in temperature influence their values ?
20. Non-ideal solutions exhibit either positive or negative deviations from Raoult's law. What are these deviations and why are they caused? Explain with one example for each type.
21. The molecular masses of polymers are determined by osmotic pressure method and not by measuring other colligative properties. Give two reasons.
22. Explain the Henry's law about dissolution of a gas in a liquid.
23. If the density of water of a lake is 1.25 g mL^{-1} and one kg of lake water contains 92 g of Na$^+$ ions, calculate the molarity of Na$^+$ ions in this lake water. [At. mass of Na = 23 g mol^{-1}]

24. 15.0 g of an unknown molecular material is dissolved in 450 g of water. The resulting solution freezes at $-0.34°C$. What is the molar mass of the material? (K_f for water = 1.86 K kg mol^{-1})

25. A solution of glycerol ($C_3H_8O_3$) in water was prepared by adding some glycerol in 500 g of water. This solution has a boiling point of 100.42°C while pure water boils at 100°C. What mass of glycerol was dissolved to make the solution?

26. 18 g of glucose, $C_6H_{12}O_6$ (Molar Mass = 180 g mol^{-1}) is dissolved in 1 kg of water in a sauce pan. At what temperature will this solution boil?
(K_b for water = 0.52 K kg mol^{-1}, boiling point of pure water = 373.15 K)

27. The partial pressure of ethane over a saturated solution containing 6.56×10^{-2} g of ethane is 1 bar. If the solution were to contains 5.0×10^{-2} g of ethane, then what will be the partial pressure of the gas?

28. Calculate the mass of compound (molar mass = 256 g mol^{-1}) to be dissolved in 75 g of benzene to lower its freezing point by 0.48 K (K_f = 5.12 K kg mol^{-1}).

29. Define an ideal solution and write one of its characteristics.

30. State Henry's Law. What is the effect of temperature on the solubility of a gas in a liquid?

31. State Raoult's law for the solution containing volatile components. What is the similarity between Raoult's law and Henry's law?

32. Calculate the freezing point of the solution when 31 g of ethylene glycol ($C_2H_6O_2$) is dissolved in 500 g of water (K_f for water = 1.86 K kg mol^{-1})

33. (i) Gas (A) is more soluble in water than Gas (B) at the same temperature. Which one of the two gases will have the higher value of K_H (Henry's constant) and why ?

(ii) In non-ideal solution, what type of deviation shows the formation of maximum boiling azeotropes ?

NCERT Exemplar

Multiple Choice Questions

1. On dissolving sugar in water at room temperature solution feels cools to touch. Under which of the following cases dissolution of sugar will be most rapid?
(a) Sugar crystals in cold water
(b) Sugar crystals in hot water
(c) Powdered sugar in cold water
(d) Powdered sugar in hot water

2. A beaker contains a solution of substance 'A'. Precipitation of substance 'A' takes place when small amount of 'A' is added to the solution. The solution is ....
(a) saturated   (b) supersaturated
(c) unsaturated   (d) concentrated

3. Maximum amount of a solid solute that can be dissolved in a specified amount of a given liquid solvent does not depend upon ....
(a) temperature
(b) nature of solute
(c) pressure
(d) nature of solvent

4. Low concentration of oxygen in the blood and tissues of people living at high altitude is due to ....
(a) low temperature
(b) low atmospheric pressure
(c) high atmospheric pressure
(d) Both low temperature and high atmospheric pressure

5. Which of the following aqueous solutions should have the highest boiling point?
(a) 1.0 M NaOH   (b) 1.0 M Na_2SO_4
(c) 1.0 M NH_4NO_3 (d) 1.0 M KNO_3

6. The unit of ebullioscopic constant is
(a) K kg mol^{-1} or K (molality)$^{-1}$
(b) mol kg K^{-1} or K^{-1} (molality)
(c) kg mol^{-1} K^{-1} or K^{-1} (molality)$^{-1}$
(d) K mol kg^{-1} or K (molality)

7. 4 L of 0.02 M aqueous solution of NaCl was diluted by adding 1 L of water. The molality of the resultant solution is ....
(a) 0.004   (b) 0.008   (c) 0.012   (d) 0.016

8. An unripe mango placed in a concentrated salt solution to prepare pickle shrivels because ....
(a) it gains water due to osmosis
(b) it loses water due to reverse osmosis
(c) it gains water due to reverse osmosis
(d) it loses water due to osmosis

9. At a given temperature, osmotic pressure of a concentrated solution of a substance ....
(a) is higher than that of a dilute solution
(b) is lower than that of a dilute solution
(c) is same as that of a dilute solution
(d) cannot be compared with osmotic pressure of dilute solution

10. Which of the following statement is false?
(a) Units of atmospheric pressure and osmotic pressure are same
(b) In reverse osmosis, solvent molecules move through a semipermeable membrane from a region of lower concentration of solute to a region of higher concentration
(c) The value of molal depression constant depends on nature of solvent
(d) Relative lowering of vapour pressure, is a dimensionless quantity

DIRECTIONS (Qs. 11-13) : *Each of these questions contains an assertion followed by reason. Read them carefully and answer the question on the basis of following options. You have to select the one that best describes the two statements.*

(a) If both Assertion and Reason are correct and the Reason is a correct explanation of the Assertion.

(b) If both Assertion and Reason are correct but Reason is not a correct explanation of the Assertion.

(c) If the Assertion is correct but Reason is incorrect.

(d) If the Assertion is incorrect but the Reason is correct.

11. **Assertion :** Molarity of a solution in liquid state changes with temperature.
    Reason : The volume of a solution changes with change in temperature.

12. **Assertion :** When methyl alcohol is added to water, boiling point of water increases.
    Reason : When a volatile solute is added to a volatile solvent elevation in boiling point is observed.

13. **Assertion :** When a solution is separated from the pure solvent by a semipermeable membrane, the solvent molecules pass through it from pure solvent side to the solution side.
    Reason : Diffusion of solvent occurs from a region of high concentration solution to a region of low concentration solution.

14. Components of a binary mixture of two liquids A and B were being separated by distillation. After sometime separation of components stopped and composition of vapour phase became same as that of liquid phase. Both the components started coming in the distillate. Explain why this happened.

15. Why are aquatic species more comfortable in cold water in comparison to warm water?

16. Why is the vapour pressure of an aqueous solution of glucose lower than that of water?

17. How does sprinkling of salt help in clearing the snow covered roads in hilly areas? Explain the phenomenon involved in the process.

18. Volatile hydrocarbons are not used in the brakes of automobile as lubricants, but non-volatile hydrocarbons are used as lubricants.

Objective Practice Exercise

DIRECTIONS : *This section contains multiple choice questions. Each question has four choices (a), (b), (c) and (d) out of which only one is correct.*

1. Which of the following units is useful in relating concentration of solution with its vapour pressure?
   (a) Mole fraction   (b) Parts per milion
   (c) Mass percentage   (d) Molality

2. A solid dissolves in water exothermically. If its saturated solution at 20°C is cooled to 0°C, then
   (a) some solid seperates out
   (b) some ice separates out
   (c) both the solid and ice separate
   (d) neither the solid nor the ice separates out

3. The molarity of pure water is
   (a) 50 M   (b) 18 M   (c) 55.6 M (d) 100 M

4. Which of the following statements, regarding the mole fraction (x) of a component in solution, is incorrect?
   (a) $0 \leq x \leq 1$ (b) $x < 1$
   (c) x is always non-negative (d) None of these

5. Considering the formation, breaking and strength of hydrogen bond, predict which of the following mixtures will show a positive deviation from Raoult's law?
   (a) Methanol and acetone
   (b) Chloroform and acetone
   (c) Nitric acid and water
   (d) Phenol and aniline

6. At equilibrium the rate of dissolution of a solid solute in a volatile liquid solvent is ....
   (a) less than the rate of crystallisation
   (b) greater than the rate of crystallisation
   (c) equal to the rate of crystallisation
   (d) zero

7. A solution of sucrose (molar mass = 342 g mol^{-1}) has been prepared by dissolving 68.5 g of sucrose in 1000 g of water. The freezing point of the solution obtained will be (K_f for water = 1.86 K kg mol^{-1}).
   (a) $- 0.372°C$ (b) $- 0.520°C$
   (d) $+ 0.372°C$ (d) $- 0.570°C$

8. The boiling point of a solution of 0.11 g of a substance in 15 g of ether was found to be 0.1°C higher than that of pure ether. The molecular weight of the substance will be ($K_b = 2.16°K$ kg mol^{-1})
   (a) 148   (b) 158   (c) 168   (d) 178

9. If the elevation in boiling point of a solution of 10 gm of solute (mol. wt. = 100) in 100 gm of water is ΔT_b, the ebullioscopic constant of water is
   (a) 10   (b) $10 \, \Delta T_b$ (c) ΔT_b (d) $\dfrac{\Delta T_b}{10}$

10. A solution of urea (mol. mass 56 g mol^{-1}) boils at 100.18°C at the atmospheric pressure. If K_f and K_b for water are 1.86 and 0.512 K kg mol^{-1} respectively, the above solution will freeze at
    (a) 0.654°C   (b) $- 0.654°C$
    (c) 6.54°C   (d) $- 6.54°C$

11. A solution containing 4.0 g of PVC in 2 litre of dioxane (industrial solvent) was found to have an osmotic pressure 3.0×10^{-4} atm at 27°C. The molar mass of the polymer (g/mol) will be :
    (a) 1.6×10^{4} (b) 1.6×10^{5}
    (c) 1.6×10^{3} (d) 1.6×10^{2}

12. Osmotic pressure of blood is 7.40 atm, at 27°C. Number of moles of glucose to be used per litre for an intravenous injection that is to have same osmotic pressure of blood is:
    (a) 0.3   (b) 0.2   (c) 0.1   (d) 0.4

13. A beaker contains a solution of substance 'A'. Precipitation of substance 'A' takes place when small amount of 'A' is added to the solution. The solution is ....
    (a) saturated   (b) supersaturated
    (c) unsaturated   (d) concentrated

14. K_H value for Ar (g), CO_2 (g), HCHO (g) and CH_4 (g) are 40.39, 1.67, 1.83×10^{-5} and 0.413 respectively. Arrange these gases in the order of their increasing solubility.
    (a) $HCHO < CH_4 < CO_2 < Ar$
    (b) $HCHO < CO_2 < CH_4 < Ar$
    (c) $Ar < CO_2 < CH_4 < HCHO$
    (d) $Ar < CH_4 < CO_2 < HCHO$

15. When the solute is present in trace quantities the following expression is used
    (a) gram per million   (b) milligram percent
    (c) microgram percent   (d) parts per million

16. The solubility of gases in liquids (water) is favoured by
    (a) increase in both pressure and temperature
    (b) decrease in both pressure and temperature
    (c) increase in pressure and decrease in temperature
    (d) decrease in pressure and increase in tempeature

17. The solubility of N_2 in water at 300 K and 500 torr partial pressure is 0.01 g L^{-1}. The solubility (in g L^{-1}) at 750 torr partial pressure is :
    (a) 0.0075   (b) 0.005   (c) 0.02   (d) 0.015

18. Equal moles of water and urea are taken in a flask. What is mass percentage of urea in the solution ?
    (a) 7.692%   (b) 769.2%
    (c) 76.92%   (d) 0.7692%

19. Maximum amount of a solid solute that can be dissolved in a specified amount of a given liquid solvent does not depend upon ....
    (a) temperature   (b) nature of solute
    (c) pressure   (d) nature of solvent

20. What is the normality of a 1 M solution of H_3PO_4 ?
    (a) 0.5 N   (b) 1.0 N   (c) 2.0 N   (d) 3.0 N

21. The statement "If 0.003 moles of a gas are dissolved in 900 g of water under a pressure of 1 atmosphere, 0.006 moles will be dissolved under a pressure of 2 atmospheres", illustrates
    (a) Dalton's law of partial pressure
    (b) Graham's law
    (c) Raoult's law
    (d) Henry's law

22. 1 M, 2.5 litre NaOH solution is mixed with another 0.5 M, 3 litre NaOH solution. Then find out the molarity of resultant solution
    (a) 0.80 M   (b) 1.0 M
    (c) 0.73 M   (d) 0.50 M

23. An X molal solution of a compound in benzene has mole fraction of solute equal to 0.2. The value of X is
    (a) 14   (b) 3.2
    (c) 1.4   (d) 2

24. Low concentration of oxygen in the blood and tissues of people living at high altitude is due to ....
    (a) low temperature
    (b) low atmospheric pressure
    (c) high atmospheric pressure
    (d) Both low temperature and high atmospheric pressure

25. On mixing 10 mL of acetone with 40 mL of chloroform, the total volume of the solution is
    (a) < 50 mL   (b) > 50 mL
    (c) $= 50$ mL   (d) Cannot be predicted

26. Each pair forms ideal solution except
    (a) C_2H_5Br and C_2H_5I (b) C_6H_5Cl and C_6H_5Br
    (c) C_6H_6 and $C_6H_5CH_3$ (d) C_2H_6I and C_2H_5OH

27. The vapour pressure of a given liquid will decrease if :
    (a) surface area of liquid is decreased
    (b) the volume of liquid in the container is decreased
    (c) the volume of the vapour phase is increased
    (d) the temperature is decreased

28. For a dilute solution, Raoult's law states that:
    (a) the lowering of vapour pressure is equal to the mole fraction of solute
    (b) the relative lowering of vapour pressure is equal to the mole fraction of solute
    (c) the relative lowering of vapour pressure is proportional to the amount of solute in solution
    (d) the vapour pressure of the solution is equal to the mole fraction of solvent

29. An azeotropic mixture of two liquids has a boiling point higher than either of them when it:
    (a) shows positive deviation from Raoult's law
    (b) shows negative deviation from Raoult's law
    (c) shows ideal behaviour
    (d) is saturated

30. A solution of sodium sulfate contains 92 g of Na^+ ions per kilogram of water. The molality of Na^+ ions in that solution in mol kg^{-1} is:
    (a) 12   (b) 4
    (c) 8   (d) 16

31. If $p°$ and p_s are vapour pressures of solvent and its solution, respectively, χ_1 and χ_2 are mole fractions of solvent and solute, respectively, then
    (a) $p_s = p°/\chi_2$ (b) $p° - p_s = p°\chi_2$
    (c) $p_s = p°\chi_2$ (d) $\dfrac{p° - p_s}{p_s} = \dfrac{\chi_1}{\chi_1 + \chi_2}$

32. The mole fraction of the solute in one molal aqueous solution is

(a) 0.027   (b) 0.036

(c) 0.018   (d) 0.019

33. For a binary ideal liquid solution, the total vapour pressure of the solution is given as:

(a) $P_{total} = P_A^{\circ} + (P_A^{\circ} - P_B^{\circ})x_B$

(b) $P_{total} = P_B^{\circ} + (P_A^{\circ} - P_B^{\circ})x_A$

(c) $P_{total} = P_B^{\circ} + (P_B^{\circ} - P_A^{\circ})x_A$

(d) $P_{total} = P_B^{\circ} + (P_B^{\circ} - P_A^{\circ})x_B$

34. The mole fraction of component A in vapour phase is χ_1 and mole fraction of component A in liquid mixture is χ_2 (p_A° = vapour pressure of pure A; p_B° = vapour pressure of pure B). Then total vapour pressure of the liquid mixture is

(a) $\dfrac{p_A^{\circ} x_2}{x_1}$ (b) $\dfrac{p_A^{\circ} x_1}{x_2}$

(c) $\dfrac{p_B^{\circ} x_1}{x_2}$ (d) $\dfrac{p_B^{\circ} x_2}{x_1}$

35. The vapour pressure of an aqueous solution of sucrose at 373 K is found to be 750 mm Hg. The molality of the solution at the same temperature will be :

(a) 0.26   (b) 0.73

(c) 0.74   (d) 0.039

36. The vapour pressure of acetone at 20°C is 185 torr. When 1.2 g of a non-volatile substance was dissolved in 100 g of acetone at 20°C, its vapour pressure was 183 torr. The molar mass (g mol^{-1}) of the substance is :

(a) 128   (b) 488

(c) 32   (d) 64

37. When common salt is dissolved in water

(a) The melting point of the solution increases.

(b) The boiling point of solution decreases.

(c) Both melting point and boiling point decrease.

(d) The boiling point of the solution increases.

38. Which statement is incorrect about osmotic pressure (π), volume (V), and temperature (T)?

(a) $\pi \propto \dfrac{1}{V}$, if T is constant.

(b) $\pi \propto T$, if V is constant.

(c) $\pi \propto V$, if T is constant.

(d) πV, is constant, if T is constant.

39. When solid SnO_2 is added to an aqueous solution of NaOH, the

(a) vapour pressure is lowered

(b) vapour pressure is raised

(c) osmotic pressure is increased

(d) boiling point is raised

40. Blood has been found to be isotonic with

(a) Normal saline solution

(b) Saturated NaCl solution

(c) Saturated KCl solution

(d) Saturated solution of a 1 : 1 mixture of NaCl and KCl

41. The molecular mass of a solute cannot be calculated by which of the following?

(a) $M_B = \dfrac{W_B \times RT}{\pi V}$

(b) $M_B = \dfrac{p^{\circ} W_B M_A}{(p^{\circ} - p) W_A}$

(c) $M_B = \dfrac{\Delta T_b W_B \times 1000}{K_b W_A}$

(d) $M_B = \dfrac{K_b W_B \times 1000}{\Delta T_b \times W_A}$

DIRECTIONS (Qs. 42-45) : *Following are the case/passage based questions.*

Boiling point or freezing point of liquid solution would be affected by the dissolved solids in the liquid phase. A soluble solid in solution has the effect of raising its boiling point and depressing its freezing point. The addition of non-volatile substances to a solvent decreases the vapor pressure and the added solute particles affect the formation of pure solvent crystals. According to many researches the decrease in freezing point directly correlated to the concentration of solutes dissolved in the solvent. This phenomenon is expressed as freezing point depression and it is useful for several applications such as freeze concentration of liquid food and to find the molar mass of an unknown solute in the solution. Freeze concentration is a high quality liquid food concentration method where water is removed by forming ice crystals. This is done by cooling the liquid food below the freezing point of the solution. The freezing point depression is referred as a colligative property and it is proportional to the molar concentration of the solution (m), along with vapor pressure lowering, boiling point elevation, and osmotic pressure. These are physical characteristics of solutions that depend only on the identity of the solvent and the concentration of the solute. The characters are not depending on the solute's identity. (Jayawardena, J. A. E. C., Vanniarachchi, M. P. G., & Wansapala, M. A. J. (2017). Freezing point depression of different Sucrose solutions and coconut water.)

[From CBSE Question Bank-2021]

42. When a non volatile solid is added to pure water it will:

(a) boil above 100°C and freeze above 0°C

(b) boil below 100°C and freeze above 0°C

(c) boil above 100°C and freeze below 0°C

(d) boil below 100°C and freeze below 0°C

43. Colligative properties are:
   (a) dependent only on the concentration of the solute and independent of the solvent's and solute's identity.
   (b) dependent only on the identity of the solute and the concentration of the solute and independent of the solvent's identity.
   (c) dependent on the identity of the solvent and solute and thus on the concentration of the solute.
   (d) dependent only on the identity of the solvent and the concentration of the solute and independent of the solute's identity.

44. Assume three samples of juices A, B and C have glucose as the only sugar present in them. The concentration of sample A, B and C are 0.1M, .5M and 0.2 M respectively. Freezing point will be highest for the fruit juice:
   (a) A
   (b) B
   (c) C
   (d) All have same freezing point

45. Identify which of the following is a colligative property :
   (a) freezing point   (b) boiling point
   (c) osmotic pressure   (d) all of the above

Chapter Test

Time : *30 Min.*   **Max. Marks : 15**

Direction :

- Questions number **1-15** carry **1 mark** each.

1. Colligative properties of the solution depend on
   (a) Nature of solute
   (b) Nature of solvent
   (c) Number of particles present in the solution
   (d) Number of moles of solvent only

2. Pressure cooker reduces cooking time because
   (a) the heat is more easily distributed
   (b) the higher pressure tenderizes the food
   (c) the boiling point of the water inside is elevated
   (d) a larger flame is used

3. Molarity of liquid HCl will be, if density of solution is 1.17 g/cc
   (a) 36.5   (b) 32.05   (c) 18.25   (d) 42.10

4. The value of Henry's constant K_H is _______.
   (a) greater for gases with higher solubility.
   (b) greater for gases with lower solubility.
   (c) constant for all gases.
   (d) not related to the solubility of gases.

DIRECTIONS (Qs. 5-7) : *Each of these questions contains an assertion followed by reason. Read them carefully and answer the question on the basis of following options. You have to select the one that best describes the two statements.*

(a) If both Assertion and Reason are correct and the Reason is a correct explanation of the Assertion.
(b) If both Assertion and Reason are correct but Reason is not a correct explanation of the Assertion.
(c) If the Assertion is correct but Reason is incorrect.
(d) If the Assertion is incorrect but the Reason is correct.

5. **Assertion :** If red blood cells were removed from the body and placed in pure water, pressure inside the cells increases.

Reason : The concentration of salt content in the cells increases.

6. **Assertion :** Azeotropic mixtures are formed only by non-ideal solutions and they may have boiling points either greater than both the components or less than both the components.

Reason : The composition of the vapour phase is same as that of the liquid phase of an azeotropic mixture.

7. **Assertion :** People taking a lot of salt or salty food experience edema which is a condition of swelling or puffiness in body.

Reason : It is a caused by water retention in tissue cells and in the intercellular spaces because of osmosis.

Case/Passage Based Questions

DIRECTIONS (Qs. 8-11) : *Following are the case/passage based questions.*

The word "colligative" has been adapted or taken from the Latin word "colligatus" which translates to "bound together". A colligative property is a property of a solution that is dependent on the ratio between the total number of solute particles (in the solution) to the total number of solvent particles. Colligative properties are not dependent on the chemical nature of the solution's components. Dilute solution containing non-volatile solute exhibit some properties which depend only on the number of solute particles present and not on the type of solute present. These properties are called colligative properties. These properties are mostly seen in dilute solutions. There are different types of colligative properties of a solution. These include, vapour pressure lowering, boiling point elevation, freezing point depression and osmotic pressure.

8. Which one of the following is a colligative property ?
   (a) Boiling point
   (b) Vapour pressure
   (c) Osmotic pressure
   (d) Freezing point

9. The relative lowering of the vapour pressure is equal to the ratio between the number of
   (a) solute molecules to the solvent molecules
   (b) solute molecules to the total molecules in the solution
   (c) solvent molecules to the total molecules in the solution
   (d) solvent molecules to the total number of ions of the solute.

10. Someone has added a non electrolyte solid to the pure liquid but forgot that among which of the two beakers he has added that solid. This problem can be solved by checking
    (a) relative lower in vapour pressure
    (b) elevation in boiling point
    (c) depression in Freezing point
    (d) all above

11. 12 g of a non-volatile solute dissolved in 108 g of water produces the relative lowering of vapour pressure of 0.1. The molecular mass of the solute is
    (a) 80 (b) 60 (c) 20 (d) 40

OR

The freezing point of 1% solution of lead nitrate in water will be
    (a) 2°C (b) 1°C
    (c) 0°C (d) below 0°C

Very Short Answer Questions

12. State Henry's Law.

13. What is the effect of temperature on the solubility of a gas in a liquid?

14. Why are soda water and soft drink bottles sealed under pressure?

15. 18 g of glucose ($C_6H_{12}O_6$) is added to 178.2 g of water. Calculate the vapour pressure of water for this aqueous solution.

Solutions

Practice Exercise-1

1. **(b)** Let total moles in solution = 1, Moles of solute = 0.2, Moles of solvent = 0.8, Mass of solvent
   $= 0.8 \times 78 \times 10^{-3}$ kg.

   $$\text{Molality X} = \frac{\text{moles of solute}}{\text{Mass of solvent}}$$

   $$= \frac{0.2}{0.8 \times 78 \times 10^{-3}} = 3.2$$

2. **(c)** Molality (m)

   $$= \frac{\text{Molarity}}{\text{Density} - \dfrac{\text{Molarity} \times \text{Molecular mass}}{1000}}$$

   $$= \frac{18}{1.8 - \dfrac{18 \times 98}{1000}} = 500 \text{ mol kg}^{-1}$$

3. **(d)** H_3PO_4 is tribasic so, N = M × nf = 1 × 3 = 3N

4. **(d)** Molarity (M) $= \dfrac{\text{wt} \times 1000}{\text{mol. wt.} \times \text{vol (mL)}}$

   $$2 = \frac{\text{wt.}}{63} \times \frac{1000}{250}$$

   $$\text{wt.} = \frac{63}{2} \text{ g} = 31.5 \text{g}$$

   $$\text{wt. of 70\% acid} = \frac{100}{70} \times 31.5 = 45 \text{ g}$$

5. **(a)** Given : w = 10 g; Mol. mass = 40
   Weight of solvent = 1250 × 0.8 g = 1000 g = 1 kg

   $$\therefore \quad \text{Molality} = \frac{10}{40 \times 1} = 0.25$$

6. **(d)** No. of millimoles = 500 × 0.2 = 100

   Thus, molarity of diluted solution $= \dfrac{100}{700}$

   (Molarity = No. of moles L^{-1} = No. of millimoles mL^{-1})
   = 0.1428 M

7. **(c)** $N_1V_1 + N_2V_2 = NV$
   $4x + 10 (1 - x) = 6 \times 1; -6x = -4 ; x = 0.67$
   Thus 0.67 litre of 4N HCl
   $1 - x = 1 - 0.67 = 0.33$ litre of 10 N HCl

8. **(b)** An increase in temperature of the solution increases the solubility of a solid solute.

   The amount of solute that dissolve depends on what type of solute it is.

   For solids and liquid solutes, changes in pressure have practically no effect on solubility.

9. **(d)** The maximum amount of solute dissolved in a given amount of solvent is its solubility.

10. **(d)** Scuba divers must cope with high concentrations of dissolved gases while breathing air at high pressure underwater. Increased pressure increases the solubility of atmospheric gases in blood. When the divers come towards surface, the pressure gradually decreases. This releases

the dissolved gases and leads to the formation of bubbles of nitrogen in the blood. This blocks capillaries and creates a medical condition known as bends, which are painful and dangerous to life. To avoid bends, as well as, the toxic effects of high concentrations of nitrogen in the blood, the tanks used by scuba divers are filled with air diluted with helium (11.7% helium, 56.2% nitrogen and 32.1% oxygen).

11. **(a)**

12. **(a)** Molar mass of glucose ($C_6H_{12}O_6$)
$= 12 \times 6 + 1 \times 12 + 16 \times 6 = 180$ g
Number of moles = Given mass/Molar mass
$= 180/180 = 1$ mol
Molality (m) = Number of moles of solute/Mass of solvent (kg) $= 1/1 = 1$ molal

13. **(c)** State of solution can be solid, liquid or gas.

14. **(a)** Solubility decreases and K_H increases with increase in temperature.

15. **(d)** To increase the solubility of CO_2 in soft drinks and soda water, the bottle is sealed under high pressure.

16. **(d)** According to Henry's law, the mass of a gas dissolved per unit volume of solvent is proportional to the pressure of the gas at constant temperature $m = K. p$ *i.e.* as the solubility increases, value of Henry's law constant decreases. Since, CO_2 is most soluble in water among the given set of gases. Therefore, CO_2 has the lowest value of Henry's law constant.

17. **(d)** According to Henry's law,
solubility $= k \times p$
$= 1.4 \times 10^{-3} \times 0.5$ mol/L
$= 7 \times 10^{-4}$ mol/L
Number of moles in 100 mL $= 7 \times 10^{-5}$
Mass of oxygen $m = 7 \times 10^{-5} \times 32g = 2.24$ mg

18. **(a)** % of N_2 in atmosphere = 78.9% by volume
% of O_2 in atmosphere = 20.95% by volume
Mole fraction = volume fraction
Partial pressure of $N_2 = 0.789$ atm = 0.799 bar
Partial pressure of $O_2 = 0.2095$ atm = 0.212 bar
According to Henry's law,

$$P_{O_2} = (K_H)_{O_2} x \Rightarrow \frac{0.212}{(34.86 \times 1000)} = x_{O_2} = 6.08 \times 10^{-6}$$

$$P_{N_2} = (K_H)_{N_2} x \Rightarrow \frac{0.799}{(76.48 \times 1000)} = x_{N_2} = 1.0447 \times 10^{-5}$$

$$\Rightarrow \left(\frac{n_{O_2}}{n_{O_2} + n_{H_2O} + n_{N_2}}\right) : \left(\frac{n_{N_2}}{n_{O_2} + n_{H_2O} + n_{N_2}}\right)$$

$$\Rightarrow n_{O_2} : n_{N_2}$$

$6.08 \times 10^{-6} : 1.04 \times 10^{-5} = 1 : 1.71$

19. Molality and mole fraction.

20. When the solute is present in very minute amounts, the concentration of the solution is expressed in parts per million.

21. No. This is because smoke consists of carbon particles suspended in air and is not homogeneous.

22. Aerated water.

23. This is because oil-water forces are not strong enough to overcome oil-oil and water-water forces.

24. Hydrated salts, contain water of crystallisation $CuSO_4 \cdot 5H_2O$.

25. Decrease in volume means stronger intermolecular forces of attraction on mixing. This implies that the solution shows negative deviation from Raoult's Law.

26. As H_2 is more soluble than helium, H_2 will have lower value of K_H than that of helium.

27. It means that 10 g of Na_2CO_3 are present in 100 g of the solution.

28. Normality $= 2 \times$ Molarity.

29. CCl_4 is a non-polar compound, whereas H_2O is a polar compound having hydrogen bonding. When CCl_4 is mixed with H_2O, CCl_4 is not able to break the hydrogen bonding of H_2O and hence remains immiscible.
However, both C_2H_5OH and H_2O are polar compounds and form hydrogen bonding. When C_2H_5OH is mixed with H_2O, the hydrogen bonding between the two takes place and thus mixing occurs.

30. Refer Theory

Practice Exercise-2 

1. **(a)** For example, decrease in the vapour pressure of water by adding 1.0 mol of sucrose to one kg of water is nearly similar to that produced by adding 1.0 mol of urea to the same quantity of water at the same temperature.

2. **(a)** Given $P_P = 80$ torr
$P_Q = 60$ torr
$P_{total} = P_P \times x_p + P_q \times x_q$
$$= \left[80 \times \frac{3}{5} + 60 \times \frac{2}{5}\right] = 16 \times 3 + 12 \times 2$$
$P_{total} = 48 + 24 = 72$ torr

3. **(a)** The solutions (liquid mixture) which boils at constant temperature and can distil as such without any change in composition are called azeotropes.
Solution of HNO_3 and H_2O will form maximum boiling point azeotrope. Maximum boiling azeotropes show negative deviation from Raoult's law.

	Composition (%)	Boiling Point
HNO_3	68.0	359 K
H_2O	32.0	373 K

Boiling point of the azeotrope of these two solutions is 393.5 K.

4. **(d)** CCl_4 is non-polar and $CHCl_3$ is polar.

5. **(b)** Positive deviations are shown by such solutions in which solvent-solvent and solute-solute interactions are stronger than the solute-solvent interactions. In such solution, the interactions among molecules becomes weaker. Therefore their escaping tendency increases which results in the increase in their partial vapour pressures.
In pure methanol, there exists intermolecular H–bonding.

$$\begin{array}{ccc} \text{---O}-\text{H---} & \text{O}-\text{H---} & \text{O}-\text{H---} \\ | & | & | \\ CH_3 & CH_3 & CH_3 \end{array}$$

On adding benzene, its molecules come between ethanol molecules, thereby breaking H-bonds which weaken intermolecular forces. This results in increase in vapour pressure.

6. **(a)** Given vapour pressure of pure solvent
$(P°) = 121.8$ mm Hg; Weight of solute $(w) = 15$ g
Weight of solvent $(W) = 250$ g; Vapour pressure of solution $(P) = 120.2$ mm Hg and Molecular weight of solvent $(M) = 78$

From Raoult's law $= \dfrac{P^o - P}{P^o} = \dfrac{w}{m} \times \dfrac{M}{W}$

$\dfrac{121.8 - 120.2}{121.8} = \dfrac{15}{m} \times \dfrac{78}{250}$

or $\quad m = \dfrac{15 \times 78}{250} \times \dfrac{121.8}{1.6} = 356.2$

7. **(c)** $\dfrac{P^o - P_s}{P^o} = \dfrac{n}{N} = \dfrac{w}{m} \times \dfrac{M}{W}$

$0.1 = \dfrac{12}{m} \times \dfrac{18}{108}$

$m = \dfrac{12 \times 18}{0.1 \times 108} = 20$

8. **(a)** $\Delta T_f = K_f \dfrac{1000 \, W_2}{M_2 W_1} = \dfrac{1.86 \times 1000 \times 68.5}{342 \times 1000} = 0.372$

$T_f = T °C_f - \Delta T_f$
$T_f = -0.372°C$

9. **(c)** $\Delta T_b = K_b \times m$
Elevation in boiling point is a colligative property, which depends upon the no. of particles (concentration of solution). Thus, greater the number of particles, greater is the elevation in boiling point and hence, greater will be its boiling point.

$Na_2SO_4 \rightleftharpoons 2Na^+ + SO_4^{2-}; \, i = 2$
$\Delta T_b = 3 \times 0.01 \times K_b$

10. **(c)** For ideal solution,

$\Delta V_{mixing} = 0$ and $\Delta H_{mixing} = 0$.

11. **(a)** Vapour pressure of liquid and solid are equal at freezing point. Reduction in V.P. occurs when solute is added.

12. **(b)**   13. **(b)**

14. This is because $Cu_2[Fe(CN)_6]$ is soluble in non-aqueous solutions.

15. The pressure required for reverse osmosis is quite high. Hence, membranes which can withstand high pressure are used.
Cellulose acetate is permeable to water, but impermeable to impurities and ions present in sea water.

16. This is because osmotic pressure depends only upon the number of solute particles per unit volume of solution and not on the nature of the solute.

17. Osmotic presence method in the most suitable method for determining the molecular weights of protein because of the use of molarities instead of molality and the change observed though very small is measurable.

18. (d) < (b) < (c) < (a)

19. To render sea water fit to drink, *i.e.,* desalination of sea water.

20. The red blood cells will expand and eventually burst as a result of water entering the cells due to osmosis.

21. This is because impurities cause a depression in freezing point. The more the impurities the lower is the freezing point.

22. An antifreeze is a substance which on adding to the cooling system of an automobile, protects the coolant from freezing in cold weather, *e.g.,* ethylene glycol.

23. Ethylene glycol $(C_2H_6O_2)$. This is because, it has lower molecular weight and hence contains more moles for the same mass of glycerine.

24. K_f represents the freezing point depression of a molal solution, i.e depression in freezing point for 1 m solution.

25. Refer Theory

26. Pure solid solvent.

27. It is the elevation in boiling point when 1 mole of a solute is dissolved in 1000 g of the solvent.

28. Refer Theory

29. It is the temperature at which its vapour pressure becomes equal to one bar.

30. The boiling point of water will also decrease.

31. No, we cannot separate the constituents of an azeotropic mixture by distillation.

32. The alcohol molecules are able to form hydrogen bonds with water molecules. As a result, alcohol and water are miscible with each other in all proportions.

33. The liquid and the vapour phase have the same composition.

34. 95% by volume of ethanol.

35. Maximum boiling point azeotrope.

36. **(a)** Ethanol – water system.
    (b) $HNO_3 – H_2O$ system.

37. $\Delta_{sol} H < 0$, *i.e.,* heat is evolved.
$\Delta_{sol} V < 0$, *i.e.,* there is a decrease in volume.

38. The formation of a non-ideal solution showing positive deviation from Raoult's Law is endothermic, *i.e.,* heat is absorbed.

39. This is because it reaches a state of equilibrium where rate of evaporation = rate of concentration.

40. This is because at lower temperature, the vapours pressure in low. Hence, lesser vapours of tear producing chemicals are produced.

41. At room temperature, the vapour pressure of liquid ammonia is very high. On cooling, vapour pressure decreases. Hence, the liquid ammonia will not splash out.

42. The weight over the lid does not allow the steam to go out. As a result, pressure inside the cooker is high. Higher the external pressure higher is the boiling point and faster is the cooking.

43. Warming up of a solution means that the process of mixing is exothermic, *i.e.*, ΔH_{mixing} = negative.
    This implies that the solution shows a negative deviation.

44. Reverse osmosis, *i.e.*, net flow of the solvent is from solution to solvent.

45. The elevation in boiling point will become four times
    because $\Delta T_b = K_b \dfrac{W_2}{M_2} \dfrac{1000}{W_1}$

46. When HgI_2 is mixed with KI (aq), a complex $K_2Hg\,I_4$ is formed and thus the number of particles in the solution are decreased.
    $$2\,KI + Hg\,I_2 \longrightarrow K_2\,[Hg\,I_4] \longrightarrow 2K^+ + [Hg\,I_4]^{2-}$$
    Due to the decrease in number of particles, vapour pressure is increased.

47. The elevation in boiling point of $0 \cdot 1$ mole of NaCl and $0 \cdot 1$ mole of sugar dissolved in water will not be same. Elevation in boiling point is a colligative property and depends upon the number of solute particles NaCl is ionic and gives more number of particles due to ionisation than sugar which consists of molecules.

48. It is due to osmosis that the dried fruits and vegetables slowly swell when placed in contact with water.
    The outer layer of the fruits and vegetable (*i.e.*, cell wall) acts as a semi-permeable membrane.
    Yes, with increase in temperature, the osmosis accelerates as the osmotic pressure of a solution increases with increase in temperature, $\pi \propto T$.

49. (a) Factors affecting the solubility of a solute are:
    (i) Nature of solute and solvent
    (ii) Temperature and pressure
    (b) 1M Na_2SO_4 has lowest freezing point because the number of effective solute particles are maximum as one molecules dissociate into three ions.

50. $P_A^o = 23 \cdot 76$ mm; $P_A = 22 \cdot 98$ mm
    Let X_B mole fraction of solute
    According to Raoult's Law, $\dfrac{P_A^o - P_A}{P_A^o} = X_B$
    $$\therefore X_B = \dfrac{23 \cdot 76 - 22 \cdot 98}{23 \cdot 76} = \dfrac{0 \cdot 78}{23 \cdot 76} = 0 \cdot 0328$$
    For dilute solutions, $X_B = n_B/n_A$ or $n_B = n_A X_B$
    If we consider 1 kg of water, then n_B becomes number of moles of solute per kg of solvent i.e., molality of solution,
    $$\therefore n_B = \dfrac{1000}{18} \times 0 \cdot 0328 = 55 \cdot 5 \times 0 \cdot 0328$$
    $$= 1 \cdot 82 \text{ mol/kg of solvent.}$$

51. Using relation, $\Delta T_f = K_f\ m = K_f \dfrac{W_B \times 1000}{M_B \times W_A}$
    $$\therefore \quad M_B = \dfrac{3 \cdot 83 \times 2 \cdot 56 \times 1000}{0 \cdot 383 \times 100} = 256 \text{ g mol}^{-1}$$

Atomic weight of sulphur = 32
$\therefore$ No. of atoms in one molecule of sulphur
$$= \dfrac{\text{Mol. wt}}{\text{At. wt}} = \dfrac{256}{32} = 8.$$
The molecular formula of sulphur is S_8

52. Let there is 100 g of solution i.e., 10 g of organic compound in 90 g of water.
    $$n_B = \dfrac{W_B}{M_B} = \dfrac{10}{60} = \dfrac{1}{6}\ ; n_A = \dfrac{W_A}{M_A} = \dfrac{90}{18} = 5.$$
    $$\dfrac{P_A^o - P_A}{P_A^o} = X_B\ ;\quad \dfrac{n_B}{n_A + n_B} = \dfrac{1/6}{5 + 1/6} = \dfrac{1}{31}$$
    $$\dfrac{23 \cdot 75 - P_A}{23 \cdot 75} = \dfrac{1}{31}$$
    $$23 \cdot 75 - P_A = \dfrac{23 \cdot 75}{31} = 0 \cdot 766 \Rightarrow P_A = 22 \cdot 98 \text{ mm Hg.}$$
    Osmotic pressure, $\pi = \dfrac{n_B}{V}\ RT = \dfrac{1 \times 0 \cdot 082 \times 298}{6 \times 0 \cdot 1}$
    $$\pi = 40 \cdot 73 \text{ atm.}$$

Past year Exercise 

1. Liquid A has higher vapour pressure.

2. If a pressure higher than osmotic pressure is applied on the solution, the solvent will flow from the solution into the pure solvent through the semipermeable membrane. Since here the flow of solvent is in the reverse direction to that observed in the usual osmosis, the process is called reverse osmosis.

3. Refer Theory

4. We know that, $\Delta T_b = K_b m$
   When, $m = 1$, $\Delta T_b = K_b$. Thus, boiling point elevation constant is equal to the elevation in boiling point when 1 mole of a solute is dissolved in 1 kg of solvent. It is also called ebullioscopic constant.

5. A liquid mixture having a definite composition and boiling like a pure liquid is called an azeotrope.

6. Both methanol and acetone are polar molecules. Hence intermolecular interactions in them are dipole-dipole interactions.

7. Refer theory

8. 5% urea solution means. 5 g urea is present in 100 mL of solution.
   $$\text{Molarity of solution } C = \dfrac{5g}{60 \text{ g/mol}} \times \dfrac{1000}{100L}$$
   $$C = \dfrac{10}{12} \text{mol/L}$$
   Osmotic pressure $\pi = CRT$
   $$= \dfrac{10}{12} \times 0.0821 \times 300 = 20.525 \text{ atm}$$

OR

It is given that the depression in freezing points of the two given aqueous solution are same.

$$(\Delta T_f)_{urea} = (\Delta T_f)_z$$

$$m_{urea} \times (K_f)_{water} = m_z \times (K_f)_{water}$$

$$\Rightarrow \frac{\dfrac{7.5}{60}}{\dfrac{100}{1000}} = \frac{\dfrac{42.75}{M_z}}{\dfrac{100}{1000}}$$

$$\Rightarrow M_z = 342 \text{ g/mol}$$

9. Let 'w' be the required mass of ascorbic acid.

Molality of ascorbic and $m = \dfrac{w/176}{75/1000}$

$$m = \frac{w}{176} \times \frac{1000}{75}$$

$$(k_f)_{acetic} = 3.9 \text{ K kg mol}^{-1}$$

$$\Delta T_f = 1.5°C$$

$$\Rightarrow \Delta T_f = 1.5 \text{ K}$$

$$\Delta T_f = m.k_f$$

$$\Rightarrow 1.5 = \frac{w}{176} \times \frac{1000}{75} \times 3.9$$

$$\Rightarrow w = 5.08 \text{ g H}" \text{ 5g}$$

10. (a) This is explained by Henry's law i.e. $P = K_H x$ or $P \propto x$ where P is pressure, x is mole fraction of gas in solution. Also, $x \propto \dfrac{1}{T}$ i.e. as temperature increases, solubility of dissolved gases in water decreases. Hence, aquatic species find difficult to breath in warm water due to decreased availability of oxygen.

(b) The effect of pressure on the solubility of a gas in a liquid is governed by Henry's Law. It states that the solubility of a gas in a liquid at a given temperature is directly proportional to the partial pressure of the gas. Mathematically, $P = K_H x$

where P is the partial pressure of the gas; and x is the mole fraction of the gas in the solution and K_H is Henry's Law constant.

At higher altitude, partial pressure of oxygen is less than that at ground level, so low O_2 in blood causes climbers to become weak and makes them unable to think clearly.

OR

Maximum boiling azeotropes mixture will be formed by mixing of acetone and chloroform. In these solutions, the A—B interactions are stronger than the A—A and B—B molecular interactions present in the two liquids forming the solution.

11. Given

T = 300K

$$C_1 = \frac{30}{180} \qquad C_2 = ?$$

$$\pi_1 = 4.98 \text{ bar} \quad \pi_2 = 1.52 \text{ bar}$$

Osmotic pressure $(\pi) = CRT$

$$\therefore \quad \pi_1 = C_1 RT$$

$$4.98 = \frac{30}{180} \times R \times 300$$

$$4.98 = 50R \qquad\qquad ....(i)$$

$$\pi_2 = C_2 RT$$

$$1.52 = C_2 \times R \times 300 \qquad ....(ii)$$

Dividing (ii) by (i)

$$C_2 = \frac{50 \times 1.52}{300 \times 4.98}$$

$$C_2 = 0.05M$$

12. Given : mass of glucose $(C_6H_{12}O_6) = w_2 = 60$ g

mass of water $w_1 = 250$ g

Molecular mass of (glucose) $(M_2) = 180$ g mol^{-1}

$K_f = 1.86$ K kg mol^{-1}

freezing point of solution, $T_f = ?$

We know,

$$\Delta T_f = K_f m$$

$$\therefore \quad \Delta T_f = K_f\, m = K_f \times \frac{w_2}{M_2} \times \frac{1000}{w_1}$$

$$\Delta T_f = 1.86 \times \frac{60}{180} \times \frac{1000}{250} = 2.48 \text{ K}$$

Now,

$$\Delta T_f = T_f^0 - T_f$$

$$2.48 = 0°C - T_f$$

$$\therefore \quad T_f = -2.48°C = 270.67 \text{ K}$$

13. (a) Osmotic pressure method is preferred for the determination of molar masses of macromoleules. This is because it is done around room temperature and molarity of solution is used instead of molality. As compared to other colligative properties, its magnitude is large even for very dilute solutions. This method is preferred for biomolecules as they are not stable at higher temperatures and polymers have poor solubility.

(b) Aquatic animals are more comfortable in cold water than in warm water. This is because as temperature increase, solubility of gases in water decreases (from Le-chatelier's principle). Thus, in warm water, the amount of oxygen available decreases. As a result, aquatic animals are more comfortable in cold water.

(c) Elevation of boiling point for 1M KCl solution is nearly double than that of 1 M sugar solution. This is because $\Delta T_b = ik_b m$. KCl being a strong electrolyte completely dissociates in water to give K^+ and Cl^- ions. Thus, i = 2 for KCl. On the other hand, sugar does not dissociate/associate in water so i = 1 for sugar solution. Hence ΔT_b (KCl) = $2\Delta T_b$ (sugar)

14. **Given:** $w_2 = 0.520$ g, $M_2 = 180$ g,

$w_1 = 80.2$ g, $K_b = 0.52$ K kg mol^{-1}

Using formula, $\Delta T_b = K_b m$

$$= K_b \times \frac{w_2}{M_2} \times \frac{1000}{w_1} = \frac{0.52 \times 0.52 \times 1000}{180 \times 80.2} = 0.018$$

Now, $\Delta T_b = T_b - T_b^\circ$

$$\Rightarrow \quad T_b = \Delta T_b + T_b^\circ = 0.018 + 100$$

$$\therefore \quad T_b = 100.018^\circ C$$

15. **Given:** $w_2 = 1.25$ g, $w_1 = 99.0$ g, $T_b = 80.31^\circ C$, $T_b^\circ = 80.10^\circ C$, $K_b = 2.53^\circ C$ kg mol^{-1}

Using formula,

$$\Delta T_b = K_b\, m = K_b \times \frac{w_2}{M_2} \times \frac{1000}{w_1}$$

$$T_b - T_b^\circ = K_b \times \frac{w_2}{M_2} \times \frac{1000}{w_1}$$

$$\Rightarrow \quad M_2 = \frac{K_b \times w_2 \times 1000}{(T_b - T_b^\circ)\, w_1}$$

$$= \frac{2.53 \times 1.25 \times 1000}{(80.31 - 80.10) \times 99}$$

$$= \frac{3162.5}{20.79} = 152.11 \approx 152 \text{ g mol}^{-1}$$

16. **Given:** $M_2 = 176$ g mol^{-1}, $\Delta T_f = 1.5^\circ C$, $w_1 = 75$ g

Using the formula,

$$\Delta T_f = K_f\, m = K_f \times \frac{w_2}{M_2} \times \frac{1000}{w_1}$$

$$1.5 = 3.9 \times \frac{w_2}{176} \times \frac{1000}{75}$$

$$\Rightarrow \quad w_2 = \frac{1.5 \times 176 \times 75}{3.9 \times 1000}$$

$$w_2 = 5.08 \text{ g}$$

17. As a result of intermolecular H-bonding between O-atom of $(CH_3)_2CO$ and H-atom of $CHCl_3$ A — B interaction becomes stronger than A — A and B — B interactions. This leads to the decrease in vapour pressure and resulting in negative deviation.

$$\begin{array}{c} H_3C \\ \\ H_3C \end{array} \!\!\! \diagdown \!\!\! C = O \cdots H - C \!\!\! \begin{array}{c} \diagup Cl \\ - Cl \\ \diagdown Cl \end{array}$$

18. Given, W_2 (unknown compound) $= 6.21$g,
W_1 ($CHCl_3$) $= 24.0$g,
T_b (b.p. of solution) $= 68.04^\circ C$,
T_b (b.p. of pure $CHCl_3$) $= 61.7^\circ C$
and $K_b = 3.63^\circ$ C/m
Elevation in boiling point

$$\Delta T_b = \frac{K_b \times W_2 \times 1000}{M_2 \times W_1}$$

or $\quad M_2 = \dfrac{K_b \times W_2 \times 1000}{\Delta T_b \times W_1}$

$$\left(\Delta T_b = T_b - T_b^\circ = 68.04^\circ C - 61.7^\circ C = 6.34^\circ C\right)$$

$$M_2 = \frac{3.63^\circ C\, m^{-1} \times 6.21g \times 1000}{6.34^\circ C \times 24.0g} = 148.15g \text{ mol}^{-1}$$

OR

Given, W_2 (mass of solute) $= 8.95$mg $= 8.95 \times 10^{-3}$g

V (Volume of solvent) $= 35.0$ mL, $= \dfrac{35}{1000} L$

π (osmotic pressure of solution)

$= 0.335$ torr $= \dfrac{0.335}{760}$ atm $\quad$ (1 torr = 1 mm of Hg)

T $= 273 + 25 = 298$ K

Molar mass of solute (gene fragment)

$$M_2 = \frac{W_2 RT}{\pi V}$$

$$= \frac{8.95 \times 10^{-3} g \times 0.082 L \text{ atm mol}^{-1} K^{-1} \times 298 K}{\dfrac{0.335}{760} \text{atm} \times \dfrac{35.0}{1000} L}$$

$$M_2 = 14193 \text{ g mol}^{-1} = 1.4193 \times 10^4 \text{ g mol}^{-1}$$

19. Refer Theory

20. Refer Theory

21. Molecular masses of polymers are best determined by osmotic pressure method. Firstly because other colligative properties give so low values that they cannot be measured accurately and secondly, osmotic pressure measurements can be made at room temperature and do not require heating which may change the nature of the polymer.

22. Refer Theory

23. Given, $\rho = 1.25$ g mL^{-1}, $W_2 = 92$g

$W_1 = 1$ kg or 1000 g

We know that,

$$\text{Denisty }(\rho) = \frac{\text{Mass}\,(m)}{\text{Volume (V)}}$$

or $\quad V = \dfrac{m}{\rho} = \dfrac{(1000 \text{ g} + 92 \text{ g})}{1.25 \text{g mL}^{-1}}$

[$\because$ Mass of solution = mass of solvent + mass of solute]

$$= \frac{1092}{1.25} \text{ mL}$$

$$\text{Molarity} = \frac{W_2 \times 1000}{M_2 \times \text{Volume of solution (mL)}}$$

$$\text{Molarity} = \frac{92 \times 1000 \times 1.25}{23 \times 1092} = 4.579 \text{ M}$$

24. **Given:** $w_2 = 15$ g

$w_1 = 450$ g

$\Delta T_f = 0 - (-0.34) = 0.34^\circ C$

Using formula,

$$\Delta T_f = K_f\, m = K_f \times \frac{w_2}{M_2} \times \frac{1000}{w_1}$$

$$M_2 = \frac{K_f \times w_2 \times 1000}{w_1 \times \Delta T_f} = \frac{1.86 \times 15 \times 1000}{450 \times 0.34} = 182.3 \text{ g mol}^{-1}$$

25. **Given:** $w_1 = 500$ g; $\Delta T_b = T_b - T_b^\circ$
$= 100.042 - 100 = 0.042°C$;

$$\Delta T_b = K_b\, m = K_b \frac{w_2}{M_2} \times \frac{1000}{w_1}$$

$$0.042 = 0.512 \times \frac{w_2}{92} \times \frac{1000}{500}$$

$$\Rightarrow \quad w_2 = \frac{0.042 \times 92 \times 500}{0.512 \times 1000} \Rightarrow w_2 = 3.77 \text{ g}$$

26. $W_2 = 18$ g
$M_2 = 180$ g mol^{-1}
$W_1 = 1$ kg $= 1000$ g
$K_b = 0.52$ K kg mol^{-1}

$$\Delta T_b = K_b \times \frac{W_2}{M_2} \times \frac{1000}{W_1}$$

$$= 0.52 \times \frac{18}{180} \times \frac{1000}{1000} = \frac{0.52}{10} = 0.052 \text{ K}$$

Now, $\Delta T_b = T_s - T^\circ \Rightarrow 0.052 = T_s - 373.15$
$\therefore \quad T_s = 373.15 + 0.052 = 373.20$ K
$\therefore \quad$ Boiling point of solution $= 373.20$ K.

27. According to Henry's law :
$m = K_H \times p$
In first case given,
$m = 6.56 \times 10^{-2}$ g, $p = 1$ bar
$\therefore \quad 6.56 \times 10^{-2}$ g $= K_H \times 1$ bar
$\therefore \quad K_H = 6.56 \times 10^{-2}$ g bar^{-1}
In second case, $m = 5.0 \times 10^{-2}$ g
$\therefore \quad 5.0 \times 10^{-2}$ g $= (6.56 \times 10^{-2}$ g bar$^{-1}) \times p$

$$\therefore \quad p = \frac{5.0 \times 10^{-2}\,\text{g}}{6.56 \times 10^{-2}\,\text{g bar}^{-1}} = 0.762 \text{ bar}$$

28. **Given :** $\Delta T_f = 0.48$ K; $M_2 = 256$ g mol^{-1}; $w_1 = 75$ g
$K_f = 5.12$ K kg mol^{-1}
To find : $w_2 = ?$
Solution: $\Delta T_f = K_f m$

$$\Delta T_f = K_f \times \frac{w_2}{M_2} \times \frac{1000}{w_1}$$

$$\Rightarrow \quad w_2 = \frac{\Delta T_f \times M_2 \times w_1}{K_f \times 1000} = \frac{0.48\text{K} \times 256\text{gmol}^{-1} \times 75\text{g}}{5.12\text{K kg mol}^{-1} \times 1000}$$

$$\Rightarrow \quad w_2 = 1.8 \text{ g}$$

29. Refer Theory.

30. Refer Theory.

31. Refer Theory.

32. $W_2 = 31$g, $W_1 = 500$ g, $K_f = 1.86$ K kg mol^{-1}
$M_2 (C_2H_6O_2) = 24 + 6 + 32 = 62$g mol^{-1}

$$\Delta T_f = \frac{1000 K_f \times W_2}{W_1 \times M_2} = \frac{1000 \times 1.86 \times 31}{500 \times 62} = 1.86 \text{ K}$$

Freezing point of pure water $= 273.15$ K
$\therefore \quad$ Freezing point of solution $= T_f^\circ - \Delta T_f$
$= 273.15 - 1.86$ K $= 271.29$ K

33. **(i)** According to Henry's law, the solubility of a gas is inversely related to the Henry's constant (K_H) for that gas. Hence, gas (B), being less soluble, would have a higher K_H value

(ii) A maximum boiling azeotrope shows negative deviation from the Raoult's law.

NCERT Exemplar 

1. **(d)** Dissolution of sugar in water will be most rapid when powdered sugar is dissolved in hot water because powder form can easily insert in the vacancies of liquid particles. Further dissolution of sugar in water in an endothermic process. Hence, high temperature will favour the dissolution of sugar in water.

2. **(b)** When solute is added to the solution three cases may arise
(i) It dissolves into solution then solution is unsaturated.
(ii) It does not dissolve in the solution then solution is known as saturated.
(iii) When solute get precipitated solution is known as supersaturated solution.

3. **(c)** Maximum amount of solid that can be dissolved in a specified amount of a given solvent does not depend upon pressure. This is because solid and liquid are highly incompressible and practically remain unaffected by change in pressure.

4. **(b)** Low concentration of oxygen in the blood and tissues of people living at high altitude is due to low atmospheric pressure. Because at high altitude, the partial pressure of oxygen is less than at the ground level. This decreased atmospheric pressure causes release of oxygen from blood.

5. **(b)** 1.0 M Na_2SO_4 has highest value of boiling point, because it will give more no of ions than other.

6. **(a)** As we know from elevation in boiling point that
$\Delta T_b = K_b m$

$$K_b = \frac{\Delta T_b}{m}$$

$$\text{Unit of } K_b = \frac{\text{unit of } \Delta T_b}{\text{unit of m}} = \frac{K}{\text{molality}}$$

$$= \frac{K}{\text{mol kg}^{-1}} = K \text{ mol}^{-1} \text{ kg}$$

7. **(d)** As we know, $M_1V_1 = M_2V_2$
On putting values, we get
$0.02 \times 4\,L = M_2 \times 5L$

$$M_2 = \frac{0.08}{5} = 0.016\,M$$

8. **(d)** When an unripe mango is placed in a concentrated salt solution to prepare pickle then mango loose water due to osmosis and get shrivel.

9. **(a)** According to definition of osmotic pressure we know that $\pi = CRT$. For concentrated solution C has higher value that dilute solution.
Hence, as concentration of solution increases osmotic pressure will also increase.

10. **(b)** In reverse osmosis, solvent molecules move through a semipermeable membrane from a region of higher concentration of solute to lower concentration.

11. **(a)** Assertion and reason both are correct statements and reason is the correct explanation of assertion.
Volume of solutions is a function of temperature which varies with temperature. Hence, molarity of solution in liquid state changes with temperature.

$$\text{Molarity} = \frac{\text{moles of solute}}{\text{volume of solution in litre}}$$

12. **(d)** Assertion is wrong statement but reason is correct statement.
When methyl alcohol is added to water, boiling point of water decreases because when a volatile solute is added to a volatile solvent elevation in boiling point is observed.

13. **(b)** Assertion and reason both are correct statements but reason is not the correct explanation of assertion.
When a solution is separation from the pure solvent by a semipermeable membrane, the solvent molecules pass through it from pure solvent side to the solution side. Solvent molecules always flow from lower concentration to higher concentration of solution.

14. Since both the components are appearing in the distillate and composition of liquid and vapour is same, this shows that liquids have formed azeotropic mixture and hence cannot be separated at this stage by distillation.

15. At a given pressure the solubility of oxygen in water increases with decrease in temperature. Presence of more oxygen at lower temperature makes the aquatic species more comfortable in cold water.

16. In pure liquid water the entire surface of liquid is occupied by the molecules of water. When a non volatile solute, for example glucose is dissolved in water, the fraction of surface covered by the solvent molecules gets reduced because some positions are occupied by glucose molecules. As a result number of solvent molecules escaping from the surface also gets reduced, consequently the vapour pressure of aqueous solution of glucose is reduced.

17. When salt is spread over snow covered roads, snow starts melting from the surface because of the depression in freezing point of water and it helps in clearing the roads.

18. The vapour pressure of volatile hydrocarbons is very high and they get evaporated leaving behind the system. Due to this they are not used as lubricants in autombles. Non-volatile hydrocarbons having *low vapour* pressure are used as lubricants.

Objective Practice Exercise 

1. **(a)** According to Henry's law partial pressure of a gas in the solution is proportional to the mole fraction of gas in the solution.
$p = K_H x$; K_H = (Henry's constant)

2. **(d)** In case of exothermic dissolution, the solubility of the solid increases on lowering the temperature. On cooling, the solution becomes unsaturated and solid solute does not separate. At $0°C$, water in the solution does not freeze.

3. **(c)** $\text{Molarity} = \dfrac{\text{Number of moles}}{\text{Volume of solution (L)}}$

$$\text{Moles of water} = \frac{\text{Mass}}{\text{Molar mass}} = \frac{1000}{18} = 55.6$$

$$\text{Molarity} = \frac{55.6}{1} = 55.6$$

4. **(a)** Mole fraction of any component A in solution

$$x = \frac{\text{No. of moles of A}}{\text{Total No. of moles of solution}}$$

As total no. of moles of solution > No. of moles of A
Thus x can never be equal to one or zero.

5. **(a)** Mixture of methanol and acetone show a positive deviation from Raoult's law. Molecules in pure methanol are hydrogen bonded. On adding acetone, its molecules enters in between the host molecules and break some of the hydrogen bonds between them.
Therefore, the intermolecular attractive forces between the solute-solvent molecules are weaker than those between the solute-solute and solvent-solvent molecules.
Other three remaining options will show negative deviation.

6. **(c)**

7. **(a)** $\Delta T_f = K_f \dfrac{1000 W_2}{M_2 W_1} = \dfrac{1.86 \times 1000 \times 68.5}{342 \times 1000} = 0.372$

$$T_f = -0.372°C$$

8. **(b)** $M = \dfrac{K_b \times w \times 1000}{\Delta T_b \times W} = \dfrac{2.16 \times 0.11 \times 1000}{0.1 \times 15} = 158.4$

9. **(c)** $\Delta T_b = \dfrac{K_b \times w \times 1000}{M \times W}$;

$$\therefore K_b = \frac{\Delta T_b \times 100 \times 100}{10 \times 1000} = \Delta T_b$$

10. **(b)** As $\Delta T_f = K_f . m$, $\Delta T_b = K_b . m$

Hence, we have $m = \dfrac{\Delta T_f}{K_f} = \dfrac{\Delta T_b}{K_b}$ or $\Delta T_f = \Delta T_b \dfrac{K_f}{K_b}$

$$\Rightarrow [\Delta T_b = 100.18 - 100 = 0.18°C]$$

$$\therefore \ \Delta T_f = 0.18 \times \frac{1.86}{0.512} = 0.654°C$$

As the freezing point of pure water is $0°C$,

$\Delta T_f = 0 - T_f \ \Rightarrow \ 0.654 = 0 - T_f \ \therefore \ T_f = -0.654$

Thus the freezing point of solution will be $-0.654°C$.

11. **(b)** $M_B = \dfrac{W_B \times R \times T}{\pi \times V} = \dfrac{4 \times 0.0821 \times 300}{3 \times 10^{-4} \times 2} \approx 1.6 \times 10^5$

12. **(a)** $7.4 = n \times 0.0821 \times 300 \ \ \therefore \ \ n = 0.3$

13. **(b)** When solute is added to the solution three cases may arise

(i) It dissolves into solution then solution is unsaturated.

(ii) It does not dissolve in the solution then solution is known as saturated.

(iii) When solute get precipitated solution is known as supersaturated solution.

14. **(c)** Value of K_H depends upon nature of gases dissolved in water. Higher the value of K_H at a given temperature, the lower is the solubility of the gas in the liquid. Hence, correct order is :

$Ar < CO_2 < CH_4 < HCHO.$

15. **(d)** For very dil. solution the concentration is expressed in ppm.

16. **(c)** Dissolution of gases in liquids is generally an exothernic process accompanied by a large decrease in volume. Follow Le chatelier's principle.

17. **(d)** According to Henry's law

$$\frac{P_1}{P_2} = \frac{S_1}{S_2} \ \ \Rightarrow \ \ \frac{500}{750} = \frac{0.01}{S_2}$$

$$\therefore S_2 = \frac{750 \times 0.01}{500} = 0.015 \ g/L$$

18. **(c)** If $H_2O = x$ mole

Mass of x mole of $H_2O = 18x$ g

Then urea $= x$ mole

Mass of x mole of $NH_2 - \overset{\overset{O}{\|}}{C} - NH_2 = 60x$ g

Total mass of the solution $= 18x + 60x = 78x$ g

Mass % of urea $= \dfrac{60x}{78x} \times 100 = 76.92\%$

19. **(c)** Maximum amount of solid that can be dissolved in a specified amount of a given solvent does not depend upon pressure. This is because solid and liquid are highly incompressible and practically remain unaffected by change in pressure.

20. **(d)** H_3PO_4 is tribasic so $N = 3M = 3 \times 1N = 3N.$

21. **(d)**

22. **(c)** From molarity equation

$M_1V_1 + M_2V_2 = M_3(V_1 + V_2)$

$1 \times 2.5 + 0.5 \times 3 = M_3 \times 5.5$

$$M_3 = \frac{4}{5.5} = 0.73M$$

23. **(b)** Relation between molality and mole fraction is

$$m = \frac{1000 \times x_2}{x_1 M_1} = \frac{1000 \times 0.2}{0.8 \times 78} = 3.2$$

Thus, $X(m) = 3.2$

24. **(b)** Low concentration of oxygen in the blood and tissues of people living at high altitude is due to low atmospheric pressure. Because at high altitude, the partial pressure of oxygen is less than at the ground level. This decreased atmospheric pressure causes release of oxygen from blood.

25. **(a)** The interparticle forces in between $CHCl_3$ and acetone increase due to H-bonding and thus $\Delta_{mixing}V$ becomes negative.

26. **(d)** C_2H_5OH show H-bonding as well as polarity both

27. **(d)** liquid $\underset{\longleftarrow}{\overset{Eq^m}{\longrightarrow}}$ vapour, $K_p = Vp$ of liq, $\Delta_r H = +ve$

$T \downarrow, Vp \downarrow$

28. **(b)** $P_{Solution} = P^°_{solution} \, x_{Solvent}$

$$\frac{P^° - P}{P^°} = x_{solute}$$

29. **(b)** Show negative deviation from Raoult's law.

30. **(b)** Number of moles in 92 g of $Na^+ = \dfrac{92}{23} = 4$ moles

$$\text{Molality } (m) = \frac{\text{Number of moles}}{\text{Mass of solvent (in kg)}}$$

$$\therefore \ m = \frac{4}{1} = 4 \ \text{mol kg}^{-1}$$

31. **(b)** $\dfrac{p^° - p_s}{p^°}$ = Mole fraction of solute = χ_2

32. **(c)**

33. **(b)** $P = P^°_A x_A + P^°_B x_B = P^°_B + x_A (P^°_A - P^°_B) [\because x_B = 1 - x_A]$

34. **(a)** $\chi_1 = \dfrac{P_A{}^° \chi_A}{P_{Total}} = \dfrac{P_A{}^° \chi_A}{P_{Total}} \ \ \therefore \ P_{Total} = \dfrac{P_A{}^° \chi_2}{\chi_1}$

35. **(c)** Given $P_A = 750$ mm Hg

$\because \ \ 373$ K is boiling point of water.

Thus, $P^°_A = 760$ mm Hg

$$m = \left(\frac{P^° - P}{P}\right) \times \frac{1000}{M_{solvent}} \ \Rightarrow \ \frac{10}{750} \times \frac{1000}{18} \Rightarrow 0.74$$

36. **(d)** Using relation,

$$\frac{p^° - p_s}{p_s} = \frac{w_2 M_1}{w_1 M_2}$$

where w_1, M_1 = mass in g and mol. mass of solvent

w_2, M_2 = mass in g and mol. mass of solute

Let $M_2 = x$

$p^° = 185$ torr

$p_s = 183$ torr

$$\frac{185-183}{183} = \frac{1.2 \times 58}{100x} \text{ (Mol. mass of acetone} = 58)$$

$x = 64$

$\therefore$ Molar mass of substance $= 64$

37. **(d)** Addition of a solute increases the boiling point of solution.

38. **(a)** $\pi \propto \dfrac{1}{V}$, and not $\pi \propto V$.

39. **(b)** $2Na^+_{(aq)} + 2OH^-_{(aq)} + SnO_{2(s)} \rightarrow 2Na^+_{(aq)}$

$$+ SnO_{3(aq)}^{2-} + H_2O$$

The number of ions decreases in the ratio of 4 to 3, and so also the colligative property.

40. **(a)** Normal saline is 0.16 M NaCl solution.

41. **(c)** $M_B = \dfrac{\Delta T_b \times W_B \times 1000}{K_b \times W_A}$ is wrong. The correct form

is $M_B = \dfrac{K_b \times W_B \times 1000}{\Delta T_b \times W_A}$

42. **(c)** When non-volatile solid is added to pure solvent the boiling point of solution increases and freezing point of solution decreases.

43. **(d)**

44. **(a)** Since the concentration of sample A is less, so it will show less depression in freezing point. Consequently, its freezing point will be higher than other solutions.

45. **(c)** Elevation in boiling point, freezing point depression and osmotic pressure are colligative properties.

Chapter Test

1. **(c)** Colligative properties of dilute solution containing non volatile solute depends upon the number of particles of the solute present in the solution.

2. **(c)** The boiling point of water inside the cooker increases above 100°C due to accumulation of steam and increase in pressure. Thus making it possible to cook food faster.

3. **(b)** Density = 1.17 g/cc (Given)

As $d = \dfrac{Mass}{Volume}$

volume = 1cc $\therefore$ mass $= d = 1.17$g

$$\text{Molarity} = \frac{\text{No. of moles}}{\text{Volume in litre}} = \frac{1.17 \times 1000}{36.5 \times 1}$$

$$= \frac{1170}{36.5} = 32.05 \text{ M}$$

4. **(b)** $x \propto 1/K_H$

5. **(c)** The pressure inside the cell increases due to osmosis. Water enters into the cell due to higher concentration inside the cell. This results in lowering of concentration of salt content inside the cell.

6. **(b)** 7. **(a)**

8. **(c)** Osmotic pressure is a colligative property.

9. **(b)** According to Raoult's law, the relative lowering in vapour pressure of a dilute solution is equal to the mole fraction of the solute present in the solution.

$$\frac{p^\circ - p}{p} = \text{Mole fraction of solute} = \frac{n}{n+N}$$

10. **(d)** All are colligative properties.

11. **(c)** $\dfrac{P^O - P_s}{P^O} = \dfrac{n}{N} = \dfrac{w}{m} \times \dfrac{M}{W}$

$$0.1 = \frac{12}{m} \times \frac{18}{108}$$

$$m = \frac{12 \times 18}{0.1 \times 108} = 20$$

OR

(d) Addition of solute to water decreases the freezing point of water (pure solvent).

$\therefore$ When 1% lead nitrate (solute) is added to water, the freezing point of water will be below 0°C.

12. Refer Theory

13. The solubility of a gas in a liquid decreases with increase in temperature.

14. To dissolve more CO_2 because solubility of CO_2 is high at higher pressure

15. **(b)** Moles of glucose $= \dfrac{18}{180} = 0.1$

Moles of water $= \dfrac{178.2}{18} = 9.9$

Total moles $= 0.1 + 9.9 = 10$

$p_{H_2O} = \text{Mole fraction} \times \text{Total pressure} = \dfrac{9.9}{10} \times 760$

$= 752.4$ Torr

3 The *p*-Block Elements

THE *p*-BLOCK ELEMENTS (GROUP 15, 16, 17 AND 18)

Group 15 Elements

- **Elements :** N, P, As, Sb, Bi, Mc
- **Electronic configuration :** ns^2np^3
- **Oxidation states :** Common oxidation states are -3, $+3$ and $+5$
- **Hydrides :** Form hydrides of type MH_3 NH_3, PH_3, AsH_3, SbH_3 and BiH_3

Basic character decreases $\rightarrow$

Thermal stability decreases $\rightarrow$

Reducing nature increases $\rightarrow$

Bond angle decreases $\rightarrow$

- **Oxides :** Form oxides of type M_2O_3, M_2O_4 and M_2O_5 Acidic character of oxides decreases down the group.
- **Halides :** Form halides of type EX_3 and EX_5

Group 16 Elements

- **Elements :** O, S, Se, Te, Po, Lv
- **Electronic configuration :** ns^2np^4
- **Oxidation states :** Oxygen shows commonly -2 and also shows $+2$ and $+1$ in OF_2 and O_2F_2 respectively S, Se, Te and Po show $+2$, $+4$ and $+6$ O.S.
- I^{st} IE of group 16 elements is lower than that of group 15 elements.
- **Hydrides :** Form hydrides of type H_2X
  * Bond angle of hydrides decreases from H_2O to H_2Po
  * The volatility of hydrides increases from H_2O to H_2S
  * Acidic strength increases from H_2O to H_2Te
  * Covalent character increases from O to Po
- **Oxides :** Form oxides of type EO_2 and EO_3
- Acidic property increases from S to Te oxides
- **Halides :** Form halides of type EX_6, EX_4, EX_2 and E_2X_2

Stability of halides decreases in order $F^- > Cl^- > Br^- > I^-$

Group 18 Elements

- **Elements :** He, Ne, Ar, Kr, Xe, Rn, Og
- **Electronic configuration :** ns^2np^6 except He $(1s^2)$
- Least reactive due to stable inert gas configuration and due to high I.E. and more positive electron gain enthalpy.
- Xe Forms 3 binary fluorides XeF_2, XeF_4 and XeF_6

These are powerful fluorinating agents.
- The only oxide of Xe is XeO_3

Group 17 Elements

- **Elements :** F, Cl, Br, I, At and Ts
- **Electronic configuration :** ns^2np^5
- **Oxidation states :** Fluorine show -1 other shows $+1$, $+3$, $+5$ and $+7$
- **Reaction with metals :**
- Ionic character : $MF > MCl > MBr > MI$
- **Displacement reaction :**

F replaces Cl, Br and I, Cl replaces Br and I
- **Oxo-acids of halogens**
  * Acid-character of oxo-acids of same halogen increases with increase in O.S.
  * Oxidising power : HOCl > HOBr > HOI
  * Thermal stability $HOCl < HClO_2 < HClO_3 < HClO_4$
- **Interhalogen compounds :**
  * Compounds of halogens with themselves.
  * These are covalent compounds
  * More reactive than halogens except F due to weaker A–X bond than X–X bond.

Topic 1   Nitrogen Family, Oxygen Family

INTRODUCTION

p-Block of the periodic table comprises six groups (group 13 to 18). The general electronic configuration of the elements present in this block is ns^2np^{1-6}.

All these groups have specific names mostly based on the first member of each group.

- **Group 13 :** Boron Family   • **Group 14 :** Carbon Family   • **Group 15 :** Nitrogen Family
- **Group 16 :** Oxygen Family   • **Group 17 :** Halogens   • **Group 18 :** Noble Gases

With the exception of the noble gases which are very little reactive chemically, the elements belonging to all these groups are reactive. This is the only block in the periodic table which includes all the three types of elements *i.e.*, metals, non-metals and semi-metals. The p-block elements are also known as the **Representative Elements**.

NITROGEN FAMILY (GROUP 15 ELEMENTS)

In group 15 of the periodic table, the elements, nitrogen ($_7$N), phosphorus ($_{15}$P), arsenic ($_{33}$As), antimony ($_{51}$Sb) and bismuth ($_{83}$Bi) are present.

Atomic and Physical Properties

(a) Electronic configuration

The general outer electronic configuration of elements of group 15 is ns^2np^3. Hence these elements belong to *p*-block.

Elements	Atomic no.	Configuration
Nitrogen [N]	7	[He] $2s^22p^3$
Phosphorus [P]	15	[Ne] $3s^2\,3p^3$
Arsenic [As]	33	[Ar] $3d^{10}\,4s^2\,4p^3$
Antimony [Sb]	51	[Kr] $4d^{10}\,5s^2\,5p^3$
Bismuth [Bi]	83	[Xe] $4f^{14}5d^{10}6s^26p^3$

(b) Atomic and ionic radii: The atomic (covalent) and ionic radii (in a particular oxidation state) of the elements of nitrogen family (group 15) are smaller than the corresponding elements of carbon family (group 14). On moving down the group, the covalent and ionic radii (in a particular oxidation state) increase with increase in atomic number. There is a considerable increase in covalent radius from N to P. However, from As to Bi, only a small increase is observed. This is due to presence of completely filled *d*-and/or *f*-orbitals in heavier members.

(c) Ionisation enthalpy: As the atomic size increases down the group, the ionisation enthalpy increases. The ionisation enthalpy of nitrogen group element is more than the corresponding elements of oxygen group. This is because more stable half filled outermost *p*-subshell of nitrogen group elements. Ionisation enthalpy decreases from N to Bi down the group due to gradual increase in atomic size.

(d) Electronegativity: Group 15 elements are more electronegative than group 14 elements. It decreases on moving down the group from N to Bi due to gradual increase in atomic size. N is the 3rd highest in periodic table.

(e) Physical state: Nitrogen is a diatomic gas while other members are solids.

(f) Metallic character: These is increase in metallic character down the group due to increase in atomic size and decrease in ionisation enthalpy.

(g) Melting and boiling points: Melting point increases from N to As and then decreases to sb and Bi. Boiling point increase down the group.

(h) Allotropy: All elements except nitrogen show allotropy.

(i) Density: Density increases down the group.

(j) Catenation

They exhibit the property of catenation but due to weak M–M bond to less extent than 14 group elements.

Bond	C–C	N–N	P–P	As–As
kJ/mol	353.3	163.7	201.6	147.4

Chemical Properties

(a) Oxidation state: The elements of this group can exhibit various oxidation states ranging between -3 to $+5$. Negative oxidation state will be exhibited when they combine with less electronegative element & positive oxidation state will be exhibited with more electronegative element. Positive oxidation state becomes more favourable as we move down the group due to increasing metallic character & electropositivity. Although due to inert pair effect the stability of $+5$ state will also decreases. The only stable compound of Bi (v) is BiF_5.

(b) **Covalency:** This is the number of covalent bonds formed by an atom. Maximum covalency of nitrogen is four because it does not have d-orbitals to expand its covalency. Whereas other elements can exhibit covalency of 5 and 6 as well by the use of their d-orbitals e.g. PCl_5, $[PCl_6]^-$

(c) **Reaction with metals:** Elements of group 15 react with metals and form binary compounds in –3 oxidation states e.g. Ca_3N_2

$$6Li + N_2 \longrightarrow 2Li_3N \; ; \quad 6Mg + P_4 \longrightarrow 2Mg_3P_2$$

(d) **Reaction with hydrogen:** All elements of group 15 form gaseous hydrides of the type MH_3. In all the hydrides the central atom is sp^3 hybridized & their shape is pyramidal due to presence of lone pair of electrons.

    (i) The basic strength of the hydrides decreases as we move down the group. Thus, NH_3 is the strongest base.

$$NH_3 > PH_3 > AsH_3 > SbH_3$$

    (ii) The thermal stability of the hydrides decreases as the atomic size increases, *i.e.,* the M – H bond strength decreases which means reducing character increases.

    (iii) In the liquid state, the molecules of NH_3 are associated due to hydrogen bonding. The molecules of other hydrides are not associated.

    (iv) NH_3 is soluble in water whereas other hydrides are insoluble.

    (v) All the hydrides, except NH_3, are strong reducing agents and react with metal ions (Ag^+, Cu^{2+}, etc.) to form phosphides, arsenides or antimonides.

Note: NH_3 PH_3 AsH_3 SbH_3 BiH_3

    Basic character, Thermal stability, Dipole moment, and Bond angle decreases from NH_3 to BiH_3 while reducing nature increases from NH_3 to BiH_3

(e) **Halides:** The elements of group 15 form two series of halides MX_3 and MX_5.

    (i) All the elements of the group form trihalides. The ionic character of trihalides increases as we move down the group. Except NCl_3, all the trihalides are hydrolysed by water. This is due to the absence of d-orbitals in nitrogen.

    (ii) PF_3 is not hydrolysed because fluorine being more electronegative than oxygen forms more stable bonds with phosphorus than P – O bonds.

    (iii) N cannot form NX_5 because of non-availability of d-orbitals. Bi cannot form a BiX_5 because of reluctance of $6s$ electrons of Bi to participate in bond formation.

    (iv) The hybridisation of M in MX_3 is sp^3 and shape is pyramidal. In MX_5 M is sp^3d hybridised and shape is trigonal bipyramid. The axial bonds in MX_5 are weaker and longer, So MX_5 are less stable and decompose on heating e.g:

$$PCl_5 \xrightarrow{\Delta} PCl_3 + Cl_2$$

(f) **Oxides**

    (i) Nitrogen forms a number of oxides. The rest of the members (P, As, Sb and Bi) of the group form two types of oxides: E_2O_3 and E_2O_5.

    (ii) The reluctance of P, As, Sb and Bi to enter into $p\pi - p\pi$ multiple bonding leads to cage structures of their oxides and they exist as dimers, E_4O_6 and E_5O_{10}.

    (iii) The basic nature of the oxides increases with increase in atomic number of the element. Thus, the oxides of nitrogen (except N_2O and NO), P (III) and As (III) are acidic, Sb (III) oxide is amphoteric and Bi (III) oxide is basic.

Anomalous Behaviour of Nitrogen

The anomalous behaviour of nitrogen is due to its :

(a) Small size   (b) High E.N. and high I.E.

(c) Non availability of vacant d-orbital   (d) Tendency to form multiple bonds.

Nitrogen differs from other elements of its own group in following properties

(a) Nitrogen is a gas while other elements are solids

(b) Nitrogen is diatomic, while other elements are tetratomic $[P_4, As_4, Sb_4]$

(c) Nitrogen can form N_3^- ion (due to small size and high E.N.)

(d) Nitrogen is chemically inert under ordinary conditions due to high dissociation energy of $N \equiv N$ bond.

(e) Nitrogen shows oxidation state from –3 to +5

(f) Hydride of nitrogen i.e., ammonia is stable and undergoes H-bonding.

Dinitrogen (N_2)

Nitrogen constitutes about 78% by volume of the atmosphere. It occurs as chile saltpetre and Indian saltpetre. It is also an essential constituent of fertilizers, explosives and proteins.

Preparation

(a) Commercially by liquefaction and fractional distillation of air.

(b) In laboratory, by treating an aqueous solution of ammonium chloride with sodium nitrite.

$$NH_4Cl \,(aq) + NaNO_2 \,(aq) \longrightarrow N_2 \,(g) + 2H_2O \,(\ell) + NaCl \,(aq)$$

(*c*) By thermal decomposition of ammonium dichromate and of sodium or barium azide.

$$(NH_4)_2Cr_2O_7 \xrightarrow{\Delta} N_2 + 4H_2O + Cr_2O_3, Ba(N_3)_2 \xrightarrow{\Delta} Ba + 3N_2$$

Physical properties

(*a*) It is a colourless, odourless, tasteless and non-toxic gas. (*b*) It has two stable isotopes : ^{14}N and ^{15}N.

(*c*) It is inert at room temperature because of high bond enthalpy of $N \equiv N$ bond but its reactivity increases rapidly with rise in temperature.

Uses

(*a*) Used in manufacture of NH_3 and other industrial chemicals containing nitrogen, *e.g.,* calcium cyanamide.

(*b*) As inert diluent for reactive chemicals in iron and steel industry.

(*c*) As a refrigerant to preserve biological materials, food items and in cryosurgery.

Ammonia

Preparation

(*a*) Decay of nitrogenous organic matter, *e.g.,* urea.

$$NH_2CONH_2 + 2H_2O \longrightarrow (NH_4)_2CO_3 \rightleftharpoons 2NH_3 + H_2O + CO_2$$

(*b*) From ammonium salts.

$$2NH_4Cl + Ca(OH)_2 \xrightarrow{Decomposes} 2NH_3 + 2H_2O + CaCl_2, (NH_4)_2SO_4 + 2NaOH \longrightarrow 2NH_3 + 2H_2O + Na_2SO_4$$

(*c*) Commercially, by Haber's process.

$$N_2(g) + 3H_2(g) \underset{700K,\ 250\ atm}{\overset{Fe,\ Mo}{\rightleftharpoons}} 2NH_3(g)$$

Iron oxide with small amount of K_2O and Al_2O_3 are used as catalysts, at a temperature of 700K and pressure of 200 atm.

Physical Properties

(*a*) Lighter than air (*b*) Easily liquefied by cooling or compression

(*c*) Highly soluble in water. The solution is alkaline (*d*) Forms H–bonding with water.

(*e*) Colourless gas with pungent odour

Chemical Properties

(*a*) It is basic and forms ammonium salts with acids.

$$NH_3 + HCl \rightarrow NH_4Cl; \quad 2NH_3 + H_2SO_4 \rightarrow (NH_4)_2SO_4$$

(*b*) **Reaction with metal salt**

$$2FeCl_3(aq) + 3NH_4OH(aq) \longrightarrow Fe_2O_3 \cdot xH_2O(s) + 3NH_4Cl(aq),$$
(Brown ppt.)

$$ZnSO_4(aq) + 2NH_4OH(aq) \longrightarrow Zn(OH)_2(s) + (NH_4)_2SO_4(aq)$$
(White ppt.)

(*c*) **Reaction with metals**

Active metals liberate H_2 with NH_3

$$2Na + 2NH_3 \longrightarrow 2NaNH_2 + H_2$$
(Sodium amide)

(*d*) **Reaction with air**

Ammonia burns in presence of catalyst to give NO

$$4NH_3(g) + SO_2(g) \xrightarrow[\Delta]{Pt} 4NO(g) + 6H_2O(l)$$

(*e*) **Complex formation**

$$Ag^+(aq) \xrightarrow{2NH_3(aq)} [Ag(NH_3)_2]^+(aq),\ Cu^{+2}(aq) \xrightarrow{4NH_3(aq)} [Cu(NH_3)_4]^{2+}(aq)$$

(*f*) **Oxidation (reducing property)**

$$3CuO + 2NH_3 \longrightarrow 3Cu + N_2 + 3H_2O,\ 4NH_3 + 5O_2 \xrightarrow[800°C]{Pt\ gauze} 4NO + 6H_2O$$

Uses:

(*a*) To produce various nitrogenous fertilisers.

(*b*) Manufacture of some inorganic nitrogen compounds like HNO_3, $(NH_4)CO_3$, Na_2CO_3 etc.

(*c*) Liquid ammonia is used as a refrigerant.

(*d*) In making artificial silk and as a laboratory reagent

Oxides of nitrogen: It forms a number of oxides in different oxidation states — N_2O, NO, N_2O_3, NO_2, N_2O_4, N_2O_5.

Nitrous Oxide (N_2O)

It is colourless neutral gas

Preparation :

$$NH_4NO_3 \xrightarrow{\Delta} N_2O + 2H_2O$$

Properties :

(a) Nitrous oxide is a colourless neutral gas with faint pleasant smell. It is heavier than air, fairly soluble in cold water but not in hot water. It is poisonous in nature; when inhaled in moderate quantities, it produces hysterical laughter, hence it is also known as *laughing gas.*

(b) *Action of heat :* $2N_2O \xrightarrow{500-900°C} 2N_2 + O_2$

Supporter of Combustion : Although nitrous oxide itself is non-combustible, it supports combustion of glowing splinter, charcoal, burning phosphorus and magnesium ribbon.

$$Mg + N_2O \longrightarrow MgO + N_2$$

Uses :

(a) It is used as the propellant gas in 'whipped' cream bombs.

(b) Mixed with oxygen, it is used as an anaesthetic for small scale operations in dentistry and surgery.

Structure:

$$:\overset{..}{\underset{..}{N}} = N^+ = \overset{..}{\underset{..}{O}} \longleftrightarrow :N \equiv \overset{+}{N} - \overset{..}{\underset{..}{O}}^-:$$

Note that N_2O is isoelectronic with CO_2.

NITRIC OXIDE OR NITROGEN MONOXIDE, [NO]

O.S. $(+2)$, colourless gas. This oxide is neutral.

Preparation

(a) By passing air through an electric arc (*Commercial method*)

$$N_2 + O_2 \rightleftharpoons 2NO$$

(b) By catalytic oxidation of ammonia (*Ostwald method*).

$$4NH_3 + 5O_2 \xrightarrow[750-900°C;\ 6atm]{Pt.\ gauze} 4NO + 6H_2O$$

(c) $3Cu(s) + 8HNO_3 (dil) \rightarrow 3Cu(NO_3)_2 + 4H_2O + 2NO$ (Lab method)

Properties : It shows oxidising as well as reducing properties. ·

Uses

(a) It is used as an intermediate in the manufacture of nitric acid.

(b) It is used as a catalyst in the lead chamber process for the manufacture of H_2SO_4.

(c) It is used in the detection of oxygen to distinguish it from nitrous oxide.

Structure

$$:N = \overset{..}{\underset{..}{O}} \longleftrightarrow = \overset{\overline{\overline{..}}}{N} = \overset{+}{O}:$$

Nitrogen Dioxide (NO_2)

O.S. $(+4)$, brown gas, acidic in nature.

Preparation

$$Pb(NO_3)_2 \xrightarrow{673K} 2PbO + 4NO_2 + O_2$$

Properties : Highly toxic, paramagnetic, reddish brown gas with choking odour, acidic

Uses :

(i) For manufacturing of HNO_3

(ii) As a catalyst in lead chamber process for sulphuric acid

Structure :

$$\underset{O}{\overset{N}{\diagdown}} \longleftrightarrow \underset{O}{\overset{N}{\diagup}} \longleftrightarrow \underset{O}{\overset{N}{\diagup}} \longleftrightarrow \underset{O}{\overset{N}{\diagdown}}$$

Dinitrogen Trioxide (N_2O_3)

Preparation

(a) $2HNO_3 + As_2O_3 + 2H_2O \longrightarrow NO + NO_2 + 2H_3AsO_4$ (b) $2Cu + 6HNO_3 \longrightarrow 2Cu(NO_3)_2 + NO + NO_2 + 3H_2O$

Properties:

The brown coloured mixture of NO and NO_2 on cooling condenses to a blue liquid which on freezing gives a blue solid of the formula N_2O_3.

$$\underbrace{NO + NO_2}_{\text{Brown}} \underset{}{\overset{-20°C \text{ room temp.}}{\rightleftharpoons}} \underset{\text{Blue}}{N_2O_3}$$

Structure of N_2O_3

It is an acidic oxide and hence dissolves in alkalies producing nitrites.

$$N_2O_3 + 2KOH \longrightarrow 2KNO_2 + H_2O$$

Thus dinitrogen trioxide is referred to as the anhydride of nitrous acid. $2HNO_2 \longrightarrow N_2O_3 + H_2O$

DINITROGEN PENTOXIDE (N_2O_5)

O.S. (+5), colourless gas, acidic in nature

Preparation :

$$4HNO_3 + P_4O_{10} \longrightarrow 4H_3PO_3 + 2N_2O_5$$

Properties :

(a) When heated above its m.p. it decomposes with explosion.

$$2N_2O_5 \xrightarrow{\text{heat}} 2N_2O_4 + O_2$$

(b) $N_2O_5 + H_2O \longrightarrow 2HNO_3$, (c) $N_2O_5 + 2NaOH \longrightarrow 2NaNO_3 + H_2O$

(d) Due to its easy decomposition, it acts as a powerful oxidising agent. It destroys all organic substances like cork, rubber etc.

Structure

In the vapour state, ionic bond structure changes to covalent structure which is a resonance hybrid of the two resonating structures.

Dinitrogen Tetraoxide (N_2O_4)

O.S. (+ 4), colourless solid/ liquid, acidic in nature.

Preparation :

$$2NO_2 \underset{\text{Heat}}{\overset{\text{Cool}}{\rightleftharpoons}} N_2O_4$$

Structure :

Note: Nitrogen forms oxyacids such as $H_2N_2O_2$ (hyponitrous acid), HNO_2 (nitrous acid) and HNO_3 (nitric acid). HNO_3 is the most important oxyacid of nitrogen.

Nitric Acid

Preparation

(*a*) Lab method: By heating KNO_3 or $NaNO_3$ and conc. H_2SO_4.

$$NaNO_3 + H_2SO_4 \longrightarrow NaHSO_4 + HNO_3$$

(*b*) Commercially, by Ostwald's process.

$$4NH_3\,(g) + 5O_2\,(g) \xrightarrow[\text{Catalyst, 500 K}]{\text{Pt/Rh gauge}} 4NO\,(g) + 6H_2O\,(g),\ 2NO\,(g) + O_2\,(g) \rightleftharpoons 2NO_2\,(g)$$

$$3NO_2\,(g) + H_2O\,(l) \longrightarrow 2HNO_3\,(aq) + NO\,(g)$$

(*c*) From air (Birkeland-Eyde electric arc process).

$$N_2 + O_2 \rightleftharpoons 2NO - 43.2 \text{ kcal.}\ \ 2NO + O_2 \xrightarrow{50°C} 2NO_2$$

$$2NO_2 + H_2O \longrightarrow HNO_2 + HNO_3,\ 3HNO_2 \longrightarrow HNO_3 + H_2O + 2NO$$

Physical Properties

(*a*) It is colourless liquid but looks yellow due to dissolved NO_2. (*b*) It freezes at 231.4 K and boils at 355.6 K.

(*c*) Fuming HNO_3 is pure HNO_3 with oxides of nitrogen dissolved in it.

Chemical Properties:

(a) $4HNO_3(aq) \xrightarrow{\text{Heat}} 4NO_2(g) + O_2(g) + 2H_2O(\ell)$

(b) It is a strong monobasic acid :

$HNO_3(aq) + H_2O(\ell) \longrightarrow H_3O^+(aq) + NO_3^-(aq)$

(c) It is a very strong oxidising agent, in concentrated as well as in dilute form :

$2HNO_3(\text{conc.}) \longrightarrow H_2O + 2NO_2 + [O]$, $2HNO_3(\text{dil.}) \longrightarrow H_2O + 2NO + 3[O]$

(d) Except gold and platinum, HNO_3 attacks all metals forming a variety of products.

(e) It oxidises many organic compounds and forms various products on reaction.

(f) Sugar on oxidation with HNO_3 gives oxalic acid.

(g) It is a strong oxidising agent and attacks most metals except noble metals such as gold and platinum. However, these dissolve in aqua regia (a mixture of 3 parts of conc. HCl and 1 part of conc. HNO_3).

Uses

(*a*) Used in manufacture of ammonium nitrate for fertilisers and other nitrates for use in explosives and pyrotechniques.

(*b*) Preparation of nitroglycerin, trinitrotoluene and other organic nitro compounds.

(*c*) Pickling of stainless steel, etching of metals and as a oxidiser in rocket fuels.

Structure

Phosphorus

Phosphorus is obtained as phosphates in nature. For e.g. phosphorite $(Ca_3(PO_4)_2)$, chlorapatite hydroxyapatite, Fluoraptite etc.

• Phosphorus occurs in bones, phosphate rocks. It is used in fertilizers.

• As, Sb, Bi, occur mostly as sulphides.

It is isolated by heating $Ca_3(PO_4)_2$ with coke and silica in an electric furnace.

$2Ca_3(PO_4)_2 + 6SiO_2 \xrightarrow{1770\ K} 6CaSiO_3 + P_4O_{10}, P_4O_{10} + 10C \rightarrow P_4 + 10CO$

Phosphorus exhibits allotropy. The various allotropes of phosphorus are white phosphorus, red phosphorus and black phosphorus. White phosphorus is the most common form whereas black phosphorus is the most stable form of phosphorus.

Allotropes of Phosphorus

White phosphorus :

(a) It is less stable and more reactive due to angular strain in the P_4 molecule where the angles are only 60°.

(b) It readily catches fire in air to give dense fumes of P_4O_{10}.

$$P_4 + 5O_2 \longrightarrow P_4O_{10}$$

(c) It consists of discrete tetrahedral P_4 molecule.

(d) White P burn in oxygen at 30°C forming trioxide and pentoxide.

(e) Reaction with caustic alkalies (NaOH and KOH) gives phosphine and sodium hypophosphite.

$$P_4 + 3NaOH + 3H_2O \longrightarrow PH_3 + 3NaH_2PO_2$$
Sodium hypophosphite

(f) White phosphorus react at ordinary temperature and on heating with chlorine it gives PCl_3 and PCl_5.

(g) White phosphorus acts as a strong reducing agent. It reduces HNO_3 to NO_2, H_2SO_4 to SO_2 and $CuSO_4$ to Cu and itself oxidised to H_3PO_4.

Red phosphorus

Red phosphorus is obtained by heating white phosphorus in an inert atmosphere for several days.

(a) It possesses iron grey lustre.

(b) It is odourless, non-poisonous, insoluble in H_2O as well as CS_2.

(c) Chemically, it is less reactive than white phosphorus.

(d) It does not glow in the dark.

(e) Red phosphorus is belived to exist as chains of P_4 tetrahedra linked together.

(f) Red phosphorus does not react with caustic alkalis.

(g) Red phosphorus react at ordinary temp. and on heating respectively with chlorine giving PCl_3 and PCl_5.

Black phosphorus

Black phosphorus has two forms : α - and β -

(a) α-black phosphorus is formed by heating red phosphorus. It has opaque monoclinic or rhombohedral crystals. It does not oxidise in air.

(b) β-black phosphorus is prepared by heating white phosphorus under high pressure. It does not burn in air upto 673 K.

Phosphine [PH_3]

Preparation

(a) $Ca_3P_2 + 6H_2O \longrightarrow 3Ca(OH)_2 + 2PH_3$ (b) $Ca_3P_2 + 6HCl \longrightarrow 3CaCl_2 + 2PH_3$

(c) $P_4 + 3NaOH + 3H_2O \longrightarrow PH_3 + 3NaH_2PO_2$

Properties

(a)   It is a colourless gas with rotten fish smell and is poisonous.

(b)   It is slightly soluble in H_2O and is weakly basic, gives phosphonium compounds with acids, e.g. : $PH_3 + HBr \longrightarrow PH_4Br$

(c)   The solution of PH_3 in water decomposes in presence of light giving red phosporus and H_2.

(d)   Phosphine when comes in contact with air, forms **vortex rings** of P_2O_5 in the form of white smoke. On the basis of this property, phosphine is used to prepare smoke screens in warfare. Calcium phosphide reacts with water forming phosphine which burns in air to give clouds of P_2O_5 which in turn acts as smoke screens.

(e) PH_3 is a powerful reducing agent.

Structures: It has a pyramidal structure with H–P–H angle of $93.6°$.

Uses :

(a)   It is used in smoke screens.

(b)   Containers containing calcium carbide and calcium phosphide are pierced and thrown in the sea when the gases evolved burn and serve as a signal. These are called Holme's signals.

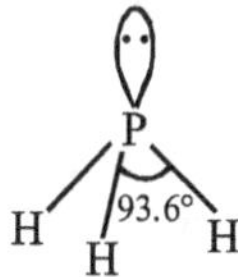

Phosphorus Halides

Phosphorus forms two types of halides, PX_3 and PX_5 (X = F, Cl, Br, I)

PX_3 (PCl_3)

Preparation

(a) $P_4 + 6Cl_2 \longrightarrow 4PCl_3$ (b) $P_4 + 8SOCl_2 \longrightarrow 4PCl_3 + 4SO_2 + 2S_2Cl_2$

Properties

(a)   It is colourless oily liquid and undergo hydrolysis in presence of moisture.

$$PCl_3 + 3H_2O \longrightarrow H_3PO_3 + 3HCl$$

(b)   It reacts with organic compounds containing – OH group

$$3CH_3COOH + PCl_3 \longrightarrow 3CH_3COCl + H_3PO_3$$

$$3C_2H_5OH + PCl_3 \longrightarrow 3C_2H_5Cl + H_3PO_3$$

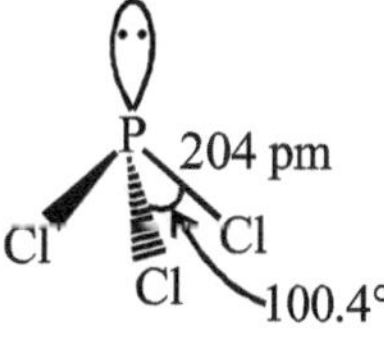

Structure: It has a pyramidal shape in which P is sp^3-hybridised.

PX_5 (PCl_5)

Preparation

(a) $P_4 + 10Cl_2 \longrightarrow 4PCl_5$ (b) $P_4 + 10SO_2Cl_2 \longrightarrow 4PCl_5 + 10SO_2$

Properties

(a)   It is a yellowish white powder.

(b)   In moist air, it hydrolysis to give $POCl_3$ and finally gets converted to H_3PO_4.

$$PCl_5 + H_2O \longrightarrow POCl_3 + 2HCl, \quad POCl_3 + 3H_2O \longrightarrow H_3PO_4 + 3HCl$$

(c)   It sublimes on heating and decomposes on stronger heating

$$PCl_5 \xrightarrow{\text{Heat}} PCl_3 + Cl_2$$

(d)   It reacts with organic compounds containing –OH group

$$C_2H_5OH + PCl_5 \longrightarrow C_2H_5Cl + POCl_3 + HCl, \quad CH_3COOH + PCl_5 \longrightarrow CH_3COCl + POCl_3 + HCl$$

(e)   Finely divided metals on heating with PCl_5 give corresponding chlorides.

$$2Ag + PCl_5 \longrightarrow 2AgCl + PCl_3, \quad Sn + 2PCl_5 \longrightarrow SnCl_4 + 2PCl_3$$

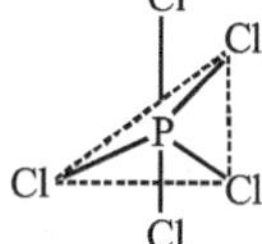

Structure : In gaseous and liquid phases, it has a trigonal bipyramidal structure. The three equatorial P–Cl bonds are equivalent, while the two axial bonds are longer than equatorial bonds. This is due to the fact that axial bonds suffer more repulsion than equatorial bonds.

In solid state, it exists as an ionic solid, $[PCl_4]^+ [PCl_6]^-$ in which the cation $[PCl_4]^+$ is tetrahedral and the anion $[PCl_6]^-$ is octahedral.

Uses : It is used in the synthesis of organic compounds like C_2H_5Cl, CH_3COCl etc. as a chlorinating agent.

Oxoacids of Phosphorus

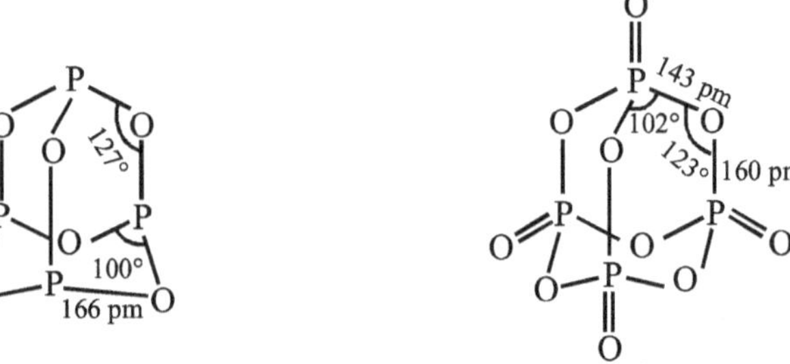

H_3PO_2
Hypophosphorous acid or phosphinic acid.
P in + 1 oxidation state Monobasic & Reducing

H_3PO_3
Orthophosphorus acid or phosphonic acid, Dibasic and reducing, P in + 3 state

$H_4P_2O_5$ Pyrophosphorus acid
Dibasic & reducing P in + 3state

$H_4P_2O_6$
Hypophosphoric Acid
Tetra basic, P in + 4 state

H_3PO_4
Orthophosphoric acid, tribasic
P in +5 state

$H_4P_2O_7$
Pyrophosphoric acid, tetra basic, P is + 5 state

Cyclotrimetaphosphoric acid tribasic, P is + 5 state

In all these acids, P – H linkages are reducing & P – OH linkages are acidic. So number of P – OH linkages is the basicity of the acid.

Oxides of Phosphorus

Structures

(a) **Phosphorus trioxide**

(b) **Phosphorus pentoxide (P_4O_6) (P_4O_{10})**

Each phosphorus atom in P_4O_6 and P_4O_{10} lie at the corners of a tetrahedron. In P_4O_6, each P is covalently bonded to three O-atoms and each O is bonded to two P-atoms. Thus, the six O-atoms lie along the edges of tetrahedron forming six P–O–P bonds.
In P_4O_{10}, each P also forms a double bond by sharing its lone pair of electrons with an O-atom.

Illustration 1 :

What is the difference between the nature of pi-bonds present in H_3PO_3 and HNO_3?

Sol. In H_3PO_3, there is $p\pi - d\pi$ bond whereas in HNO_3 there is $p\pi - p\pi$ bond. $p\pi - p\pi$ bond in HNO_3 is stronger than $p\pi - d\pi$ bond in H_3PO_3.

OXYGEN FAMILY (GROUP 16 ELEMENTS)

In group 16 of the periodic table, elements, oxygen ($_8O$), sulphur ($_{16}S$), selenium ($_{34}Se$), tellurium ($_{52}Te$) and polonium ($_{84}Po$) are present.

Atomic and Physical Properties

(a) **Electronic configuration :** The elements have the structure ns^2np^4 for their valence shells. The first element of the group 16 differs in its chemical behaviour from that of other members of the group due to its small size and high electronegativity.

(b) **Metallic character :** The metallic character increases with increase in atomic number. The first four elements are non-metallic in character. Non-metallic character is strongest in O and S, weaker in Se and Te while Po is metallic.

(c) **Atomic and ionic radii :** Atomic and ionic radii increases from top to bottom, due to increase in the number of shells.

(d) **Ionisation enthalpy :** Ionisation enthalpy decreases down the group, due to increase in size. Elements of group 16 have lower ionisation enthalpy values as compared to group 15 in the corresponding periods. This is due to the fact that group 15 elements have extra stable half-filled p-orbital electronic configurations.

(e) **Electron gain enthalpy :** Oxygen has less negative electron gain enthalpy than sulphur due to compact nature of oxygen atom. From sulphur onwards, electron gain ethalpy becomes less negative upto Po.

(f) **Electronegativity :** Next to F, O has highest electronegativity value among the elements. Within the group, electronegativity decreases with increase in atomic number.

(g)   **Catenation :** The tendency for catenation decreases markedly as we go down the group. Sulphur has a strong tendency for catenation. This is evident from the formation of polysulphides S_n^{2-}, polysulphonic acids, $HO_3S - S_n - SO_3H$ and sulphanes, $H - S_n - H$.

(h)   **Density :** Increases down the group regularly.

(i)   **Melting point and boiling point :** Both show a regular increase down the group due to increase in molecular weight and Van der Waal's forces of attraction.

(j)   **Atomicity :** Oxygen is diatomic, sulphur and selenium octa atomic with puckered ring structure

$$\text{Ring} \qquad S_6$$

(k)   **Allotropy :** All the elements exhibit allotropy.

Chemical Properties

(a)   **Oxidation state :** Oxygen shows oxidation state of –2 but in case of OF_2 and O_2F_2 oxidation state is +2 and +1 respectively. Sulphur, selenium, tellurium and polonium shows +2, +4 and +6 oxidation states. Stability of +6 oxidation state decreases down the group and +4 oxidation state increases down the group due to inert pair effect.

O	S	Se	Te	Po
–1, –2	–2 to +6	–2 to +6	–2 to +6	–2 to +6

In OF_2 the oxidation state of oxygen is +2

(b)   **Reaction with hydrogen:** All the elements of the group form volatile hydrides.

    (a)   The volatility increases markedly from water to hydrogen sulphide and then declines. This is evident in their boiling point. Increasing order of boiling points of hydrides is $H_2S < H_2Se < H_2Te < H_2O$. Down the group boiling point increases because of increasing molecular weight which increases the van der Waal's interaction. H_2O has abnormally high b.p. due to hydrogen bonding.

    (b)   The thermal stability of the hydrides decreases in the order: $H_2O > H_2S > H_2Se > H_2Te > H_2Po$.

    (c)   The strength of the hydrides as acids increases in the order: $H_2O < H_2S < H_2Se < H_2Te$.

    (d)   The reducing power of the hydrides increases from H_2O to H_2Po.

(c)   **Reaction with halogens**

Group 16 elements form number of halides of type EX_4 and EX_6. Where E is an group 16 element and X is a halogen. Stability of halides decrease in the order $F^- > Cl^- > Br^- > I^-$.

    (a)   **Hexahalides** - These are formed by fluorine only (not by Cl, Br, I) where elements exhibit maximum valency of +6. SF_6, SeF_6, TeF_6 are colourless gases with sp^3d^2 hybridisation and octahedral structure. These are covalent in nature. Due to bigger size of Cl, Br and I the coordination number of 6 is not achieved.

    (b)   **Tetrahalides** - With the exception of SBr_4, SI_4 and SeI_4 all tetrahalides are known. They have trigonal bipyramidal shape with sp^3d hybridiation.

    (c)   **Dihalides** - The dihalides eg SCl_2, OF_2, $TeBr_2$ are sp^3, hybridised and have distorted bond angles due to electron pair repulsions

    (d)   **Dimeric monohalides** - The dimeric monohalides are given by sulphur and selenium eg S_2F_2, S_2Cl_2, Se_2Cl_2 S_2Br_2, Se_2Br_2.

(d)   **Reaction with oxygen**

Group 16 elements form oxides of type EO_2 and EO_3 type. O_3 and SO_2 are gases while SeO_2 is solid.

These oxides become less acidic as we go down the group. Reducing property of dioxides decreases from SO_2 to TeO_2.

S, Se and Te form trioxides of the formula MO_3. In the gaseous phase, SO_3 exist as a planar triangular molecule.

Element	Mono-Oxide	Dioxide	Tri-Oxide
S	SO	SO_2	SO_3
Se	-	SeO_2	SeO_3
Te	TeO	TeO_2	TeO_3
PO	PoO	PoO_2	-

Reducing property of dioxides decreases from SO_2 to TeO_2, SO_2 is a reducing agent while TeO_2 is a oxidizing agent.

Dioxygen

Preparation

(a)   By heating oxygen containing salts, such as chlorates, nitrates and permanganates.

$$2KClO_3 \xrightarrow[MnO_2]{\Delta} 2KCl + 3O_2$$

(b)   By thermal decomposition of the oxides of metals low in the electrochemical series and higher oxides of some metals.

$$2Ag_2O \, (s) \longrightarrow 4Ag \, (s) + O_2 \, (g)$$

(*c*) By catalytic decomposition of H_2O_2.
$$2H_2O_2\,(aq) \longrightarrow 2H_2O\,(l) + O_2\,(g)$$
(*d*) From water by electrolysis. Hydrogen is released at cathode and oxygen at anode.
(*e*) **Industrial preparation:** By liquefaction of air followed by its fractional distination. Carbon and water vapour are removed before liquifaction of the air.

Properties:
(*a*) Colourless and odourless gas soluble in water.
(*b*) It has three stable isotopes: ^{16}O, ^{17}O and ^{18}O.
(*c*) It reacts with nearly all metals and non-metals except Au, Pt and some noble gases. Some reactions with metals, non-metals and other compounds are given as:

$$2Ca + O_2 \longrightarrow 2CaO; \quad 2Mg + O_2 \rightarrow 2MgO; \quad 3Fe + 2O_2 \rightarrow Fe_3O_4; \quad C + O_2 \rightarrow CO_2; \quad P_4 + 5O_2 \rightarrow 2P_2O_5;$$

$$S + O_2 \rightarrow SO_2; \quad 4HCl + O_2 \xrightarrow{Cu_gCl_2} 2Cl_2 + 2H_2O \textbf{ (Deacon's process)};$$

$$2ZnS + 3O_2 \longrightarrow 2ZnO_2 + 2SO_2; \quad 4NH_3 + 5O_2 \xrightarrow{Pt} 4NO + 6H_2O \textbf{ (Ostwald's process)}$$

$$2SO_2 + O_2 \xrightarrow{V_2O_5} 2SO_3 \qquad \textbf{(Contact process)}$$

Oxides

Binary compounds of oxygen with another element are called oxides. Oxides are of two types.

(a) Simple oxides - MgO, Al_2O_3.   (b) Mixed oxides - Fe_3O_4, Al_2O_3.

Simple oxides are of four types.

(i) Acidic (Non-metal oxides)   (ii) Basic (Metal oxides)   (iii) Amphoteric   (iv) Neutral

- Oxides which give an acid with water are called acidic oxides. General non-metal are acidic. e.g. SO_2, PO_5, SO_3, I_2O_5. Oxides of some metals in high oxidation state are also acidic. e.g., Mn_2O_7, Cr_2O_3, V_2O_5, etc.
- Oxides which give a base with water are basic oxides. Generally metal oxides are basic e.g., Na_2O, CaO, BaO, etc.
- Oxides which exhibit dual behaviour i.e., show properties of both acidic and basic oxides are called amphoteric oxides. e.g., ZnO, Al_2O_3, SnO
- Oxides which are neither acidic nor basic are called neutral oxides. e.g., CO, NO and N_2O.

Uses:
(*a*) In respiration and combustion processes.
(*b*) In oxyacetylene welding and manufacture of steel.
(*c*) As oxygen cylinders in hospitals, high altitude flying and in mountaineering.

Ozone

Ozone is an allotrope of ozone. It is formed from atmospheric oxygen in presence of sunlight.

Preparation : When a slow dry stream of oxygen is passed through a silent electrical discharge in a special type of apparatus called ozoniser (Siemen's and Brodie's ozonisers) conversion of oxygen to ozone occurs. The product is known as ozonised oxygen :

$$3O_2 \longrightarrow 2O_3, \quad \Delta H°(298\,K) = +68kcal; \quad 3O_2 \longrightarrow 2O_3; \Delta H° = +142kJ/mol$$

Properties
(*a*) It is a pale-blue gas with a characteristic smell. It changes to dark blue liquid and violet-black solid.
(*b*) It is harmless in small concentrations. In higher concentrations it can be explosive and can damage body tissues.
(*c*) It is heavier than air.
(*d*) O_3 is neutral to litmus.
(*e*) It is thermodynamically unstable, it is endothermic i.e. its standard heat of formation is positive.
(*f*) It acts as a powerful oxidising agent due to the ease with which it liberates atoms of nascent oxygen $(O_3 \longrightarrow O_2 + O)$. Some of the examples of its oxidizing action are :

    (i) $PbS + 4O_3 \rightarrow PbSO_4 + 4O_2$ (ii) $2HCl + O_3 \rightarrow Cl_2 + H_2O + O_2$ (iii) $2KI + H_2O + O_3 \rightarrow 2\,KOH + I_2 + O_2$

(*g*) Nitrogen oxides (emitted from jet aeroplanes) combine rapidly with ozone resulting in its depletion in upper atmosphere.

$$NO(g) + O_3(g) \longrightarrow NO_2(g) + O_2(g)$$

Note:
(*a*) This reaction forms the basis of quantitative analysis of O_3. O_3 oxidizes I^- in a solution buffered with borate buffer having pH 9.2. The I_2 formed is further reduced by a standard solution of $Na_2S_2O_3$. The amount of $Na_2S_2O_3$ gives the amount of I_2 produced in oxidation which is then related to amount of O_3 used in oxidizing I^-.

(*b*) Ozone layer in stratosphere protects earth from UV radiations but now it is under threat from nitrogenous oxides emitted from exhaust system of supersonic jets which are slowly depleting the concentration of ozone layer via reaction $NO + O_3 \rightarrow NO_2 + O_2$

Structure

$$\ddot{O} \overset{\ddot{O}}{\diagup} \quad \longleftrightarrow \quad \overset{\ddot{O}}{\diagup} \ddot{O}$$

Uses:

(*a*)   As germicide, disinfectant and for sterilising water.

(*b*)   Bleaching oils, ivory, flour, starch, etc.

(*c*)   Acts as an oxidising agent in the manufacture of $KMnO_4$.

Allotropes of Sulphur

Important allotropes of sulphur are yellow rhombic (α – sulphur) and monoclinic (β - sulphur).

Yellow or rhombic sulphur (α-Sulphur)

(a)   It is stable form of sulphur at room temperature.   (b)   Its m.p. is 385.8K

(c)   Its specific gravity is 2.06

(d)   It is insoluble in water, somewhat soluble in benzene, alcohol, ether & readily soluble in CS_2.

Monoclinic sulphur (β-Sulphur)

(a)   It is prepared by melting rhombic sulphur in a dish and cooling it.   (b)   Its m.p. is 393 K

(c)   Its specific gravity is 1.98   (d)   It is soluble in CS_2

(e)   It is stable only above 369K

(f)   Both α and β sulphur have S_8 molecules. α-sulphur is stable below 369K and β-sulphur is stable above 369K and at 369K both the forms are stable.

(g)   Other modifications of sulphur has 6–20 sulphur atoms per ring. In cyclo-S_6 the ring adopts chair form.

(h)   In vapour state at higher temperatures sulphur exists as S_2 molecule which has two unpaired electrons in the antibonding π orbitals like O_2 and hence, exhibits paramagnetism.

Sulphur Dioxide

Preparation

(*a*) $S(s) + O_2(g) \longrightarrow SO_2(g)$

(*b*)   In laboratory, by treating a sulphite with dil. H_2SO_4.

$$SO_3^{2-}(aq) + 2H^+(aq) \longrightarrow H_2O(l) + SO_2(g)$$

(*c*)   Industrially, as a by product of roasting of sulphide ores.

$$4FeS_2(s) + 11O_2(g) \longrightarrow 2Fe_2O_3(s) + 8SO_2(g)$$

Properties

(*a*)   Colourless gas with pungent smell and highly soluble in water.

(*b*) SO_2 with water forms sulphurous acid. Thus it is acidic in nature

$$SO_2(g) + H_2O(l) \rightleftharpoons \underset{\text{Sulphurous acid}}{H_2SO_3(aq)}$$

(*c*) $2NaOH + SO_2 \longrightarrow \underset{\text{Sodium sulphite}}{Na_2SO_3} + H_2O$

Sodium sulphite reacts with more SO_2 to form sodium hydrogen sulphite.

$$Na_2SO_3 + H_2O + SO_2 \longrightarrow 2NaHSO_3$$

(*d*)   Reaction with chlorine in presence of charcoal as catalyst:

$$SO_2(g) + Cl_2(g) \longrightarrow SO_2Cl_2(l)$$

(*e*)   Sulphur dioxide reacts with oxygen in the presence of vanadium (V) oxide.

$$2SO_2(g) + O_2(g) \xrightarrow{V_2O_5} 2SO_3(g)$$

(*f*)   In moist condition, acts as reducing agent.

For example :

$$2Fe^{3+} + 2H_2O + SO_2 \rightarrow 2Fe^{2+} + SO_4^{2-} + 4H^+$$

It is an oxidising agent also.

Example of its oxidizing action are :

$$2H_2S + SO_2 \rightarrow 2H_2O + 3S$$

$$5SO_2 + 2MnO_4^- + 2H_2O \rightarrow 5SO_4^{2-} + 4H^+ + 2Mn^{2+}$$

Structure : It is angular and is a resonance hybrid of two canonical forms.

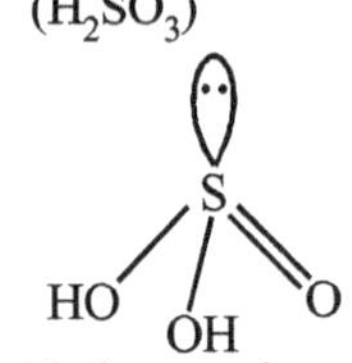

Uses:

(a) In refining petroleum and sugar.

(b) In bleaching wool and silk.

(c) As an anti-chlor, disinfectant and preservatives.

(d) In manufacture of $NaHSO_3$, calcium hydrogen sulphite.

(e) As a solvent.

Oxo-Acids of Sulphur

S, Se and Te forms a number of oxo-acids. Among the oxo-acids of S, sulphuric acid is most important. Other oxoacids of sulphur are $H_2SO_3, H_2S_2O_3, H_2S_2O_4, H_2S_2O_5, H_2S_xO_6$ ($x = 2$ to 5) etc. Sulphurous acid (H_2SO_3) and thiosulfuric acid ($H_2S_2O_3$) are unstable and cannot be isolated. They exist only in aqueous solutions or in the form of their salts.

Structure of some important oxoacids of sulphur is as following :

(i) Sulphurous acid (H_2SO_3)

(ii) Sulphuric acid or oil of vitriol(H_2SO_4)

(iii) Thiosulphuric acid ($H_2S_2O_3$)

(iv) Pyrosulphurous acid ($H_2S_2O_5$)

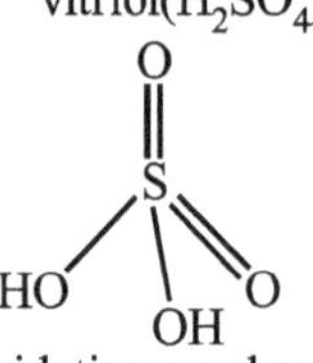

(oxidation number of S = +4)

(Oxidation number of S = 6)

(Oxidation number of S = −2, + 6 contains S = S linkage)

(Oxidation number of S = +4)

(v) Peroxodisulphuric acid or Marshall's acid ($H_2S_2O_8$)

(vi) Dithionic acid ($H_2S_2O_6$)

(vii) Pyrosulphuric acid (oleum) ($H_2S_2O_7$)

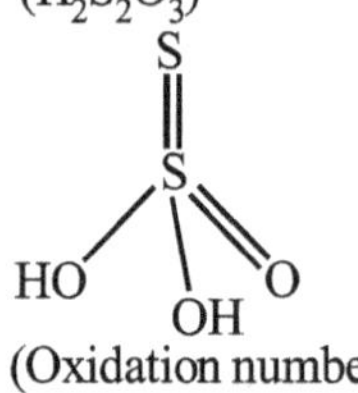

(Oxidation number of S = +6; contains one peroxy group)

(Oxidation no of S = +5 contains one S − S bond)

(Oxidation number of S = +6, contains S − O − S linkage)

Sulphuric Acid

Physical characteristics

(a) H_2SO_4 is colourless, dense, oily liquid.

(b) Freezing point and boiling point are 10.5°C and 340°C respectively.

(c) Density is 1.84 gm cm^{-3}.

(d) Forms hydrate with the evolution of heat :

$H_2SO_4.H_2O$ [monohydrate], $H_2SO_4.2H_2O$ [dihydrate], $H_2SO_4.3H_2O$ [trihydrate]

(e) It has strong affinity for water and acts as oxidizing agent.

(f) High b.p. and viscosity of H_2SO_4 is due to H–bonding.

Chemical characteristics

(a) Acid character (dibasic acid)

$$H_2SO_4 \rightarrow H^+ + HSO_4^-, \quad HSO_4^- \rightarrow H^+ + SO_4^{2-}$$

(b) Forms two type of salts (normal and acidic) :

$$NaOH + H_2SO_4 \rightarrow NaHSO_4 + H_2O, \quad NaHSO_4 + NaOH \rightarrow Na_2SO_4 + H_2O$$

(c) Dehydrating agent [due to high affinity for water]

$$C_{12}H_{22}O_{11} \xrightarrow{\text{conc. } H_2SO_4} 12C + 11H_2O, \quad HCOOH \xrightarrow{\text{conc. } H_2SO_4} CO + H_2O, \quad C_2H_5OH \xrightarrow{\text{conc. } H_2SO_4} C_2H_4 + H_2O$$

(d) **Acts as an oxidizing agent**

$$P_4 + 10H_2SO_4 \longrightarrow P_4O_{10} + 10SO_2 + 10H_2O, \quad C + 2H_2SO_4 \rightarrow CO_2\uparrow + 2SO_2\uparrow + 2H_2O,$$

$$2HBr + H_2SO_4 \rightarrow 2H_2O + SO_2\uparrow + Br_2, H_2S + H_2SO_4 \rightarrow 2H_2O + SO_2\uparrow + S$$

(e) **Displaces more volatile acids :**

$$NaCl + H_2SO_4 \rightarrow NaHSO_4 + HCl, \quad NaNO_3 + H_2SO_4 \rightarrow NaHSO_4 + 2HNO_3$$

$$FeS + H_2SO_4 \rightarrow FeSO_4 + H_2S, \quad Ca_3(PO_4)_2 + 3H_2SO_4 \rightarrow 3CaSO_4 + 2H_3PO_4$$

(f) **Reaction with metals :** Zn, Mg, Fe gives hydrogen

$$Zn + H_2SO_4(dil) \rightarrow ZnSO_4 + H_2$$

Cu gives SO_2.

$$Cu + 2H_2SO_4 (conc.) \rightarrow CuSO_4 + 2H_2O + SO_2$$

Note: Metals like Cu, Pb, Hg, Bi and noble metals are not attacked by dil. H_2SO_4.

(g) **Formation of insoluble sulphates :**

$$BaCl_2 + H_2SO_4 \rightarrow BaSO_4\downarrow + 2HCl, \quad Pb(NO_3)_2 + H_2SO_4 \rightarrow PbSO_4\downarrow + 2HNO_3$$

(h) **Reaction with PCl_5 and $KClO_3$:**

$$PCl_5 + H_2SO_4 \rightarrow ClSO_2OH + POCl_3 + HCl, \quad 3KClO_3 + 3H_2SO_4 \rightarrow 3KHSO_4 + HClO_4 + 2ClO_2 + H_2O$$

Uses:

(*a*) Manufacture of fertilisers.	(*b*) Used in petroleum refining.
(*c*) Manufacture of pigments, paints and dyestuff intermediates.	(*d*) Used in detergent industry.
(*e*) Metallurgical application.	(*f*) Used in storage batteries.
(*g*) Manufacture of nitrocellulose products.	(*h*) Laboratory reagent.

Illustration 2 :

Sulphur forms SF_6 while oxygen does not form OF_6. Why?

Sol. S atom has vacant *d*-orbitals and it can have six electrons unpaired in its configuration due to excitation of paired electrons in s and *p*-orbitals of its valence shell into *d*-orbital. O atom does not have vacant *d*-orbitals in its configuration.

Practice Exercise-1

Multiple Choice Questions

1. Concentrated nitric acid, upon long standing, turns yellow brown due to the formation of
   (a) NO (b) NO_2 (c) N_2O (d) N_2O_4

2. In the reaction

   $$HNO_3 + P_4O_{10} \rightarrow HPO_3 + X, \text{ the product X is}$$

   (a) N_2O_5 (b) N_2O_3 (c) NO_2 (d) H_2O

3. Ammonia on catalytic oxidation gives an oxide from which nitric acid is obtained. The oxide is :
   (a) N_2O_3 (b) NO (c) NO_2 (d) N_2O_5

4. The correct decreasing order of basic strength is:
   (a) $AsH_3 > SbH_3 > PH_3 > NH_3$
   (b) $SbH_3 > AsH_3 > PH_3 > NH_3$
   (c) $NH_3 > PH_3 > AsH_3 > SbH_3$
   (d) $PH_3 > AsH_3 > SbH_3 > NH_3$

5. When orthophosphoric acid is heated to 600°C, the product formed is
   (a) PH_3 (b) P_2O_5
   (c) H_3PO_3 (d) HPO_3

Assertion & Reason Questions

DIRECTIONS (Qs. 6-8) : *Each of these questions contains an assertion followed by reason. Read them carefully and answer the question on the basis of following options. You have to select the one that best describes the two statements.*

(a) If both Assertion and Reason are correct and the Reason is a correct explanation of the Assertion.

(b) If both Assertion and Reason are correct but Reason is not a correct explanation of the Assertion.

(c) If the Assertion is correct but Reason is incorrect.

(d) If the Assertion is incorrect but the Reason is correct.

6. **Assertion :** When a metal is treated with conc. HNO_3 it generally yields a nitrate, NO_2 and H_2O.
   Reason : Conc. HNO_3 reacts with metal and first produces a metal nitrate and nascent hydrogen. The nascent hydrogen then further reduces HNO_3 to NO_2.

7. **Assertion :** Dinitrogen is inert at room temperature.
   Reason : Dinitrogen directly combines with lithium to form ionic nitrides.

8. **Assertion :** Both rhombic and monoclinic sulphur exist as S_8 but oxygen exists as O_2.

Reason : Oxygen forms $p\pi - p\pi$ multiple bond due to small size and small bond length but $p\pi - p\pi$ bonding is not possible in sulphur.

Case/Passage Based Questions

DIRECTIONS (Qs. 9-13) : *Following are the case/passage based questions. Attempt any 4 out of 5 questions.*

Phosphorus is known to form a number of oxoacids. In oxoacids of phosphorus, it is tetrahedrally surrounded by other atoms. Generally, all these acids are known to form at least one $P = O$ bond and one P–OH bond, for example: H_3PO_4, H_3PO_3, etc. P–P or P–H bonds are also found in addition to $P = O$ bonds and P–OH bonds in oxoacids of phosphorus where the oxidation state of phosphorus is less than +5. These acids are generally seen too disproportionate to either lower and higher oxidation states. The P – H bonds in oxoacids cannot go through ionization to give H^+ ions whereas the H atoms which are attached with oxygen in P–OH form are ionizable. Hence, we can say that only the H atoms attached with oxygen cause basicity.

9. Among the oxyacids of phosphorus, the dibasic acid is
   (a) $H_4P_2O_7$ (b) H_3PO_2 (c) HPO_3 (d) H_3PO_3
10. The structural formula of hypophosphorous acid is

11. P_2O_5 is heated with water to give
    (a) hypophosphorous acid (b) phosphorous acid
    (c) hypophosphoric acid (d) orthophosphoric acid

DIRECTIONS (Qs. 12-13) : *Each of these questions contains an assertion followed by reason. Read them carefully and answer the question on the basis of following options. You have to select the one that best describes the two statements.*
(a) If both Assertion and Reason are correct and the Reason is a correct explanation of the Assertion.
(b) If both Assertion and Reason are correct but Reason is not a correct explanation of the Assertion.
(c) If the Assertion is correct but Reason is incorrect.
(d) If the Assertion is incorrect but the Reason is correct.

12. **Assertion:** H_3PO_4 is a tribasic acid.
    Reason: H_3PO_4 contain three P–OH groups.
13. **Assertion:** hypophosphorus acid is a good reducing agent.
    Reason: oxidation state of P is +1

Very Short Answer Questions

14. Mention an important property of hydrazine.
15. NO_2 is coloured but its dimer is colourless. Why?
16. CO_2 and SO_2 are not iso-structural. Explain.
17. Why does the tendency to show –2 oxidation state diminishes from S to Po?
18. Why does oxygen not show an oxidation state of + 4 and + 6 like sulphur?
19. N atom possesses 5 valence electrons but does not form NCl_5. Why?
20. Write one chemical reaction to show that conc. H_2SO_4 can act as an oxidising agent.
21. Name allotropes of oxygen.
22. What is laughing gas? How is it prepared?
23. Name allotropes of phosphorus. Which of these is most reactive?
24. H_2S is acidic while H_2O is neutral. Why?

Short Answer Questions

25. Molecular nitrogen N_2 is not particularly reactive. Explain.
26. H_3PO_3 is diprotic. Explain.
27. Water has a higher boiling point than H_2S.
28. CO_2 and NO_2 are not isostructural. Explain.
29. Both PCl_4^+ and $SiCl_4$ have tetrahedral structures. Explain.
30. Orthophosphoric acid (H_3PO_4) is tribasic but phosphorus acid (H_3PO_3) is dibasic. Explain.
31. Thermal stability of water is much higher than that of H_2S. Explain.
32. H_2S has a stronger reducing behaviour in comparison to that of water. Explain.
33. Oxygen shows covalency of two whereas sulphur shows covalency upto six. Why?
34. NH_3 is more basic than PH_3. Explain.
35. Why do hydrides of oxygen and sulphur differ in physical state?
36. NF_3 is not a base but NCl_3 is base. Why?

Topic 2   Halogen Family, Noble Gases

HALOGEN FAMILY GROUP 17 ELEMENTS

The group 17 of the periodic table contain fluorine ($_9F$), chlorine ($_{17}Cl$), bromine ($_{35}Br$), iodine ($_{53}I$) and astatine ($_{55}At$). They are collectively called halogens as their salts are present in sea water. At is radioactive, artificially prepared and unstable. They have a strong tendency to accept one electron to acquire stable inert gas configuration. Hence exhibit nonmetallic behaviour.
High electronegativity makes them very reactive and they are not available in free state. Except At, the other members are found in combined state in suitable quantities in nature.

Atomic and Physical Properties

(a) Electronic configuration: Electronic configuration is $ns^2\,np^5$ for valence shells.

Element	Atomic number	Configuration
Fluorine [F]	9	[He] $2s^2 2p^5$
Chlorine [Cl]	17	[Ne] $3s^2 3p^5$
Bromine [Br]	35	[Ar] $3d^{10}4s^2 4p^5$
Iodine [I]	53	[Kr] $4d^{10}5s^2 5p^5$
Astatine [At]	85	[Xe] $4f^{14}\,5d^{10}\,6s^2 6p^5$

(b) Atomic and ionic radii : Halogens have the smallest atomic radii in their respective periods due to maximum effective nuclear charge. Down the group atomic and ionic radii increases from F to I due to increase in the number of quantum shells.

(c) Ionisation enthalpy : The first ionisation energies are relatively high but decreases down the group. Iodine can lose an electron and form I^+ ion.

(d) Electron gain enthalpy: The electron affinities are high, increases from F to Cl and then decreases down the group. The electron affinity of F is less than that of Cl due to its small size with high electron density.Electron affinity varies as $Cl > F > Br > I$

(e) Electronegativity : Halogens have high electronegativities F is most electronegative element known. Electronegativity decreases on moving down the group.

(f) Physical state : Fluorine and chlorine are gases, bromine is a liquid while iodine is a solid.

(g) Melting and soiling points : Their melting and boiling points steadily increase with atomic number.

(h) Bond energy : Actually, the bond energy should have decreased from F – F to I – I but in practice it starts decreasing from Cl – Cl to I – I.

$$\begin{array}{cccc} F-F & Cl-Cl & Br-Br & I-I \\ \text{38 kcal/mole} & \text{57 kcal/mole} & \text{45.5 kcal/more} & \text{35.6 kcal/mole} \end{array}$$

The lower value of bond dissociation energy of F – F bond than Cl – Cl bond is due to larger inter-electronic (electron-electron) repulsion between the non-bonding electrons in the $2p$-orbitals of fluorine atom than those in the $3p$-orbitals of chlorine atoms. Moreover, the X – X bond in Cl_2, Br_2 and I_2 is much stronger due to hybridisation of p- and d-orbitals.

(i) Non-metallic character : There is a gradual decline in the non-metallic character as we move down the group with decrease in electronegativity hence iodine shows some metallic character, viz. presence of metallic lustre and formation of positive ion, I^+.

(j) Density: It increases down the group in a regular fashion and follows the order $F > Cl > Br > I$

Chemical Properties

(a) Oxidation state: All halogens exhibit –1 oxidation state. Other halogens except fluorine also exhibit +1, +3, +5 and +7 oxidation state.

(b) Oxidising nature: Fluorine does not has d-orbital in its valence shell and hence cannot expand its octet. Therefore shows only –1 oxidation state. Halogens are good oxidising agents. The tendency of oxidising power decreases down the group. F_2 is the strongest oxidizing agent and oxidizes other halide ions. A halogen oxidizes halide ions of higher atomic number.

(c) Reaction with metals and non-metals: X_2 reacts with metals to give halides. The ionic character of the halides decreases in the order

$$MF > MCl > MBr > MI$$

Halides of metals having low IE are more ionic in comparison to halides of metals having high IE. For metals exhibiting more than one oxidation states, the halide with higher oxidation state of metal is more covalent in comparison to halide having metal with lower oxidation state. X_2 react with non metals like S, P, As etc.

(d) Reaction with hydrogen: All halogens react with hydrogen to form volatile H – X, which dissolve in water to form hydrohalic acids. Acidic strength of hydrogen halides varies as:

$$HF < HCl < HBr < HI$$

The stability of these halides decreases down the group due to decrease in bond dissociation enthalpy in the order.

$$H\text{-}F > H\text{-}Cl > H\text{-}Br > H\text{-}I$$

Also volatility decreases from HCl to HI.

The order of b.p is $HCl < HBr < HI < HF$

(e) Reaction with oxygen: Chlorine forms oxides Cl_2O, ClO_2, Cl_2O_6 & Cl_2O_7. These oxides are highly reactive and strong oxidising agents and tend to explode. ClO_2 is used as bleaching agent for paper and pulp industries. It is also used in textiles and in water treatment.

Among the halogen oxides, bromine oxides Br_2O, BrO_3 are least stable due to middle row anomaly. These are stable only at low temperature. These are powerful oxidants. Iodine forms I_2O_4, I_2O_5 and I_2O_7. These are insoluble solids. They decomposes in heating I_2O_5 is a good reducing agent. I_2O_5 is used in the estimaton of CO.

(f) **Reaction with metal:** Halogens forms metal halides with metals. Ionic character of M-X bond decreases in the order $M - F > M - Cl > M - Br > M - I$

Halides in higher oxidation state are more covalent whereas halides in lower oxidation state are ionic

(g) **Reaction with halogen:** Halogens combine amongst themselves to form a number of compounds known as interhalogen of type XX', XX_3', XX_5' and XX_7

(h) **Reaction with alkalies:** Cl_2, Br_2 and I_2 behave similarly when treated with alkali (they undergo disproportionation reaction)

    (a) Cold and dilute alkali :

$$X_2 + 2NaOH \rightarrow NaX + NaOX + H_2O$$

    (b) Hot and concentrated alkali :

$$3X_2 + 6NaOH \rightarrow 5NaX + NaXO_3 + 3H_2O$$

    F_2 behaves differently with alkalies :

$$F_2 + 2NaOH\,(dil) \rightarrow 2NaF + OF_2 + H_2O,\ 2F_2 + 4NaOH\,(conc) \rightarrow 4NaF + O_2 + 2H_2O$$

Anomalous Behaviour of Fluorine

Anomalous behaviour of fluorine is due to its small size, highest electronegativity, non-availability of d-orbitals, low F–F bond dissociation energy and highest positive reduction potential.

Main points of difference are :

(a) Fluorine shows only -1 oxidation state. This is due to its most electronegative nature.

(b) Fluorine has a covalency of 1.

(c) Fluorine forms inter and intramolecular H–bonds.

(d) HF is a weak acid as compared to HCl, HBr and HI.

(e) Fluorine forms two series of salts $NaHF_2$ and Na_2F_2.

(f) AgF is soluble in water while AgCl, AgBr and AgI are insoluble.

(g) Fluorine does not forms oxo acids while oxo acids of other halogens are well known, ex : $HClO_3$, $HOBr$, HIO_4 etc.

(h) Fluorine is the most reactive amongst halogens (due to low F–F energy).

(i) Fluorine forms SF_6 whereas no other halogen forms SX_6.

(j) CaF_2 is insoluble in water whereas $CaCl_2$, $CaBr_2$ and CaI_2 are soluble.

Chlorine

Preparation:

(a) By heating MnO_2 with conc. HCl.

$$MnO_2 + 4HCl \rightarrow MnCl_2 + Cl_2 + 2H_2O$$

(b) By action of HCl or $KMnO_4$.

$$2KMnO_4 + 16HCl \rightarrow 2KCl + 2MnCl_2 + 8H_2O + 5Cl_2$$

Commercial manufacture

(a) In the Deacon process HCl is oxidised by air in presence of $CuCl_2$ as catalyst at 400°C

$$4HCl + O_2 \xrightarrow{\ CuCl_2\ } 2Cl_2 + 2H_2O$$

(b) In the electrolytic process, it is obtained at anode in the electrolysis of concentrated solution of brine (NaCl).

$$NaCl \rightleftharpoons Na^+ + Cl^-$$

$$2Na^+ + 2e^- \rightarrow 2Na + 2H_2O \rightarrow 2NaOH + H_2\ (\text{at cathode})\ ;\ 2Cl^- - 2e^- \longrightarrow 2Cl \longrightarrow Cl_2\ (\text{at anode})$$

Properties

(a) Greenish-yellow gas with pungent and suffocating odour.

(b) Cl_2 is 2-5 times heavier than air.

(c) Soluble in water its aqueous solution is known as chlorine water which on careful cooling gives chlorine hydrate $Cl_2.8H_2O$.

(d) Reacts with metals and non-metals to form chlorides.

For example : $2Fe + 3Cl_2 \longrightarrow 2FeCl_3$; $P_4 + 6Cl_2 \longrightarrow 4PCl_3$

(e) Chlorine has great affinity for hydrogen and react with hydrogen containing compounds to form HCl

For e.g : $H_2S + Cl_2 \longrightarrow 2HCl + S$; $H_2 + Cl_2 \longrightarrow 2HCl$

(f) Reaction with NH_3 :

$$\underset{\text{(excess)}}{8NH_3} + 3Cl_2 \longrightarrow 6NH_4Cl + N_2\ ,\quad NH_3 + \underset{\text{(excess)}}{3Cl_2} \longrightarrow NCl_3 + 3HCl$$

(g) Reaction with NaOH

$$\underset{\text{(Cold and dilute)}}{2NaOH} + Cl_2 \longrightarrow NaCl + NaOCl + H_2O\ ;\quad \underset{\text{(Hot and conc.)}}{6NaOH} + 3Cl_2 \longrightarrow 5NaCl + NaClO_3 + 3H_2O$$

(h)   Acts as oxidising and bleaching agent.

Oxidising action of Cl$_2$

$$2FeSO_4 + H_2SO_4 + Cl_2 \longrightarrow Fe_2(SO_4)_3 + 2HCl$$

Bleaching action :

Bleaching action is due to oxidation

$$Cl_2 + H_2O \longrightarrow 2HCl + O, \text{ Coloured substance} + O \longrightarrow \text{Colourless substance}$$

Uses:

(*a*)   For bleaching pulp, cotton and textiles.

(*b*)   Extraction of Au and Pt.

(*c*)   Manufacture of dyes, drugs and organic compounds like CCl_4, $CHCl_3$, DDT, refrigerants, etc.

(*d*)   Sterilising drinking water.

(*e*)   Preparation of poisonous gases such as phosgene ($COCl_2$), tear gas (CCl_3NO_2), mustard gas ($ClCH_2CH_2SCH_2CH_2Cl$).

Hydrogen Chloride

Preparation

In laboratory by heating NaCl with conc. H_2SO_4.

$$NaCl + H_2SO_4 \xrightarrow{420K} NaHSO_4 + HCl; \quad NaHSO_4 + NaCl \xrightarrow{823K} Na_2SO_4 + HCl$$

Properties:

(*a*)   Colourless and pungent smelling gas, easily liquefied to a colourless liquid and freezes to a white crystalline solid.

(*b*)   Extremely soluble in water. Its b.p. is 189 K and f.p. is 159 K

(*c*)   Reacts with NH_3 and gives white fumes of NH_4Cl

$$NH_3 + HCl \longrightarrow NH_4Cl$$

(*d*)   When 3 parts conc. HCl and 1 part conc. HNO_3 are mixed, aqua regia is formed which is used for dissolving noble metals like Au, Pt.

Uses:

(*a*)   Manufacture of Cl_2, NH_4Cl and glucose (from corn starch)

(*b*)   For extracting glue from bones and purifying bone black.

(*c*)   In medicine and as a laboratory reagent.

Oxoacids of Halogens

(a)   **Acid–character:** The acid–character of the oxo acids of same halogen increases with the increase in the oxidation number of the halogen.

Example : $HClO_4 > HClO_3 > HClO_2 > HClO$

Acid strength of oxoacids of different halogens in same O.S. decreases with increase in atomic number of the halogen atom.

Example : $HOCl > HOBr > HOI$

(b)   **Oxidising power :** Oxidizing power of the oxo acids of same halogen decreases with the increase in O.S. of halogen atom.

Example : $HOCl > HClO_2 > HClO_3 > HClO_4$

The order of oxidizing power of different perhalic acids (or their salts) follows the order : $ClO_4^- < BrO_4^- < IO_4^-$

(c)   **Thermal stability:** Thermal stability of oxoacid of chlorine follows the order : $HOCl < HClO_2 < HClO_3 < HClO_4$

(d)   **Stability of conjugate bases:** ClO^-, ClO_2^-, ClO_3^-, ClO_4^- are the conjugate bases of the acids HClO, $HClO_2$, $HClO_3$ and $HClO_4$.

Conjugate bases $[HX + H_2O \rightleftharpoons H_3O^+ + X^-]$

The strength of an acid is related to the strength of its conjugate base, i.e., *stronger the acid, the weaker will be its conjugate base and vice versa.* In other words, the strength of the conjugate bases of the above four acids follows the following order.

$ClO_4^- < ClO_3^- < ClO_2^- < ClO^-$ (Relative basic character)

Thus ClO_4^- is the weakest base and hence $HClO_4$ (conjugate acid of ClO_4^-) is the strongest acid.

(e)   **Structure**

Oxoacids of chlorine :

(a) Hypochlorous acid   (b) Chlorous acid   (c) Chloric acid   (d) Perchloric acid.
   (HOCl)   ($HClO_2$)   ($HClO_3$)   ($HClO_4$)

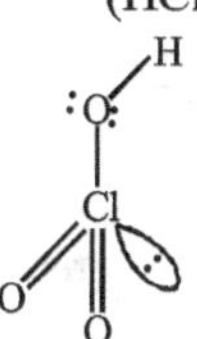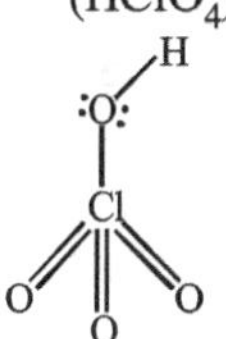

Interhalogen Compounds

The compounds of halogens among themselves are known as **interhalogen compounds**. The main reason for the formation of these compounds is the large electronegativity and size differences among the halogens. Thus fluorine, the most electronegative element and the smallest halogen, forms the maximum number of interhalogens (halogen fluorides).

Preparation

Interhalogen compounds are prepared by direct combination or by the action of halogen on lower interhalogen compounds. Example:

$$I_2 + 2Cl_2 \underset{\text{Excess}}{\longrightarrow} 2ICl_3; \quad \underset{\text{equimolar}}{Cl_2} + F_2 \xrightarrow{437K} 2ClF; \quad Br_2 + 3F_2 \underset{\text{(Diluted with water)}}{\longrightarrow} 2BrF_3$$

Properties

(*a*)   They are strong oxidising agents.

(*b*)   More reactive than the halogen except F_2.

(*c*)   They are covalent compounds.

(*d*)   Their stability increases as the size of central atom increase.

(*e*)   In these compounds, the smaller and the more electronegative atom is assigned a negative oxidation state.

There are four types of interhalogen compounds. The less electronegative halogen A is always written first.

Type	Interhalogen	Shapes
AB	ClF, BrF, BrCl	Linear
AB$_3$	ClF, BrF$_3$, IF$_3$, ICl$_3$	T shaped, distored trigonal pyramidal due to 2 lone pairs of electrons (sp^3d)
AB$_5$	ClF$_5$, BrF$_5$	Distorted octahedral, square pyramidal due to 1 lone pair of electrons (sp^3d^2)
AB$_7$	IF$_7$	Pentagonal bipyramidal (sp^3d^3)

Uses

(a)   Used as fluorinating agents

(b)   ClF$_3$ and BrF$_3$ are used for the production of UF$_6$ in the enrichment of U-235

Illustration 3 :

Why is HF the weakest acids among hydrohalo acids inspite of the fact that F is most electronegative?

Sol. Due to widespread H-bonding in HF, H^+ is not easily formed. Due to small bond length of H – F, bond dissociation energy is high.

Group 18 Elements : The Noble Gases

Zero group or group-18 contains six gaseous elements He, Ne, Ar, Kr, Xe and Rn. First five elements are present in small quantities in atmosphere and are called rare gases. Radon is obtained as a decay product of radium and is radioactive.

$$^{226}_{88}Ra \longrightarrow {}^{222}_{86}Rn + {}^{4}_{2}He$$

Due to stable outer configuration of s^2p^6 (octet), these gases exhibit inert character and are called inert gases. Under specific conditions, these gases can form compounds [XeF_2, XeF_4 etc.].

These elements occupy position between the most electronegative (halogens) and the most electropositive (alkali metals) elements. Thus zero group elements are neither electro positive nor electronegative in nature.

Atomic and Physical Properties

(a)   **Electronic configuration**

General E.C. : ns^2np^6

Element	Atomic number	Electronic Configuration
Helium [He]	2	$1s^2$
Neon [Ne]	10	[He] $2s^2\,2p^6$
Argon [Ar]	18	[Ne] $3s^2\,3p^6$
Krypton [Kr]	36	[Ar] $3d^{10}\,4s^2\,4p^6$
Xenon [Xe]	54	[Kr] $4d^{10}\,5s^2\,5p^6$
Radon [Rn]	86	[Xe] $4f^{10}\,5d^{10}\,6s^2\,6p^6$

(b)   **Ionisation enthalpy:** Due to stable electronic configuration, these gases exhibit very high I.E. It decreases down the group with increase in size.

(c)   **Atomic radii**: They have the largest radii in their respective periods. This is because they have van der Waal's radii while others have covalent radii. And, Van der Waal radii is greater than the covalent radii.

(d) **Electron gain enthalpy (EGE):** They have large positive values of EGE due to stable electronic configurations. As a result, they have no tendency to accept electron.

(e) **Physical Properties**
  (i)   All the noble gases are monoatomic.
  (ii) They are colourless, odourless and tasteless.
  (iii) They have very low m.pts. and b.pts. due to weak dispersion forces (or, van der Waal's forces) holding the atoms of these elements.
  (iv) These gases cannot be easily liquefied because their atoms are held together by weak van der Waal's forces of attraction. Ease of liquefication increases down the group due to increase in magnitude of van der Waal's forces with the increase in atomic size.
  (v)   They are very slightly soluble in water.

Chemical Properties

Noble gases are the least reactive because :
(a) of stable inert gas configuration.
(b) of high I.E. and more positive electron gain enthalpy.

The first noble gas compound was isolated by **Neil Bartlett**. He prepared a red compound of Xe which was formulated as Xe^+PtF_6 (prepared by mixing PtF_6 and Xe). After this, a number of compounds mainly with most electronegative elements like F and O, have been synthesised.

Xe-F compounds
Preparation :

$$Xe(g) + F_2(g) \xrightarrow[1\,bar]{673K} XeF_2(s); \quad Xe(g) + 2F_2(g) \xrightarrow[7\,bar]{873K} XeF_4(s); \quad Xe(g) + 3F_2(g) \xrightarrow[60\text{-}70\,bar]{573K} XeF_6(s);$$
$$\text{(excess)} \qquad\qquad\qquad\qquad (1\!:\!5) \qquad\qquad\qquad\qquad (1\!:\!20)$$

$$XeF_4 + O_2F_2 \longrightarrow XeF_6 + O_2$$

Reactions :

(a) They react readily even with traces of water :   (b) $XeF_2 + PF_5 \longrightarrow [XeF]^+[PF_6]^-$

  Ex: $2XeF_2(s) + 2H_2O(\ell) \longrightarrow 2Xe(g) + 4HF(aq) + O_2(g)$

(c) $XeF_4 + SbF_5 \longrightarrow [XeF_3]^+[SbF_6]^-$ (d) $XeF_6 + MF \longrightarrow M^+[XeF_7]^-$ (M = Na, K, Rb or Cs)

Xe-O compounds
Preparation :
(i) Hydrolysis of XeF_4 and XeF_6 with water gives XeO_3.

  $$6XeF_4 + 12H_2O \longrightarrow 4Xe + 2XeO_3 + 24HF + 3O_2; \quad XeF_6 + 3H_2O \longrightarrow XeO_3 + 6HF$$

(ii) Partial hydrolysis of XeF_6 gives oxyfluorides, $XeOF_4$ and XeO_2F_2.

  $$XeF_6 + H_2O \longrightarrow XeOF_4 + 2HF; \quad XeF_6 + 2H_2O \longrightarrow XeO_2F_2 + 4HF$$

Properties :
(i) XeO_3 is a colourless explosive solid and has pyramidal molecular structures.
(ii) $XeOF_4$ is a colourless volatile liquid and has square pyramidal molecular structure.

Structure of fluorides and oxides of Xenon :

(a) **XeF_2**   (b) **XeF_4**   (c) **XeF_6**   (d) **$XeOF_4$**   (e) **XeO_3**

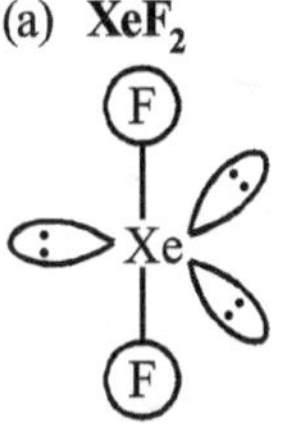 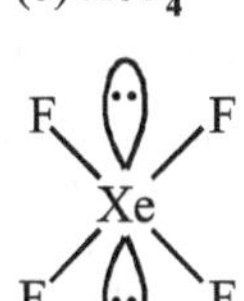 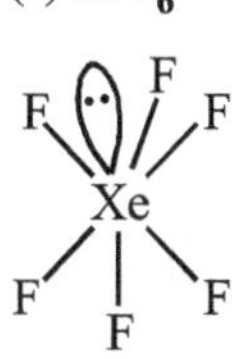 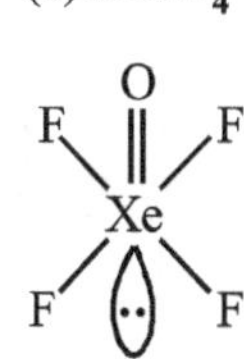 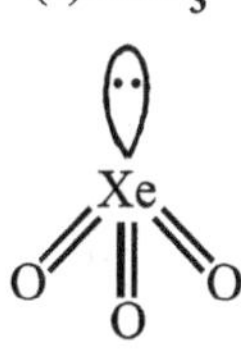

Linear   Square planar   Distorted octahedral   Square pyramidal   Pyramidal

Uses of Noble Gases

Noble gases are widely used to provide inert atmosphere in metallurgical processes (e.g. Ti), in welding and cutting (antioxidant), in electric bulbs (prolongs filament life), etc. They are also used as coolants for low temperature work. Amongst the noble gases only helium and argon are easily available and hence these are most widely used.

Helium :

(a) Used in balloons and airships as it is light and non-inflammable.

(b) Used in creating inert atmosphere in metallurgy and welding metals.

(c) Used in filling tungsten lamps required for signaling.

(d) A mixture of He and O_2 is used for respiration by divers in deep sea. Since He is much less soluble in the blood than nitrogen at high pressure.

(e) Used for filling vacuum tubes and radio tubes.

(f) Liquid helium (b.p. 4.1 K) is used as a cryogenic fluid to provide low temperatures for studying scientific phenomena occuring near the absolute zero. It is also used in gas thermometers required for low temperature measurements.

Neon :

(a) Neon lamps are used in green houses as it is effective in the growth of chlorophyll.

(b) Neon lamps are used in botanical gardens.

(c) Neon lights are visible in fog and mist and there fore neon lights are used for making signals in night for pilots.

(d) Neon is also used in discharge tubes required for decorative and advertising purpose.

(e) Neon tubes are used in various fields of electro technology for rectifiers, voltage, regulators, inductors, etc.

Argon :

(a) Used for creating inert atmosphere for welding.

(b) Ar plus He mixture is used for signal electrical device.

(c) Ar plus Ne are used in filling fluorescent tubes, radio–valves etc.

(d) Used in bulbs to enhance the life of filament.

Krypton and Xenon :

Used in filling up bulbs containing incandescent filaments.

Radon : (a) Used in radio therapy of cancer.

         (b) Used to check the defects in steel sheets.

In group 18 of the Periodic table, elements helium ($_2$He), neon ($_{10}$Ne), argon ($_{18}$Ar), krypton ($_{36}$Kr), xenon ($_{54}$Xe) and radon ($_{86}$Rn) are present. They are collectively called as **noble gases**.

Illustration 4 :

Fluorine does not undergo disproportionation reactions but other halogens do. Explain why?

Sol. Disproportionation means simultaneous oxidation – reduction. F being the most electronegative element undergoes only reduction but not oxidation. As a result, it shows +1 oxidation state while other halogens show both negative (–1) and positive (+1, +3, +5, +7) oxidation states. Thus, F does not show disproportionation reactions while other halogen do.

Practice Exercise-2

Multiple Choice Questions

1. Which of the following on thermal decomposition gives oxygen gas ?
   (a) Ag_2O (b) Pb_3O_4
   (c) PbO_2 (d) All of these

2. The correct order of increasing oxidising power is
   (a) $F_2 > Br_2 > Cl_2 > I_2$ (b) $F_2 < Cl_2 < Br_2 < I_2$
   (c) $Cl_2 > Br_2 > F_2 > I_2$ (d) $I_2 < Br_2 < Cl_2 < F_2$

3. The correct order of heat of formation of halogen acids is
   (a) $HI > HBr > HCl > HF$
   (b) $HF > HCl > HBr > HI$
   (c) $HCl > HF > HBr > HI$
   (d) $HCl > HBr > HF > HI$

4. Which one is most stable to heat –
   (a) $HClO$ (b) $HClO_2$ (c) $HClO_3$ (d) $HClO_4$

5. The noble gas which was discovered first in the sun and then on the earth
   (a) argon   (b) xenon   (c) neon   (d) helium

Assertion & Reason Questions

DIRECTIONS (Qs. 6-8) : *Each of these questions contains an assertion followed by reason. Read them carefully and answer the question on the basis of following options. You have to select the one that best describes the two statements.*

(a) If both Assertion and Reason are correct and the Reason is a correct explanation of the Assertion.
(b) If both Assertion and Reason are correct but Reason is not a correct explanation of the Assertion.
(c) If the Assertion is correct but Reason is incorrect.
(d) If the Assertion is incorrect but the Reason is correct.

6. **Assertion :** Inert gases are monoatomic.
   Reason : Inert gases have stable configuration.

7. **Assertion :** Fluorine exists only in -1 oxidation state.
   Reason : Fluorine has $2s^2 2p^5$ configuration.
8. **Assertion :** The fluorine has lower reactivity.
   Reason : F – F bond has low bond dissociation energy.

Very Short Answer Questions

9. Why are halogens strong oxidising agents?
10. Why is fluorine most reactive among halogens?
11. Why is HF stored in wax-coated glass bottles?
12. Why is iodine more soluble in KI than in H_2O?
13. NF_3 is an exothermic compound but NCl_3 is an endothermic compound. Explain.
14. Why is helium used in inflating aeroplane tyres?
15. Why are the interhalogens compounds more reactive than the halogens (except F_2)?
16. With what the neutral molecule is ClO^- is iso-structural?
17. Show that Cl_2 gas can be obtained from bleaching powder.
18. Why is OF_6 compound not known?

Short Answer Questions

19. Arrange the following in the decreasing order of property indicated.
    (*i*) F_2, Cl_2, Br, I_2 – Bond energy
    (*ii*) HF, HCl, HBr, HI – Acid strength (in water)
    (*iii*) M–F, M–Cl, M–Br, M–I – Ionic character of the bond.
    (*iv*) ClO_4^-, BrO_4^-, IO_4^- – Oxidizing power
20. Give equations for the following :
    (*i*) $XeF_2 + H_2O \longrightarrow$ (*ii*) $XeF_6 + H_2O \longrightarrow$
    (*iii*) $XeF_6 + PF_5 \longrightarrow$ (*iv*) $XeF_6 + NaF \longrightarrow$
21. Solubility of noble gases in water increases as we more down the group. Explain.
22. Xenon does not form fluorides, such as XeF_3 and XeF_5. Why?
23. Why is perchloric acid, $HClO_4$ a stronger acid than sulphuric acid?
24. Among the noble gases, Xe forms maximum noble gas compounds with fluorine. Why is it so?
25. ClF_3 exists whereas FCl_3 does not. Give reasons.

Important Tips & Formulae

- Hydracid of halogens HF forms two series of salts (**$NaHF_2$ and NaF**).

- Silver halide insoluble in ammonia : AgI

- Asthma patient for respiration uses a mixture of
  Helium + Oxygen

- Metals and non-metals react with HNO_3 under different conditions to give NO or NO_2.

- In laboratory, dioxygen is prepared by heating $KClO_3$ in presence of MnO_2.

- XeF_2 is linear, XeF_4 is square planar and XeF_6 is distorted octahedral.

- XeF_2, XeF_4, and XeF_6 are powerful fluorinating agents.

- Xe form two oxides such as XeO_3 and XeO_4.

- Freshly prepared phosphorous is colourless. On standing acquires pale lemon colour due to formation of red phosphorus on the surface. It is therefore called yellow phosphorous. Due to its poisonous nature the jaw bones decay and disease is known as **"Phossy jaw"**

- **Smoke screen :** Ca_3P_2 is used smoke screen. PH_3 obtained from it catches fire to give the needed smoke.

- **Rat poison :** Zinc phosphide Zn_3P_2 is a rat poison, which gives PH_3.

- In solid state, PCl_5 exists as an ionic solid, $[PCl_4]^+ [PCl_6]^-$ in which the cation $[PCl_4]^+$ is tetrahedral and the anion $[PCl_6]^-$ is octahedral.

- **SO_3.** is a gas, sp^2 hybridised and planar in nature.

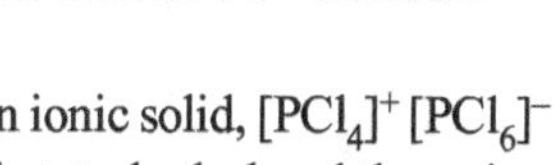

In solid state it exist as a **cyclic trimer** $(SO_3)_3$ γ-form or as a **linear** chain cross linked sheets

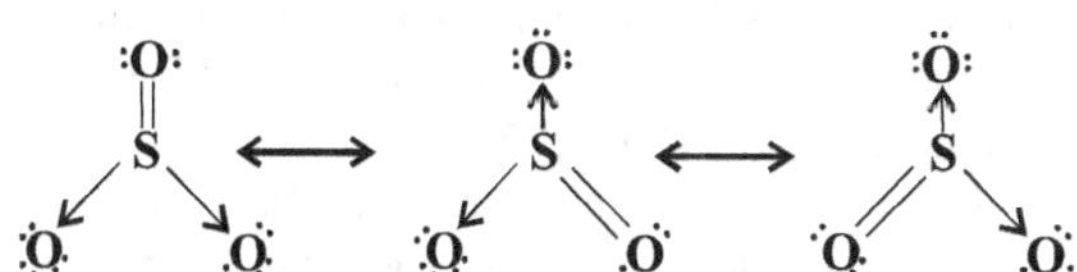

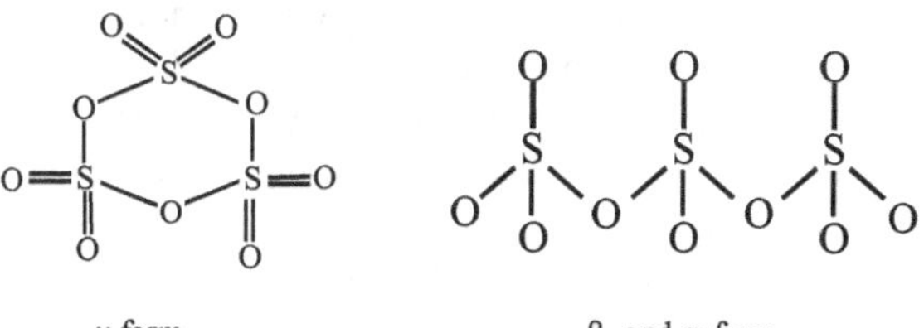

γ-form   β- and α-form

- SF_6 is used in high voltage tranformers because of its insulating property.

- Liquid oxygen mixed with finely divided carbon is used in place of dynamite in coal mining.

- A mixture of ozone and cyanogen is used as a rocket fuel.

- Gun powder is a mixture of sulphur, charcoal and KNO_3.

- S_2Cl_2 is used in the vulcanisation of rubber. The process was discovered by, **Charles Goodyear** in 1839.

- Electrical conductivity of Se is negligible in dark but increases on exposure to light. Due to this property, Se is used in photo-electric cells and as a photoconductor in photocopying (Xerox) machines.

- **Euchlorine**

  It is a mixture of chlorine and chlorine dioxide and obtained by heating $KClO_3$ with conc. HCl

  $$2KClO_3 + 4HCl \rightarrow 2KCl + Cl_2 + 2ClO_2 + 2H_2O$$

- $NaClO_3$ is a powerful weed killer and $KClO_3$ *(Berthelot's salt)* is used in fire works and matches as oxidising agent.

- **Clathrates**

  A number of organic and inorganic compounds having gases trapped into the cavities of crystal lattices are *enclosure* or *clathrate* compounds. They are known as *cage compounds* also. The clathrates are non stoichiometric compounds. He and Ne do not form clathrates due to their small size.

NCERT Questions

1. Discuss the general characteristics of Group 15 elements with reference to their electronic configuration, oxidation state, atomic size, ionisation enthalpy and electronegativity.

Sol. In group 15 of the Periodic Table, the elements, nitrogen ($_7$N), phosphorus ($_{15}$P), arsenic ($_{33}$As), antimony ($_{51}$Sb) and bismuth ($_{83}$Bi) are present.

The elements of this group can exhibit various oxidation states ranging between -3 to $+5$. Negative oxidation state will be exhibited when they combine with less electronegative element and positive oxidation state will be exhibited with more electronegative element. Positive oxidation state becomes more favourable as we more down the group due to increasing metallic character & electropositivity. Although due to inert pair effect the stability of +5 state will also decrease. The only stable compound of Bi (V) is BiF_5.

The atomic (covalent) and ionic radii (in a particular oxidation state) of the elements of nitrogen family (group 15) are smaller than the corresponding elements of carbon family (group 14). On moving down the group, the covalent and ionic radii (in a particular oxidation state) increase with increase in atomic number. There is a considerable increase in covalent radius from N to P. However, from As to Bi, only a small increase is observed. As the size increases on moving down the group, the ionisation enthalpy increases. The ionisation enthalpy of nitrogen group elements is more than the corresponding elements of oxygen group. This is because of more stable half filled outermost *p*- subshell of nitrogen group elements. Electronegativity decreases down the group with increase in atomic size.

2. Why does the reactivity of nitrogen differ from phosphorus?

Sol. N_2 exist as a diatomic molecule containing triple bond between two N-atoms. Due to the presence of triple bond between the two N-atoms, the bond dissociation energy is large ($941 \cdot 4$ kJ mol^{-1}). As a result of this, N_2 is inert and unreactive whereas, phosphorus exists as a tetratomic molecule, containing P $-$ P single bond. Due to the presence

of single bond, the bond dissociation energy is weaker (213 kJmol^{-1}) than $N \equiv N$ triple bond ($941 \cdot 4$ kJ mol^{-1}) and moreover due to presence of angular strain in P_4 tetrahedra. As a result of this, phosphorus is much more reactive than nitrogen.

3. Discuss the trends in chemical reactivity of group 15 elements.

Sol. **Hydrides :** All elements of group 15 form gaseous hydrides of the type MH_3.

In all the hydrides the central atom is sp^3 hybridized and their shape is pyramidal due to presence of lone pair of electrons.

(a) The basic strength of the hydrides decreases as we move down the group. Thus, NH_3 is the strongest base.
$$NH_3 > PH_3 > AsH_3 > SbH_3$$

(b) The thermal stability of the hydrides decreases as the atomic size increases, *i.e.,* the M $-$ H bond strength decreases which means reducing character increases.

(c) In the liquid state, the molecules of NH_3 are associated due to hydrogen bonding. The molecules of other hydrides are not associated.

(d) NH_3 is soluble in water whereas other hydrides are insoluble.

(e) All the hydrides, except NH_3, are strong reducing agents and react with metal ions (Ag^+, Cu^{2+}, etc.) to form phosphides, arsenides or antimonides.

  Halides : The elements of group 15 form two series of halides MX_3 and MX_5.

(a) All the elements of the group form trihalides. The ionic character of trihalides increases as we move down the group. Except NCl_3 all the trihalides are hydrolysed by water. This is due to the absence of *d*-orbitals in nitrogen.

(b) PF_3 is not hydrolysed because fluorine being more electronegative than oxygen forms more stable bonds with phosphorus than P $-$ O bonds.

(c) N cannot form NX_5 because of non-availability of *d*-orbitals. Bi cannot form BiX_5 because of reluctance of $6s$ electrons of Bi to participate in bond formation.

(d) The hybridisation of M in MX_3 is sp^3 and shape is pyramidal. M in MX_5 is sp^3d as hybridised and shape is trigonal pyramidal. The axial bonds in MX_5 are weaker and longer, So MX_5 are less stable and decompose on heating eg:

$$PCl_5 \xrightarrow{\Delta} PCl_3 + Cl_2$$

Oxides :

(a) Nitrogen forms a number of oxides. The rest of the members (P, As, Sb and Bi) of the group form two types of oxides: E_2O_3 and E_2O_5.

(b) The reluctance of P, As, Sb and Bi to enter into $p\pi - p\pi$ multiple bonding leads to cage structures of their oxides and they exist as dimers, E_4O_6 and E_5O_{10}.

(c) The basic nature of the oxides increases with increase in atomic number of the element. Thus, the oxides of nitrogen (except N_2O and NO), P (III) and As (III) are acidic, Sb (III) oxide is amphoteric and Bi (III) oxide is basic.

4. Why does NH_3 form hydrogen bond but PH_3 does not?

Sol. Nitrogen has an electronegativity value $3\cdot0$, which is much higher than that of H $(2\cdot1)$. As a result, $N-H$ bond is quite polar and hence NH_3 undergoes intermolecular $H-$ bonding.

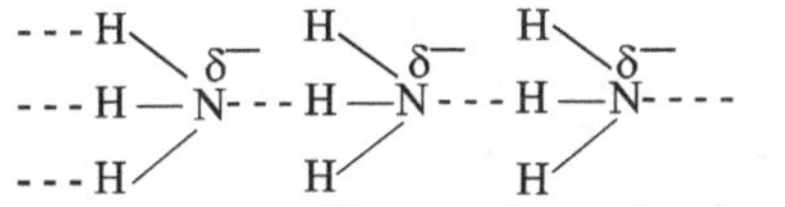

Phosphorus have an electronegativity value $2\cdot1$. Thus, $P-H$ bond is not polar and hence PH_3 does not undergo $H-$ bonding.

5. How is nitrogen prepared in the laboratory? Write the chemical equations of the reactions involved.

Sol. In laboratory, nitrogen is prepared by heating an equimolar aqueous solution of ammonium chloride and sodium nitrite. As a result of double decomposition reaction, ammonium nitrite is formed. Ammonium nitrite is unstable and decompose to form nitrogen gas.

$$NH_4Cl\,(aq) + NaNO_2\,(aq) \longrightarrow NH_4NO_2\,(aq) + NaCl\,(aq)$$

$$NH_4NO_2\,(aq) \xrightarrow{Heat} N_2\,(g) + 2H_2O\,(l)$$

6. How is ammonia manufactured industrially?

Sol. Commercially, by Haber's process.

$$N_2\,(g) + 3H_2\,(g) \underset{\Delta}{\overset{*}{\rightleftharpoons}} 2NH_3\,(g); \; \Delta_f H = -46.1\,kJ\,mol^{-1}$$

* iron oxide, K_2O, Al_2O_3

The optimum conditions for the production of NH_3 are pressure of 200 atm and temperature of 100 K.

7. Illustrate how copper metal can give different products on reaction with HNO_3.

Sol. On heating with dil HNO_3, copper gives copper nitrate and nitric oxide.

$$3Cu + 8HNO_3\,(dil) \xrightarrow{Heat} 3Cu\,(NO_3)_2 + 4H_2O + 2NO$$

With concentrated HNO_3, copper gives NO_2 instead of NO.

$$Cu + 4HNO_3(conc.) \xrightarrow{Heat} Cu(NO_3)_2 + 2H_2O + 2NO_2$$

8. Give the resonating structures of NO_2 and N_2O_5.

Sol. Resonating structures of NO_2 are:

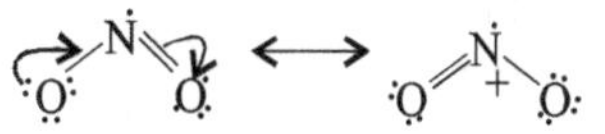

Resonating structures of N_2O_5 are:

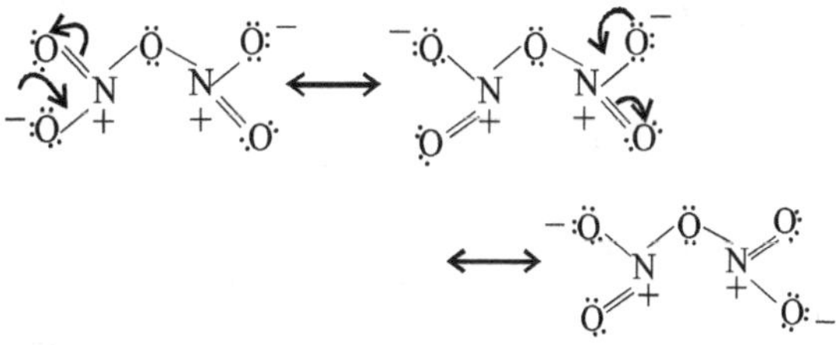

9. The HNH angle value is higher than HPH, HAsH and HSbH angles. Why?

[Hint : Can be explained on the basis of sp^3 hybridisation in NH_3 and only s-p bonding between hydrogen and other elements of the group].

Sol. In all these cases, the central atom is sp^3 hybridized. Three of the four sp^3 orbitals form three σ-bonds, while the fourth contains the lone pair of electrons. On moving down from N to Sb, the electronegativity of the central atom goes on decreasing. As a result of this, bond pairs of electrons lie away and away from the central atom. This is because of the force of repulsion between the adjacent bond pairs goes on decreasing and the bond angles keep on decreasing from NH_3 to SbH_3. Thus, bond angles are in the order:

HNH		HPH		HAsH		HSbH
$(107\cdot8°)$	>	$(93\cdot6°)$	>	$(91\cdot8°)$	>	$(91\cdot3°)$

10. Why does $R_3P = O$ exist but $R_3N = O$ does not (R = alkyl group)?

Sol. Nitrogen does not contains d-orbitals. As a result, it cannot expand its covalency beyond four and cannot form $p\pi - d\pi$ multiple bonds. In constrast, P contains the d-orbitals, and can expand its covalency beyond 4 and can form $p\pi - d\pi$ multiple bonds.

Hence $R_3P = O$ exist but $R_3N = O$ does not.

11. Explain why NH_3 is basic while BiH_3 is only feebly basic.

Sol. In both NH_3 and BiH_3, N and Bi have a lone pair of electrons on the central atom and hence should behave as Lewis bases. But NH_3 is much more basic than BiH_3. Since the atomic size of N is much smaller than that of Bi, therefore, electron density on N-atom is much higher than that on Bi-atom. Thus, the tendency of N in NH_3 to donate its lone pair of electrons is much more in comparison to tendency of Bi in BiH_3. Hence, NH_3 is more basic than BiH_3.

12. Nitrogen exists as diatomic molecule and phosphorus as P_4. Why?

Sol. Nitrogen exists as a diatomic molecule having a triple bond between the two N-atoms. This is due its small size that it forms $p\pi - p\pi$ multiple bonds with itself and with carbon / oxygen as well. On the other hand, phosphorus due to its larger size does not form multiple $p\pi - p\pi$ bonds with itself. It prefers to form $P-P$ single bonds and hence it exists as tetrahedral P_4 molecule.

13. **Write main differences between the properties of white phosphorus and red phosphorus.**

Sol. Structure of white and red phosphorus are given below:

	Property	White Phosphorus	Red Phosphorus
(i)	State	Translucent	Brittle, substance
(ii)	Colour	White gets yellowish on exposure to light	Red
(iii)	Odour	Garlic like odour	Odourless
(iv)	Hardness	Soft like wax and can be cut by knife	Hard
(v)	Poisonous nature	Poisonous	Non-poisonous
(vi)	Solubility	Soluble in CS_2	Insoluble in CS_2
(vii)	Chemiluminescence	Glows in dark	Dose not glow in dark.
(viii)	Density	1.8	2.1
(ix)	Reactivity	Very reactive	Less reactive
(x)	Action of oxygen	Burns with greenish glow to form P_4O_{10}	Combines with O_2 only on heating to form P_4O_{10}

14. **Why does nitrogen show catenation properties less than phosphorus?**

Sol. The extent of catenation depends upon the strength of the element−element bond. The $N-N$ bond strength ($159\,kJ\,mol^{-1}$) is weaker than $P-P$ bond strength ($213\,kJ\,mol^{-1}$). Thus, nitrogen shows less catenation properties than phosphorus.

15. **Give the disproportionation reaction of H_3PO_3.**

Sol. On heating, H_3PO_4 undergoes self-oxidation reduction, *i.e.,* disproportionation to form PH_3.

$$\underset{\text{Phosphorus acid}}{\overset{+3}{4H_3PO_3}} \overset{\Delta}{\longrightarrow} \underset{\text{Phosphine}}{\overset{-3}{PH_3}} + \underset{\substack{\text{Orthophosphoric} \\ \text{acid}}}{\overset{+5}{3H_3PO_4}}$$

16. **Can PCl_5 act as an oxidising as well as a reducing agent. Justify.**

Sol. The oxidation state of P in PCl_5 is $+5$. Since P has five electrons in its valence shell, therefore, it cannot donate electron and cannot increase its oxidation state beyond $+5$, Thus, PCl_5 cannot act as a reducing agent. It can act as oxidizing agent by itself undergoing reduction.

$$\overset{+5}{P}\overset{}{Cl_5} + \overset{0}{H_2} \longrightarrow \overset{+3}{P}\overset{}{Cl_3} + \overset{+1}{2HCl}$$

$$\overset{0}{2Ag} + \overset{+5}{P}Cl_5 \longrightarrow \overset{+1}{2Ag}Cl + \overset{+3}{P}Cl_3$$

17. **Justify the placement of O, S, Se, Te and Po in the same group of the periodic table in terms of electronic configuration, oxidation state and hydride formation.**

Sol. **(1)** **Electronic configuration:**

O (At. no. = 8) = [He] $2s^2\,2p^4$

S (At. no. = 16) = [Ne] $3s^2\,3p^4$

Se (At. no. = 34) = [Ar] $3d^{10}\,4s^2\,4p^4$

Te (At. no. = 52) = [Kr] $4d^{10}\,5s^2\,5p^4$

Po (At. no. = 84) = [Xe] $4f^{14}\,5d^{10}\,6s^2\,6p^4$

Thus, all these elements have the same $ns^2\,np^4$ ($n = 2$ to 6) valence shell electronic configuration, hence are justified to be placed in group 16 of the Periodic Table.

(2) **Oxidation state :** Two more electrons are needed to acquire the nearest noble gas configuration. Thus, the minimum oxidation state of these elements should be -2.

O and to some extent S show -2 oxidation state. Other element being more electropositive than O and S, do not show negative oxidation state. As these contain six electrons, thus, maximum oxidation state shown by them is $+6$. Other oxidation state shown by them are $+2$ and $+4$. O do not show $+4$ and $+6$ oxidation state, due to the absence of d-orbitals. Thus, on the basis of maximum and minimum oxidation states, these elements are justified to be placed in the same group 16 of the periodic table.

(3) **Hydride formation:** All these elements share two of their valence electrons with $1s-$ orbital of hydrogen to form hydrides of the general formula EH_2, *i.e.,* H_2O, H_2S, H_2Se, H_2Te and H_2Po. Thus, on the basis of hydride formation, these elements are justified to be placed in the same group 16 of the Periodic Table.

18. **Why is dioxygen a gas but sulphur a solid?**

Sol. Refer Theory.

19. **Knowing the electron gain enthalpy values of $O \to O^-$ and $O \to O^{2-}$ as -141 and $702\,kJ\,mol^{-1}$ respectively, how can you account for the formation of a large number of oxides having O^{2-} species and not O^-?**

Sol. Let us consider the reaction of oxygen with monopositve metal, we can have two compounds MO(O in -1 state) and M_2O (O in -2 state). The energy required for formation of O^{-2} is compensated by increased coulombic attraction between M^+ and O^{-2}. Coulombic force of attraction, F_A is proportional to product of charges on ions i.e.

$$F_A \propto \frac{q_1 q_2}{r^2}$$ where q_1 and q_2 are charges on ions and r is distance between ions. Same logic can be applied if metal is dispositive.

20. **Which aerosols deplete ozone?**

Sol. Aerosols like chlorofluorocarbons (CFC's), *i.e.,* freon (CCl_2F_2), depletes the ozone layer by supplying $Cl^{\cdot}$ free radicals which convert O_3 to O_2.

$$\underset{\text{Freon}}{CCl_2F_2\,(g)} \overset{hv}{\longrightarrow} {}^{\bullet}Cl(g) + {}^{\bullet}CClF_2\,(g)$$

$${}^{\bullet}Cl\,(g) + O_3\,(g) \longrightarrow ClO^{\bullet}(g) + O_2\,(g)$$

$$ClO^{\bullet}(g) + {}^{\bullet}O\,(g) \longrightarrow {}^{\bullet}Cl\,(g) + O_2\,(g)$$

21. How is SO_2 an air pollutant?

Sol. Refer Theory.

22. Why are halogens strong oxidising agents?

Sol. The halogens are strong oxidising agents due to low bond dissociation enthalpy, high electronegativity and large negative electron gain enthalpy.

23. Explain why fluorine forms only one oxoacid, HOF.

Sol. Cl, Br and I form four series of oxo acids of general formula HOX, HOXO, $HOXO_2$ and $HOXO_3$. In these oxo-acids, the oxidation states of halogens are $+1, +3, +5,$ and $+7$ respectively. However, due to high electronegativity, small size and absence of d-orbitals, F does not form oxo-acids with $+3, +5$ and $+7$, oxidation states. It just forms one oxo-acid (HOF).

24. Explain why inspite of nearly the same electronegativity, nitrogen forms hydrogen bonding while chlorine does not.

Sol. Both nitrogen (N) and chlorine (Cl) have electronegativity of 3.0. However, only nitrogen is involved in the hydrogen bonds (e.g., NH_3) and not chlorine. This is due to smaller atomic size of nitrogen (atomic radius $=70$ pm) as compared to chlorine (atomic radius $=99$) pm). therefore, N can cause greater polarisation of N–H bond than Cl in case of Cl—H bond. Consequently, N atom is involved in hydrogen bonding and not chlorine.

25. Write two uses of ClO_2.

Sol. (1) ClO_2 is an excellent bleaching agent. It is 30 times stronger bleaching agent then the Cl_2. It is used as a bleaching agent for paper pulp in paper industry and in textile industry.

(2) ClO_2 is also a powerful oxidising agent and chlorinating agent. It acts as a germicide for disinfecting water. It is used for purifying drinking water.

26. Why are halogens coloured?

Sol. The halogens are coloured because their molecules absorb light in the visible region. As a result of which their electrons get excited to higher energy levels while the remaining light is transmitted. The color of halogens is the color of this transmitted light.

27. Write the reactions of F_2 and Cl_2 with water.

Sol. $2F_2(g) + 2H_2O(l) \longrightarrow 4H^+(aq) + 4F^-(aq) + O_2(g)$
$3F_2(g) + 3H_2O(l) \longrightarrow 6H^+(aq) + 6F^-(aq) + O_3(g)$
$Cl_2(g) + H_2O(l) \longrightarrow HCl(aq) + HOCl(aq)$
F_2 oxidises water, whereas Cl_2 undergoes disproportion in water.

28. How can you prepare Cl_2 from HCl and HCl from Cl_2? Write reactions only.

Sol. $\underset{\substack{\text{Oxidising} \\ \text{agent}}}{MnO_2} + 4HCl \longrightarrow MnCl_2 + Cl_2 + 2H_2O$

We can also used $KMnO_4, K_2Cr_2O_7,$ etc., in place of MnO_2.

$H_2 + Cl_2 \xrightarrow{\text{Diffused sunlight}} 2HCl$

29. What inspired N. Bartlett for carrying out reaction between Xe and PtF_6?

Sol. N. Bartlett observed that PtF_6 reacts with O_2 to give an compound $O_2^+[PtF_6]^-$.
$PtF_6(g) + O_2(g) \longrightarrow O_2^+[PtF_6]^-$

Since the first ionization enthalpy of Xe (1170 kJ mol^{-1}) is fairly close to that of O_2 molecule (1175 kJ mol^{-1}), he thought that PtF_6 should also oxidise Xe to Xe$^+$. This inspired Bartlett to carryout the reaction between Xe and PtF_6. When PtF_6 and Xe were made to react, a rapid reaction took place and a red solid, $Xe^+[PtF_6]^-$ was obtained.

$Xe + PtF_6 \xrightarrow{278\ K} Xe^+[PtF_6]^-$

30. What are the oxidation states of phosphorus in the following:

(*i*) H_3PO_3 (*ii*) PCl_3
(*iii*) Ca_3P_2 (*iv*) Na_3PO_4
(*v*) POF_3

Sol. (*i*) H_3PO_3 (*ii*) PCl_3
$\quad 3(+1) + x + 3(-2) = 0 \qquad\ x + 3(-1) = 0$
$\quad \therefore\ x = +3 \qquad\qquad\qquad\qquad x = +3$

(*iii*) Ca_3P_2 (*iv*) Na_3PO_4
$\quad 3(+2) + 2x = 0 \qquad\quad 3(+1) + x + 4(-2) = 0$
$\quad x = -3 \qquad\qquad\qquad\qquad\ x = +5$

(*v*) POF_3
$\quad x + 1(-2) + 3(-1) = 0$
$\quad x = +5.$

31. Write balanced equations for the following:

(*i*) **NaCl is heated with sulphuric acid in the presence of MnO_2.**

(*ii*) **Chlorine gas is passed into a solution of NaI in water.**

Sol. (*i*)

$$\begin{array}{l} NaCl + H_2SO_4 \longrightarrow NaHSO_4 + HCl] \times 4 \\ 4HCl + MnO_2 \longrightarrow MnCl_2 + Cl_2 + 2H_2O \\ \hline 4NaCl + MnO_2 + 4H_2SO_4 \longrightarrow MnCl_2 + 4NaHSO_4 + Cl_2 + 2H_2O \end{array}$$

i.e Cl^- is oxidized by MnO_2

(*ii*) $Cl_2(g) + 2NaI(aq) \longrightarrow 2NaCl(aq) + I_2(s)$
i.e. I^- is oxidized by Cl_2.

32. How are xenon fluorides XeF_2, XeF_4 and XeF_6 obtained?

Sol. XeF_2, XeF_4 and XeF_6 are obtained by direct reaction between Xe and F_2 as follows:

$\underset{\text{excess}}{Xe(g)} + F_2(g) \xrightarrow[\text{Ni tube}]{673\ K,\ 1bar} XeF_2(s)$

$\underset{(1n\ 1:5\ \text{ratio})}{Xe(g)} + 2F_2(g) \xrightarrow{873\ K,\ 7\ bar} XeF_4(s)$

$\underset{(1n\ 1:20\ \text{ratio})}{Xe(g)} + 3F_2(g) \xrightarrow{573\ K,\ 60-70bar} XeF_6(s)$

33. With what neutral molecule is ClO^- isoelectronic? Is that molecule a Lewis base?

Sol. ClO^- has $17 + 8 + 1 = 26$ electrons.
Also, OF_2 has $(8 + 2 \times 9) = 26$ electrons.
and ClF has $(17 + 9) = 26$ electrons.
Out of these, ClF can act as Lewis base. The chlorine atom has three lone pair of electrons which it donates to form compounds like ClF_3, ClF_5 and ClF_7

34. How are XeO_3 and $XeOF_4$ prepared?

Sol. (*i*) $6XeF_4 + 12H_2O \xrightarrow{\text{Hydrolysis}} 4Xe + 2XeO_3 + 24HF + 3O_2$

$\quad XeF_6 + 3H_2O \xrightarrow{\text{Hydrolysis}} XeO_3 + 6HF$

(*ii*) $XeF_6 + H_2O \xrightarrow{\text{Hydrolysis}} XeOF_4 + 2HF$

35. Arrange the following in the order of property indicated for each set:
(i) F_2, Cl_2, Br_2, I_2 – increasing bond dissociation enthalpy.
(ii) HF, HCl, HBr, HI – increasing acid strength.
(iii) NH_3, PH_3, AsH_3, SbH_3, BiH_3 – increasing base strength.

Sol. *(i)* Bond dissociation enthalpy decreases as the bond distance increases from F_2 to I_2 due to increase in the size of the atom, on moving from F to I.
F – F bond dissociation enthalpy is smaller then the Cl – Cl and even smaller than Br – Br. This is because F atom is very small and have large electron-electron repulsion among the lone pairs of electrons in F_2 molecule where they are much closer to each other than in case of Cl_2. The increasing order of bond dissociation enthalphy is
$$I_2 < F_2 < Br_2 < Cl_2$$

(ii) Acid strength of HF, HCl, HBr and HI depends upon their bond dissociation enthalpies. Since the bond dissociation enthalpy of H – X bond decreases from H – F to H – I as the size of atom increases from F to I. Thus, the acid strength order is
$$HF < HCl < HBr < HI$$
The weak acidic strength of HF is also due to H-bonding due to which release of H^+ becomes difficult.

(iii) NH_3, PH_3, AsH_3, SbH_3 and BiH_3 behaves as Lewis bases due to the presence of lone pair of electrons on the central atom. As we move from N to Bi, size of atom increases. Electron density on central atom decreases and hence the basic strength decreases from NH_3 to BiH_3. Thus basic strength order is
$$BiH_3 < SbH_3 < AsH_3 < PH_3 < NH_3$$

36. Which one of the following does not exist ?
(i) $XeOF_4$ *(ii)* NeF_2
(iii) XeF_4 *(iv)* XeF_6

Sol. NeF_2 does not exist. This is because the sum of first and second ionization enthalpies of Ne are much higher than those of Xe. Consequently, F_2 can oxidise Xe to Xe^{2+} but cannot oxidise Ne to Ne^{2+}.

37. Give the formula and describe the structure of a noble gas species which is isostructural with:
(i) ICl_4^- *(ii)* IBr_2^- *(iii)* BrO_3^-

Sol. *(i)* ICl_4^-: In ICl_4^-, central atom I has seven valence electrons and one due to negative charge. Four out of these 8 electrons are utilized in forming four single bonds with four Cl atoms. Four remaining electrons constitutes the two lone pairs. It is arranged in square planar structure. ICl_4^- has 36 valence electrons. A noble gas species having 36 valence electrons is XeF_4 ($8 + 4 \times 7 = 36$). XeF_4 is also square planar.

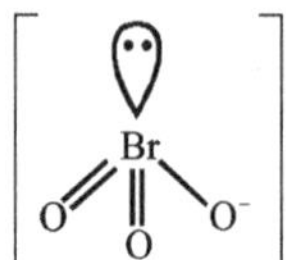

(ii) **IBr_2^-:** In IBr_2^-, central atom I has eight electrons. Two of these are utilized in forming two single bonds with two Br atom. Six remaining electrons constitutes three lone pairs. It is arranged in linear structure.

IBr_2^- has 22 valence electrons. A noble gas species having 22 valence electrons is XeF_2 ($8 + 2 \times 7 = 22$). XeF_2 is also linear.

(iii) In BrO_3^- ion the central Br atom has 8 valence electrons ($7 + 1$). Out of these, it shares 4 with two atoms of O forming Br = O bonds. Out of the remaining four electrons, 2 are donated to the third O atom which accounts for its negative charge. The remaining 2 electrons constitute one lone pair. In order to minimise the force of repulsion, the structure of BrO_3^- ion must be pyramidal. BrO_3^- ion has ($7 + 3 \times 6 + 1$) = 26 valence electrons and is isoelectronic as well as iso-structural with noble gas species XeO_3 which has also 26($8 + 3 \times 6$) electrons.

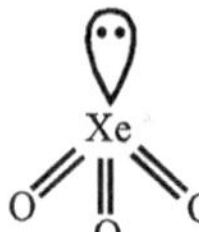

38. Why do noble gases have comparatively large atomic sizes?
Sol. This is because noble gases have only van der Waal's radii while others have covalent radii. van der Waal's radii are larger than covalent radii.

39. List the uses of neon and argon gases.
Sol. Refer Theory.

Past year Exercise

1. **Assertion:** F – F bond in F_2 molecule is weak.
Reason: F atom is small in size.
(a) If both Assertion and Reason are correct and the Reason is a correct explanation of the Assertion.
(b) If both Assertion and Reason are correct but Reason is not a correct explanation of the Assertion.
(c) If the Assertion is correct but Reason is incorrect.
(d) If the Assertion is incorrect but the Reason is correct.

2. Write the formula of the compound of iodine which is obtained when conc. HNO_3 oxidises I_2.

3. Elements of group 16 generally show lower value of first ionisation enthalpy as compared to the corresponding elements of group 15. Explain why?

4. Why does fluorine not play the role of a central atom in interhalogen compounds?

5. Explain in aqueous medium, HCl is stronger acid than HF.
6. Arrange F_2, Cl_2, Br_2 and I_2 in the order of increasing bond dissociation enthalpy.
7. Complete the following chemical equation
$$XeF_4 + SbF_5 \longrightarrow$$
8. Complete the following reaction equation
$$XeF_2 + PF_5 \longrightarrow$$
9. Which one of PCl_4^+ and PCl_4^- is not likely to exist and why?
10. NF_3 is an exothermic compound, whereas NCl_3 is not. Explain.
11. Of PH_3 and H_2S which is more acidic and why?
12. ICl is more reactive than I_2.
13. Despite having greater polarity, hydrogen fluoride boils at a lower temperature than water.
14. Predict the shape and the asked angle (90° or more or less) in the following case:
XeF_2 and the angle F—Xe—F
15. Draw the molecular structure of $XeOF_4$.
16 Why helium forms no real chemical compound?
17. Complete the following chemical reaction equation
$$P_4 + SO_2Cl_2 \longrightarrow$$
18. Which is a stronger reducing agent, SbH_3 or BiH_3 and why?
19. Phosphorus has greater tendency for catenation than nitrogen. Why?

OR

Nitrogen shows weaker tendency for catenation than phosphorus. Explain.
20. All the bonds in SF_4 are not equivalent. Explain, why?
21. Draw the structure of $H_2S_2O_7$.
22. SF_6 is kinetically an inert substance. Explain.
23. Explain the following by giving an appropriate reason.
O_2 and F_2 both stabilise higher oxidation states of metals but O_2 exceeds F_2 in doing so.
24. Despite lower value of its electron gain enthalpy with negative sign, fluorine (F_2) is a stronger oxidising agent than Cl_2.
25. Complete the following equation
$$NaOH \text{ (hot and conc.)} + Cl_2 \longrightarrow$$
26. Explain the following giving an appropriate reason in case. Structures of xenon fluorides cannot be explained by valence bond approach.
27. Complete the following chemical equation.
$$XeF_4 + O_2F_2 \xrightarrow{143K}$$
28. Name two poisonous gases which can be prepared from chlorine gas.
29. What is the basicity of H_3PO_3 and why?
30. What inspired N. Bartlett for carrying out reaction between Xe and PtF_6?

Short Answer Questions

31. Draw the shape of the following molecules:
   (a) $XeOF_4$ (b) BrF_3

32. Account for the following:
   (a) Sulphurous acid is a reducing agent.
   (b) Fluorine forms only one oxoacid.
   (c) Boiling point of noble gases increases from He to Rn.

OR

Complete the following chemical reactions:
   (a) $MnO_2 + 4HCl$ (b) $XeF_6 + KF$
   (c) $I^-(aq) + H^+(aq) + O_2(g)$

33. When dilute ferrous sulphate solution is added to an aqueous solution containing nitrate ion followed by careful addition of concentrated sulphuric acid along the sides of the test tube, a brown ring is formed at the interface between the solution and sulphuric acid layers. Which anion is confirmed by the appearance of brown ring? What is the composition of the brown ring?

OR

How can you prepare Cl_2 from HCl and HCl from Cl_2? Write reactions only.

34. Among the hydrides of Group - 15 elements, which have the
   (a) lowest boiling point?
   (b) maximum basic character?
   (c) highest bond angle?
   (d) maximum reducing character?

35. Draw the structures of the following
   (a) XeF_4 (b) BrF_5

36. Give reasons for the following:
   (a) Red phoshorus is less reactive than white phosphorus.
   (b) Electron gain enthalpies of halogens are largely negative
   (c) N_2O_5 is more acidic than N_2O_3.

37. Draw the structures of the following molecules :
   (i) N_2O_5 (ii) XeF_2

38. Give reasons for the following :
   (i) Though nitrogen exhibits +5 oxidation state, it does not form pentahalide.
   (ii) Electron gain enthalpy with negative sign of fluorine is less than that of chlorine.
   (iii) The two oxygen-oxygen bond lengths in ozone molecule are identical.

39. What happens when :
   (i) PCl_5 is heated?   (ii) H_3PO_3 is heated?
Write the reactions involved.

40. Account for the following :
   (i) NF_3 is an exothermic compound but NCl_3 is an endothermic compound.
   (ii) HF is not stored in glass bottles but is kept in wax-coated bottles.
   (iii) Bleaching of flowers by Cl_2 is permanent while that of SO_2 is temporary.

41. Explain the following :
   (a) NO_2 readily forms a dimer.
   (b) $BiCl_3$ is more stable than $BiCl_5$.

42. Complete the following equations:
   (i) $P_4 + H_2O \rightarrow$ (ii) $XeF_4 + O_2F_2 \rightarrow$

43. Give reasons for the following:
    (i) $(CH_3)_3P=O$ exists but $(CH_3)_3N=O$ does not.
    (ii) Oxygen has less electron gain enthalpy with negative sign than sulphur.
    (iii) H_3PO_2 is a stronger reducing agent than H_3PO_3.
44. Complete the following equations:
    (i) $Ag+PCl_5 \rightarrow$ (ii) $CaF_2+H_2SO_4 \rightarrow$
45. Draw the structures of the following:
    (i) XeF_4 (ii) $HClO_4$
46. Complete the following equations:
    (i) $C + conc. H_2SO_4 \rightarrow$ (ii) $XeF_2 + H_2O \rightarrow$
47. Draw the structures of the following:
    (i) XeO_3 (ii) H_2SO_4
48. Complete the following chemical equations :
    (i) $Ca_3P_2 + H_2O \rightarrow$ (ii) $Cu + H_2SO_4 (conc.) \rightarrow$
    OR
    Arrange the following in the order of property indicated against each set :
    (i) HF, HCl, HBr, HI - increasing bond dissociation enthalpy.
    (ii) H_2O, H_2S, H_2Se, H_2Te - increasing acidic character.
49. (a) Draw the structures of the following molecules.
    (i) $XeOF_4$ (ii) H_2SO_4
    (b) Write the structural differences between white phosphorus and red phosphorus.

50. Account for the following :
    (i) PCl_5 is more covalent than PCl_3.
    (ii) Iron on reaction with HCl forms $FeCl_2$ and not $FeCl_3$
    (iii) The two O-O bond lengths in the ozone molecule are equal.
51. (a) Draw the structures of the following:
    (i) XeF_2 (ii) BrF_3
    (b) Write the structural difference between white phosphorus and red phosphorus.
52. Account for the following :
    (i) Bi(V) is a stronger oxidizing agent than Sb(V).
    (ii) N–N single bond is weaker than P–P single bond.
    (iii) Noble gases have very low boiling points.
53. (a) Draw the structures of the following compounds :
    (i) XeF_4 (ii) N_2O_5
    (b) Write the structural difference between white phosphorous and red phosphorous.
54. Account for the following :
    (i) Sulphur in vapour form exhibits paramagnetic behaviour.
    (ii) $SnCl_4$ is more covalent than $SnCl_2$.
55. Give reasons :
    (i) SO_2 is reducing while TeO_2 is an oxidizing agent.
    (ii) Nitrogen does not form pentahalide.
    (iii) ICl is more reactive than I_2.

NCERT Exemplar

Multiple Choice Questions

1. Affinity for hydrogen decreases in the group from fluorine to iodine. Which of the halogen acids should have highest bond dissociation enthalpy?
   (a) HF (b) HCl (c) HBr (d) HI
2. In the preparation of HNO_3, we get NO gas by catalytic oxidation of ammonia. The moles of NO produced by the oxidation of two moles of NH_3 will be ....
   (a) 2 (b) 3 (c) 4 (d) 6
3. The oxidation state of central atom in the anion of compound NaH_2PO_2 will be ....
   (a) +3 (b) +5 (c) +1 (d) −3
4. Which of the following is isoelectronic pair?
   (a) ICl_2, ClO_2 (b) BrO_2^-, BrF_2^+
   (c) ClO_2, BrF (d) CN^-, O_3
5. Which of the following elements can be involved in $p\pi - d\pi$ bonding?
   (a) Carbon (b) Nitrogen
   (c) Phosphorus (d) Boron
6. In the preparation of compounds of Xe, Bartlett had taken $O_2^+ PtF_6^-$ as a base compound. This is because
   (a) both O_2 and Xe have same size.
   (b) both O_2 and Xe have same electron gain enthalpy.
   (c) both O_2 and Xe have almost same ionisation enthalpy.
   (d) both Xe and O_2 are gases.

7. Which of the following statements is wrong?
   (a) Single N — N bond is stronger than the single P — P bond.
   (b) PH_3 can act as a ligand in the formation of coordination compounds with transition elements.
   (c) NO_2 is paramagnetic in nature.
   (d) Covalency of nitrogen in N_2O_3 is four.
8. In solid state PCl_5 is a ....
   (a) covalent solid
   (b) octahedral structure
   (c) ionic solid with $[PCl_6]^+$ octahedral and $[PCl_4]^-$ tetrahedral
   (d) ionic solid with $[PCl_4]^+$ tetrahedral and $[PCl_6]^-$ octahedral
9. A brown ring is formed in the ring test for NO_3^- ion. It is due to the formation of
   (a) $[Fe(H_2O)_5(NO)]^{2+}$
   (b) $FeSO_4 . NO_2$
   (c) $[Fe(H_2O)_4(NO)_2]^{2+}$
   (d) $FeSO_4 . HNO_3$
10. Elements of group- 15 form compounds in +5 oxidation state. However, bismuth forms only one well characterised compound in +5 oxidation state. The compound is
    (a) Bi_2O_5 (b) BiF_5
    (c) $BiCl_5$ (d) Bi_2S_5

Assertion & Reason Questions

DIRECTIONS (Qs. 11-13) : *Each of these questions contains an assertion followed by reason. Read them carefully and answer the question on the basis of following options. You have to select the one that best describes the two statements.*

(a) If both Assertion and Reason are correct and the Reason is a correct explanation of the Assertion.

(b) If both Assertion and Reason are correct but Reason is not a correct explanation of the Assertion.

(c) If the Assertion is correct but Reason is incorrect.

(d) If the Assertion is incorrect but the Reason is correct.

11. **Assertion:** N_2 is less reactive than P_4.
Reason: Nitrogen has more electron gain enthalpy than phosphorus.

12. **Assertion:** HNO_3 makes iron passive
Reason: HNO_3 forms a protective layer of ferric nitrate on the surface of iron.

13. **Assertion:** HI cannot be prepared by the reaction of KI with concentrated H_2SO_4.
Reason: HI has lowest $H — X$ bond strength among halogen acids.

Short Answer Questions

14. PH_3 forms bubbles when passed slowly in water but NH_3 dissolves. Explain why?

15. On reaction with Cl_2, phosphorus forms two types of halides 'A' and 'B'. Halide A is yellowish-white powder but halide 'B' is colourless oily liquid. Identify A and B and write the formulas of their hydrolysis products.

16. White phosphorus reacts with chlorine and the product hydrolyses in the presence of water. Calculate the mass of HCl obtained by the hydrolysis of the product formed by the reaction of 62 g of white phosphorus with chlorine in the presence of water.

Objective Practice Exercise

Multiple Choice Questions

DIRECTIONS : *This section contains multiple choice questions. Each question has four choices (a), (b), (c) and (d) out of which only one is correct.*

1. Which one of the following halide does not hydrolyse
(a) $SbCl_3$　(b) $AsCl_3$　(c) PCl_3　(d) NF_3

2. Catalytic oxidation of NH_3 (passing a mixture of NH_3 and air over heated Pt gauge) gives
(a) NO　(b) N_2O　(c) N_2O_3　(d) N_2O_5

3. By mixing ammonium chloride to potassium nitrite and heating, we get
(a) Ammonium nitrate　　(b) $KNH_4(NO_3)_2$
(c) Nitrogen　　　　　　(d) Nitrogen dioxide

4. If phosphorous acid is allowed to react with sufficient quantity of KOH, the product obtained is
(a) K_3PO_3　(b) KH_2PO_3　(c) K_2HPO_3　(d) $KHPO_3$

5. Which of the following statements is wrong?
(a) Single $N — N$ bond is stronger than the single $P — P$ bond.
(b) PH_3 can act as a ligand in the formation of coordination compounds with transition elements.
(c) NO_2 is paramagnetic in nature.
(d) Covalency of nitrogen in N_2O_3 is four.

6. Which one of the following pairs is obtained on heating ammonium dichromate?
(a) N_2 and H_2O　　　(b) N_2O and H_2O
(c) NO and H_2O　　　(d) NO and NO_2

7. Which of the following properties of white phosphorus are shared by red phosphorus?
(a) It phosphorescences in air
(b) It burns when heated in air
(c) It dissolves in CS_2
(d) It reacts with NaOH to give PH_3

8. Which of the following orders regarding thermal stability of hydrides MH_3 of group 15 is correct?
(a) $NH_3 > PH_3 > AsH_3$　　(b) $NH_3 < PH_3 < AsH_3$
(c) $NH_3 > PH_3 < AsH_3$　　(d) $NH_3 < PH_3 > AsH_3$

9. Incorrect statement about PH_3 is:
(a) It is produced by hydrolysis of Ca_3P_2
(b) It gives black ppt. (Cu_3P_2) with $CuSO_4$ solution
(c) Spontaneously burns in presence of P_2H_4
(d) It does not react with B_2H_6

10. Sulphuric acid has great affinity for water because it
(a) Decomposes water
(b) Forms hydrate with water
(c) Hydrolyse the acid
(d) Decomposes the acid

11. Which one of the following statements is wrong?
(a) SO_2 dissolves in water and forms sulphurous acid
(b) SO_2 acts as a bleaching agent
(c) SO_2 has pungent odour
(d) SO_2 acts only as oxidising agent

12. Which one of the following is wrong?
(a) Oxygen and sulphur belong to the same group of periodic table
(b) Oxygen is a gas while sulphur is solid
(c) Both oxygen and sulphur show +2, +4 and +6 oxidation states
(d) H_2S has no hydrogen bonding

13. Sulphur does not exist as S_2 molecule because
(b) It is less electronegative
(b) It has ability to exhibit catenation

(c) It is not able to constitute $p\pi$-$p\pi$ bond

(d) It has the tendency to show variable oxidation states

14. Which of the following solutions does not change its colour on passing ozone through it?

(a) Starch iodide solution

(b) Alcoholic solution of benzidine

(c) Acidic solution of $K_2Cr_2O_3$

(d) Acidified solution of $FeSO_4$

15. In case of hydride of oxygen family, which of the following physical property change regularly on moving down the group.

(a) Melting point   (b) Thermal stability

(c) Boiling point   (d) Critical temperature

16. The correct sequence of decreasing number of π-bonds in the structures of H_2SO_3, H_2SO_4 and $H_2S_2O_7$ is :

(a) $H_2SO_3 > H_2SO_4 > H_2S_2O_7$

(b) $H_2SO_4 > H_2S_2O_7 > H_2SO_3$

(c) $H_2S_2O_7 > H_2SO_4 > H_2SO_3$

(d) $H_2S_2O_7 > H_2SO_3 > H_2SO_4$

17. The number of S—S bonds in SO_3, $S_2O_3^{2-}$, $S_2O_6^{2-}$ and $S_2O_8^{2-}$ respectively are

(a) 1, 0, 0, 1   (b) 1, 0, 1, 0   (c) 0, 1, 1, 0   (d) 0, 1, 0, 1

18. When SO_2 gas is passed through an acidified solution of $K_2Cr_2O_7$

(a) the solution becomes blue

(b) the solution becomes colourless

(c) SO_2 is reduced

(d) green $Cr_2(SO_4)_3$ is formed

19. Volatile nature of halogens is because

(a) The halogen molecules are more reactive

(b) The force existing between the molecules are only weak van der Waal forces

(c) Halogen molecules are bounded by strong forces

(d) Halogen molecules are bounded by electrostatic forces.

20. In the reaction:

$3Br_2 + 6OH^{\ominus} \rightarrow 5Br^{\ominus} + BrO_3^{\ominus} + 3H_2O$. Br_2 is

(a) Oxidised   (b) Reduced

(c) Disintegrated   (d) Disproportionated

21. The products of the chemical reaction between $Na_2S_2O_3$, Cl_2 and H_2O are

(a) S, HCl, Na_2SO_4 (b) S, HCl, Na_2S

(c) S, HCl, Na_2SO_3 (d) S, $NaClO_3$

22. Electron gain enthalpy with negative sign of fluorine is less than that of chlorine due to :

(a) High ionization enthalpy of fluorine

(b) Smaller size of chlorine atom

(c) Smaller size of fluorine atom

(d) Bigger size of $2p$ orbital of fluorine

23. In the case of alkali metals, the covalent character decreases in the order:

(a) $MF > MCl > MBr > MI$ (b) $MF > MCl > MI > MBr$

(c) $MI > MBr > MCl > MF$ (d) $MCl > MI > MBr > MF$

24. Of the interhalogen AX_3 compounds, ClF_3 is most reactive but BrF_3 has higher conductance in liquid state. This is because

(a) BrF_3 has higher molecular mass

(b) ClF_3 is more volatile

(c) BrF_3 dissociates into BrF_2^+ and BrF_4^- most easily

(d) Electrical conductance does not depend on concentration

25. XeF_6 on partial hydrolysis with water produces a compound 'X'. The same compound 'X' is formed when XeF_6 reacts with silica. The compound 'X' is :

(a) XeF_2 (b) XeF_4

(c) $XeOF_4$ (d) XeO_3

26. Which compound is prepared by the following reaction?

$$\underset{\text{(1:5 volume ratio)}}{Xe + 2F_2} \xrightarrow[\text{673 K, 5–6 atm}]{\text{Ni vessel}}$$

(a) XeF_2 (b) XeF_6 (c) XeF_4 (d) $XeOF_2$

27. What are the products formed in the reaction of xenon hexafluoride with silicon dioxide?

(a) $XeSiO_4 + HF$ (b) $XeF_2 + SiF_4$

(c) $XeOF_4 + SiF_4$ (d) $XeO_3 + SiF_2$

28. Liquid flow from a higher to a lower level. Which of the following liquids can climb up the wall of the glass vessel in which it is placed?

(a) Alcohol   (b) Liquid He

(c) Liquid N_2 (d) Water

29. Helium-oxygen mixture is used by deep sea divers in preference to nitrogen-oxygen mixture because

(a) Nitrogen is much less soluble in blood than helium

(b) Helium is much less soluble in blood than nitrogen

(c) Nitrogen is highly soluble in water

(d) Due to high pressure deep under the sea nitrogen and oxygen react to give poisonous nitric oxide.

30. XeF_6 dissolves in anhydrous HF to give a good conducting solution which contains:

(a) H^+ and XeF_7^- ion   (b) HF_2^- and XeF_5^+ ions

(c) $HXeF_6^+$ and F^- ions   (d) None of these

31. Incorrect statement regarding following reactions is:

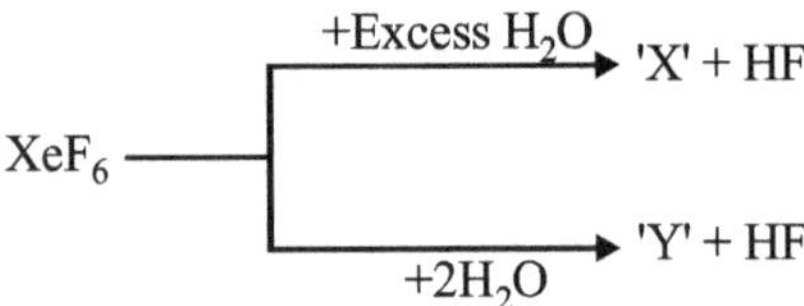

(a) 'X' is explosive

(b) 'Y' is an oxyacid of xenon

(c) Both are example of non-redox reaction

(d) XeF_6 can undergo partial hydrolysis.

Case/Passage Based Questions

DIRECTIONS : *Following are the case/passage based questions.*

In the last 10 years much has been learned about the molecular structure of elemental sulfur. It is now known that many different types of rings are sufficiently metastable to exist at room temperature for several days. It is known that at high temperature, the equilibrium composition allows for a variety of rings and chains to exist in comparable concentration, and it is known that at the boiling point and above, the vapor as well as the liquid contains small species with three, four, and five atoms. The sulfur atom has the same number of valence electrons as oxygen. Thus, sulfur atoms S_2 and S_3 have physical and chemical properties analogous to those of oxygen and ozone. S_2 has a ground state of 38 $\sigma 3s^2 \sigma^* 3s^2 \sigma 3p_z^2 \pi 3p_x^2 = \pi 3p_y^2 \pi^* 3p_x^1 = \pi^* 3p_y^1$. S_3, thiozone has a well-known uv spectrum, and has a bent structure, analogous to its isovalent molecules O_3, SO_2, and S_2O. The chemistry of the two elements, sulphur and oxygen, differs because sulfur has a pronounced tendency for catenation. The most frequently quoted explanation is based on the electron structure of the atom. Sulfur has low-lying unoccupied $3d$ orbitals, and it is widely believed that the $4s$ and $3d$ orbitals of sulfur participate in bonding in a manner similar to the participation of $2s$ and $2p$ orbitals in carbon.

(**Source:** Meyer, B. (1976). *Elemental sulfur. Chemical Reviews, 76(3), 367-388.* doi:10.1021/cr60301a003)

[From CBSE Question Bank-2021]

In the following questions, a statement of assertion followed by a statement of reason is given. Choose the correct answer out of the following choices on the basis of the above passage.

(a) Assertion and reason both are correct statements and reason is correct explanation for assertion.

(b) Assertion and reason both are correct statements but reason is not correct explanation for assertion.

(c) Assertion is correct statement but reason is wrong statement.

(d) Assertion is wrong statement but reason is correct statement.

32. **Assertion:** Sulphur belongs to same group in the periodic table as oxygen.
    Reason: S_2 has properties analogous to O_2.

33. **Assertion:** Thiozone has bent structure like ozone.
    Reason: Ozone has a lone pair which makes the molecule bent.

34. **Assertion:** S_2 is paramagnetic in nature.
    Reason: The electrons in $\pi^* 3p_x$ and $\sigma^* 3p_y$ orbitals in S_2 are unpaired.

35. **Assertion:** Sulphur has a greater tendency for catenation than oxygen.
    Reason: $3d$ and $4s$ orbitals of Sulphur have same energy.

Chapter Test

Time : *30 min* **Max. Marks : *15***

Direction :

- Questions number **1-15** carry **1 mark** each.

1. The sequence of acidic character is
   (a) $SO_2 > CO_2 > CO > N_2O_5$
   (b) $SO_2 > N_2O_5 > CO > CO_2$
   (c) $N_2O_5 > SO_2 > CO > CO_2$
   (d) $N_2O_5 > SO_2 > CO_2 > CO$

2. The structure of XeF_6 is
   (a) Distorted octahedral
   (b) Pyramidal
   (c) Telrahedral
   (d) None of the above.

3. The hydrolysis or trialylchlorosilanc R_3SiCl, yields ....
   (a) R_2SiO
   (b) $Si(OH)_4$
   (c) $R_3–Si–O–SiR_3$
   (d) $R_2Si(OH)_2$

4. Oxidation states of P in $H_4P_2O_5$, $H_4P_2O_6$, and $H_4P_2O_7$, are respectively:
   (a) $+3, +5, +4$
   (b) $+5, +3, +4$
   (c) $+5, +4, +3$
   (d) $+3, +4, +5$

DIRECTIONS (Qs. 5-7) : *Each of these questions contains an assertion followed by reason. Read them carefully and answer the question on the basis of following options. You have to select the one that best describes the two statements.*

(a) If both Assertion and Reason are correct and the Reason is a correct explanation of the Assertion.

(b) If both Assertion and Reason are correct but Reason is not a correct explanation of the Assertion.

(c) If the Assertion is correct but Reason is incorrect.

(d) If the Assertion is incorrect but the Reason is correct.

5. **Assertion :** Iodine is more soluble in water than in carbon tetrachloride.
   Reason : Iodine is a non-polar compound.

6. **Assertion :** Atoms in S_8 molecule undergo sp^3 hybridization and contain two tone pair on each atom.
   Reason : S_8 has a V-shape.

7. **Assertion:** A mixture of He and O_2 is used for respiration for deep sea divers.
   Reason : He is soluble in blood.

Case/Passage Based Questions

DIRECTIONS (Qs. 8-11) : *Following are the case/passage based questions.*

The discovery and preparation of several of the interhalogen compounds followed shortly after the discovery of the elements themselves. Since the halogens are all relatively strongly electronegative elements, each lacking one electron to complete its outer shell, they form diatomic molecules with a shared electron-pair bond between them:

$$:\overset{..}{\underset{..}{F}}\cdot\overset{\times\times}{\underset{\times\times}{F}}\times \qquad :\overset{..}{\underset{..}{Cl}}\cdot\overset{\times\times}{\underset{\times\times}{Cl}}\times \qquad :\overset{..}{\underset{..}{Br}}\cdot\overset{\times\times}{\underset{\times\times}{Br}}\times \qquad :\overset{..}{\underset{..}{I}}\cdot\overset{\times\times}{\underset{\times\times}{I}}\times$$

In a very similar manner, interhalogen molecules are formed, the simplest type being represented by CIF, BrCl, 1Br, etc., whose physical properties are intermediate between those of the two elements involved. However, these properties are not necessarily the average of those of the two parent elements.

Of the six possible uni-univalent halogen halides, five, all except iodine fluoride, are known to exist; the latter is probably too unstable, since in the known iodine-fluorine compounds, iodine always has a valence greater than 1.

Considerably more interest from a structural standpoint are the interhalogen compounds in which one of the halogens has a valence greater than 1. Three such series exist: AB_3, AB_5 and AB_7. No compounds are known where an even number of atoms of one halogen combine with an odd number of another; such a molecule would have an unpaired electron.

8. Interhalogen compounds are more reactive than the individual halogen because
    (a) two halogens are present in place of one
    (b) they are more ionic
    (c) their bond energy is less than the bond energy of the halogen molecule
    (d) they carry more energy

9. Which of the following statements are correct?
    (i) Among halogens, radius ratio between iodine and fluorine is maximum.
    (ii) Leaving F—F bond, all halogens have weaker X—X bond than X—X′ bond in interhalogens.
    (iii) Among interhalogen compounds maximum number of atoms are present in iodine fluoride.
    (iv) Interhalogen compounds are more reactive than halogen compounds.
    (a) (i) and (ii)   (b) (i), (ii) and (iii)
    (c) (ii) and (iii)   (d) (i), (iii) and (iv)

10. Which of the following is not the characteristic of interhalogen compounds ?
    (a) They are more reactive than halogens
    (b) They are quite unstable but none of them is explosive
    (c) They are covalent in nature
    (d) They have low boiling points and are highly volatile.

Assertion & Reason Questions

DIRECTION (Q. 11) : *Each of these questions contains an assertion followed by reason. Read them carefully and answer the question on the basis of following options. You have to select the one that best describes the two statements.*
(a) If both Assertion and Reason are correct and the Reason is a correct explanation of the Assertion.
(b) If both Assertion and Reason are correct but Reason is not a correct explanation of the Assertion.
(c) If the Assertion is correct but Reason is incorrect.
(d) If the Assertion is incorrect but the Reason is correct.

11. **Assertion:** interhalogen compounds are more reactive than halogens(except F)
    Reason: bond strength in interhalogen compounds is weaker than halogen molecule except F–F.
    OR
    Assertion: ClF_3 is used for the production of UF_6 in the enrichment of U_{235}.
    Reason: ClF_3 is hypergolic in nature.

Very Short Answer Questions

12. Which compound led to the discovery of noble gas compounds.
13. Which is more covalent – $SbCl_3$ or $SbCl_5$?
14. What is the oxidation state of cyclo trimetaphosphoric acid.
15. Can FCl_3 exist ? Comment.

Solutions

Practice Exercise-1

1. **(b)** The slow decomposition of HNO_3 is represented by the equation
   $$4HNO_3 \rightarrow 4NO_2 + 2H_2O + O_2$$
   (yellow-brown)

2. **(a)** $4HNO_3 + P_4O_{10} \longrightarrow 4HPO_3 + 2N_2O_5$

3. **(b)** $4NH_3(g) + 5O_2(g) \xrightarrow{\text{Catalyst}} 4NO(g) + 6H_2O(g)$
   $2NO(g) + O_2(g) \rightleftharpoons 2NO_2(g)$
   $3NO_2(g) + H_2O(l) \longrightarrow 2HNO_3(aq) + NO(g)$

4. **(c)** As the size of central atom increases, the lone pair of electrons occupies a larger volume. In other words, electron density on the central atom decreases and consequently its tendency to donate a pair of electrons decreases along with basic character from NH_3 to BiH_3.

5. **(d)** $2H_3PO_4 \xrightarrow[-2H_2O]{600°C} 2HPO_3$

6. **(a)** $\underset{\text{(Metal)}}{M} + \underset{\text{(Conc.)}}{HNO_3} \longrightarrow \underset{\text{(Metal nitrate)}}{MNO_3} + \underset{\text{(Nascent hydrogen)}}{H}$
   $2HNO_3 + \underset{\text{(Nascent hydrogen)}}{2H} \longrightarrow 2NO_2 + 2H_2O$

7. **(c)** At higher temperatures, dinitrogen combines with metals to form ionic nitrides.

8. **(a)**   9. **(d)**

10. **(a)** We know that empirical formula of hypophosphorus acid is H_3PO_2. In this only one ionisable hydrogen atom is present *i.e.* it is monobasic. Therefore, option (a) is correct structural formula of it.

11. **(d)** $P_2O_5 + 3H_2O \xrightarrow{\Delta} 2H_3PO_4$

12. (a)

13. (b) hypophosphorus acid has two P–H bond.

14. It is a weak base and burns in presence of oxygen.
$$NH_2 - NH_2 + O_2 \xrightarrow{Burn} N_2 + 2H_2O$$

15. NO_2 has unpaired electron and due to this, it has brown colour. N_2O_4 does not have unpaired electrons and thus it is colourless.

16. In CO_2 is sp hybridised and thus is linear molecule. SO_2 is sp^2 hybridised and thus is a bent molecule. Thus, they are not iso-structural.

17. Electropositive character (metallic character) increases from top to bottom in the group. Due to increase in atomic size, the tendency to gain two electrons decreases down the group.

18. Oxygen do not have vacant d-orbitals. It cannot have 4 and 6 electrons unpaired due to excitation of $2s$ and $2p$ electrons to d-orbitals.

19. N atom does not have d-orbitals and thus it cannot have all five valence electrons as unpaired.

20. $C + 2H_2SO_4 \text{ (conc.)} \xrightarrow{\Delta} CO_2 + 2SO_2 + 2H_2O$.

21. Dioxygen (O_2) and ozone (O_3).

22. N_2O is laughing gas prepared by heating NH_4NO_3.
$$NH_4NO_3 \xrightarrow{\Delta} N_2O + 2H_2O$$

23. White red and black phosphorus are three allotropes of phosphorus. White phosphorus is most reactive.

24. The S – H bond is weaker than O – H bond because the size of S-atom is bigger than that of O-atom. Hence, H_2S can dissociate to give H^+ ions in aqueous solution.

25. N_2 is not reactive, particularly at ordinary conditions of temperature because there is triple covalent bond $(N \equiv N)$ between two N-atoms. To break this bond to form N-atoms, a large amount of energy is required which is hardly available from enthalpies of reactions under ordinary conditions. In N_2 molecule octet of each N atom is already complete and it cannot expand its octet as there is no vacant d-orbital in its valence shell.

26. H_3PO_3 is diprotic as its structure involves only two replaceable H-atoms linked to P through O–H groups. The third H-atom is directly linked to P-atom of H_3PO_3 molecule and is thus not ionisable.

$$H - O - \overset{\displaystyle O}{\underset{\displaystyle OH}{\overset{\|}{P}}} - H$$

27. This is due to strong intermolecular H-bonding between water molecules which is not present in H_2S. It is because of high polarity of O–H bond as compared to S– H bond. Oxygen atom is highly electronegative and very small in size as compared to sulphur atoms.

28. C is sp hybridised in CO_2 and thus it is linear in shape. In NO_2, N is sp^2 hybridised and it has odd electrons therefore, it is a bent molecule. The structure of two are :

$$O = C = O \quad \text{and} \quad \overset{\cdot\cdot}{O} \overset{\displaystyle \overset{\cdot\cdot}{N}}{\underset{134°}{\diagup \diagdown}} \overset{\cdot\cdot}{O}$$

29. In PCl_4^+ phosphorous exists as P^+ and has 14 electrons similar to Si. Therefore, P in PCl_4^+ and Si in $SiCl_4$ are sp^3 hybridised and therefore, both are tetrahedral.

30. Refer Theory

31. Thermal stability of H_2O is more than that of H_2S. This is because of H – O bond energy being higher than that of H – S bond energy. H – O bond energy is 463 kJ/mol & H – S bond energy is 347 kJ/mol. The reason for stronger H–O bond is less bond length in H –O (96 pm) than in H–S (134 pm). So water dissociates between 2073 – 2270 K & H_2S dissociate between 673 K – 873 K.

32. H_2S is a stronger reducing agent as compared to water. This is because S – H bond is weaker than O – H bond.

33. This is because oxygen cannot expand its octet due to the non-availability of d-orbitals in oxygen. Sulphur has vacant d-orbitals which can be utilized to form covalent compounds in which the octet of S-atom can be expanded.

34. The basic character of hydrides of group 15 elements is due to presence of lone pair of electrons on central atom in them. Due to small size of N as compared to P there is higher electron density at N in NH_3 as compared to P in PH_3. Lone pair of electron is more easily available in NH_3 than PH_3.

35. H_2O, a hydride of oxygen undergoes inter-molecular H-bonding. As a result, it exists as an associated molecule and hence is a liquid at room temperature. However, H_2S, a hydride of sulphur does not undergo H-bonding. As a result, it exists as discrete molecule and hence is a gas at room temperature.

36. Due to the presence of a non-bonded electron pair on the central atom nitrogen halides act as bases. NF_3 is not an electron donor because fluorine being most electronegative tends to draw electron density away from N-atom and thus makes it a poor electron donor.

Practice Exercise-2 

1. (d) $2Ag_2O\,(s) \rightarrow 4Ag\,(s) + O_2\,(g)$
$2Pb_3O_4\,(s) \rightarrow 6PbO\,(s) + O_2\,(g)$
$2PbO_2\,(s) \rightarrow 2PbO\,(s) + O_2\,(g)$

2. (d) Oxidising power decreases down the group.

3. (b) On moving from top to bottom of halogen group the bond dissociation energy of hydrogen halides decreases and so the heat of formation of halogen acids also decreases.

4. (d) As the oxidation state of the central halogen atom increases, the halogen-oxygen bond becomes more and more covalent. As a result, the thermal stability of the oxoacid increases. Thus, $HClO_4$ is most stable to heat, whereas $HClO$ is least stable to heat.

5. (d) He was observed in the spectrum of the sun.

6. (a) Inert gases are monoatomic because they have stable configuration as their octet is complete.

7. (a) Fluorine exists in only –1 oxidation state due to the absence of vacant d-orbital.

8. (e) Fluorine is a highly reactive non-metal due to its low bond dissociation energy.

9. Refer Theory

10. It is most electronegative and is smallest in its atomic size, and has relatively less bond energy.

11. HF reacts with silica (SiO_2) present in glass and forms water soluble acid.
$$SiO_2 + 4HF \longrightarrow SiF_4 + 2H_2O$$

$$SiF_4 + 2HF \longrightarrow \underset{\text{(Water soluble)}}{H_2SiF_4}$$

12. It forms a complex with KI.

$$I_2 + I^- \longrightarrow I_3^-$$

13. F is highly electronegative and $N-F$ bond energy is higher than $N-Cl$ bond energy.

14. Inspite of its low density, it is non-flammable.

15. This is because $A-X$ bond in interhalogens is weaker than the $X-X$ bond in halogens.

16. In ClO^- there are $17+8+1=26$ electrons. A neutral molecule with 26 electrons is OF_2 $(8+2\times9=26)$.

17. $CaOCl_2 + H_2SO_4 \longrightarrow CaSO_4 + H_2O + Cl_2$.

18. Refer Theory

19. (*i*) $Cl-Cl > Br-Br > F-F > I-I$
(*ii*) $HI > HBr > HCl > HF$
(*iii*) $M-F > M-Cl > M-Br > M-I$
(*iv*) $BrO_4^- > ClO_4^- > IO_4^-$

20. (*i*) $2XeF_2 + 2H_2O \longrightarrow 2Xe + 4HF + O_2$
(*ii*) $XeF_6 + 3H_2O \longrightarrow XeO_3 + 6HF$
(*iii*) $XeF_6 + PF_5 \longrightarrow [XeF_5]^+ [PF_6]^-$
(*iv*) $XeF_6 + NaF \longrightarrow Na^+ [XeF_7]^-$

21. Refer Theory.

22. All the filled orbitals of Xe have paired electrons. The promotion of one, two or three electrons from the $5p$ filled orbitals to the $5d$ vacant orbitals will give rise to two, four and six half-filled orbitals. So Xe can combine with even but not odd number of F atoms. Hence, it cannot form XeF_3 and XeF_5.

23. In perchloric acid, $HClO_4$, oxidation state of Cl is $+7$ while that of S in sulphuric acid is $+6$.

$$H-O-\overset{O}{\overset{\|}{\underset{\|}{\overset{+7}{Cl}}}}=O \qquad H-O-\overset{O}{\overset{\|}{\underset{\|}{\overset{+6}{S}}}}-OH$$

The more positive charge on Cl creates more δ^+ on H. And also the conjugate base of $HClO_4$ is more stable because the negative charge will be spread over four oxygens in ClO_4^-.

24. Xe has relatively lowest ionisation energy among noble gases. Also, there is maximum electronegativity difference between Xe and F (as F is most electronegative). The large electronegativity difference enables to excite the Xe atom to various excited states where unpaired electrons become available for bonding.

25. Cl has vacant d-orbitals and thus can show a valency of $+3$ and thus ClF_3 is formed. On the other hand, F atom does not have d-orbitals and can show only an oxidation state of -1. F can not show a covalency of more than one due to non-availability of d-orbitals.

Past year Exercise

1. (a) Because of small size of F atoms, their is repulsion of electrons in F_2 molecule. Thus, F-F bond in F_2 molecule is weak.

2. Iodine is oxidised to iodic acid when it reacts with conc. HNO_3.

$$I_2 + 10\,HNO_3 \rightarrow 2\,HIO_3 + 10\,NO_2 + 4\,H_2O$$

3. Elements of group 16 have lower ionisation enthalpy values as compared to group 15 in the corresponding periods. This is due to the fact that group 15 elements have extra stable half-filled p-orbital electronic configurations.

4. Due to absence of vacant d-orbitals and small size fluorine does not show higher oxidation state.

5. Since the bond dissociation enthalpy of $H-X$ bond decreases from $H-F$ to $H-I$ as the size of atom increases from F to I. Thus, the acid strength order is $HF < HCl < HBr < HI$

6. Refer Theory

7. $XeF_4 + SbF_5 \longrightarrow [XeF_3]^+ [SbF_6]^-$

8. $XeF_2 + PF_5 \longrightarrow [XeF]^+ [PF_6]^-$

9. PCl_4^- is not likely to exist because here the oxidation state of P is $+3$, which is less stable.

10. N—F bond strength is greater than F—F bond strength, therefore, formation of NF_3 is spontaneous and reaction occur with release of energy. In case of NCl_3, N—Cl bond strength is lesser than Cl—Cl bond strength. Thus, energy has to be supplied during the formation of NCl_3.

11. Electronegativity increases on moving left to right in a period thus S is more electronegative than P. So, $S-H$ bond is more polar than $P-H$ bond resulting in easier removal of H^+ ion. Hence H_2S is more acidic than PH_3.

12. Interhalogen compounds are more reactive than halogens (except flourine) ICl being interhalogen is more reactive than I_2 because of lower bond dissociation energy.

13. H – bonding occurs in both H_2O and HF. Higher boiling point of H_2O is due to the extensive H-bonding than HF.

14. 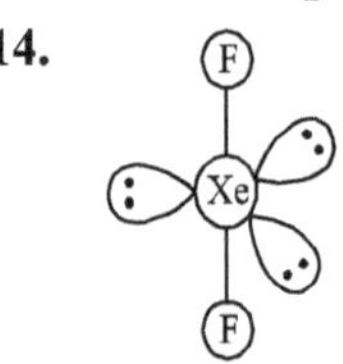

Linear

Shape : linear
Angle $F-Xe-F$: $180°$

15.

$$\overset{O}{\overset{\|}{\underset{\underset{\displaystyle F}{/\ \backslash}}{\underset{F}{\overset{F\backslash\ /F}{Xe}}}}}$$

Square pyramidal

16. Due to its small size and high IE, helium is chemically unreactive. Therefore it forms no real chemical compound.

17. $P_4 + 10SO_2Cl_2 \longrightarrow 4PCl_5 + 10SO_2$

18. In MH_3 the thermal stability of the hydrides decreases as the atomic size of central metal atom increases, *i.e.*, the $M-H$ bond strength decreases which means reducing character increases. Thus BiH_3 is the stronger reducing agent than the SbH_3.

19. Since P—P bond strength $(213\ \text{kJ mol}^{-1})$ is more than N—N bond strength $(159\ \text{kJ mol}^{-1})$. Hence, phosphorus shows marked catenation properties than nitrogen.

20. In SF_4, sulphur is sp^3d hybridised. It has trigonal bipyramidal structure in which one of the equatorial positions is occupied by a lone pair of electrons (see-saw geometry). Hence all the bonds in SF_4 are not equal.

21. Refer Theory

22. In SF_6, S is sterically protected by six F atoms therefore is an inert substance.

23. O_2 and F_2 both stabilise higher oxidation states of metals but O_2 exceeds F_2 in doing so due to ability of oxygen to form multiple bonds with metals.

24. It is due to
   (i)   low enthalpy of dissociation of F—F bond.
   (ii) high hydration enthalpy of F^-.

25. $3Cl_2 + \underset{\text{(Hot and Conc.)}}{6NaOH} \longrightarrow 5NaCl + NaClO_3 + 3H_2O$

26. On the basis of VBT covalent bonds are formed by the overlapping of half-filled atomic orbitals. But xenon has fully-filled electronic configuration. Hence, the structure of xenon fluorides cannot be explained by VBT.

27. $XeF_4 + O_2F_2 \xrightarrow{143K} XeF_6 + O_2$

28. Phosgene ($COCl_2$), tear gas (CCl_3NO_2).

29. Refer Theory

30. Refer NCERT Question 29.

31. (a) Refer answer 15.

(b) 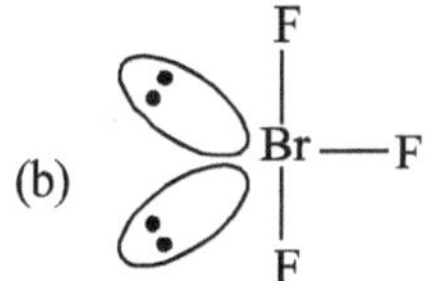

   T-shape

32. (a) Sulphurous acid can be oxidized to sulphuric acid and therefore can act as a reducing agent.
   (b) Due to small size and high electronegativity, fluorine cannot remain in higher oxidation state and therefore, cannot act as a central atom in higher oxoacids. It forms only one oxoacid HOF.
   (c) Only weak dispersion forces act as interatomic attraction in noble gases. Thus, as the atomic mass increases, boiling point increases from He to Rn.

OR

(a) $MnO_2 + 4HCl \longrightarrow MnCl_2 + Cl_2 + 2H_2O$
(b) $XeF_6 + KF \longrightarrow K^+[XeF_7]^-$
(c) $4I^-(aq) + 4H^+(aq) + O_2(g) \longrightarrow 2I_2 + 2H_2O$

33. Nitrate ion is confirmed by the appearence of brown ring.

$NO_3^- + Fe^{2+} + H^+ \longrightarrow Fe^{3+} + NO + H_2O$

$\left[Fe(H_2O)_6\right]^{2+} + NO \longrightarrow \left[Fe(H_2O)_5 NO\right]^{2+} + H_2O$

(brown ring)

OR

$4HCl + O_2 \xrightarrow{CaCl_2} 2Cl_2 + 2H_2O$

$2Cl_2 + 2H_2O \longrightarrow 4HCl + O_2$

34. The Hydrides of group 15 elements are:
$NH_3, PH_3, AsH_3, SbH_3, BiH_3$
(a) PH_3 has the lowest boiling point.
(This is because boiling point depends on mass. Down the group, atomic mass of central atom increases, so boiling point increases. However, NH_3 has higher boiling point than PH_3 due to hydrogen bonding).

(b) NH_3 has the maximum basic character.
(This is because basic character depends on the ease of release of lone pair on the central atom (lewis base), which is turn depends upon the charge density on the central atom. Smaller the size of the central atom, more is the charge density, easier is the availability of lone pair and hence more is the basicity).

(c) NH_3 has the highest bond angle.
(This is because in NH_3, N being small in size and highly electronegative, pulls the electron pair of the N–H bond towards itself. As a result, the bond pairs get closer resulting in increased repulsions between them. So, to minimize the repulsion, the bond pairs move away from each other giving a bond angle of $107.8°$.

(d) BiH_3 has the maximum reducing character.
Down the group, size of the central atom increases, bond length increases and hence, bond strength decreases. Thus, it becomes easier to release H. Hence, reducing character increases).

35. (a) XeF_4 (b) BrF_5

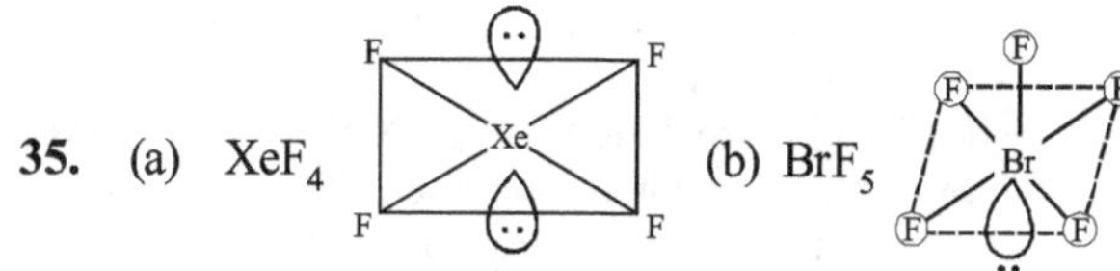

36. (a) Presence of angular strain in any molecule make it reactive. Such angular strain is found in the white phosphorus P_4 molecule where the angles are only $60°$ making it more reactive. White phosphorous is made of discrete tetrahedral P_4 molecules while red phosphorus is consist of chains of P_4 tetrahedra linked together. Due to these facts it can be concluded that red phosphorus is less reactive than white phosphorus.

(b) Halogens have largely negative electron gain enthalpies because they have only one electron less than stable noble gas configurations.

(c) Oxidation state of N in $N_2O_5 = +5$
Oxidation state of N in $N_2O_3 = +3$
In N_2O_5 nitrogen is present in highest oxidation state of $+5$. The oxide of an element in its highest oxidation state is least stable and most strongly acidic. Thus N_2O_5 is more acidic than N_2O_3.

37. (i) 

(ii) 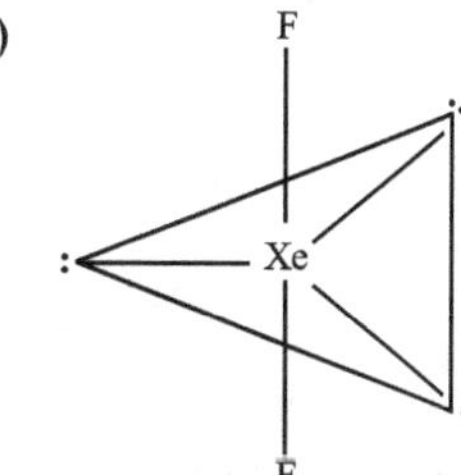

38. (i) Electronic configuration of N is $1s^2 2s^2 2p_x^1 2p_y^1 2p_z^1$. It has no vacant d-orbitals so it can not expand its valency. Nitrogen can only form $p\pi$ - $p\pi$ multiple bonds hence NX_5 is not possible.

(ii) In halogens electron affinity decreases in group except chlorine $Cl > F > Br > I$.

The electron gain enthalpy of F is less negative than that of Cl because of its small size as a result of which inter-electronic repulsions between electrons present in its $2p$ subshell are comparatively large.

(iii) Ozone molecule is a resonance hybrid of following contributing structure :

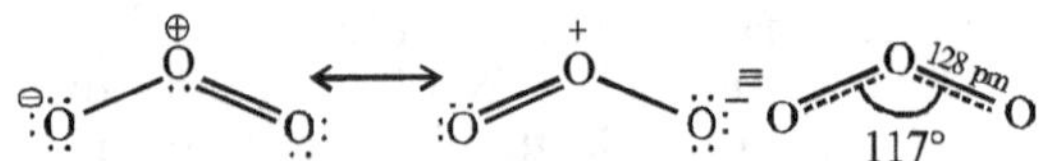

Due to resonance, both the oxygen-oxygen bonds have partial double bond character and equal bond length (128 pm).

39. (i) When heated, PCl_5 sublimes but decomposes on stronger heating into PCl_3 and Cl_2

$$PCl_5 \rightleftharpoons PCl_3 + Cl_2$$

(ii) $4 \overset{+3}{H_3PO_3} \xrightarrow{\Delta} \overset{-3}{PH_3} + 3 \overset{+5}{H_3PO_4}$

This reaction is called disproportionation.

40. (i) Due to smaller size of F as compared to Cl, the N – F bond is much stronger than N – Cl bond, while bond dissociation energy of F_2 is much lower than that of Cl_2. Therefore, energy released during the formation of NF_3 molecule is more than the energy neded to break N_2 and F_2 molecules into individual atoms. In other words, formation of NF_3 is an exothermic reaction or NF_3 is an exothermic compound. In contrast energy released during the formation of NCl_3 molecule is less than the energy needed to break N_2 and Cl_2 into individual atoms. In other words, formation of NCl_3 is an endothermic reaction or NCl_3 is an endothermic compound.

(ii) HF reacts with silica (SiO_2) present in glass and forms water soluble acid.

$$SiO_2 + 4HF \longrightarrow SiF_4 + 2H_2O$$
$$SiF_4 + 2HF \longrightarrow \underset{\text{(Water soluble)}}{H_2SiF_4}$$

Thus wax coated bottles are used as HF does not attack wax.

(iii) Cl_2 bleaches coloured material by oxidation.

$$Cl_2 + H_2O \longrightarrow 2HCl + [O]$$
$$\text{Coloured material} + [O] \longrightarrow \text{colourless}$$

Therefore, bleaching is permanent.

On the other hand, SO_2 bleaches coloured material by reduction and hence the bleaching is temporary effect and when the bleached colourless material is exposed to air, it gets oxidised and colour is restored.

$$SO_2 + 2H_2O \longrightarrow H_2SO_4 + 2[H]$$
$$\text{Coloured material} + [H]$$
$$\longrightarrow \underset{\text{material}}{\text{Colourless}} \xrightarrow[\text{oxidation}]{\text{Aerial}} \underset{\text{material}}{\text{Coloured}}$$

41. (a) In NO_2 an odd electron is present on N-atom. In order to become more stable, the two odd electrons pair up to form a dimer.

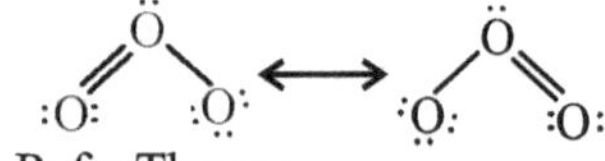

42. (i) $P_4 + 6H_2O \longrightarrow 2PH_3 + 2H_3PO_3$

(ii) $XeF_4 + O_2F_2 \longrightarrow XeF_6 + O_2$

43. (i) Refer NCERT Question 10.

(ii) Due to very small size of O, interelectronic repulsions in its atom are high and hence, it does not accept electrons with ease. On the other hand, S is much larger in size than O, so no interelectronic repulsions and hence, it can accept electron with much ease than O. Thus, O has less negative electron gain enthalpy than sulphur.

(iii) H_3PO_2 has two P–H bonds while H_3PO_3 has only one. As a result, H_3PO_2 acts as a stronger reducing agent than H_3PO_3.

44. (i) $2Ag + PCl_5 \rightarrow 2AgCl + PCl_3$

(ii) $CaF_2 + H_2SO_4 \rightarrow CaSO_4 + 2HF$

45. (i) XeF_4 (ii) $HClO_4$

46. (i) $C + 2H_2SO_4 \rightarrow 2SO_2 + CO_2 + 2H_2O$

(ii) $2XeF_2 + 2H_2O \rightarrow 2Xe\,(g) + 4HF\,(aq) + O_2(g)$

47. (i) Refer Theory

48. (i) $Ca_3P_2 + 6H_2O \longrightarrow 3Ca(OH)_2 + 2PH_3$

(ii) $Cu + 2H_2SO_4(\text{Conc.}) \longrightarrow CuSO_4 + SO_2 + 2H_2O$

OR

(i) Refer Theory   (ii) Refer Theory

49. (a) Refer Theory

(b)

White P	Red P
Consists of discrete tetrahedral P_4 molecule	it is polymeric, consisting of chains of P_4 tetrahedra

50. (i) PCl_5 is more covalent than PCl_3. This is because ionization energy required for the formation of P^{5+} is very high. Hence, rather than forming ionic bonds, P in +5 oxidation state forms covalent bonds.

(ii) Iron on reaction with HCl forms $FeCl_2$ instead of $FeCl_3$ because hydrogen produced in the reaction reacts with the available oxygen thus Fe^{2+} does not get the chance to oxidize to Fe^{3+}.

(iii) The two O–O bond lengths in ozone are equal due to resonance. Ozone is a resonance hybrid of two forms shown below and the molecule is angular with a bond angle of about $117°$.

51. (a) Refer Theory

(b) Refer Theory

52. (i) Down the group, stability of +5 oxidation state decreases and that of +3 oxidation state increases due to inert pair effect. As a result, Bi (V) is strongly oxidising in nature and hence it is a stronger oxidising agent than Sb (V).

(ii) N-N single bond is very weak due to large interelectronic repulsions between the lone pairs of electrons on the N-atoms because of small bond length. Down the group from N to P, size increases, interelectronic repulsions decrease and hence stability of P-P single bond increases.

(iii) Noble gases have very low boiling points. This is because the atoms of these elements are held together by weak van der Waal forces of attraction in liquid as well as in solid states.

53. (a) Refer Theory   (b) Refer Theory

54. (i) Sulphur exhibits paramagnetic behaviour in vapour state due to the presence of unpaired electron in anti-bonding orbitals.

(ii) In $SnCl_4$, Sn is in + 4 oxidation state while in $SnCl_2$, it is in + 2 O.S. Sn in + 4 O.S. has less tendency to lose electrons than in + 2.O.S. and thus in + 4 O.S, it has more tendency to share electrons than in + 2.O.S. Hence, $SnCl_4$ is more covalent than $SnCl_2$.

55. (i) SO_2 is a reducing agent because sulphur has empty *d*-orbitals and it can easily expand its +4 oxidation state to +6 oxidation state. However, as Te is a heavy element; therefore, due to inert pair effect, its lower oxidation state is more stable, and TeO_2 acts as oxidising agent.

(ii) Due to unavailability of empty *d*-orbitals in nitrogen, it cannot expand its valency. Hence, nitrogen does not form pentahalide.

(iii) In general, interhalogen compounds are more reactive because of lower bond dissociation energy than halogen molecules (except F_2)

NCERT Exemplar 

1. (a) On moving down the group, size of halogen atom increases hence, the H–X bond length increases. As a result, bond dissociation enthalpy decreases. Hence, the correct order of bond enthalpy is :
$$H-F > H-Cl > H-Br > H-I.$$

2. (a) $4NH_3(g) + 5O_2(g) \xrightarrow[\text{500K, 9 bar}]{\text{Pt/Rh gauge catalyst}}$
$$4NO(g) + 6H_2O(l)$$
$\therefore$ Two moles of NH_3 will produce 2 moles of NO on catalytic oxidation.

3. (c) Let oxidation state of P in NaH_2PO_2 is x.
$$1 + 2 \times 1 + x + 2 \times (-2) = 0 \implies x = +1$$

4. (b) Isoelectronic pair have same number of electrons
Total number of electrons for the given compounds :

BrO_2^-	BrF_2^+
$35 + 2 \times 8 + 1 = 52$	$35 + 9 \times 2 - 1 = 52$

ICl_2	ClO_2	BrF
$53 + 2 \times 17 = 87$	$17 + 16 = 33$	$35 + 9 = 44$

CN^-	O_3
$6 + 7 + 1 = 14$	$8 \times 3 = 24$

5. (c) Among carbon, nitrogen, phosphorus and boron only phosphorus has vacant *d*-orbital hence, only phosphorus has the ability to form $p\pi - d\pi$ bonding.

6. (c) Bertlett had taken $O_2^+ Pt F_6^-$ as a base compound because O_2 and Xe both have almost same ionisation enthalpy.

7. (a) The single N — N bond is weaker than the single P — P bond. This is why phosphorus show allotropy but nitrogen does not.

8. (d) In solid state PCl_5 exists as an ionic solid with the cation $[PCl_4]^+$ (tetrahedral) and the anion $[PCl_6]^-$ (octahedral).

9. (a) $NO_3^- + 3Fe^{2+} + 4H^+ \longrightarrow NO + 3Fe^{3+} + 2H_2O$
$$\left[Fe(H_2O)_6\right]^{2+} + NO \longrightarrow \left[Fe(H_2O)_5(NO)\right]^{2+} + H_2O$$
Brown ring

10. (b) The only well characterised compound having + 5 oxidation state of Bi is BiF_5. It is due to smaller size and high electronegativity of fluorine.

11. (c) N_2 is less reactive than P_4 due to high value of bond dissociation energy which is due to presence of triple bond between two N-atoms of N_2 molecule.

12. (c) HNO_3 makes iron passive due to formation of passive form of oxide on the surface. Hence, Fe does not dissolve in conc HNO_3 solution.

13. (b) HI cannot be prepared by the reacton of KI with concentrated H_2SO_4 because HI is converted into I_2 on reaction with H_2SO_4.

14. NH_3 forms hydrogen bonds with water therefore it is soluble in it but PH_3 cannot form hydrogen bond with water so it escapes as gas.

15. A is PCl_5 (It is yellowish white powder)
$$P_4 + 10Cl_2 \longrightarrow 4PCl_5$$
B is PCl_3 (It is a colourless oily liquid)
$$P_4 + 6Cl_2 \longrightarrow 4PCl_3$$
Hydrolysis products are formed as follows :
$$PCl_3 + 3H_2O \longrightarrow H_3PO_3 + 3HCl$$
$$PCl_5 + 4H_2O \longrightarrow H_3PO_4 + 5HCl$$

16. $P_4 + 6Cl_2 \longrightarrow 4PCl_3$
$PCl_3 + 3H_2O \longrightarrow H_3PO_3 + 3HCl] \times 4$
$P_4 + 6Cl_2 + 12H_2O \longrightarrow 4H_3PO_3 + 12HCl$
Moles of white phosphorus = 62/124 = 0.5 mol
1 mol of white phosphorus produces 12 mol of HCl.
$\therefore$ 0.5 moles of P_4 produces = 6 moles HCl
Mass of 6 mol HCl = 6 × 36.5 = 219.0 g HCl

Objective Practice Exercise 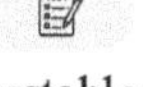

1. (d) Due to high N—F bond strength, NF_3 is highly stable and hence inert towards hydrolysis.

2. (a) $2NH_3 + 5/2 O_2 \xrightarrow[\Delta]{Pt} 2NO + 3H_2O$

3. (c) $NH_4Cl + KNO_2 \xrightarrow{\Delta} KCl + N_2 + 2H_2O$

4. (c) $H_3PO_3 + 2KOH \rightarrow K_2HPO_3 + 2H_2O$

5. (a) The single N — N bond is weaker than the single P — P bond. This is why phosphorus show allotropy but nitrogen does not.

6. (a) $(NH_4)_2 Cr_2O_7 \xrightarrow{\Delta} N_2 + 4H_2O + Cr_2O_3$

7. (b)   **8.** (a)

9. (d) PH_3 (Lewis base) can react with B_2H_6 (Lewis acid).

10. (b)

11. **(d)** SO_2 acts as an oxidising agent as well as reducing agent.
12. **(c)** Oxygen does not show oxidation state +4 and +6.
13. **(c)**
14. **(c)** Ozone does not react with acidified solution of $K_2Cr_2O_7$.
15. **(b)** Order of M.P. of B.P. or critical temperature : $H_2O > H_2Te > H_2Se > H_2S$
16. **(c)**
17. **(c)**

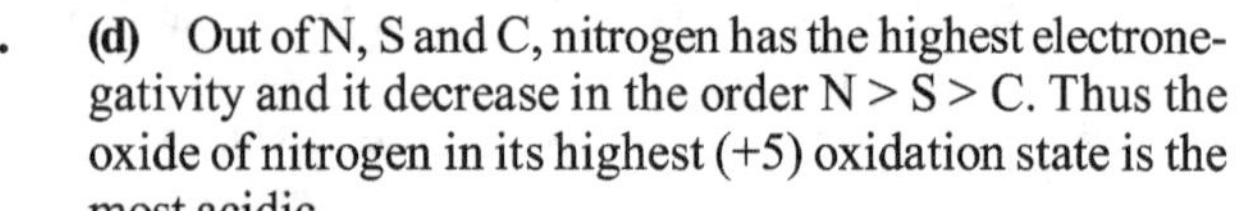

(SO_3) , $(S_2O_3^{2-})$, $(S_2O_6^{2-})$, $(S_2O_8^{2-})$

Hence (c) is the correct option.

18. **(d)** $K_2Cr_2O_7 + H_2SO_4 + 3SO_2 \longrightarrow$
$$K_2SO_4 + Cr_2(SO_4)_3 + H_2O$$
(Green)

19. **(b)**
20. **(d)** $3Br_2 + 6OH^{\ominus} \rightarrow 5Br^{\ominus} + BrO_3^{\ominus} + 3H_2O$. (0) (–1) (+5)
21. **(a)** $Na_2S_2O_3 + H_2O + Cl_2 \rightarrow Na_2SO_4 + S + 2HCl$
22. **(c)** The electron gain enthalpy order for halogens is $Cl > F > Br > I$
Due to small size of fluorine the extra electron to be added feels more electron-electron repulsion. Therefore fluorine has less value for electron affinity than chlorine.
23. **(c)** $MI > MBr > MCl > MF$. As the size of the anion decreases covalency decreases.
24. **(c)** In liquid state BrF_3 dissociates into BrF_2^+ and BrF_4^- ions most easily.
25. **(c)** $XeF_6 + H_2O \longrightarrow XeOF_4 + 2HF$ (Partial hydrolysis)
$XeF_6 + 2H_2O \longrightarrow XeO_2F_2 + 4HF$
$SiO_2 + 2XeF_6 \longrightarrow 2XeOF_4 + SiF_4$
(Xenon oxy tetra fluoride)
26. **(c)**
27. **(c)** $2XeF_6 + SiO_2 \rightarrow 2XeOF_4 + SiF_4$
28. **(b)**   29. **(b)**
30. **(b)** $HF + XeF_6 \longrightarrow XeF_5^+ + HF_2^-$
31. **(b)** XeF_6 — $\xrightarrow{+\text{Excess } H_2O} XeO_3 + HF$ (X) ; $\xrightarrow{+2H_2O} XeO_2F_2 + HF$ (Y)

Y is not an oxyacid of xenon.
32. **(b)** Sulphur and oxygen both belong to group 16 of the periodic table.
33. **(b)** Ozone   Thiozone

Ozone molecule is found to have bent shape because lone pair present on central oxygen atom repels the electrons of the two bonds.

34. **(a)**
35. **(c)** Sulphur has a greater tendency for cateration than oxygen because lone pair of oxygen repel the bond $O – O$ bond to a greater extent than the lone pairs of $S – S$ bond. According to aufbau principle, the $4s$ orbital is lower in energy than the $3d$ orbital.

Chapter Test

1. **(d)** Out of N, S and C, nitrogen has the highest electronegativity and it decrease in the order $N > S > C$. Thus the oxide of nitrogen in its highest (+5) oxidation state is the most acidic.
Next to N_2O_5 in the decreasing order of acidity will be SO_2 then CO_2 and finally CO which is neutral.
2. **(a)** sp^3d^3 hybridization will give pentagonal bipyramid geometry with one trans position occupied by a lone pair and shape of the molecule will be distorted octahedral.

XeF_6 sp^3d^3 hybridisation

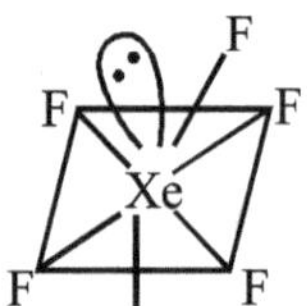

3. **(c)** The hydrolysis of R_3SiCl, yields $R_3Si(OH)$ which condenses to give $R_3Si – O – SiR_3$
$$R_3\,Si\,O -[H + H - O]- Si\,R_3 \longrightarrow R_3 – Si – O – Si – R_3$$
4. **(d)** $H_4P_2O_5 : 4 + 2x + 5(-2) = 0 \Rightarrow x = +3$
$H_4P_2O_6 : 4 + 2x + 6(-2) = 0 \Rightarrow x = +4$
$H_4P_2O_7 : 4 + 2x + 7(-2) = 0 \Rightarrow x = +5$
5. **(d)** Iodine, being a non-polar compound is more soluble in CCl_4 (non-polar compound) than in water as "like dissolves like".
6. **(c)** S_8 has puckered ring type structure.
7. **(c)** A mixture of He and O_2 is used for respiration by deep sea divers but Helium is not soluble in blood.
8. **(c)** The bond energy of interhalogen compounds is less than the bond energy of halogens.
9. **(d)** All halogens (leaving F-F) have stronger bond then that in interhalogens.
10. **(d)** Interhalogen compounds are not highly volatile.
11. **(a)**

OR

(b) Interhalogen compounds are useful fluorinating agents.
12. Formation of $O_2^+ [PtF_6]^-$ led to the discovery of first noble gas compound $Xe[PtF_6]$.
13. $SbCl_5$, due to higher oxidation state. In higher oxidation state, polarsing power of Sb increases.
14. Formula of Cyclotrimetaphosphoric acid is $(HPO3)_3$. Oxidatin ste of P is
$3[+1 + x + 3(-2)] = 0 \quad \Rightarrow \quad x = +5$
15. No, because F cannot exhibit valency more than one. Further three big sized Cl atoms cannot be accommodated around a small F atom.

4 Haloalkanes and Haloarenes

HALOALKANES AND HALOARENES

Haloalkanes — **Haloarenes**

Haloalkanes

Preparation

From alcohols:

- $ROH + HX \longrightarrow RX + H_2O$
- $ROH + PCl_5 \longrightarrow PCl + POCl + HCl$
- $ROH + SOCl_2 \longrightarrow RCl + SO_2 + HCl$

From hydrocarbons:

- $CH_2 = CH_2 + HX \longrightarrow CH_3CH_2X$
- Order of reactivity $HI > HBr > HCl > HF$

In case of unsymmetrical alkenes addition occurs according to Markownikoff's rule only in case of HBr in presence of peroxides addition occurs according to anti Markownikoff's rule

- $CH_2 = CH_2 + Br_2 \xrightarrow{CCl_4} BrCH_2CH_2Br$
- $CH_4 \xrightarrow[hv]{Cl_2} CH_3Cl + CH_2Cl + CHCl_3 + CCl_4$

From Halogen Exchange

With NaI (Finkelstein reaction):

$$\underset{(X=Cl, Br)}{R-X} + NaI \xrightarrow{Acetone} \underset{Iodoalkane}{R-I} + NaX$$

With AgF (Swarts reaction):

$$C_2H_5Cl + AgF \longrightarrow \underset{Flouroetane}{C_2H_5F} + AgCl$$

Properties

- **Nucleophilic substitution**

$$RX + KOH \longrightarrow ROH + KX$$
$$RX + H_2O \longrightarrow ROH + HX$$
$$RX + NaOR' \longrightarrow ROR' + NaX$$
$$RCl - NaI \xrightarrow{Acetone} RI + NaCl$$
$$RX + LiAlH_4 \longrightarrow RH + LiX + AlX_3$$

- **Elimination reaction**

$$CH_2CH_2Br \xrightarrow{OH^-} CH_2CH_2 + H_2O + Br^-$$

- **Reaction with metal**

$$CH_3CH_2Br + Mg \xrightarrow{Dry\ Ether} CH_2CH_2MgBr$$

- **Wurtz reaction :**

$$2RX + 2Na \longrightarrow RR + 2NaX$$

Haloarenes

Preparation

- **From arenes**

$$C_6H_6 + Cl_2 \xrightarrow[dark]{Fe} C_6H_5Cl$$

- **Sandmeyer's reaction**

$$C_6H_5 \overset{+}{N}_2Cl^- \xrightarrow{Cu_2Cl_2/HCl} C_6H_5Cl + N_2$$

- **By Gattermann reaction**

$$C_6H_5 \overset{+}{N}_2Cl^- \xrightarrow{Cu/HCl} C_6H_5Cl + N_2$$

- **Hunsdiecker reaction**

$$C_6H_5COOAg + Br_2 \xrightarrow[Reflux]{CCl_4} C_6H_5Br + CO_2 + AgBr$$

Properties
Nucleophilic substitution reactions

Electron withdrawing group present at o-and p-position increases the reactivity towards nucleophilic substitution.

Nucleophilic substitution involves replacement of $-X$ group with $-OH$, $-NH_2$ and $-CN$ groups.

Electrophilic and o, p-directing, due to $+ I$ effect of halogen group electron density increases at ortho and para positions.

(a) Halogenation   (b) Nitration
(c) Sulphonation   (d) Friedel-crafts reaction

| **Topic 1** | **Classification, Nomenclature and Methods of Preparation of Haloalkanes and Haloarenes** |  |

INTRODUCTION

The replacement of one or more hydrogen atoms of hydrocarbons by equal number of halogen atoms give rise to halogen derivatives or halides. The halogen derivatives of alkanes, alkenes, alkynes and arenes are known as alkyl halide, alkenyl halides, alkynyl halides and aryl halides respectively. Monohaloalkanes are commonly known as **alkyl halides** (represented by RX) and monohaloarenes as **aryl halides** (represented by ArX).

Haloalkanes are halogen derivatives of alkanes. Their general formula is $C_nH_{2n+1}X$ where X = F, Cl, Br or I and n = 2, 3, 4 .... etc.

For example, C_2H_5Cl C_3H_7Br
                        Ethylchloride   Propyl bromide

Haloalkenes or alkenyl halides are the halogen derivatives of alkenes. Their general formula is $C_nH_{2n-1}X$ where X = F, Cl, Br or I and n = 2, 3, 4, ..., etc. For example,

$$CH_2{=}CH{-}Cl \qquad Cl{-}CH_2{-}CH{=}CH_2$$
                    (Vinylchloride)   (Allylchloride)

Haloalkynes or alkynyl halides are the halogen derivatives of alkynes. Their general formula is $C_nH_{2n-3}X$ where X = F, Cl, Br or I and n = 2, 3, 4, ..., etc. For example,

$$H{-}C{\equiv}C{-}Cl \qquad CH_3{-}C{\equiv}C{-}Cl$$
                    chloroethyne   1–chloro prop–1–yne

Halogen derivatives of aromatic hydrocarbons in which the halogen atom is linked to one of the carbon atoms of the side chain carrying the aryl group are called **aralkyl halides**.

CLASSIFICATION OF HALOALKANES AND HALOARENES

Haloalkanes are classified as fluoro, chloro, bromo or iodo compounds according to the type of halogen present. Haloalkanes and haloarenes have been broadly classified in two ways depending upon the number of halogen atoms present as well as upon the nature of C–X bond.

On the Basis of No. of Halogen Atoms

Mono, di, tri, tetra, etc. depending on whether they contain one, two, three, four halogen atoms in structures.

$$
\begin{array}{ccc}
C_2H_5X & CH_2X & CH_2X \\
 & | & | \\
 & CH_2X & CHX \\
 & & | \\
 & & CH_2X \\
\text{mono} & \text{di} & \text{tri}
\end{array}
$$

Classification Based on Nature of C – X Bond

(a) **Compounds containing sp^3 hybridised C–X bond**

   (i) **Alkyl halides or haloalkanes :**
$$RCH_2X \quad R_2CHX \quad R_3CX$$
$$1° \qquad\quad 2° \qquad\quad 3°$$

   (ii) **Allylic halides :** In these compounds the halogen atom is linked to an sp^3 hybridised carbon atom which has a C = C bond attached to it.

   (iii) **Benzylic halides :** The tetrahedral carbon involved in C – X bond is linked to an aromatic ring.

(b) **Compounds containing sp^2 hybridised C–X bond**

   (i) **Vinylic halides :** The halogen atom is attached to sp^2 hybridised carbon atom of C = C bond.

(ii) **Aryl halides :** The halogen atom is attached directly to the carbon atom of the benzene ring.

Alkyl halides are further classified as primary (1°), secondary (°) and tertiary (3°) according to the halogen atom attached to primary, secondary and tertiary carbon atoms, respectively. For example,

$$CH_3 — CH_2 — CH_2 — Cl \qquad CH_3 — \overset{\overset{\displaystyle CH_3}{|}}{CH} — Cl \qquad CH_3 — \overset{\overset{\displaystyle CH_3}{|}}{\underset{\underset{\displaystyle CH_3}{|}}{C}} — Cl$$

(Primary)   (Secondary)   (Tertiary)

Dihalides and their Classification (General Formula: $C_nH_{2n}X_2$)

The dihaloalkanes having the same type of halogen atoms are named as alkylidene or alkalene di-halides. The dihalo-compounds having same type of halogen atoms are further classified as geminal halides (halogen atoms are present on the same carbon atom) and vicinal halides (halogen atoms are present on the adjacent carbon atoms). In IUPAC system, they are named as dihaloalkanes.

IUPAC NOMENCLATURE

Alkyl halides are named as halo substituted hydrocarbons in the IUPAC system of nomenclature. Haloarenes are the common as well as IUPAC names of aryl halides. For dihalogen derivatives, the prefixes o –, m –, p – are used in common system but in IUPAC system, the numerals 1, 2 ; 1, 3, and 1, 4 are used.

NATURE OF C–X BOND

Due to electronegativity difference between the carbon and the halogen, the shared pair of electron lies closer to the halogen atom. As a result, the halogen carries a small negative charge, while the carbon carries a small positive charge. Consequently, C – X bond is a polar covalent bond.

As the size of halogen atom increases on moving down the group the carbon - halogen bond length also increases from C–F to C–I.

METHODS OF PREPARATION OF HALOALKANES

From Alcohols

(a) **From halogen acids (Grove's Process) :** $R — OH + HX \longrightarrow R — X + H_2O$
                                    Alcohol   Halogen   Haloalkane
                                         acid

For a given alcohol, the reactivity of the halogen acids in the above reaction decreases in the order: HI > HBr > HCl and that of alcohols for a given halogen acids follow the order: 3° > 2° > 1°.

(b) **From phosphorus pentachloride:** $R—OH + PCl_5 \longrightarrow R—Cl + POCl + HCl$
                                    Phosphorus   Haloalkane   Phosphorus
                                    pentachloride   oxychloride

(c) **From thionyl chloride:** $R — OH + \overset{Cl}{\underset{Cl}{>}}S = O \xrightarrow{Pyridine} R—Cl + SO_2\uparrow + HCl\uparrow$
                                                         Haloalkanes
                         Thionyl chloride

Thionyl chloride method is preferred over hydrogen chloride or phosphorus pentachloride method since both the by-products (SO_2 and HCl) in this reaction being gases escape leaving the chloroalkanes in almost pure state.

(d) **By action of PCl_3 :**

$$\begin{matrix} R—OH \\ R—OH \\ R—OH \end{matrix} + P\begin{matrix} Cl \\ Cl \\ Cl \end{matrix} \longrightarrow 3R–Cl + H_3PO_3$$

                                         Chloroalkane   Phosphorous acid
Alcohol

Bromoalkanes and iodoalkanes are prepared by the action of PBr_3 and PI_3 on suitable alcohols. But since PBr_3 and PI_3 are not very stable compounds, they are generally prepared in situ by the action of red P on bromine and iodine.

From Alkenes

(a) **By addition of halogen acids:** $CH_2 = CH_2 + HX \longrightarrow CH_3 — CH_2 — X$
                                                         Iodoethane

The order of reactivity is HI > HBr > HCl > HF. The addition of hydrogen halides to an unsymmetrical alkene takes place according to Markovnikov's rule. When an unsymmetrical alkene or alkyne reacts with unsymmetrical reagent, then negative part of reagent attach with that carbon atom which contains lesser number of hydrogen atom during the addition.

In presence of peroxides such as benzoyl peroxide ($(C_6H_5COO)_2$), the addition of HBr (but not HCl or HI) to unsymmetrical alkenes takes place contrary to Markovnikov's rule. This is known as Peroxide effect or Kharasch effect.

(b) **By addition of halogens:** $CH_2=CH_2+Br_2 \xrightarrow{CCl_4} BrCH_2-CH_2Br$
$\qquad\qquad\qquad$ 1,2–Dibromoethane

(c) **By allylic halogenation :** When alkenes are heated with Cl_2 or Br_2 to a high temperature of about 773K, hydrogen atom of the allylc carbon which is next to the double bonded carbon gets substituted.

$$CH_3-CH=CH_2+Cl_2 \xrightarrow{773K} Cl-CH_2-CH=CH_2 + HCl$$
$\qquad\qquad\qquad\qquad\qquad$ 3–chloroprop–1–ene

From Alkanes

$$R-H+X-X \xrightarrow{Sunlight} R-X \ + \ H-X$$
$\qquad$ Alkane $\qquad\qquad\qquad\qquad\qquad$ Monohaloalkane

It is very difficult to stop the reaction at the formation of monohalogen stage. The reaction continues till all hydrogens in alkane are replaced one by one by chlorine or bromine and a mixture of mono, di, tri, tetra etc. halogen derivatives is obtained, which cannot be separated easily.

Note:
1. Chlorination and bromination can be achieved by above method while iodination is done in presence of oxidising agent (i.e., HNO_3 or HIO_3). Direct fluorination is highly exothermic. Thus, it is done by heating alkyl chlorides with inorganic fluorides (Hg_2F_2, AgF, SbF_3 etc.).
2. Benzylic hydrogens (hydrogen present on C attached directly to benzene) are more reactive, hence easily replaced than 1°, 2° or 3° hydrogens.

The reactivity of the alkanes follows the following order :
Tertiary alkane > Secondary alkane > Primary alkane
However, compounds containing only one type of hydrogen atom can be converted into monohalogenated products in good yield by taking excess of the concerned hydrocarbon; examples of such compounds are CH_4, CH_3CH_3, $(CH_3)_4C$, $C_6H_5CH_3$ etc.

$$CH_4 \xrightarrow[hv\ or\ 520-670K]{Cl_2} CH_3Cl+CH_2Cl_2+CHCl_3+CCl_4$$
$\ $ Methane

By Halogen Exchange

Swarts reaction
Alkyl chloride/ bromide is heated in presence of a metallic fluoride such as AgF, Hg_2F_2, CoF_2 or SbF_3
$$CH_3-Br+AgF \rightarrow CH_3F+AgBr$$

For alkyl iodides : (Finkelstein reaction)

$$CH_3CHXCH_3 \ + \ NaI \xrightarrow{acetone} CH_3CHICH_3 + \ NaX \downarrow \quad ; R-Cl+NaI \xrightarrow{Acetone,\ \Delta} R-I+NaCl$$
$\ $ (X=Cl, Br) $\qquad$ Soluble in acetone $\qquad\qquad\qquad\qquad$ Insoluble in acetone

From Silver Salt of Fatty Acids (Borodine Hundsdiecker Reaction)

$$CH_3CH_2COOAg+Br_2 \xrightarrow{CCl_4,\ Reflux} CH_3-CH_2-Br+CO_2+AgBr$$
$\qquad\qquad\qquad\qquad\qquad\qquad$ Bromoethane

Reaction involves free radical mechanism and gives an alkyl halide having one carbon atom less.
Yield of alkyl bromides follows the order : 1° > 2° > 3°.
Yield is very low in case of chlorides, while iodine in such cases react differently. $2RCOOAg+I_2 \longrightarrow RCOOR+CO_2+2AgI$

METHODS OF PREPARATION OF HALOARENES

By Aromatic Hydrocarbons

(a) **Nuclear halogenation**

   (i)   Nuclear halogenation is an electrophilic substitution reaction.

  (ii)   Fluorination is difficult to control, while iodination is too slow to be useful. Moreover, iodination being reversible (because of reducing character of HI), the reaction requires the use of an oxidising agent like HNO_3, HIO_3, HgO etc.

$$5HI+HIO_3 \longrightarrow 3I_2+3H_2O$$

 (iii)   Introduction of second –Cl is difficult as compared to first, because of electron withdrawing character of chlorine (deactivating nature of halogens).

(b) **Side chain halogenation**

Halogenation of higher arenes, *i.e.* other than benzene, in presence of light or heat and in the absence of a halogen carrier introduces halogen in the side chain.

Toluene $\xrightarrow[\text{Sunlight} -HCl]{383\,K, +Cl_2}$ Benzylchloride $\xrightarrow[\text{Sunlight} -HCl]{Cl_2, 383K}$ Benzalchloride $\xrightarrow[\text{Sunlight} -HCl]{Cl_2\, 383K}$ Benzotrichloride

Side chain halogenation occurs by free radical mechanism. In case, the side chain is larger than methyl group, side chain halogenation mainly occurs at the benzylic carbon (carbon directly attached to benzene nucleus). This is due to stability of benzylic free radical due to resonance.

$\xrightarrow[\text{Sunlight}]{Br_2,\ heat}$ 2-phenylethyl radical (less stable, 1° free radical, 2° benzylic radical)   or   Benzylic free radical (more stable) $\xrightarrow{Br_2}$ 1-Bromo-1-phenylethane **(Major product)**

From Diazonium Salts

Benzene diazonium chloride

$\xrightarrow[\substack{\text{Sandmeyer} \\ \text{reaction}}]{CuCl/HCl}$ Chlorobenzene $+ N_2$

$\xrightarrow[\substack{\Delta \\ \text{Gattermann} \\ \text{reaction}}]{Cu/HCl}$ $+ N_2$

$\xrightarrow[\substack{\text{Belz-Schiemann} \\ \text{reaction}}]{HBF_4}$ $[N_2BF_4]$ $\xrightarrow{Heat}$ $+ N_2 + BF_3$

Advantages of Preparation from Diazonium Salts Over Direct Halogenation

(a) Fluorides and iodides can be easily prepared.

(b) Halogenation gives a mixture of o- and p- isomers which are difficult to separate.

From Silver Salt of Aromatic Acids – Hunsdiecker Reaction

COOAg $+ Br_2$ $\xrightarrow{CCl_4,\ Reflux}$ Br $+ CO_2 + AgBr$

Illustration 1 :

Explain why thionyl chloride method is preferred for preparing alkyl chlorides from alcohols?

Sol. It is because the by products of the reaction, *i.e.*, SO_2 and HCl being gases escape into the atmosphere leaving behind alkyl chloride in almost pure state.

Illustration 2 :

Write the structure of the main product of chlorination of benzene in presence of UV light.

Sol. Benzene hexachloride (BHC) is formed.

$\xrightarrow[\text{UV light}]{3Cl_2}$

Practice Exercise-1

Multiple Choice Questions

1. When two halogen atoms are attached to same carbon atom then it is :
   (a) *vic*-dihalide
   (b) *gem*-dihalide
   (c) α, ω-halide
   (d) α, β-halide

2. A compound is formed by substitution of two chlorine for two hydrogens in propane. The number of possible isomeric compounds is
   (a) 4 (b) 3 (c) 5 (d) 2

3. Which one of the following is not an allylic halide?
   (a) 4-Bromopent-2-ene
   (b) 3-Bromo-2-methylbut-1-ene
   (c) 1-Bromobut-2-ene
   (d) 4-Bromobut-1-ene

4. IUPAC name of $CH_3CH_2C(Br) = CH - Cl$ is
   (a) 2-bromo-1-chlorobutene
   (b) 1-chloro-2-bromobutene
   (c) 3-chloro-2-bromobutene
   (d) None of the above

5. Halogenation of alkanes is
   (a) a reductive process
   (b) an oxidative process
   (c) an isothermal process
   (d) an endothermal process

6. In the preparation of chlorobenzene from aniline, the most suitable reagent is
   (a) chlorine in the presence of ultraviolet light
   (b) chlorine in the presence of $AlCl_3$
   (c) nitrous acid followed by heating with Cu_2Cl_2
   (d) HCl and Cu_2Cl_2

7. Aryl halides can not be prepared by the reaction of aryl alcohols with PCl_3, PCl_5 or $SOCl_2$ because
   (a) phenols are highly stable compounds.
   (b) carbon-oxygen bond in phenols has a partial double bond character
   (c) carbon-oxygen bond is highly polar
   (d) all of these.

8. Ethyl alcohol reacts with thionyl chloride in the presence of pyridine to give
   (a) $CH_3CH_2Cl + H_2O + SO_2$
   (b) $CH_3CH_2Cl + HCl$
   (c) $CH_3CH_2Cl + HCl + SO_2$
   (d) $CH_3CH_2Cl + SO_2 + Cl_2$

9. Ethylene dichloride can be prepared by adding HCl to
   (a) ethane
   (b) ethylene
   (c) acetylene
   (d) ethylene glycol

10. The best method for the conversion of an alcohol into an alkyl chloride is by treating the alcohol with
   (a) PCl_5
   (b) dry HCl in the presence of anhydrous $ZnCl_2$
   (c) $SOCl_2$ in presence of pyridine
   (d) none of these

Assertion & Reason Questions

DIRECTIONS (Qs. 11-15) : *Each of these questions contains an assertion followed by reason. Read them carefully and answer the question on the basis of following options. You have to select the one that best describes the two statements.*

(a) If both Assertion and Reason are correct and the Reason is a correct explanation of the Assertion.
(b) If both Assertion and Reason are correct but Reason is not a correct explanation of the Assertion.
(c) If the Assertion is correct but Reason is incorrect.
(d) If the Assertion is incorrect but the Reason is correct.

11. **Assertion :** Alkyl fluorides are prepared by heating AgF with alkyl chloride.
    Reason : Because direct fluorination of alkanes occurs very slowly with rupture of $C = C$ bonds.

12. **Assertion :** Neopentyl chloride is prepared by free radical chlorination of neopentane.
    Reason : This is because free radicals normally do not rearrange.

13. **Assertion :** Iodoalkanes are formed by Finkelstein reaction.
    Reason : Because NaI is soluble in acetone or methanol.

14. **Assertion :** Anti Markovnikov's rule is not applicable for HF, HCl or HI except HBr.
    Reason : Addition of HCl, HF or HI to alkenes forms only Markovnikov's products.

15. **Assertion :** Alkyl iodides cannot be prepared by Hunsdiecker reaction.
    Reason : This is because iodine reacts with silver salt of carboxylic acids to give esters and silver salts.

Very Short Answer Questions

16. What happens when chlorine is passed through toluene in presence of sunlight?
17. How is vinyl chloride prepared? Give its one important use.
18. How is allyl halide prepared?
19. Write IUPAC name of 'westron'. Mention its important use.
20. Draw possible isomers of C_4H_9Cl.

Short Answer Questions

21. Illustrate the following giving an example:
    (a) Markownikoff's rule
    (b) Kharasch effect (or peroxide effect or anti-Markownikoff's addition)
22. How will you prepare fluorobenzene?
23. Identify X, Y and Z in the following reactions:

    (i) $C_6H_5NH_2 \xrightarrow{NaNO_2 + del.HCl} X \xrightarrow[HBr]{CuBr} Y \xrightarrow[623\,K,\,Pressure]{NaOH} Z$

    (ii) $C_6H_5CH_3 \xrightarrow{Cl_2,\,FeCl_3} X \xrightarrow{Cl_2/h\nu} Y \xrightarrow{aq\,KOH}$

    (iii) $C_6H_5N_2^+Cl^- \xrightarrow[Warm]{KI} X \xrightarrow{Cu} Y$

24. Give the IUPAC names of isomers of $C_2H_4Cl_2$. Give one test to distinguish these.

25. How will you prepare *m*-bromoiodobenzene from benzene?

26. Identify all the possible monochloro structural isomers that would be expected to form on free radical chlorination of $(CH_3)_2CHCH_2CH_3$.

27. How will you carry out the following conversions:
   (*i*)   1-Iodobutane from 1-butene
   (*ii*) Sec-propyl bromide from isobutyric acid
   (*iii*) Fluoroethane from ethanol

28. Write the products of the following reactions:

(*i*)  + HBr $\longrightarrow$

(*ii*) $CH_3 CH_2 CH = CH_2 + HCl$

(*iii*) $C_6H_5 - CH_2 - CH = CH_2 + HI \xrightarrow{\text{Peroxide}}$

Topic 2   Properties of Haloalkanes and Haloarenes

PHYSICAL PROPERTIES OF HALOALKANES

Colour and Physical State

Alkyl halides are colourless when pure but bromides and iodides develop colour when exposed to light. Methyl chloride, methyl bromide, ethyl chloride, ethyl bromide and some chlorofluoromethanes are gases at room temperatures. Higher chloro, bromo, iodo compounds are either liquids or solids. The members containing upto eighteen carbon atoms (C_{18}) are generally liquids while the higher members of the family are solids at room temperature.

Boiling Points

(a) Due to greater polarity as well as higher molecular mass as compared to corresponding hydrocarbons, the intermolecular forces of attraction are stronger in the halogen derivatives. That is why, the boiling points of chlorides, bromides and iodides are comparatively higher than comparable mass hydrocarbons.

(b) For the same alkyl group, the boiling points of haloalkanes decrease in the order :
   $RI > RBr > RCl > RF.$

(c) For isomeric alkyl halides, the boiling points decreases with branching.

(d) The boiling points of chloro, bromo and iodo compounds increases as the number of halogen atoms increases.

Density

Alkyl fluorides and chlorides are generally lighter than water whereas alkyl bromides and iodides and polyhalides are heavier. The density increase with increase in the number of halogen atoms whereas the density decreases with increase in size of alkyl group. Their relative densities follow the order.
   $RI > RBr > RCl$

Solubility

Even though haloalkanes and haloarenes are polar molecules still they are insoluble in water. However, they are quite soluble in organic solvents of low polarity such as petroleum, ether, benzene, chloroform, ether, carbon tetrachloride, etc. This is because less energy is released when new interactions are set up between haloalkane and water molecules and these are not as strong as original H-bonds in water.

Dipole Moment

Except fluoride, dipole moment decreases with the decrease in electronegativity from Cl to I. Fluorides, although having highest electronegativity have lower dipole moment than chloride due to the very small size of F and hence very small C–F bond length which outweighs the effect of electronegativity (recall that $m = d \times e$). Thus the order for dipole moment is $CH_3Cl > CH_3F > CH_3Br > CH_3I$.

PHYSICAL PROPERTIES OF HALOARENES

Melting and Boiling Points

Their boiling points are low due to absence of hydrogen bonding. These values increase with the increase in size of the halogen atom from flourine to iodine. Although, the three isomeric dihalobenzenes have nearly same boiling points, the *p*-isomer has higher melting point than the *o*- and *m*-isomers. This is due to symmetrical nature of the *para* isomer due to which it is better packed in the crystal lattice. This explains why only the *para* isomer crystallises on cooling a solution containing *ortho* and *para* isomers.

Solubility

Haloarenes are less polar than haloalkanes because in aryl halides, halogen is present on sp^2 hybridised carbon which is more electronegative than the sp^3 hybridised carbon of alkyl halides or halocyclohexanes. Consequently, the electronegativity difference between C and Cl is low in aryl halides than in alkyl halides. Thus they are also insoluble in water.

Density

Haloarenes are heavier than water and their densities increase from fluorobenzene to iodobenzene

CHEMICAL PROPERTIES OF HALOALKANES

Nucleophilic Substitution Reactions

$C-X$ bond in alkyl halide is more polar due to electron repelling nature of alkyl group (–) and thus readily undergo nucleophilic substitution reaction. They are of two types:

(a) S_N1 **Reaction (Substitution Nucleophilic Unimolecular)**

This reaction occurs in two steps. In first step, a carbocation is formed from alkyl halide molecule. First step is slow step so it is also rate determining step. In second step, an attacking nucleophile attacks on this carbocation and forms the final product. In this reaction, rate of reaction is dependent on the concentration of alkyl halide molecule only and not on the concentration of nucleophile. So the reaction is called as *unimolecular substitution reaction*. Molecularity of reaction is two but the order of reaction is one. Polar medium is necessary for the reaction. The reactivity of alkylhalides in S_N reaction is : $3° > 2° > 1°$

Example :

$$CH_3-\underset{\underset{CH_3}{|}}{\overset{\overset{CH_3}{|}}{C}}-X + \overset{\oplus}{K}-\overset{\ominus}{OH} \xrightarrow{H-OH} CH_3-\underset{\underset{CH_3}{|}}{\overset{\overset{CH_3}{|}}{C}}-OH + KX$$

tertiary butylhalide   tertiary butylalcohol

Mechanism :

(i) $CH_3-\underset{\underset{CH_3}{|}}{\overset{\overset{CH_3}{|}}{C}}-X \xrightarrow{\text{Slow step}} CH_3-\underset{\underset{CH_3}{|}}{\overset{\overset{CH_3}{|}}{\overset{\oplus}{C}}} + \overset{\ominus}{X}$

Ter. butyl carbocation

(ii) $CH_3-\underset{\underset{CH_3}{|}}{\overset{\overset{CH_3}{|}}{\overset{\oplus}{C}}} + \overset{\ominus}{OH} \xrightarrow{\text{Fast step}} CH_3-\underset{\underset{CH_3}{|}}{\overset{\overset{CH_3}{|}}{C}}-OH$

Rate of reaction $\propto [(CH_3)_3C-X]$

(b) S_N2 **Reactions (Substitution Nucleophilic Bimolecular) :**

This reaction occurs in a single step. In this reaction, an attacking nucleophile attacks from back side of the central carbon atom of alkyl halide. When nucleophile attacks on central atom, then a transition state is formed in which attacking nucleophile and halogen atom both are linked with half bonds to the central atom. This stage is an unstable stage, after sometime halogen atom attract bonded electrons towards itself and leaves in the form of halide ion while attacking nucleophile forms complete bond with central carbon. In this reaction, bond breaking and bond forming processes both take place simultaneously and rate of reaction is dependent on the concentration of alkyl halide and concentration of attacking nucleophile both. So the reaction is called biomolecular substitution reaction. Molecularity of reaction is two and the order of reaction is also two. In this reaction complete inversion of configuration takes place. This inversion of configuration is called **Walden Inversion.** Polar medium is not necessary for this type of reaction. The reactivity of alkyl halides in S_N2 reactions is : $1° > 2° > 3°$.

The order of reactivity among various 1° alkyl halides is

$$CH_3X > C_2H_5X > n-C_3H_7X, \text{ etc.}$$

Bulkier the alkyl group, more is the steric hindrance in the formation of transition state and less is the reactivity of alkyl halide (remember that it is contrary to the stability of the carbonium ion : $n-C_3H_7^+ > C_2H_5^+ > CH_3^+$; but here carbonium ion is not formed as an intermediate).

Remember that in case alkyl halide is optically active, S_N2 **reactions lead to Walden inversion.** Thus in short, 3° alkyl halides react by S_N^1, 1° by S_N^2 and 2° by either or both of these mechanism depending upon the nature of the alkyl halide and the reagent.

For a given alkyl group, the order of reactivity is

$$R-I > R-Br > R-Cl > R-F$$

Increasing bond energy ; Decreasing halogen reactivity.

This is in accordance with the carbon – halogen bond energy; the carbon – fluorine bond energy is maximum and thus fluorides are the least reactive while carbon – iodine bond energy is minimum and hence iodides are the most reactive.

Example : $CH_3-X + K-OH \longrightarrow CH_3-OH + KX$

$$\underset{H}{\overset{H}{\diagdown}}\overset{\delta+}{C}\text{---}X^{\delta-} + OH^- \longrightarrow \left[\overset{\ominus}{HO}\text{----}\underset{\underset{H \quad H}{|}}{C}\text{----}X^{\ominus}\right] \longrightarrow HO\text{----}C\underset{H}{\overset{H}{\diagup}}H + X^-$$

transition state

Rate of reaction $\propto [CH_3X][OH^-]$

Some important nucleophilic substitution reactions of alkyl halides are listed below

(a) Hydrolysis :

(i) With aqueous KOH : Alkyl halides are hydrolysed to corresponding alcohols by boiling with aqueous alkali solution.

$$R\text{–}X + K\text{–}OH \longrightarrow \underset{\text{Alcohol}}{R\text{–}OH} + K\text{–}X$$

(ii) Using moist Ag_2O : $2R\text{–}X + Ag_2O + H_2O \longrightarrow \underset{\text{Alcohol}}{2R\text{–}OH} + 2AgX$

(b) Ether synthesis :

(i) Reaction with NaOR : $R\text{–}X + NaOR \longrightarrow \underset{\text{Ether}}{R\text{–}O\text{–}R} + NaX$

The above reaction is called "**Williamson's ether synthesis**".

(ii) Using dry Ag_2O : $2R\ X + Ag_2O \longrightarrow \underset{\text{Ether}}{R\text{–}O\text{–}R} + 2AgX$

(c) Reaction with Na_2S :

$$\begin{array}{c} R\text{–}X \quad Na \\ + \qquad \quad \diagdown S \longrightarrow \underset{\text{dialkyl sulphide}}{R\text{–}S\text{–}R} \quad + 2NaX \\ R\text{–}X \quad Na \diagup \end{array}$$

(d) Reaction with KSH : $R\text{–}X + K\text{–}SH \longrightarrow \underset{\text{Alkane thiol}}{R\text{–}SH} + KX$

(e) Reaction with KCN : $R\text{–}X + KCN \longrightarrow \underset{\text{Alkane nitrile}}{R\text{–}C\equiv N} + KX$

Alkane nitrile is an important compound which gives following products.

(i) $R\text{–}C\equiv N \xrightarrow{\text{LiAlH}_4 / \text{Reduction}} \underset{\text{Alkyl amine}}{R\text{–}CH_2\text{–}NH_2}$

(ii) $R\text{–}C\equiv N \xrightarrow[\text{partial hydrolysis}]{H_2O} \underset{\substack{\| \\ O \\ \text{Alkane amide}}}{R\text{–}C\text{–}NH_2}$

(iii) $R\text{–}C\equiv N \xrightarrow[\text{Complete hydrolysis}]{H_3O^+} \underset{\substack{\| \\ O \\ \text{Carboxylic acid}}}{R\text{–}C\text{–}O\text{–}H} + NH_3$

(f) Reaction with AgCN :

$$R\text{–}X + AgCN \longrightarrow \underset{\text{Alkane isocynide}}{R\text{–}N\overset{\rightarrow}{\equiv} C} + AgX$$

$$R\text{–}N\overset{\rightarrow}{\equiv} C \xrightarrow{\text{Hydrolysis}} \underset{\text{Alkane amine}}{R\text{–}NH_2} + HCOOH$$

$$R\text{–}N\overset{\rightarrow}{\equiv} C \xrightarrow{\text{Reduction}} \underset{\substack{\\ \text{Secondary amine}}}{R\text{–}\overset{\overset{\textstyle H}{|}}{N}\text{–}CH_3}$$

(g) Reaction with KNO_2 : $R\text{–}X + \overset{+}{K}\text{–}\overset{-}{O}\text{–}N{=}O \longrightarrow \underset{\text{alkyl nitrite}}{R\text{–}O\text{–}N{=}O} + KX$

(h) Reaction with $AgNO_2$: $R\text{–}X + Ag\text{–}O\text{–}N{=}O \longrightarrow \underset{\text{nitro alkane}}{R\text{–}N\diagdown^{\diagup O}_{\diagdown O}} + AgX$

(i) Reaction with Na_2SO_3 : $R\text{–}X + Na_2SO_3 \longrightarrow \underset{\text{Alkyl sodium sulphonate}}{RSO_3Na} + NaX$

(j) Reaction with silver acetate (Esterification) : $R\text{–}X + Ag\text{–}O\text{–}\underset{\substack{\| \\ O \\ \text{silver acetate}}}{C}\text{–}CH_3 \longrightarrow \underset{\substack{\| \\ O \\ \text{ester}}}{CH_3\text{–}C}\text{–}O\text{–}R + AgX$

(k) Reaction with benzene (Friedel-Craft Reaction) : $C_6H_5\text{–}H + X\text{–}R \xrightarrow[180°C]{\text{AlCl}_3} \underset{\text{Alkyl benzene}}{C_6H_5\text{–}R} + H\text{–}X$

Alkyl halide shows electrophilic substitution in the above reaction, which is exception in alkyl halide.

Elimination Reaction

When a haloalkane is heated with alcoholic solution of potassium hydroxide, there is elimination of hydrogen atom from β-carbon and a halogen atom from the α-carbon atom. An alkene is formed as a product, also called β-elimination or dehydrohalogenation

$$\underset{\text{1-Bromopropene}}{CH_3CH_2CH_2Br} \text{ or } \underset{\text{2-Bromopropene}}{CH_3CHBrCH_3} \xrightarrow[\text{Heat}]{\text{alc. KOH}} \underset{\text{Propene}}{CH_3-CH=CH_2} + HBr$$

If the structure of alkyl halide is such that it can undergo elimination in two different ways, due to the availability of different types of β-hydrogens, then the more highly substituted alkene (*i.e.,* having lesser number of hydrogen atoms on the doubly bonded carbon atoms) is the major product of dehydrohalogenation. This is called **Saytzeff's rule.**

$$\underset{\text{2-Bromobutane}}{CH_3CH_2CHBrCH_3} \xrightarrow[\text{heat}]{\text{alc. KOH}} \underset{\text{1-Butene (minor)}}{CH_3CH_2CH=CH_2} + \underset{\text{2-Butene (major)}}{CH_3CH=CHCH_3}$$

Ease of dehydrohalogenation among halides is : $3° > 2° > 1°$

An alkyl halide which gives a more stable or more alkyl substituted alkene as a result of dehydrohalogenation reacts faster as compared to the alkyl halide which gives less substituted alkene.

Ease of formation of alkenes is $CH_2=CH_2 < CH_3-CH=CH_2 < (CH_3)_2C=CH_2$

Ease of dehydrohalogenation of alkyl halides is $CH_3CH_2Br < (CH_3)_2CHBr < (CH_3)_3CBr$

Note: Elimination and substitution reactions normally compete with each other. The reaction which actually predominates depends upon:
(a) Nature of the alkyl halide, (b) strength and size of the base or nucleophile and (c) reaction conditions.

Reaction with Metals

(a) Most of the organic chlorides, bromides and iodides react with certain metals to form compounds containing carbon metal bond. Such compounds are called **organometallic compounds.**

$$\underset{\substack{\text{Alkyl} \\ \text{halides}}}{R-X} + Mg \xrightarrow{\text{Dry ether}} \underset{\text{Grignard reagent}}{R-Mg-X}$$

$$R-X+2Li \xrightarrow{\text{dry ether}} R-Li+LiX, \quad 2C_2H_5Br+2Zn \rightarrow 2C_2H_5ZnBr \xrightarrow{\Delta} (C_2H_5)_2Zn+ZnBr_2$$

(b) **Wurtz reaction:** Alkyl halides react with metallic sodium in presence of dry ether to form symmetrical alkanes containing double the number of carbon atoms present in the alkyl halide.

$$R \overbrace{-X+2\,Na+X-} R \xrightarrow{\text{Dry ether}} \underset{\text{Alkane}}{R-R} + 2Na^+X^-$$

(c) Alkyl lithiums react with copper halides to form higher alkanes **(Corey-House synthesis)**

$$2RLi \xrightarrow[(-LiI)]{CuI} R_2CuLi \xrightarrow[(1° \text{ halide})]{R'X} R-R'$$

Reduction of Alkyl Halides

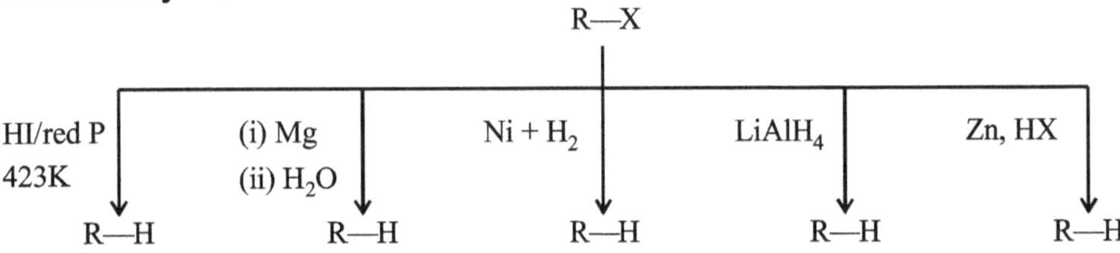

(When $X = I$)

Halogenation

$$CH_3Cl \xrightarrow{Cl_2,\ hv} CH_2Cl_2 \xrightarrow{Cl_2,\ hv} CHCl_3 \xrightarrow{Cl_2,\ hv} CCl_4$$

Isomerisation

$$\underset{\text{1-Bromopropane}}{CH_3CH_2CH_2Br} \xrightarrow[\text{anhy. AlCl}_3]{573\ K} \underset{\text{2-Bromopropane}}{CH_3CHBrCH_3}$$

CHEMICAL PROPERTIES OF HALOARENES

Nucleophilic Substitution

Aryl halides are extremely less reactive towards nucleophilic substitution reaction due to following reasons :

(*a*) **Resonance effect:** In haloarenes, the lone pair of electron on the halogen atom are delocalized on the benzene ring as:

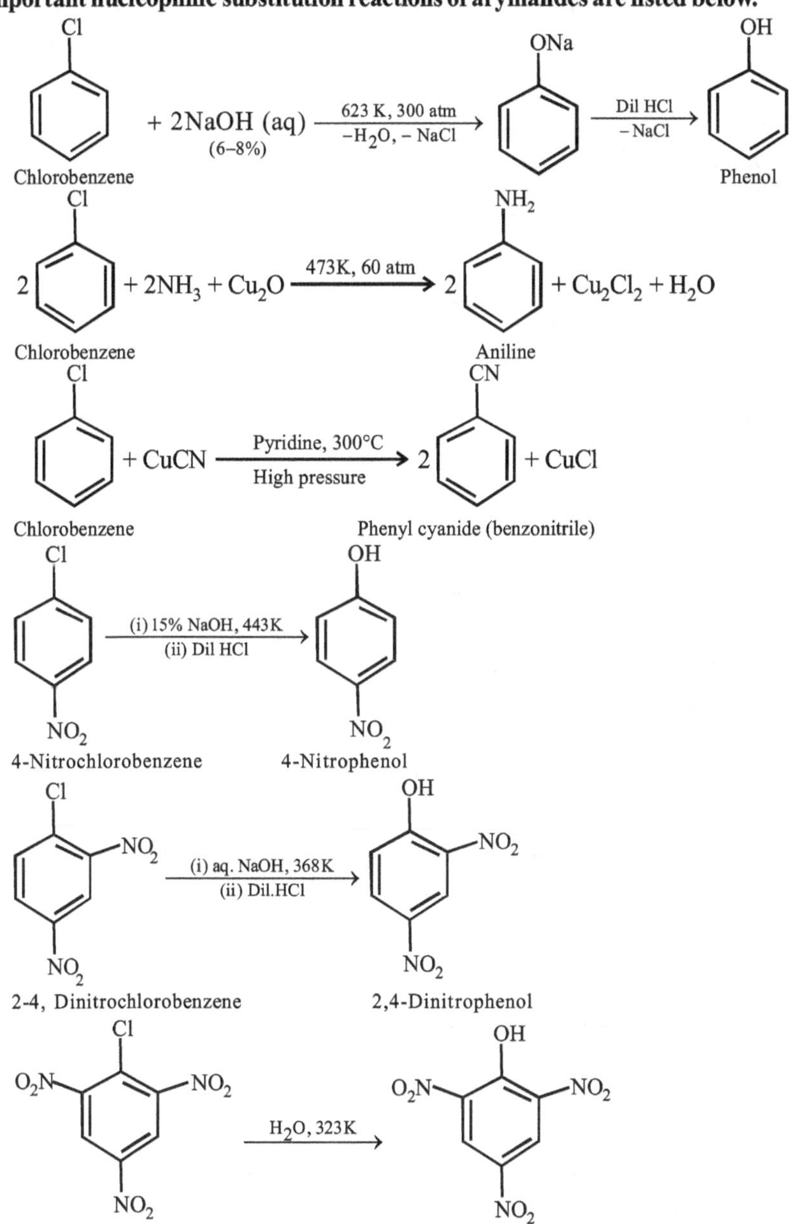

As a result, C – Cl bond acquires some double bond character. Consequently, C – X bond in aryl halides is little stronger than in alkyl halides, and hence cannot be easily broken.

(b)   In haloalkane, the halogen is attached to sp^3-hybridized carbon while in haloarenes the halogen is attached to sp^2-hybridized carbon. Since sp^2-hybridized orbital is smaller in sizes as compared to sp^3-carbital of carbon, therefore, the C – Cl bond in haloarenes should be shorter and hence stronger than in methyl chloride.

(c)   In haloarenes, the phenyl cation formed as a result of self-ionisation will not be stabilised by resonance and therefore, S_N1 mechanism is ruled out.

(d)   Also because of possible repulsion, it is less likely for the electron rich nucleophile to approach electron rich arenes.

Some important nucleophilic substitution reactions of arylhalides are listed below.

However, aryl halides having electron-withdrawing groups (like –NO_2, –CN, –$COOH$, –SO_3H etc.) in ***ortho*** and ***para*** positions undergo nucleophilic substitution very easily. Further, greater the number of such groups in *o*- and *p*- positions, more rapid is the reaction and hence less vigorous conditions are required.

Electrophilic Substitution Reactions

Haloarenes undergo the usual electrophilic substitution reactions of the benzene ring such as halogenation, nitration, sulphonation and Friedel crafts reactions. Halogen atom is slightly deactivating and o, p-directing. For example,

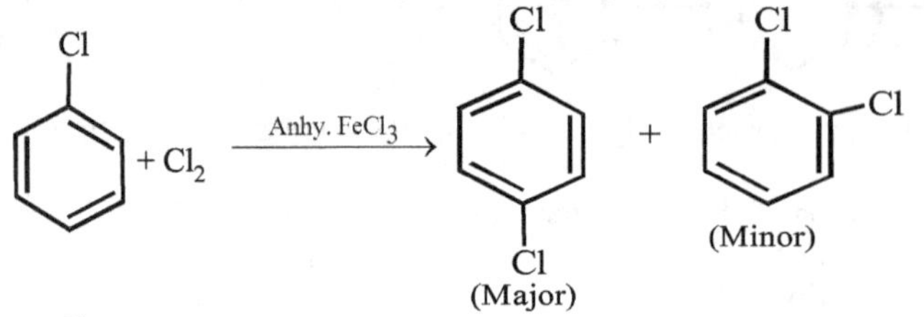

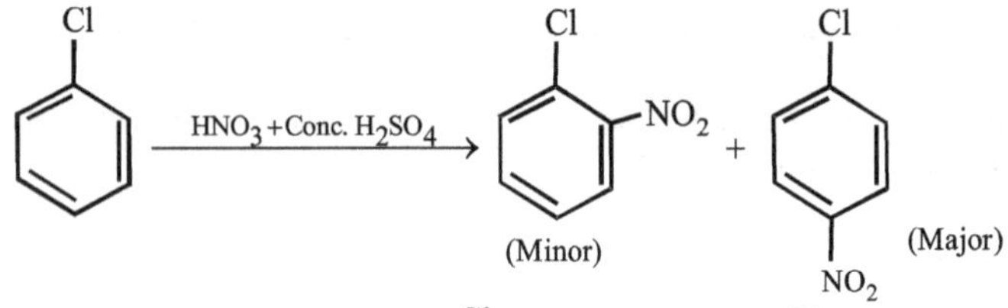

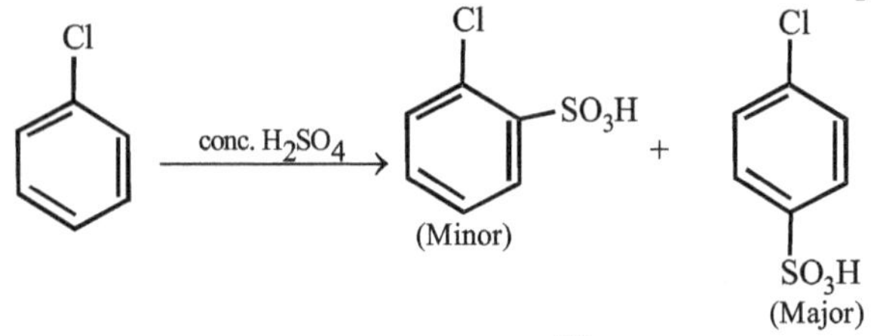

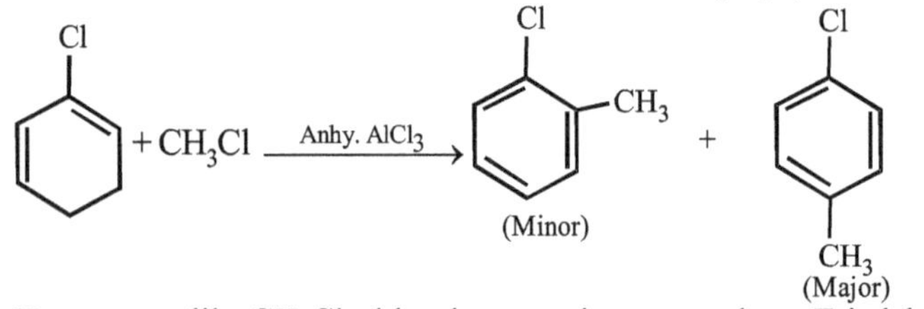

Note: However, unlike CH_3Cl, chlorobenzene does not undergo Friedel-Craft reaction with benzene. This is because of unstability of $C_6H_5^+$ cation.

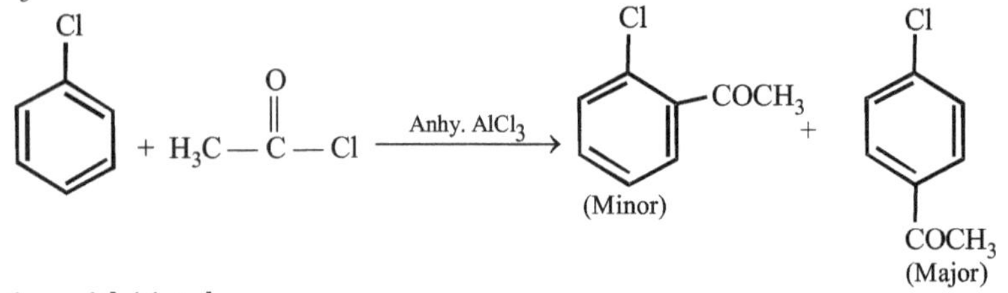

Reaction with Metals

(a) **Wurtz - Fittig reaction:** A mixture of an alkyl halide and aryl halide gives an alkylarene when treated with sodium in dry ether and is called Wurtz - Fittig reaction.

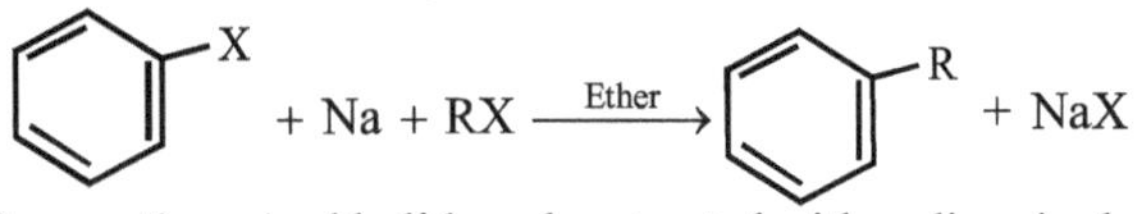

(b) **Fittig reaction:** Aryl halides when treated with sodium in dry ether gives a joint product of two aryl groups.

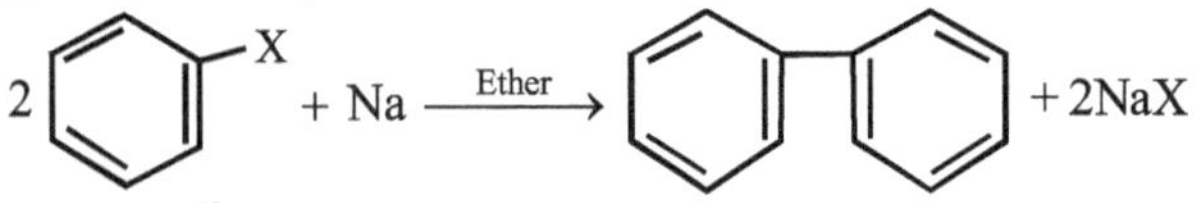

(c) **Ullmann reaction**

Chloro and bromo benzenes do not give this reaction. But when there is an electron withdrawing group present at the ortho and/or para position of the halogen atom, Ullmann reaction occurs.

Reduction

Illustration 3 :

How will you convert chlorobenzene into benzene?

Sol.

Illustration 4 :

Which is more easily hydrolysed: bromoethane or bromobenzene?

Sol. Bromoethane.

Practice Exercise-2

Multiple Choice Questions

1. Which one is most reactive towards S_N1 reaction?
   (a) $C_6H_5CH(C_6H_5)Br$
   (b) $C_6H_5CH(CH_3)Br$
   (c) $C_6H_5C(CH_3)(C_6H_5)Br$
   (d) $C_6H_5CH_2Br$

2. The order of reactivities of the following alkyl halides for a S_N2 reaction is
   (a) $RF > RCl > RBr > RI$
   (b) $RF > RBr > RCl > RI$
   (c) $RCl > RBr > RF > RI$
   (d) $RI > RBr > RCl > RF$

3. Which among MeX, RCH_2X, R_2CHX and R_3CX is most reactive towards S_N2 reaction?
   (a) MeX
   (b) RCH_2X
   (c) R_2CHX
   (d) R_3CX

4. $Br\text{—}\square\text{—}Cl \xrightarrow{Mg\ ether} A \xrightarrow{D_2O} B \xrightarrow{Na\ ether} C$, C is
   (a)
   (b)
   (c)
   (d) None of these.

5. Haloarenes are ortho and para directing due to
   (a) Resonance in aryl halide
   (b) –I effect of halogen atom
   (c) +I effect of halogen atom
   (d) Both (a) and (b)

6. Consider the reactions :
   (i) $(CH_3)_2CH-CH_2Br \xrightarrow{C_2H_5OH} (CH_3)_2CH-CH_2OC_2H_5 + HBr$
   (ii) $(CH_3)_2CH-CH_2Br \xrightarrow{C_2H_5O^-} (CH_3)_2CH-CH_2OC_2H_5 + Br^-$
   The mechanisms of reactions (i) and (ii) are respectively :
   (a) S_N1 and S_N2
   (b) S_N1 and S_N1
   (c) S_N2 and S_N2
   (d) S_N2 and S_N1

7. $>\text{—}Br + NaOH \xrightarrow{Solvent} >\text{—}OH$
   For which solvent rate of S_N2 will be maximum?
   (a) Benzene
   (b) 100% H_2O
   (c) 100% acetone
   (d) 75% H_2O + 25% acetone

8. Chlorobenzene is formed by reaction of chlorine with benzene in the presence of $AlCl_3$. Which of the following species attacks the benzene ring in this reaction?
   (a) Cl^-
   (b) Cl^+
   (c) $AlCl_3$
   (d) $[AlCl_4]^-$

9. Uses of dichloromethane is
   (a) paint remover
   (b) solvent in drugs manufacturing
   (c) metal cleansing and finishing solvent
   (d) All of the above
10. Haloforms are trihalogen derivatives of
    (a) Ethane   (b) Methane
    (c) Propane   (d) Benzene

Assertion & Reason Questions

DIRECTIONS (Qs. 11-14): *Each of these questions contains an assertion followed by reason. Read them carefully and answer the question on the basis of following options. You have to select the one that best describes the two statements.*
   (a) If both Assertion and Reason are correct and the Reason is a correct explanation of the Assertion.
   (b) If both Assertion and Reason are correct but Reason is not a correct explanation of the Assertion.
   (c) If the Assertion is correct but Reason is incorrect.
   (d) If the Assertion is incorrect but the Reason is correct.

11. **Assertion :** The boiling points of alkyl halides RX (X = Cl, Br or I) are considerably higher than those of the hydrocation of comparable molecular mass.
    Reason : Due to greater polarity as well as higher molecular mass than that of parent hydrocarbon.
12. **Assertion :** The C-X bond length increases from C-F to C-I.
    Reason : Since the size of halogen atom increases as we go down the group in the periodic table.
13. **Assertion :** High concentration of nucleophile favour $S_N I$ mechanism.
    Reason : 2° alkyl halides are more reactive than 1° alkyl halides towards $S_N I$ reactions.
14. **Assertion :** Boiling point of isomeric haloalkanes is $CH_3CH_2CH_2Br > CH_3CH_2CHBrCH_3 > (CH_3)_3CBr$.
    Reason : The boiling point of isomeric haloalkanes decreases with increase in branching.

Case/Passage Based Questions

DIRECTIONS (Qs. 15-19): *Following are the case/passage based questions.*

It is typical of aryl halides that they undergo nucleophilic substitution only with extreme difficulty. Except for certain industrial processes where very severe conditions are feasible, one does not ordinarily prepare phenols (ArOH), ethers (ArOR), amines (ArNH$_2$), on nitriles (ArCN) by nucleophilic attack on aryl halides. The aryl halides cannot be used in the Friedel-Crafts's alkylation reaction just like alkyl halides, which can be used. However, aryl halides do undergo nucleophilic substitution readily if the aromatic ring contains, in addition to halogen, certain other properly placed groups. The presence of electron withdrawing groups like $-NO_2$, $-CF_3$ at ortho or para position to the halogen atom makes the aryl halides more susceptible to nucleophilic attack.

15. Benzene reacts with *n*-propyl chloride in the presence of anhydrous AlCl$_3$ to give
    (a) 3 – propyl – 1 – chlorobenzene
    (b) n-Propylbenzene
    (c) No reaction
    (d) Isopropylbenzene

16. Which one of the following is most reactive towards nucleophilic substitution reaction?
    (a) $CH_2 = CH - Cl$ (b) C_6H_5Cl
    (c) $CH_3CH = CH - Cl$ (d) $ClCH_2 - CH = CH_2$
17. Read the following statements and choose the correct code
    (i) $S_N 2$ reactions follows a second order kinetics whereas $S_N 1$ reactions follows the first order kinetics
    (ii) $S_N 1$ reactions follows the second order kinetics whereas $S_N 2$ follows the first order kinetics
    (iii) $S_N 2$ reactions take place in a single step whereas $S_N 1$ reactions take place in two steps
    (iv) Tertiary alkyl halides are least reactive towards $S_N 2$ reactions but we observe high reactivity towards $S_N 1$ reaction.
    (a) (ii) and (iv) are correct
    (b) (i), (iii) and (iv) are correct
    (c) (i), (ii) and (iv) are correct
    (d) (ii), (iii) and (iv) are correct
18. Which of the following pair represent incorrect match of reactivity towards $S_N 2$ reaction?
    (a) $CH_3CH_2Cl > (CH_3)_3Cl$
    (b) $(CH_3)_2CHCl > (CH_3)_3Cl$
    (c) $CH_3 - CH = CH_2 > CH_3Cl$
    (d) None of these
19. Consider the following bromides :

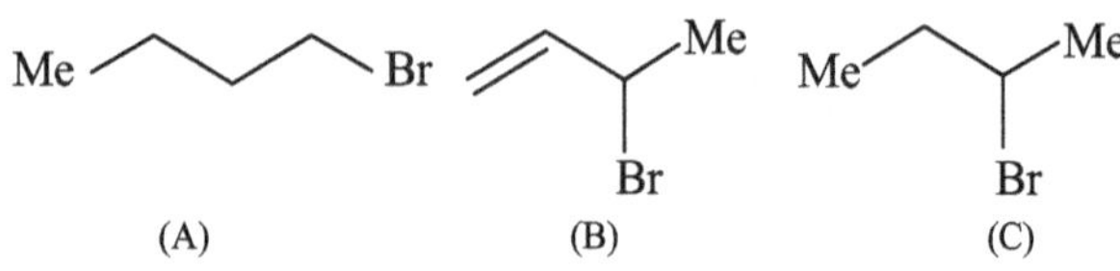

The correct order of $S_N 1$ reactivity is
    (a) B > C > A   (b) B > A > C
    (c) C > B > A   (d) A > B > C

Very Short Answer Questions

20. Which of the following compounds show optical isomerism and why?
    (*a*) 1 - Bromobutane   (*b*) 2-Bromobutane
21. Chloroalkanes are used as industrial solvents and not bromo and iodo compounds. Explain why.
22. Write various isomers of $C_6H_4Cl_2$. Indicate the isomer which has highest melting point.
23. What type of isomerism is shown by 1, 2-dichloroethene? Write the structure of its various isomers.
24. Arrange the following in order of increasing boiling point:

$$CH_3CH_2CH_2CH_2Br \;;\; (CH_3)_3CBr \;;\; CH_3\underset{\underset{CH_3}{|}}{C}HCH_2Br$$

25. Arrange the following in order of increasing boiling point: C_2H_5Br, C_2H_5I, C_2H_5Cl.
26. Arrange the following in the order of decreasing polarity: CH_3Br, CH_3I, CH_3Cl.
27. Which out of *o*-chloronitrobenzene and 2, 4, 6-trinitrochlorobenzene is more reactive towards nucleophilic substitution?
28. Write the structure of an alkene (C_4H_8) which adds on HBr in presence and in the absence of peroxide to give the same product C_4H_9Br.
29. What is westrosol? Give its important uses.

30. Complete the following reactions (giving major products):

$$CH_3-\underset{\underset{CH_3}{|}}{CH}I \xrightarrow{Na, Dry\ other} ?$$

31. How will you test the formation of phosgene in a chloroform sample?

32. Why a small amount of ethyl alcohol is added to chloroform bottles during storage of chloroform?

33. Why is chlorine atom is vinyl chloride $(CH_2 = CH - Cl)$ is less reactive as compared to ethyl chloride?

34. Allyl chloride $(CH_2 = CH - CH_2Cl)$ is hydrolysed more readily than n-propyl chloride. Explain.

35. *p*-isomers is less soluble in a given solvent than *o*-and *m*-isomer. Why ?

36. Ethyliodide is colourless when freshly prepared but changes to brown gradually when lying on shelf for a long time. Explain.

37. Identify X, Y and Z in the following sequence of reactions?

$$CH_3CH_2CH_2Br \xrightarrow{Alk.\ KOH} (X) \xrightarrow{H_2O/H^+} (Y) \xrightarrow{PCl_5} (Z)$$

38. Out of chlorobenzene and chloromethane, which is more reactive towards nucleophilic substitution reactions?

39. What effect should the following resonance of vinyl chloride have on its dipole moment ?

$$CH_2 = CH - \ddot{C}l: \longleftrightarrow CH_2^- = CH - \overset{+}{C}l$$

40. Which alkyl halide has the highest density and why?

41. Give the structure of an optically active hydrocarbon (C_5H_{12}) which on catalytic hydrogenation gives an optically inactive compound (C_6H_{14}).

42. Haloalkanes undergo nucleophilic substitution reactions. Why?

43. Why haloarenes undergo electrophilic substitution reaction?

44. What happens when chloroform is warmed with silver powder?

45. Haloarenes and haloalkanes are polar compounds but insoluble in water. Why?

46. Write reactions to indicate the formation of main product when chloroform reacts with following:
(*a*) Ethylamine   (*b*) Acetone   (*c*) Nitric acid

47. An organic compound 'A' on heating with NH_3 and cuprous oxide at high pressure gives compound 'B'. The compound 'B' on treatment with ice cold solution of $NaNO_2$ and HCl gives compound 'C', which on heating with copper turnings and HCl gives 'A' again. Identify A, B, and C.

Important Tips & Formulae

- **Nucleophilicity of some common nucleophiles in water and alcohol**

Class of nucleophile	Nucleophile	Relative reactivity
Very good	$R_3P:, I^-, HS^-, RS^-$	$> 10^5$
Good	$R_2NH, HO^-, RO^-, CN^-, N_3^-$	10^4
Fair	$Br^-, NH_3, Cl^-, RCOO^-$	10^3
Weak	F^-, H_2O, ROH	1
Very weak	$RCOOH$	10^{-2}

▸ **Trends in nucleophilicity :**

(*i*) A species with a negative charge is a stronger nucleophile than a similar neutral species. In particular, a base is a stronger nucleophile than its conjugate acid.

$$:\!\ddot{O}H > H_2\ddot{O}: \ ; \quad :\!\ddot{S}H > H_2\ddot{S}: \ ; \quad :\!\ddot{N}H_2 > \ddot{N}H_3$$

(*ii*) With increase in electronegativity, nucleophilicity decreases from left to right in the periodic table.

$$:\!\ddot{O}H > \ddot{F}:^- \ ; \quad :NH_3 > H_2\ddot{O}: \ ; \quad R_3P: > R_2\ddot{S}:$$

(*iii*) Nucleophilicity increases down the periodic table, following the increase in size and polarizability.

$$I^- > Br^- > Cl^- > F^-; ^-SeH > ^-SH > ^-OH;$$

$$R_3P: > R_3N:$$

The rate of S_N1 is independent of the nature of the nucleophile (stronger or weaker) because here the nucleophile attacks on the carbocation (a fast step). The net result is that, other things being equal, a strong nucleophile favours the S_N2 reaction, and a weak nucleophile favours the S_N1 reaction.

▸ **Intermolecular versus intramolecular nucleophilic substitution**

A molecule having two functional groups one of which acts as nucleophile and other leaving group can undergo intermolecular or intramolecular nucleophilic substitution. If the two such groups are separated from each other by four or five carbon atoms, intramolecular reaction occurs leading to the formation of five or six membered (stable) rings (intramolecular S_N).

Since three- and four-membered rings are strained (unstable) when the two groups are separated by one, two or three carbon atoms, intermolecular nucleophilic substitution takes place.

NCERT Questions

1. Name the following halides according to IUPAC system and classify them as alkyl, allyl, benzyl (primary, secondary, tertiary), vinyl or aryl halides:

(*i*) $(CH_3)_2CHCH(Cl)CH_3$

(*ii*) $CH_3CH_2CH(CH_3)CH(C_2H_5)Cl$

(*iii*) $CH_3CH_2C(CH_3)_2CH_2I$

(*iv*) $(CH_3)_3CCH_2CH(Br)C_6H_5$

(*v*) $CH_3CH(CH_3)CH(Br)CH_3$

(*vi*) $CH_3C(C_2H_5)_2CH_2Br$

(*vii*) $CH_3C(Cl)(C_2H_5)CH_2CH_3$

(*viii*) $CH_3CH=C(Cl)CH_2CH(CH_3)_2$

(*ix*) $CH_3CH=CHC(Br)(CH_3)_2$

(*x*) $p\text{-}ClC_6H_4CH_2CH(CH_3)_2$

(*xi*) $m\text{-}ClCH_2C_6H_4CH_2C(CH_3)_3$

(*xii*) $o\text{-}Br\text{-}C_6H_4CH(CH_3)CH_2CH_3$

Sol. (*i*) 2-Chloro-3methylbutane , 2° alkyl halide

(*ii*) 3-Chloro-4methyl hexane , 2° alkyl halide

(*iii*) 1-Iodo-2,2-dimethylbutane, 1° alkyl halide

(*iv*) 1-Bromo-3,3-dimethyl-1-phenylbutane, 2° benzylic halide

(*v*) 2-Bromo-3-methylbutane , 2° alkyl halide

(*vi*) 1-Bromo-2-ethyl-2-methylbutane, 1° alkyl halide

(*vii*) 3-Chloro-3-methylpentane, 3° alkyl halide

(*viii*) 3-Chloro-5-methylhex-2-ene, vinylic halide

(*ix*) 4-Bromo-4-methylpent-2-ene, allylic halide

(*x*) 1-Chloro-4-(2-methylpropyl) benzene, aryl halide

(*xi*) 1-Chloromethyl-3- (2,2-dimethylpropyl) benzene, 1° benzylic halide.

(*xii*) 1-Bromo-2-(1-methylpropyl) benzene, aryl halide.

2. Give the IUPAC names of the following compounds:

(*i*) $CH_3CH(Cl)CH(Br)CH_3$

(*ii*) $CHF_2CBrClF$

(*iii*) $ClCH_2C\equiv CCH_2Br$

(*iv*) $(CCl_3)_3CCl$

(*v*) $CH_3C(p\text{-}ClC_6H_4)_2CH(Br)CH_3$

(*vi*) $(CH_3)_3CCH=C(Cl)C_6H_4I\text{-}p$

Sol. (*i*) 2-Bromo-3-chlorobutane

(*ii*) 1-Bromo-1-chloro-1,2,2-trifluoroethane

(*iii*) 1-Bromo-4-chlorobut-2-yne

(*iv*) 2-(Trichloromethyl)–1, 1,1,2,3,3,3heptachloropropane

(*v*) 2-Bromo-3,3-bis-(4-chlorophenyl) butane

(*vi*) 1-Chloro-1-(4-iodophenyl)-3,3-dimethylbut-1-ene.

3. Write the structures of the following organic halogen compounds:

(*i*) **2-Chloro-3-methylpentane**

(*ii*) **p-Bromochlorobenzene**

(*iii*) **1-Chloro-4-ethylcyclohexane**

(*iv*) **2- (2-Chlorophenyl) -1- iodooctane**

(*v*) **2-Bromobutane**

(*vi*) **4-tert-Butyl-3-iodoheptane**

(*vii*) **1-Bromo-4-sec-butyl-2-methylbenzene**

(*viii*) **1, 4-Dibromobut-2-ene**

Sol. (*i*) $CH_3 - CH - CH - CH_2CH_3$

$\quad\quad\quad\quad\quad | \quad\quad |$

$\quad\quad\quad\quad Cl \quad\; CH_3$

(*ii*) Br—⟨benzene⟩—Cl

(*iii*) H_5C_2—⟨cyclohexane⟩—Cl

(*iv*) $ICH_2 - CH - (CH_2)_5 - CH_3$ with ortho-Cl phenyl substituent

(*v*) $CH_3 - CH_2 - CH - CH_3$

$\quad\quad\quad\quad\quad\quad |$

$\quad\quad\quad\quad\quad\; Br$

(*vi*) $CH_3 - CH_2 - CH - CH - CH_2CH_2CH_3$

$\quad\quad\quad\quad\quad\quad\; | \quad\quad\; |$

$\quad\quad\quad\quad\quad\quad\; I \quad\; C(CH_3)_3$

(*vii*) $CH_3 - CH_2 - CH$—⟨benzene with CH₃ and Br⟩

(*viii*) $BrCH_2 - CH=CH - CH_2Br$

4. Which one of the following has the highest dipole moment?

(*i*) CH_2Cl_2 (*ii*) $CHCl_3$ (*iii*) CCl_4

Sol. The three dimensional structures of the three compounds along with the direction of dipole moment in each of their bonds are given below:

CCl_4 being symmetrical has zero dipole moment. In $CHCl_3$, the resultant of two $C-Cl$ dipole moments is opposed by the resultant of $C-H$ and $C-Cl$ bonds. Since the dipole moment of latter resultant is expected to be smaller than the former, $CHCl_3$ has a finite dipole (1·03 D) moment.

In CH_2Cl_2, the resultant of two $C-Cl$ dipole moments is reinforced by resultant of two $C-H$ dipoles, therefore, CH_2Cl_2 (1·62 D) has a dipole moment higher than that of $CHCl_3$.

Thus, CH_2Cl_2 has highest dipole moment.

5. A hydrocarbon C_5H_{10} does not react with chlorine in dark but gives a single monochloro compound C_5H_9Cl in bright sunlight. Identify the hydrocarbon.

Sol. The hydrocarbon with molecular formula C_5H_{10} can either a cycloalkane or an alkene.

Since the compound does not react with Cl_2 in the dark, therefore it cannot be an alkene but must be a cycloalkane.

Since the cycloalkane reacts with Cl_2 in the presence of bright sunlight to give a single monochloro compound, C_5H_9Cl, therefore, all the ten hydrogen atoms of the cycloalkanes must be equivalent. Thus, the cycloalkane is cyclopentane.

$$\text{No reaction} \xleftarrow[\text{dark}]{Cl_2} \text{⬠} \xrightarrow[\text{Sunlight}]{Cl_2}$$

Cyclopentane
(C_5H_{10})

$$\text{Monochloro-cyclopentane}$$
$$(C_5H_9Cl)$$

6.　Write the isomers of the compound having formula C_4H_9Br.

Sol.　Double bond equivalent (DBE) for C_4H_9Br

$$= \frac{4\,(4-2) + 9\,(1-2) + 1(1-2)}{2} + 1 = 0$$

So none of the isomer has a ring or unsaturation, so the isomers are position or chain isomers

(i)　$CH_3CH_2CH_2CH_2Br$　(ii)　$CH_3 - \overset{\overset{\displaystyle CH_3}{|}}{CH} - CH_2Br$
　1-Bromo butane　　　　　　1–Bromo–2–methylpropane

(iii)　$CH_3 - CH_2 - \overset{\overset{}{|}}{\underset{\underset{Br}{|}}{CH}} - CH_3$　(iv)　$CH_3 - \overset{\overset{\displaystyle CH_3}{|}}{\underset{\underset{\displaystyle CH_3}{|}}{C}} - Br$
　2-Bromo butane　　　　　　　2–Bromo–2–methylpropane

7.　Write the equations for the preparation of 1-iodobutane from

(i)　1-butanol　(ii) 1-chlorobutane　(iii) but-1-ene.

Sol.　(i)　$CH_3CH_2CH_2CH_2OH + KI + H_3PO_4 \rightarrow$
　　　　$CH_3CH_2CH_2CH_2I + H_2O + KH_2PO_4$

(ii)　$CH_3CH_2CH_2CH_2Cl + KI$

$\xrightarrow{Acetone} CH_3CH_2CH_2CH_2I + KCl \downarrow$

(iii)　$CH_3CH_2 - CH = CH_2 + HBr$

$\xrightarrow{Peroxide} CH_3CH_2CH_2CH_2Br$
$\downarrow NaI\,/\,Acetone$
$CH_3CH_2CH_2CH_2 - I + NaBr$

8.　What are ambident nucleophiles ? Explain with an example.

Sol.　Nucleophiles which can attack through two different sites are called ambident nucleophiles. For example, cyanide ion is a resonance hybrid of the following two structures:

$$: C \equiv N: \longleftrightarrow :C = \ddot{N} :$$

It can attack through carbon to form cyanide and through N to form isocyanide.

9.　Which compound in each of the following pairs will react faster in S_N2 reaction with ^-OH?

(i) CH_3Br or CH_3I

(ii) $(CH_3)_3CCl$ or CH_3Cl

Sol.　(i)　Since I^- ion is a better leaving group than Br^- ion, therefore, CH_3I reacts faster CH_3Br in S_N2 reaction with OH^- ion.

(ii) On steric grounds, $1°$ alkyl halides are more reactive than tert-alkyl halides in S_N2 reactions. Therefore, CH_3Cl will react at a faster rate than $(CH_3)_3CCl$ in a S_N2 reaction with OH^- ion.

10.　Predict all the alkenes that would be formed by dehydrohalogenation of the following halides with sodium ethoxide in ethanol and identify the major alkene:

(i)　1-Bromo-1-methylcyclohexane　　(ii)　2-Chloro-2-methylbutane　　(iii)　2, 2, 3-Trimethyl-3-bromopentane.

Sol.

(i)　[structure: $\xrightarrow{C_2H_5ONa/\,C_2H_5OH}$ giving Major (methylcyclohexene) + Minor (methylenecyclohexane)]

Major　　　　Minor

(ii)　$CH_3 - CH - C - CH_2 \xrightarrow{C_2H_5ONa/\,C_2H_5OH} CH_3 - CH = \overset{\overset{\displaystyle CH_3}{|}}{C} - CH_3 +\ CH_3 - CH_2 - \overset{\overset{\displaystyle CH_3}{|}}{C} = CH_2$
　　　　　　　　　　　　　　　　　　　　　　(Major)　　　　　　　　　(Minor)

(iii)　$CH_3 - \overset{\overset{\displaystyle CH_3}{|}}{\underset{\underset{\displaystyle CH_3}{|}}{C}} - \overset{\overset{\displaystyle CH_2 H}{|}}{\underset{\underset{\displaystyle Br\ H}{|}}{C}} - CH - CH_3 \xrightarrow{C_2H_5ONa/\,C_2H_5OH} CH_3 - \overset{}{\underset{\underset{\displaystyle CH_3}{|}}{C}} - \overset{\overset{\displaystyle CH_2}{||}}{C} - CH_2 - CH_3 + CH_3 - \overset{\overset{\displaystyle CH_3}{|}}{\underset{\underset{\displaystyle CH_3}{|}}{C}} - C = CH - CH_3$
　　　　　　　　　　　　　　　　　　　　　　　　　　(Minor)　　　　　　　　　(Major)

11.　How will you bring about the following conversions?

(i)　Ethanol to but-1-yne　　　　　　**(ii)　Ethane to bromoethene**

(iii) Propene to 1-nitropropane　　　　**(iv) Toluene to benzyl alcohol**

(v)　Propene to propyne　　　　　　　**(vi) Ethanol to ethyl fluoride**

(vii) Bromomethane to propanone　　　**(viii) But-1-ene to but-2-ene**

(ix) 1-Chlorobutane to n-octane　　　　**(x) Benzene to biphenyl**

Sol.　(i)　$CH_3CH_2OH \xrightarrow[-SO_2,-HCl]{SOCl_2,\,Pyridine} CH_3CH_2 - Cl$,　$CH \equiv CH + NaNH_2 \xrightarrow{Liq\,NH_3,\,196\,K} HC = C^- Na^+$
　　　　　Ethanol　　　　　　　　　　　Chloroethane (I)　　　　　　　　　　　　　　　　　　Sodium acetylide (II)

　　　　$CH_3 - CH_2 - Cl + HC \equiv C^- Na^+ \longrightarrow CH_3CH_2 - C \equiv CH + NaCl$
　　　　　　　　(I)　　　　　　　(II)

(ii)　$CH_3 - CH_3 + Br_2 \xrightarrow{hv,\,520-670\,K} CH_3CH_2 - Br + HBr$
　　　Ethane　　　　　　　　　　　Bromoethane

$$\xrightarrow[-HBr]{KOH(alc)} CH_2 = CH_2 \xrightarrow{Br_2/CCl_4} BrCH_2CH_2Br \xrightarrow[-HBr]{\Delta/KOH(alc)} CH_2 = CHBr$$
Bromoethene

(iii) $CH_3 — CH = CH_2 \xrightarrow[Peroxide\ effect]{HBr, ROOR} CH_3CH_2CH_2Br \xrightarrow{AgNO_2, C_2H_5OH/H_2O} CH_3CH_2CH_2NO_2$
Propene $\qquad$ 1–Bromopropane $\qquad$ 1-nitropropane

(iv) Toluene $\xrightarrow[-HCl]{Cl_2/773K}$ Benzyl chloride $\xrightarrow[-KCl]{Aq.\ KOH,\ \Delta}$ Benzyl alcohol

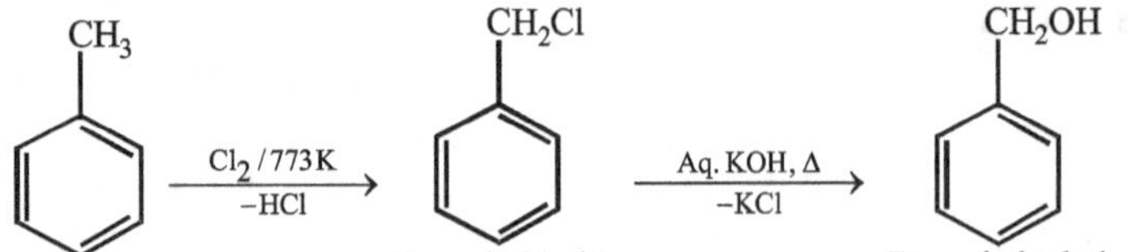

(v) $CH_3 — CH = CH_2 \xrightarrow{Br_2/CCl_4} CH_3 — \underset{\underset{Br}{|}}{CH} — \underset{\underset{Br}{|}}{CH_2} \xrightarrow[-2KBr, -2H_2O]{KOH\ (alc.),\ \Delta} CH_3 – C \equiv CH$
Propene $\qquad\qquad\qquad$ 1,2–Dibromo propane $\qquad$ Propyne

(vi) $CH_3CH_2OH \xrightarrow[-SO_2, -HCl]{SOCl_2,\ Pyridine} CH_3CH_2Cl \xrightarrow[-Hg_2Cl_2]{Hg_2F_2} CH_3CH_2F$
Ethanol $\qquad$ Ethyl chloride $\qquad$ Ethyl fluoride

(vii) $CH_3 — Br \xrightarrow[-KBr]{KCN\ (alc)} CH_3CN \xrightarrow{CH_3MgBr/ether} \left[CH_3 — \underset{\underset{CH_3}{|}}{C} = NMgBr \right] \xrightarrow[-NH_3, -Mg(OH)Br]{H^+/H_2O} CH_3 — \underset{\underset{CH_3}{|}}{C} = O$
Bromoethane $\qquad$ Acetonitrile $\qquad\qquad\qquad\qquad\qquad\qquad\qquad\qquad\qquad\qquad$ Propanone

(viii) $CH_3CH_2CH = CH_2 \xrightarrow[Markownikoff's\ addition]{HBr} CH_3CH_2\underset{\underset{Br}{|}}{CH} — CH_3 \xrightarrow[HBr]{KOH(alc.)\Delta} CH_3 — CH = CH — CH_3$
But–1–ene $\qquad\qquad\qquad\qquad\qquad$ 2-Bromobutane $\qquad\qquad$ But–2–ene (Major product)

(ix) $2CH_3CH_2CH_2CH_2Cl + 2Na \xrightarrow[Wurtz\ reaction]{Dry\ ether} CH_3CH_2CH_2CH_2CH_2CH_2CH_2CH_3 + 2NaCl$
1–chlorobutane $\qquad\qquad\qquad\qquad\qquad\qquad$ n–Octane

(x) Benzene $\xrightarrow{Br_2/FeBr_3}$ Bromobenzene—Br $\xrightarrow[Fittig\ reaction]{2Na, Dry\ ether, \Delta}$ Biphenyl $+ 2NaBr$

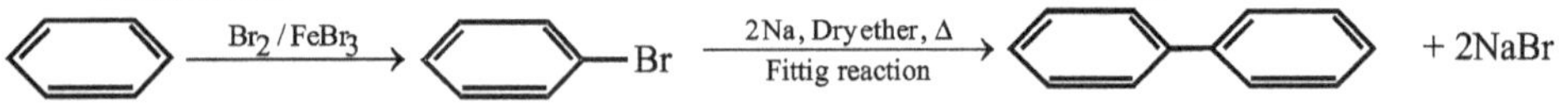

12. **Explain why**
 (i) **the dipole moment of chlorobenzene is lower than that of cyclohexyl chloride?**
 (ii) **alkyl halides, though polar, are immiscible with water?**
 (iii) **Grignard reagents should be prepared under anhydrous conditions?**

Sol. (i) sp^2-hybrid carbon in chlorobenzene is more electronegative than a sp^3-hybrid carbon in cyclohexylchloride, due to greater s-character. Thus, C atom of chlorobenzene has less tendency to release electrons to Cl than carbon atom of cyclohexylchloride. As a result, C – Cl bond in chlorobenzene is less polar than in cyclohexylchloride. Further, due to delocalization of lone pairs of electrons of the Cl atom over the benzene ring, C–Cl bond in chlorobenzene acquires some double bond character while the C – Cl in cyclohexyl chloride is a pure single bond. In other words, C–Cl bond in chlorobenzene is shorter than in cyclohexyl chloride.

Since dipole moment is a product of charge and distance, therefore, chlorobenzene has lower dipole moment than cyclohexylchloride due to lower magnitude of negative charge on the Cl atom and shorter C – Cl distance.

(ii) Alkyl halides are polar molecules, therefore, their molecules are held together by dipole-dipole attraction. The molecules of H_2O are held together by H-bonds. Since the new forces of attraction between water and alkyl halide molecules are weaker than the forces of attraction already existing between alkyl halide – alkyl halide molecules and water-water molecules, therefore, alkyl halides are immiscible (not soluble) in water. Alkyl halide are neither able to form H– bonds with water nor are able to break the H–bounding network of water.

(iii) Grignard reagents are very reactive. They react with moisture present in the apparatus to form alkanes

$$R — Mg — X + H — OH \longrightarrow R — H + Mg(OH)X$$

Thus, Grignard reagents must be prepared under anhydrous conditions.

13. **Write the structure of the major organic product in each of the following reactions:**
 (i) $CH_3CH_2CH_2Cl + NaI \xrightarrow{Acetone,\ heat}$
 (ii) $(CH_3)_3CBr + KOH \xrightarrow{Ethanol, heat}$
 (iii) $CH_3CH(Br)CH_2CH_3 + NaOH \xrightarrow{Water}$
 (iv) $CH_3CH_2Br + KCN \xrightarrow{aq.\ ethanol}$
 (v) $C_6H_5ONa + C_2H_5Cl \longrightarrow$
 (vi) $CH_3CH_2CH_2OH + SOCl_2 \longrightarrow$
 (vii) $CH_3CH_2CH = CH_2 + HBr \xrightarrow{Peroxide}$
 (viii) $CH_3CH = C(CH_3)_2 + HBr \longrightarrow$

Sol. (*i*) $CH_3CH_2CH_2Cl + NaI \xrightarrow[\text{(Finkelstein reaction)}]{\text{acetone, heat}} CH_3CH_2CH_2I + NaCl$

  1–Chloropropane   1–Iodopropane

(*ii*) $(CH_3)_3CBr + KOH \xrightarrow[\text{Dehydrohalogenation}]{\text{Ethanol, heat}} CH_3-\underset{\underset{CH_3}{|}}{C}=CH_2 + KBr + H_2O$

  2–Bromo–2–methylpropane   2–Methylpropene

(*iii*) $CH_3-\underset{\underset{Br}{|}}{CH}-CH_2CH_3 + NaOH \xrightarrow[\text{(Hydrolysis)}]{\text{Water}} CH_3-\underset{\underset{OH}{|}}{CH}-CH_2CH_3 + NaBr + H_2O$

(*iv*) $CH_3CH_2Br + KCN \xrightarrow[\text{(Nucleophilic substitution)}]{\text{aq. ethanol}} CH_3CH_2CN + KBr$

  Pr opanenitrile

(*v*) $C_6H_5O^-Na^+ + C_2H_5Cl \xrightarrow[\text{synthesis}]{\text{Williamson's}} C_6H_5-O-C_2H_5 + NaCl$

  Sodium phenoxide   Ethylchloride   Phenetole

(*vi*) $CH_3CH_2CH_2OH + SOCl_2 \xrightarrow[\text{substitution}]{\text{Nucleophilic}} CH_3CH_2CH_2Cl + HCl + SO_2$

  Pr opan–1–ol   1–Chloropropane

(*vii*) $CH_3CH_2CH=CH_2 + HBr \xrightarrow[\text{(Anti–Markownikoff's addition)}]{\text{Peroxide}} CH_3CH_2CH_2CH_2Br$

  But–1–ene   1–Bromobutane

(*viii*) $CH_3-CH=\underset{\underset{CH_3}{|}}{C}-CH_3 + HBr \xrightarrow[\text{addition}]{\text{Markownikoff's}} CH_3-CH_2-\underset{\underset{Br}{\overset{\overset{CH_3}{|}}{|}}}{C}-CH_3$

  2–Bromo–2–methylbutane

14. **Write the mechanism of the following reaction:**

$$n\text{-BuBr} + KCN \xrightarrow{\text{EtOH–H}_2\text{O}} n\text{-BuCN}$$

Sol. KCN is a resonance hybrid of the following two contributing structures:

$$K^+[^-:C\equiv N: \longleftrightarrow :C=N:^-]$$

Thus, CN^- ion is an ambident nucleophile. Therefore, it can attack the carbon atom of C-Br bond in n-BuBr either through C or N. Since $C-C$ bond is stronger than $C-N$ bond, therefore, attack occurs through C to form n-butyl cyanide.

$$K^+CN^- + CH_3CH_2CH_2\overset{\delta^+}{CH_2}-\overset{\delta^-}{Br} \longrightarrow CH_3CH_2CH_2CH_2CN + KBr$$

  n-Butyl bromide   n-Butyl cyanide

15. **Arrange the compounds of each set in order of reactivity towards S_N2 displacement:**

  (*i*) **2-Bromo-2-methylbutane, 1-Bromopentane, 2-Bromopentane.**

  (*ii*) **1-Bromo-3-methylbutane, 2-Bromo-2-methylbutane, 3-Bromo-2-methylbutane.**

  (*iii*) **1-Bromobutane, 1-Bromo-2, 2-dimethylpropane, 1-Bromo-2-methylbutane, 1-Bromo-3-methyl butane.**

Sol. The S_N2 reactions reactivity depends upon steric hindrance. More the steric hindrance slower the reaction.

Thus the order of reactivity will be $1° > 2° > 3°$

1– Bromopentane > 2–Bromopentane > 2–Bromo-2–methylbutane

1-Bromo-3-methylbutane > 2-Bromo-3-methylbutane > 2-Bromo -2-methyl butane

Since in case of 1° alkyl halides steric hindrance increases in the order, *n*-alkyl halides, alkyl halides with a substituent at any position other than the β-position, one substituent at the β-position, two substituents at the β-position, therefore, the reactivity decreases in the same order. Thus, the reactivity of the given alkyl bromides decreases in the order:

1-Bromobutane > 1-Bromo-3-methylbutane > 1-Bromo-2-methylbutane > 1-Bromo-2,2-dimethyl propane.

16. **Out of $C_6H_5CH_2Cl$ and $C_6H_5CHClC_6H_5$ which is more easily hydrolysed by aqueous KOH.**

Sol. $C_6H_5CH_2Cl$ is 1° aryl halide while $C_6H_5CH(Cl)C_6H_5$ is a 2° aryl halide. In S_N1 reactions, the reactivity depends upon the stability of carbocations.

$$C_6H_5\underset{\underset{Cl}{|}}{CH}C_6H_5 \xrightarrow{\text{Ionization}} C_6H_5-\overset{+}{CH}-C_6H_5 + Cl^-$$

  Carbocation is stabilized by delocalization over two C_6H_5 rings

$$C_6H_5CH_2Cl \xrightarrow{\text{Ionization}} C_6H_5\overset{+}{CH}_2 + Cl^-$$

  Carbocation is stabilized by delocalization over one C_6H_5 ring

Since the $C_6H_5\overset{+}{CH}C_6H_5$ carbocation is more stable than $C_6H_5\overset{+}{CH}_2$ carbocation, therefore, $C_6H_5CHClC_6H_5$ gets hydrolysed more easily than $C_6H_5CH_2Cl$ under S_N1

conditions. However, under S_N2 conditions, the reactivity depends on steric hindrance, therefore, under S_N2 conditions, $C_6H_5CH_2Cl$ gets hydrolysed more easily than $C_6H_5CHClC_6H_5$.

17. ***p*-Dichlorobenzene has higher m.p. and lower solubility than those of *o*-and *m*-isomers. Discuss.**

Sol. The *p*-isomer being more symmetrical fits closely in the crystal lattice and thus has stronger inter- molecular forces of attraction than *o*- and *m*-isomers. Since during melting or dissolution, the crystal lattice breaks, therefore, a large amount of energy is needed to melt or dissolve the *p*-isomer than the corresponding *o*-and *m*-isomers. In other words, the melting point of the *p*-isomer is higher and its solubility lower than the corresponding *o*- and *m*-isomers.

18. **How the following conversions can be carried out:**

(*i*)	Propene to propan-1-ol	(*ii*)	Ethanol to but-1-yne
(*iii*)	1-Bromopropane to 2-bromopropane	(*iv*)	Toluene to benzyl alcohol
(*v*)	Benzene to 4-bromonitrobenzene	(*vi*)	Benzyl alcohol to 2-phenylethanoic acid
(*vii*)	Ethanol to propanenitrile	(*viii*)	Aniline to chlorobenzene
(*ix*)	2-Chlorobutane to 3, 4-dimethylhexane	(*x*)	2-Methyl-1-propene to 2-chloro-2-methylpropane
(*xi*)	Ethyl chloride to propanoic acid	(*xii*)	But-1-ene to *n*-butyliodide
(*xiii*)	2-Chloropropane to 1-propanol	(*xiv*)	Isopropyl alcohol to iodoform
(*xv*)	Chlorobenzene to p-nitrophenol	(*xvi*)	2-Bromopropane to 1-bromopropane
(*xvii*)	Chloroethane to butane	(*xviii*)	Benzene to diphenyl
(*xix*)	tert-Butyl bromide to isobutyl bromide	(*xx*)	Aniline to phenylisocyanide

Sol. (*i*) $CH_3CH=CH_2 \xrightarrow{\text{HBr/Peroxide}} CH_3CH_2CH_2Br \xrightarrow[\text{Hydrolysis}]{\text{Aq.KOH,}\Delta} CH_3CH_2CH_2OH$

Propene   Propan-1-ol

(*ii*) $CH_3CH_2OH \xrightarrow{\text{P/I}_2,\Delta} CH_3CH_2I \xrightarrow[\text{Dehydrohalogenation}]{\text{KOH (alc),}\Delta} CH_2=CH_2$

Ethanol

$\xrightarrow[\text{addition}]{\begin{array}{c}Br_2/CCl_4\\ \text{electrophilic}\end{array}}$

$Na^+C\equiv C\ Na^+ \xleftarrow[196\ K]{\text{NaNH}_2,\ \text{Liq. NH}_3} CH\equiv CH \xleftarrow[\text{halogenation}]{\text{KOH (alc),}\Delta\ \text{Dehydro}} \underset{\overset{|}{Br}\ \ \ \overset{|}{Br}}{CH_2-CH_2}$

$\underset{(\text{excess})}{CH_3I}\Big\vert \begin{array}{c}\text{Nucleophilic}\\ \text{substitution}\end{array}$

$\longrightarrow \underset{\text{But-2-yne}}{CH_3-C\equiv C-CH_3}$

(*iii*) $CH_3CH_2CH_2Br \xrightarrow[\text{Dehydrohalogenation}]{\text{KOH(alc),}\Delta} CH_3CH=CH_2 \xrightarrow[\text{Mark. addition}]{\text{HBr}} \underset{\text{2-Bromopropane}}{CH_3-CHBr-CH_3}$

(*iv*)

Toluene $\xrightarrow[-HCl]{Cl_2/383K, hv}$ (CH$_2$Cl) $\xrightarrow[-KCl]{\text{Aq. KOH,}\Delta}$ (CH$_2$OH) Benzylalcohol

(*v*)

Benzene $\xrightarrow[\begin{array}{c}\text{Electrophilic}\\ \text{substitution}\end{array}]{Br_2/FeBr_3}$ (Br) $\xrightarrow[(\text{Nitration})]{\text{Conc.HNO}_3+\text{Conc.H}_2\text{SO}_4}$ O_2N—(ring)—Br   4-Bromonitrobenzene

(*vi*)

Benzyl alcohol (CH$_2$OH) $\xrightarrow[-SO_2,-HCl]{SOCl_2}$ (CH$_2$Cl) $\xrightarrow[\begin{array}{c}(\text{Nucleophilic}\\ \text{substitution})\end{array}]{\text{KCN, Et-OH-H}_2O}$ (CH$_2$CN) $\xrightarrow[\text{Hydrolysis}]{H^+/H_2O}$ (CH$_2$COOH)

2-Phenylethanoic acid

(*vii*) $CH_3CH_2OH \xrightarrow{\text{P/I}_2,\Delta} CH_3CH_2I \xrightarrow[\begin{array}{c}(\text{Nucleophilic}\\ \text{substitution})\end{array}]{\text{KCN, Et-OH-H}_2O} \underset{\text{Propanenitrile}}{CH_3CH_2CN}$

Ethanol

(*viii*)

Aniline (NH$_2$) $\xrightarrow[\text{Diazotisation}]{\text{NaNO}_2/\text{HCl},273-278K}$ (ring)$-\overset{+}{N}\equiv NCl^-$ $\xrightarrow[\begin{array}{c}\text{Sandmeyer}\\ \text{reaction}\end{array}]{\text{CuCl/HCl}}$ (Cl) Chlorobenzene

(ix) $2CH_3-CH(Cl)-CH_2CH_3 + 2Na \xrightarrow[\text{Wurtz reaction}]{\text{Dry ether}} CH_3CH_2-CH(CH_3)-CH(CH_3)-CH_2CH_3 + 2NaCl$

2-Chlorobutane   3,4–Dimethylhexane

(x) $CH_3-C(CH_3)=CH_2 \xrightarrow[\text{Mark. addition}]{\text{HCl}} CH_3-C(CH_3)(Cl)-CH_3$

2–Methyl–1–propene   2–Chloro–2–methylpropane

(xi) $CH_3CH_2Cl \xrightarrow[\substack{\text{(Nucleophilic} \\ \text{subsitution)}}]{\text{KCN, EtOH–H}_2\text{O}} CH_3CH_2CN \xrightarrow[\text{Hydrolysis}]{H^+/H_2O} CH_3CH_2COOH$

Ethyl chloride   Propanenitrite   Propanoic acid

(xii) $CH_3CH_2CH=CH_2 \xrightarrow[\text{Anti–Mark. Addition}]{\text{HBr/RCOOR}} CH_3CH_2CH_2CH_2Br \xrightarrow[\text{Finkelstein reaction}]{\text{NaI, acetone}} CH_3CH_2CH_2CH_2I$

But–1–ene   n–Butyliodide

(xiii) $CH_3-CH(Cl)-CH_3 \xrightarrow[\text{Dehydrohalogenation}]{\text{KOH(alc), }\Delta} CH_3-CH=CH_2 \xrightarrow[\substack{\text{Anti–Mark.} \\ \text{addition}}]{\text{HBr, Peroxide}} CH_3CH_2CH_2Br \xrightarrow[]{\text{KOH(aq), }\Delta} CH_3CH_2CH_2OH$

2–Chloropropane   Propene   1–Bromo–propane   1-Propanol

(xiv) $CH_3-CH(OH)-CH_3 + 4I_2 + 6NaOH \xrightarrow[\substack{\text{Iodoform} \\ \text{reaction}}]{\Delta} CHI_3 + CH_3COONa + 5NaI + 5H_2O$

Iso propyl alcohol   Iodoform

(xv) Chlorobenzene$-Cl \xrightarrow[\text{(Nitration)}]{\text{Conc. HNO}_3 + \text{Conc. H}_2\text{SO}_4} O_2N-$p-Nitrochlorobenzene$-Cl \xrightarrow[\text{(ii) Dil HCl}]{\text{(i)15\% NaOH, 433K}} O_2N-$$-OH$

Chlorobenzene   p-Nitrochlorobenzene (Major isomer)   p-nitrophenol

(xvi) $CH_3-CH(Br)-CH_3 \xrightarrow[\text{Dehydrohalogenation}]{\text{KOH(alc), }\Delta} CH_3CH=CH_2 \xrightarrow[\text{Peroxide effect}]{\text{HBr/Peroxide}} CH_3CH_2CH_2Br$

2–Bromopropane   1–Bromopropane

(xvii) $2CH_3CH_2-Cl + 2Na \xrightarrow[\text{Wurtz reaction}]{\text{Dry ether}} CH_3CH_2-CH_2CH_3 + 2NaCl$

Chloroethane   Butane

(xviii) Benzene $\xrightarrow[]{\text{Br}_2/\text{FeBr}_3}$ $-Br \xrightarrow[\text{Fittig reaction}]{2Na, \text{Dry ether}, \Delta}$ Biphenyl $+ 2NaBr$

Benzene   Biphenyl

(xix) $CH_3-C(CH_3)(Br)-CH_3 \xrightarrow[\text{Dehydrohalogenation}]{\text{KOH(alc.), }\Delta} CH_3-C(CH_3)=CH_2 \xrightarrow[\substack{\text{Anti Mark.} \\ \text{Addition}}]{\text{HBr, Peroxide}} CH_3-CH(CH_3)-CH_2Br$

tert–Butylbromide   Isobutyl bromide

(xx) Aniline$-NH_2 + CHCl_3 + 3KOH \xrightarrow[\substack{\text{Carbylamine} \\ \text{reaction}}]{\text{Warm}}$ $-N\equiv C + 3KCl + 3H_2O$

Aniline

19. The treatment of alkyl chlorides with aqueous KOH leads to the formation of alcohols but in the presence of alcoholic KOH, alkenes are major products. Explain.

Sol. In aqueous solution, KOH is almost completely ionized to give OH^- ions which being a strong nucleophile brings about a substitution reaction on alkyl halides to form alcohols. Further in the aqueous solution, OH^- ions are highly solvated (hydrated). This solvation reduces the basic character of OH^- ions which, therefore, fails to abstract a hydrogen from the β-carbon of the alkyl chloride to form alkenes. In contrast, an alcoholic solution of KOH contains alkoxide (RO^-) ion which being a much stronger base than OH^- ions perferentially eliminates a molecule of HCl from an alkyl chloride to form alkenes.

20. Primary alkyl halide C_4H_9Br (a) reacted with alcoholic KOH to give compound (b) Compound (b) is reacted with HBr to give (c) which is an isomer of (a). When (a) is reacted with sodium metal it give compound (d), C_8H_{18} which is different from the compound formed when n-butyl bromide is reacted with sodium. Give the structural formula of (a) and write the equations for all the reactions.

Sol. (*i*) There are two primary alkyl halides having the molecular formula, C_4H_9Br.

$$CH_3CH_2CH_2CH_2Br \text{ and } \underset{\text{Isobutyl bromide}}{CH_3\overset{\displaystyle \overset{CH_3}{|}}{CH}-CH_2Br}$$
$$\underset{n-\text{Butyl bromide}}{}$$

(*ii*) Since compound (*a*) when reacted with Na metal gave a compound (*d*) with molecular formula C_8H_{18} which was different from the compound obtained when *n*-butyl bromide was reacted with Na metal, therefore, (*a*) must be isobutyl bromide and compound (*d*) must be 2,5-dimethylhexane.

$$2CH_3\,CH_2\,CH_2\,CH_2\,Br + 2Na \xrightarrow{\text{Wurtz reaction}} \underset{n\text{-Octane}}{CH_3CH_2\,CH_2CH_2CH_2\,CH_2CH_2CH_3}$$

$$2CH_3-\overset{\overset{\displaystyle CH_3}{|}}{CH}-CH_2Br + 2Na \xrightarrow{\text{Wurtz reaction}} \underset{\text{2,5-dimethylhexane \ (d)}}{CH_3-\overset{\overset{\displaystyle CH_3}{|}}{CH}-CH_2-CH_2-\overset{\overset{\displaystyle CH_3}{|}}{CH}-CH_3}$$

(*iii*) If compound (*a*) is isobutyl bromide, than the compound (*b*) which it gives on treatment with alcoholic KOH must be 2-methyl-1-propane.

$$\underset{\text{Isobutyl bromide}}{CH_3-\overset{\overset{\displaystyle CH_3}{|}}{CH}-CH_2Br} \xrightarrow[\text{Dehydrohalogenation}]{\text{KOH (alc), }\Delta} \underset{\text{2-Methyl-1-propane (b)}}{CH_3-\overset{\overset{\displaystyle CH_3}{|}}{C}=CH_2}$$

(*iv*) The compound (*b*) on treatment with HBr gives compound (*c*) in accordance with Markownikoff rule. Therefore, compound (*c*) is tert-butyl bromide which is an isomer of compound (*a*) ,*i.e.*, isobutyl bromide.

$$CH_3-\overset{\overset{\displaystyle CH_3}{|}}{C}=CH_2 \xrightarrow{\text{HBr}} CH_3-\overset{\overset{\displaystyle CH_3}{|}}{\underset{\underset{\displaystyle Br}{|}}{C}}-CH_3$$
$$\underset{\substack{\text{tert}-\text{Butylbromide (c)}\\ (\text{an isomer of compound (a)})}}{}$$

Thus
(*a*) is isobutyl bromide,   (*b*) is 2-methyl-1-propane,
(*c*) is tert-butylbromide, and   (*d*) is 2, 5-dimethylhexane.

21.   **What happens when**
(*i*) n-butyl chloride is treated with alcoholic KOH.
(*ii*) bromobenzene is treated with Mg in the presence of dry ether.
(*iii*) chlorobenzene is subjected to hydrolysis.
(*iv*) ethyl chloride is treated with aqueous. KOH.
(*v*) methyl bromide is treated with sodium in the presence of dry ether.
(*vi*) methyl chloride is treated with KCN.

Sol.

(*i*) $\underset{n-\text{Butylchloride}}{CH_3CH_2-CH_2-CH_2-Cl} + KOH\text{ (alc)} \xrightarrow[\text{Dehydrohalogenation}]{\Delta} \underset{\text{But}-1-\text{ene}}{CH_3CH_2CH=CH_2} + KCl + H_2O$

(*ii*) $\underset{\text{Bromobenzene}}{\boxed{}-Br} + Mg \xrightarrow{\text{Dry ether}} \underset{\text{Phenylmagnesium bromide}}{\boxed{}-MgBr}$

(*iii*) $\underset{\text{Chlorobenzene}}{\boxed{}-Cl} + NaOH\ (aq) \xrightarrow[\text{(ii) Dil. HCl}]{\text{(i)}6-8\%\text{ NaOH, 623K, 300 atm}} \boxed{}-OH$

(*iv*) $\underset{\text{Ethyl chloride}}{CH_3CH_2-Cl} + KOH\text{ (aq)} \xrightarrow[\Delta]{\text{Hydrolysis}} \underset{\text{Ethyl alcohol}}{CH_3CH_2-OH} + KCl + H_2O$

(*v*) $\underset{\text{Methylbromide}}{CH_3-Br + 2Na + Br-CH_3} \xrightarrow[\text{(wurtz reaction)}]{\text{Dry ether}} CH_3-CH_3 + 2NaBr$

(*vi*) $\underset{\substack{\text{Methyl}\\\text{chloride}}}{CH_3-Cl} + KCN \xrightarrow[\text{Nucleophilic substitution}]{\text{Et}-OH-H_2O,\ \Delta} \underset{\text{Methyl cyanide}}{CH_3C\equiv N} + KCl$

Past year Exercise

Case/Passage Based Questions

DIRECTIONS (Qs. 1-5) : *Following are the case/passage based questions.*

The substitution reaction of alkyl halide mainly occurs by S_N1 or S_N2 mechanism. Whatever mechanism alkyl halides follow for the substitution reaction to occur, the polarity of the carbon halogen bond is responsible for these substitution reactions. The rate of S_N1 reactions are governed by the stability of carbocation whereas for S_N2 reactions steric factor is the deciding factor. If the starting material is a chiral compound, we may end up with an inverted product or racemic mixture depending upon the type of mechanism followed by alkyl halide. Cleavage of ethers with HI is also governed by steric factor and stability of carbocation, which indicates that in organic chemistry, these two major factors help us in deinding the kind of product formed.

1. Predict the stereochemistry of the product formed if an optically active alkyl halide undergoes substitution reaction by S_N1 mechanism.
2. Name the instrument used for measuring the angle by which the plane polarised light is rotated.
3. Predict the major product formed when 2-Bromopentane reacts with alcoholic KOH.
4. Give one use of CHI_3.
5. Write the structures of the products formed when anisole is treated with HI.

Very Short Answer Questions

6. Write the IUPAC name of

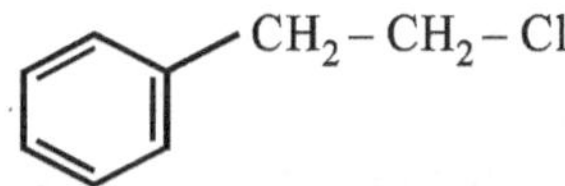

7. Out of chlorobenzene and benzyl chloride, which one gets easily hydrolysed by aqueous NaOH and why?

8. Out of 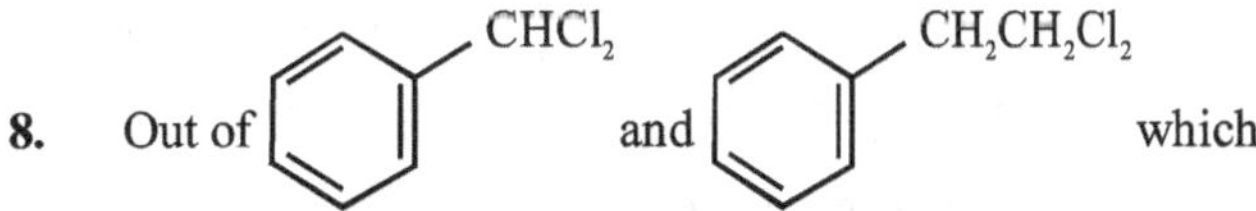 and which is an example of benzylic halide?

9. Write the structure of the following compound 3-(4-chlorophenyl)-2-methylpropane.

10. Which will react faster in S_N2 displacement, 1-bromopentane or 2-bromopentane and why?

11. What happens when bromine attacks

$$CH_2 = CH - CH_2 - C \equiv CH ?$$

12. Write the IUPAC name of the following compound :

$$CH_3 - \underset{\underset{CH_3}{|}}{\overset{\overset{CH_3}{|}}{C}} - \underset{\underset{Cl}{|}}{CH} - CH_3$$

13. Which aerosol depletes ozone layer ?

14. Write the IUPAC name of the following compound :

$$CH_3 - \underset{\underset{Br}{|}}{CH} - CH_2 - \underset{\underset{Cl}{|}}{CH} - CH_3$$

15. Write the IUPAC name of $CH_3\underset{\underset{Cl}{|}}{CH} - CH_2CH = CH_2$.

16. What happens when $CH_3 - Br$ is treated with KCN?

17. Write the IUPAC name of $CH_3CH = CH - \underset{\underset{Br}{|}}{\overset{\overset{CH_3}{|}}{C}} - CH_3$.

18. What happens when ethyl chloride is treated with aqueous KOH?

19. Write the IUPAC name of $(CH_3)_2CHCH(Cl)CH_3$

20. Which compound in the following pair undergoes faster S_N1 reaction?

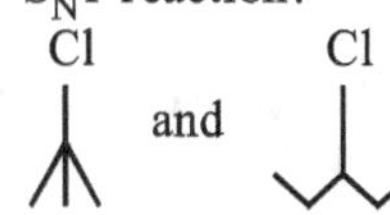

21. How may methyl bromide be preferentially converted to methyl isocyanide?

22. Identify the chiral molecule in the following pair:

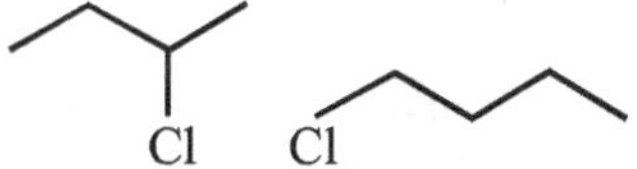

23. Which would undergo S_N1 reaction faster in the following pair?

$$CH_3 - CH_2 - Br \text{ and } CH_3 - \underset{\underset{Br}{|}}{\overset{\overset{CH_3}{|}}{C}} - CH_3$$

Short Answer Questions

24. Give reasons for the following :
    (a) The presence of $- NO_2$ group at ortho or para position increases the reactivity of haloarenes towards nucleophilic substitution reactions.
    (b) *p*-Dichlorobenzene has higher melting point than that of ortho or meta isomer.
    (c) Thionyl chloride method is preferred for preparing alkyl chloride from alcohols.

    OR

    (a) Write equation for preparation of l-iodobutane from l-chlorobutane.
    (b) Out of 2-bromopentane, 2-bromo-2-methylbutane and 1-bromopentane, which compound is most reactive towards elimination reaction and why?
    (c) Give IUPAC name of $CH_3 - CH = CH - \underset{\underset{Br}{|}}{\overset{\overset{CH_3}{|}}{C}} - CH_3$

25. (a) Identify the chiral molecule in the following pair :

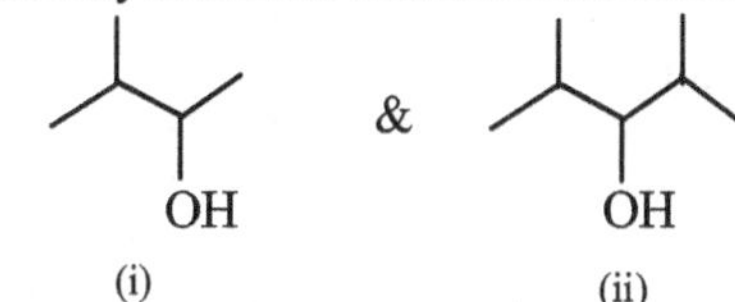

    (b) Write the structure of the product when chlorobenzene is treated with methyl chloride in the presence of sodium metal and dry ether.

(c)   Write the structure of the alkene formed by dehydrohalogenation of 1-bromo-1 methylcyclohexane with alcoholic KOH.

26. Write the structures of the main products in the following reactions:

(i) 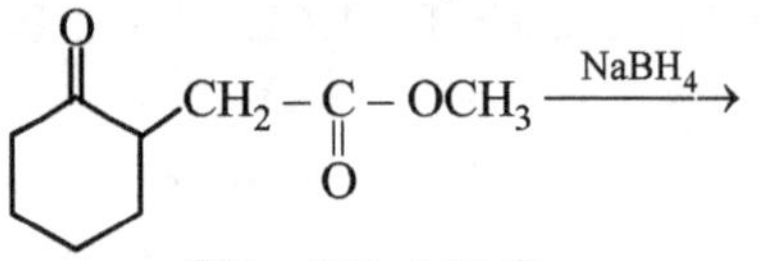 [cyclohexanone structure] $CH_2 - \underset{\underset{O}{\|}}{C} - OCH_3 \xrightarrow{NaBH_4}$

(ii) 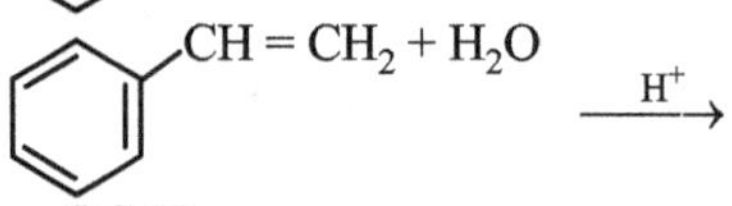 [benzene ring] $CH = CH_2 + H_2O \xrightarrow{H^+}$

(iii) 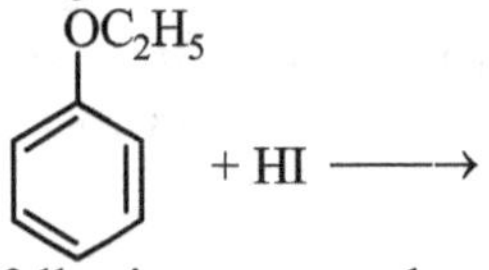 [benzene ring with OC_2H_5] $+ HI \longrightarrow$

27. The following compounds are given to you:
2-Bromopentane, 2-Bromo-2-methylbutane, 1-Bromopentane
(a)   Write the compound which is most reactive towards S_N2 reaction.
(b)   Write the compound which is optically active.
(c)   Write the compound which is most reactive towards β-elimination reaction.

28. Answer the following
(i)   Haloalkanes easily dissolve in organic solvents.
(ii)   What is known as racemic mixture? Give an example.
(iii)   Of the two bromo derivatives $C_6H_5CH(CH_3)Br$ and $(C_6H_5)CH(C_6H_5)Br$, which one is more reactive in S_N1 substitution reaction and why?

29. (i)   Write the mechanism of the following reaction.
$$n-BuBr + KCN \xrightarrow[H_2O]{C_2H_5OH} n-BuCN$$
(ii)   Why chlorobenzene has lower dipole moment than cyclohexyl chloride.

30. Answer the following questions:
(i)   What is meant by chirality of a compound?
(ii)   Which one of the following compounds is more easily hydrolysed by KOH and why? $CH_3CHClCH_2CH_3$ or $CH_3CH_2CH_2CH_2Cl$
(iii)   Which one undergoes S_N2 substitution reaction faster and why?

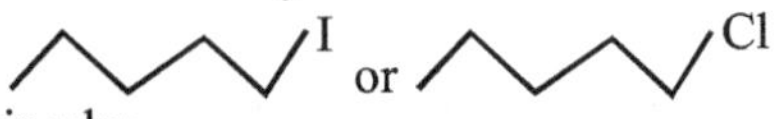

[zigzag structure with I] or [zigzag structure with Cl]

31. Explain why
(i)   alkyl halides are polar yet they are immiscible with water.
(ii)   Grignard reagents are prepared strictly under anhydrous conditions.

32. Although chlorine is highly electronegative, it undergoes electrophilic aromatic substitution in o- and p- position.

33. Give reasons for the following :
(i)   Ethyl iodide undergoes S_N2 reaction faster than ethyl bromide
(ii)   (±) 2-Butanol is optically inactive.
(iii)   C – X bond length in halobenzene is smaller than C – X bond length in $CH_3 – X$.

34. Chlorobenzene is extremely less reactive towards a nucleophilic substitution reaction. Give two reasons for the same.

35. Why does p-dichlorobenzene have a higher m.p. than its o- and m-isomers?

36. Account for the following :
(a)   The C – Cl bond length in chlorobenzene is shorter than that in $CH_3 – Cl$.
(b)   Chloroform is stored in closed dark brown bottles.

37. Give chemical tests to distinguish between the following pairs of compounds :
(i)   Benzyl chloride and Chlorobenzene
(ii)   Chloroform and Carbon tetrachloride

38. Explain why :
(i)   The dipole moment of chlorobenzene is lower than that of cyclohexyl chloride.
(ii)   Alkyl halides, though polar, are immiscible with water.

39. Explain the following :
(a)   The dipole moment of chlorobenzene is lower than that of cyclohexyl chloride.
(b)   Alkyl halides, though polar, are immiscible with water.
(c)   Grignard reagents should be prepared under anhydrous condition.

40. (a)   Draw the structures of major monohalo products in each of the following reactions :
(i) 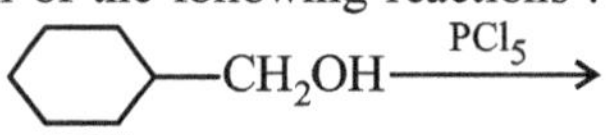 [cyclohexane ring]$-CH_2OH \xrightarrow{PCl_5}$
(ii) 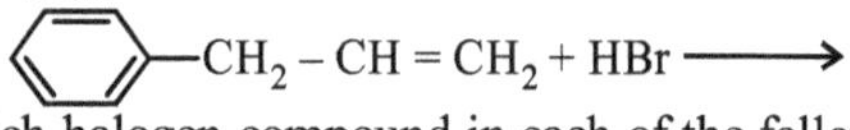 [benzene ring]$-CH_2 - CH = CH_2 + HBr \longrightarrow$
(b)   Which halogen compound in each of the following pairs will react faster in S_N2 reaction:
(i) CH_3Br or CH_3I (ii) $(CH_3)_3C–Cl$ or $CH_3–Cl$

41. Draw the structure of major monohalo product in each of the following reactions :
(i) 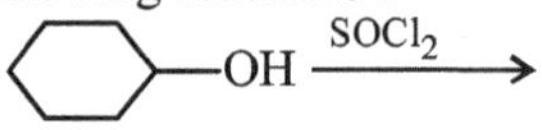 [cyclohexane ring]$-OH \xrightarrow{SOCl_2}$
(ii) 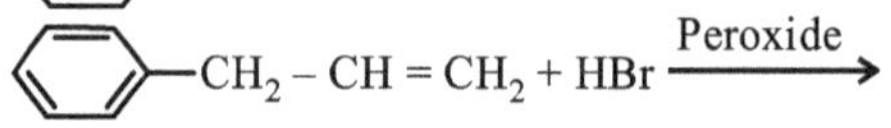 [benzene ring]$-CH_2 - CH = CH_2 + HBr \xrightarrow{Peroxide}$

42. Give reasons:
(a)   n-Butyl bromide has higher boiling point than t-butyl bromide.
(b)   The presence of nitro group ($–NO_2$) at o/p positions increases the reactivity of haloarenes towards nucleophilic substitution reactions.

43. How do you convert :
(i)   Chlorobenzene to biphenyl
(ii)   Propene to 1-iodopropane
(iii)   2-bromobutane to but-2-ene

OR

Write the major product(s) in the following :

(i) 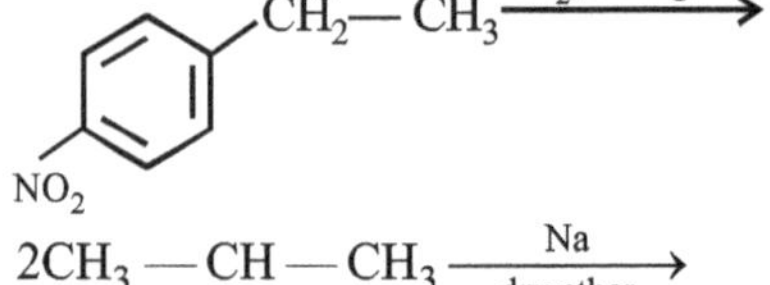 [benzene ring with NO_2]$CH_2 — CH_3 \xrightarrow{Br_2,UV\ light}$

(ii) $2CH_3 — \underset{\underset{Cl}{|}}{CH} — CH_3 \xrightarrow[dry\ ether]{Na}$

(iii) $CH_3 — CH_2 — Br \xrightarrow{AgCN}$

NCERT Exemplar

Multiple Choice Questions

1. Toluene reacts with a halogen in the presence of iron (III) chloride giving ortho and para halo compounds. The reaction is
   (a) electrophilic elimination reaction
   (b) electrophilic substitution reaction
   (c) free radical addition reaction
   (d) nucleophilic substitution reaction

2. Arrange the following compounds in the increasing order of their densities.

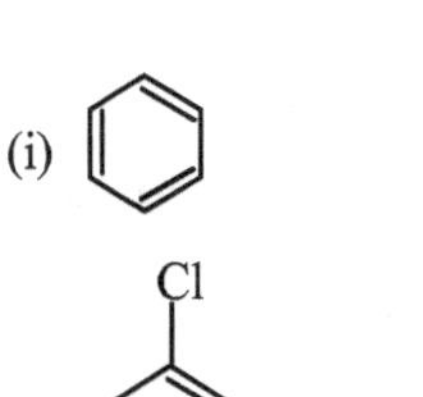

(i)

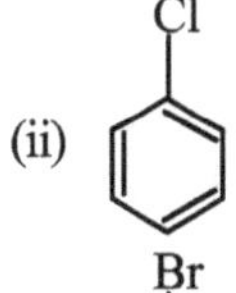

(ii)

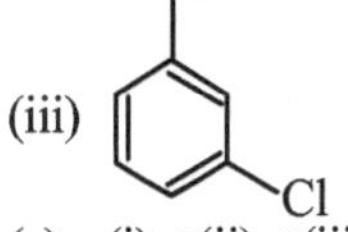

(iii)

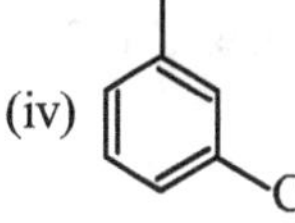

(iv)

   (a) (i) < (ii) < (iii) < (iv)
   (b) (i) < (iii) < (iv) < (ii)
   (c) (iv) < (iii) < (ii) < (i)
   (d) (ii) < (iv) < (iii) < (i)

3. The position of Br in the compound $CH_3CH = CHC(Br)(CH_3)_2$ can be classified as ....
   (a) allyl   (b) aryl
   (c) vinyl   (d) secondary

4. Chloromethane on treatment with excess of ammonia yields mainly
   (a) N, N-dimethylmethanamine $\left(CH_3 —N\begin{smallmatrix}CH_3\\CH_3\end{smallmatrix}\right)$
   (b) N - methylmethanamine $(CH_3 — NH — CH_3)$
   (c) methanamine (CH_3NH_2)
   (d) mixture containing all these in equal proportion

5. Reaction of $C_6H_5CH_2Br$ with aqueous sodium hydroxide follows ....
   (a) S_N1 mechanism
   (b) S_N2 mechanism
   (c) Any of the above two depending upon the temperature of reaction
   (d) Saytzeff rule

6. Which is the correct increasing order of boiling points of the following compounds?
   1 - bromoethane, 1 - bromopropane, 1 - bromobutane, Bromobenzene
   (a) Bromobenzene < 1 - bromobutane < 1 bromopropane < 1- bromoethane
   (b) Bromobenzene < 1 - bromobutane < 1 - bromopropane < 1- bromobutane
   (c) 1 - bromopropane < 1 - bromorpropane < 1 - bromoethane < Bromobenzene
   (d) 1 - bromoethane < 1 - bromopropane < 1 - bromobutane < Bromobenzene

Assertion & Reason Questions

DIRECTIONS (Qs. 7-9) : *Each of these questions contains an assertion followed by reason. Read them carefully and answer the question on the basis of following options. You have to select the one that best describes the two statements.*
   (a) If both Assertion and Reason are correct and the Reason is a correct explanation of the Assertion.
   (b) If both Assertion and Reason are correct but Reason is not a correct explanation of the Assertion.
   (c) If the Assertion is correct but Reason is incorrect.
   (d) If the Assertion is incorrect but the Reason is correct.

7. **Assertion :** Phosphorus chlorides (tri and penta) are preferred over thionyl chloride for the preparation of alkyl chlorides from alcohols.
   Reason : Phosphorus chlorides give in pure alkyl halides.

8. **Assertion :** tert-butyl bromide undergoes Wurtz reaction to give 2, 2, 3, 3-tetramethylbutane.
   Reason : In Wurtz reaction, alkyl halides react with sodium in dry ether to give hydrocarbon containing double the number of carbon atoms present in the halide.

9. **Assertion :** Nitration of chlorobenzene leads to the formation of *m*-nitrochlorobenzene.
   Reason (R) : $–NO_2$ group is a *m*-directing group.

Short Answer Questions

10. Which of the following compounds will have the highest melting point and why?

(I)   (II)   (III)

11. How do polar solvents help in the first step in S_N1 mechanism?

12. How can you obtain iodoethane from ethanol when no other iodine containing reagent except NaI is available in the laboratory?

13. Cyanide ion acts as an ambident nucleophile. From which end it acts as a stronger nucleophile in aqueous medium? Give reason for your answer.

Objective Practice Exercise

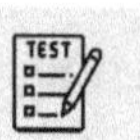

Multiple Choice Questions

DIRECTIONS : *This section contains multiple choice questions. Each question has four choices (a), (b), (c) and (d) out of which only one is correct.*

1. Which of the following is a primary halide?
  (a) Isopropyl iodide   (b) Secondary butyl iodide
  (c) Tertiary butyl bromide   (d) Neohexyl chloride

2. Among the following compounds, which one has the shortest C – Cl bond?

  (a) 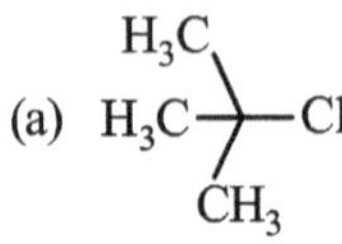   (b) 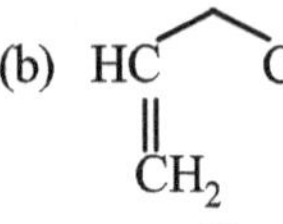

  (c) 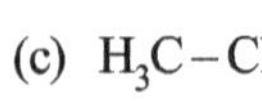   (d) 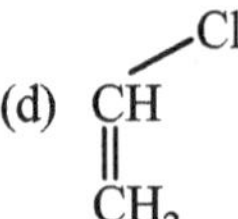

3. When two halogen atoms are attached to adjacent carbon atom then it is :
  (a) *vic*-dihalide   (b) *gem*-dihalide
  (c) α, ω-halide   (d) α, β-halide

4. The order of reactivity of the given haloalkanes towards nucleophile is :
  (a) $RI > RBr > KCl$ (b) $RCl > RBr > RI$
  (c) $RBr > RCl > RI$ (d) $RBr > RI > RCl$

5. Which one of the following is not an allylic halide?
  (a) 4-Bromopent-2-ene
  (b) 3-Bromo-2-methylbut-1-ene
  (c) 1-Bromobut-2-ene
  (d) 4-Bromobut-1-ene

6. An organic compound A (C_4H_9Cl) on reaction with Na/diethyl ether gives a hydrocarbon which on monochlorination gives only one chloro derivative, then A is
  (a) tert-butyl chloride   (b) sec-butyl chloride
  (c) iso-butyl chloride   (d) n-butyl chloride

7. Which chloride is least reactive with the hydrolysis point of view?
  (a) CH_3Cl (b) CH_3CH_2Cl
  (c) $(CH_3)_3CCl$ (d) $CH_2 = CH - Cl$

8. How many structural isomers are possible for a compound with molecular formula C_3H_7Cl ?
  (a) 2   (b) 5   (c) 7   (d) 9

9. For the compounds
  CH_3Cl, CH_3Br, CH_3I and CH_3F,
  the correct order of increasing C-halogen bond length is:
  (a) $CH_3F < CH_3Cl < CH_3Br < CH_3I$
  (b) $CH_3F < CH_3Br < CH_3Cl < CH_3I$
  (c) $CH_3F < CH_3I < CH_3Br < CH_3Cl$
  (d) $CH_3Cl < CH_3Br < CH_3F < CH_3I$

10. A set of compounds in which the reactivity of halogen atom in the ascending order is

  (a) chlorobenzene, vinyl chloride, chloroethane
  (b) chloroethane, chlorobenzene, vinyl chloride
  (c) vinyl chloride, chlorobenzene, chloroethane
  (d) vinyl chloride, chloroethane, chlorobenzene

11. The compound which contains all the four 1°, 2°, 3° and 4° carbon atoms is
  (a) 2, 3-dimethylpentane
  (b) 3-chloro-2, 3-dimethylpentane
  (c) 2, 3, 4-trimethylpentane
  (d) 3,3-dimethylpentane

12. Identify Z in the following series
$$C_2H_5I \xrightarrow{\text{Alc. KOH}} X \xrightarrow{Br_2} Y \xrightarrow{KCN} Z$$
  (a) CH_3CH_2CN (b) $NCCH_2–CH_2CN$
  (c) $BrCH_2–CH_2CN$ (d) $BrCH=CHCN$

13. Benzene hexachloride is
  (a) 1, 2, 3, 4, 5, 6-hexachlorocyclohexane
  (b) 1, 1, 1, 6, 6, 6-hexachlorocyclohexane
  (c) 1, 6-phenyl-1, 6-chlorohexane
  (d) 1, 1-phenyl-6, 6-chlorohexane

14. In the following groups :
  $–OAc$ (I) $–OMe$ (II)
  $– OSO_2 Me$ (III) $–OSO_2CF_3$ (IV)
  the order of leaving group ability is
  (a) $I > II > III > IV$ (b) $IV > III > I > II$
  (c) $III > II > I > IV$ (d) $II > III > IV > I$

15. Which of the following is most reactive toward S_N2 reaction?
  (a) $CH_2{=}CH - CH_2 - Cl$ (b) $Ph - CH_2 - Cl$
  (c) $Me - O \frown Cl$ (d) $Ph - \underset{\underset{O}{\|}}{C} - CH_2 - Cl$

16. The major product formed when 1, 1, 1-trichloro-propane is treated with aqueous potassium hydroxide is:
  (a) Propyne   (b) 1-Propanol
  (c) 2-Propanol   (d) Propionic acid

17. Arrange the following halides in the decreasing order of S_N1 reactivity :
  $CH_3CH_2CH_2Cl,$ $CH_2 = CHCH(Cl)CH_3,$
      (I)   (II)
  $CH_3CH_2CH(Cl)CH_3$
      (III)
  (a) $I > II > III$ (b) $II > I > III$
  (c) $II > III > I$ (d) $III > II > I$

18. Which of the following will give vinyl chloride ?
  (a) $CH_2 = CH_2 + Cl_2 \xrightarrow{600°C}$
  (b) $ClCH_2 – CH_2Cl \xrightarrow[\text{ethanol}]{KOH}$
  (c) $CH \equiv CH + HCl \xrightarrow{Hg^{2+}}$
  (d) All of these

19. Comment on the following reactions
    (i) $CH_3OH + NaCl \longrightarrow$
    (ii) $CH_3OH + HCl \longrightarrow$
    (a) Both reactions take place easily
    (b) Only reaction (ii) takes place
    (c) Reaction (ii) takes places faster than (i)
    (d) None of the two reactions in possible

20. Conant Finkelstein reaction for the preparation of alkyl iodide is based upon the fact that
    (a) Sodium iodide is soluble in methanol, while sodium chloride is insoluble in methanol
    (b) Sodium iodide is soluble in methanol, while NaCl and NaBr are insoluble in methanol
    (c) Sodium iodide is insoluble in methanol, while NaCl and NaBr are soluble
    (d) The three halogens differ considerably in their electronegativity

21. When chlorine is passed through propene at 400°C, which of the following is formed ?
    (a) PVC
    (b) Allyl chloride
    (c) Alkyl chloride
    (d) 1, 2-Dichloroethane

22. 2-Bromopentane is heated with potassium ethoxide in ethanol. The major product obtained is
    (a) 2-ethoxypentane
    (b) pentene-1
    (c) *trans*-2-pentene
    (d) *cis*-pentene-2

23. When $CH_3CH_2CHCl_2$ is treated with $NaNH_2$, the product formed is
    (a) $CH_3 - CH = CH_2$
    (b) $CH_3 - C \equiv CH$
    (c) $CH_3CH_2CH \diagdown \begin{smallmatrix} NH_2 \\ NH_2 \end{smallmatrix}$
    (d) $CH_3CH_2CH \diagdown \begin{smallmatrix} Cl \\ NH_2 \end{smallmatrix}$

24. Aryl fluoride may be prepared from arene diazonium chloride using :
    (a) HBF_4/Δ
    (b) $HBF_4/NaNO_2, Cu, \Delta$
    (c) CuF/HF
    (d) Cu/HF

25. When *m*-chloronitrobenzene is treated with sodamide in presene of liquid ammonia, main product is
    (a) *o*-Nitroaniline
    (b) *p*-Nitroaniline
    (c) *m* - Nitroaniline
    (d) All of these

26. Bromination of toluene gives
    (a) only *m*-substituted product
    (b) only *p*-substituted product
    (c) mixture of *o*-and *p*-substituted products
    (d) mixture of *o*-and *m*-substituted products

27. What is the product of the following reaction ?

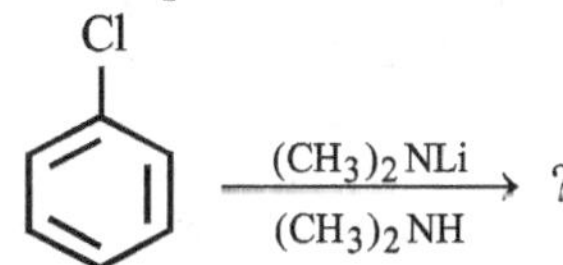

    (a) N, N-dimethylaniline
    (b) phenyllithium (C_6H_5Li)
    (c) *para*-chloro-N, N-dimethylaniline
    (d) *meta*-chloro-N, N-dimethylaniline

28. Chlorobenzene can be prepared by reacting aniline with :
    (a) hydrochloric acid
    (b) cuprous chloride
    (c) chlorine in presence of anhydrous aluminium chloride
    (d) nitrous acid followed by heating with cuprous chloride

29. Aryl halides are extremely less reactive towards nucleophilic substitution than alkylhalides. Which of the following accounts for this ?
    (i)   Due to resonance in aryl halides.
    (ii) In alkyl halides carbon atom in C–X bond is sp^2 hybridised whereas in aryl halides carbon atom in C–X bond is sp^3 hybridized.
    (iii) Due to stability of phenyl cation.
    (iv) Due to possible repulsion there are less chances of nucleophile to approach electron rich arenes.
    (a) (i), (ii) and (iv)
    (b) (i), (ii) and (iii)
    (c) (i) and (iv)
    (d) (ii), (iii) and (iv)

30. Which of the following synthetic schemes would be the best for the synthesis of the compound, 2-bromo-1-chloro-4-nitrobenzene?

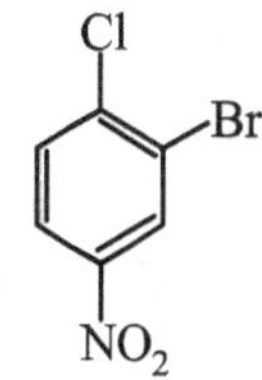

    2-bromo-1-chloro-4-nitrobenzene

    (a) $\xrightarrow[FeBr_3]{Br_2} \xrightarrow[H_2SO_4]{HNO_3} \xrightarrow[AlCl_3]{Cl_2}$
    (b) $\xrightarrow[FeBr_3]{Br_2} \xrightarrow[AlCl_3]{Cl_2} \xrightarrow[H_2SO_4]{HNO_3}$
    (c) $\xrightarrow[AlCl_3]{Cl_2} \xrightarrow[H_2SO_4]{HNO_3} \xrightarrow[FeBr_3]{Br_2}$
    (d) $\xrightarrow[AlCl_3]{Cl_2} \xrightarrow[FeBr_3]{Br_2} \xrightarrow[H_2SO_4]{HNO_3}$

31. The correct kinetic rate equation for the addition-elimination mechanism of nucleophilic aromatic substitution
    (a) rate = k [aryl halide] [nucleophile]
    (b) rate = k [aryl halide]
    (c) rate = k [aryl halide] [nucleophile]^2
    (d) rate = k [nucleophile]

32. When hydrochloric acid gas is treated with propene in presence of benzoyl peroxide, it gives
    (a) 2-chloropropane
    (b) allyl chloride
    (c) *n*-propyl chloride
    (d) No reaction occurs

33. Elimination of bromine from 2-bromobutane results in the formation of –
    (a) predominantly 2-butyne
    (b) predominantly 1-butene
    (c) predominantly 2-butene
    (d) equimolar mixture of 1- and 2-butenes

34. $C_3H_8 + Cl_2 \xrightarrow{\text{Light}} C_3H_7Cl + HCl$ is an example of

    (a) substitution   (b) elimination

    (c) addition   (d) rearrangement reaction

35. $CH_3 - CH_2 - CH_2 - Cl \xrightarrow[\text{KOH}]{\text{alc.}} B \xrightarrow{\text{HBr}} C \xrightarrow[\text{ether}]{\text{Na}} D$

In the above sequence of reactions, the product D is

    (a) propane   (b) 2, 3-dimethylbutane

    (c) hexane   (d) allyl bromide

36. In the following sequence of reactions

$C_2H_5Br \xrightarrow{\text{AgCN}} X \xrightarrow{\text{Reduction}} Y$; Y is

    (a) *n*-propyl amine   (b) isopropyl amine

    (c) ethyl amine   (d) ethylmethyl amine

37. The reaction conditions leading to the best yield of C_2H_5Cl are :

    (a) C_2H_6 (excess) $+ Cl_2 \xrightarrow{\text{UV light}}$

    (b) $C_2H_6 + Cl_2 \xrightarrow[\text{room temperature}]{\text{dark}}$

    (c) $C_2H_6 + Cl_2$ (excess) $\xrightarrow{\text{UV light}}$

    (d) $C_2H_6 + Cl_2 \xrightarrow{\text{UV light}}$

38. On sulphonation of C_6H_5Cl

    (a) *m*-chlorobenzenesulphonic acid is formed.

    (b) benzenesulphonic acid is formed.

    (c) *o*-chlorobenzenesulphonic acid is formed.

    (d) mixture of *o*- and *p*-chlorobenzene sulphonic acid is formed.

39. When chlorobenzene is reacted with acetyl chloride in the presence of anhydrous $AlCl_3$, the major product formed is

    (a) 2-chloroacetophenone   (b) 3-chloroacetophenone

    (c) 4-chloroacetophenone   (d) 1, 4-dichlorobenzene

40. Which of the following compounds will give racemic mixture on nucleophilic substitution by OH^- ion?

    (i) $CH_3 - \underset{\underset{C_2H_5}{|}}{CH} - Br$ (ii) $CH_3 - \underset{\underset{C_2H_5}{|}}{\overset{\overset{Br}{|}}{C}} - CH_3$

    (iii) $CH_3 - \underset{\underset{C_2H_5}{|}}{CH} - CH_2Br$

    (a) (i)   (b) (i), (ii) and (iii)

    (c) (ii) and (iii)   (d) (i) and (iii)

41. Ethanol can be prepared more easily by which reaction ?

    (i) $CH_3CH_2Br + H_2O \longrightarrow CH_3CH_2OH$

    (ii) $CH_3CH_2Br + Ag_2O$ (in boiling water)

                   $\longrightarrow CH_3CH_2OH$

    (a) by (i) reaction

    (b) by (ii) reaction

    (c) Both reactions proceed at same rate

    (d) by none

42. The best method for the conversion of an alcohol into an alkyl chloride is by treating the alcohol with

    (a) PCl_5

    (b) dry HCl in the presence of anhydrous $ZnCl_2$

    (c) $SOCl_2$ in presence of pyridine

    (d) None of these

43. *n*-Propyl bromide on treatment with ethanolic potassium hydroxide produces

    (a) propane   (b) propene

    (c) propyne   (d) propanol

44. Gem dihalides on treatment with alcoholic KOH give :

    (a) alkyne   (b) alkene

    (c) alkane   (d) all of these

45. Which of the following reactions is an example of nucleophilic substitution reaction?

    (a) $2\,RX + 2\,Na \rightarrow R - R + 2\,NaX$

    (b) $RX + H_2 \rightarrow RH + HX$

    (c) $RX + Mg \rightarrow RMgX$

    (d) $RX + KOH \rightarrow ROH + KX$

46. Which one of the following is not an allylic halide?

    (a) 4-Bromopent-2-ene

    (b) 3-Bromo-2-methylbut-1-ene

    (c) 1-Bromobut-2-ene

    (d) 4-Bromobut-1-ene

47. Which of the following alkyl halides will undergo S_N1 reaction most readily?

    (a) $(CH_3)_3C - F$ (b) $(CH_3)_3C - Cl$

    (c) $(CH_3)_3C - Br$ (d) $(CH_3)_3C - I$

48. Which of the following is the correct method of preparation of methyl fluoride?

    (a) $CH_4 + HF \rightarrow$ (b) $CH_3OH + HF \rightarrow$

    (c) $CH_4 + F_2 \rightarrow$ (d) $CH_3Br + AgF \rightarrow$

Case/Passage Based Questions

DIRECTIONS (Qs. 49-53) : *Following are the case/passage based questions.*

Nucleophilic substitution reaction of haloalkane can be conducted according to both S_N^1 and S_N^2 mechanisms. However, which mechanism it is based on is related to such factors as the structure of haloalkane, and properties of leaving group, nucleophilic reagent and solvent.

Influences of halogen: No matter which mechanism the nucleophilic substitution reaction is based on, the leaving group always leave the central carbon atom with electron pair. This is just the opposite of the situation that nucleophilic reagent attacks the central carbon atom with electron pair. Therefore, the weaker the alkalinity of leaving group is, the more stable the anion formed is and it will be more easier for the leaving group to leave the central carbon atom; that is to say, the reactant is more easier to be substituted. The alkalinity order of halogen ion is $I^- < Br^- < Cl^- < F^-$ and the order of their leaving tendency should be $I^- > Br^- > Cl^- > F^-$. Therefore, in four halides with the same alkyl and different halogens, the order of substitution reaction rate is $RI > RBr > RCl > RF$. In addition, if the leaving group is very easy to leave, many carbocation intermediates are generated in the reaction and the reaction is based on S_N^1 mechanism. If the leaving group is not easy to leave, the reaction is based on S_N^2 mechanism.

Influences of solvent polarity: In S_N^1 reaction, the polarity of the system increases from the reactant to the transition state, because polar solvent has a greater stabilizing effect on the transition state than the reactant, thereby reduce activation energy and accelerate the reaction. In S_N^2 reaction, the polarity of the system generally does not change from the reactant to the transition state and only charge dispersion occurs. At this time, polar solvent has a great stabilizing effect on Nu than the transition state, thereby increasing activation energy and slow down the reaction rate. For example, the decomposition rate (S_N^1) of tertiary chlorobutane in 25°C water (dielectric constant 79) is 300000 times faster than in ethanol (dielectric constant 24). The reaction rate (S_N^2) of 2-bromopropane and NaOH in ethanol containing 40% water is twice slower than in absolute ethanol. In a word, the level of solvent polarity has influence on both S_N^1 and S_N^2 reactions, but with different results. Generally speaking, weak polar solvent is favorable for S_N^2 reaction, while strong polar solvent is favorable for S_N^1 reaction, because only under the action of polar solvent can halogenated hydrocarbon dissociate into carbocation and halogen ion and solvents with a strong polarity is favorable for solvation of carbocation, increasing its stability. Generally speaking, the substitution reaction of tertiary haloalkane is based on S_N^1 mechanism in solvents with a strong polarity (for example, ethanol containing water).

(Ding, Y. (2013). A Brief Discussion on Nucleophilic Substitution Reaction on Saturated Carbon Atom. In *Applied Mechanics and Materials* (Vol. 312, pp. 433-437). Trans Tech Publications Ltd.)

[From CBSE Question Bank-2021]

49. S_N^1 mechanism is favoured in which of the following solvents:
    (a) benzene
    (b) carbon tetrachloride
    (c) acetic acid
    (d) carbon disulphide

50. Nucleophilic substitution will be fastest in case of:
    (a) 1-Chloro-2,2-dimethyl propane
    (b) 1-Iodo-2,2-dimethyl propane
    (c) 1-Bromo-2,2-dimethyl propane
    (d) 1-Fluoro-2,2-dimethyl propane

51. S_N^1 reaction will be fastest in which of the following solvents?
    (a) Acetone (dielectric constant 21)
    (b) Ethanol (dielectric constant 24)
    (c) Methanol (dielectric constant 32)
    (d) Chloroform (dielectric constant 5)

52. Polar solvents make the reaction faster as they:
    (a) destabilize transition state and decrease the activation energy
    (b) destabilize transition state and increase the activation energy
    (c) stabilize transition state and increase the activation energy
    (d) stabilize transition state and decrease the activation energy

53. S_N^1 reaction will be fastest in case of:
    (a) 1-Chloro-2-methyl propane
    (b) 1-Iodo-2-methyl propane
    (c) 1-Chlorobutane
    (d) 1-Iodobutane

Chapter Test

Time : 30 Min.   **Max. Marks : 15**

Direction :

• Questions number **1-15** carry **1 mark** each.

1. An organic compound A (C_4H_9Cl) on reaction with Na/diethyl ether gives a hydrocarbon which on monochlorination gives only one chloro derivative, then A is
   (a) tert-butyl chloride
   (b) sec-butyl chloride
   (c) isobutyl chloride
   (d) n-butyl chloride

2. $CH_3 - CH_2 - \underset{\underset{Cl}{|}}{CH} - CH_3$ obtained by chlorination of n-butane, will be
   (a) *l*-form
   (b) *d*-form
   (c) Meso form
   (d) Racemic mixture

3. Which of the statement(s) is/are true, regarding following reaction?

$$\underset{\underset{R''}{\overset{R}{|}}}{R'-CBr} \xrightarrow{Nu^-} \underset{\underset{R''}{\overset{R}{|}}}{R'-CNu} + Br^-$$

   (i) The reaction involves the formation of transition state.
   (ii) Higher the nucleophilic character of the nucleophile, faster will be the reaction.
   (iii) The product is always optically inactive.
   (a) (ii) only
   (b) (ii) and (iii)
   (c) (i), (ii) and (iii)
   (d) Neither (i), (ii) nor (iii)

4. Which of the following is most reactive towards S_N2 reaction?
   (a) CH_3X
   (b) CH_3CH_2X
   (c) $(CH_3)_2CHX$
   (d) $(CH_3)_3CX$

DIRECTIONS (Qs. 5-7) : *Each of these questions contains an assertion followed by reason. Read them carefully and answer the question on the basis of following options. You have to select the one that best describes the two statements.*

(a) If both Assertion and Reason are correct and the Reason is a correct explanation of the Assertion.
(b) If both Assertion and Reason are correct but Reason is not a correct explanation of the Assertion.
(c) If the Assertion is correct but Reason is incorrect.
(d) If the Assertion is incorrect but the Reason is correct.

5. **Assertion :** Chloral reacts with phenyl chloride to form DDT.
   Reason : It is an electrophilic substitution reaction.

6. **Assertion :** Alkyl iodide can be prepared by treating alkyl chloride/bromide with NaI in acetone.
Reason : NaCl/NaBr are soluble in acetone while NaI is not.

7. **Assertion :** Alkylbenzene is not prepared by Friedel-Crafts alkylation of benzene.
Reason : Alkyl halides are less reactive than acyl halides.

Case/Passage Based Questions

DIRECTIONS (Qs. 8-11) : *Following are the case/passage based questions.*

Alkyl halides are insoluble in water but soluble in organic solvents. The insolubility in water is due to their inability to form hydrogen bonds with water. Alkyl bromides and iodides are denser than water whereas alkyl chlorides and fluorides are lighter than water. Alkyl halides have higher boiling points than alkanes of comparable molecular weight. For a given halogen atom, the boiling points of alkyl halides increase with the increase in the size of the alkyl group.

8. Which of the following is liquid at room temperature (b.p. is shown against it)?
(a) CH_3I (42 °C)
(b) CH_3Br (3 °C)
(c) C_2H_5Cl (12 °C)
(d) CH_3F (–78 °C)

9. Which of the following possesses highest melting point?
(a) Chlorobenzene
(b) *m*-dichlorobenzene
(c) *o*-dichlorobenzene
(d) *p*-dichlorobenzene

10. Read the following statements and choose the correct answer
(i) The boiling points of isomeric haloalkanes decrease with increase in branching.
(ii) Among isomeric dihalobenzenes the para-isomers have higher melting point than their ortho and meta-isomers.
(iii) The isomeric dihalobenzenes have large difference in their boiling and melting points
(iv) The isomeric dihalobenzenes have nearly same boiling point.

(a) (i), (ii) and (iii) are correct
(b) (i) and (iii) are correct
(c) (ii) and (iv) are correct
(d) (i), (ii) and (iv) are correct

11. The decreasing order of boiling points of alkyl halides is
(a) $RF > RCl > RBr > RI$
(b) $RBr > RCl > RI > RF$
(c) $RI > RBr > RCl > RF$
(d) $RCl > RF > RI > RBr$

OR

Which of the following options correctly represent the increasing order of B.Pt.
(a) 1 chloropropone < 1 chlorobutane < Isopropyl
(b) Isopropyl < 1 chloropropone < 1 chlorobutane
(c) Isopropyl < 1 chlorobutane < 1 chloropropone
(d) 1 chloropropone < Isopropyl < 1 chlorobutane

Very Short Answer Questions

12. Give the IUPAC name for $C_6H_5CH_2CH_2Br_5$

13. Which is a better nucleophile, a bromide ion or an iodide ion?

14. Write IUPAC names of the following:

(a)
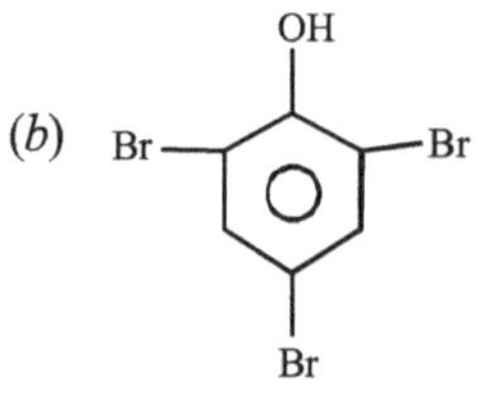

(b)

15. Arrange the following in order of increasing ease towards nucleophilic substitution:
2, 4, 6-Trinitrochlorobenzene, 4-Nitrochlorobenzene, Chlorobenzene, 2,4-Dinitrochlorobenzene.

Solutions 

Practice Exercise-1

1. **(b)**

$$\underset{CH_2Cl}{\overset{CH_2Cl}{|}} \qquad \underset{CH_3}{\overset{CHCl_2}{|}}$$

(*vic*-dihalide)   (*gem*-dihalide)

2. **(c)** The compound is $C_3H_6Cl_2$ and the number of possible isomeric compunds is 5.

3. **(d)** 4-Bromobut-l-ene is not an allylic halide

$$\underset{\text{4-Bromobut-l-ene}}{BrH_2C—CH_2—CH=CH_2}$$

4. **(a)**
$$\underset{\substack{4 \quad 3 \quad 2}}{CH_3CH_2\overset{\overset{Br}{|}}{C}=CH-Cl}$$
2-Bromo-1-chloro but-1-ene

5. **(b)** $RH + Cl_2 \xrightarrow{\text{UV light}} RCl + HCl$

Oxidation No. of Cl is decreasing from 0 (in Cl_2) to –1 (in RCl)

6. **(c)**

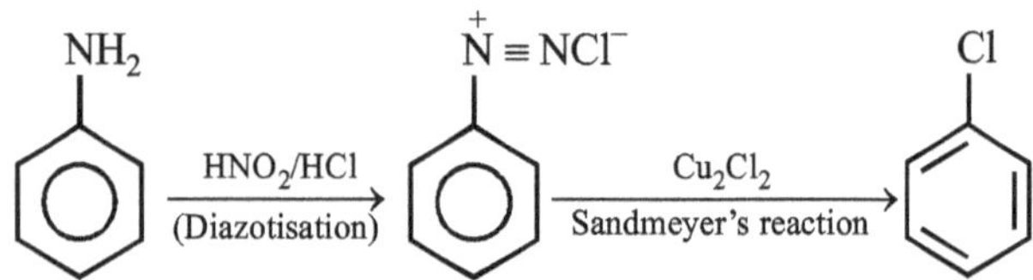

7. **(b)** This method is not applicable for the preparation of aryl halides because the C–O bond in phenol has a partial double bond character and is difficult to break being stronger than a single bond.

8. **(c)** Ethyl alcohol forms ethyl chloride with thionyl chloride in presence of pyridine.

$$CH_3CH_2OH + SOCl_2 \xrightarrow{Pyridine} CH_3CH_2Cl + SO_2 + HCl$$

9. **(d)** Ethylene dichloride can be prepared by adding HCl to ethylene glycol ($CH_2OH \cdot CH_2OH$).

10. **(c)** $R-OH + SOCl_2 \xrightarrow{Pyridine} RCl + SO_2\uparrow + HCl\uparrow$
SO$_2$ and HCl being gases escape leaving behind pure alkyl halide.
Direct fluorination of alkane is highly exothermic process.

11. **(c)** alkyl fluorides are obtained by heating alkyl chloride or bromide in the presence of metallic fluorides like AgF or SbF$_3$. the reaction is known as Swartz reaction.
$$R-X + AgF/Hg_2F_2 \rightarrow R-F + AgX/Hg_2X_2$$

12. **(a)** Free radical substitution reaction
$$(CH_3)_4C + Cl_2 \xrightarrow{Sunlight} (CH_3)_3C-CH_2-Cl$$
Free radicals normally do not rearrange.

13. **(a)** NaI is soluble in acetone or methanol, gives I which undergoes S_NI reaction with RBr or RCl to form todoalkanes. I has lower reactivity as a nucleophile, therefore iodoalkane cannot be prepared by direct iodination. Finkeistein reaction is best method for the preparation of iodoalkanes.

14. **(a)** H-F and H-Cl bonds are stronger than H–Br bond. H–F or H–Cl bonds are not broken by the alkoxy free radicals obtained from peroxides, while HI is weaker than HBr as it is broken by the alkoxy free radicals obtained from peroxides, but the iodine atoms so, formed readily combine with each other to give iodine molecules, rather than attack the double bond of alkenes.

15. **(a)** Iodine forms esters with the silver salts, this is known as the Birnbaun-Simonini reaction.
$$2RCO_2Ag + I_2 \rightarrow RCOOR + CO_2 + 2AgI$$

16. When chlorine is passed through toluene in presence of sunlight, side chain halogenation takes place in toluene. Benzyl chloride is formed.

17. Vinyl chloride is prepared by addition of HCl to acetylene in presence of HgCl$_2$.
$$CH \equiv CH + HCl \xrightarrow{HgCl_2} H_2C = CHCl$$
It is widely used in manufacturing PVC (polyvinyl chloride).

18. Allyl chloride ($CH_2 = CH - CH_2Cl$) is prepared by chlorination of propene at high temperature.
$$CH_2 = CH - CH_3 \xrightarrow[\text{Traces of peroxide}]{475\,K,\,light,\,SO_2Cl_2}$$
$$CH_2 = CH - CH_2Cl + SO_2 + HCl$$
$$\text{Allyl chloride}$$
$$CH_2 = CH - CH_3 + Br_2 \xrightarrow{800\,K} CH_2 = CH - CH_2Br + HBr$$
$$\text{Allyl bromide}$$

19. The westron is CHCl$_2$–CHCl$_2$ and it can be named as 1, 1, 2, 2-tetrachloroethane. It is used as a solvent for paints and varnishes in paint industries.

20. $CH_3-CH_2-CH_2-CH_2-Cl$, $CH_3-CH_2-CH-CH_3$
1–chlorobutane
$$\underset{\underset{Cl}{|}}{CH_3-CH_2-CH-CH_3}$$
2–chlorobutane

$$\underset{\underset{CH_3}{|}}{CH_3-CH-CH_2\,Cl}\,,\quad \underset{\underset{CH_3}{|}}{\overset{\overset{CH_3}{|}}{CH_3-C-Cl}}$$
1–chloro–2–methyl propane   2–chloro–2–methyl propane

21. (a) Refer Theory
(b) Refer Theory

22. Fluorobenzene is prepared from aniline. Aniline is first subjected to diazotisation with NaNO$_2$/HBF$_4$ to form $C_6H_5N_2^+BF_4^-$ and then it is heated to decompose it to form C_6H_5F.

$$\text{Fluorobenzene}$$

23. (i) $X = C_6H_5N_2^+Cl^-$; $Y = C_6H_5Br$; $Z = C_6H_5OH$.
(ii) $X = pClC_6H_4CH_3$; $Y = pClC_6H_4CH_2Cl$;
$Z = pClC_6H_4CH_2OH$.
(iii) $X = C_6H_5I$, $Y = C_6H_5 - C_6H_5$.

24. IUPAC names of isomers : 1, 2-Dichlorethane and 1, 1-Dichloroethane.
Hydrolysis of 1, 2-Dichlorethane with aqueous NaOH gives ethylene glycol while the hydrolysis of 1, 1-Dichloroethane gives ethanal. Which will give positive iodoform test.

25.

26. (i) $Cl\,CH_2 - \underset{\underset{CH_3}{|}}{CH} - CH_2 - CH_3$
1-chloro-2-methylbutane

(ii) $CH_3 - \underset{\underset{CH_3}{|}}{\overset{\overset{Cl}{|}}{C}} - CH_2 - CH_3$
2-chloro-2-methylbutane

(*iii*) $CH_3 - CH - CH - CH_3$
         | |
        CH_3 Cl

2-chloro-3-methylbutane

(*iv*) $CH_3 - CH - CH_2 - CH_2Cl$
              |
             CH_3

1-chloro-3-methylbutane

27. (*i*) $CH_3CH_2CH=CH_2 \xrightarrow[\substack{(Anti-Mark. \\ Addition)}]{HBr, Peroxide} CH_3CH_2CH_2CH_2 - Br \xrightarrow{NaI/acetone} CH_3CH_2CH_2CH_2 - I$

1-Butene ... 1-Iodo-butane

(*ii*)
$CH_3 - \underset{\underset{\text{Isobutyric acid}}{}}{\overset{\overset{CH_3}{|}}{CH}} - COOH \xrightarrow[-CO_2, -H_2O]{Ag_2CO_3} CH_3 - \overset{\overset{CH_3}{|}}{CH} - COOAg \xrightarrow{Br_2/CCl_4, reflux}$

$CH_3 - \overset{\overset{CH_3}{|}}{CH} - Br$
Sec-propylbromide

(*iii*) $CH_3CH_2OH \xrightarrow[-SO_2, HCl]{SOCl_2} CH_3CH_2Cl \xrightarrow[-Hg_2Cl_2]{Hg_2F_2, \Delta} CH_3CH_2F$

Ethanol ... Fluoroethane

28. (*i*)

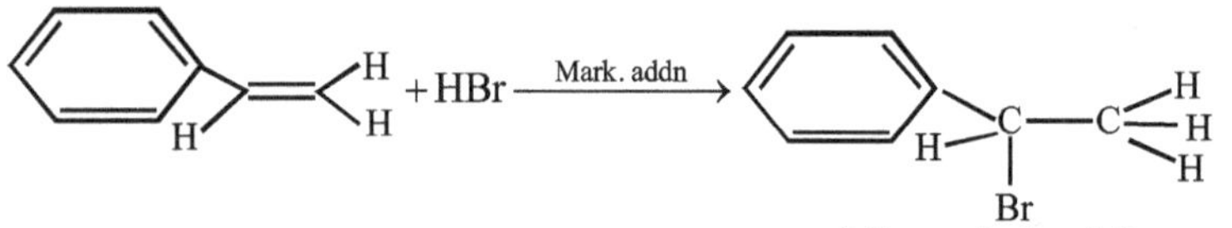

1-Bromo-1-phenylethane

(*ii*) $CH_3CH_2 - CH=CH_2 + HCl \xrightarrow{Mark. \; addn} CH_3 - CH_2 - \overset{}{CH} - CH_3$
                                                              |
                                                             Cl
2-chlorobutane

(*iii*) 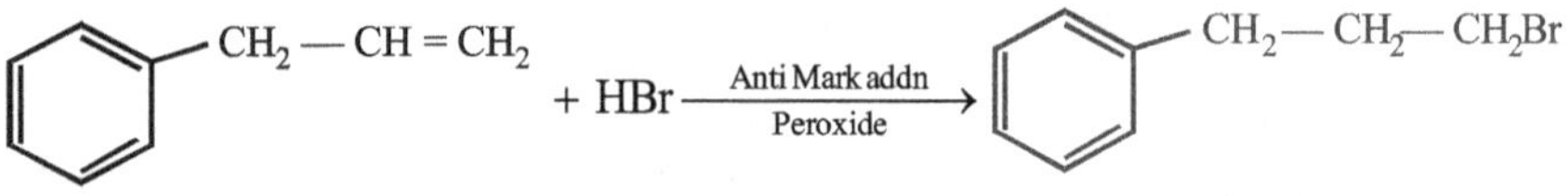 ... $+ HBr \xrightarrow[Peroxide]{Anti \; Mark \; addn}$ ...

1-Bromo-3-phenylpropane

Practice Exercise-2 

1. **(c)** S_N1 reactions involve the formation of carbocations, hence higher the stability of carbocation, more will be reactivity of the parent alkyl halide. Thus tertiary carbocation formed from (c) is stabilized by two phenyl groups and one methyl group, hence most stable.

2. **(d)** Weaker the C–X bond, greater is the reactivity.

3. **(a)** 1° Alkyl halides (having least steric hindrance at α-carbon atom) are most reactive towards S_N2 reaction.

4. **(b)** $Cl-\langle\rangle-Br \xrightarrow{Mg/ether} Cl-\langle\rangle-MgBr$ (A)

$\downarrow D_2O$

$D-\langle\rangle-\langle\rangle-D \xleftarrow{Na/ether} Cl-\langle\rangle-D$ (C) ... (B)

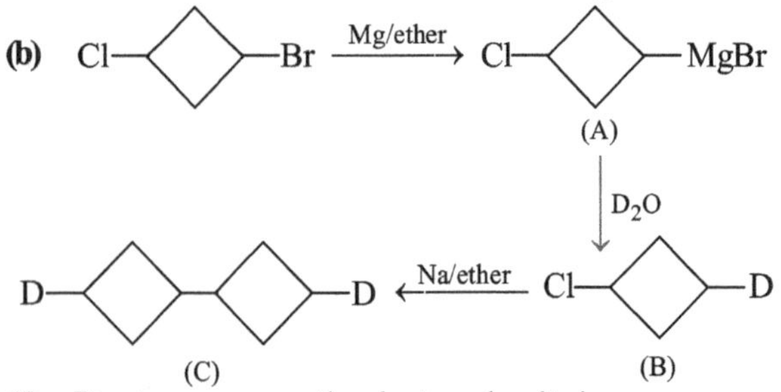

5. **(d)** Due to resonance, the electron density increases more at ortho- and para-positions than at meta-positions. Further, the halogen atom because of its – I effect has some tendency to withdraw electrons from the benzene ring. As a result, the ring gets somewhat deactivated as compared to benzene and hence the electrophilic substitution reactions in haloarenes occur slowly and require more drastic conditions as compared to those in benzene.

6. **(a)** A strong nucleophile favours the S_N2 reaction and a weak nucleophile favours the S_N1 reaction.
First reaction is S_N1 reaction because C_2H_5OH is used as solvent which is a weak nucleophile.
Second reaction is S_N2 reaction because $C_2H_5O^-$ is strong nucleophile.

7. **(c)** For S_N2 reaction polar aprotic solvent is needed.

8. **(b)** $AlCl_3 + Cl_2 \longrightarrow \left[AlCl_4\right]^- + Cl^+$

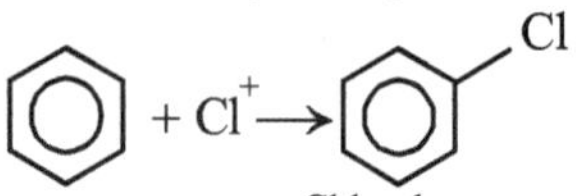

Chlorobenzene

9. **(d)** Dichloromethane is widely used as solvent as a paint remover, as a propellant in aerosols and as a process solvent in the manufacture of drugs. It is also used as a metal cleansing and finishing solvent.

10. **(b)** Haloforms (CHX_3) are trihalogen derivatives of methane. Example : Chloroform $CHCl_3$.

11. **(a)** Alkyl halides are polar in nature and have dipole-dipole interaction, while hydrocarbons are non-polar in nature and have only weak van der Waal's forces. Therefore, alkyl halides have higher boiling point than hydrocarbons.

12. **(a)** C–X bond length increases and bond dissociation enthalpy decreases, therefore, reactivity order is $RI > RBr > RCl > RF$.

13. **(d)** S_N1 mechanism does not depend on the concentration of nucleophile. 2° alkyl halides are more reactive than 1° alkyl halides towards S_N1 mechanism, because 2° carbocation is more stable than 1° carbocation.

14. **(a)** As the branching increases in isomeric alkyl groups, contact surface area of molecule decreases; therefore, van der Waal forces decrease reducing intermolecular interactions and hence the boiling points.

15. **(d)** $C_6H_6 + CH_3CH_2CH_2Cl \xrightarrow[\text{AlCl}_3]{\text{Anhyd.}} C_6H_5\overset{\overset{\displaystyle CH_3}{|}}{C}HCH_3$ (Isopropyl benzene)

16. **(d)** More the stability of the carbocation, higher will be the reactivity of the parent chloride. Allyl chloride > vinyl chloride > chlorobenzene.

17. **(b)** S_N2 reaction follow a 2nd order kinetic, i.e., the rate depends upon the concentration of both the reactants, where in S_N1 reactions rate depends only upon the concentration of only one reactant.
The order of reactivity order of alkyl halides for S_N1 reaction $3° > 2° > 1°$ and for S_N2 reactions $3° < 2° < 1°$

18. **(c)**

19. **(a)** Since S_N1 reactions involve the formation of carbo-cation as intermediate in the rate determining step, more is the stability of carbocation higher will be the reactivity of alkyl halides towards S_N1 route. Now we know that stability of carbocations follows the order : $3° > 2° > 1°$, so S_N1 reactivity should also follow the same order.
$3° > 2° > 1° >$ Methyl **(S_N1 reactivity)**

20. 2-Bromobutane, it contains chiralcarbon atoms.

21. Chlorocompounds are most stable, most volatile and are most polar among chloro, bromo and iodo alkanes.

22. The various isomers are:

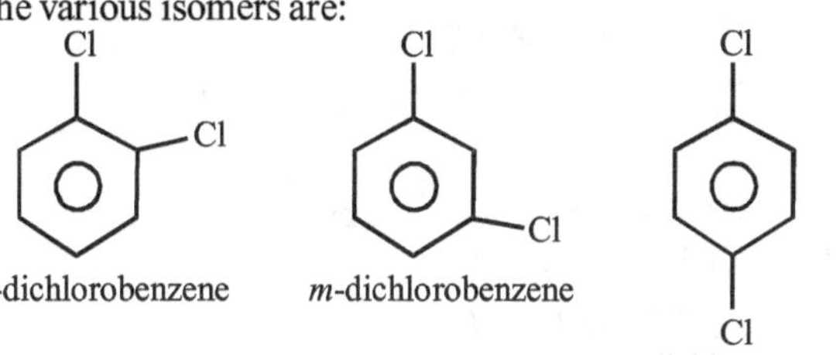

o-dichlorobenzene　　m-dichlorobenzene　　p-dichlorobenzene

p-dichlorobenzene has highest melting point.

23. It shows cis-trans (geometrical) isomerism.

Cis 1, 2-dichloroethene　　　Trans 1, 2-dichloroethene

24. $(CH_3)_3CBr < CH_3\overset{\overset{\displaystyle CH_3}{|}}{C}HCH_2Br < CH_3CH_2CH_2CH_2Br$

The boiling point decreases with increase in branching of alkyl group.

25. The boiling points are in the order: $C_2H_5Cl < C_2H_5Br < C_2H_5I$. The boiling point increases with increase in molecular mass.

26. CH_3Cl is most polar and CH_3I is least polar as Cl is most electronegative and iodine is least electronegative. $CH_3Cl > CH_3Br > CH_3I$

27. 2, 4, 6-trinitrocholorobenzene.

28. Symmetrical alkene gives the same products. Here, $CH_3 - CH = CH - CH_3$ is an isomer of C_4H_8 which is symmetrical alkene.

29. Westrosol is $CHCl = CCl_2$ and its IUPAC name is 1, 1, 2-trichloroethene. It is used in dry cleaning of clothes in laundries.

30. $2CH_3\overset{\overset{\displaystyle }{}}{C}H - I \xrightarrow{2\,Na,\,Dry\,ether} CH_3 - CH - CH - CH_3$ with CH_3 on the first carbon and CH_3, CH_3 branches on the product.

31. The formation of white precipitates on addition of $AgNO_3$ indicates the presence of phosgene in the sample of chloroform.

32. Addition of ethyl alcohol slows down the oxidation of chloroform and converts the poisonous phosgene into non-poisonous ethyl carbonate.

$$2C_2H_5OH + \underset{\text{Ethyl alcohol}}{\overset{\text{Cl}}{\underset{\text{Cl}}{>}}C=O} \longrightarrow \overset{C_2H_5O}{\underset{C_2H_5O}{>}}C=O + 2HCl$$

Phosgene　　　　　　Ethyl carbonate

33. It is because of the double bond character of $C = Cl$ bond in vinyl chloride due to the resonance in vinyl chloride whereas in ethyl chloride, there is a weaker $C - Cl$ single bond.

$$CH_2 = CH - \ddot{C}l: \longleftrightarrow \overset{\ominus}{C}H_2 = CH - \overset{\oplus}{C}l:$$

34. Allyl carbonium ion is more stable due to the possible resonance as shown below and Cl^- is lost as a good leaving group due to weak $C - Cl$ bond. n-propyl carbonium ion is not stabilised as no resonance is possible and thus $C - Cl$ bond in n-propyl chloride is stronger.

$$\underset{\text{allyl chloride}}{CH_2 = CH\,CH_2\,Cl} \xrightarrow{Cl} CH_2 = CH - \overset{\oplus}{C}H_2 \longleftrightarrow \overset{\oplus}{C}H_2 - CH = CH_2$$
Stablised by resonance

$$CH_3 - CH_2 - CH_2 - Cl \xrightarrow{-Cl} CH_3 - CH_2 - \overset{\oplus}{C}H_2$$
not stabilised

35. Para isomer has higher lattice energy as it is more symmetric than ortho and meta-isomer. Higher the lattice energy, lower is the solubility.

36. Ethyliodide is not very stable compound and decomposes slowly to form I_2 which gets dissolved in C_2H_5I imparts colour and forms brown colour in solution.

37. X is $CH_3 - CH = CH_2$
Y is $CH_3 - \overset{\overset{\displaystyle }{|}}{\underset{\displaystyle OH}{C}}H - CH_3$, Z is $CH_3 - \overset{\overset{\displaystyle }{|}}{\underset{\displaystyle Cl}{C}}H - CH_3$

38. Chloromethane since it is an alkyl halide.

39. This resonance effect decreases the dipole moment of vinyl chloride relative to ethyl chloride.

40. CH_3I, because of its smallest carbon content and heaviest halogen, i.e., I.

41. $\underset{\substack{\text{3–methylpent–1–ene} \\ \text{(Optically active)}}}{CH_2 = CH - \overset{\overset{\displaystyle CH_3}{|}}{C}H - CH_2\,CH_3} \xrightarrow{H_2/Ni}$

$$\underset{\substack{\text{3–Methylpentane} \\ \text{(Optically inactive)}}}{CH_3\,CH_2\,\overset{\overset{\displaystyle CH_3}{|}}{C}HCH_2\,CH_3}$$

42. This is because haloalkanes are polar in nature and carbon atom in C – X bond has partial positive charge, *i.e.,* $C^{\delta+} - X^{\delta-}$

43. Refer theory.

44. Ethyne is formed.

$$CHCl_3 + 6Ag + Cl_3CH \longrightarrow CH \equiv CH + 6AgCl$$
Ethyne

45. Although haloarenes and haloalkanes are polar but they are unable to form hydrogen bond with water, therefore these are insoluble in water.

46. (*a*) $CHCl_3$ reacts with ethylamine on warming in presence of alcoholic KOH.
$$CHCl_3 + C_2H_5NH_2 + 3KOH \,(alc)$$
$$\longrightarrow C_2H_5N \equiv C + 3KCl + 3H_2O$$
Ethylisocyanide

(*b*) $CH_3COCH_3 + CHCl_3$

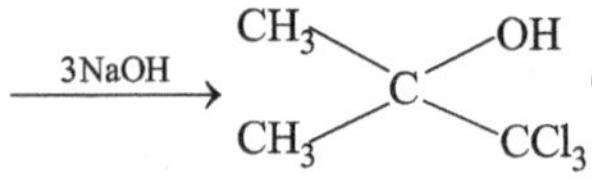

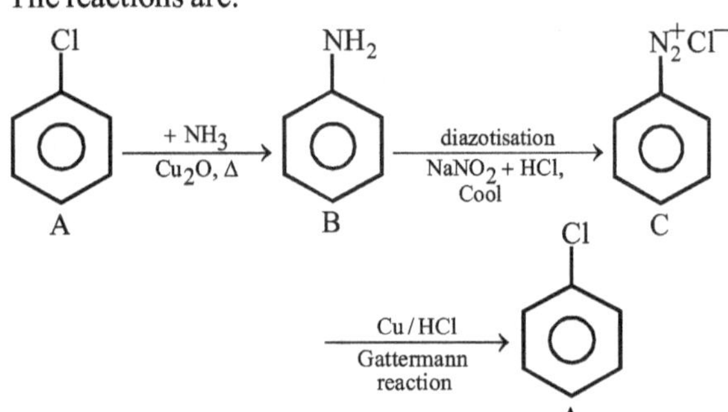

(*c*) $CHCl_3 + HONO_2 \xrightarrow{\Delta}$

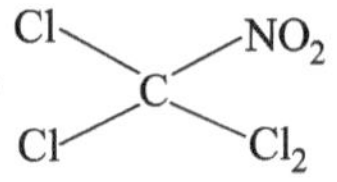

Chloropicrin

47. The compound 'A' is chlorobenzene, B is aniline and C is benzene diazonium chloride.
The reactions are:

1. Inversion occurs more than retention, leading to partial racemization.

2. Polarimeter

3.

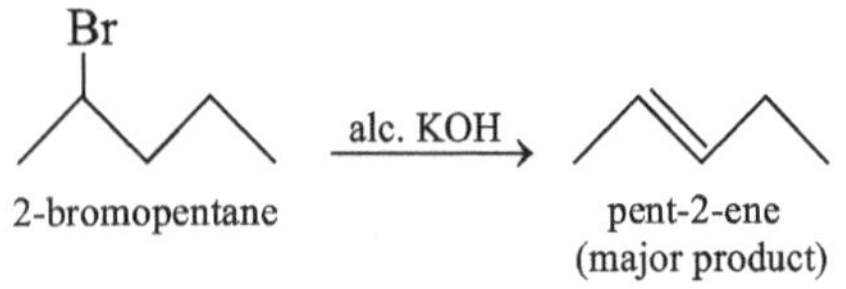

Br

alc. KOH →

2-bromopentane → pent-2-ene (major product)

4. Iodoform (CHI_3) is used as a disinfectant.

5.

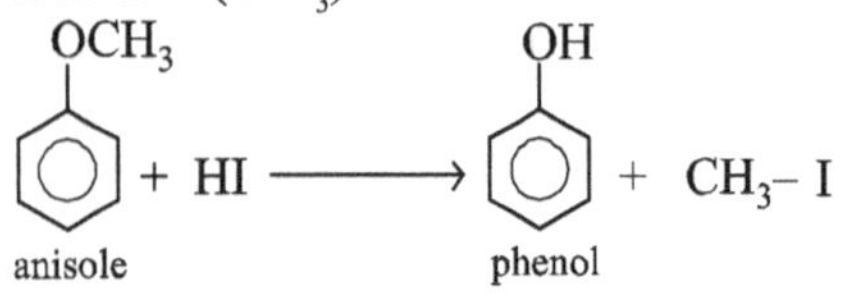

OCH_3 + HI $\longrightarrow$ OH + CH_3– I

anisole → phenol

6.

$\overset{1}{C}H_2 - \overset{2}{C}H_2 - Cl$

1-Phenyl-2-chloroethane

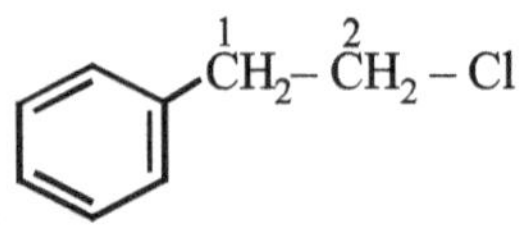

7. Out of chlorobenzene and benzyl chloride, **benzyl chloride** gets easily hydrolysed. This is because in benzyl chloride $(C_6H_5CH_2Cl)$ Cl is attached to sp^3 hybridised carbon and the C–Cl bond is easier to break as compared to chlorobenzene (C_6H_5Cl) where the C is sp^2 hybridised and the C–Cl bond has a partial double bond, character due to resonance.

8. The example of benzylic halide is

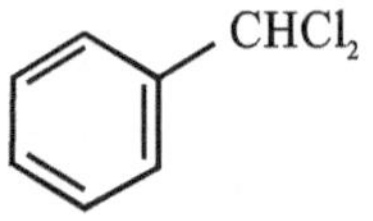

$CHCl_2$

In benzylic halides the halogen atom is bonded to an sp^3-hybridised carbon atom which is directly attached with an aromatic ring.

9.

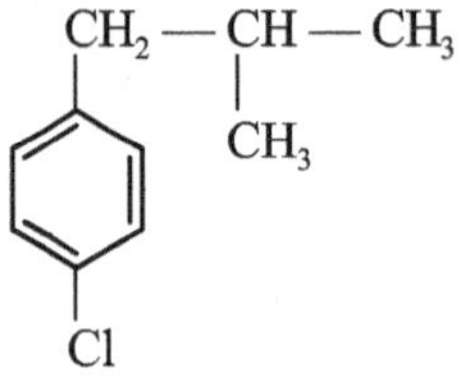

$CH_2 - CH - CH_3$
$\quad\quad\quad |$
$\quad\quad CH_3$

Cl

3-(4-chlorophenyl)-2-methyl propane

10. 1-bromopentane reacts faster in S_N2 displacement because it is a primary halide, i.e., less hindered.

11. If Br_2 is used in excess

$$CH_2 - CH - CH_2 - \overset{Br}{\underset{Br}{C}} - \overset{H}{\underset{Br}{C}} - Br \text{ is formed}$$

But if only one mole of Br_2 is used, then
$$CH_2 = CH - CH_2 - C = CH - Br \text{ will be formed.}$$
$$\quad\quad\quad\quad\quad\quad\quad\quad |$$
$$\quad\quad\quad\quad\quad\quad\quad\quad Br$$

12. 2-Chloro-3, 3-dimethylbutane.

13. Freon.

14. 2-Bromo-4-chloropentane.

15. 4-Chloropent-1-ene.

16. $CH_3Br + KCN \longrightarrow CH_3CN + KBr$
Ethanenitrile

17. 4-Bromo-4-methylpent-2-ene.

18. Ethyl alcohol is formed

$$CH_3CH_2Cl + KOH\,(aq) \longrightarrow CH_3CH_2OH + KCl$$
Ethyl chloride $\quad\quad\quad\quad\quad\quad\quad$ Ethanol

19.

$$\overset{4}{C}H_3 - \overset{3}{\underset{CH_3}{C}H} - \overset{2}{\underset{Cl}{C}H} - \overset{1}{C}H_3$$
2-Chloro-3-methylbutane

20. S_N1 reactions involve the formation of carbocations, order of stability of carbocation is $3° > 2° > 1°$ hence higher the stability of carbocation, more will be the reactivity of the parent alkyl halide. Thus

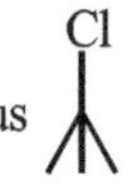

Cl

undergoes S_N1 reaction faster in comparison to

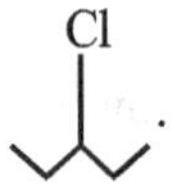

Cl .

21. By reaction of methyl bromide with alcoholic solution of AgCN.

$$CH_3Br + AgCN \xrightarrow[\text{D}]{C_2H_5OH/H_2O} CH_3-N\cong C + AgBr$$

Methyl bromide   Methyl isocyanide

22. A chiral molecule has atleast one C-atom in which all the four groups are different.

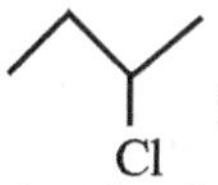

is a chiral molecule.

23. S_N1 reactions involve the formation of carbocations, order of stability of carbocations is $3° > 2° > 1°$ hence higher the stability of carbocation, more will be the reactivity of the parent alkyl halide. Thus $(CH_3)C-Br$ undergoes S_N1 reaction faster in comparison to C_2H_5Br.

24. (a) The presence of electron-withdrawing groups such as $-NO_2$, $-CN$, etc. at o-and p-positions (but not at m-position) w.r.t. the halogen greatly activates the halogen towards nucleophilic displacemnt. Further, greater the number of such groups at o- and p-positions w.r.t. the halogen, more reactive is the haloarene. The NO_2 group at o- and p- positions withdraws electrons from the benzene ring and thus makes the ring electron deficient and facilitates the attack of the nucleophile (OH) on haloarenes. The carbanion thus formed is stabilized by resonance as shown below.

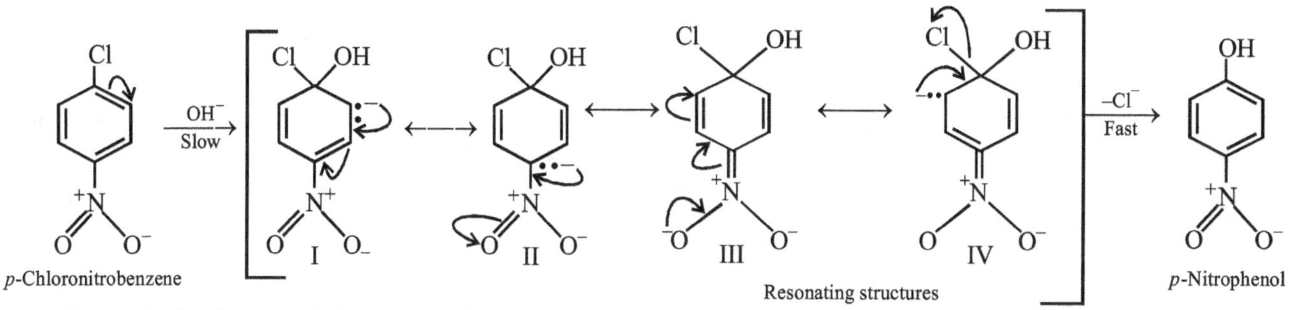

p-Chloronitrobenzene   Resonating structures   *p*-Nitrophenol

(b) p-Dichlorobenzene, being symmetrical, fits tightly in its crystal lattice. Thus the intermolecular forces of attraction in the p-isomer are stronger than those in the o-and m- isomers; which requires larger amount of energy to melt or dissolve the p-isomer than the o- and m-isomers. Consequently, the melting point of the p-isomer will be higher and its solubility lower than the corresponding o- and m-isomers.

(c) Thionyl chloride method is preferred over hydrogen chloride or phosphorus pentachloride method since both the by-products (SO_2 and HCl) in this reaction being gases escape leaving the chloroalkanes in almost pure state.

$$R-OH + \underset{\text{Thionyl chloride}}{\begin{array}{c}Cl\\ Cl\end{array}\!\!\!>\!S=O} \xrightarrow{\text{Pyridine}} \underset{\text{Haloalkane}}{R-Cl} + SO_2\uparrow + HCl\uparrow$$

OR

(a) $$\underset{\text{1-Chlorobutane}}{CH_3CH_2CH_2CH_2Cl} \longrightarrow \underset{\text{1-Iodobutane}}{CH_3CH_2CH_2CH_2I}$$

$$CH_3CH_2CH_2CH_2Cl + \underset{\substack{\text{soluble}\\\text{in acetone}}}{NaI} \xrightarrow{\text{acetone}} CH_3CH_2CH_2CH_2I + \underset{\substack{\text{insoluble}\\\text{in acetone}}}{NaCl\downarrow}$$

(b) 2-Bromo-2-methyl butane is most reactive towards elimination reaction.

$$\underset{\text{1-Bromopentane}}{CH_3-CH_2CH_2CH_2CH_2-Br} \qquad 1° \text{ alkyl halide}$$

$$\underset{\text{2-Bromopentane}}{CH_3-CH_2-CH_2-\overset{\overset{\displaystyle Br}{|}}{C}H-CH_3} \qquad 2° \text{ alkyl halide}$$

$$\underset{\text{2-Bromo-2-methylbutane}}{CH_3CH_2-\underset{\underset{\displaystyle CH_3}{|}}{\overset{\overset{\displaystyle Br}{|}}{C}}-CH_3} \qquad 3° \text{ alkyl halide}$$

$3°$ Alkyl halide is most reactive towards elimination reaction due to the formation of more stable $3°$ carbocation which loses proton to form alkene.

$$\underset{3° \text{ Carbocation}}{CH_3CH_2-\underset{\underset{\displaystyle CH_3}{|}}{\overset{+}{C}}-CH_3} \xrightarrow{-H^+} \underset{\text{Saytzeff's product}}{CH_3-CH=\underset{\underset{\displaystyle CH_3}{|}}{C}-CH_3}$$

(c) 4-Bromo-4-methylpent-2-ene.

The presence of electron-withdrawing groups such as $-NO_2$, $-CN$, etc. at o-and p-positions (but not at m-position) w.r.t. the halogen greatly activates the halogen towards nucleophilic displacemnt. Further, greater the number of such groups at o-and p-positions w.r.t. the halogen, more reactive is the haloarene.

The presence of NO_2 groups at o- and p- positions withdraws electrons from the benzene ring and thus facilitates the attack of the nucleophile on haloarenes. The carbanion thus formed is stabilized by resonance as shown below:

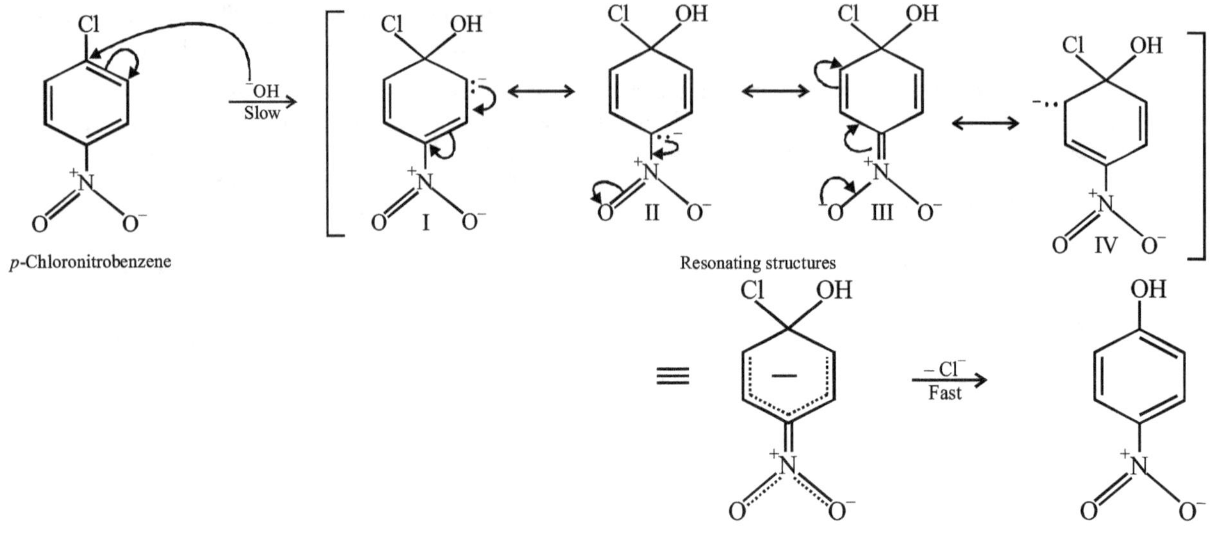

p-Chloronitrobenzene

Resonating structures

Resonance hybrid

p-Nitrophenol

25. (a)

(i)   (ii)

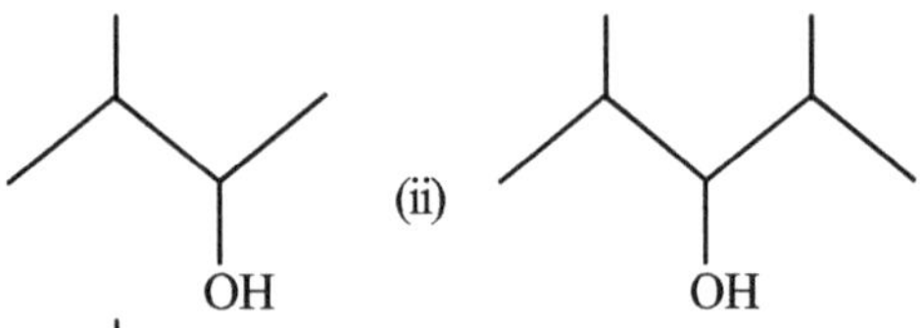

(i) 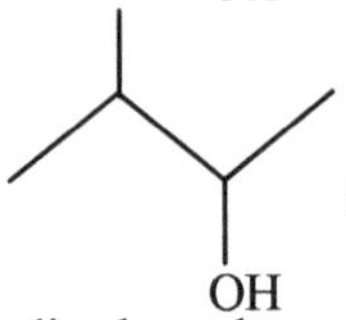   is the chiral molecule

(Chirality depends on presence of asymmetric carbon atom.

in (i)   *C is asymmetric whereas in (ii) there is

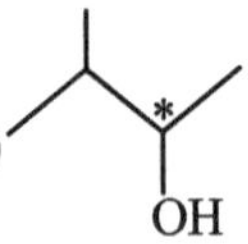

no asymmetric carbon)

(b)

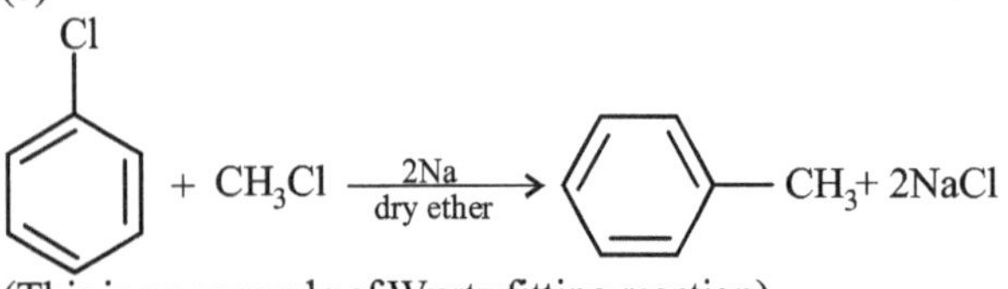

+ CH_3Cl $\xrightarrow[\text{dry ether}]{2Na}$ CH_3+ $2NaCl$

(This is an example of Wurtz fitting reaction)

(c)

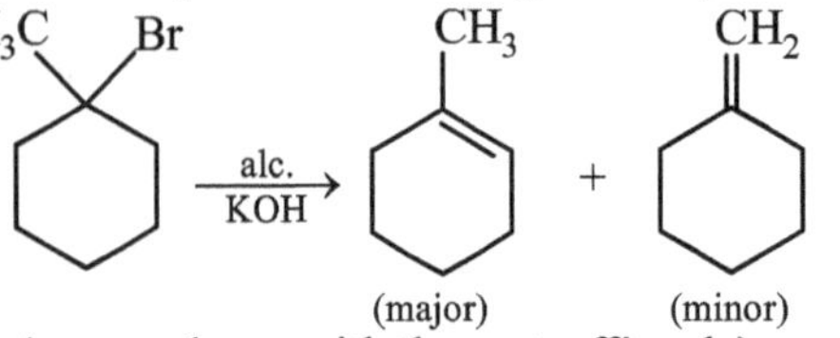

$\xrightarrow[\text{KOH}]{\text{alc.}}$

(major)   (minor)

(This is in accordance with the saytzeff's rule)

26. (i)

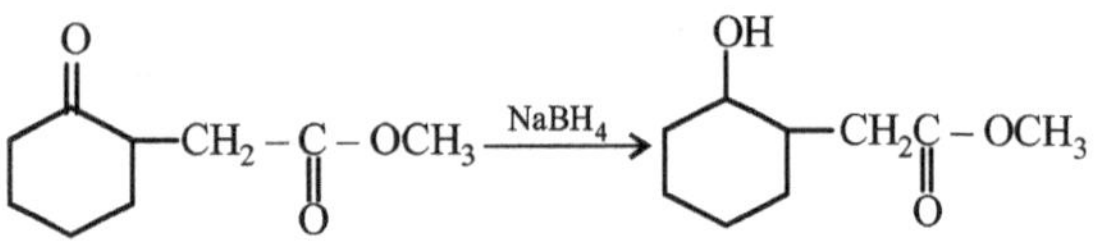

$\xrightarrow{NaBH_4}$

(NaBH$_4$ does not reduce the ester group, so only ketonic group gets reduced to alcohol)

(ii)

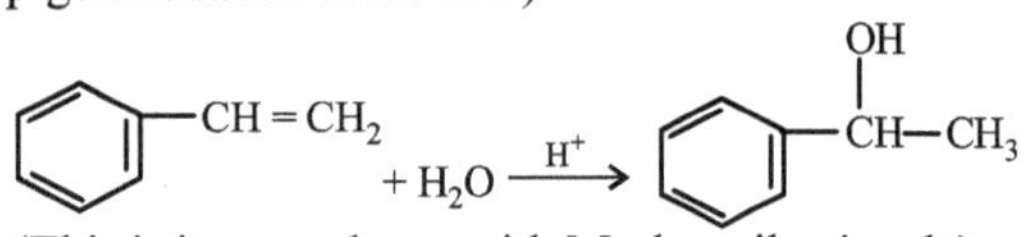

$\xrightarrow[+ H_2O]{H^+}$

(This is in accordance with Markovnikov's rule)

(iii)

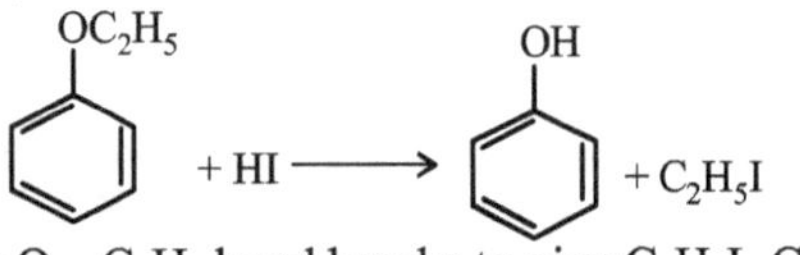

$+ HI \longrightarrow$ $+ C_2H_5I$

(The $O-C_2H_5$ bond breaks to give C_2H_5I. C_6H_5-O does not break due to partial double bond character)

27. Structure of the given compounds are :

$$H_3C - CH_2 - CH_2 - CH_2 - CH_2 - Br$$

1-Bromopentane
(A)

$$H_3C - CH_2 - CH_2 - CH - CH_3$$
$$\overset{|}{Br}$$

2-Bromopentane
(B)

$$H_3C - CH_2 - \overset{\overset{\displaystyle Br}{|}}{C} - CH_3$$
$$\underset{CH_3}{|}$$

2-Bromo-2-methylbutane
(C)

(i) As we can see in the above figures, (A), contains the least steric hindrance so towards the S_N2 reaction 1-bromopentane will be most reactive.

(ii) 2-bromopentane (Figure B) contain chiral carbon in it. So, this compound is optically active.

(iii) 2-bromo-2-methylbutane will be most reactive towards the β-elimination since it will form most stable alkene (on account of highest no of α-hydrogens)

28. (i) Interactions between (a) haloalkane – organic solvent, (b) haloalkane-haloalkane, and (c) organic solvent-organic solvent are almost similar. Hence molecules of the haloalkane gradually mix with the molecules of the organic solvent.

(ii) A mixture containing two enantiomers in equal proportion will have zero optical rotation. Such mixtures are called racemic mixtures, e.g., (±) butan-2-ol.

(iii) The carbocation intermediate from $C_6H_5CH(C_6H_5)Br$ is more stable because it is stabilised by two phenyl groups due to resonance, so $C_6H_5CH(C_6H_5)Br$ is more reactive in S_N1 reaction.

29. (i) KCN ionises to give CN^- which is ambident nucleophile and thus can attack on the carbon of alkyl halide through its carbon or nitrogen. However, since the C–C bond is stronger than the C–N bond, attack occurs through carbon to form n–BuCN.

$$:\overset{-}{C}{\equiv}N: \longleftrightarrow :C{\equiv}\overset{..}{N}:^-$$

$$:\overset{-}{C}{\equiv}N: + CH_3CH_2CH_2-\overset{\delta+}{CH_2}\overset{\delta-}{Br}\longrightarrow$$

$$CH_3CH_2CH_2CH_2CN + KBr$$

(ii) Refer Q.-12 (i) NCERT Questions.

30. (i) This term is used to describe such molecules which have no elements of symmetry, thus asymmetrical molecules are also called chiral molecules *e.g.*, lactic acid, $CH_3CH(OH)COOH$.

$$\begin{array}{ccc}
H_3C & & CH_3 \\
| & & | \\
H-C-OH & \quad HO-C-H \\
| & & | \\
COOH & & COOH \\
\end{array}$$

Mirror

(ii) $CH_3CHClCH_2CH_3$ is more reactive than $CH_3CH_2CH_2CH_2Cl$ as the former one gives more stable carbocation intermediate.

$$\underset{H_3CCH_2}{\overset{H_3C}{>}}\overset{H}{\underset{|}{C}}Cl \longrightarrow \underset{H_3CCH_2}{\overset{H_3C}{>}}\overset{H}{\underset{|}{C^+}}\overset{OH^-}{\longrightarrow}\underset{H_3CH_2C}{\overset{H_3C}{>}}\overset{H}{\underset{|}{C}}-OH$$

(iii) An ∧∧∧I, as iodide is a better leaving group because of its larger size therefore, it undergoes S_N2 reaction faster.

31. Refer Q. - 12 NCERT Questions.

32. Chlorine in chlorobenzene undergoes +E and +M effects, which increase electron density in *o*- and *p*-positions. However, –I effect of chlorine decreases electron density on benzene nucleus, thus retarding electrophilic substitution. However, the combined effect of +E and +M is greater than the –I effect of Cl with the result electrophilic substitution in chlorobenzene is difficult (due to –I effect

of Cl) but takes place in *o*- and *p*-positions (due to +E and +M effects of Cl).

33. (i) Ethyl iodide undergoes S_N2 reaction faster than ethyl bromide because I^- is a better leaving group than Br^-.

(ii) (±) 2-Butanol represents a racemic mixture of two enantiomers. Two enantiomers always show opposite optical activities. i.e., they rotate the plane of polarized light by equal amounts in opposite directions. The optical rotation of an equimolar mixture of a pair of enantiomers is zero because the optical rotations of the enantiomers cancel out.

(iii) C atom bearing halogen in halobenzene is sp^2 hybridised while in $CH_3 - X$ it is sp^3 hybridised. As sp^2 hybrid orbital is smaller than an sp^3 hybrid orbital due to greater s-character, the C–X bond length in halobenzene is smaller than in $CH_3 - X$.

34. Aryl halides (like vinyl halides) are less reactive towards nucleophilic substitutions under ordinary conditions (difference from alkyl halides). This low reactivity is due to *(a)* resonance effect, *(b)* sp^2 hybridisation of carbon atom holding the halogen atom and *(c)* less polarity of the C–X bond.

35. The symmetry of the para isomer allows the molecules in the solid to pack much more closely than possible for the meta or ortho isomers.

36. (a) This is due to partial double bond character of C – Cl bond in chlorobenzene.

(b) Chloroform in the presence of air gets oxidised to phosgene. Phosgene is carbonyl chloride and is represented as $COCl_2$. To prevent the formation of phosgene, chloroform is stored in dark coloured bottles. The reaction is represented as.

$$CHCl_3 + \frac{1}{2}O_2 \longrightarrow COCl_2 + HCl.$$

37. Chemical tests to distinguish between :

(i) Benzyl chloride and Chlorobenzene

Benzyl chloride and chlorobenzene can be distinguished by $AgNO_3$ test. Benzyl chloride upon boiling with aq. KOH followed by acidification with dil. HNO_3 and addition of $AgNO_3$ solution produces white ppt. of $AgCl$.

$$CH_2Cl\text{-}C_6H_5 + KOH(aq) \xrightarrow{Boil} CH_2OH\text{-}C_6H_5 + K^+Cl^-$$

(Benzyl Chloride → Benzyl alcohol)

$$K^+Cl^- + AgNO_3 \longrightarrow AgCl\downarrow + K^+NO_3^-$$

(White ppt)

Chlorobenzene upon similar treatment does not give white ppt. of $AgCl$.

$$C_6H_5Cl \xrightarrow[(ii)\ AgNO_3]{(i)\ KOH(aq),\ Boil} \text{No white ppt.}$$

(Chlorobenzene)

(ii) Chloroform and Carbon tetrachloride

Chloroform and carbon tetrachloride can be distinguished by carbylamine test. Carbon tetrachloride does not give this test. Chloroform on warming with an alcoholic solution of aniline and KOH gives carbylamine having offensive smell.

$$CHCl_3 + C_6H_5NH_2 + 3KOH \xrightarrow{\text{Warm}}$$

Chloroform

$$C_6H_5N \overset{=}{\equiv} C + 3KCl + 3H_2O$$

Phenylisocyanide

$$CCl_4 + C_6H_5NH_2 + KOH \longrightarrow \text{No reaction}$$

38. (i) Refer Q. - 12(i) NCERT Questions.

39. Refer Q. - 12 NCERT Questions.

40. (a)

(i) $\langle\text{cyclohexyl}\rangle-CH_2OH \xrightarrow{PCl_5} \langle\text{cyclohexyl}\rangle-CH_2Cl$

(ii) $\langle\text{phenyl}\rangle-CH_2CH = CH_2 + HBr \longrightarrow$

$\langle\text{phenyl}\rangle-CH_2\underset{|}{C}HCH_3$ with Br

(b) (i) CH_3Br or CH_3I

CH_3I reacts faster by S_N2 reaction because I^- is a better leaving group than Br^-

(ii) $(CH_3)_3C-Cl$ or CH_3Cl

CH_3Cl being $1°$ alkyl halide reacts faster by S_N2 reaction due to less steric hindrance.

41. (i) $\langle\text{cyclohexyl}\rangle-OH \xrightarrow{SOCl_2} \langle\text{cyclohexyl}\rangle-Cl$

(ii) $\langle\text{phenyl}\rangle-CH_2-CH=CH_2 + HBr \xrightarrow{\text{Peroxide}}$

$\langle\text{phenyl}\rangle-CH_2-CH_2-\underset{|}{C}H_2$ with Br

42. (a) *n*-Butyl bromide has higher boiling point than *t*-butyl bromide as the boiling point decreases with branching. This is due to the reason that with branching the surface area of alkyl halide decreases and hence the magnitude of the van der Waal's forces of attraction also decreases.

(b) Refer Theory.

43. (i)

$2 \langle\text{chlorobenzene}\rangle + 2Na \xrightarrow{\text{Dry either}} \langle\text{biphenyl}\rangle + 2NaCl$

(Chlorobenzene)   (Biphenyl)

(ii)

$$H_2C = CH-CH_3 + BH_3 \xrightarrow{Et_2O} HO-CH_2-CH_2-CH_3 + HI$$

(Propene)

$$\xrightarrow{NaOH, H_2O_2}$$

$$I-CH_2-CH_2-CH_3 + H_2O$$

(1–Iodopropane)

(iii)

$$CH_3-\underset{|}{C}H-CH_2-CH_3 \xrightarrow{\text{alc KOH}} CH_3-CH = CH-CH_3$$

with Br   (But-2-ene)

OR

(i)

$\langle\text{4-nitro, CH}_2-CH_3\rangle \xrightarrow[\text{UV light}]{Br_2}$

$\langle\text{4-nitro, CH}_2-CH_2Br\rangle + HBr$

(ii) $2CH_3-\underset{|}{C}H-CH_3 \xrightarrow[\text{Wurtz Reaction}]{\underset{\text{dry ether}}{Na}}$ with Cl

$$CH_3-\underset{|}{C}H-CH_3$$
$$CH_3-\overset{|}{C}H-CH_3$$

(iii) $CH_3-CH_2-Br \xrightarrow{AgCN} CH_3-CH_2-NC$

1. (b) As electrophile Cl^+ attacks on electron rich benzene ring and substitutes hydrogen on ortho and para position w.r.to. $-CH_3$ group. So, the reaction is electrophilic substitution reaction.

2. (a) Density is directly related to molecular mass. Higher the molecular mass, higher will be the density of the compound. The order of molecular mass is benzene < chlorobenzene < dichlorobenzene < bromochlorbenzene

3. (a) Compounds in which the halogen atom is bonded to sp^3 hybridised carbon atom next to carbon carbon-double bond are known as allyl halides.

$$CH_3CH = CHC(Br)(CH_3)_2$$

4. (c) $CH_3Cl + NH_3 \rightarrow CH_3NH_2 + HCl$

     Excess   Methanamine

However, if the two reactants are present in the same amount, then the mixture of amines (i.e., primary, secondary and tertiary) are obtained.

5. (a) In $C_6H_5CH_2Br$ carbocation is $C_6H_5\overset{\oplus}{C}H_2$ which is stable due to resonance.

6. (d) Boiling point is directly proportional to size of the molecule. All contains same halogen atom but different hydrocarbon part. Larger the different hydrocarbon part larger the boiling point.

7. (d) Thionyl chloride is preferred over PCl_3 and PCl_5 for the preparation of alkyl chlorides from alcohols because Thionyl chloride gives pure alkyl halide as other two products $(SO_2 + HCl)$ are escapable gases.

8. (b) $(CH_3)_3CBr \xrightarrow[\text{Dry ether}]{Na}$

$$CH_3-\underset{\underset{CH_3}{|}}{\overset{\overset{CH_3}{|}}{C}}-\underset{\underset{CH_3}{|}}{\overset{\overset{CH_3}{|}}{C}}-CH_3 + 2\,NaBr$$

9. (d) Chlorination of nitrobenzene leads to the formation of *m*-nitrochlorobenzene because $-NO_2$ group deactivates the ring because it is *meta* directing.

10.   II, due to symmetry of para-positions; it fits into crystal lattice better than other isomers.

11.   In first step in S_N1 tert-alkyl halide undergoes ionization to produce tert-alkyl carbocation and halide ion. The energy needed for cleavage of the $C - X$ bond is obtained through the solvation of halide ion with proton of protic solvent. Thus polar solvents help in solvation of carbocation.

12. $C_2H_5OH + HCl \xrightarrow{ZnCl_2} C_2H_5Cl \xrightarrow{NaI} C_2H_5I$.

13.   It acts as a stronger nucleophile from the carbon end because it will lead to the formation of $C - C$ bond which is more stable than the $C - N$ bond.

Objective Practice Exercise

1.   **(d)**   Neohexyl chloride is a primary halide as in it Cl-atom is attached to a primary carbon.

$$CH_3 - \overset{\overset{\displaystyle CH_3}{|}}{\underset{\underset{\displaystyle CH_3}{|}}{C}} - CH_2 - CH_2Cl$$

2.   **(d)**   Due to conjugation of lonepair of Cl with π bond, partial double bond character decreases bond length that's why compound (d) has shortest C–Cl bond length.

3.   **(a)** $\underset{\underset{\displaystyle CH_3}{|}}{CHCl_2} \quad \underset{\underset{\displaystyle CH_2Cl}{|}}{CH_2Cl}$

     (*gem*-dihalide)   (*vic*-dihalide)

4.   **(a)**   For a given alkyl group, the order of reactivity is

$$\underset{\text{increasing bond energy}}{R - I > R - Br > R - Cl > R - F} \rightarrow \text{decreasing halogen}$$

reactivity.

This order depends on the carbon-halogen bond energy; the carbon-fluorine bond energy is maximum and thus fluorides are least reactive while carboniodine bond energy is minimum hence iodides are most reactive.

5.   **(d)**   4-Bromobut-1-ene is not an allylic halide

$$\underset{\text{4–Bromobut–1–ene}}{BrH_2C - CH_2 - CH = CH_2}$$

6.   **(a)**

$$CH_3 - \overset{\overset{\displaystyle CH_3}{|}}{\underset{\underset{\displaystyle CH_3}{|}}{C}} - Cl + 2Na + Cl - \overset{\overset{\displaystyle CH_3}{|}}{\underset{\underset{\displaystyle CH_3}{|}}{C}} - CH_3$$

     t-Butyl chloride   Wurtz Rxn $\downarrow$

$$CH_3 - \overset{\overset{\displaystyle CH_3}{|}}{\underset{\underset{\displaystyle CH_3}{|}}{C}} - \overset{\overset{\displaystyle CH_3}{|}}{\underset{\underset{\displaystyle CH_3}{|}}{C}} - CH_2Cl \xleftarrow[\text{Clorination}]{\text{Mono}} CH_3 - \overset{\overset{\displaystyle CH_3}{|}}{\underset{\underset{\displaystyle CH_3}{|}}{C}} - \overset{\overset{\displaystyle CH_3}{|}}{\underset{\underset{\displaystyle CH_3}{|}}{C}} - CH_3$$

7.   **(d)**   The non-reactivity of chlorine atom in vinyl chloride is due to resonance stabilisation.

$$CH_2 = CH - \overset{..}{\underset{..}{Cl}} \longrightarrow \overset{-}{C}H_2 - CH = \overset{+}{\underset{..}{Cl}}$$

8.   **(a)**

9.   **(a)**   The correct order of increasing bond length is $CH_3F < CH_3Cl < CH_3Br < CH_3I$

10.   **(a)** $CH_3CH_2Cl > CH_2 = CHCl > C_6H_5Cl$

11.   **(b)**

$$\underset{\underset{\displaystyle Cl}{|}}{CH_3 - \overset{1°}{CH} - \overset{2°}{\underset{4°}{C}} - CH_2 - CH_3}$$

$$\overset{1°}{CH_3} \quad \overset{1°}{CH_3}$$

3-chloro-2,3-dimethylpentane

12.   **(b)** $C_2H_5I \xrightarrow{\text{alc. KOH}} CH_2 = CH_2 \xrightarrow{Br_2}$

$$BrCH_2 - CH_2Br \xrightarrow{KCN} NCCH_2.CH_2CN$$

13.   **(a)**

14.   **(b)**   Weaker the base, better the leaving group. Hence

$$\xrightarrow{\text{Decreasing order of basicity}}$$

$$\underset{\text{(II)} \quad \text{(I)} \quad \text{(III)} \quad \text{(IV)}}{OMe \quad OAc \quad OSO_2Me \quad OSO_2CF_3}$$

$$\xleftarrow{\text{Decreasing order of leaving group}}$$

15.   **(d)**

16.   **(d)** $Cl_3C - CH_2CH_3 + KOH \xrightarrow{\text{heat}}$

$$(OH)_3C - CH_2CH_3 + 3KCl$$

$$\overset{\overset{\displaystyle O}{\|}}{CH_3CH_2C} - OH \longleftarrow$$

17.   **(c)**   Stability of the three corresponding carbocations

$$CH_2 = CH\overset{+}{C}HCH_3 > CH_3CH_2\overset{+}{C}HCH_3 > CH_3CH_2\overset{+}{C}H_2$$

   Allyl Carbocation   2° Carbocation   1° Carbocation

18.   **(d)**   All given reactions give the vinyl chloride by substitution (a), by dehydrohalogenation (b) and by addition (c)

19.   **(b)**   Reaction (i) is not possible because OH^- is a stronger base than Cl^-; hence it can't be replaced by Cl^-. However, in reaction (ii) OH group is first protonated to form $R\overset{+}{O}H_2$ in which H_2O, being a very weak base, is easily replaced by Cl^-.

20.   **(b)** $R - X + NaI \xrightarrow{\text{acetone}} R - I + NaX \downarrow$

     Soluble in   Insoluble in

     (CH_3OH, Me_2CO) (CH_3OH, Me_2CO)

     (where $X = Cl$ or Br)

21.   **(b)**   At high temp. i.e., 400°C substitution occurs in preference to addition.

$$CH_3CH = CH_2 \xrightarrow[-HCl]{Cl_2, 400°C} ClCH_2CH = CH_2$$

22.   **(c)**   Potassium ethoxide is a strong base, and 2-bromopentane is a 2° bromide, so elimination reaction predominates

$$CH_3CH(Br)CH_2CH_2CH_3 \xrightarrow{OC_2H_5^-}$$

$$CH_3CH = CHCH_2CH_3 + CH_2 = CHCH_2CH_2CH_3$$

   Pentene - 2(major) *trans*   Pentene–1(minor) *cis*

Since *trans*- alkene is more stable than *cis*, thus *trans*-pentene -2 is the main product.

23.   **(b)** $CH_3 - CH_2 - CHCl_2 \xrightarrow[\Delta]{NaNH_2}$

$$CH_3 - CH = CHCl \xrightarrow[\Delta]{NaNH_2} CH_3 - C \equiv CH$$

                              Final Product

24. (a)

$$C_6H_5-N=NCl \xrightarrow[\Delta]{HBF_4} C_6H_5-F + N_2 + BF_3 + NaCl$$

(Balz-Schiemann's reaction)

25. (c)

26. (c) $-CH_3$ group is *o, p*–directing.

27. (a)

$$C_6H_5Cl + (CH_3)_2 NLi \xrightarrow{(CH_3)_2 NH} C_6H_5 N(CH_3)_2 + LiCl$$

28. (d) $C_6H_5NH_2 \xrightarrow[HCl]{HONO} C_6H_5N_2Cl \xrightarrow{CuCl} C_6H_5Cl$

29. (c)   **30. (d)**

31. (a)

Rate $\propto$ $[C_6H_5Cl]\,[\overline{Nu}:]$

32. (a) Peroxide effect is observed only in case of HBr. Therefore, addition of HCl to propene even in the presence of benzoyl peroxide occurs according to Markonikov's rule:

$$CH_3 - CH = CH_2 \xrightarrow[\substack{Benzoyl \\ peroxide}]{HCl} CH_3 - CHCl - CH_3$$

33. (c)

$$CH_3 - \overset{\overset{\displaystyle Br}{|}}{C}H - CH_2 - CH_3 \xrightarrow{Alc.\ KOH}$$

$$CH_3 - CH = CH - CH_3 + HBr$$

The formation of 2-butene is in accordance to **Saytzeff's rule** according to which more substituted alkene is formed in major quantity.

34. (a) It is an example of substitution reaction

35. (b) $CH_3 - CH_2 - CH_2 - Cl \xrightarrow[KOH]{alc.} \underset{(B)}{CH_3CH = CH_2}$

$$\xrightarrow{HBr} \underset{(C)}{CH_3 - \overset{\overset{\displaystyle Br}{|}}{C}H - CH_3} \xrightarrow[ether]{Na} \underset{(D)}{\overset{1}{C}H_3\overset{2}{C}H - \overset{3}{C}H\overset{4}{C}H_3}$$

(with CH_3 groups on C2 and C3)

36. (d) $\underset{Ethyl\ bromide}{C_2H_5Br} \xrightarrow{AgCN} \underset{Ethyl\ isocyanide}{C_2H_5NC} \xrightarrow{Reduction}$

$$\underset{Ethyl\ methyl\ amine}{C_2H_5NHCH_3}$$

37. (a) $C_2H_6\ (excess) + Cl_2 \xrightarrow{UV\ light} C_2H_5Cl + HCl$

38. (d) $-Cl$ is *o, p*–directing.

39. (c)

$$\underset{Chlorobenzene}{C_6H_5Cl} \xrightarrow[anhy.AlCl_3]{CH_3COCl} \underset{2\text{-Chloroacetophenone}}{} + \underset{\substack{4\text{-Chloroaceto-} \\ phenone\ (Major)}}{}$$

Ortho-Product is minor because of steric hindrance.

40. (a) All those compounds which follow S_N1 mechanism during nucleophilic subsitution reaction will give racemic mixture.

Order of reactivity of alkyl halides for S_N1.

$$3° > 2° > 1°\ CH_3\ X$$

Thus, $CH_3 - \overset{\overset{\displaystyle |}{C_2H_5}}{C}H - Br$ contains a 2° chiral carbon, so

it gives a racemic product.

41. (b) Heavy metal ions, particularly Ag^+, catalyse S_N1 reaction because of presence of empty orbital.

42. (c) $R - OH + SOCl_2 \xrightarrow{Pyridine} RCl + SO_2\uparrow + HCl\uparrow$

SO_2 and HCl being gases escape leaving behind pure alkyl halide.

43. (b) $\underset{n-Propyl\ bromide}{CH_3 - CH_2 - CH_2Br} \xrightarrow[-HBr]{ethanolic\ KOH} \underset{Propene}{CH_3 - CH = CH_2}$

44. (a) Gem dihalides on treatment with alcoholic KOH gives alkyne as follows :

$$R - \overset{\overset{\displaystyle CX_2}{|}}{C}H_2 \ \ \xrightarrow[-2HX]{alc.KOH} RC \equiv CH$$

(shown as $R-CH_2CX_2$ with H substituent)

45. (d)

46. (d) 4-Bromobut-l-ene is not an allylic halide

$$\underset{4-Bromobut-1-ene}{BrH_2C - CH_2 - CH = CH_2}$$

$$\underset{4-Bromopent-2-ene}{CH_3 - CH = CH - \overset{\overset{\displaystyle Br}{|}}{C}H - CH_3} \quad \underset{3-Bromo-2-methylbut-1-ene}{CH_2 = \overset{\overset{\displaystyle CH_3}{|}}{C} - \overset{\overset{\displaystyle Br}{|}}{C}H - CH_3}$$

$$\underset{1-Bromobut-2-ene}{BrCH_2 - CH = CH - CH_3} \quad \underset{4-Bromobut-1-ene}{CH_2 = CH - CH_2 - CH_2Br}$$

47. (d) All compounds have tertiary alkyl group but bond between carbon and iodine (C — I) is weakest bond due to higher difference in size of carbon and iodine.

48. (d) Fluoroalkanes are difficult to prepare directly because flourination of hydrocarbons with pure F_2 gas occurs explosively. Therefore these are prepared by treating alkyl chloride or bromide with salts such as Hg_2F_2, AgF. The reaction is called swarts reaction.

$$CH_3Br + AgF \rightarrow CH_3F + AgBr$$

49. **(c)** S_N1 mechanism is favoured by polar protic solvent.

50. **(b)** Iodine is a better leaving group than Cl, Br and F.

51. **(c)** Methanol has higher dielectric constant (32) than other given compounds.

52. **(d)**

53. **(b)** Since I is a better leaving group, and upon leaving, it will form seconday carbocation (stable) in the compound I-Iodo-2 methyl propane.

Chapter Test

1. **(a)**

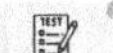

2. **(d)** Chlorination of *n*-butane takes place via free radical formation i.e., $Cl_2 \xrightarrow{h\nu} \overset{\bullet}{Cl} + \overset{\bullet}{Cl}$

$$CH_3 - CH_2 - CH_2 - CH_3 \xrightarrow{Cl_2/h\nu}$$

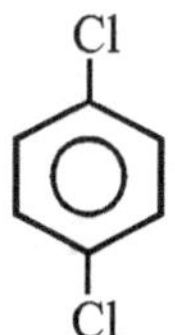

Racemic mixture
50% *d* form + 50% *l* form

$Cl^{\bullet}$ may attack on either side and give a racemic mixture of 2-chlorobutane which contain 50% *d* form and 50% *l*-form.

3. **(d)** (ii) and (iii)

4. **(a)** 1° Alkyl halides (having least steric hindrance at α-carbon atom) are most reactive towards S_N2 reaction.

5. **(c)** Chloral Cl_3CCHO reacts with phenyl chloride to form D.D.T. in presence of conc. H_2SO_4 and a H_2O molecule is eliminated in this reaction. Hence, it is an elimination reaction

6. **(c)** Alkyl iodide can be prepared by treating alkyl halides with NaI in presence of acetone. It is called Finkelstein reaction.

$$R-X + NaI \xrightarrow{acetone} R-I + NaX$$

Also, NaI is soluble in acetone but NaBr/NaCl are not soluble.

7. **(b)** Alkylbenzene can not be prepared by Friedal Crafts alkylation of benzene as di, tri alkylated benzenes are also formed.

8. **(a)** Boiling point of CH_3I is 42°C which indicates that it is liquid at room temperature. CH_3I is larger molecule so it has stronger vander Waal's force of attraction than others.

9. **(d)** Para-dichlorobenzene has most symmetrical structure than others. It is found as crystalline lattice form, therefore, it has highest melting point (52°C) due to symmetrical structure.

10. **(d)** (i) (ii) and (iv) are correct.

11. **(c)** For the same alkyl group, the boiling points of alkyl halides decrease in the order :

RI > RBr > RCl > RF

This is because with the increase in size and mass of halogen atom, the magnitude of van der Waal's forces increases.

OR

(b)

12. 1-Chloro-2-phenylethane.

13. Iodide ion because of its bigger size and lower electronegativity.

14. (*a*) 1, 1, 1-Trichloro -2, 2-diphenylethane.
(*b*) 2, 4, 6-tribromophenol.

15. Chlorobenzene < 4-nitrochlorobenzene
< 2, 4- dinitrochlorobenzene < 2, 4, 6-trinitrochlorobenzene

5 Alcohols, Phenols and Ethers

ALCOHOLS, PHENOLS AND ETHERS

Alcohols — **Phenols** — **Ethers**

Alcohols

Preparation

(a) **By acid catalysed hydration :** Alkenes reacts with H_2O in presence of H_3O^+

(b) **By Hydroboration-Oxidation :** Diborane with alkene gives trialkyl boride which gives alcohol with H_2O_2/OH^-

(c) **Reduction of Aldehydes and Ketones**

Aldehyde $\xrightarrow{H_2/Pd}$ 1° Alcohol

Ketone $\xrightarrow{NaBH_4}$ 2° Alcohol

(d) **Reduction of carboxylic acids**

$RCOOH \xrightarrow[(ii)\,H_2O]{(i)\,LiAlH_4} RCH_2OH$

Properties

(a) $2ROH + 2M \rightarrow 2R\text{-}\overset{+}{O}\overset{-}{M} + H_2$

(b) $RCOOH + H\text{-}OR' \rightarrow RCOOR' + H_2O$

(c) $RCOCl + H\text{-}OR' \rightarrow RCOOR' + HCl$

(d) $ROH + R'MgX \rightarrow R'\text{-}H + ROMgX$

(e) $ROH + PCl_5 \rightarrow RCl + POCl_3 + HCl$

(f) $R\text{-}OH + HCl \xrightarrow{Anh.ZnCl_2} CH_3CH_2\text{-}Cl + H_2O$

(g) $CH_3CH_2OH \xrightarrow{Conc.H_2SO_4} CH_2=CH_2 + H_2O$

(h) $RCH_2OH \xrightarrow{[O]} R\text{-}\underset{H}{C}=O \xrightarrow{[O]} R\text{-}\overset{O}{\underset{}{C}}\text{-}OH$

Ethers

Preparation

(a) **Dehydration of alcohol**

$2CH_3CH_2OH \xrightarrow{H_2SO_4} C_2H_5OC_2H_5 + H_2O$

(b) **Williamson's synthesis**

$R\text{-}X + R'\text{-}ONa \rightarrow ROR' + NaX$

Properties

(a) $R\text{-}O\text{-}R' + HX \rightarrow RX + R'OH$

(b) **Methoxy benzene**

$\xrightarrow[\text{Ethanoic acid}]{Br_2}$ *o*- and, *p*-bromo Methoxy benzene

$\xrightarrow[CH_3Cl]{Anhy.AlCl_3}$ *o*- and *p*-methyl methoxy benzene

$\xrightarrow{H_2SO_4 + HNO_3}$ *o*- and *p*-nitro methoxy benzene

Phenols

Preparation

(a) Chlorobenzene + NaOH $\xrightarrow[(ii)\,HCl]{(i)\,623K,\,300\,atm}$ Phenol

(b) Benzene $\xrightarrow[(ii)\,NaOH,\,H^+]{(i)\,Oleum}$ Phenol

(c) Aniline $\xrightarrow[273-278K]{NaNO_2 + HCl}$ Diazonium salt $\xrightarrow{H_2O}$ Phenol

(d) Cumene $\xrightarrow[(ii)\,H^+/H_2O]{(i)\,O_2}$ Phenol

Properties

(a) Nitration give *o*- and *p*-nitrophenol

(b) With Br_2/H_2O it gives 2, 4, 6- tribromophenol

(c) In presence of low polarity solvents like $CHCl_3$ and CS_2 on bromination it gives *o*, and *p*-bromophenol

(d) Phenol $+ CO_2 \xrightarrow{400K,\,4-7atm}$ Salicylic acid

(e) Phenol $+ CHCl_3 \xrightarrow{NaOH}$ Salicylaldehyde

| Topic 1 | Classification and Structure of Alcohols, Phenols and Ethers, Preparation and Properties of Alcohols and Phenols |

Alcohols are the hydroxy derivatives of aliphatic hydrocarbons and **phenols** are the hydroxy derivatives of aromatic hydrocarbons in which the hydroxyl group is directly attached to the carbon atom of the aromatic ring.

CLASSIFICATION OF ALCOHOLS, PHENOLS AND ETHERS

Classification of Alcohols and phenols

According to the number of –OH groups
Alcohols and phenols may be classified as **monohydric, dihydric, trihydric or polyhydric** according as they contain one, two, three or many hydroxyl groups respectively in their molecules.

(a) Monohydric [one – OH] $\longrightarrow CH_3CH_2 – OH$;

(b) Dihydric [two – OH] $\longrightarrow$ $CH_2 – CH_2$;
with OH OH

(c) Trihydric [three – OH] $\longrightarrow$ $CH_2 – CH – CH_2$;
with OH OH OH

(d) Polyhydric[n–OH] $\longrightarrow CH_2 –CH–CH_2$;
with OH OH OH

Monohydric alcohols are further classified according to hybridisation of C-atom to which –OH is attached.

Alcohols having C_{sp^3}–OH bond
(a) **Primary (1°), secondary (2°) and tertiary (3°) alcohols** according as the OH group is attached to a primary, secondary and tertiary carbon atoms respectively.
    (i) *primary* or 1° alcohol $\longrightarrow CH_3CH_2 – OH$ (ii) *Secondary* or 2° alcohol $\longrightarrow (CH_3)_2CH – OH$
    (iii) *Tertiary* or 3° alcohol $\longrightarrow (CH_3)_3C – OH$
(b) **Allylic alcohol:** – OH group is attached to a sp^3 hybridised carbon next to the C=C double bond.

For *e.g.,* $CH_2 = CH – CH_2OH$; $CH_2 = CH – \overset{\displaystyle H}{\underset{\displaystyle CH_3}{C}} – OH$

(c) **Benzylic alcohol:** – OH group is attached to a sp^3-hybridised C-atom next to an aromatic ring.

For *e.g.,*

Alcohols having C_{sp^2} – OH bond : – OH group containing vinylic carbon or aryl carbon.
$CH_2 = CH – OH$

vinyl alcohol (unstable)

Phenol   Catechol

Classification of Ethers

Ethers are classified as **simple** or **symmetrical** ethers if the alkyl or aryl groups attached to the oxygen atom are same, and **mixed** or **unsymmetrical** ethers if the two groups are different.

NOMENCLATURE

Alcohols

The name of an alcohol is derived from the name of the alkane from which the alcohol is derived by substituting 'e' of alkane with the suffix 'ol'. The position of the substituents are indicated by numerals. Cyclo alcohols are named using the prefix cyclo and considering the – OH group attached to C–1

Phenols

The simplest hydroxy derivative of benzene is phenol. It is its common name and also an accepted IUPAC name. As structure of phenol involves a benzene ring in its substituted compounds, the terms ortho (1, 2- disubstituted), meta (1, 3- disubstituted) and para (1, 4-disubstituted) are often used in the common names.

Ethers

Common names of ethers are derived from the names of alkyl or aryl groups written as separate words in alphabetical order and adding the word 'ether' at the end. General, IUPAC name of ethers is alkoxy alkane where alkoxy is smaller alkyl group attached to oxygen.

STRUCTURE OF FUNCTIONAL GROUPS

Structure of Alcoholic –OH Group

Alcohols are bent molecules. The carbon atom (linked with O atom of – OH group) is sp^3 hybridised. The central O atom is also in sp^3 state of hybridisation. The bond angle is 108.9°. Two of the four sp^3-hybridised orbitals of O overlap separately with $1s$ orbital of H and sp^3-orbital of C to form O–H and C–O, bonds while remaining two sp^3-orbitals contain lone pairs of electrons. Due to lone pair–lone pair repulsions, the C–O–H bond angle is less than normal tetrahedral structure (109°28').

Structure of Phenolic – OH Group

In phenols, –OH group is attached to sp^2 hybridised C of aromatic ring. The C–O bond length in phenols is less than methanol. This is because of

(i) partial double bond character of C–O bond

(ii) sp^2 – hybridised state of C to which O is attached.

Structure of Ethers

Hybridisation state of oxygen is sp^3

In ethers, 2 bond pairs and 2 lone pairs on O are arranged approximately tetrahedrally. The bond angle is slightly greater than tetrahedral angle due to repulsive interaction between bulky –R groups. The C–O bond length is almost same as that in alcohols.

METHODS OF PREPARATION OF ALCOHOLS

(I) From Alkenes

(a) **By acid catalysed hydration:** Alkenes react with water in the presence of acid as catalyst to form alcohols. In case of unsymmetrical alkenes, the addition reaction takes place in accordance with Markovnikov's rule.

$$e.g., \quad CH_3C = CH_2 + H_2O \underset{\overset{H^+}{\longrightarrow}}{\rightleftharpoons} CH_3 - CH - CH_3$$

Mechanism of hydration

(i) Electrophilic attack of H_3O^+

$$H_2O + H^+ \longrightarrow H_3O^+$$

(from acid)

$$>C = C< + H_3O^+ \longrightarrow -\overset{+}{C} - \overset{|}{C} - H + H_2O$$

(*ii*) Nucleophilic attack of water on carbocation

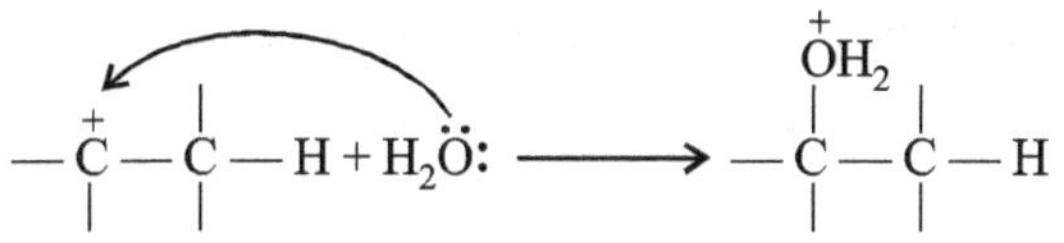

$$-\overset{+}{C}-\overset{|}{C}-H + H_2\overset{..}{O}: \longrightarrow -\overset{\overset{+}{O}H_2}{\underset{|}{C}}-\overset{|}{C}-H$$

(*iii*) Deprotonation

$$-\overset{\overset{H\ \ H}{\diagdown\overset{+}{O}}}{\underset{|}{C}}-\overset{|}{C}-H \xrightarrow{H_2\overset{..}{O}:} -\overset{OH}{\underset{|}{C}}-\overset{|}{C}-H + H_3O^+$$

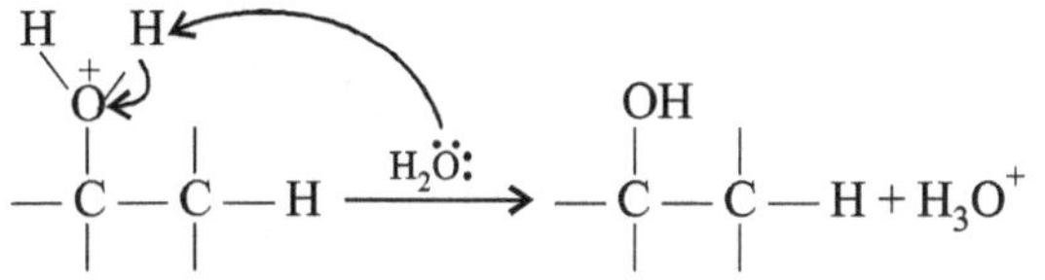

(b) **By hydroboration–oxidation:** Diborane $(BH_3)_2$ reacts with alkenes to give trialkyl boranes as addition product. Which is oxidised to alcohol by hydrogen peroxide in the presence of aqueous sodium hydroxide.

$$CH_3-CH=CH_2 + (H-BH_2)_2 \longrightarrow CH_3-\underset{\underset{H}{|}}{CH}-\underset{\underset{BH_2}{|}}{CH_2} \xrightarrow{CH_3-CH=CH_2} (CH_3-CH_2-CH_2)_2BH$$

$$\Big\downarrow CH_3-CH=CH_2$$

$$B(OH)_3 + 3CH_3CH_2CH_2OH \xleftarrow[\underset{Propan\text{-}1\text{-}ol}{3H_2O_2}]{H_2O/OH^-} (CH_3-CH_2-CH_2)_3B$$

(II) From Carbonyl Compounds

(a) **By reduction of aldehydes and ketones :** Aldehydes give $1°$ alcohols and ketones give $2°$ alcohols.

$$RCHO + H_2 \xrightarrow{Pd} \underset{1°\ alcohol}{RCH_2OH}; \qquad RCOR' \xrightarrow{NaBH_4} \underset{\underset{\underset{2°\ alcohol}{OH}}{|}}{R-CH-R'}$$

Note: $3°$ alcohol cannot be obtained by this method. $LiAlH_4$ does not reduce carbon carbon double bond, hence it is used to prepare unsaturated alcohols from unsaturated aldehydes and ketones.

(b) **By reduction of carboxylic acids and their derivatives:**

$$e.g., RCOOH \xrightarrow[(ii)H_2O]{(i)LiAlH_4} RCH_2OH; \quad \underset{\underset{O}{||}}{R-C-X} + 4H \xrightarrow{LiAlH_4} RCH_2OH + HX$$

$$\underset{Acid\ halide}{}$$

$$\underset{\underset{O}{||}}{R-C-OR'} + 4H \xrightarrow{LiAlH_4} \underset{Alcohol}{RCH_2OH + R'OH}; \qquad \underset{Acid\ anhydride}{(RCO)_2O} + 8H \xrightarrow{LiAlH_4} \underset{Alcohol}{2RCH_2OH + H_2O}$$

$$\underset{Ester}{}$$

Acid amide on reduction forms primary amine as major product and not alcohol.

Commercially acids are converted to alcohols as following :

$$RCOOH \xrightarrow[H^+]{R'OH} RCOOR' \xrightarrow[Catalyst]{H_2} RCH_2OH + R'OH$$

(III) From Grignard Reagents

$$HCHO + RMgX \longrightarrow RCH_2OMgX \xrightarrow{H_2O} RCH_2OH + Mg(OH)X$$

$$RCHO + R'MgX \longrightarrow \underset{\underset{R'}{|}}{R-CH-OMgX} \xrightarrow{H_2O} \underset{\underset{R'}{|}}{R-CH-OH} + Mg(OH)X$$

$$RCOR + R'MgX \longrightarrow \underset{\underset{R}{|}}{R-C-OMgX} \xrightarrow{H_2O} \underset{\underset{R'}{|}}{R-C-OH} + Mg(OH)X$$

Primary alcohols can also be prepared by

$$R-Mg-X + H_2C\overset{\diagup\diagdown}{\underset{O}{\text{———}}}CH_2 \longrightarrow R-CH_2-CH_2-O-Mg-X \xrightarrow{H_2O} \underset{Alcohol}{R-CH_2CH_2OH + Mg(X)OH}$$

(ethylene oxide)

(IV) From Alkyl Halides (Hydrolysis)

Alkyl halides on hydrolysis with aq. KOH/moist Ag_2O or AgOH form alcohols. The hydrolysis occurs by nucleophilic substitution reaction.

$$R-CH_2-X + AgOH(aq.) \longrightarrow R-CH_2-OH + AgX$$
$$1° Alcohol$$

$$R-\underset{}{\overset{R}{CH}}-X + K-OH\,(aq.) \longrightarrow R-\underset{}{\overset{R}{CH}}-OH + KX \,; \qquad R-\underset{R}{\overset{R}{C}}-X + H-OH \longrightarrow R-\underset{R}{\overset{R}{C}}-OH + HX$$

Alkyl halide $\qquad\qquad\qquad\qquad$ 2° Alcohol $\qquad\qquad\qquad\qquad\qquad\qquad\qquad$ 3° Alcohol

(V) From Primary Amines

Primary alcohols are formed when primary amines are treated with nitrous acid (HNO_2)

$$R-NH_2 + HNO_2 \xrightarrow{\;HCl\;} R-OH + N_2 + H_2O$$

METHODS OF PREPARATION OF PHENOLS

Phenols also known as carbolic acid. They are prepared from following methods:

(I) From Haloarenes (Dow's Process)

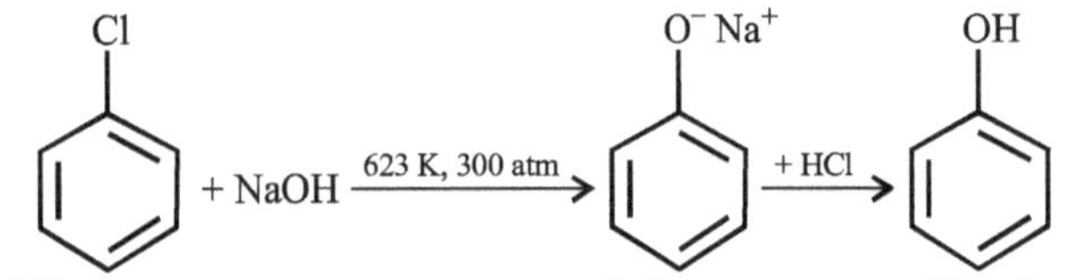

Chlorobenzene + NaOH $\xrightarrow{623\ K,\ 300\ atm}$ Sodium phenoxide $\xrightarrow{+\ HCl}$ Phenol

(II) From Benzenesulphonic Acid

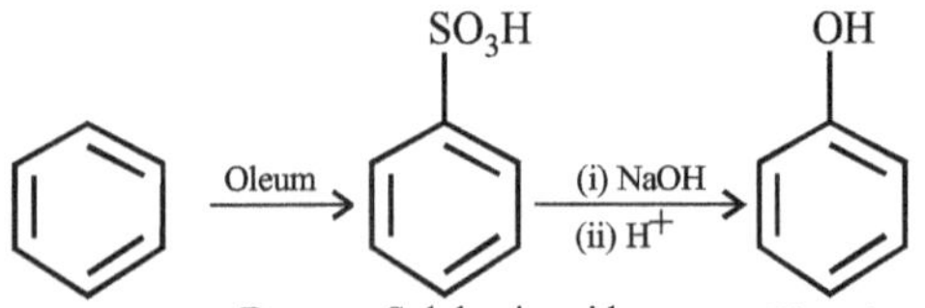

Benzene $\xrightarrow{Oleum}$ Benzene Sulphonic acid $\xrightarrow[(ii)\ H^+]{(i)\ NaOH}$ Phenol

(III) From Diazonium Salts

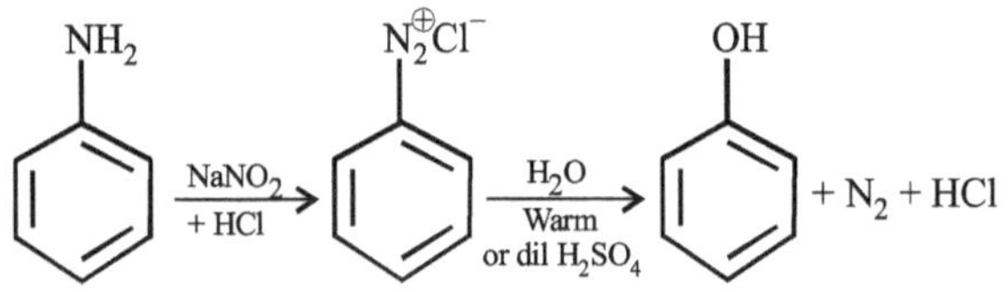

Aniline $\xrightarrow[+\ HCl]{NaNO_2}$ Benzene diazonium chloride $\xrightarrow[\substack{Warm \\ or\ dil\ H_2SO_4}]{H_2O}$ Phenol $+ N_2 + HCl$

(IV) From Cumene

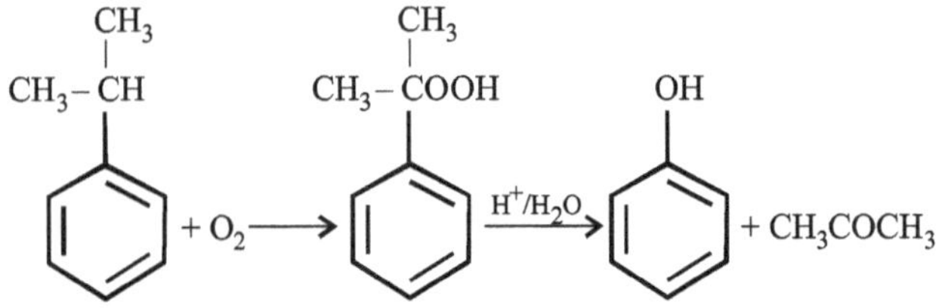

Cumene $+ O_2 \longrightarrow$ Cumene hydroperoxide $\xrightarrow{H^+/H_2O}$ Phenol $+ CH_3COCH_3$

(V) By Distilling a Phenolic Acid with Soda Lime (Decarboxylation)

Salicylic acid $+ NaOH \xrightarrow[\Delta]{CaO}$ Phenol $+ Na_2CO_3$

PHYSICAL PROPERTIES OF ALCOHOLS AND PHENOLS

Physical State

At ordinary temperature lower alcohols are colourless liquids with distinct smell and burning taste. The higher members are colourless, odourless waxy solids. Pure phenols are either colourless liquids or solids. But they usually turn reddish-brown due to atmospheric oxidation.

Boiling Points

The boiling points of alcohols and phenols are much higher than the corresponding aliphatic hydrocarbons and haloalkanes because they form intermolecular hydrogen bonds.

Boiling points of alcohols and phenols increases with increase in the number of carbon atoms due to increase in van der Wall's forces. In alcohols, the boiling points decrease with increase of branching in carbon chain.

$$\text{Boiling point} \propto \text{Molecular mass} \propto \frac{1}{\text{No. of branches}}$$

Solubility

The lower alcohols are highly soluble in water but the solubility decreases with the increase in molecular mass of the alcohol. Among isomeric alcohols, the solubility increases with branching. Phenols also form hydrogen bonds with water and hence should be soluble in water.

CHEMICAL PROPERTIES OF ALCOHOLS AND PHENOLS :

(I) Reactions Involving the Cleavage of the O – H Bond

(a) **Reaction with metals :** Alcohols and phenols gives alkoxides / phenoxides and hydrogen with active metals:

$$2ROH + 2M \longrightarrow 2R-O^-M^+ + H_2; \quad 2ROH + M \longrightarrow (RO)_2M + H_2 \, (M = Ca^{2+} \text{ or } Mg^{2+})$$

$$6(CH_3)_3COH + 2Al \longrightarrow 2\left((CH_3)_3CO\right)_3Al + 3H_2 ;$$

OH $+ NaOH \longrightarrow$ ONa $+ H_2O$

Above reactions shows that alcohol and phenols are Bronsted acids i.e., they can donate a proton to a stronger base. $(M = Na^+ \text{ or } K^+)$

Acidity of alcohols: They are acidic due to polar O–H bond. Alkyl groups increases the e^- density on O atom of the O–H bond. As a result, the electrons of the O–H bond are not sufficiently attracted towards the oxygen atom thereby decreasing the polarity of O–H bond. Thus tending to decrease the acid strength. Acid strength order of alcohols will be $1° > 2° > 3°$. Due to same reason, alcohols are weaker acids than water. Basic strength order of alkoxides.

$$R_3CO^- > R_2CHO^- > RCH_2O^-$$

Acidity of phenols

The most characteristic property of phenols is their acidity. Phenols are more acidic than alcohols which are even more weakly acidic than water, but phenols are less acidic than carboxylic acids.

$$R-COOH > Ar-OH > H-OH > R-OH \qquad \textbf{(Acidic character)}$$

(i) Greater acidity of a phenol than an alcohol is due to possibility of resonance in phenol which leads to electron-deficient oxygen atom. Presence of electron-deficient oxygen atom (see structures II, III and IV) in turn weakens the $-\overset{+}{O} \longleftarrow H$ bond, and thus facilitates release of proton.

I   II   III   IV

Such structures are not possible in alcohols.

(ii) Once hydrogen atom is removed from phenol, the ion (phenoxide) is very much stabilized due to delocalization of its negative charge.

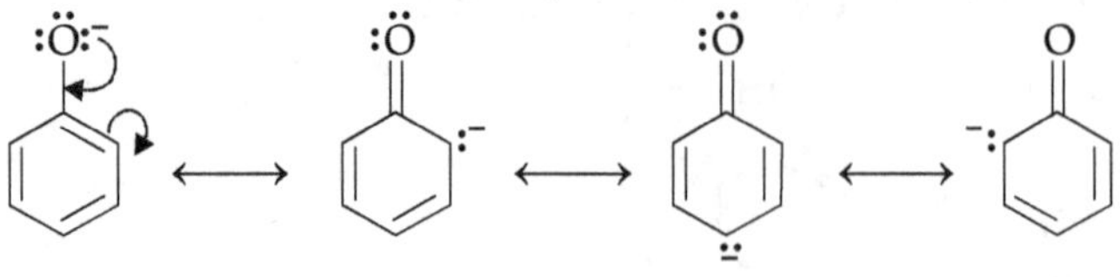

V   VI   VII   VIII

Resonance in phenoxide ion (note that structures VI to VIII are equivalent)

Remember that phenoxide ion is very much more stable than the parent compound phenol because phenoxide ion does not involve charge separation, while in phenol three equivalent resonanting structures (II to IV) involve charge separation.

Note: Electron-withdrawing substituents increase the acidity of phenols ; while electron-releasing substituents decrease acidity.

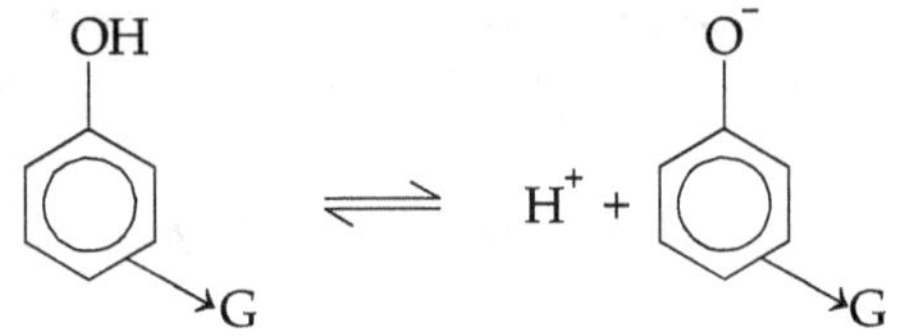

G withdraws electrons, thus disperses the –ve charge of the ion, stabilises it and hence increases ionization of the parent phenol.

(where $G = -NO_2, -CN, -CHO, -COOH, -\overset{+}{N}R_3, -X$)

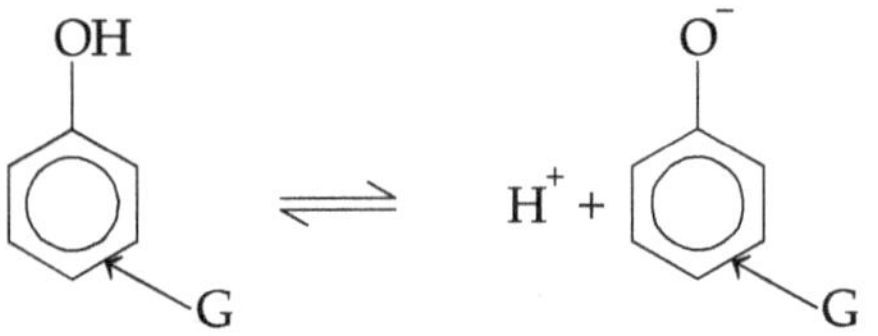

G releases electrons, thus intensifies the -ve charge of the ion, destabilises it and hence decreases ionization of the parent phenol.

(where $G = -R, -OR, -NR_2$)

(b)   **Reaction with carboxylic acids**

$$Ar/RCO\underbrace{-OH+H-}OR' \underset{}{\overset{conc.H_2SO_4}{\rightleftharpoons}} RCO-OR'+H_2O$$
Ester

Conc. H_2SO_4 is used to remove water formed in the reaction and shifts the equilibrium towards right.

Mechanism : $H_2SO_4 \longrightarrow H^+ + HSO_4^-$

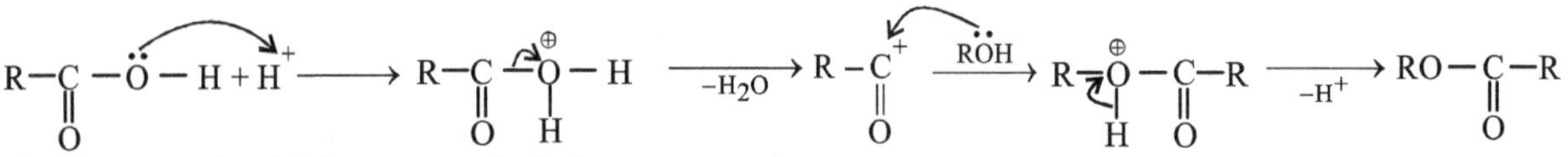

The above reaction is laboratory method of ester preparation.

(c)   **Reaction with acid chlorides and anhydrides:**

$$Ar/RCO-Cl+H-OR' \longrightarrow RCOOR'+HCl \; ; \; R-OH+(CH_3CO)_2O \longrightarrow CH_3COOR+CH_3COOH$$

(d)   **Reaction with Grignard reagents:**

$$Ar/R-OH+R'-MgX \longrightarrow R'-H+ROMgX$$

(II)   **Reactions Involving the Cleavage of C – OH Bond**

(a)   **Reaction with halogen acids:** Alcohols (but not phenols) react with halogen acids to form haloalkanes (alkyl halides) and water.

$$CH_3CH_2-OH+H-Cl \xrightarrow[\Delta]{Anhy.ZnCl_2} CH_3CH_2-Cl+H_2O$$

$$\begin{matrix} CH_3 \\ CH_3 \end{matrix}\!\!\!\!CH-OH+H-Cl \xrightarrow[\Delta]{Anhy.\,ZnCl_2} \begin{matrix} CH_3 \\ CH_3 \end{matrix}\!\!\!\!CHCl+H_2O$$

$$CH_3-\overset{\overset{\displaystyle CH_3}{|}}{\underset{\underset{\displaystyle CH_3}{|}}{C}}-OH+H-Cl \xrightarrow{Room\,temp} CH_3-\overset{\overset{\displaystyle CH_3}{|}}{\underset{\underset{\displaystyle CH_3}{|}}{C}}-Cl+H_2O$$

The difference in reactivity of three classes of alcohols with HCl distinguishes them from one another (Lucas test)

(b)   **Reaction with phosphorus halides:**

$$R-OH+PCl_5 \longrightarrow R-Cl+POCl_3+HCl \; ; \; 3R-OH+PCl_3 \longrightarrow 3R-Cl+H_3PO_3$$

(c) Reaction with thionyl chloride:

$$R-OH + SOCl_2 \xrightarrow{\text{Pyridine}} R-Cl + SO_2\uparrow + HCl\uparrow$$

(d) Reaction with ammonia:

$$R-OH + NH_3 \xrightarrow[\substack{300°C \\ \text{or} \\ Al_2O_3}]{\text{anhy. ZnCl}_2} \underset{\text{Alkylamine}}{RNH_2} + H_2O$$

(III) Reactions Involving the Alcohol Molecule as a Whole

(a) Dehydration:

$$CH_3-CH_2OH \xrightarrow[433-443K]{\text{conc.}H_2SO_4} CH_2=CH_2 + H_2O$$

Secondary and tertiary alcohols dehydrate under milder conditions.

$$CH_3CH(OH)CH_3 \xrightarrow[440K-H_2O]{85\%H_2SO_4} CH_3CH=CH_2; \quad (CH_3)_3C-OH \xrightarrow[358K,-H_2O]{20\%H_2SO_4} CH_3-\overset{\overset{\textstyle CH_3}{|}}{C}=CH_2$$

The relative ease of dehydration of alcohols follows the order:

$$3° > 2° > 1°$$

Reaction with H_2SO_4 at diferent temperatures:

(i) $\quad C_2H_5OH + H_2SO_4 \xrightarrow{110°C} \underset{\text{Ethyl hydrogen sulphate}}{CH_3CH_2OSO_3H}$

(ii) $\quad 2CH_3CH_2OSO_3H \xrightarrow{170°C} \underset{\text{Diethyl sulphate}}{(C_2H_5)_2SO_4 + H_2SO_4}$

(iii) $\quad CH_3CH_2OSO_3H + HOC_2H_5 \text{ (excess)} \xrightarrow{140°C} \underset{\text{Diethyl ether}}{CH_3-CH_2-\overset{\cdot\cdot}{\underset{\cdot\cdot}{O}}-CH_2-CH_3 + H_2SO_4}$

(iv) $\quad \underset{\text{Ethyl hydrogen sulphate}}{CH_3CH_2OSO_3H} \xrightarrow[170°C]{\text{Conc.}H_2SO_4 \text{(excess)}} \underset{\text{Ethene}}{CH_2=CH_2 + H_2SO_4}$

Mechanism of dehydration

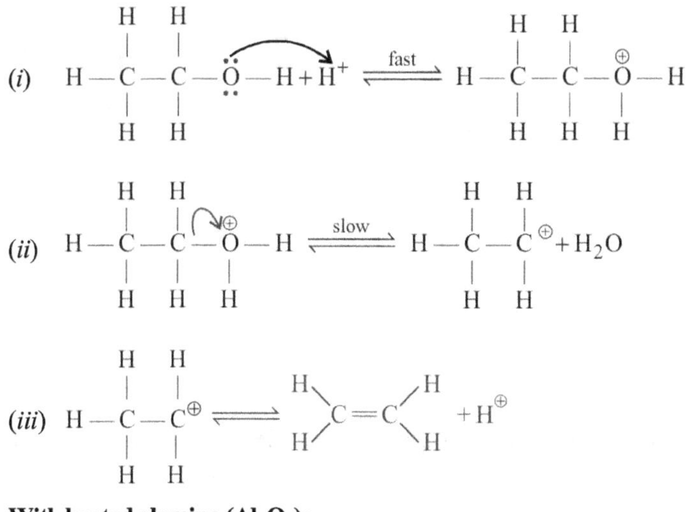

(i) $H-\overset{\overset{\textstyle H}{|}}{\underset{\underset{\textstyle H}{|}}{C}}-\overset{\overset{\textstyle H}{|}}{\underset{\underset{\textstyle H}{|}}{C}}-\overset{\cdot\cdot}{\underset{\cdot\cdot}{O}}-H + H^+ \overset{\text{fast}}{\rightleftharpoons} H-\overset{\overset{\textstyle H}{|}}{\underset{\underset{\textstyle H}{|}}{C}}-\overset{\overset{\textstyle H}{|}}{\underset{\underset{\textstyle H}{|}}{C}}-\overset{\oplus}{O}-H$

(ii) $H-\overset{\overset{\textstyle H}{|}}{\underset{\underset{\textstyle H}{|}}{C}}-\overset{\overset{\textstyle H}{|}}{\underset{\underset{\textstyle H}{|}}{C}}-\overset{\oplus}{O}-H \overset{\text{slow}}{\rightleftharpoons} H-\overset{\overset{\textstyle H}{|}}{\underset{\underset{\textstyle H}{|}}{C}}-\overset{\oplus}{\underset{\underset{\textstyle H}{|}}{C}} + H_2O$

(iii) $H-\overset{\overset{\textstyle H}{|}}{\underset{\underset{\textstyle H}{|}}{C}}-\overset{\oplus}{C} \rightleftharpoons \underset{H}{\overset{H}{}}C=C\overset{H}{\underset{H}{}} + H^{\oplus}$

(b) With heated alumina (Al_2O_3):

$$2CH_3CH_2OH \xrightarrow[513-523K]{Al_2O_3} CH_3CH_2-O-CH_2CH_3 + H_2O, \quad CH_3CH_2OH \xrightarrow[623K]{Al_2O_3} CH_2=CH_2 + H_2O$$

$$CH_3-\overset{\overset{\textstyle CH_3}{|}}{\underset{\underset{\textstyle CH_3}{|}}{C}}-OH \xrightarrow[423K]{Al_2O_3} CH_3-\overset{\underset{\underset{\textstyle CH_3}{|}}{}}{C}=CH_2 + H_2O$$

(c) Oxidation:

(i) Primary alcohol initially forms aldehyde on oxidation and on further oxidation forms respective acid.

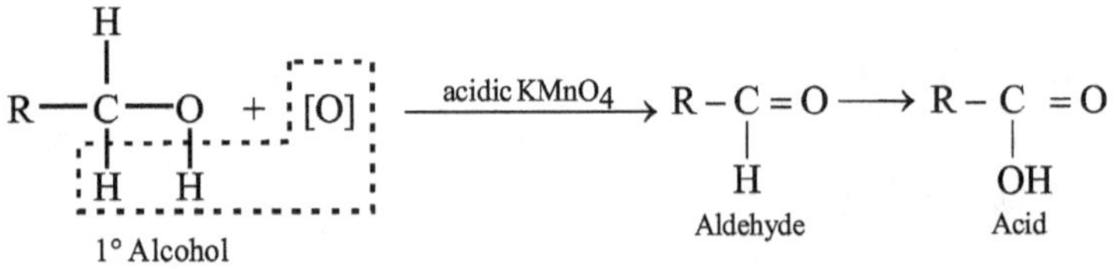

$$R \overset{\overset{\displaystyle H}{|}}{\underset{\underset{\displaystyle H}{|}}{C}} \!-\! O \overset{|}{\underset{\displaystyle H}{}} + [O] \xrightarrow{\text{acidic KMnO}_4} R-\underset{\underset{\displaystyle H}{|}}{C}=O \longrightarrow R-\underset{\underset{\displaystyle OH}{|}}{C}=O$$

1° Alcohol   Aldehyde   Acid

(ii) Secondary alcohol initially forms respective ketone on oxidation which on further oxidation forms acid with less no. of carbon atoms. Oxidation of ketone is slightly difficult than aldehyde due to stability so, we use strong oxidising agent for oxidation.

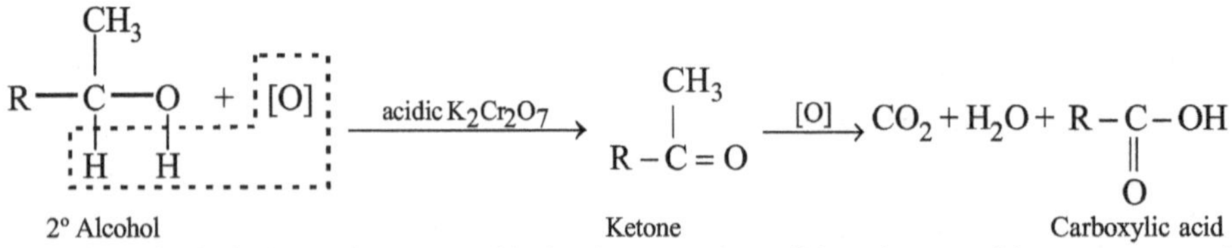

$$R \overset{\overset{\displaystyle CH_3}{|}}{\underset{\underset{\displaystyle H}{|}}{C}} \!-\! O \overset{|}{\underset{\displaystyle H}{}} + [O] \xrightarrow{\text{acidic K}_2\text{Cr}_2\text{O}_7} \underset{R-\underset{\underset{\displaystyle }{}}{C}=O}{\overset{CH_3}{|}} \xrightarrow{[O]} CO_2 + H_2O + R-\underset{\underset{\displaystyle O}{\|}}{C}-OH$$

2° Alcohol   Ketone   Carboxylic acid

(iii) Tertiary alcohols are resistant to oxidation in normal conditions but on taking strongest oxidising agent like chromic acid in dilute nitric acid they form less carbon ketone.

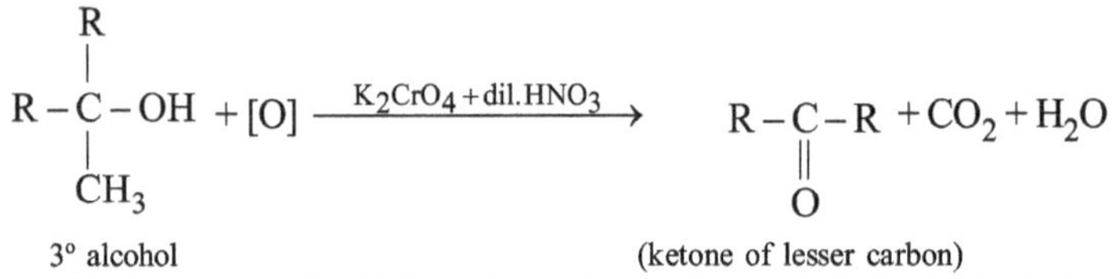

$$R-\overset{\overset{\displaystyle R}{|}}{\underset{\underset{\displaystyle CH_3}{|}}{C}}-OH + [O] \xrightarrow{\text{K}_2\text{CrO}_4 + \text{dil. HNO}_3} R-\underset{\underset{\displaystyle O}{\|}}{C}-R + CO_2 + H_2O$$

3° alcohol   (ketone of lesser carbon)

Note: For oxidation of 1° alcohol, acidic $KMnO_4$ is used as oxidant while for 2° alcohol acidic $K_2Cr_2O_7$ is used.

(d) Action of hot copper:

1° and 2° alcohol undergo dehydrogenation on reaction with hot copper at 573K to form aldehydes and ketones respectively.

$$CH_3CH_2OH \xrightarrow{\text{Cu/573K}} CH_3CHO + H_2; \quad \underset{CH_3}{\overset{CH_3}{>}}\!C\!\overset{H}{\underset{OH}{<}} \xrightarrow{\text{Cu, 573 K}} \underset{CH_3}{\overset{CH_3}{>}}C=O + H_2$$

3° alcohols undergo dehydration reaction with hot copper to form alkene

$$CH_3 - \overset{\overset{\displaystyle CH_3}{|}}{\underset{\underset{\displaystyle CH_3}{|}}{C}} - OH \xrightarrow{\text{Cu/573K}} CH_3 - \overset{\overset{\displaystyle CH_3}{|}}{C} = CH_2 + H_2O$$

Reactions of Phenols

(a) Electrophilic aromatic substitution reactions

   (i) Nitration: with dil. HNO_3

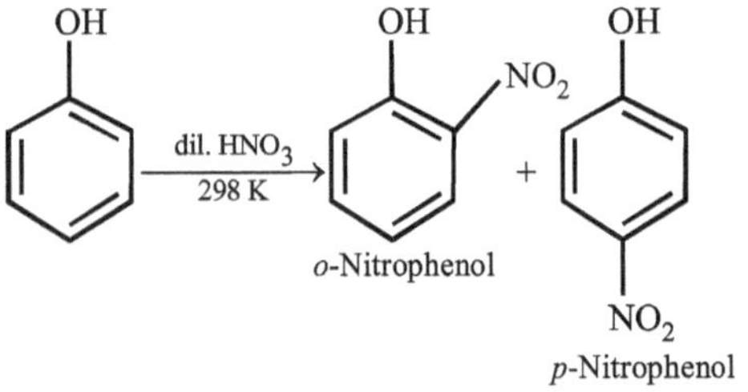

o-Nitrophenol

+

p-Nitrophenol

o-Nitrophenol is more volatile due to intramolecular hydrogen bonding, while p-nitrophenol is less volatile due to intermolecular hydrogen bonding.

Nitration with conc. HNO_3:

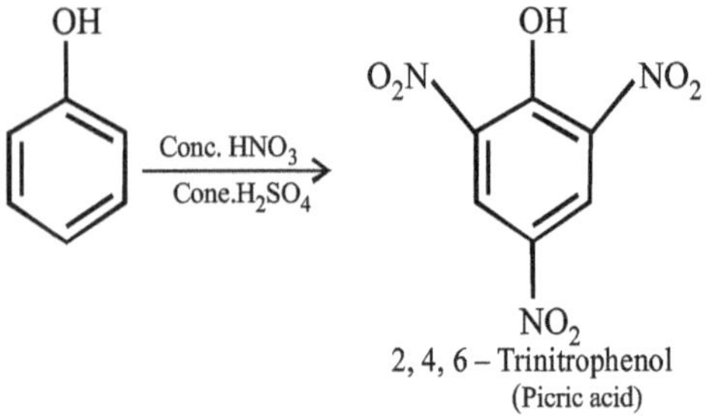

2, 4, 6 – Trinitrophenol
(Picric acid)

(ii) Halogenation: In presence of solvent of high polarity such as H_2O :

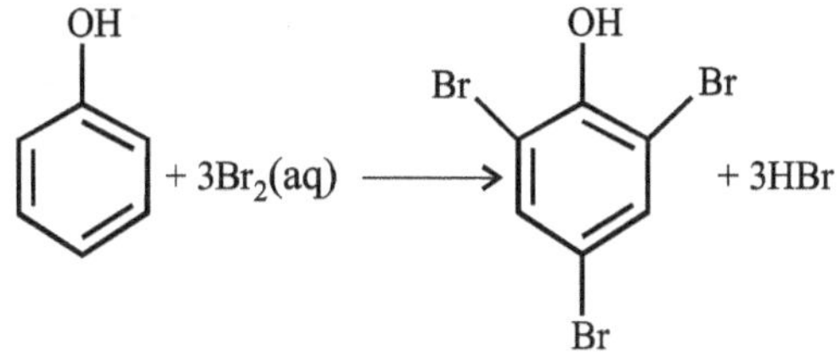

$$\text{Phenol} + 3Br_2(aq) \longrightarrow \text{2, 4, 6 Tribromophenol} + 3HBr$$

2, 4, 6 Tribromophenol

Polyhalogenation takes place when water is used as a solvent because of the fact that water (a highly polar solvent) facilitates the ionisation of phenol to phenoxide ion which is more reactive than phenol towards electrophilic substitution.

In presence of solvents of low polarity such as $CHCl_3$ or CS_2:

These non-polar solvents (CS_2, CCl_4) decreases the electrophilic character of Br_2 and minimizes ionization of phenol.

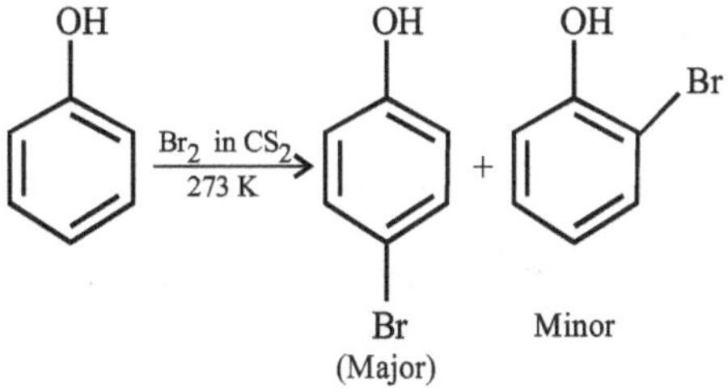

$$\xrightarrow[273 \text{ K}]{Br_2 \text{ in } CS_2}$$

Br (Major) + Br Minor

(iii) Sulphonation : o-Isomer predominates at low temperature while p-isomer at high temperature.

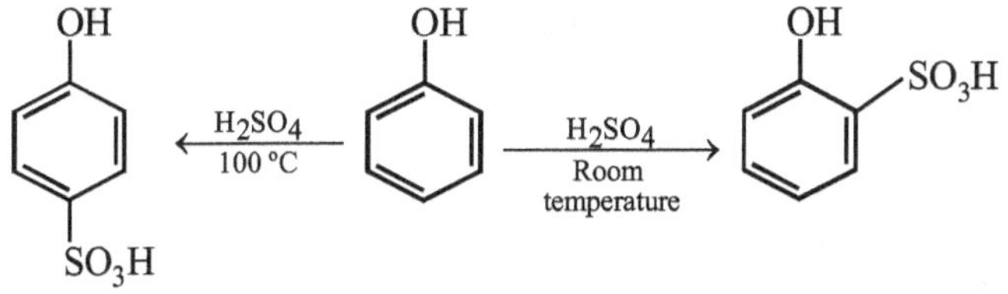

$$\xleftarrow[100\,°C]{H_2SO_4} \qquad \xrightarrow[\substack{Room \\ temperature}]{H_2SO_4}$$

p-Phenolsulphonic acid   Phenol o-Phenolsulphonic acid

(iv) Friedel - Craft's alkylation and acylation :

Alkylation

$$\xrightarrow[\text{anhy. } AlCl_3]{RX}$$

+ ;

Acylation

$$\xrightarrow[\text{anhy. } AlCl_3]{RCOX}$$

+

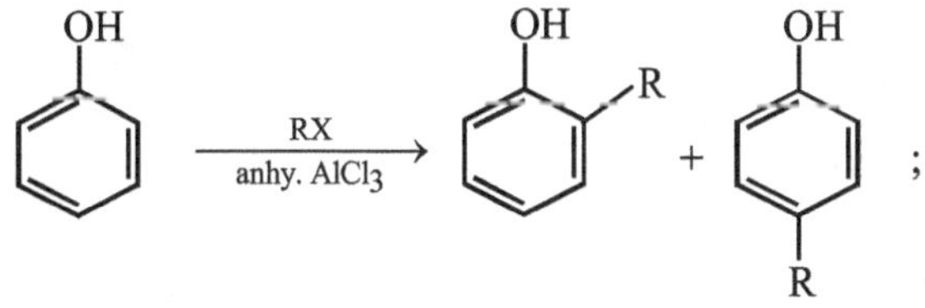

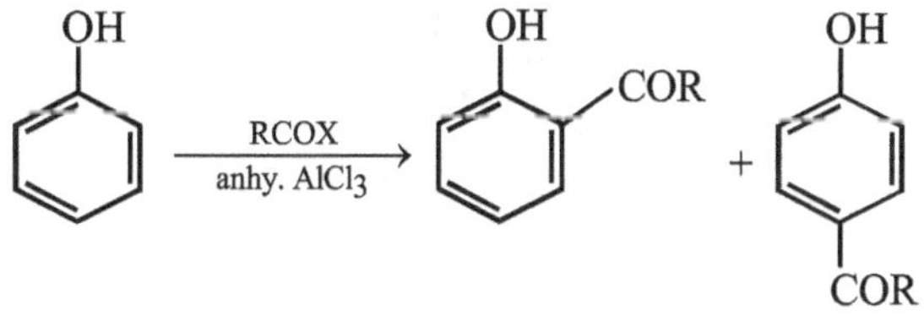

(b) Kolbe's reaction:

$$\xrightarrow{NaOH} \qquad + CO_2 \xrightarrow[\text{4-7 atm}]{400 \text{ K}} \qquad \xrightarrow[- NaCl]{\text{dil. HCl}}$$

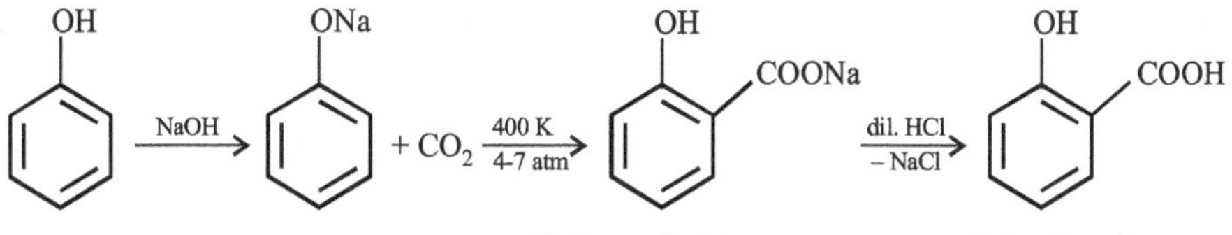

Sodium salicylate   Salicyclic acid

If the reaction is carried out at high temperature, p-isomer is the main product.

(c) Reimer-Tiemann reaction:

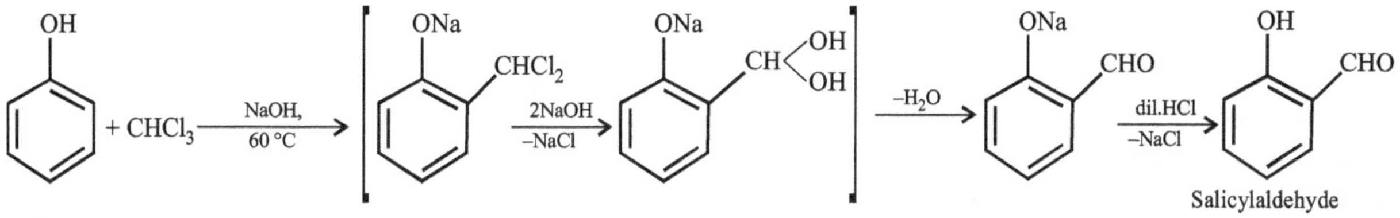

$$+ CHCl_3 \xrightarrow[60\,°C]{NaOH,} \qquad \xrightarrow[-NaCl]{2NaOH} \qquad \xrightarrow{-H_2O} \qquad \xrightarrow[-NaCl]{\text{dil.HCl}}$$

Salicylaldehyde

(d) Reaction of phenol with Zn dust:

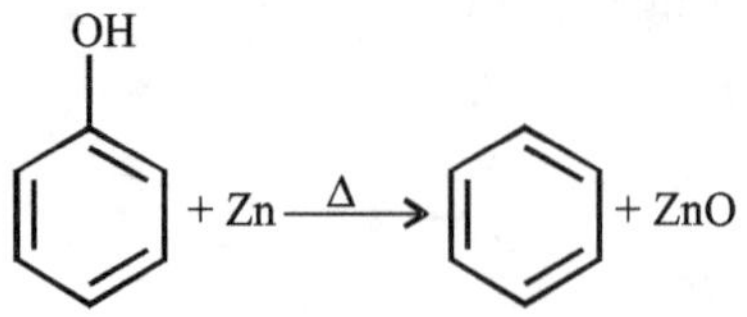

Phenol $+ Zn \xrightarrow{\Delta}$ Benzene $+ ZnO$

(e) Oxidation:

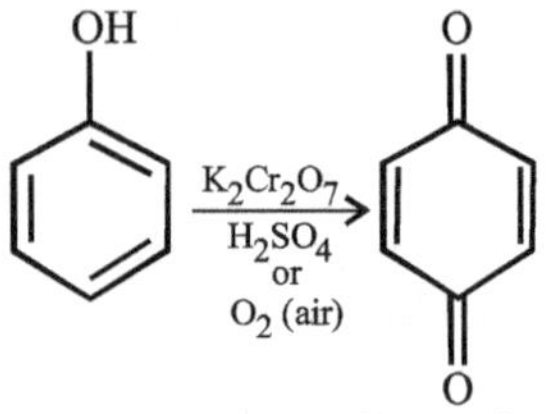

Phenol $\xrightarrow[\substack{H_2SO_4 \\ \text{or} \\ O_2 \text{ (air)}}]{K_2Cr_2O_7}$ Benzoquinone

(f) Gattermann's reaction:

$$HCl + H-C \equiv N \xrightarrow{AlCl_3} Cl-HC=NH$$

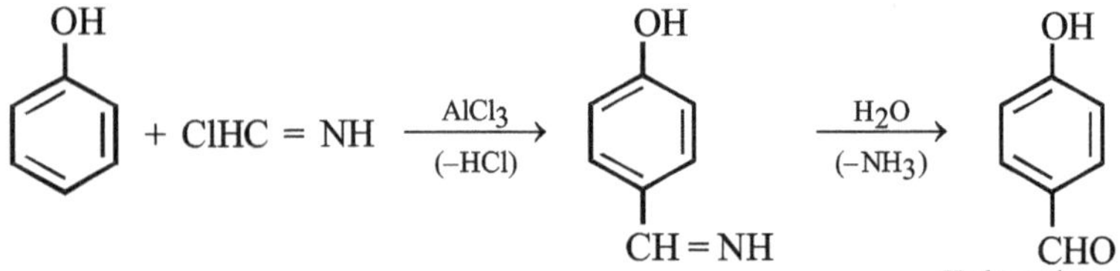

Phenol $+ ClHC=NH \xrightarrow[(-HCl)]{AlCl_3}$ (p-substituted, $CH=NH$) $\xrightarrow[(-NH_3)]{H_2O}$ p-Hydroxy benzaldehyde (CHO)

(g) Phthalein reaction : Phenol reacts with phthalic anhydride in presence of concentrated H_2SO_4 to form phenolphthalein.

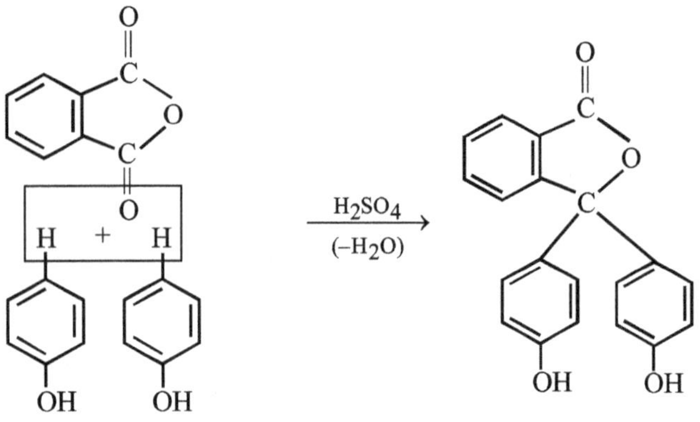

Phenol (2 molecules) $\xrightarrow[(-H_2O)]{H_2SO_4}$ Phenolphthalein (a dye)

Illustration 1 :

Name the phenol with molecular formula C_7H_8O which on treatment with Br_2-water readily gives a precipitate of $C_7H_5OBr_3$.

Sol. m-Cresol.

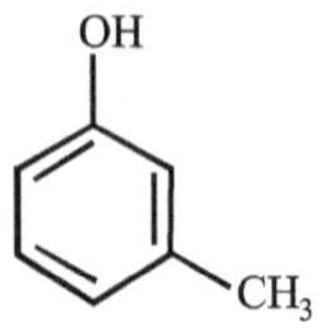

Illustration 2 :

Give the IUPAC name of $[(CH_3)_2CH]_3COH.$
Sol. 2, 4-Dimethyl-3-(methylethyl) pentan-3-ol.

Illustration 3 :

How will you convert ethanol into ethylene?
Sol. By heating with conc. H_2SO_4 at 433-443 K.

Practice Exercise-1

Multiple Choice Questions

1. Isopropyl alcohol is obtained by reacting which of the following alkenes with concentrated H_2SO_4 followed by boiling with H_2O?
   (a) Ethylene
   (b) Propylene
   (c) 2-Methylpropene
   (d) Isoprene

2. Which statement is not correct about alcohol?
   (a) Molecular weight of alcohol is higher than water
   (b) Alcohol of less no. of carbon atoms is less soluble in water than alcohol of more no. of carbon atoms
   (c) Alcohol evaporates quickly
   (d) All of the above

3. Which of the following is not true in case of reaction with heated copper at 300°C?
   (a) Phenol $\longrightarrow$ Benzyl alcohol
   (b) Secondary alcohol $\longrightarrow$ Ketone
   (c) Primary alcohol $\longrightarrow$ Aldehyde
   (d) Tertiary alcohol $\longrightarrow$ Olefin

4. When phenol is treated with excess bromine water, it gives:
   (a) *m*-bromophenol
   (b) *o*- and *p*-bromophenol
   (c) 2, 4-dibromophenol
   (d) 2, 4, 6-tribromophenol

5. Which of the following statements are correct ?
   (i) In phenols, the —OH group is attached to sp^2 hybridised carbon of an aromatic ring
   (ii) The carbon – oxygen bond length (136 pm) in phenol is slightly more than that in methanol
   (iii) Partial double bond character is due to the conjugation of unshared electron pair of oxygen with the aromatic ring.
   (iv) Phenol has sp^2 hybridised state of carbon to which oxygen is attached.
   (a) (i), (ii) and (v)
   (b) (i), (ii) and (iii)
   (c) (i), (iii) and (iv)
   (d) (i) and (iv)

6. Propene, $CH_3CH = CH_2$ can be converted into 1-propanol by oxidation. Indicate which set of reagents amongst the following is ideal to effect the above conversion?
   (a) $KMnO_4$ (alkaline)
   (b) Osmium tetraoxide (OsO_4/CH_2Cl_2)
   (c) B_2H_6 and alk. H_2O_2
   (d) O_3/Zn

7. The reagent used for dehydration of an alcohol is
   (a) phosphorus pentachloride
   (b) calcium chloride
   (c) aluminium oxide
   (d) sodium chloride

Assertion & Reason Questions

DIRECTIONS (Qs. 8-10) : *Each of these questions contains an assertion followed by reason. Read them carefully and answer the question on the basis of following options. You have to select the one that best describes the two statements.*

(a) If both Assertion and Reason are correct and the Reason is a correct explanation of the Assertion.

(b) If both Assertion and Reason are correct but Reason is not a correct explanation of the Assertion.

(c) If the Assertion is correct but Reason is incorrect.

(d) If the Assertion is incorrect but the Reason is correct.

8. **Assertion :** Small armount of ingestion of methanol causes blindness and death.
   Reason : This is because methanol is oxidised first to methanal and then to methanoic acid which may cause blindness and death.

9. **Assertion :** Lower alcohols are soluble in water.
   Reason : Lower alcohols do not form hydrogen bonding with water molecules.

10. **Assertion :** Lucas reagent [$HCl + ZnCl_2$ (anhydrous)] on reaction with tertiary alcohols immediately produces turbidity.
    Reason : This is because tertiary alcohols easily form halides which are immiscribe in water.

Case/Passage Based Questions

DIRECTIONS (Qs. 11-15) : *Following are the case/passage based questions. Attempt any 4 out of 5 questions.*

Alcohols and phenols are the most important compounds used in our daily life. Alcohols are prepared by hydration of alkenes, fermentation of glucose, reduction of aldehydes, ketones, carboxylic acids, and esters. Alcohols are soluble in water. Boiling points increase with the increase in molar mass and decrease with branching. Alcohols on dehydration give alkene at 443K, follow carbocation mechanism. Excess of alcohol at 413K on dehydration with conc. H_2SO_4 also follows the carbocation mechanism but gives diethyl ether. Alcohols undergo nucleophilic substitution reactions, esterification with carboxylic acids, and derivatives like amides, acid halides, acid anhydride. Phenol is prepared from cumene, diazonium salts, anisole, and chlorobenzene. Phenol is used to prepare salicylaldehyde, salicylic acid, aspirin, methyl salicylate, *p*-benzoquinone. Phenol undergoes electrophilic substitution reaction at *o* & *p*-position.

11. The IUPAC name of $CH_3 - \underset{\underset{OH}{|}}{CH} - CH_2 - \underset{\underset{OH}{|}}{\overset{\overset{CH_3}{|}}{C}} - CH_3$ is
    (a) 1, 1-dimethyl-1, 3-butanediol
    (b) 2-methyl-2, 4-pentanediol
    (c) 4-methyl-2, 4-pentanediol
    (d) 1, 3, 3-trimethyl-1, 3-propanediol

12. Acid catalyzed hydration of alkenes except ethene leads to the formation of
    (a) primary alcohol
    (b) secondary or tertiary alcohol
    (c) mixture of primary and secondary alcohols
    (d) mixture of secondary and tertiary alcohols

13. Which of the following statements are correct ?
   (i) Alcohols react as nucleophiles in the reactions involving cleavage of O–H bond.
   (ii) Alcohols react as electrophiles in the reactions involving cleavage of O–H bond.
   (iii) Alcohols react as nucleophile in the reaction involving cleavage of C–O bond.
   (iv) Alcohols react as electrophiles in the reactions involving C–O bond.
   (a) (i) only
   (b) (i) and (iv)
   (c) (ii) and (iii)
   (d) (ii) only

14. Consider the following reaction:

$$Phenol \xrightarrow{Zn\ dust} X \xrightarrow[Anhydrous\ AlCl_3]{CH_3Cl} Y$$

$$\xrightarrow{Alk.\ KMnO_4} Z$$

The product Z is
   (a) benzaldehyde
   (b) benzoic acid
   (c) benzene
   (d) toluene

15.
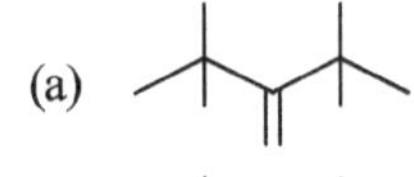 $\xrightarrow[\Delta]{H^{\oplus}}$ Major product

   (a) 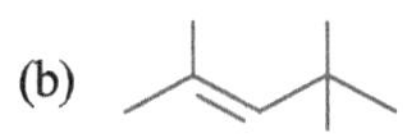
   (b)
   (c) 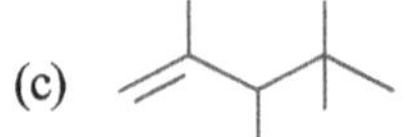
   (d)

Very Short Answer Questions

16. What is Lucas reagent?
17. What is the role of anhydrous $ZnCl_2$ is following reaction:

$$CH_3CH_2OH + HCl \xrightarrow{anhyd.ZnCl_2} CH_3CH_2Cl + H_2O$$

18. What happens when glycerol is treated with periodic acid?
19. Glycerol is highly soluble in both, water and alcohol. How?

20. Why does phenol get coloured on long standing?
21. Why is glycerol used widely in cosmetics?
22. How is the C — OH bond in phenol stabilised?
23. Arrange the n-butyl, sec-butyl and tert-butyl alcohols in order of decreasing acidic character.
24. Arrange HCl, HBr and HI in order of decreasing reactivity with alcohols.
25. What is methylated spirit (or denatured spirit)?
26. What is power alcohol?
27. Differentiate between alcohol and inorganic hydroxides.
28. Why is glycerine used as preservative for fruits, vegetables and other eatables?
29. Define fermentation. Mention one important use of this process in industry.
30. How will you find whether a given (OH) group is alcoholic or phenolic in nature?
31. Arrange the following in order of decreasing acid strength: H_2O, C_2H_5OH, C_6H_5OH.

Short Answer Questions

32. Give a chemical test to distinguish 1-propanol and 2-propanol.
33. Phenol is more acidic than alcohol while both contain hydroxyl group. Why?
34. Alcohols act as weak bases. Explain.
35. Phenol has a smaller dipole moment than methanol. Explain.
36. Phenols do not give protonation reactions readily. Explain.
37. What will be the main product of action of excess of Br_2 on phenol in aqueous medium?
38. Write equations when
   (a) thionyl chloride acts upon 1-propanol.
   (b) cumene hydroperoxide is treated with dil H_2SO_4.
39. Explain o-nitrophenol is more acidic than m-nitrophenol.
40. Why o-nitrophenol has lower boiling point than p-nitrophenol?

Topic 2   Preparation and Properties of Ethers

METHODS OF PREPARATION OF ETHERS

By Dehydration of Alcohols

(for simple ethers)

$$2\ CH_3CH_2OH \xrightarrow[413K]{H_2SO_4} C_2H_5OC_2H_5 + H_2O$$

Mechanism: The formation of ether is S_N2 reaction (nucleophilic bimolecular)

Step 1: $C_2H_5 - \overset{..}{\underset{..}{O}} - H + H^+ \longrightarrow C_2H_5 - \overset{\overset{H}{|+}}{\underset{..}{O}} - H$
    Step 2: $C_2H_5 - \overset{..}{\underset{..}{O}} - H + C_2H_5 - \overset{\overset{H}{|+}}{\underset{..}{O}} - H \longrightarrow C_2H_5 - \overset{\overset{H}{|+}}{\underset{..}{O}} - C_2H_5 + H_2O$

Step 3: $C_2H_5 - \overset{\overset{H}{|+}}{\underset{..}{O}} - C_2H_5 \longrightarrow C_2H_5 - \overset{..}{\underset{..}{O}} - C_2H_5 + H^{\oplus}$
Diethyl ether

$$CH_3CH_2OH \xrightarrow[443K]{H_2SO_4} CH_2 = CH_2$$

Mechanism

Step 1: $C_2H_5 - \overset{..}{\underset{..}{O}} - H + \overset{\oplus}{H} \xrightleftharpoons{\text{Fast}} C_2H_5 - \overset{H}{\underset{..}{\overset{|+}{O}}} - H$ **Step 2:** $C_2H_5 - \overset{H}{\underset{..}{\overset{|+}{O}}} - H \xrightleftharpoons{\text{Slow}} C_2H_5^+ + H_2O$

Ethyl oxoniumion   Carbocation

Step 3: $H - \overset{\overset{H}{|}}{\underset{\underset{H}{|}}{C}} \overset{\overset{H}{|+}}{\underset{\underset{H}{|}}{C}} \rightleftharpoons CH_2 = CH_2 + \overset{\oplus}{H}$

Ethylene

This method is suitable for the preparation of ethers having primary alkyl groups only. Moreover at slightly high temperature yield of ether will be low due to formation of alkene.

Williamson Synthesis

(For mixed ethers)

$$R - X + R' - \overset{..}{\underset{..}{O}} Na \longrightarrow R - \overset{..}{\underset{..}{O}} - R' + NaX$$

Williamson synthesis can be applied for the synthesis of symmetrical as well as unsymmetrical ethers. It follows S_N^2 path, hence it is most successful when the alkyl halide, sulphonate, or sulphate is primary (or methyl). If the alkyl halide (substrate) is tertiary or secondary they react with alkoxide base by E2 elimination rather than by S_N^2 substitution. Thus if we want to prepare *tert*-butyl ether, we must take *tert*-butyl group in the form of alkoxide rather than halide,

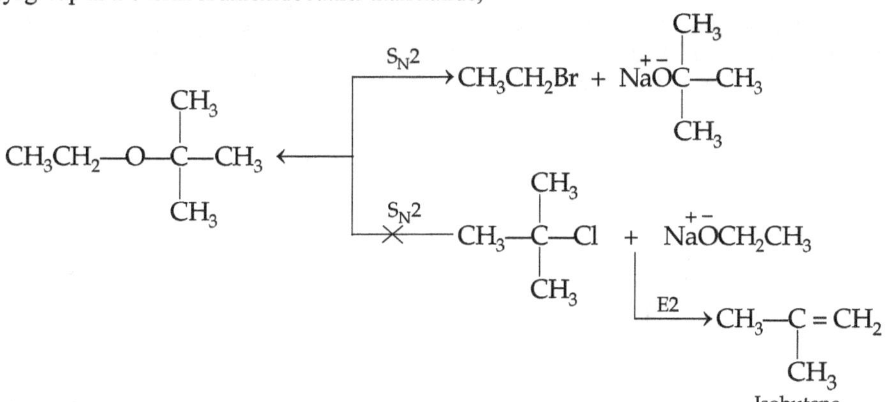

For aryl ethers: (sodium phenoxide reacts with RX)

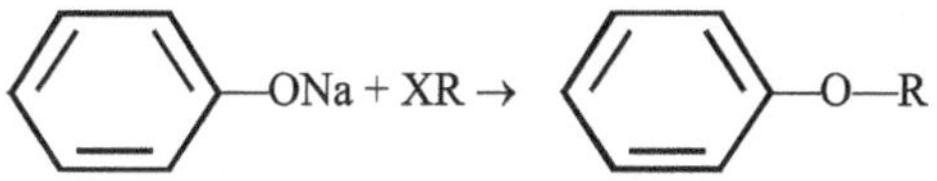

PHYSICAL PROPERTIES OF ETHERS

(a) Dimethyl ether and ethyl methyl ethers are gases at ordinary temperature while the other lower homologous of ether are colourless liquids with characteristic 'ether smell'.
(b) Because of the greater electronegativity of oxygen than carbon, the C – O bonds are slightly polar and thus have a dipole moment.
(c) Boiling points of ethers are much lower than those of the isomeric alcohols, because ethers do not form intermolecular H-bonding.
(d) The solubility of lower ethers in water is due to the formation of hydrogen bonds between water and other molecules.
(e) All ethers are lighter than water.

CHEMICAL PROPERTIES

Cleavage of C-O Bond in Ethers

$$R - O - R' + HX \longrightarrow RX + R' - OH \xrightarrow[\text{(excess)}]{H-X} R' - X + H_2O$$

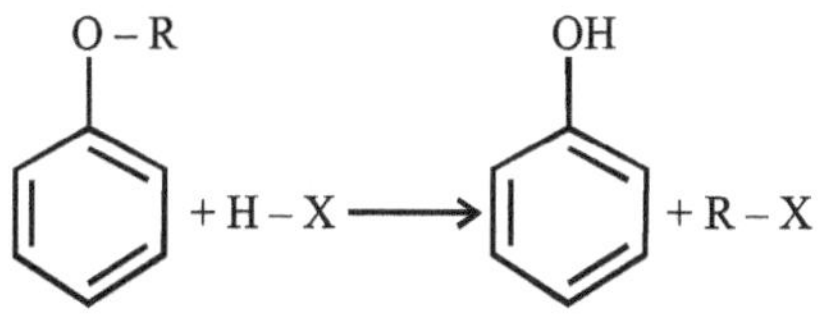

The order of reactivity of hydrogen halides is as following : HI > HBr > HCl

Mechanism

Step 1: Protonation

$$CH_3 - \ddot{O} - CH_2.CH_3 + H - I \rightleftharpoons CH_3 - \overset{+}{\underset{\cdot\cdot}{O}}H - CH_2CH_3 + I^-$$

Step 2: Nucleophilic attack of I^- (S_N2 reaction)

$$\overset{-}{I} + CH_3 - \underset{\oplus}{\overset{H}{O}} - CH_2 - CH_3 \rightarrow [I \cdots CH_3 \cdots \underset{\oplus}{\overset{H}{O}} \cdots CH_2CH_3] \rightarrow CH_3I + CH_3CH_2OH$$

When 1° or 2° alkyl gps. are present the lower alkyl iodide is formed.

In case of mixed ether, lower alkyl group form halide and higher will form an alcohol.

$$CH_3 - O - C_2H_5 + HI \rightarrow CH_3I + CH_3CH_2OH$$

This is because iodide ion prefers to attack on the least substituted smaller alkyl group.

When one of the alkyl group is tertiary than tertiary halides is formed.

$$\underset{\underset{CH_3}{|}}{\overset{\overset{CH_3}{|}}{CH_3 - C - O - CH_3}} + HI \longrightarrow CH_3OH + \underset{\underset{CH_3}{|}}{\overset{\overset{CH_3}{|}}{CH_3 - C - I}}$$

This is because of the formation of a more stable tertiary carbocation, which combines with halide ion to give alkyl halide.

When Ar–O–R etherd are reacted with HI Alkyl aryl ethers are cleaved at weaker O – R bond to give phenols and alkyl iodide. Ar – O bond is stronger because the carbon atom of phenyl group is sp^2 hybridized and there is partial double bond character.

Electrophilic Substitution

Alkoxy group (–OR) is ortho, para directing and activates the aromatic ring towards electrophilic substitution reaction.

(a) Halogenation:

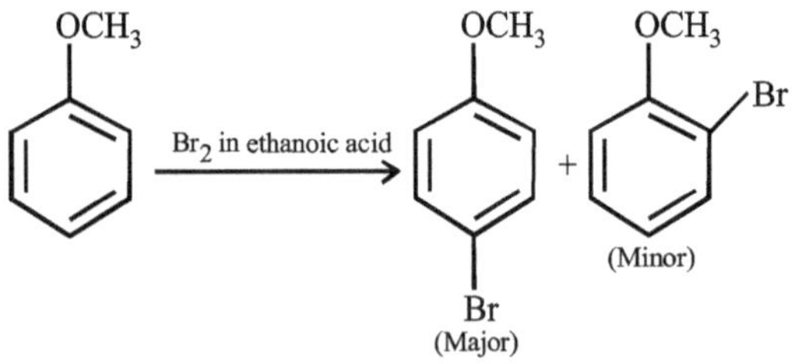

(b) Friedel-Crafts reaction:

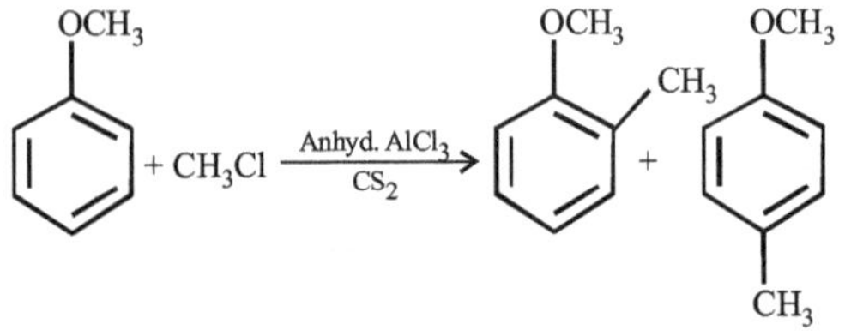

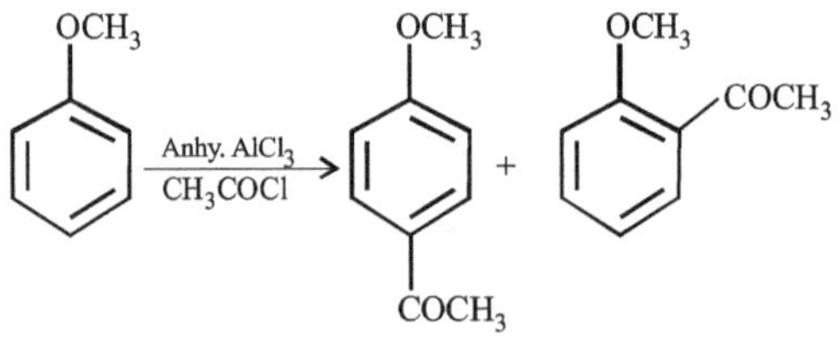

(c) Nitration:

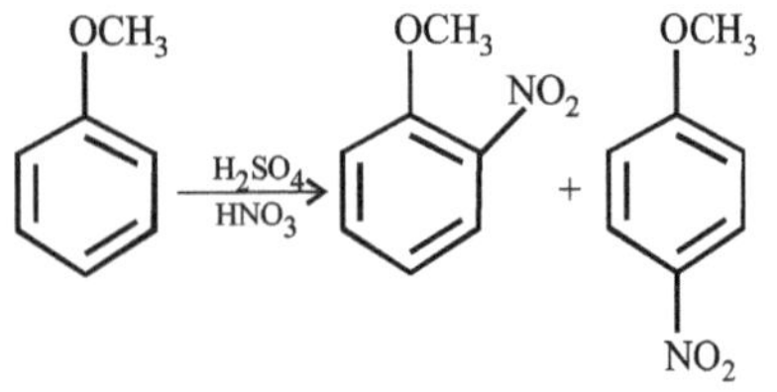

Reaction with PCl₅

$$C_2H_5 - O - C_2H_5 + PCl_5 \longrightarrow 2C_2H_5Cl + POCl_3$$

Reaction with H₂SO₄

(a) With conc. H₂SO₄

$$C_2H_5 - O - C_2H_5 + H_2SO_4 \xrightarrow{\Delta} C_2H_5OSO_2OH + C_2H_5OH$$

Ethyl hydrogen sulphate

(b) With dil. H_2SO_4 :

$$C_2H_5-O-C_2H_5 + H-OH \xrightarrow{\text{dil.}H_2SO_4} 2C_2H_5OH$$

(c) $R-O-R' + H_2O \xrightarrow[\substack{\text{heat under} \\ \text{pressure}}]{\text{dil. }H_2SO_4} R-OH + R'-OH$

Illustration 4 :

Complete the following reaction:

$$(CH_3)_2 CH-OCH_3 + \underset{\text{(excess)}}{HI} \xrightarrow{\Delta} - + -$$

Sol. $(CH_3)_2 CH-OCH_3 + \underset{\text{(excess)}}{HI} \xrightarrow{\Delta} CH_3-\underset{\underset{CH_3}{|}}{CH}-OH + CH_3I$

Illustration 5 :

What happens when ethers are directly subjected to distillation?

Sol. Explosion may take place if ether got converted to ether peroxide by aerial oxidation.

Illustration 6 :

How do diethylether react with carbon monoxide under pressure?

Sol. Ester is formed according to the following equations:

$$C_2H_5-O-C_2H_5 + CO \xrightarrow[\Delta]{\text{High pressure}} C_2H_5-\overset{\overset{O}{\|}}{C}-OC_2H_5$$
$$\text{Ethylpropanoate}$$

Illustration 7 :

Why Williamson's synthesis for preparing ethers is not applicable to tertiary alkylhalides?

Sol. This because the alkoxide ion being both a powerful nucleophile and a base will dehydrogenate the tertiary alkylhalides to form an alkene.

Practice Exercise-2

Multiple Choice Questions

1. Which of the following cannot be made by using Williamson's synthesis?
(a) Methoxybenzene
(b) Benzyl *p*-nitrophenyl ether
(c) Methyl tertiary butyl ether
(d) Di-tert-butyl ether

2. Ethanol and dimethyl ether form a pair of functional isomers. The boiling point of ethanol is higher than that of dimethyl ether, due to the presence of
(a) H-bonding in ethanol
(b) H-bonding in dimethyl ether
(c) CH_3 group in ethanol
(d) CH_3 group in dimethyl ether

3. An ether is more volatile than an alcohol having the same molecular formula. This is due to
(a) dipolar character of ethers
(b) alcohols having resonance structures
(c) inter-molecular hydrogen bonding in ethers
(d) inter-molecular hydrogen bonding in alcohols

4. Which of the following has strongest hydrogen bonding?
(a) Ethyl amine
(b) Ethanal
(c) Ethyl alcohol
(d) Diethyl ether

5. An aromatic ether is not cleaved by HI even at 525 K. The compound is
(a) $C_6H_5OCH_3$
(b) $C_6H_5OC_6H_5$
(c) $C_6H_5OC_3H_7$
(d) Tetrahydrofuran

6. Which of the following compounds is resistant to nucleophilic attack by hydroxyl ions?
(a) Methyl acetate
(b) Acetonitrile
(c) Acetamide
(d) Diethyl ether

Assertion & Reason Questions

DIRECTIONS (Qs. 7-9) : *Each of these questions contains an assertion followed by reason. Read them carefully and answer the question on the basis of following options. You have to select the one that best describes the two statements.*

(a) If both Assertion and Reason are correct and the Reason is a correct explanation of the Assertion.

(b) If both Assertion and Reason are correct but Reason is not a correct explanation of the Assertion.

(c) If the Assertion is correct but Reason is incorrect.

(d) If the Assertion is incorrect but the Reason is correct.

7. Assertion : Symmetric and unsymmetric ethers can be prepared by Williamson's synthesis.

Reason : Williamson's synthesis is an example of nucleophilic substitution reaction.

8. Assertion : When alkyl aryl ethers react with excess of hydrogen halides, phenol and alkyl halide are produced.

Reason : Alkyl aryl ethers are cleaved at the alkyl-oxygen due to more stable aryl-oxygen bond.

9. Assertion : $(CH_3)_3C - \overset{..}{\underset{..}{O}} - CH - CH_3$
$\qquad\qquad\qquad\qquad\quad |$
$\qquad\qquad\qquad\qquad\; C_2H_5$

cannot be prepared by Williamson's synthesis.

Reason : Only primary alkyl halide reacts with sodium alkoxide ($1°$, $2°$ or $3°$) to give ether.

Very Short Answer Questions

10. How does a sample of ether made free from peroxides?

11. Diethylether does not react with sodium but ethanol and phenol react with it. Explain.

12. Write IUPAC names of following:

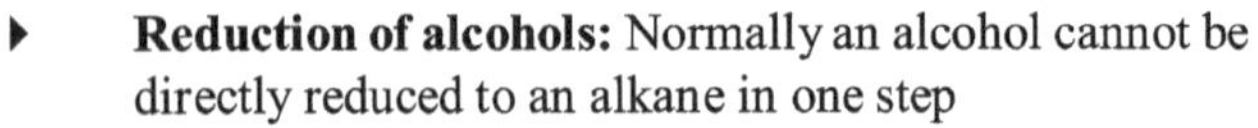

13. Name the alkylhalide and sodium alkoxide used to synthesize tert-butylethyl ether.

14. Name the products obtained when anisole is treated with HI.

15. Write the structure of perchlorodiethyl ether.

16. Name the reagent used to convert bromoethane to ethoxy ethane or diethylether.

Short Answer Questions

17. Give two important uses of ethers in industry.

18. What happens when:

(a) ethyl alcohol vapours are passed over heated alumina?

(b) monochlorodimethyl ether is treated with methyl magnesium bromide?

19. Why sodium metal can be used for drying of ether but not ethanol?

20. How is the presence of peroxide in ether detected? How are peroxides removed from ethers?

21. What is the IUPAC name of methyl tert-butyl ether? Describe one method for its preparation.

22. Why are Grignard reagents soluble in ether but not in benzene?

23. Why are ethers inert?

24. Under what conditions do ethers form oxonium salts?

25. Which of the following is the correct method for synthesizing methyl-tert.butyl ether and why?

(i) $(CH_3)_3CBr + NaOMe \longrightarrow$

(ii) $CH_3Br + NaO\text{-tert.butyl} \longrightarrow$

Give the name of the reaction selected. Which type of mechanism is involved in this reaction?

Important Tips & Formulae

▸ **Reduction of alcohols:** Normally an alcohol cannot be directly reduced to an alkane in one step

The $-OH$ group is a poor leaving group. It is converted into other superior leaving groups e.g. tosylate group.

Cyclohexyl tosylate

▸ **Methylated spirit:** The rectified spirit rendered poisonous by addition of 4-5% methyl alcohol, traces of pyridine and some copper sulphate is known as methylated spirit or denatured alcohol.

▸ **Power alcohol:** When alcohol is mixed with petrol and used in internal combustion engines then, it is known as power alcohol.

▸ **Proof-spirit:** An aqueous solution of 57.1% alcohol by volume or 49.3% alcohol by volume called proof spirit.

▸ **Condensation with HCHO (Lederer-Manasse reaction):** Phenol react with HCHO in weak acidic or alkaline medium to form a mixture of o- and p-hydroxy benzyl alcohol. Reaction is called Lederer-Manasse reaction. Condense to give a crossed linked polymer as **bakelite**.

▸ **Tests of Phenols**

(i) **Ferric chloride test:** Phenol + 1% $FeCl_3$ solution $\rightarrow$ Violet colour

(ii) **Bromine water:** Phenol + bromine water $\rightarrow$ Curdy precipitate

(iii) **Phenolphthalein test :** (Phenol + phthalic anhydride + conc. H_2SO_4) + NaOH $\xrightarrow{\text{heat}}$ Pink colour

▸ **Test for peroxide linkage in ether**

[Ether + freshly prepared $FeSO_4$ solution + Few drops of KCNS] $\rightarrow$ Red colour $[Fe(CNS)_3]$

Appearance of red colour confirms the presence of peroxide, i.e.,

$Fe^{2+} \xrightarrow{\text{peroxide}} Fe^{3+} \xrightarrow{3KCNS}$ Red colour $[Fe(CNS)_3]$

▸ **Reaction of Ether with HX**

(a) **If HX is cold :**

$CH_3 - O - CH_2 - CH_3 + HX \text{ (cold)} \longrightarrow$
$\qquad\qquad\qquad\qquad\qquad\qquad CH_3 - X + C_2H_5OH$

If we take unsymmetrical ether with cold H—X, then smaller alkyl group forms alkyl halide.

(b) **If HX is hot :**

$$CH_3-CH_2-O-CH_2-CH_3+2H-X \xrightarrow{\Delta} 2CH_3-CH_2-X+H_2O$$

$$CH_3-O-CH_2-CH_3+2H-X \xrightarrow{\Delta} CH_3-X+C_2H_5X+H_2O$$

The above reaction is called **'Ziesel's method** estimation'.

▸ In presence of sodium hydroxide, phenol generates phenoxide ion which is even more reactive than phenol. Thus, in alkaline medium, phenol undergoes Kolbe's reaction.

▸ The C–O bond in ethers can be cleaved by hydrogen halides.

▸ **Dehydration :**
When vapours of ether are passed at 380 °C over heated alumina, then alkene is formed by the elimination of water.

▸ % of –OCH_3 group $= \dfrac{31\times \text{Wt. of AgI}\times 100}{\text{Mol. mass of AgI}\times \text{Wt. of ether}}$

▸ **Distinction Between Primary, Secondary and Tertiary Alcohols**

(i) **Lucas test.** Lucas reagent (a mixture of conc HCl and zinc chloride) reacts with alcohols to form corresponding alkyl chlorides which are insoluble. Formation of a chloride from an alcohol is indicated by the cloudiness that appars when the chloride separates from the solution. Hence the time required for cloudiness to appear is a measure of reactivity of the alcohol.

A tertiary alcohol reacts immediately, a secondary alcohol reacts within five minutes, and a primary alcohol does not react appreciably at room temperature. However, remember that allyl alcohol, $CH_2 = CHCH_2OH$ reacts as rapidly as tertiary alcohols with the Lucas reagent to form *soluble* allyl chloride.

(ii) **Victor Meyer test.** This test is based upon the fact that the three types ($1°$, $2°$ or $3°$) of nitroalkanes (formed by alcohols) react differently with nitrous acid followed by sodium hydroxide. The three types of alcohols are first converted to corresponding nitro compounds.

$$\underset{}{\text{C}}\text{—OH} \xrightarrow{P/I_2} \underset{}{\text{C}}\text{—I} \xrightarrow{AgNO_2} \underset{}{\text{C}}\text{—NO_2}$$

Nitroalkane

Nitroalkane, so obtained, is treated first with nitrous acid and then with sodium hydroxide to get different colours at the end.

$$CH_3CH_2NO_2 \xrightarrow{HONO} CH_3\underset{\substack{\| \\ NOH}}{C}NO_2 \xrightarrow{NaOH} CH_3\underset{\substack{\| \\ NOHa}}{C}NO_2$$

1° Nitroalkane **(red)**   Nitrolic acid (blue)   Sod. nitrolate (from 1° alcohol)

$$(CH_3)_2CHNO_2 \xrightarrow{HONO} (CH_3)_2\underset{\substack{| \\ NO}}{C}NO_2 \xrightarrow{NaOH} \text{No reaction}$$

2° Nitroalkane (from 2° alcohol)   Pseudonitrol **(blue)**

$$(CH_3)_3CNO_2 \xrightarrow{NaOH} \text{No reaction (no colour)}$$

3° Nitroalkane

NCERT Questions

1. **Write IUPAC names of the following compounds:**

(i) $CH_3-CH-CH-\underset{\underset{CH_3}{|}}{\overset{\overset{CH_3}{|}}{C}}-CH_3$
$\quad\quad\ \ \underset{CH_3\ \ OH}{}$

(ii) $CH_3-\underset{\underset{OH}{|}}{CH}-CH_2-\underset{\underset{OH}{|}}{CH}-\underset{\underset{C_2H_5}{|}}{CH}-CH_2-CH_3$

(iii) $CH_3-\underset{\underset{OH}{|}}{CH}-\underset{\underset{OH}{|}}{CH}-CH_3$

(iv) $HOCH_2-CHOH-CH_2OH$

(v)   (2-methylphenol structure)

(vi)   (4-methylphenol structure)

(vii)   (2,5-dimethylphenol structure)

(viii)   (2,6-dimethylphenol structure)

(ix) $CH_3-O-CH_2-\underset{\underset{CH_3}{|}}{CH}-CH_3$

(x) $C_6H_5-O-C_2H_5$

(xi) $C_6H_5-O-C_7H_{15}(n-)$

(xii) $CH_3-CH_2-O-\underset{\underset{CH_3}{|}}{CH}-CH_2-CH_3$

Sol. *(i)* $2, 2, 4-\text{Trimethylpentan}-3-\text{ol}$
     (ii) 5-Ethylheptane-2, 4-diol
     (iii) Butane-2, 3-diol
     (iv) Propane-1, 2, 3-triol
     (v) 2-Methylphenol

(*vi*) 4-Methylphenol

(*vii*) 2, 5-Dimethylphenol

(*viii*) 2,6-Dimethylphenol

(*ix*) 1-Methoxy-2-methylpropane

(*x*) Ethoxybenzene

(*xi*) 1-Phenoxyheptane

(*xii*) 2-Ethoxybutane

2. **Write structures of the compounds whose IUPAC names are as follows:**

(*i*) **2-Methylbutan-2-ol**

(*ii*) **1-Phenylpropan-2-ol**

(*iii*) **3, 5-Dimethylhexane-1, 3, 5-triol**

(*iv*) **2, 3-Diethylphenol**

(*v*) **1-Ethoxypropane**

(*vi*) **2-Ethoxy-3-methylpentane**

(*vii*) **Cyclohexylmethanol**

(*viii*) **3-Cyclohexylpentan-3-ol**

(*ix*) **Cyclopent-3-en-1-ol**

(*x*) **4-Chloro-3-ethylbutan-1-ol**

Sol. (*i*) $CH_3 - \underset{\underset{OH}{|}}{\overset{\overset{CH_3}{|}}{C}} - CH_2 - CH_3$

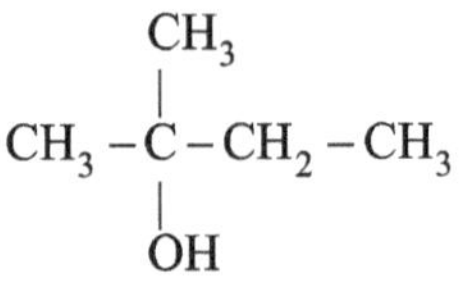

(*ii*) $\langle\ \rangle - CH_2 - \underset{\underset{OH}{|}}{CH} - CH_3$

(*iii*) $\underset{\underset{OH}{|}}{CH_2} - CH_2 - \underset{\underset{OH}{|}}{\overset{\overset{CH_3}{|}}{C}} - CH_2 - \underset{\underset{OH}{|}}{\overset{\overset{CH_3}{|}}{C}} - CH_3$

(*iv*) (structure: phenol with OH, and two C_2H_5 groups)

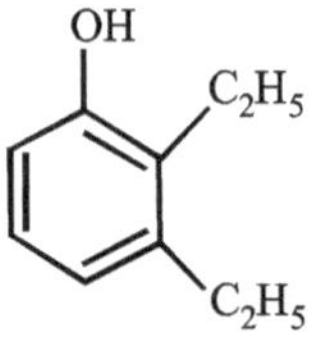

(*v*) $CH_3CH_2 - O - CH_2CH_2CH_3$

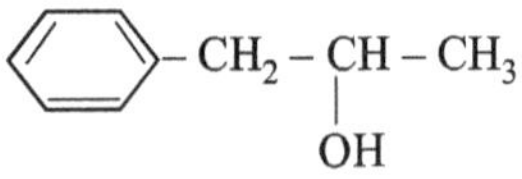

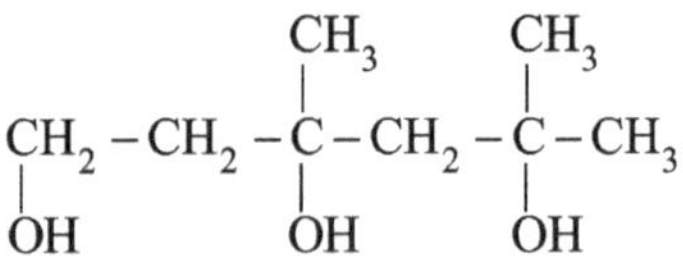

(*vi*) $CH_3 - CH_2 - \overset{\overset{\displaystyle CH_3 - CH - CH - CH_2CH_3}{|}}{O} \quad CH_3$

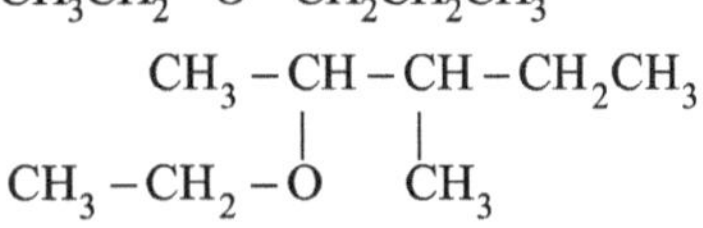

(*vii*) (cyclohexane ring with CH_2OH)

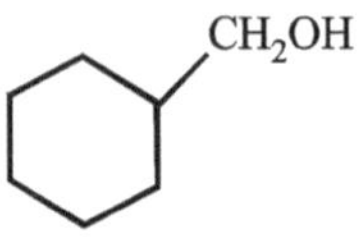

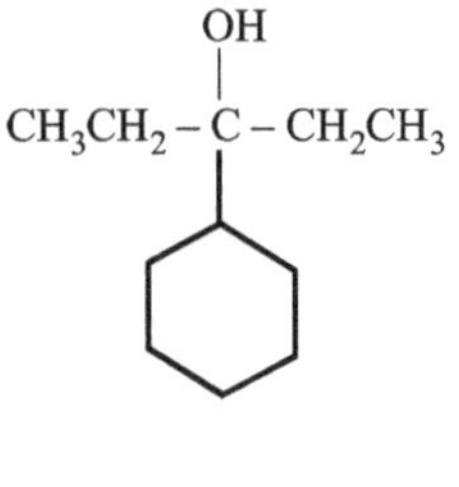

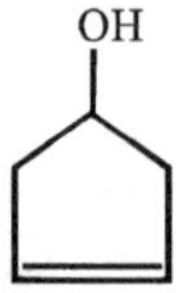

(*viii*) $CH_3CH_2 - \underset{\underset{(cyclohexane)}{|}}{\overset{\overset{OH}{|}}{C}} - CH_2CH_3$

(*ix*) (cyclopentene ring with OH)

(*x*) $ClCH_2 - \underset{\underset{C_2H_5}{|}}{CH} - CH_2 - CH_2OH$

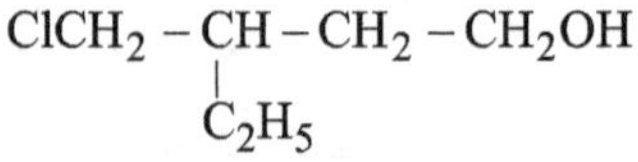

3. (*i*) **Draw the structures of all isomeric alcohols of molecular formula $C_5H_{12}O$ and give their IUPAC names.**

(*ii*) **Classify the isomers of alcohols in question 11.3 (*i*) as primary, secondary and tertiary alcohols.**

Sol. Eight isomers are possible. These are:

(*i*) $CH_3CH_2CH_2CH_2CH_2OH$
Pentan-1-ol
(1°)

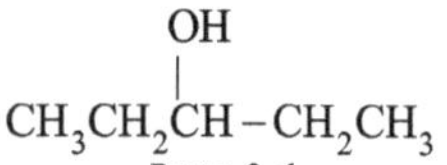

(*ii*) $CH_3CH_2CH_2 - \underset{\underset{OH}{|}}{CH}CH_3$
Pentan-2-ol
(2°)

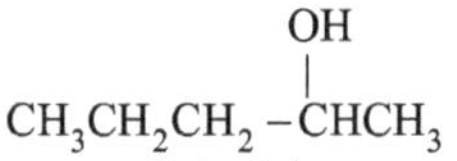

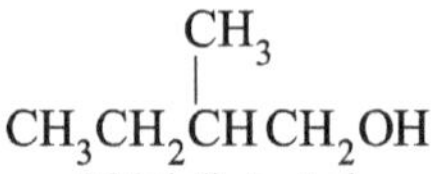

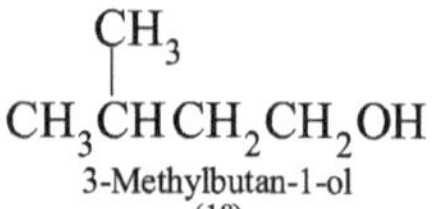

(*iii*) $CH_3CH_2\underset{\underset{OH}{|}}{CH} - CH_2CH_3$
Pentan-3-ol
(2°)

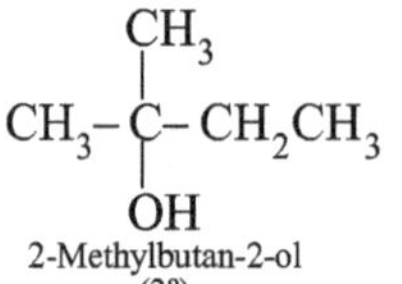

(*iv*) $CH_3CH_2\underset{\underset{CH_3}{|}}{CH}CH_2OH$
2-Methylbutan-1-ol
(1°)

(*v*) $CH_3\overset{\overset{CH_3}{|}}{CH}CH_2CH_2OH$
3-Methylbutan-1-ol
(1°)

(*vi*) $CH_3 - \underset{\underset{OH}{|}}{\overset{\overset{CH_3}{|}}{C}} - CH_2CH_3$
2-Methylbutan-2-ol
(3°)

(*vii*) $CH_3 - \underset{\underset{CH_3}{|}}{\overset{\overset{CH_3}{|}}{C}} - CH_2OH$
2,2-Dimethylpropan–1–ol
(1°)

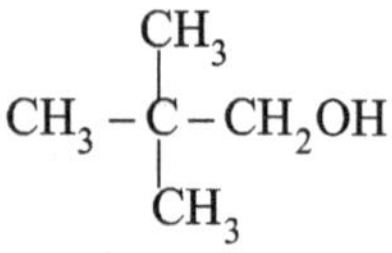

(*viii*) $CH_3 - \underset{\underset{CH_3}{|}}{CH} - \underset{\underset{OH}{|}}{CH} - CH_3$
3-Methylbutan-2-ol
(2°)

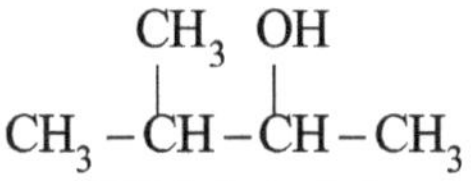

4. **Explain why propanol has higher boiling point than that of the hydrocarbon, butane?**

Sol. The molecules of butane are held together by weak van der Waal's forces of attraction while those of propanol are held together by stronger intermolecular hydrogen bonding.

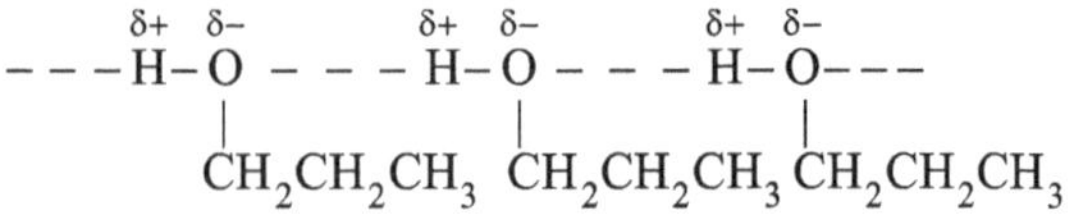

$$- - - \overset{\delta+}{H} - \overset{\delta-}{\underset{\underset{CH_2CH_2CH_3}{|}}{O}} - - - - \overset{\delta+}{H} - \overset{\delta-}{\underset{\underset{CH_2CH_2CH_3}{|}}{O}} - - - - \overset{\delta+}{H} - \overset{\delta-}{\underset{\underset{CH_2CH_2CH_3}{|}}{O}} - - -$$

Therefore, the boiling point of propanol is much higher than that of butane.

5. **Alcohols are comparatively more soluble in water than hydrocarbons of comparable molecular masses. Explain this fact.**

Sol. Alcohols can form hydrogen bonds with water and by breaking the hydrogen bonds already existing between water molecules. Therefore, they are soluble in water.

$$\overset{\delta-}{R-\overset{|}{\underset{H}{O}}}----\overset{\delta+}{H}-\overset{\delta-}{\underset{H}{O}}----\overset{\delta+}{H}-\overset{\delta-}{\underset{R}{O}}$$

On the other hand, hydrocarbons cannot from hydrogen bonds with water and hence are insoluble in water.

6. What is meant by hydroboration-oxidation reaction? Illustrate it with an example.

Sol. The addition of diborane to alkenes to form trialkyl boranes followed by their oxidation with alkaline hydrogen peroxide to form alcohols is called hydroboration-oxidation. For example,

$$CH_3 - CH = CH_2 \xrightarrow[BH_3]{Dry\ ether}$$

$$CH_3 - \underset{H}{\overset{|}{C}}H - \underset{BH_2}{\overset{|}{C}}H_2 \xrightarrow{CH_3CH=CH_2} (CH_3CH_2CH_2)_2\ B-H$$

$$(CH_3CH_2CH_2)_3\ B \longleftarrow CH_3-CH=CH_2$$

$$(CH_3CH_2CH_2)_3\ B + 3H_2O_2 \xrightarrow{OH^-,H_2O} \underset{Propan-1-ol}{3CH_3CH_2CH_2OH} + \underset{Boric\ acid}{B(OH)_3}$$

Hydroboration oxidation amounts to anti Markonikov addition of water to the unsymmetrical alkene.

7. Give the structures and IUPAC names of monohydric phenols of molecular formula, C_7H_8O.

Sol. The three isomers are:

2-methylphenol
o-Cresol

3-methylphenol
m-Cresol

4-methylphenol
p-Cresol

8. While separating a mixture of ortho and para nitrophenols by steam distillation, name the isomer which will be steam volatile. Give reason.

Sol. o-Nitrophenol is steam volatile due to chelation (intramolecular H – bonding) and hence can be separated by steam distillation from p-nitrophenol which is not steam volatile because of intermolecular H-bonding.

o-nitrophenol
(intramolecular H-bonding)

p-nitrophenol
(intermolecular H-bonding)

9. Give the equations of reactions for the preparation of phenol from cumene.

Sol.

Cumene

Cumene hydroperoxide

Phenol

$+ CH_3CCH_3$
Propanone
(Acetone)

10. Write chemical reaction for the preparation of phenol from chlorobenzene.

Sol.

Chlorobenzene

$+ 2NaOH \xrightarrow[-NaCl,\ -H_2O]{623\ K,\ 300\ atm}$

Sodium phenoxide

$\xrightarrow[-NaCl]{HCl}$

Phenol

11. Write the mechanism of hydration of ethene to yield ethanol.

Sol. Direct addition of H_2O to ethene in presence of an acid does not occur. Indirectly, ethene is first passed through concentrated H_2SO_4, when ethyl hydrogen sulphate is formed.

$$H_2SO_4 \longrightarrow H^+ + {}^-OSO_2OH$$

$$\underset{Ethene}{CH_2 = CH_2} + H^+ \longrightarrow \underset{Ethylcarbonation}{CH_3 - CH_2^+} \xrightarrow[Fast]{{}^-OSO_2OH}$$

$$\underset{\substack{Ethyl\ hydrogen\\sulphate}}{CH_3CH_2OSO_2OH}$$

Ethylhydrogen sulphate is then boiled with water undergoes hydrolysis to form ethanol.

$$H_2\ddot{O} + \underset{\substack{Ethylhydrogen\\sulphate}}{CH_3 - CH_2 - OSO_2OH} \longrightarrow$$

$$CH_3 - CH_2 - \overset{+}{\underset{}{\ddot{O}}} \longleftarrow CH_3 - CH_2 - OH + H_3\overset{+}{O}$$
$$\underset{Ethanol}{}$$

12. You are given benzene, conc. H_2SO_4 and NaOH. Write the equations for the preparation of phenol using these reagents.

Sol.

$$\underset{Benzene}{C_6H_6} \xrightarrow[Sulphonation]{conc.H_2SO_4,\Delta} \underset{\substack{Benzene\\sulphonic\ acid}}{C_6H_5SO_3H} \xrightarrow[573K]{NaOH,\ fuse}$$

$$\underset{\substack{Sodium\\phenoxide}}{C_6H_5ONa} \xrightarrow[-NaCl]{Dil\ HCl} \underset{Phenol}{C_6H_5OH}$$

13. Show how will you synthesise
(i) 1-phenylethanol from a suitable alkene.
(ii) cyclohexylmethanol using an alkyl halide by an S_N2 reaction.
(iii) Pentan-1-ol using a suitable alkyl halide?

Sol. (i) Addition of H_2O to ethenylbenzene is presence of dil H_2SO_4.

$$+ H-OH \xrightarrow{Dil.\ H_2SO_4}$$

1-phenylethanol

(*ii*) Hydrolysis of cyclohexylmethyl bromide by aqueous NaOH gives cyclohexylmethanol.

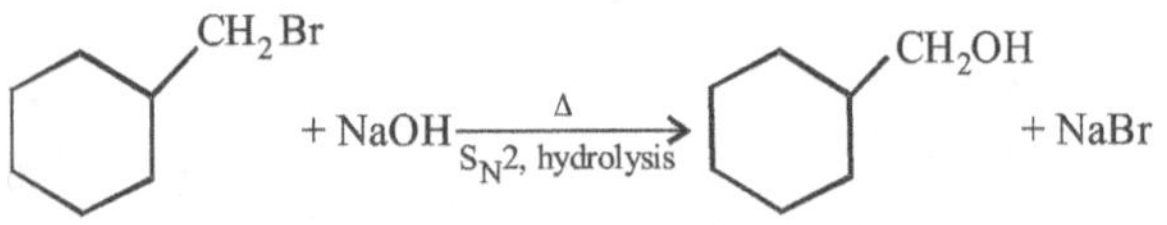

$$\text{Cyclohexyl-CH}_2\text{Br} + \text{NaOH} \xrightarrow[\text{S}_N2,\text{ hydrolysis}]{\Delta} \text{Cyclohexyl-CH}_2\text{OH} + \text{NaBr}$$

Cyclohexyl-
methanol

(*iii*) Hydrolysis of 1-bromopentane by aqueous NaOH gives pentan-1-ol.

$$\text{CH}_3\text{CH}_2\text{CH}_2\text{CH}_2\text{CH}_2\text{Br} + \text{NaOH}$$

$$\xrightarrow[\text{S}_N2,\text{Hydrolysis}]{\Delta} \text{CH}_3\text{CH}_2\text{CH}_2\text{CH}_2\text{CH}_2\text{—OH} + \text{NaBr}$$

Propan-1-ol

14. **Give two reactions that show the acidic nature of phenol. Compare its acidity with that of ethanol.**

Sol. The reactions showing acidic nature of phenol are:

(a) **Reaction with sodium:** Phenol reacts with active metals like sodium to liberate H_2 gas.

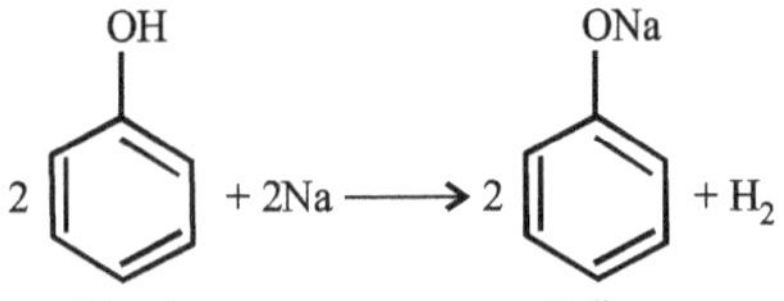

$$2 \text{ Phenol (OH)} + 2\text{Na} \longrightarrow 2 \text{ Sodium phenoxide (ONa)} + \text{H}_2$$

(b) **Reaction with NaOH:** Phenol dissolves in NaOH to form sodium phenoxide and water.

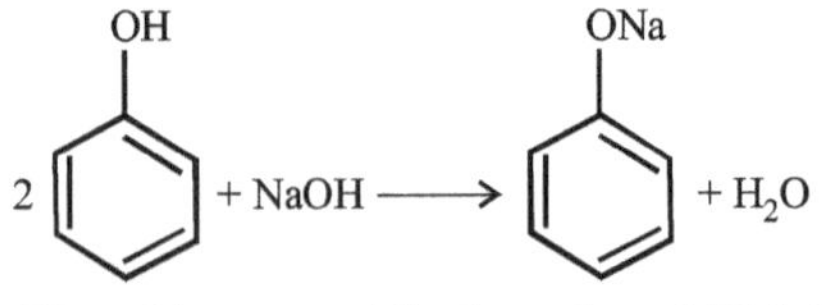

$$2 \text{ Phenol (OH)} + \text{NaOH} \longrightarrow \text{(ONa)} + \text{H}_2\text{O}$$

Phenol is more acidic than ethanol. This is due to the reason that phenoxide ion left after the loss of a proton from phenol is stabilized by resonance, while ethoxide ion left after less of a proton from ethanol, is not.

15. **Explain why is ortho-nitrophenol more acidic than ortho-methoxyphenol?**

Sol. Refer Theory

16. **Explain how does the –OH group attached to a carbon of benzene ring activate it towards electrophilic substitution?**

Sol. Phenol may be regarded as a resonance hybrid of structures I-V, shown below.

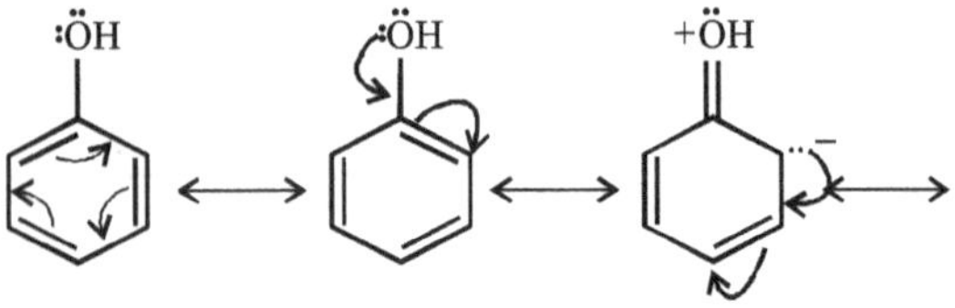

I   II   III

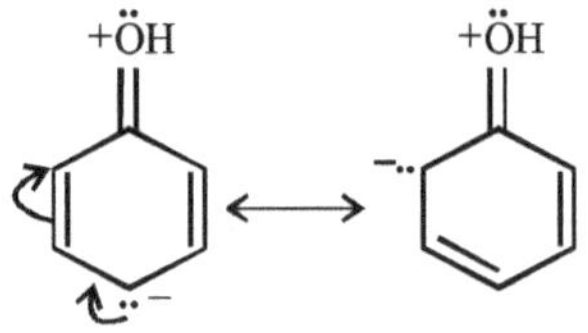

IV   V

As a result of +R effect of the –OH group, the electron density in the benzene ring increases thereby facilitating the attack of an electrophile. In other words, presence of –OH group, activates the benzene ring towards electrophilic substitution reactions. Further, since the electron density is relatively higher at the two *o*-and one *p*-position, therefore electrophilic substitution occurs mainly at *o*-and *p*-positions.

17. **Give equations of the following reactions:**
   (*i*) **Oxidation of propan-1-ol with alkaline KMnO$_4$ solution.**
   (*ii*) **Bromine in CS$_2$ with phenol.**
   (*iii*) **Dilute HNO$_3$ acid with phenol.**
   (*iv*) **Treating phenol with chloroform in presence of aqueous NaOH.**

Sol. (*i*) $\text{CH}_3\text{CH}_2\text{CH}_2\text{OH} + 2\,[\text{O}]$

$$\xrightarrow[\text{Oxidation}]{\text{Alk.KMnO}_4} \text{CH}_3\text{CH}_2\text{COOH} + \text{H}_2\text{O}$$

Propanoic acid

(*ii*) Phenol $\xrightarrow{\text{Br}_2 \text{ in CS}_2}$ 2-Bromophenol (Minor) + 4-Bromophenol (Major)

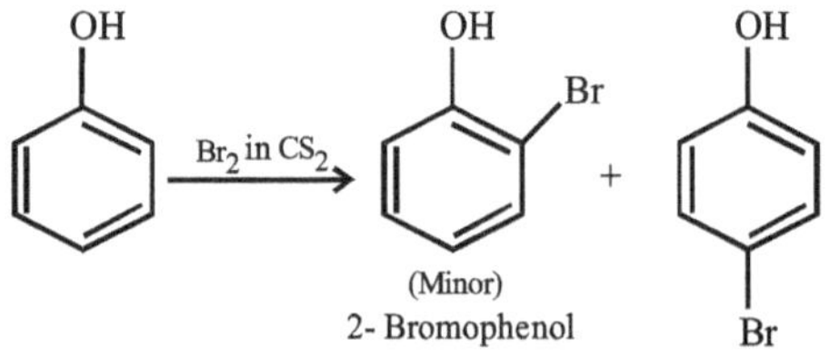

(*iii*) Phenol $\xrightarrow{\text{Dil HNO}_3}$ 2-Nitrophenol (Major) + 4-Nitrophenol (Minor)

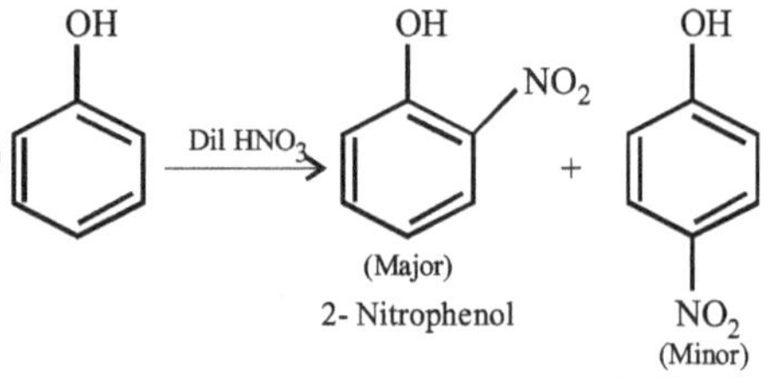

(*iv*) Phenol $\xrightarrow{\text{CHCl}_3, \text{NaOH, 343K}}$ (ONa, CHO) $\xrightarrow{\text{H}^+, \text{H}_2\text{O}}$ 2-Hydroxybenzaldehyde (salicylaldehyde)

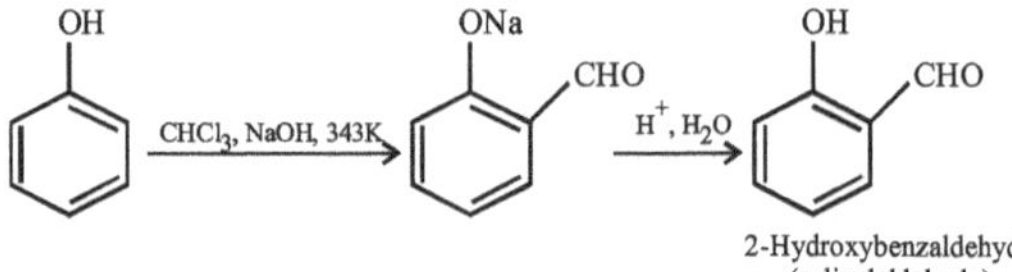

18. **Explain the following with an example**
   (*i*) **Kolbe's reaction**
   (*ii*) **Reimer - Tiemann reaction**
   (*iii*) **Williamson ether synthesis**
   (*iv*) **Unsymmetrical ether**

Sol. Refer Theory

19. **Write the mechanism of acid dehydration of ethanol to yield ethene.**

Sol. The mechanism of dehydration of alcohols to form alkenes occur by the following three steps:
   (*a*) Formation of protonated alcohol:

$$\text{CH}_3\text{CH}_2\text{—}\ddot{\text{O}}\text{—H} + \text{H}^+ \rightleftharpoons \text{CH}_3\text{CH}_2\text{—}\overset{+}{\text{O}}\overset{H}{\underset{H}{\diagup}}$$

(Oxonium Salt)

(*b*) Formation of carbocation :

$$CH_3CH_2 - \overset{+}{O}\overset{H}{\underset{H}{<}} \xrightarrow{\text{Slow}} CH_3\overset{+}{CH_2} + H_2O$$
$$\text{Ethylcarbocation}$$

(*c*) Elimination of a proton to form ethene:

$$H - CH_2 - \overset{+}{CH_2} \rightleftharpoons CH_2=CH_2 + H^+$$
$$\text{Ethene}$$

20. How are the following conversions carried out?
(*i*) **Propene → Propan-2-ol**
(*ii*) **Benzyl chloride → Benzyl alcohol**
(*iii*) **Ethyl magnesium chloride → Propan-1-ol**
(*iv*) **Methyl magnesium bromide → 2-Methylpropan-2-ol**

Sol. (*i*) $CH_3 - CH = CH_2 + \text{Conc. } H_2SO_4 \longrightarrow$
$\quad\quad\quad$ Propene

$$CH_3 - CH - CH_3 \xrightarrow[-H_2SO_4]{H_2O,\ \Delta} CH_3-CH-CH_3$$
$$\overset{|}{OSO_3H} \quad\quad\quad\quad\quad \overset{|}{OH}$$
$$\text{propan-2-ol}$$

(*ii*)

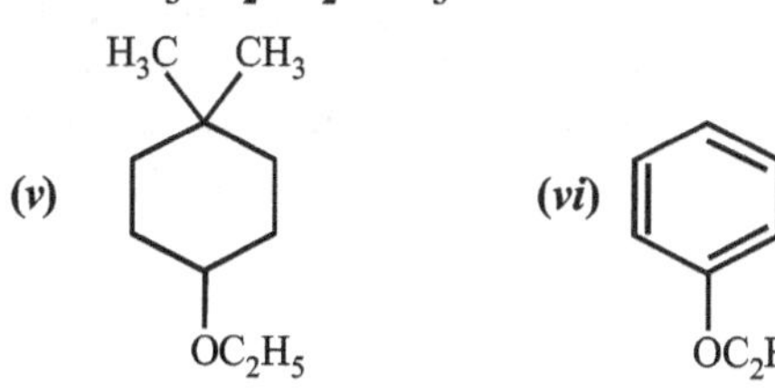

Benzyl chloride $\quad + NaOH\ (aq) \xrightarrow{\text{Hydrolysis}}$ Benzyl alcohol $+ NaCl$

(*iii*)

$$\overset{H}{\underset{H}{>}}\overset{\delta+ \ \delta-}{C = O} + CH_3\ CH_2 \overset{\delta-}{-} MgCl \xrightarrow{\text{Dry ether}}$$
$$\text{Formaldehyde} \quad\quad \text{Ethyl magnesium}$$
$$\text{chloride}$$

$$[CH_3\ CH_2\ CH_2\ OMgCl] \xrightarrow[-Mg(OH)Cl]{H_3O^+} CH_3CH_2CH_2OH$$
$$\text{Addition product} \quad\quad\quad\quad\quad\quad \text{Propan-1-ol}$$

(*iv*)

$$\overset{CH_3}{\underset{H}{>}}\overset{\delta+ \ \delta-}{C = O} + CH_3 \overset{\delta-}{-} \overset{\delta+}{MgBr} \xrightarrow{\text{Dry ether}}$$
$$\text{Acetaldehyde} \quad\quad \text{Methyl magnesium}$$
$$\text{bromide}$$

$$\begin{bmatrix} CH_3 \\ CH_3 \end{bmatrix} C \begin{matrix} CH_3 \\ OMgBr \end{matrix} \xrightarrow[Mg(OH)Br]{H_2O/H^+} (CH_3)_3C-OH$$
$$\quad\quad\quad\quad\quad\quad\quad\quad\quad \text{2-Methylpropan-2-ol}$$
$$\text{Methylmagnesiumbromide}$$

21. Name the reagents used in the following reactions:
(*i*) **Oxidation of a primary alcohol to carboxylic acid.**
(*ii*) **Oxidation of a primary alcohol to aldehyde.**
(*iii*) **Bromination of phenol to 2, 4, 6 – tribromophenol**
(*iv*) **Benzyl alcohol to benzoic acid.**
(*v*) **Dehydration of propan-2-ol to propene.**
(*vi*) **Butan-2-one to butan-2-ol.**

Sol. (*i*) Acidified potassium dichromate or neutral/ acidic/ alkaline potassium permanganate.
(*ii*) Pyridinium chlorochromate (PCC), $(C_5H_5NH)^+$ $ClCrO_3^-$ in CH_2Cl_2
or Pyridinium dichromate (PDC), $[(C_5H_5NH)_2]^{2+}$ $Cr_2O_7^{2-}$ in CH_2Cl_2
(*iii*) Aqueous bromine, *i.e.,* Br_2/H_2O.

(*iv*) Acidified or alkaline potassium permanganate.
(*v*) 85% H_2SO_4 at 440 K.
(*vi*) Ni/H_2 or $NaBH_4$ or $LiAlH_4$.

22. Give reason for the higher boiling point of ethanol in comparison to methoxymethane.

Sol. Ethanol undergoes intermolecular H-bonding due to the presence of a hydrogen atom attached to the electronegative oxygen atom. As a result, ethanol exists as associated molecules.

$$---H-O---H-O---H-O---$$
$$\quad\quad\quad \overset{|}{CH_2CH_3} \quad \overset{|}{CH_2CH_3} \quad \overset{|}{CH_2CH_3}$$

Consequently, a large amount of energy is required to break these hydrogen bonds. Therefore, the boiling point of ethanol is higher than that of methoxymethane which does not form H-bonds.

23. Give IUPAC names of the following ethers.

(*i*) $C_2H_5OCH_2 - \overset{|}{\underset{CH_3}{CH}} - CH_3$

(*ii*) $CH_3 - O - CH_2CH_2Cl$
(*iii*) $O_2N - C_6H_4 - OCH_3 (p)$
(*iv*) $CH_3CH_2CH_2OCH_3$

(*v*) (*vi*)

Sol. (*i*) 1-Ethoxy-2-methylpropane
(*ii*) 2-Chlorlo-1-methoxyethane
(*iii*) 4-Nitroanisole
(*iv*) 1-Methoxypropane
(*v*) 1-Ethoxy-4-4-dimethylcyclohexane
(*vi*) Ethoxybenzene

24. Write the names of reagents and equations for the preparation of the following ethers by Williamson's synthesis:
(*i*) **1-Propoxypropane**
(*ii*) **Ethoxybenzene**
(*iii*) **2-Methoxy-2-methylpropane**
(*iv*) **1-Methoxyethane**

Sol. (*i*) $CH_3CH_2CH_2O^-Na^+ + CH_3CH_2CH_2Br \xrightarrow{\Delta}$
$\quad\quad$ Sodium propoxide $\quad$ 1–Bromopropane

$$CH_3CH_2CH_2 - O - CH_2CH_2CH_3 + NaBr$$
$$\text{1–Propoxypropane}$$

(*ii*) Sodium phenoxide (O^-Na^+) $+ CH_3CH_2Br \longrightarrow$ Ethoxybenzene (OCH_2CH_3) $+ NaBr$
$\quad\quad\quad\quad\quad\quad\quad$ Bromoethane

(iii)
$$CH_3 - \underset{\underset{CH_3}{|}}{\overset{\overset{CH_3}{|}}{C}} - O^- Na^+ + CH_3 - Br \xrightarrow{\Delta}$$

Sodium–2–methyl–2–propoxide, Bromoethane

$$CH_3 - \underset{\underset{CH_3}{|}}{\overset{\overset{CH_3}{|}}{C}} - OCH_3 + NaBr$$

2–methyl–2–methoxypropane

(iv) $CH_3CH_2O^- Na^+ + CH_3 - Br \xrightarrow{\Delta}$

Sodium ethoxide, Bromoethane

$$CH_3CH_2OCH_3 + NaBr$$

1–Methoxyethane

25. Illustrate with examples the limitations of Willamson synthesis for the preparation of certain types of ethers.

Sol. Williamson's synthesis is a versatile method for the synthesis of both symmetrical and unsymmetrical ethers. However, for the synthesis of unsymmetrical ethers, a proper choice of reactants is necessary. Since Williamson's synthesis occurs by S_N2 mechanism and primary alkyl halides are most reactive in S_N2 reaction, therefore, best yields of unsymmetrical ethers are obtained when the alkyl halides are primary and the alkoxide may be primary, secondary or tertiary. For example, tert-butylethyl ether is prepared by treating ethyl bromide with sodium tert-butoxide.

$$CH_3 - \underset{\underset{CH_3}{|}}{\overset{\overset{CH_3}{|}}{C}} - O^- Na^+ + CH_3\overset{\delta+}{CH_2} - \overset{\delta-}{Br} \xrightarrow{\Delta}$$

(3° Alkoxide)

$$CH_3 - \underset{\underset{CH_3}{|}}{\overset{\overset{CH_3}{|}}{C}} - OCH_2CH_3 + Na^+Br^-$$

The above ether cannot be prepared by treating sodium ethoxide with tert-butyl chloride or bromide since under these condition an alkene, *i.e.,* isobutylene is the main product.

$$(CH_3)_3 - C - Br + C_2H_5O^- Na^+ \longrightarrow$$

$$CH_3 - \underset{CH_3}{\overset{|}{C}} = CH_2 + NaBr + C_2H_5OH$$

2–Methylpropene

Aryl and vinyl halides cannot be used as substrates because they are less reactive in nucleophilic substitution.

26. How is 1-propoxypropane synthesised from propan-1-ol? Write the mechanism of this reaction.

Sol. (a) Williamson's synthesis

(i) $3CH_3CH_2CH_2OH + PBr_3 \longrightarrow$

Propan–1–ol

$$3CH_3CH_2CH_2Br + H_3PO_3$$

1–Bromoprapane

(ii) $2CH_3CH_2CH_2OH + 2Na \longrightarrow$

Propan–1–ol

$$2CH_3CH_2CH_2O^- Na^+ + H_2$$

Sodium propoxide

$$CH_3CH_2CH_2O^- \overset{+}{Na} + CH_3CH_2CH_2 - \overset{\delta+}{\underset{}{}}\overset{\delta-}{Br}$$

$$\xrightarrow[\text{Heat}]{\text{Dry ether}} CH_3CH_2CH_2 - O - CH_2CH_2CH_3 + NaBr$$

1–propoxypropane

(b) By dehydration of 1-propanol with conc. H_2SO_4 at 413 K.

$$CH_3CH_2CH_2OH + H^+ \longrightarrow CH_3CH_2CH_2 - \overset{+}{O}\underset{H}{\overset{H}{\diagdown}}$$

Propan -1- ol, Protonated-1-propanal

$$CH_3CH_2CH_2 - \ddot{O}H + CH_3CH_2CH_2 - \overset{+}{O}\underset{H}{\overset{H}{\diagdown}} \xrightarrow[-H_2O]{413K}$$

$$CH_3CH_2CH_2 - \overset{+}{\underset{H}{O}} \diagdown CH_2CH_2CH_3 + H - \ddot{O} - CH_2CH_2CH_3 \longrightarrow$$

$$CH_3CH_2CH_2 - O - CH_2CH_2CH_3 +$$

$$CH_3CH_2CH_2\overset{+}{O}H_2$$

27. Preparation of ethers by acid dehydration of secondary or tertiary alcohols is not a suitable method. Give reason.

Sol. Acid catalysed dehydration of primary alcohols to ethers occurs by S_N2 reaction involving nucleophilic attack by the alcohol molecule on the protonated alcohol molecule.

$$CH_3CH_2CH_2\ddot{O}H + CH_3CH_2CH_2 - \overset{+}{O}H_2 \xrightarrow[-H^+, -H_2O]{S_N2}$$

$$CH_3CH_2CH_2 - O - CH_2CH_2CH_3$$

Under these conditions, 2° and 3° alcohols, however, give alkenes rather than ethers. The reason being that due to steric hindrance, nucleophilic attack by the alcohol molecule on the protonated alcohol molecule does not occur. Instead protonated 2° and 3° alcohols lose a molecule of water to form stable 2° and 3° carbocation. These carbocations prefer to lose a proton to form alkenes rather than undergoing nucleophilic attack by alcohol molecules to form ethers.

$$CH_3 - \underset{(2°\text{ Alcohol})}{\overset{\overset{CH_3}{|}}{CH}} - OH \xrightarrow{H^+} CH_3 - \overset{\overset{CH_3}{|}}{CH} - \overset{+}{O}H_2 \xrightarrow{-H_2O} CH_3 - \overset{\overset{CH_3}{|}}{CH}^{\oplus}$$

$$CH_3 - \overset{\overset{CH_3}{|}}{CH} - O - \overset{\overset{CH_3}{|}}{CH} - CH_3 \underset{-H^+}{\overset{CH_3CHOHCH_3}{\longleftarrow}} \times \overset{}{\underset{-H^+}{\longrightarrow}} CH_3 - CH = CH_2$$

Similarly, 3° alcohols give alkenes rather than ethers.

$$(CH_3)_3C - OH \xrightarrow{+H^+} (CH_3)_3 - C - \overset{+}{O}H_2 \xrightarrow{-H_2O} (CH_3)_3 - C^+$$

(3° Alcohol)

$$CH_3 - \underset{\underset{CH_3}{|}}{\overset{\overset{CH_3}{|}}{C}} - O - \underset{\underset{CH_3}{|}}{\overset{\overset{CH_3}{|}}{C}} - CH_3 \underset{-H^+}{\overset{(CH_3)_3COH}{\longleftarrow}} \times \overset{}{\underset{-H^+}{\longrightarrow}} CH_3 - \overset{\overset{CH_3}{|}}{C} = CH_2$$

28. Write the equation of the reaction of hydrogen iodide with
   (*i*) **1-propoxypropane**
   (*ii*) **methoxybenzene, and**
   (*iii*) **benzyl ethyl ether**

Sol. (*i*) $CH_3CH_2CH_2OCH_2CH_2CH_3$
       1–propoxypropane

$$\xrightarrow[373\,K]{HI} CH_3CH_2CH_2 - OH + CH_3CH_2CH_2I$$
              Propan–1–ol   Iodopropane

(*ii*) Methoxybenzene $\xrightarrow{HI,\ 373\ K}$ Phenol $+ CH_3 - I$ (Iodomethane)

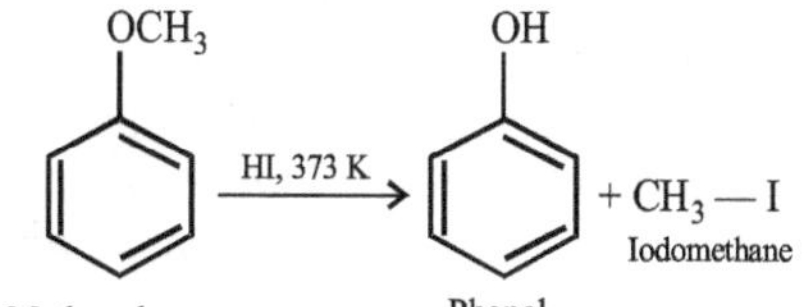

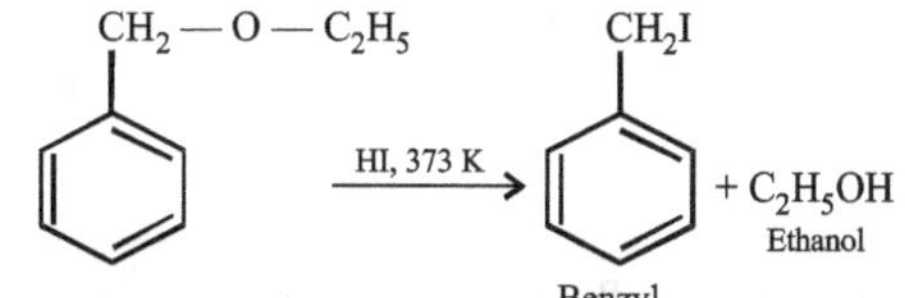

(*iii*) Benzyl ethyl ether $\xrightarrow{HI,\ 373\ K}$ Benzyl Iodide $+ C_2H_5OH$ (Ethanol)

29. Explain the fact that in aryl alkyl ethers
   (*i*) the alkoxy group activates the benzene ring towards electrophilic substitution and
   (*ii*) it directs the incoming substituents to ortho and para positions in benzene ring.

Sol. In aryl alkyl ethers, the +R-effect of the alkoxy (OR) group increases the electron density in the benzene ring, thereby activating the benzene ring towards electrophilic substitution reaction.

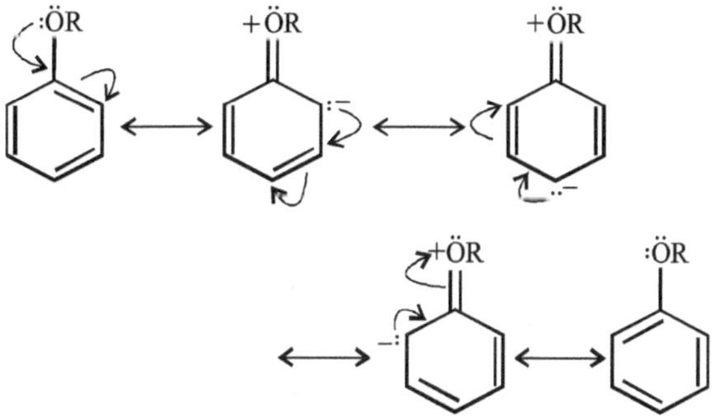

Since the electron density increases more at the two ortho and one para position as compared to meta position therefore, electrophilic substitution reactions mainly occur at *o*-and *p*-positions.

30. **Write the mechanism of the reaction of HI with methoxymethane.**

Sol. When equimolar amounts of HI and methoxy methane are reacted, a mixture of methyl alcohol and methyl iodide is formed by the following mechanism:

(*a*) $CH_3 - \ddot{O} - CH_3 + H - I \xrightarrow[Fast]{Protonation} CH_3 - \overset{+}{O} - CH_3 + I^-$ (Oxonium ion)

(*b*) $I^- + CH_3 - \overset{+}{O} - CH_3 \xrightarrow[Slow]{S_N2} CH_3 - I + CH_3OH$

If however, excess of HI is used, methyl alcohol formed in step (b) is also converted into methyl iodide by following mechanism:

(*c*) $CH_3 - \ddot{O} - H + H - I \xrightarrow[Fast]{Protonation} CH_3 - \overset{+}{O} - H + I^-$

(*d*) $I^- + CH_3 - \overset{+}{O} - H \xrightarrow[Slow]{S_N2} CH_3I + H_2O$

31. **Write equations of the following reactions:**
   (*i*) **Friedel-Crafts reaction –alkylation of anisole**
   (*ii*) **Nitration of anisole.**
   (*iii*) **Bromination of anisole in ethanoic acid medium**
   (*iv*) **Friedel-Craft's acetylation of anisole.**

Sol. (*i*) Anisole $+ CH_3Cl \xrightarrow{Anhy.\ AlCl_3}$ *o*-Methylanisole (Minor) $+$ *p*-Methylanisole (major)

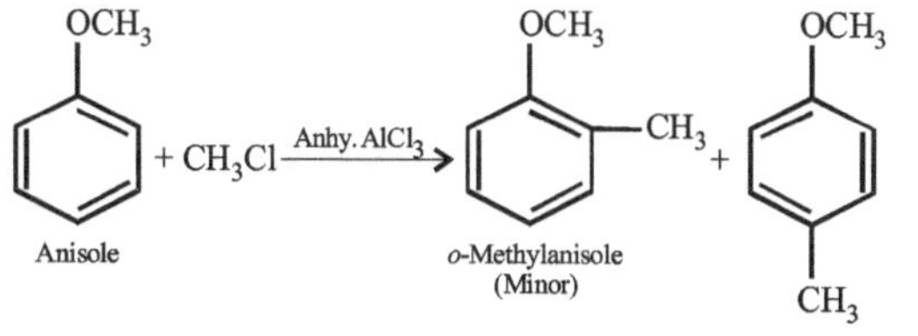

(*ii*) Anisole $\xrightarrow[+conc.\ H_2SO_4]{conc.\ HNO_3}$ *o*-nitroanisole (Minor) $+$ *p*-nitroanisole (Major)

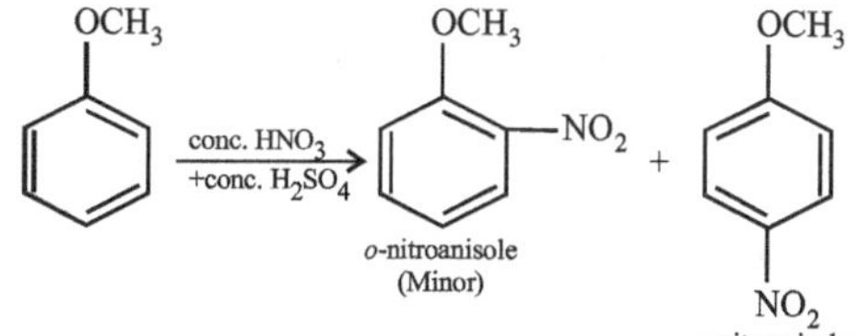

(*iii*) Anisole $+ Br_2 \xrightarrow{CH_3COOH}$ *o*-Bromoanisole (Minor) $+$ *p*-Bromoanisole (Major)

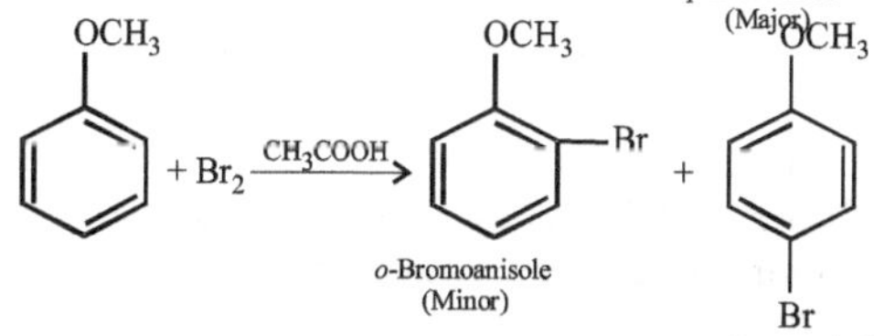

(*iv*) Anisole $+ CH_3COCl \xrightarrow{Anhy.\ AlCl_3}$ *o*-methoxy acetophenone (Minor) $+$ *p*-methoxy acetophenone (Major)

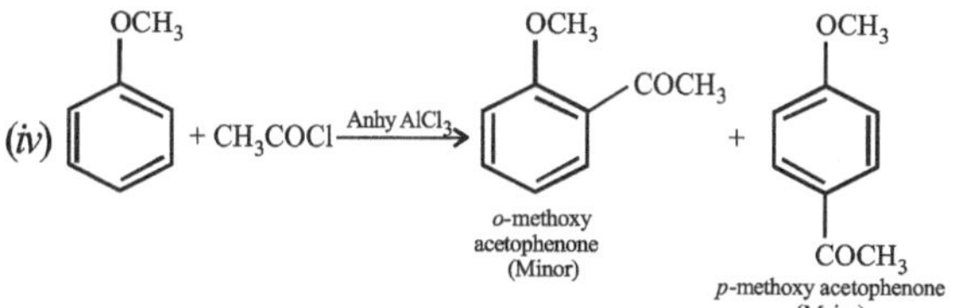

32. **Show how would you synthesise the following alcohols from appropriate alkanes?**

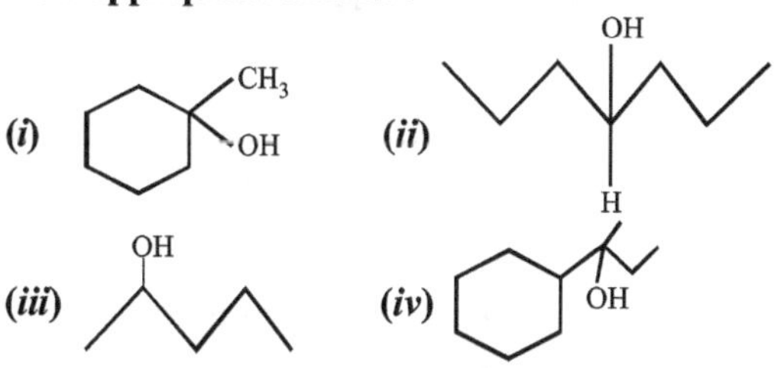

   (*i*)   (*ii*)

   (*iii*)   (*iv*)

Sol. Refer Theory

33. When 3-methylbutant 2-ol is treated with HBr, the following reaction takes place:

$$CH_3 - CH - CH - CH_3 \xrightarrow{HBr} CH_3 - \underset{\underset{CH_3}{|}}{\overset{\overset{Br}{|}}{C}} - CH_2CH_3$$
$$\underset{CH_3 \quad OH}{}$$

Give a mechanism for this reaction.

(Hint : The secondary carbocation formed in step II rearranges to a more stable tertiary carbocation by a hydride ion shift from 3rd carbon atom.)

Sol.

$$CH_3 - \underset{\underset{CH_3}{|}}{CH} - \underset{\underset{OH}{|}}{CH} - CH_3 \xrightarrow{H^+} CH_3 - \underset{\underset{CH_3}{|}}{CH} - \underset{\underset{\overset{+}{OH_2}}{|}}{CH} - CH_3 \xrightarrow{-H_2O} CH_3 - \underset{\underset{CH_3}{|}}{\overset{H}{C}} - \overset{+}{CH} - CH_3$$

2° carbocation
(I) Less stable

1-2-hydride shift

$$CH_3 - \underset{\underset{CH_3}{|}}{\overset{\overset{Br}{|}}{C}} - CH_2 - CH_3 \xleftarrow[\underset{attack}{Nucleophilic}]{Br^-} CH_3 - \underset{\underset{CH_3}{|}}{\overset{+}{C}} - CH_2 - CH_3$$

3° carbocation
(II) more stable

Protonation of the given alcohol followed by loss of water gives a 2° carbocation(I), which being unstable rearranges by 1, 2-hydride shift to form the more stable 3° carbocation (II). Nucleophilic attack by Br⁻ ion on this carbocation (II) gives the final product.

Past year Exercise

Very Short Answer Questions

1. Draw the structure of Hex-1-en-3-ol.

2. Write the IUPAC name of the following compound.

$$\underset{\quad\quad\quad\quad\quad\underset{OH}{|}}{CH_3CH = CH - CH - CH_2CH_3}$$

3. Write IUPAC name of the following:

$$CH_3 - \underset{\underset{CH_3}{|}}{C} = \underset{\underset{Br}{|}}{C} - CH_2OH$$

4. Of the two hydroxy organic compounds ROH and R'OH, the first one is basic and other is acidic in behaviour. How is R different from R' ?

5. Which of the following isomers is more volatile : o-nitrophenol or p-nitrophenol

6. Write the IUPAC name of the following compound:

$$CH_3 - O - \underset{\underset{CH_3}{|}}{\overset{\overset{CH_3}{|}}{C}} - CH_3$$

7. Write the IUPAC name of the following :

$$CH_3 - \underset{\underset{C_2H_5}{|}}{\overset{\overset{CH_3}{|}}{C}} - \underset{\underset{OH}{|}}{CH} - CH_3$$

Short Answer Questions

8. A compound A (C_2H_6O) on oxidation by PCC gave B, which on treatment with aqueous alkali and subsequent heating furnished C. B on oxidation by $KMnO_4$, forms a monobasic carboxylic acid with molar mass 60 g mol⁻¹. Deduce the structure A, B and C.

9. Explain the following giving one example for each.
(i) Reimer-Tiemann reaction
(ii) Friedel-Crafts acetylation of anisole

10. Explain the following behaviours.
(i) Alcohols are more soluble in water than the hydrocarbons of comparable molecular masses.
(ii) *o*-Nitrophenol is more acidic than *ortho*-methoxyphenol.

11. Draw the structure and name the product formed if the following alcohols are oxidised. Assume that an excess of oxidising agent is used.
(i) $CH_3CH_2CH_2CH_2OH$
(ii) 2-butanol
(iii) 2-methyl-1-propanol

12. State the products of the following reactions
(i) $CH_3CH_2CH_2OCH_3 + HBr \longrightarrow$

(ii) ⟨benzene ring⟩ $- OC_2H_5 + HBr \longrightarrow$

(iii) $(CH_3)_3C - O - C_2H_5 + HI \longrightarrow$

13. Explain the mechanism of acid catalysed hydration of an alkene to form corresponding alcohol.

14. Explain the mechanism of the following reaction:

$$CH_3 - CH_2 - OH \xrightarrow[443\,K]{H^+} CH_2 = CH_2 + H_2O$$

15. Write the equations involved in the following reactions :
(i) Reimer – Tiemann reaction
(ii) Williamson's ether synthesis

16. Explain the mechanism of the following reaction:

$$2CH_3 - CH_2 - OH \xrightarrow[413K]{H^+} CH_3CH_2 - \overset{..}{O} - CH_2 - CH_3 + H_2O$$

17. How will you convert :
(i) Propene to Propan-2-ol?
(ii) Phenol to 2, 4,6-trinitrophenol?

18. How will you convert the following ?
(i) Propan-2-ol to propanone
(ii) Phenol to 2,4,6-tribromophenol.

19. How will you convert.
    (a) Propene to Propan-1-ol?
    (b) Ethanal to Propan-2-ol?
20. Write the mechanism of the following reaction:
    $$CH_3CH_2OH \xrightarrow{HBr} CH_3CH_2Br + H_2O$$
21. Write the final product(s) in each of the following reactions :

    (a) $CH_3 - \underset{\underset{CH_3}{|}}{\overset{\overset{CH_3}{|}}{C}} - O - CH_3 + HI \longrightarrow$

    (b) $CH_3 - CH_2 - \underset{\underset{OH}{|}}{CH} - CH_3 \xrightarrow{Cu/573K}$

    (c) $C_6H_5 - OH \xrightarrow[\text{(ii)}\quad H^+]{\text{(i) } CHCl_3 + aq.NaOH}$

22. What happens when
    (a) Phenol reacts with conc. HNO_3 ?
    (b) Ethyl chloride reacts with $NaOC_2H_5$?
    Write the chemical equations involved in the above reactions.
23. (a) Butan-1-ol has a higher boiling point than diethyl ether. Why?
    (b) Write the mechanism of the following reaction:
    $$2CH_3CH_2OH \xrightarrow[413K]{H^+} CH_3CH_2 - O - CH_2 - CH_3$$

24. Write the structures of the main products in the following reactions:

    (i) 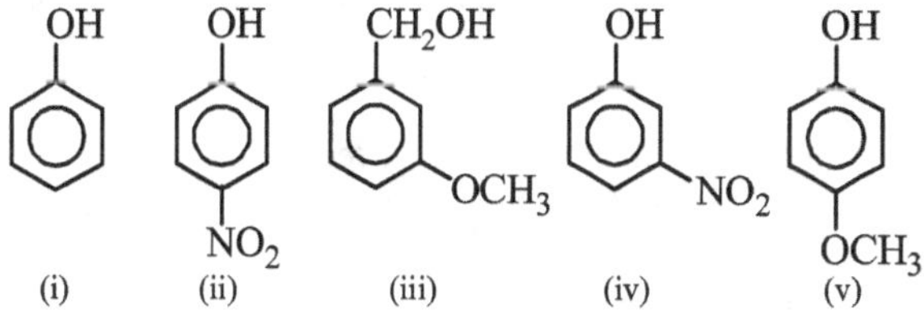

    (ii) (benzene ring) $CH = CH_2 + H_2O \xrightarrow{H^+}$

    (iii) (benzene ring with OC_2H_2) $+ HI \longrightarrow$

25. (a) Arrange the following compounds in the increasing order of their acid strength:
    p-cresol, p-nitrophenol, phenol
    (b) Write the mechanism (using curved arrow notation) of the following reaction:
    $$CH_2 = CH_2 \xrightarrow{H_2O^+} CH_3 - \overset{+}{C}H_2 + H_2O$$

    OR

    Write the structures of the products when Butan–2 – ol reacts with the following
    (a) CrO_3 (b) $SOCl_2$

NCERT Exemplar 

Multiple Choice Questions

1. How many alcohols with molecular formula $C_4H_{10}O$ are chiral in nature?
   (a) 1   (b) 2   (c) 3   (d) 4
2. What is the correct order of reactivity of alcohols in the following reaction?
   $$R - OH + HCl \xrightarrow{ZnCl_2} R - Cl + H_2O$$
   (a) $1° > 2° > 3°$ (b) $1° < 2° < 3°$
   (c) $3° > 2° > 1°$ (d) $3° > 1° > 2°$
3. The process of converting alkyl halides into alcohols involves ....
   (a) addition reaction   (b) substitution reaction
   (c) dehydrohalogenation (d) rearrangement reaction
4. Give IUPAC name of the compound given below.
   $$CH_3 - \underset{\underset{Cl}{|}}{CH} - CH_2 - CH_2 - \underset{\underset{OH}{|}}{CH} - CH_3$$
   (a) 2-chloro-5-hydroxyhexane
   (b) 2-hydroxy-5-chlorohexane
   (c) 5-chlorohexan-2-ol
   (d) 2-chlorohexan-5-ol
5. Phenol is less acidic than ....
   (a) ethanol   (b) o - nitrophenol
   (c) o-methylphenol   (d) o-methoxyphenol

6. Mark the correct order of decreasing acid strength of the following compounds.

   (i) (phenol, OH)   (ii) (OH, para-NO_2)   (iii) (CH_2OH, OCH_3)   (iv) (OH, NO_2)   (v) (OH, para-OCH_3)

   (a) $V > IV > II > I > III$ (b) $II > IV > I > III > V$
   (c) $IV > V > III > II > I$ (d) $V > IV > III > II > I$
7. Arrange the following compounds in increasing order of boiling point.
   Propan - 1- ol, butan - 1 - ol, butan - 2 - ol, pentan - 1 - ol
   (a) Propan-1-ol, butan-2-ol, butan-1-ol, pentan-1-ol
   (b) Propan-1-ol, butan-1-ol, butan-2-ol, pentan-1-ol
   (c) Pentan-1-ol, butan-2-ol, butan-1-ol, propan-1-ol
   (d) Pentan-1-ol, butan-1-ol, butan-2-ol, propan-1-ol

Assertion & Reason Questions

DIRECTIONS (Qs. 8-10) : *Each of these questions contains an assertion followed by reason. Read them carefully and answer the question on the basis of following options. You have to select the one that best describes the two statements.*

(a) If both Assertion and Reason are correct and the Reason is a correct explanation of the Assertion.

(b) If both Assertion and Reason are correct but Reason is not a correct explanation of the Assertion.

(c) If the Assertion is correct but Reason is incorrect.

(d) If the Assertion is incorrect but the Reason is correct.

8. **Assertion :** p-nitrophenol is more acidic than phenol.
Reason : Nitro group helps in the stabilisation of the phenoxide ion by dispersal of negative charge due to resonance.

9. **Assertion :** Boiling points of alcohols and ethers are high.
Reason : Alcohols can form intermolecular hydrogen-bonding.

10. **Assertion :** o-nitrophenol is less soluble in water than the m and p-isomers.
Reason : m and p-nitrophenols exist as associated molecules.

11. What is denatured alcohol?

12. Out of o-nitrophenol and p-nitrophenol, which is more volatile? Explain.

13. Nitration is an example of aromatic electrophilic substitution and its rate depends upon the group already present in the benzene ring. Out of benzene and phenol, which one is more easily nitrated and why?

14. In Kolbe's reaction, instead of phenol, phenoxide ion is treated with carbon dioxide. Why?

Objective Practice Exercise

DIRECTIONS : *This section contains multiple choice questions. Each question has four choices (a), (b), (c) and (d) out of which only one is correct.*

1. Molecular formula of amyl alcohol is
(a) $C_7H_{14}O$ (b) $C_6H_{13}O$
(c) $C_5H_{12}O$ (d) $C_5H_{10}O$

2. Methylated spirit is
(a) methanol   (b) methanol + ethanol
(c) methanoic acid   (d) methanamide

3. The compound $HOCH_2 - CH_2OH$ is
(a) ethane glycol   (b) ethylene glycol
(c) ethylidene alcohol   (d) dimethyl alcohol

4. The IUPAC name of 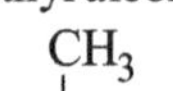 $CH_3 - CH - CH_2 - CH - CH_3$ is :
(with CH_3 on the second carbon and OH on the fourth carbon)
(a) 1, 1-dimethyl-1, 3-butanediol
(b) 2-methyl-2-pentanol
(c) 4-methyl-2, 4-pentanediol
(d) 1, 3, 3-trimethyl-1, 3-propanediol

5. Alcoholic beverages contain :
(a) isopropyl alcohol   (b) n-propyl alcohol
(c) ethyl alcohol   (d) methyl alcohol

6. Which of the following are isomers ?
(a) Methyl alcohol and dimethyl ether
(b) Ethyl alcohol and dimethyl ether
(c) Acetone and acetaldehyde
(d) Propionic acid and propanone

7. The characteristic grouping of secondary alcohols is
(a) $-CH_2OH$ (b) $>CHOH$
(c) $-\overset{|}{\underset{|}{C}}-OH$ (d) $>C\overset{OH}{\underset{OH}{\diagdown}}$

8. The C–O–H bond angle in ethanol is nearly
(a) 90°   (b) 104°   (c) 120°   (d) 109°

9. Which is oxidized most easily?
(a) $CH_3 - CHOH - CH_3$
(b) a benzene ring with $-OH$
(c) $CH_3 - CH_2 - O - CH_2 - CH_3$
(d) a cyclohexane ring with CH_3 and $-OH$

10. Which is the best reagent to convert isopropyl alcohol to isopropyl bromide?

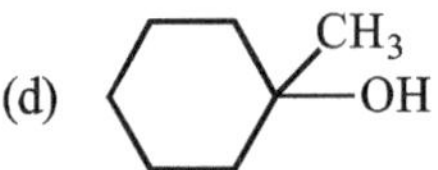

$$CH_3 - \overset{\overset{\displaystyle CH_3}{|}}{CH} - OH \xrightarrow{?} CH_3 - \overset{\overset{\displaystyle CH_3}{|}}{CH} - Br$$

(a) HBr   (b) $SOBr_2$
(c) Br_2 (c) CH_3MgBr

11. Which are not cleaved by HIO_4?
I. glycerol   II. glycol
III. 1, 3 propenediol
IV. methoxy-2-propanol
(a) I, II, III, IV   (b) I, II
(c) II, III   (d) III, IV

12. Which of the esters shown, after reduction with $LiAlH_4$ and aqueous workup, will yield two molecules of only a single alcohol?
(a) $CH_3CH_2CO_2CH_2CH_3$ (b) $C_6H_5CO_2CH_2C_6H_5$
(c) $C_6H_5CO_2C_6H_5$ (d) None of these

13. Which of the following reagents would carry out the following transformation? $(D = {}^2H)$

$$\text{(phenyl)}-\overset{\overset{\displaystyle O}{\|}}{C}CH_3 \xrightarrow{?} \text{(phenyl)}-\overset{\overset{\displaystyle OH}{|}}{\underset{\underset{\displaystyle D}{|}}{C}}CH_3$$

(a) $NaBD_4$ in CH_3OH (b) $LiAlH_4$, then D_2O
(c) $NaBD_4$ in CH_3OD (d) $LiAlD_4$, then D_2O

14. In which of the following group, each member gives positive iodoform test?
    (a) methanol, ethanol, propanone
    (b) ethanol, isopropanal, methanal,
    (c) ethanol, ethanal isopropyl alcohol
    (d) propanal, propanol 2, propanone

15. 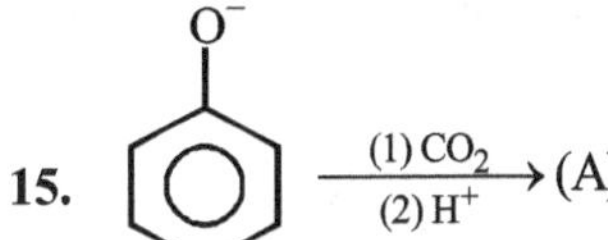 $\xrightarrow[(2)\,H^+]{(1)\,CO_2}$ (A)

    Which of the following is true statement about the reaction?
    (a) Ortho isomer is major if PhONa is used
    (b) Para isomer is major if PhOK is used
    (c) Product formed is further used for preparation of drug aspirin
    (d) All of these

16. The major reason that phenol is a better Bronsted acid than cyclohexanol is that:
    (a) it is a beter proton donor.
    (b) the cyclohexyl group is an electron donating group by induction, which destabilizes the anion formed in the reaction by resonance.
    (c) phenol is able to stabilize the anion formed in the reaction.
    (d) the phenyl group is an electron withdrawing group by induction, which stabilizes the anion formed in the reaction.

17. Which one of the following substituents at *para*-position is most effective in stabilizing the phenoxide ion?

    (a) $-CH_3$ (b) $-OCH_3$ (c) $-COCH_3$ (d) $-CH_2OH$

18. Phenol undergoes electrophilic substitution more easily than benzene because
    (a) –OH group exhibits +M effect and hence increases the electron density on the *o*- and *p*-positions.
    (b) oxocation is more stable than the carbocation.
    (c) both (a) and (b).
    (d) –OH group exhibits acidic character.

19. Which of the following is the correct order of the acidity of the three compounds ?

    CH₂CH₃ / OH (I)   COCH₃ / OH (II)   OH / OCH₃ (III)

    (a) II > III > I
    (b) III > II > I
    (c) II > I > III
    (d) III > I > II

20. Give the best conditions for this transformation:

    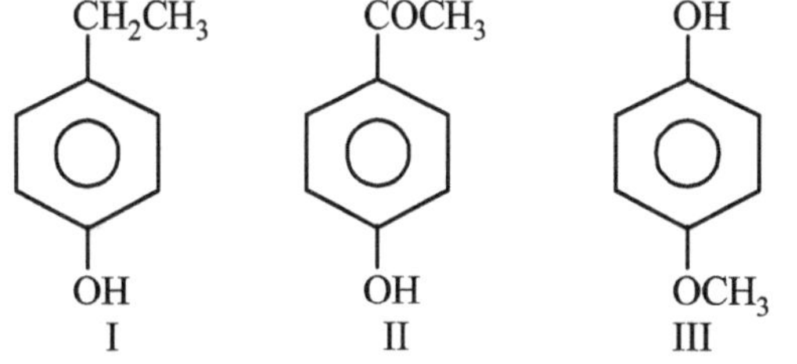

    (a) $CH_3OH, H^+(cat)$, heat   (b) $H_2O, H^+(cat.)$, heat
    (c) Mg, ether, CH_3OH (d) $SOCl_2, CH_3OH$

21. An organic compound of molecular formula $C_4H_{10}O$ does not react with sodium. With excess of HI, it gives only one type of alkyl halide. The compound is
    (a) Ethoxyethane   (b) 2-Methoxypropane
    (c) 1-Methoxypropane   (d) 1-Butanol

22. Which yields isopropyl methyl ether with little or no by products ?

    (a) $(CH_3)_2CHO^-Na^+ + CH_3I \longrightarrow$

    (b) $CH_3O^-Na^+ + (CH_3)_2CHI \longrightarrow$

    (c) $(CH_3)_2CHOH + CH_3OH \xrightarrow{H_2SO_4}$

    (d) All of these

23. What is X in the following reaction ?

    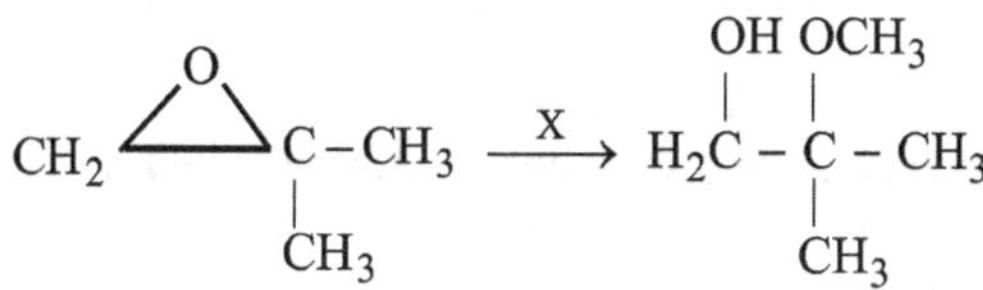

    (a) CH_3OH, H_2SO_4
    (b) $CH_3OH, CH_3O^-\overset{+}{Na}$
    (c) H_2O/H_2SO_4 followed by CH_3OH
    (d) $CH_3MgBr/$ether followed by H_3O^+

24. In Williamson synthesis of mixed ether having a primary and a tertiary alkyl group if tertiary halide is used, then :
    (a) Rate of reaction will be slow due to slow cleavage of carbon-halogen bond.
    (b) Alkene will be the main product.
    (c) Simple ether will form instead of mixed ether.
    (d) Expected mixed ether will be formed.

25. Allyl phenyl ether can be prepared by heating:
    (a) $C_6H_5Br + CH_2=CH-CH_2-ONa$
    (b) $CH_2=CH-CH_2-Br + C_6H_5ONa$
    (c) $C_6H_5-CH=CH-Br + CH_3-ONa$
    (d) $CH_2=CH-Br + C_6H_5-CH_2-ONa$

26. Which of the following reactions will not result in the formation of anisole?
    (a) Phenol + dimethyl sulphate in presence of a base
    (b) Sodium phenoxide is treated with methyl iodide
    (c) Reaction of diazomethane with phenol
    (d) Reaction of methylmagnesium iodide with phenol

27. The process of converting alkyl halides into alcohols involves ....
    (a) addition reaction   (b) substitution reaction
    (c) dehydrohalogenation   (d) rearrangement reaction

28. The compound which reacts fastest with Lucas reagent at room temperature is
    (a) $CH_3CH_2-CHOH.CH_3$ (b) $CH_3CH_2CH_2OH$
    (c) CH_3COHCH_3 / CH_3 (d) CH_3CHCH_2OH / CH_3

29. Which of the following compounds is oxidised to prepare methyl ethyl ketone?
(a) 2-Propanol   (b) 1-Butanol
(c) 2-Butanol   (d) t-Butyl alcohol

30. IUPAC name of *m*-cresol is ....
(a) 3-methylphenol
(b) 3-chlorophenol
(c) 3-methoxyphenol
(d) benzene-1,3-diol

31. Which one of the following will most readily be dehydrated in acidic conditions ?

(a)   (b)

(c)   (d)

32. Which of the following compounds will react with sodium hydroxide solution in water?
(a) C_6H_5OH (b) $C_6H_5CH_2OH$
(c) $(CH_3)_3COH$ (d) C_2H_5OH

33. Which of the following is most acidic?
(a) Benzyl alcohol   (b) Cyclohexanol
(c) Phenol   (d) *m*-chlorophenol

34. Mark the correct increasing order of reactivity of the following compounds with HBr/HCl.

(I)   (II)   (III)

(a) I < II < III   (b) II < I < III
(c) II < III < I   (d) III < II < I

35. Which of the following species can act as the strongest base?
(a) $^\ominus OH$ (b) $^\ominus OR$
(c) $^\ominus OC_6H_5$ (d) $^\ominus O$—$\langle\rangle$—NO_2

36. How many alcohols with molecular formula $C_4H_{10}O$ are chiral in nature?
(a) 1   (b) 2   (c) 3   (d) 4

37. *tert*-Butyl ethyl ether can't be prepared by which reaction?
(a) *tert* – Butanol + ethanol $\xrightarrow{H^+}$
(b) *tert*-Butyl bromide + sodium ethoxide $\rightarrow$
(c) Sodium *tert*-butoxide + ethyl bromide $\rightarrow$
(d) Isobutene + ethanol $\xrightarrow{H^+}$

DIRECTIONS : *Following are the case/passage based questions.*

An efficient, aerobic catalytic system for the transformation of alcohols into carbonyl compounds under mild conditions, copper-based catalyst has been discovered. This copper-based catalytic system utilizes oxygen or air as the ultimate, stoichiometric oxidant, producing water as the only by-product

$$R^2\!\!-\!\!\overset{R_1}{\underset{H}{C}}\!\!-\!\!OH \xrightarrow[\substack{5\%\ DBADH_2;\ O_2 \\ Toluene;\ 70°\ to\ 90°C}]{\substack{5\%\ CuCl;\ 5\%\ Phen; \\ 2\ equiv.\ K_2CO_3;}} R^2\!\!\underset{}{\overset{R_1}{C}}\!\!=\!\!O$$

A wide range of primary, secondary, allylic, and benzylic alcohols can be smoothly oxidized to the corresponding aldehydes or ketones in good to excellent yields. Air can be conveniently used instead of oxygen without affecting the efficiency of the process. However, the use of air requires slightly longer reaction times.

This process is not only economically viable and applicable to large-scale reactions, but it is also environmentally friendly. (*Reference:Ohkuma, T., Ooka, H., Ikariya, T., & Noyori, R. (1995). Preferential hydrogenation of aldehydes and ketones. Journal of the American Chemical Society, 117(41), 10417-10418.*) **[CBSE Sample 2021]**

38. The Copper based catalyst mention in the study above can be used to convert:
(a) propanol to propanonic acid
(b) propanone to propanoic acid
(c) propanone to propan-2-ol
(d) propan-2-ol to propanone

39. The carbonyl compound formed when ethanol gets oxidised using this copper-based catalyst can also be obtained by ozonolysis of:
(a) But-1-ene   (b) But-2-ene
(c) Ethene   (d) Pent-1-ene

OR

Which of the following is a secondary allylic alcohol?
(a) But-3-en-2-ol   (b) But-2-en-2-ol
(c) Prop-2-enol   (d) Butan-2-ol

40. Benzyl alcohol on treatment with this copper-based catalyst gives a compound 'A' which on reaction with KOH gives compounds 'B' and 'C'. Compound 'B' on oxidation with $KMnO_4$ - KOH gives compound 'C'. Compounds 'A', 'B' and 'C' respectively are :
(a) Benzaldehyde, Benzyl alcohol, potassium salt of Benzoic acid
(b) Benzaldehyde, potassium salt of Benzoic acid, Benzyl alcohol
(c) Benzaldehyde, Benzoic acid, Benzyl alcohol
(d) Benzoic acid, Benzyl alcohol, Benzaldehyde

41. An organic compound 'X' with molecular formula C_3H_8O on reaction with this copper based catalyst gives compound 'Y' which reduces Tollen's reagent. 'X' on reaction with sodium metal gives 'Z' . What is the product of reaction of 'Z' with 2-chloro-2-methylpropane?
(a) $CH_3CH_2CH_2OC(CH_3)_3$ (b) $CH_3CH_2OC(CH_3)_3$
(c) $CH_2{=}C(CH_3)_2$ (d) $CH_3CH_2CH{=}C(CH_3)_2$

Chapter Test

Time : *30 Min.*   **Max. Marks : *15***

Direction :

- Questions number **1-15** carry **1 mark** each.

1. The compound which reacts fastest with Lucas reagent at room temperature is
   - (a) butan-1-ol
   - (b) butan-2-ol
   - (c) 2-methylpropan-1-ol
   - (d) 2-methylpropan-2-ol

2. Which of the following compounds is oxidised to prepare methyl ethyl ketone?
   - (a) 2-Propanol
   - (b) 1-Butanol
   - (c) 2-Butanol
   - (d) t-Butyl alcohol

3. Which one of the following will most readily be dehydrated in acidic conditions ?

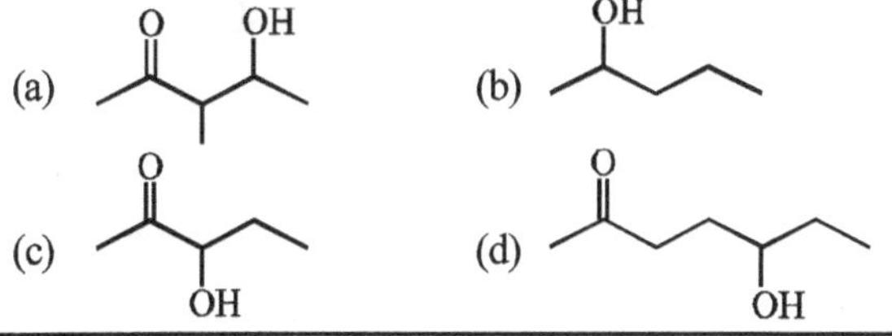

DIRECTIONS (Qs. 4-7) : *Each of these questions contains an assertion followed by reason. Read them carefully and answer the question on the basis of following options. You have to select the one that best describes the two statements.*

(a) If both Assertion and Reason are correct and the Reason is a correct explanation of the Assertion.

(b) If both Assertion and Reason are correct but Reason is not a correct explanation of the Assertion.

(c) If the Assertion is correct but Reason is incorrect.

(d) If the Assertion is incorrect but the Reason is correct.

4. **Assertion :** Cresols are less acidic than phenols.
   Reason : Alkyl group present on the cresols does not favour the formation of phenoxide ion.

5. **Assertion:** The ease of dehydration of the following alcohols is

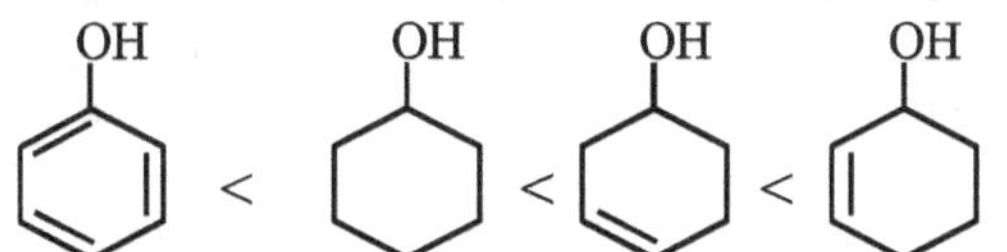

   Reason: Alcohols leading to conjugated alkenes are dehydrated to a greater extent.

6. **Assertion:** *ter*-butyl methyl ether is not prepared by the reaction of *ter*-butyl bromide with sodium methoxide.
   Reason: Sodium methoxide is a strong nucleophile.

7. **Assertion:** Phenol undergo Kolbe reaction, ethanol does not.
   Reason: Phenoxide ion is more basic than ethoxide ion.

Case/Passage Based Questions

DIRECTIONS : *Following are the case/passage based questions.*

The dehydration of phenols and alkylation of phenols by alcohols over thorium were studied at 400–500 °C and atmospheric pressure. Phenol and cresols, when dehydrated gave diaryl ethers as main products. With *para*-substituted phenols such as *p*-methoxy, *p*-*t*-butyl, *p*-chloro, and *p*-nitrophenol no ether formation was noticed. All the reactions were accompanied by a considerable amount of coke formation. Alkylation of phenols by alcohols gave a mixture of O- and C-alkylated products under the same reaction conditions. O-alkylation and C-alkylation are parallel reactions.

DIRECTIONS (Qs. 8-11) : *Each of these questions contains an assertion followed by reason. Read them carefully and answer the question on the basis of following options. You have to select the one that best describes the two statements.*

(a) If both Assertion and Reason are correct and the Reason is a correct explanation of the Assertion.

(b) If both Assertion and Reason are correct but Reason is not a correct explanation of the Assertion.

(c) If the Assertion is correct but Reason is incorrect.

(d) If the Assertion is incorrect but the Reason is correct.

8. **Assertion :** Phenoxide ion is more stable than alkoxide ion.
   Reason : The delocalisation of negative charge in phenols makes them more stable.

   OR

   Assertion : Phenols do not react with metal carbonates and metal hydrogen carbonates.
   Reason : Metal carbonates and metal hydrogen carbonates are basic in nature.

9. **Assertion :** Phenols when react directly with carboxylic acids produce ester.
   Reason : Electron withdrawing groups increases the acidic character of phenols.

10. **Assertion :** *p*-Nitrophenol is less acidic than *m*-nitrophenol.
    Reason : Phenol is a weaker acid than carbonic acid.

11. **Assertion :** Value of pka is higher for ethanol than phenol.
    Reason : Phenoxide ion is more stable than alkoxide ion.

Very Short Answer Questions

12. Give the IUPAC name of
$$CH_3 - CH_2 - CH - CH - CH - CH_3$$
$$\qquad\qquad\qquad | \qquad\quad | \qquad\quad |$$
$$\qquad\qquad\quad CH_2Cl \; CH_2OH \; CH_3$$

13. Draw the structure of hex-1-en-3-ol.

14. What is wood alcohol? Why is it so called?

15. Vapours of an organic compound 'X' when passed over hot reduced copper chips at 575 K give acetone. Name the compound 'X'.

Solutions 

Practice Exercise-1 

1. **(b)** Since the compound is formed by hydration of an alkene, to get the structure of alkene remove a molecule of water from the alcohol.

$$CH_3\underset{\underset{OH}{|}}{C}HCH_3 \xrightarrow{-H_2O} CH_2{=}CHCH_3$$

Isopropyl alcohol   Propylene

2. **(b)** The solubility of alcohols depend on number of C-atoms of alcohols. The solubility of alcohols in water decreases with the increase in number of C-atoms of alcohol. As resulting molecular weight increases, the polar nature of – OH bond decreases and hence strength of hydrogen bond decreases.

3. **(a)** When primary (1°) alcohols are treated with copper at 300°C, then aldehydes are obtained by dehydrogenation of alcohols. Similarly secondary (2°) alcohols form ketone and alkene is obtained by dehydration of tertiary (3°) - alcohols. But phenol does not respond to this test.

4. **(d)**

2, 4,6-Tribromophenol

Note : The –OH group in phenol, being activating group, facilitates substitution in the *o-* and *p*-positions.

5. **(c)** The C—O bond length (136 pm) in phenol is slightly less than that in methanol (142 pm).

6. **(c)** $KMnO_4$ (alkaline) and OsO_4 / CH_2Cl_2 are used for hydroxylation of double bond while O_3 /Zn is used for ozonolysis. Therefore, the right option is (c), i.e.,

$$3CH_3CH = CH_2 \xrightarrow{BH_3 \text{ in THF}} (CH_3CH_2CH_2)_3B$$

$$\xrightarrow[NaOH]{3H_2O_2} 3CH_3CH_2CH_2OH + H_3BO_3$$

1-propanol

7. **(c)** $CH_2 = CH_2 \xleftarrow[650\,K]{Al_2O_3} CH_3CH_2OH \xrightarrow[525\,K]{Al_2O_3}$

$$CH_3CH_2OCH_2CH_3$$

8. **(a)** Methanol is injurious to the nervous system. It mainly damages central nervous system and optic nerve, therefore, ingestion of small amount of methanol cause blindness and death.

9. **(c)** Alcohols are highly polar in nature, threfore, they show intermolecular hydrogen bonding and are miscrible with water.

10. **(a)**

11. **(b)**

$$\overset{5}{C}H_3 - \overset{4}{C}H - \overset{3}{C}H_2 - \overset{2}{\overset{|}{C}} - \overset{1}{C}H_3$$

2-Methyl-2, 4-pentanediol.

12. **(b)**

13. **(b)** Alcohols are versatile compounds. They react both as nucleophiles and electrophiles. The bond between

14. **(b)**   **15. (d)**

16. The mixture of HCl and anhydrous $ZnCl_2$ is known as Lucas reagent (HCl + anhydrous $ZnCl_2$). It is used to convert alcohol into haloalkane.

17. It acts as dehydration agent and absorbs H_2O, one of the product of the given reaction. It favours the forward reaction (Le – chateliar Principle).

18. $$CH_2 - CH - CH_2 + HIO_4 \xrightarrow[\text{Periodic acid}]{\text{Heated}}$$

with OH groups (Glycerol)

$$2HCHO + HCOOH$$

Formaldehyde   Formic acid

19. It can form hydrogen bonds with water as well as with alcohol.

20. On long standing in contact with air, phenol gets slowly oxidised.

21. Glycerol is hygroscopic and thus it keeps the skin moisturised.

22. Due to resonance in phenol molecule, C — O bond acquires double bond character and gets stabilised.

23. The acidic character of given alcohols follows the order:

$$CH_3CH_2CH_2CH_2OH > CH_3 - CH_3 - CH - CH_3 > CH_3 - \underset{CH_3}{\overset{CH_3}{C}} - OH$$

n – Butylalcohol   *sec*–Butyl alcohol   *tert*–Butylalcohol

24. HI is most reactive and HCl is least reactive as H – I bond energy is least. HI > HBr > HCl.

25. Industrial ethyl alcohol is made unfit for drinking purposes by addition of small quantity of poisonous substance generally methanol. It is known as methylated spirit or denatured alcohol. The denaturation of ethyl alcohol can also be done by other poisonous substances like pyridine, copper sulphate. etc.

26. Refer Theory

27. Alcohols (ROH) are practically unionised and neutral organic substances whereas inorganic hydroxides, *e.g.,* NaOH, KOH, Ca(OH)$_2$, ionise to give OH⁻ ions and are thus alkaline. These are of mineral origin and turn red litmus blue.

28. This is because of its hygroscopic nature, it keeps the fruits, vegetables, etc., moist.

29. It is the process of breaking down large molecules into smaller ones in the presence of biocatalyst called enzymes. This process is used widely in manufacture of ethanol from molasses or starch. It is also used in bakery preparations and fast food industries.

30. By treating the substance with neutral $FeCl_3$ solution, phenolic (OH) group gives blue or violet colouration while alcoholic (OH) group does not give any characteristic colour.

31. Phenol is more acidic than water while ethanol is less acidic than water.
$$C_6H_5OH > H_2O > C_2H_5OH$$

32. Lucas regent (anhyd. $ZnCl_2$ + HCl) is added to both and shaken. 2-propanol produces cloudiness in about 3-5 minutes at room temperature while 1-propanol does not give cloudiness even after a long time at room temperature.

33. Refer Theory

34. It is due to the presence of lone pair of electrons on oxygen atoms of alcohol, these act as weak bases (Lewis bases).

35. It is due to the electron withdrawing nature of benzene ring attached to oxygen atom in phenol and electron repelling nature of methyl group attached to oxygen atom in methanol. The difference in electronegativity of sp^2–C and oxygen in phenol is less than that is sp^3–C and oxygen in methanol.

36. C — OH bond in phenol is stabilised due to resonance and electron pair at oxygen atom in phenol is not easily available to proton, therefore, it does not give protonation reactions readily.

37. 2, 4, 6 – tribromo phenol is formed

OH + $3Br_2$ (aq) ⟶ 2,4,6-tribromophenol + 3HBr

38. (a) $CH_3CH_2CH_2OH + SOCl_2 \xrightarrow{\Delta} CH_3CH_2CH_2Cl + SO_2 + HCl$

(b)

$H_3C - \overset{\overset{\displaystyle CH_3}{|}}{C} - O - OH \xrightarrow[H_2SO_4]{H_2O/H^+}$ phenol (OH) $+ CH_3COCH_3$

39. When an electron withdrawing group like nitro group ($-NO_2$) is present at ortho-(or para) position to phenolic group, it is more effective in increasing the acidic character of phenol than when it is present at meta-position. The dispersal of negative charge becomes easier.

40. Due to intramolecular H-bonding in o-nitrophenol inter-molecular forces of attraction are weaker while in p-nitrophenol there is no intramolecular H-bonding. The inter-molecular forces are stronger in p-nitrophenol. Thus, o-nitrophenol has lower boiling point than p-nitrophenol. p-Nitrophenol undergoes intermolecular hydrogen bounding.

Practice Exercise-2

1. **(d)** The two components should be $(CH_3)_3CONa$ + $(CH_3)_3CBr$. However, tert-alkyl halides tend to undergo elimination reaction rather than substitution leading to the formation of an alkene, $Me_2C = CH_2$

2. **(a)** Due to H-bonding, the boiling point of ethanol is much higher than that of the isomeric diethyl ether.

3. **(d)** Due to inter-molecular hydrogen bonding in alcohols boiling point of alcohols is much higher than ether.

4. **(c)** Ethyl alcohol has strongest hydrogen bonding due to large electronegativity difference.

5. **(b)** Due to greater electronegativity of sp^2-hybridized carbon atoms of the benzene ring, diaryl ethers are not attacked by nucleophiles like I^-.

6. **(d)** Diethyl ether, being a Lewis base, is not attacked by nucleophiles, while all others contain electrophilic carbon, hence attacked by nucleophiles like OH^- ions.

$$CH_3 - \overset{\overset{\displaystyle O\delta-}{||}}{\underset{\delta+}{C}} - OCH_3 \qquad CH_3 - \overset{\delta+ \quad \delta-}{C \equiv N}$$

$$CH_3 - \overset{\overset{\displaystyle O\delta-}{||}}{\underset{\delta+}{C}} - NH_2 \qquad C_2H_5 - \ddot{O} - C_2H_5$$

7. **(b)** In Williamson's synthesis, only primary alkyl halides (RX) react with sodium alkoxide (RONa 1° or 2° or 3°) giving ether, therefore, both symmetrical and unsymmetrical ethers can be prepared.

8. **(a)** Aryl-oxygen bond is highly stable due to stabilisation of lone pair of electrons on oxygen atom due to resonance effect and sp^2 hybridization of the carbon atom.

$$C_6H_5 - \ddot{O} - R + HX \longrightarrow C_6H_5OH + RX$$
$$(x–Cl, Br)$$

9. **(a)** Limitation of Williamson's synthesis is that only primary alkyl halide reacts with 1° or 2° or 3° sodium alkoxide to give ethers.

10. By shaking the sample of ether with an aqueous solution of ferrous sulphate or KI.

11. Diethylether (C_2H_5 — O — C_2H_5) does not contains an active hydrogen atom attached to oxygen like in ethanol (C_2H_5OH) and phenol (C_6H_5OH).

12. (i) 2-Bromomethoxy benzene
    (ii) Bromomethoxy benzene

13. Ethylbromide and sodium-tert-butoxide.

14. Phenol and methyliodide.

15. $CCl_3 — CCl_2 — O — CCl_2 — CCl_3$

16. Sodium ethoxide ($CH_3CH_2O^-Na^+$).

17. (a) These are used as industrial solvents for paints, gums, resins and oil, etc.
    (b) Lower ethers like diethyl ether is used as a refrigerant and an anaesthetic agent in surgical operations, etc.

18. (a) Diethyl ether is formed due to dehydration of ethylalcohos.

$$2C_2H_5OH \xrightarrow[\text{Dehydration}]{Al_2O_3, 525 K} C_2H_5OC_2H_5 + H_2O$$

(b) A higher homologue of ether is formed, i.e., ethylmethyl ether.

$$CH_3 — O — CH_2Cl + CH_3MgBr \longrightarrow CH_3OCH_2CH_3 + MgClBr$$

19. Sodium metal reacts with ethanol to form sodium ethoxide (C_2H_5ONa) but does not react with ether ($C_2H_5OC_2H_5$).

20. The presence of peroxides is detected by addition of freshly prepared $FeSO_4$ and KCNS. Appearance of blood red colour confirms the presence of peroxides in ether. Peroxides can be removed by shaking ethers well with ferrous sulphate solution.

21. The structure is
$$CH_3 - O - \underset{\underset{CH_3}{|}}{\overset{\overset{CH_3}{|}}{C}} - CH_3$$

IUPAC name is 2-methoxy-2-methyl propane. It is prepared by following reaction:

$$CH_3Br + \underset{\substack{\text{Sodium salt of} \\ \text{tertiary butyl alcohol}}}{(CH_3)_3CONa} \longrightarrow \underset{\substack{\text{Methyl tert-butyl} \\ \text{ether}}}{CH_3 - O - C(CH_3)_3} + NaBr$$

22. Grignard reagents form coordination complexes with ethers but not with benzene since the former has lone pairs of electrons but the latter does not.

23. Ethers are inert due to the absence of active groups and multiple bonds from their molecules.

24. Ethers are weakly basic and react with strong acids (*e.g.*, H_2SO_4 HBr, etc.) to form oxonium salts.
$$C_2H_5 - O - C_2H_5 +$$

$$H_2SO_4 \xrightarrow{\text{Ice-cold}} \left[C_2H_5 - \underset{\underset{H}{|}}{\overset{+}{O}} - C_2H_5 \right] HSO_4^-$$

25. Method (ii) is the correct method for the formation of methyl-tert.butyl ether.
In method (i) the product obtained will be an alkene.
The reaction (ii) is known as **Williamson's synthesis**. It involves S_N^2 **mechanism.**

Past year Exercise

1.
$$\overset{1}{H_3C} - \overset{2}{\underset{\underset{Cl}{|}}{CH}} - \overset{3}{\underset{\underset{CH_3}{|}}{CH}} - \overset{4}{CH_2} - \overset{5}{CH_3}$$

2-Chloro-3-methylpentane

2. Hex-4-en-3-ol.

3. 2-Bromo-3-methylbut-2-en-l-ol.

4. ROH is $R_1\overset{+}{N}H_3OH$ (alkylammonium hydroxide). On ionisation it gives OH^- and is, therefore, basic.
$$R_1\overset{+}{N}H_3OH^- \rightleftharpoons R_1\overset{+}{N}H_3 + OH^-$$
$\therefore$ R is $R_1\overset{+}{N}H_3$

R'OH is 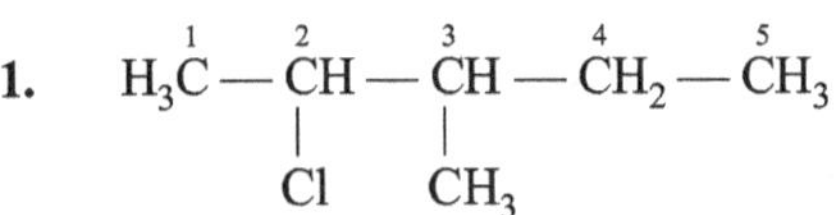—OH (phenol). It gives H_3O^+ ion in aqueous solution and is, therefore, acidic.

$$\text{⬡} - OH + H_2O \longrightarrow \text{⬡} - \ddot{O}^{\cdot-} + H_3O^+$$
$\therefore$ R' is $\text{⬡}-$

5. Refer Theory

6. IUPAC name of the given compound is 2-methoxy-2-methylpropane.

7.
$$CH_3 - \underset{\underset{C_2H_5}{|}}{\overset{\overset{CH_3}{|}}{C}} - \underset{\underset{OH}{|}}{CH} - CH_3$$
3, 3 – Dimethylpentan-2-ol

8. A monobasic carboxylic acid has the formula RCOOH.
Given, molar mass of RCOOH $= 60$ g mol^{-1}
$$x + 12 + 16 + 16 + 1 = 60$$
$$x = 60 - 45 = 15$$
Thus, $R = CH_3$ (molar mass 15) and the acid is CH_3COOH. The acid is obtained by the oxidation of aldehyde, so B is an aldehyde, *i.e.*, CH_3CHO and A is CH_3CH_2OH (an alcohol). The reaction are as

$$\underset{\underset{(C_2H_6O)}{}}{\underset{(A)}{CH_3CH_2OH}} \xrightarrow[PCC]{[O]} \underset{(B)}{CH_3CHO}$$

9. (i) Refer Theory
   (ii) Refer Theory

10. (i) Alcohols have polar group, hence they can form H–bonds with water, the H–bond between –OH group of alcohols and H–O–H is stronger than the H–bonds between water–water and between alcohol–alcohol, hence alcohols (essentially lower) easily become miscible with water molecules.

$$\cdots \overset{\delta+}{H} - \underset{\underset{R}{|}}{\overset{\delta-}{O}} \cdots \overset{\delta+}{H} - \underset{\underset{H}{|}}{\overset{\delta-}{O}} \cdots \overset{\delta+}{H} - \underset{\underset{R}{|}}{\overset{\delta-}{O}} \cdots$$

Hydrocarbons have no polar group, hence can't form H–bonds with water and thus remain insoluble in water.
(ii) Electron-withdrawing substituents increase the acidity of phenols; while electron-releasing substituents decrease acidity. Thus substituents affect acidity of phenols in the same way as they affect acidity of carboxylic acids; it is of course, opposite to the way these groups affect basicity of amines.

G withdraws electrons, thus disperses the –ve charge of the ion due to $-I, -R$ or both effects, stabilises it and hence increases ionization of the parent phenol.

(where G $= -NO_2, -CN, -CHO, -COOH, -\overset{+}{N}R_3, -X$)

G release electrons, thus disperses the –ve charge of the ion due to $+I, +R$ or both effects, destabilises it and hence increases ionization of the parent phenol.

(where G $= -R, OR, NR_2$)

11. (i) $CH_3CH_2CH_2CH_2OH \xrightarrow[\text{Oxidation}]{[O]} CH_3CH_2CH_2COOH$

$\underset{\text{Butanoic acid}}{}$

(ii) $CH_3-\underset{\underset{\text{2-butanol}}{|}}{\overset{}{\underset{OH}{C}H}}-CH_2CH_3 \xrightarrow[\text{Oxidation}]{[O]} CH_3-\underset{\underset{\text{2-butanone}}{\overset{\|}{O}}}{C}-CH_2CH_3$

(iii) $CH_3-\underset{\underset{CH_3}{|}}{\overset{\overset{H}{|}}{C}}-CH_2OH \xrightarrow[\text{Oxidation}]{[O]} CH_3-\underset{\underset{CH_3}{|}}{\overset{\overset{H}{|}}{C}}-COOH$

$\underset{\text{2-methylpropanoic acid}}{}$

12. (i) $CH_3CH_2CH_2OCH_3 + HBr \longrightarrow$

$CH_3CH_2CH_2Br + CH_3OH$

$CH_3CH_2\overset{+}{C}H_2$ is more stable than $CH_3{}^+$ due to inductive effect $(CH_3CH_2 \rightarrow -CH_2{}^+)$ as well as hyperconjugation.

(ii)

⬡–OC_2H_5 + HBr $\longrightarrow$ ⬡–OH + C_2H_5Br

(iii) $(CH_3)_3C-O-C_2H_5 + HI \longrightarrow (CH_3)_3CI + C_2H_5OH$

$(CH_3)_3C^+$ (a 3° carbocation) is more stable than the $C_2H_5{}^+$, hence it is easily formed.

13. Mechanism :

(i) Protonation of alkene :

$$H_2O + H^+ \rightarrow H_3O^+$$

$$\text{>}C=C\text{<} + H\overset{\overset{H}{|}}{\underset{\cdot\cdot}{O}}-H \rightarrow -\overset{|}{C}-\overset{\overset{H}{|}}{\underset{|}{C}}\text{<} + H_2\overset{\cdot\cdot}{\underset{\cdot\cdot}{O}}$$

(ii) Nucleophilic attack of $H_2\overset{\cdot\cdot}{O}$

$$-\overset{\overset{H}{|}}{\underset{|}{C}}-\overset{+}{\underset{|}{C}}\text{<} + H_2\overset{\cdot\cdot}{O} \rightarrow -\overset{\overset{H}{|}}{\underset{|}{C}}-\overset{\overset{H}{|}}{\underset{\underset{\oplus}{|}}{C}}-O-H$$

(iii) Deprotonation:

$$-\overset{\overset{H}{|}}{\underset{|}{C}}-\overset{\overset{H}{|}}{\underset{\underset{\cdot\cdot}{|}}{C}}-\overset{\oplus}{O}-H + H_2\overset{\cdot\cdot}{O} \rightarrow -\overset{\overset{H}{|}}{\underset{|}{C}}-\overset{\overset{OH}{|}}{\underset{|}{C}}- + H_3O^+$$

14. **Step 1.** Formation of protonated alcohol :

$$CH_3CH_2-\overset{\cdot\cdot}{\underset{\cdot\cdot}{O}}-H + H^+ \rightleftharpoons CH_3-CH_2-\overset{\nearrow H}{\underset{\searrow H}{\underset{\cdot\cdot}{O}}}$$

Step 2. Formation of carbocation

$$CH_3-CH_2-\overset{\oplus}{\underset{\cdot\cdot}{O}}\overset{\nearrow H}{\underset{\searrow H}{}} \underset{\text{Slow}}{\rightleftharpoons} \overset{\oplus}{CH_3}-CH_2 + H_2O$$

$\underset{\substack{\text{Ethyl} \\ \text{carbocation}}}{}$

It is the rate determining step.

Step 3. Elimination of a proton to form Ethene

$$H-CH_2-\overset{\oplus}{CH_2} \underset{\text{Fast}}{\rightleftharpoons} CH_2=CH_2 + H^+$$

$\underset{\text{Ethene}}{}$

15. (i) Refer Theory

(ii) Refer Theory

16. (i) $C_2H_5-\overset{\cdot\cdot}{\underset{\cdot\cdot}{O}}-H + H^+ \longrightarrow C_2H_5-\overset{\overset{H}{|}\oplus}{\underset{\cdot\cdot}{O}}-H$

(ii) $C_2H_5-\overset{\cdot\cdot}{\underset{\cdot\cdot}{O}}-H + C_2H_5-\overset{\overset{H}{|}\oplus}{\underset{\cdot\cdot}{O}}-H \longrightarrow C_2H_5-\overset{\overset{H}{|}\oplus}{\underset{\cdot\cdot}{O}}-C_2H_5 + H_2O$

(iii) $C_2H_5-\overset{\overset{H}{|}\oplus}{\underset{\cdot\cdot}{O}}-C_2H_5 \longrightarrow C_2H_5-\overset{\cdot\cdot}{\underset{\cdot\cdot}{O}}-C_2H_5 + H^{\oplus}$

$\underset{\text{Diethyl ether}}{}$

17. (i) $\underset{\text{Propene}}{CH_3-CH=CH_2} + H_2SO_4 \xrightarrow[\text{Addition}]{\text{Markownikoff's}}$

$CH_3-\underset{\underset{OSO_2OH}{|}}{CH}-CH_3 \xrightarrow[-H_2SO_4]{-H_2O,\, \Delta} CH_3-\underset{\underset{\underset{\text{Propan-2-ol}}{}}{\overset{|}{OH}}}{CH}-CH_3$

(ii)

⬡–OH (Phenol) $\xrightarrow[\text{conc.}H_2SO_4]{\text{conc.}HNO_3}$

$\underset{\text{2, 4, 6-Trinitrophenol}}{}$ (2,4,6-trinitrophenol structure with O_2N, NO_2, and NO_2 groups)

18. (i) $CH_3-\underset{\underset{\text{Propan-2-ol}}{}}{\overset{\overset{OH}{|}}{C}H}-CH_3 \xrightarrow{Cu, 573\,K}$

$\underset{\text{Pr opan}-2-\text{one}}{CH_3-\overset{\overset{\|}{O}}{C}-CH_3} + H_2$

(ii)

⬡–OH (Phenol) $+ 3Br_2 \xrightarrow{H_2O}$ (2,4,6-tribromophenol with Br, Br, Br) $+ 3HBr$

$\underset{\text{2, 4, 6-Tribromophenol}}{}$

19. (a)

$\underset{\text{Pr opene}}{CH_3CH=CH_2} + HBr \xrightarrow{\text{Peroxide}} CH_3CH_2CH_2Br$

$\xrightarrow{\text{aq.KOH},\Delta} \underset{\text{Propan}-1-\text{ol}}{CH_3CH_2CH_2OH}$

(b) $\overset{CH_3}{\underset{H}{\diagup}}C=O \xrightarrow{CH_3MgI} \underset{\underset{H\quad CH_3}{|\quad|}}{\overset{\overset{CH_3\,\,OMgI}{|\quad\quad|}}{C}} \xrightarrow{H^+, H_2O} \underset{\underset{\underset{\text{2-Propanol}}{}}{H\quad CH_3}}{\overset{\overset{CH_3\,\,OH}{|\quad|}}{C}}$

20. $CH_3CH_2OH \xrightarrow{HBr} CH_3CH_2Br + H_2O$

Since the alkyl group is 1°, thus the above reaction will follow S_N2 mechanism as shown below:

$$HBr \longrightarrow H^+ + Br^-$$

Step 1: $CH_3CH_2OH + H^+ \rightleftharpoons CH_3CH_2\overset{\oplus}{O}H_2$

Step 2:

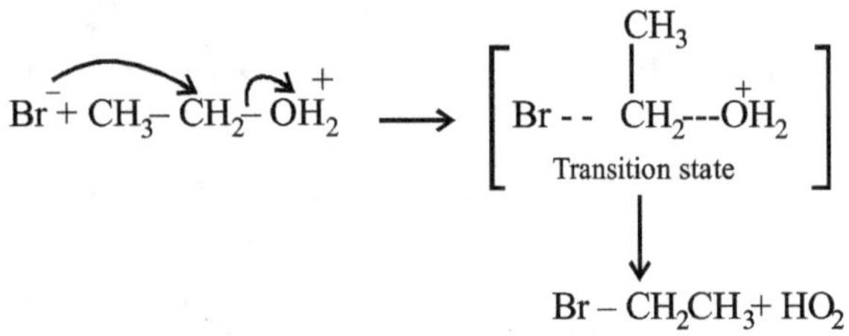

$$Br^- + CH_3\!-\!CH_2\!-\!\overset{+}{O}H_2 \longrightarrow \left[Br\text{-}\text{-} \ \overset{CH_3}{\underset{}{CH_2}}\text{-}\text{-}\text{-}\overset{+}{O}H_2 \right]$$

Transition state

$$Br - CH_2CH_3 + HO_2$$

21. The final products of the given reactions are :

(a)

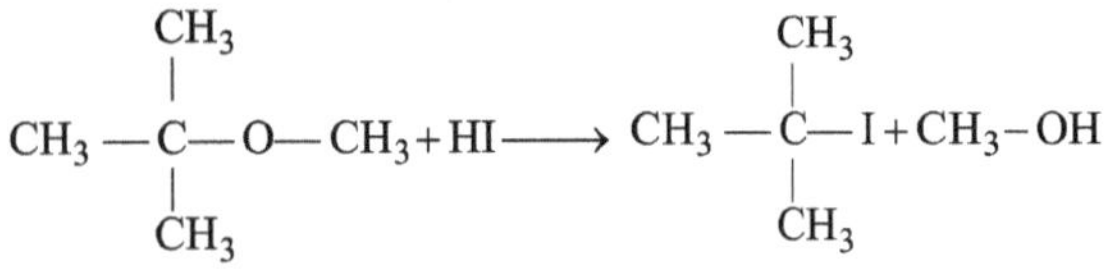

$$CH_3 - \underset{\underset{CH_3}{|}}{\overset{\overset{CH_3}{|}}{C}} - O - CH_3 + HI \longrightarrow CH_3 - \underset{\underset{CH_3}{|}}{\overset{\overset{CH_3}{|}}{C}} - I + CH_3 - OH$$

(b) $CH_3 - CH_2 - \underset{\underset{OH}{|}}{CH} - CH_3 \xrightarrow{Cu/573K}$

$$CH_3 - CH_2 - \underset{\underset{O}{\|}}{C} - CH_3 + H_2$$

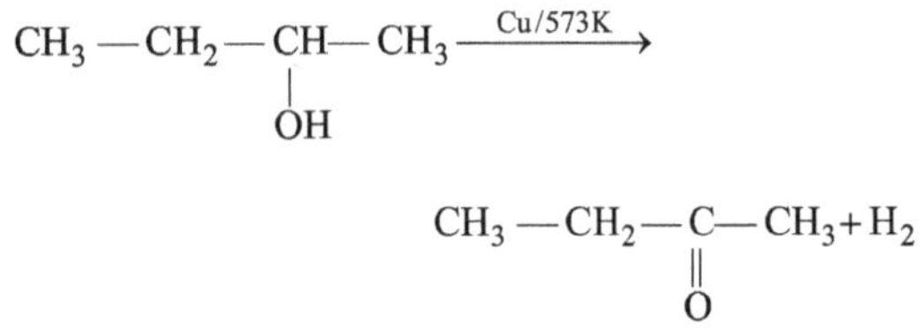

(c) Phenol $\xrightarrow{\text{(i) } CHCl_3 + \text{ aq. NaOH}}$ (2-hydroxybenzaldehyde sodium salt, ONa with CHO)

Salicylaldehyde (with OH and CHO) $\xleftarrow{H^+}$

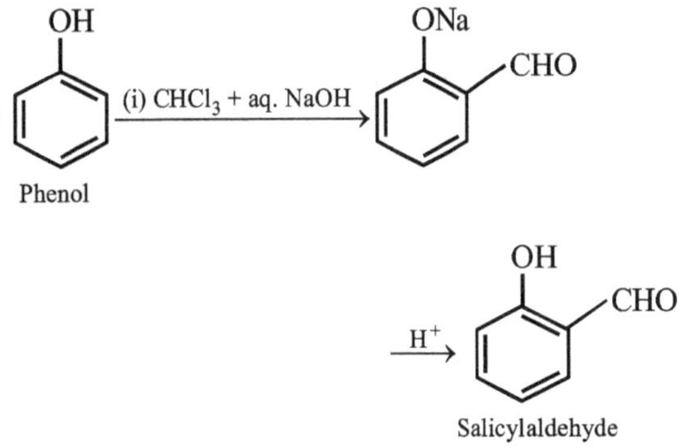

22. (a) Phenol $\xrightarrow[HNO_3]{Conc.}$ 2, 4, 6 Tritritrophenol (Picric acid)

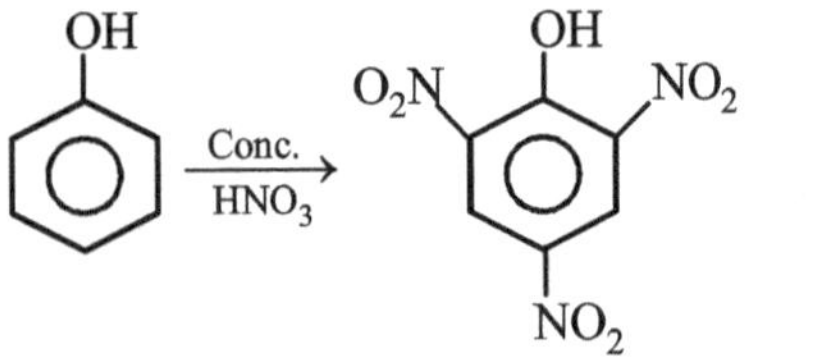

(b) $CH_3CH_2Cl + NaOC_2H_5 \xrightarrow{S_N2} CH_3CH_2OC_2H_5$ (Diethyl ether)

23. (a) Refer theory

(b) $CH_3CH_2OH \xrightarrow{H^+} CH_3CH_2\overset{+}{O}H_2 \xrightarrow{(-H_2O)}$

$$CH_3\overset{+}{C}H_2 \xrightarrow[\text{(2nd molecule)}]{CH_3CH_2OH}$$

$$CH_3CH_2\!-\!\overset{+}{\underset{\underset{H}{|}}{O}}\!-\!CH_2CH_3 \xrightarrow{(-H^+)} CH_3CH_2\!-\!O\!-\!CH_2CH_3$$

Diethyl ether

24. (i) (cyclohexanone with $-CH_2-\overset{O}{\underset{\|}{C}}-OCH_3$) $\xrightarrow{NaBH_4}$ (cyclohexanol with $-CH_2\overset{O}{\underset{\|}{C}}-OCH_3$)

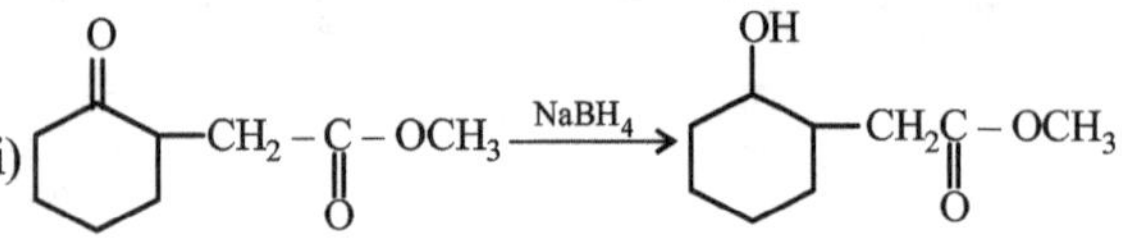

($NaBH_4$ does not reduce the ester group, so only ketonic group gets reduced to alcohol)

(ii) (styrene, $-CH=CH_2$) $+ H_2O \xrightarrow{H^+}$ (1-phenylethanol, $\overset{OH}{\underset{}{CH}}-CH_3$)

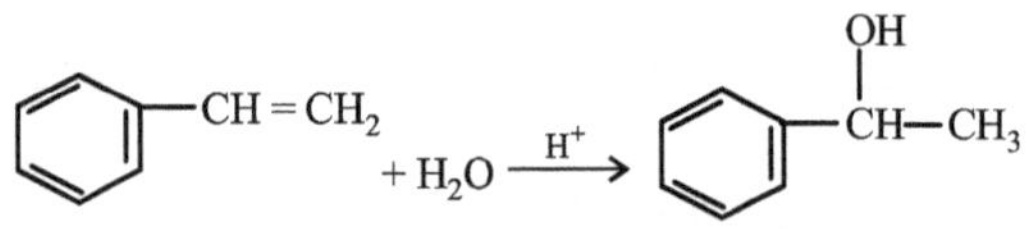

(This is in accordance with Markovnikov's rule)

(iii) (phenetole, OC_2H_5) $+ HI \longrightarrow$ (phenol, OH) $+ C_2H_5I$

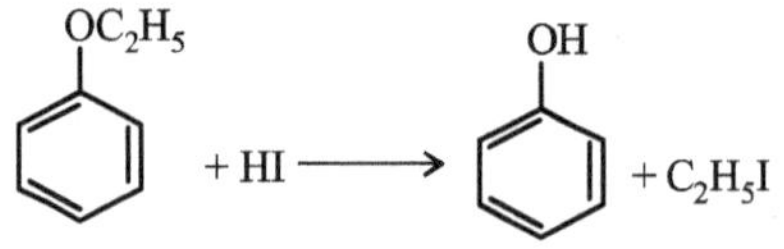

(The $O - C_2H_5$ bond breaks to give C_2H_5I. $C_6H_5 - O$ does not break due to partial double bond character)

25. (a) Increasing order of acid strength is

p-cresol < phenol < p-nitrophenol

(b) Reaction :

$$CH_2 = CH_2 \xrightarrow{H_3O^+} CH_3 - \overset{+}{C}H_2 + H_2O$$

Mechanism :

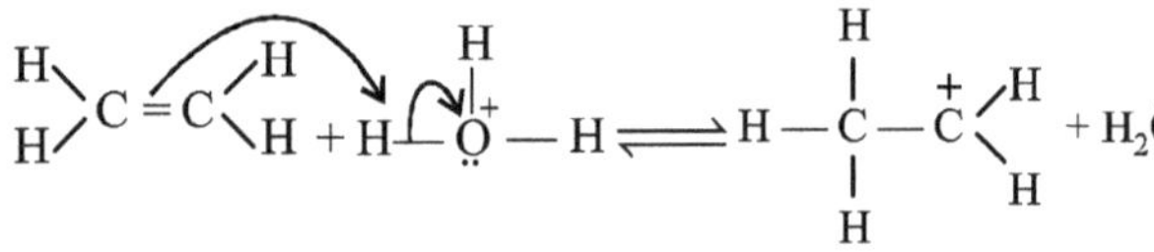

$$\underset{H}{\overset{H}{}}C = C\underset{H}{\overset{H}{}} + H - \underset{\underset{H}{.}}{\overset{H}{\underset{..}{O}}} - H \rightleftharpoons H - \underset{\underset{H}{|}}{\overset{\overset{H}{|}}{C}} - \overset{+}{C}\underset{H}{\overset{H}{}} + H_2\overset{..}{O}$$

OR

(a) Secondary alcohol (Butan-2-ol) on reaction with chromic anhydride (CrO_3) oxidises to ketone (Butan-2-one).

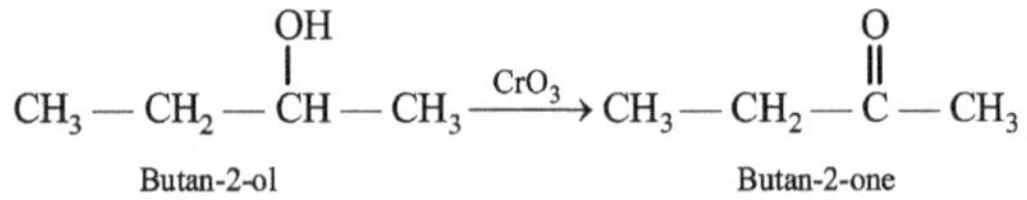

$$CH_3 - CH_2 - \underset{\underset{OH}{|}}{CH} - CH_3 \xrightarrow{CrO_3} CH_3 - CH_2 - \underset{\underset{O}{\|}}{C} - CH_3$$

Butan-2-ol   Butan-2-one

(b) Butan-2-ol on treating with $SOCl_2$ forms 2-chlorobutane

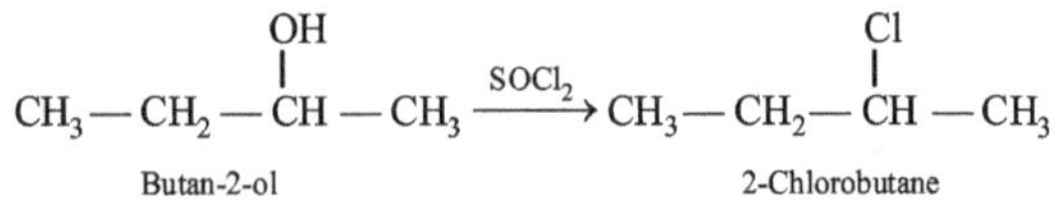

$$CH_3 - CH_2 - \underset{\underset{OH}{|}}{CH} - CH_3 \xrightarrow{SOCl_2} CH_3 - CH_2 - \underset{\underset{Cl}{|}}{CH} - CH_3$$

Butan-2-ol   2-Chlorobutane

NCERT Exemplar

1. (a) Following are the three possible isomers of butanol

(i) $CH_3CH_2 - CH_2 - CH_2OH$

Butan–1–ol

no chiral carbon

(ii) $CH_3 - CH_2 - \overset{*}{CH} - CH_3$ with OH below

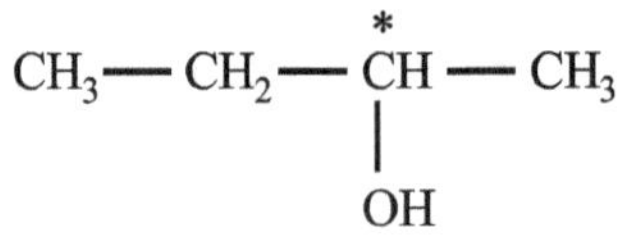

Butan –2 – ol

(iii)

1-Chiral Carbon

$$CH_3$$
$$|$$
$$H_3C - C - CH_3$$
$$|$$
$$OH$$

2 – methylpropan – 2 – ol

No Chiral Carbon

2. **(c)** $HCl + An.\ ZnCl_2$ is known as lucas reagent. It is used to determine degree of an alcohol.

The reaction follow nucleophilic substitution reaction in which — OH group is replaced by — Cl. In this reaction carbocation is formed as intermediate. Higher the stability of intermediate carbocation higher will be the reactivity of reactant molecule. Since 3° carbocation is more stable than 2° carbocation as well as 1° carbocation, so the order of reactivity of alcohols is $3° > 2° > 1°$.

3. **(b)** The process of conversion of alkyl halides into alcohols involves substitution reaction.

$$R - X \xrightarrow{\ OH^-\ } R - OH$$

Alkyl halide Alcohol

4. **(c)**

$$\overset{6}{CH_3} - \overset{5}{CH} - \overset{4}{CH_2} - \overset{3}{CH_2} - \overset{2}{CH} - \overset{1}{CH_3}$$
$$\qquad\quad | \qquad\qquad\qquad\qquad |$$
$$\qquad\quad Cl \qquad\qquad\qquad\qquad OH$$

5-Chlorohexan-2-ol

5. **(b)** Presence of electron withdrawing group at ortho position increase the acidic strength. In o-nitrophenol, nitro group is present at ortho position. On the other hand, in o-methylphenol and in o-methoxyphenol, electron releasing group ($—CH_3$, $—OCH_3$) are present.

Presence of these groups at ortho and para positions of phenol decreases the acidic strength of phenols. So, phenol is less acidic than o-nitrohenol.

6. **(b)** Electron withdrawing substituents increase the acidic strength of phenols. so, p-nitrophenol (II) and m-nitrophenol (IV) are stronger acid than phenol (I). If— NO_2 group is present at p-position, then it exerts both — I and — R effect, but if it is present at meta position, then it exerts only–I effect. Therefore, p-nitrophenol is stronger than m-nitrophenol.

On the other hand, electron releasing substituents decreases the acidic strength of phenol. If — OCH_3 group is present at meta position, it will exert – I effect only.

But, if it is present at para position, it will exert + R and – I effect. Thus, m - methoxy benzyl alcohol is more acidic than p- methoxy phenol. Hence, the correct order of decreasing acidic strength will be : $II > IV > I > III > V$.

7. **(a)** With increase in molecular mass boiling point increases. Thus the b.p. of pentan-1-ol will be more than other given compounds. Now, among isomeric alcohols 1° alcohols have higher boiling points than 2° alcohols due to higher surface area in 1° alcohols.

Hence, increasing order of b.p. will be

Propan-1-ol < butan-2-ol < butan-1-ol < pentan-1-ol.

8. **(a)** p-nitrophenol is more acidic than phenol because nitro group helps in the stabilisation of the phenoxide ion by dispersal of negative charge due to resonance.

9. **(d)** Boiling points of alcohols are higher than that of ethers of comparable molecular mass. Alchols can form intermalecular hydrogen bonding while ethers.

10. **(b)** Due to the presence of intramolecular hydrogen bonding. o-nitrophenol does not form hydrogen bonds with H_2O but m and p-nitrophenol form hydrogen bonds with water.

11. Alcohol is made unfit for drinking by mixing some copper sulphate and pyridine in it. This is called denatured alcohol.

12. Ortho nitrophenol, is more volatile due to the presence of intramolecular hydrogen bonding in o-nitrophenol while intermolecular hydrogen bonding is present in p-nitrophenol.

13. Phenol is more easily nitrated than benzene as the presence of —OH group in phenol increases the electron density at ortho and para positions in benzene ring by +R effect. The nitration, being an electrophilic substitution reaction is more facile where the electron density is more.

14. Phenoxide ion is more reactive than phenol towards electrophilic aromatic substitution and hence undergoes electrophilic substitution with carbon dioxide which is a weak electrophile.

Objective Practice Exercise

1. **(c)**

2. **(b)** 5-10 % methanol and remaing ethanol is called methylated spirit. It is also known as denatured alcohol because it is unfit for drinking.

3. **(b)**   **4.** **(b)**

5. **(c)** Alcoholic beverages contain ethyl alcohol (C_2H_5OH) which is drinking alcohol. CH_3OH is poisonous alcohol.

6. **(b)** C_2H_5OH and $CH_3 – O – CH_3$ are isomers.

7. **(b)**

8. **(d)** In C_2H_5OH,

$$CH_3 - CH_2 \overset{\ddot{O}}{\underset{109°}{\frown}} H$$

Due to presence of lone pair of electrons on oxygen, there occurs a small decrease in bond angle from the normal tetrahedral bond angle ($109°28'$).

9. **(a)**

$$CH_3-CH-CH_3 \xrightarrow{[O]} CH_3-\overset{\overset{\displaystyle O}{\|}}{C}-CH_3$$
$$\qquad\quad |$$
$$\qquad\quad OH$$

2° alcohol more easily oxidised than 3° alcohol.

10. **(b)**

$$CH_3-\overset{\overset{\displaystyle CH_3}{|}}{CH}-OH \xrightarrow{SOBr_2} CH_3-\overset{\overset{\displaystyle CH_3}{|}}{CH}-Br + SO_2 + HBr$$

Side products are gases.

In case of HBr elimination also favours to produce alkene.

11. **(d)** HIO_4 will not oxidise, diol from 1, 3 atom and not used for cleavage of ether.

12. (b) $Ph-\overset{O}{\underset{}{C}}-O-CH_2-Ph \xrightarrow[H_2O]{LiAlH_4} Ph-CH_2OH$ (2 mole)

13. (a)

$C_6H_5-\overset{O}{\underset{}{C}}CH_3 \xrightarrow[CH_3OH]{NaBD_4} C_6H_5-\overset{OH}{\underset{D}{C}}CH_3$

(Nucleophilic addition takes place)

14. (c)   15. (d)   16. (d)

17. (c) Electron withdrawing group stabilises the benzene ring due to delocalisation of charge.
$-CH_3$ and $-CH_2OH$ are electron donating group and hence decrease the stability of benzene ring $-OCH_3$ is weaker electron withdrawing group than $-COCH_3$. Hence $-COCH_3$ group more stabilize the phenoxide ion at p-position.

18. (c)

+ M effect in phenol
activates benzene ring

Oxonium ion
(more stable)

Carbonium ion
(less stable)

High stability of oxonium ion (oxocation) is because here every atom (except H) has a complete octet of electrons, while in carbocations, carbon bearing positive charge is having six electrons.

19. (c)

20. (a)

$\xrightarrow[H^+]{CH_3OH}$

$\xrightarrow[H^+]{CH_3OH}$ (Acetal)

21. (a) $C_4H_{10}O \xrightarrow{\text{excess of HI}} \text{only RI}$

Since the compound ($C_4H_{10}O$) does not react with sodium, oxygen must be in the form of ether (R–OR). Further since a single alkyl halide is formed, the two alkyl groups must be same, hence ether is $C_2H_5OC_2H_5$.

22. (a) $(CH_3)_2CHO^- \overset{+}{Na} + CH_3I \longrightarrow$

$(CH_3)_2CH-O-CH_3 + NaI$

23. (a)

$CH_2\overset{O}{\diagup\!\diagdown}\underset{CH_3}{\overset{}{C}}-CH_3 \xrightarrow[H_2SO_4]{CH_3OH} H_2C-\underset{CH_3}{\overset{OH\ OCH_3}{C}}-CH_3$

24. (b) The tertiary alkyl halide undergo elimination reaction to give alkenes

$CH_3-\underset{CH_3}{\overset{CH_3}{C}}-X + NaOC_2H_5 \longrightarrow CH_3-\underset{}{\overset{CH_3}{C}}=CH_2$
2-methyl propene

25. (a) $C_6H_5Br + NaO-CH_2-CH=CH_2 \longrightarrow$
$C_6H_5-O-CH_2-CH=CH_2 + NaBr$
Allyl phenyl ether

26. (d) Phenol has active (acidic) hydrogen so it reacts with CH_3MgI to give CH_4, and not anisole
$C_6H_5OH + CH_3MgI \longrightarrow CH_4 + C_6H_5OMgI$

27. (b) The process of conversion of alkyl halides into alcohols involves substitution reaction.
$R-X \xrightarrow{OH^-} R-OH$
Alkyl halide   Alcohol

28. (c) The order of reactivity of alcohol with Lucas reagent is $tert. > sec. > pri.$

29. (c) Secondary alcohols oxidise to produce kenone.
$CH_3CHOHCH_2CH_3 \xrightarrow{(O)} CH_3COCH_2CH_3$
2-Butanol   Ethyl methyl ketone

30. (a)

m-Cresol

Its IUPAC name is 3-methylphenol.

31. (d)

32. (a) Phenol, being more acidic in nature, reacts with sodium hydroxide solution gives phenoxide ion. This phenoxide ion is resonance stabilised.

33. (d) Presence of electron withdrawing group increases the acidic strength. So, *m*-chlorophenol is most acidic among all the given compounds.

34. (c) Nucleophilic substitution reaction depend upon the stability of carbocation. As, presence of electron withdrawing group decreases the stability of carbocation in compounds (II) and (III), therefore, will give less stable carbocation than (I).
Further NO_2 group is a stronger EWG than $-Cl$.

Thus, p-$NO_2 - C_6H_4 - \overset{+}{C}H_2$ will be less stable than

$pCl - C_6H_4 - \overset{+}{C}H_2$

Hence, the order of stability of carbocations, and thus reactivity of parent alcohol will be:

$O_2N-C_6H_4-\overset{+}{C}H_2 < Cl-C_6H_4-\overset{+}{C}H_2 < C_6H_5-\overset{+}{C}H_2$

35. (b) Weakest acid has the strongest conjugate base. Among all these acids, ROH is the weakest acid. Therefore, the strongest base is RO^-.

36. **(a)** Following are the three possible isomers of butanol

(i) $CH_3CH_2 — CH_2 — CH_2OH$

Butan–1–ol

no chiral carbon

(ii) $CH_3 — CH_2 — \overset{*}{CH} — CH_3$
$|$
OH

Butan –2 – ol

1-Chiral Carbon

(iii)
CH_3
$|$
$H_3C — C — CH_3$
$|$
OH

2 – methylpropan – 2 – ol

No Chiral Carbon

37. **(b)** $(CH_3)_3CBr + NaOC_2H_5$ can't be applied for synthesising the ether because sod. ethoxide, being a strong base, will preferentially cause elimination reaction.

$(CH_3)_3CBr \xrightarrow{^-OC_2H_5} (CH_3)_2C = CH_2 + HBr$

In isobutene + ethanol, isobutene will form *tert*-butyl cation which reacts with ethanol, a nucleophile to form ether.

$(CH_3)_2C = CH_2 \xrightarrow{H^+} (CH_3)_2\overset{+}{C}CH_3$

$\xrightarrow[\text{(ii) }-H^+]{\text{(i) }CH_3CH_2OH} (CH_3)_3COCH_2CH_3$

38. **(d)**   **39.** **(b) OR (a) 40. (a)**   **41.** **(c)**

Chapter Test

1. **(d)** The order of reactivity of alcohol with Lucas reagent is *tert.* > *sec.* > *pri.*

2. **(c)** Secondary alcohols oxidise to produce kenone.

$CH_3CHOHCH_2CH_3 \xrightarrow{(O)} CH_3COCH_2CH_3$
2-Butanol   Ethyl methyl ketone

3. **(a)**   **4.** **(a)**

5. **(a)** 2-Cyclohexenol is dehydrated more readily than 3-cyclohexenol because the carbocation formed from the former is more stable than the latter.

6. **(b)** *Ter*-butyl bromide and sodium methoxide reacts to form 2-methylpropene and ethanol (elimination reaction).

CH_3
$|$
$CH_3 — C — Br + CH_3ONa \longrightarrow CH_3 — C = CH_2$
$|$
CH_3

with CH_3 group above the $C=CH_2$

7. **(c)** Sodium phenoxide (sodium salt of phenol) and CO_2 on heating form sodium salicylate which is known as Kolbe's reaction. Ethanol does not respond to this reaction. Phenoxide ion is more less basic than ethoxide ion. Because the lone pair of e⁻s is not easily available for protonation due to the conjugation.

8. **(a)** In alkoxides, the $R \rightarrow O^-$ ion is unstable due to high charge density on oxygen atom ($+ I$ effect) and sp^3 hybridisation. This phenoxide io ($C_6H_5 – O^-$) is stabilised by resonance and sp^2 hybridisation of the carbon atom, therefore, it is more stable due to less charge density on oxygen atom.

OR

(b) Phenols are weaker acids ($K_a = 1.3 \times 10^{-10}$) than carboxylic acids ($K_a = 10^{-5}$) and carbonic acids ($K_a = 10^{-7}$). Therefore, phenols do not react with carbonates and bicarbonates.

9. **(d)** Phenols cannot react directly with carboxylic acid and does not form ester, as oxygen of phenoxide ion has less charge density due to resonance, hence, the phenoxide ion ($C_6H_5 – O^-$) is stable and does not favour esterification. electron withdrawing character increases acidic nature of phenol.

10. **(d)** *p*-Nitrophenol is more acidic than *m*-nitrophenol due to – I, and – m character of NO_2 group. At m-position only -I effect is considered.

11. **(a)**

12. 3-Chloromethyl-2-isopropylpentan-1-ol.

13. $H_2C = CH — CH — CH_2CH_2CH_3$
$|$
OH

14. Methanol (CH_3OH) is known as wood alcohol. It is so called as it was earlier prepared by heating wood in absence of air.

15. The compound 'X' is isopropyl alcohol (or 2-propanol). It undergoes de-hydrogenation.

$CH_3 — CH — CH_3 \xrightarrow{Cu\,chips} CH_3 — C — CH_3$
$|$ $||$
OH O
2–Propanol   Acetone

6 Biomolecules

Concept Map

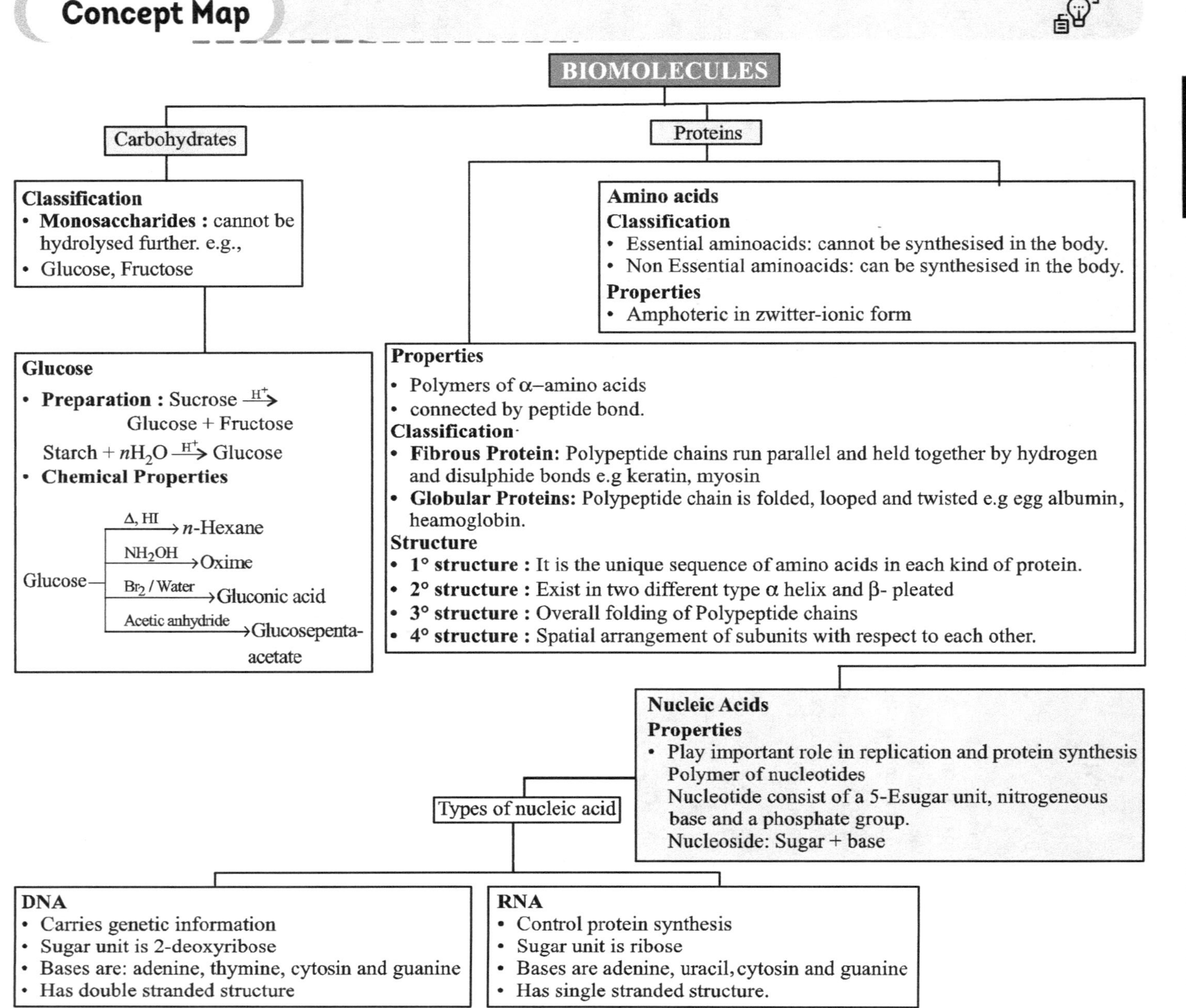

Topic 1   Carbohydrates, Amino Acids and Proteins 

INTRODUCTION

All common activities of a living organism (bioactivity) involve reactions of certain organic compounds (mostly organic). Such compounds are called biomolecules. The important biomolecules are carbohydrates, lipids, proteins vitamins, hormones, nucleic acids, etc. They not only build up living system, but are also responsible for their growth maintenance and their ability to reproduce.

CARBOHYDRATES

Carbohydrates are defined as the optically active polyhydroxy aldehydes or ketones or substances which yield these on hydrolysis.

Carbohydrates constitute one of the most important groups of natural products. Earlier of, carbohydrates were defined as compounds containing carbon, hydrogen and oxygen, the latter two elements being present in the same ratio as in water, i.e., they were regarded as the hydrates of carbon (carbo-carbon; hydrates-hydrates) and thus corresponded to the formula $C_x(H_2O)_y$, Later on it was discovered that these compounds were not hydrates of carbon as they did not contain free water molecules

$$C_6H_{12}O_6 \qquad C_{12}H_{22}O_{11} \qquad (C_6H_{10}O_5)_n$$

Glucose and Fructose   Sucrose   Cellulose and Starch

Carbohydrates corresponding to general formula $C_x(H_2O)_y$

But later on it was found that certain carbohydrates do not correspond to this formula, e.g.,

$$C_6H_{12}O_5 \qquad C_7H_{14}O_6$$

Rhamnose   Rhamnohexose

Carbohydrates not corresponding to general formula $(C_x(H_2O)_y$

Classification of Carbohydrates

Based on Molecular Size

(a) **Monosaccharides**
    (i) In these $n = 3$ to 7
    (ii) Their naming is of the following type:

n	Formula	Group	Aldoses	Ketose
n = 3	$C_3H_6O_3$	Triose	Glyceraldehyde	Dihydroxy acetone.
n = 4	$C_4H_8O_4$	Tetrose	Erythrose	Erythrulose
n = 5	$C_5H_{10}O_5$	Pentose	Ribose	Ribulose
n = 6	$C_6H_{12}O_6$	Hexose	Glucose	Fructose

    (iii) In aldoses aldehyde group is present and all central carbon atoms are asymmetrical (chiral).
    (iv) In ketose, ketone group is present and except 2nd carbon all atom are asymmetrical (chiral).

(b) **Oligosaccharides:** They yield 2-10 monosaccharide units on hydrolysis. They are further classified as di-, tri, tetra-, saccharides etc. depending upon the number of monosaccharides formed by them on hydrolysis ex: sucrose on hydrolysis gives one molecule each of glucose and fructose whereas maltose gives two molecules of glucose only.

(c) **Polysaccharides:** They yield a large number of monosaccharide units (more than ten) upon hydrolysis. For ex: starch,, cellulose, glycogen, gums etc.

Based on Nature

Carbohydrates are also classified as reducing and non-reducing sugars depending on whether they reduce Fehling's and Tollen's reagent or not.

(a) All monosaccharides whether aldose or ketose are reducing sugars.

(b) In disaccharides, if reducing groups of monosaccharides, i.e., aldehydic or ketone groups are bonded, these are non-reducing sugars, ex:- sucrose. If, however these groups are free in the sugar, then it is reducing sugar ex: maltose and lactose

Based on Taste

Carbohydrates with sweet taste are called sugars while those without a sweet taste are called non-sugars. Mono and oligosaccharides are sugars while polysaccharides are non-sugars.

Glucose ($C_6H_{12}O_6$)

Glucose is an aldohexose. It is a monomer of many of the larger carbohydrates such as starch, cellulose.

Preparation of Glucose

(a) By hydrolysis of cane-sugar: In laboratory, glucose can be prepared by hydrolysis of cane-sugar in the presence of alcohol using dilute hydrochloric acid. Glucose and fructose are formed in equal amounts. Glucose, being less soluble in ethyl alcohol than fructose, crystallizes out.

$$\underset{\text{Sucrose}}{C_{12}H_{22}O_{11}} + H_2O \xrightarrow{\;H^+\;} \underset{\text{Glucose}}{C_6H_{12}O_6} + \underset{\text{Fructose}}{C_6H_{12}O_6}$$

(b) By hydrolysis of starch: Glucose is obtained, **on commercial scale**, by hydrolysis of starch by boiling it with dilute sulphuric acid at 393 K under a pressure of 2–3 bar.

$$\underset{\text{Starch}}{(C_6H_{10}O_5)_n} + nH_2O \xrightarrow[\text{393K; 2–3bar}]{H^+} \underset{\text{Glucose}}{nC_6H_{12}O_6}$$

Structure of Glucose:

The reactions of glucose indicate that its molecule contains one primary ($-CH_2OH$) and four secondary ($>CHOH$) hydroxyl groups.

$$\begin{array}{c} CHO \\ | \\ (CHOH)_4 \\ | \\ CH_2OH \end{array}$$

Evidences in Support of the Open Chain Structure of Glucose

(a) Reduction : $\underset{\text{Glucose}}{HOH_2C\,.\,(CHOH)_4\,.\,CHO} + 2[H] \xrightarrow[H_2O]{Na-Hg} \underset{\text{Sorbito}}{HOCH_2.(CHOH)_4\,.\,CH_2OH}$

(b) Reaction with hydrogen iodide : $HOCH_2-(CHOH)_4-CHO \xrightarrow[\text{red P}]{HI} \underset{\text{n-Hexane}}{H_3C-CH_2-CH_2-CH_2-CH_2-CH_3}$

(c) Oxidation : $\underset{\text{Glucose}}{HOH_2C\,.\,(CHOH)_4\,.\,CHO} + [O] \xrightarrow{Br_2/H_2O} \underset{\text{Gluconic acid}}{HOCH_2\,.(CHOH)_4\,.\,COOH}$

Since glucose is readily oxidised, it acts as a strong reducing agent and reduces Tollen's reagent (ammonical silver nitrate) and Fehling solution to metallic silver and cuprous oxide (red) respectively.
Glucose on oxidation by dil. HNO_3 gives a dicarboxylic acid, saccharic acid

$$\underset{\text{Glucose}}{\begin{array}{c} CHO \\ | \\ (CHOH)_4 \\ | \\ CH_2OH \end{array}} \xrightarrow{\text{dil. } HNO_3} \underset{\text{Saccharic acid}}{\begin{array}{c} COOH \\ | \\ (CHOH)_4 \\ | \\ COOH \end{array}}$$

(d) Acetylation: $OHC\,.\,(CHOH)_4\,.\,CH_2OH + 5Ac_2O \longrightarrow \underset{\text{Glucose penta-acetate or penta-acetyl glucose}}{OHC.\,(CHOAc)_4\,.\,CH_2OAc}$

(e) Formation of osazone: Like the normal aldehydes, glucose reacts with phenylhydrazine in equimolecular proportion to form phenylhydrazone but unlike the normal aldehydes, glucose reacts with excess of phenylhydrazine (three molecular proportions) to form glucosazone.

$$\begin{array}{c} CHO \\ | \\ CHOH \\ | \\ (CHOH)_3 \\ | \\ CH2OH \end{array} \xrightarrow[-H_2O]{\underset{(\text{excess})}{C_6H_5NHNH_2}} \underset{\text{Glucosazone}}{\begin{array}{c} CH=N.NHC_6H_5 \\ | \\ C=N.NHC_6H_5 \\ | \\ (CHOH)_3 \\ | \\ CH_2OH \end{array}}$$

Glucosazone is a yellow crystalline compound, sparingly soluble in water and has a sharp melting point. On account of these properties, it is used in the identification of glucose.
Glucose, fructose and mannose form the same osazone (glucosazone). Osazone formation involves only first two carbon atoms.

(f) Reaction with hydroxylamine: $HOCH_2 - (CHOH)_4 - CHO + NH_2OH \longrightarrow HOCH_2 - (CHOH)_4 - CH = N - OH + H_2O$

(Glucose oxime)

(g) Formation of cyanohydrin

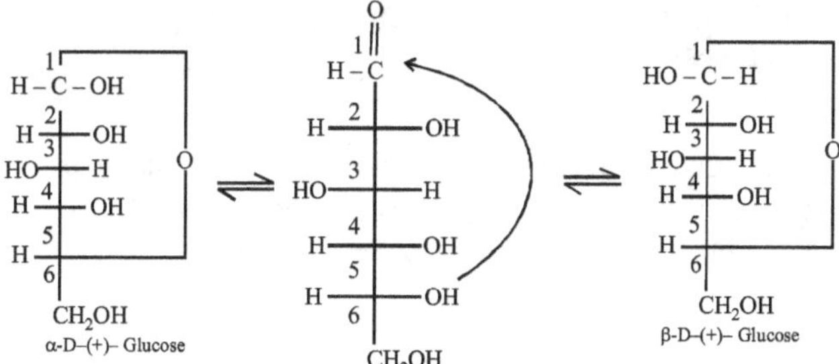

Limitation of Open Chain Structure of D (+) Glucose :

The following reactions of glucose could not be explained on the basis of its open chain structure.
(a) Glucose does not give, 2, 4-DNP test, Schiff's test and does not form addition product with $NaHSO_3$.
(b) The penta acetate of glucose does not react with hydroxylamine indicating the absence of free –CHO group.
(c) It is found to exist in 2 forms: α and β.

Cyclic Structure of D (+) Glucose

In this structure, the aldehyde (–CHO) group is involved in the form of a ring with the –OH group attached to C_5 carbon. It is a six membered ring, often called δ-oxide ring. The ring accounts for the two isomeric forms α and β as shown below :

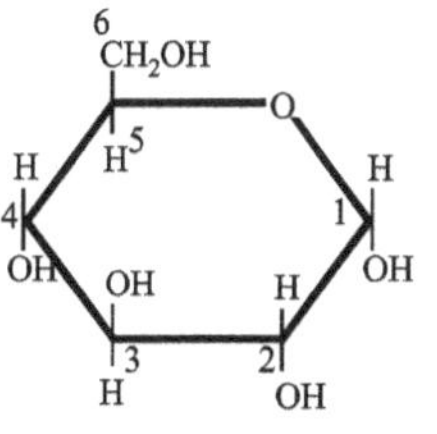

The two cyclic hemi acetal forms of glucose differ only in configuration of –OH at C_1. Such isomers (α and β) are called **anomers.**
Note: Both the forms are optically active, α-D- glucose has specific rotation + 111.5° and β-D-glucose has specific rotation + 19.5°.

Mutarotation

When either of the two forms of glucose is dissolved in water there is change in rotation till the equilibrium value of + 52.5°. This is known as mutarotation.

$$\alpha–D(+)Glucose \rightleftharpoons Equilibrium\ Mixture \rightleftharpoons \beta–D–(+)Glucose$$
$$+111.5° \qquad\qquad +52.5° \qquad\qquad +19.5°$$

Haworth Structure of Glucose

The two cyclic structures for D (+) glucose shown in the pyranose form as :

Fructose (Laevulose), $C_6H_{12}O_6$

The D (laevo-) fructose, also known as laevulose or fruit sugar is found in many fruits and in honey. It occurs in combination with glucose in cane and beet sugars. The most important source of fructose is the polysaccharide, inulin (a polymer of fructose).

Commercially, fructose is obtained by the hydrolysis of inulin. It melts at 104°C, and sweetest of all sugars, but is seldom used in pure form. It exhibits mutarotation, the specific rotation values of α-, β- and equilibrium mixture are –21°, 133.5° and –92.3° respectively. Fructose responds most of the usual reactions of the ketonic and hydroxyl groups. Two important properties of fructose are oxidation and reduction.

Oxidation

Fructose, although, has no aldehydic group, it reduces Fehling's solution and Tollen's reagent. This reducing property of fructose is said to be due to the presence of an α-hydroxy ketonic group which is readily oxidised by Fehling solution and Tollen's reagent.

$$\underset{\text{Fructose}}{\begin{array}{c} CH_2OH \\ | \\ CO \\ | \\ CHOH \\ | \\ (CHOH)_2 \\ | \\ CH_2OH \end{array}} \xrightarrow{\text{Oxidation}} \underset{\text{Tartaric acid}}{\begin{array}{c} CH_2OH \\ | \\ COOH \\ \text{Glycolic acid} \\ + \\ COOH \\ | \\ (CHOH)_2 \\ | \\ COOH \end{array}}$$

Reduction

Reduction of fructose with Na-Hg and water gives two alcohols, sorbitol and mannitol (difference from glucose which gives only sorbitol on reduction).

$$\underset{\text{Fructose}}{\begin{array}{c} CH_2OH \\ | \\ CO \\ | \\ (CHOH)_3 \\ | \\ CH_2OH \end{array}} \xrightarrow[\text{Water}]{\text{Na – Hg}} \underset{\text{Sorbtol and Mannitol}}{\begin{array}{c} CH_2OH \\ | \\ HCOH \\ | \\ (CHOH)_3 \\ | \\ CH_2OH \end{array} + \begin{array}{c} CH_2OH \\ | \\ HOCH \\ | \\ (CHOH)_3 \\ | \\ CH_2OH \end{array}}$$

Structure of Fructose

Fructose has the molecular formula $C_6H_{12}O_6$ and on the basis of its reactions it was found to contain a ketonic functional group at C—2 and six carbon atoms in straight chain as in case of glucose. It belongs to D-series and is a laevorotatory compound. Therefore, fructose is correctly named as D-(–)-fructose. Its open chain structure may be written as:

$$\begin{array}{c} CH_2OH \\ | \\ C = O \\ OH-\!\!-H \\ H-\!\!-OH \\ H-\!\!-OH \\ | \\ CH_2OH \end{array}$$

D-(–)Fructose

Fructose also exists in two cyclic forms which are obtained by the addition of –OH at C–5 to the ($>C = O$) group. The ring thus formed is a five membered ring and is named as furanose with analogy to the compound furan.

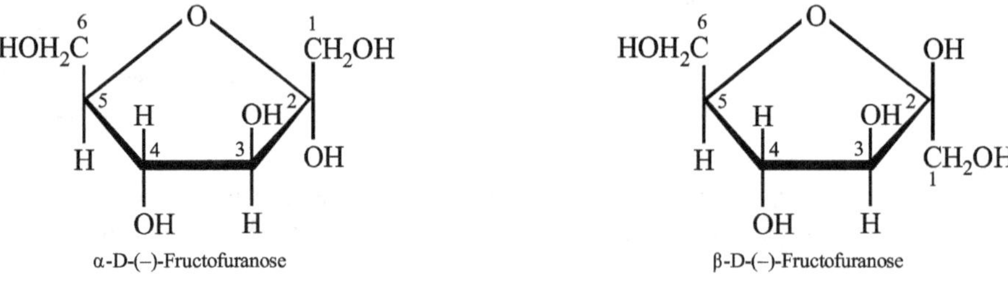

α-D-(–)-Fructofuranose   β-D-(–)-Fructofuranose

The cyclic structures of two anomers of fructose are represented by **Haworth structures** as given:

α-D-(–)-Fructofuranose   β-D-(–)-Fructofuranose

Biological Importance of Carbohydrates

(a) It is the main source of energy (1 g carbohydrate gives about 4.1 k cal of energy).
(b) Cell wall is made up of cellulose.
(c) Ribose sugar (carbohydrate) is the structural component of DNA and RNA.

Illustration 1 :

What are anomers ?

Sol. Anomers are those stereoisomers of sugars which differ from each other in the stereochemistry at $C - 1$.

AMINO ACIDS AND PROTEINS

Amino acids are the compounds having one or more amino groups and one or more carboxyl groups in the same molecule. They are usually classified into α, β, γ, etc. according to the relative positions of the two functional groups, viz.

$$\overset{\overset{\displaystyle NH_2}{|}}{CH_3CH\,COOH}$$
α-Aminopropionic acid
(an α-amino acid)

$$\overset{\overset{\displaystyle NH_2}{|}}{CH_2CH_2COOH}$$
β-Aminopropionic acid
(a β-amino acid)

Chemical Structure

(a) Amino acids are presented by the general formula:

$$H_2N-\overset{\overset{\displaystyle R}{|}}{\underset{\underset{\displaystyle H\ O}{}}{C}}-\overset{}{\underset{}{C}}-OH \quad \text{or} \quad H_2N-\overset{\overset{\displaystyle R}{|}}{\underset{\underset{\displaystyle H}{|}}{C}}-COOH$$

R = Alkyl group.

(b) If 'R' changes, amino acid formed also changes.
   e.g. If $R = H \rightarrow$ Glycine (Simplest Amino Acid), If $R = CH_3 \rightarrow$ Alanine, If $R = CH_2OH \rightarrow$ Serine.

$$NH_2-\overset{\overset{\displaystyle H}{|}}{\underset{\underset{\displaystyle H}{|}}{C}}-COOH \quad \text{or} \quad NH_2-CH_2-COOH$$
Glycine

$$NH_2\ \overset{\overset{\displaystyle CH_2OH}{|}}{\underset{\underset{\displaystyle H}{|}}{C}}\ COOH$$
Serine

$$NH_2\ \overset{\overset{\displaystyle CH_3}{|}}{\underset{\underset{\displaystyle H}{|}}{C}}\ COOH$$
Alanine

(c) **Zwitter ions:** Due to the presence of an acidic and a basic group in the same molecule, most of the amino-acids are neutral and exist largely as dipolar or zwitterions or inner salts in which proton from the carboxyl group has been transferred to the amino group and thus a dipolar ion containing both a positive and a negative charge is formed.

$$R-\overset{\overset{\displaystyle NH_2}{|}}{CH}-COOH \rightleftharpoons R-\overset{\overset{\displaystyle NH_3^+}{|}}{CH}-COO^-$$
Amino acid   Zwitterion

Classification of Amino Acids

Amino acids are classified into three types basic, acidic and neutral amino acids. The amino acids having equal number of amino and carboxyl groups are called neutral amino acids. If amino groups are more in number than carboxyl groups, then the amino acids are basic and if number of carboxyl groups are more than amino groups the amino acids are acidic.

Nearly 30 amino acids have been obtained from the hydrolysis of proteins. Except two (proline and hydroxyproline) all are amino acids, while the exceptional two are imino acids.

Among the 30 known (natural) amino-acids certain may be synthesised in the body while others can't be synthesised in the body at a rate necessary for normal growth and hence must be supplied in the diet. Therefore, the first category of amino acids are called dispensable or non-essential amino acids, while those of the second category are known as indispensable or essential amino acids.

(a) **Essential amino acids :**

   These are as follows :

(i) Leucine	(ii) Isoleucine	(iii) Lysine	(iv) Methionine
(v) Phenyl alanine	(vi) Threonine	(vii) Tryptophan	(viii) Valine

   Arginine and Histidine are **semi-essential** amino acids i.e. they are partly synthesized in tissues.

(b) Non-essential amino acids :

These are as follows :

(i) Alanine	(ii) Aspargine	(iii) Aspartic acid	(iv) Cistine
(v) Glutamic acid	(vi) Glutamine	(vii) Hydroxy proline	(viii) Glycine
(ix) Proline	(x) Serine	(xi) Tyrosine	

Except glycine (the first member of the series) which is optically inactive, all of the amino acids contain at least one asymmetric carbon atom and hence they are optically active and can exist in d and l forms.

Configuration of α-amino acids

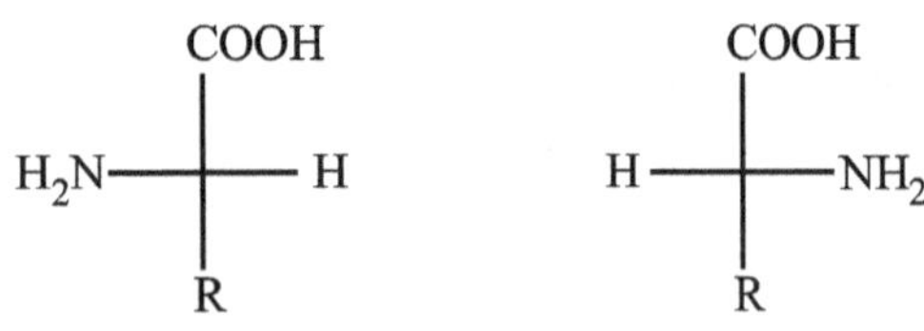

L-Amino acid   D-Amino acid
(NH_2 on L.H.S.)   (NH_2 on R.H.S.)

But it is very important to note that in nature they never exist in racemic form, i.e., in nature they are always present in optically active form.

Peptide Bond

(a) Two or more than two amino acids link to form a peptide.

(b) The bond present between peptides is called peptide bond.

It is of 3 types

Dipeptide	Tripeptide	Polypeptide
($n_{AA} = 2$)	($n_{AA} = 3$)	($n_{AA} > 3$)

(c) A peptide bond is formed between $-NH_2$ group of one amino acid and $-COOH$ group of another amino acid with the elimination of a water molecule.

$$H-N-\underset{\underset{H}{|}}{\overset{\overset{R}{|}}{C}}-\underset{\underset{O}{||}}{C}-\boxed{O-H+H}-N-\underset{\underset{H}{|}}{\overset{\overset{R}{|}}{C}}-\underset{\underset{O}{||}}{C}-OH \xrightarrow{-H_2O} H-N-\underset{\underset{H}{|}}{\overset{\overset{R}{|}}{C}}-\boxed{\underset{\underset{O}{||}}{C}-N}-\underset{\underset{H}{|}}{\overset{\overset{R}{|}}{C}}-\underset{\underset{O}{||}}{C}-OH$$

Amino acid   Amino Acid   **Peptide Bond**

Proteins

Proteins are highly complex, natural compounds, composed of a large number of different α-amino-acids joined together with peptide linkage, i.e., they are naturally occuring polypeptides.

The biological importance of proteins can be judged by the fact that the animals can live for a long time without fat or carbohydrate, but not without protein. Proteins mainly supply new tissues, repair working parts and make up the loss (e.g., as gland secretions) in the vital processes. Only the plants can build up proteins from inorganic materials like nitrates, ammonium sulphate, carbon dioxide and water, while most of the animals derive them mainly from plants and some other animals.

Configuration of Proteins

Biological nature or function of protein was confirmed by its conformation.

This conformation is of 4 types

(a) Primary structure : This type of structure was given by **Fredric Sanger** in 1953 in Insulin (of one chain). Primary structure refers to the number, nature and sequence of the amino acids in protein molecule. Primary structure is conformed by a single polypeptide chain in a linear manner.

All amino acids are attached in a straight chain by peptide bond. It is important as the replacement of just one amino acid in the sequence of a protein destroys its biological activity.

(b) Secondary structure : The conformation which the polypeptide chains acquire as a result of H-bonding is called secondary structure of protein. H-bonds along with peptide bond are present in secondary structure.

The H-bonds are present between hydrogen of amino group and oxygen atom of carboxylic acid group.

The structure is of two types :

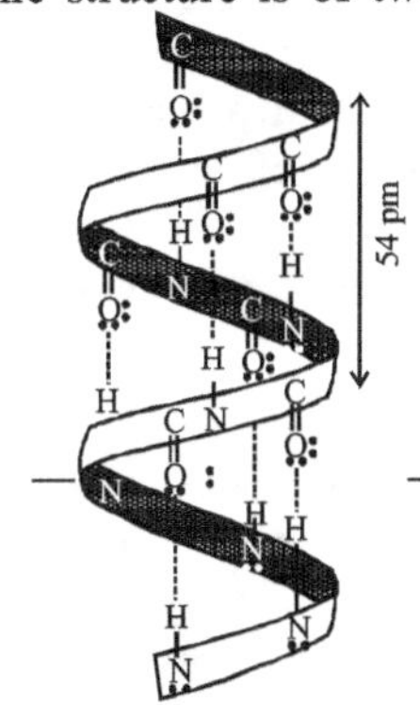

(i) α - **helix**	**(ii)** β -**pleated sheet**
1. Chain is spiral	1. Structure of protein is not arranged in a sequence.
2. 3.7 amino acids in one coiling	2. Polypeptide chain are parallel to each other.
3. Right handed circular.	3. Intermolecular H-bonds hold together the neighbouring polypeptide chains.
4. Intermolecular H-bonds are present	
Eg. → Myosin, Keratin etc.	Eg.→ Silk fibres.

(c) Tertiary structure : α – helix bend, twist and fold leading to the final three dimensional structure.

Tertiary structure refers to its three dimensional structure, i.e., folding and bonding of the long peptide chains. Three types of bonds are responsible for tertiary structure, viz. hydrogen, ionic and hydrophobic.

This structure is formed by four type of bonds which makes a regularity in it. These are :

(i) Hydrogen bond :

$$\overset{|}{C} = O \cdots\cdots H - \overset{|}{\underset{H}{N}} -$$

Hydrogen bond

They are formed between oxygen of acidic amino acid and –H of basic amino acid.

(ii) Hydrophobic bond :

Non - polar side chains of neutral amino acid tends to be closely associated with one another in proteins. They are present in between the amino acids. These are not true bonds.

(iii) Ionic bond : $-COO^-.....H_3^+N-$

Ionic bond

These are salt bonds formed between oppositely charged groups in side chains of amino acids

(iv) Disulphide bonds : $|$ ------ S - S ---- $|$

Relatively stable bond and thus is not broken readily under usual conditions of denaturation. Formed between the -SH group of amino acid Ex. Cystine and Methionine.

(d) Quaternary Structure: When two or more polypeptide chains unite by forces other than covalent bonds (i.e., not peptide and disulphide bonds) we get quaternary structure of protein. It is most stable structure.

Ex. Haemoglobin

Types of Proteins

Classification of proteins is based upon three general properties:shape, solubility and chemical composition.

(a) Simple proteins: The simple proteins are those which yield only amino acids on hydrolysis.

(b) Conjugated proteins: Conjugated proteins on hydrolysis yield α-amino acids and other non-proteinous substances in addition to α-amino acids. The non-proteinous moiety is usually referred to prosthetic group.

(c) Derived proteins: Derived proteins are the products formed by the action of physical (such as heat), chemical or enzymatic agents on natural proteins. The derived proteins are thus intermediate hydrolysis products of proteins.

Alternatively, proteins are of two types depending upon their shape and functions.

(i) Fibrous proteins: These have thread like molecules which lie side by side to form fibres. The various molecules are held together by hydrogen bonds. These are insoluble in water but soluble in concentrated acids and alkalies. Examples are keratin of hair, nails, wood, feathers and horn, myosin of muscles, and fibroin of silk.

(ii) Globular proteins: This type of protein has molecule folded into compact units which often acquire spheroidal shape. Such proteins are soluble in water, dilute acids and alkalis. Examples are insulin, haemoglobin, albumin, etc.

Denaturation of Proteins

When a protein, in its native form, is subjected to a physical change like change in temperature, or a chemical change like change in pH, the native conformation of the molecule is disrupted and proteins so formed are called **denaturated proteins**.

The denaturation may be reversible or irreversible. The coagulation of egg on boiling is an example of irreversible protein denaturation.

However, it has been shown now that in some cases, the process is actually reversible. The reverse process is called **renaturation**.

Test of Proteins

(a)   With conc. HNO_3 on heating give yellow ppt. Which on more heating give solution. This yellow colour is same that is formed on the skin when the latter comes in contact with the conc. nitric acid. It is **Xanthoprotic test**.

(b)   The protein is warmed gently with 10% solution of sodium hydroxide and then a drop of very dilute copper sulphate solution is added, the formation of reddish-violet colour indicates the presence of peptide link, –CO–NH–. The test is also positive for the compound biuret, $H_2N.CONH.CONH_2$, obtained from urea by heating This is **Biurete test.**

BIOLOGICAL IMPORTANCE OF PROTEINS

(a)   Component of plasma membrane.
(b)   All enzymes are proteins.
(c)   Many hormones are proteins.
(d)   Antigen and antibody are proteins.
(e)   Actin and myosin proteins are important in muscle contraction.
(f)   Proteins are important in growth, regeneration and repairing.
(g)   Calorific value: 4.0 kcal.

Illustration 2 :

What are proteins?

Sol.   Proteins are biopolymers containing a large number of amino acids joined to each other by peptide linkages having three dimensional structure.

Illustration 3 :

How many different dipeptides can be formed from alanine and glycine ? Name them.

Sol. $2^2 = 4$ dipeptides are possible.

The names of the four dipeptides are Ala – Ala, alanylalanine, Ala – Gly, alanylglycine ; Gly – Gly, glycylglycine, and Gly–Ala, glycylalanine.

Practice Exercise-1

Multiple Choice Questions

1.   The symbols D and L represent
    (a)   the optical activity of compounds.
    (b)   the relative configuration of a particular stereoisomer.
    (c)   the dextrorotatory nature of molecule.
    (d)   the levorotatory nature of molecule

2.   The α-D glucose and β-D glucose differ from each other due to difference in carbon atom with respect to its
    (a)   conformation   (b)   configuration
    (c)   number of OH groups   (d)   size of hemiacetal ring

3.   For osazone formation, the effective structural unit necessary is

(a) CH_2OCH_3
      |
     CO
      |

(b) CH_2OH
      |
     CO
      |

(c) CH_2OH
      |
    $CHOCH_3$
      |

(d) CHO
      |
    $CHOCH_3$
      |

4.   Denaturation of proteins leads to loss of its biological activity by
    (a)   Formation of amino acids
    (b)   Loss of primary structure
    (c)   Loss of both primary and secondary structures
    (d)   Loss of both secondary and tertiary structures

5.   Proteins are condensation polymers of
    (a) α-amino acids   (b) β-amino acids
    (c) α-hydroxy acids   (d) β-hydroxy acids

Assertion & Reason Questions

DIRECTIONS (Qs. 6-8) : *Each of these questions contains an assertion followed by reason. Read them carefully and answer the question on the basis of following options. You have to select the one that best describes the two statements.*

(a) If both Assertion and Reason are correct and the Reason is a correct explanation of the Assertion.

(b) If both Assertion and Reason are correct but Reason is not a correct explanation of the Assertion.

(c) If the Assertion is correct but Reason is incorrect.

(d) If the Assertion is incorrect but the Reason is correct.

6. **Assertion :** Proteins are made up of α-amino acids.
   Reason : During denaturation, secondary and tertiary structures of proteins are destroyed.

7. **Assertion:** Tyrosine behaves as an acid at pH = 7.
   Reason: pK_a of phenol is more than 7.

8. **Assertion :** Oxidation of glucose by Br_2 water gives saccharic acid.
   Reason : Br_2 water oxidizes –CHO and alcohol.

Case/Passage Based Questions

DIRECTIONS (Qs. 9-13) : *Following are the case/passage based questions. Attempt any 4 out of 5 questions.*

The word protein is derived from Greek word, "proteios" which means primary. As the name shows, the proteins are of paramount importance for biological systems. Out of the total dry body weight, 3/4th are made up of proteins. Proteins are used for body building; all the major structural and functional aspects of the body are carried out by protein molecules. Abnormality in protein structure will lead to molecular diseases with profound alterations in metabolic functions. Proteins contain Carbon, Hydrogen, Oxygen and Nitrogen as the major components while Sulfur and Phosphorus are minor constituents. Nitrogen is characteristic of proteins. On an average, the nitrogen content of ordinary proteins is 16% by weight. All proteins are polymers of amino acids. Alpha carboxyl group of one amino acid reacts with alpha amino group of another amino acid to form a peptide bond or CO-NH bridge. Proteins are synthesized by polymerization of amino acids through peptide bonds. Two amino acids combined to form a dipeptide; three amino acids form a tripeptide; four will make a tetrapeptide; a few amino acids together will make an oligopeptide; and combination of 10-50 amino acids is a polypeptide. By convention, long polypeptide chains containing more than 50 amino acids are called proteins.

9. Two functional groups that are present in all amino acids are the
   (a) hydroxy, amine
   (b) hydroxy, amide
   (c) carboxyl, amino
   (d) carboxyl, amide

10. Amino acids generally exist in the form of Zwitter ions. This means they contain
    (a) basic—NH_2 group and acidic —COOH group
    (b) the basic— $\overset{+}{N}H_3$ group and acidic —COO^- group
    (c) basic—NH_2 and acidic —H^+ group
    (d) basic –COO^- group and acidic — $\overset{+}{N}H_3$ group

11. Simplest proteins has one peptide linkage. It is
    (a) tripeptide
    (b) dipeptide
    (c) tetrapeptide
    (d) oligopeptide

12. One of essential α-amino acids is
    (a) lysine
    (b) serine
    (c) glycine
    (d) proline

13. Proteins are polypeptides of
    (a) β-amino acids
    (b) α-hydroxy acids
    (c) D-α-amino acids
    (d) L-α-amino acids

Very Short Answer Questions

14. Which type of bonds are responsible for secondary structure of proteins?
15. Give an example of 'anomer'.
16. Write the structure of simplest amino acids, glycine.
17. Name the linkage which holds together two monosaccharide units in a polysaccharide?
18. How do amino acids form proteins?
19. How is excess glucose stored in our body?
20. Name the protein which stores oxygen in the muscle tissues.
21. How many molecules of ATP are consumed for the synthesis of one molecule of glucose?
22. What is ATP?
23. What type of bonding occurs in a α-helix configuration?
24. In what respect, do the two naturally occurring amino acid, differ from each other?
25. How many tripeptides are possible using three alanine, glycine and tyrosine?
26. Name the building blocks of proteins.
27. What happens when protein is denatured?

Short Answer Questions

28. What are peptides?
29. Why is glucose generally given to patients under exhaustion?
30. Name the anomers of glucose. How do they differ and what is the chief consequence of this difference ?
31. What are the differences between a globular and fibrous protein?
32. What are the differences between α-helix structure and β-pleated sheet structure?
33. Define native state of protein.
34. What are the three main classes of organic molecules that account for the molecular complexity of cells?
35. What are the two major forms of secondary structures in proteins? What kinds of bonds stabilise these structures?
36. Why does glucose reacts with Fehling's solution and phenyl hydrazine, but not with $NaHSO_3$?
37. Give the appropriate term to describe the following:
    (a) A molecule with a full positive charge and a full negative charge on different parts of the molecules.
    (b) A compound formed by condensing together of a number of 2-amino acid molecules.
    (c) The change which occurs when a solution of a protein is heated.
    (d) The class of proteins to which keratin belongs.

Topic 2 — Nucleic Acids 

NUCLEIC ACIDS

Nucleic acids are colourless, complex, amorphous, compounds made up of three units: bases, sugar and phosphoric acid. These are obtained by the hydrolysis of nucleoproteins which is a class of conjugated proteins. Nucleic acid constitutes the prosthetic group of the nucleoproteins. These are macro-molecules of high molecular weight and are present in every living cell. Nucleic acids are of two types:

(a) Pentose nucleic acids or ribonucleic acids (R.N.A.)

(b) Deoxypentose nucleic acids or deoxyribonucleic acids (D.N.A.)

Nucleic acids can be hydrolysed in stages to nucleotides, nucleosides and phosphoric acid and ultimately to base and sugar.

Nucleic acid $\rightarrow$ Nucleotides $\rightarrow$ Nucleosides + H_3PO_4 $\rightarrow$ Base + Sugar

Sugars

Two sugars are found to be present in nucleic acids, namely D-ribose in R.N.A. and 2-deoxyribose in D.N.A.

Bases

Two types of bases have been isolated from the hydrolysis products of nucleosides; viz. purines and pyrimidines. Important purine bases are adenine and guanine; while pyrimidine bases are uracil, thymine and cytosine. Adenine, guanine and cytosine are present in RNA as well as in DNA, while thymine is present only in DNA and uracil only in RNA.

Nucleosides

These are condensation products of a base with sugar. The five important nucleosides are named as adenosine, guanosine, cytidine, uridine and thymidine.

Nucleotides

These are condensation products of nucleosides with phosphoric acid. The five important nucleotides are named as adenylic acid, guanylic acid, cytidylic acid, uridylic acid and thymidylic acid. In nucleotides and hence in nucleic acids the three important units are present as

Base-Sugar-Phosphate

The double stranded helical structure was given by **Watson and Crick**. The two polynucleotide chains of DNA molecule are twisted around a common axis but run in opposite directions to form a right-handed helix. The two chains are joined together by specific hydrogen bonds (adenine to thymine and guanine to cytosine).

Deoxyribose Nucleic Acid (D.N.A.)

(a) It is found in nucleus.

(b) DNA is made up of 3 units-

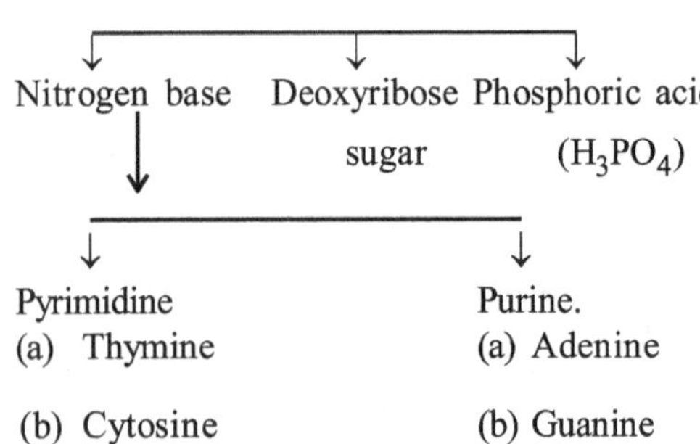

S.No.	Deoxyribonucleoside
(a)	Adenine + Deoxyribose $\rightarrow$ Deoxyadenosine
(b)	Guanine + Deoxyribose $\rightarrow$ Deoxyguanosine
(c)	Cytosine + Deoxyribose $\rightarrow$ Deoxycytidine
(d)	Thymine + Deoxyribose $\rightarrow$ Deoxythymidine

Structure of DNA

(a) Double Helical model of DNA was proposed by biochemist **J.D.Watson**, British chemist **FHC Crick** in 1953.

(b) DNA has a double helix structure and is made up of two chains of polynucleotides.

(c) DNA is a polymer of Nucleotide.

(d) The two strands are joined by 3' $\rightarrow$ 5' phosphodiester bonds.

(e) Sugar and phosphates are alternately arranged.

(f) In both chains, in between A and T, 2 hydrogen bonds are present while in C and G, 3 H-bonds are present. (A = T) (C≡ G)

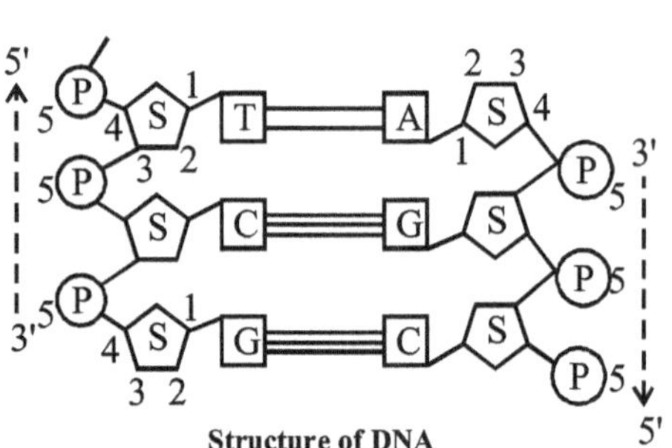

Structure of DNA

(g) A always attaches with T while C always attaches with G.

(h) Purine and pyrimidine are found in ratio 1 : 1. cells.

(i) DNA is attached with histone protein.

(j) DNA is present in prokaryotic cell and mitochondria.

Functions of DNA

(a) Self - replication or self -duplication

DNA has the property of self - replication . It is therefore a reproducing molecule. This unique property of DNA is at the root of all reproduction. Through its replication, **DNA acts as the key to heredity**. In the replication of DNA, the two strands of a double helix unwind and separate as a template for the formation of a new complementary strand.

(b) Protein synthesis

The specific sequence of base pair in DNA represents coded information for the manufacture of specific proteins. These code instructions first are **transcribed** into the matching nitrogen- base sequences within mRNA and the instructions in such RNA subsequently are translated into particular sequence of amino acid units within the polypeptide chains and proteins.

The major steps in the utilization of the genetic information can be represented as :

$$DNA \xrightarrow{\text{Replication}} DNA \xrightarrow{\text{Transcription}} RNA \xrightarrow{\text{Translation}} Protein$$

Ribonucleic Acid (RNA)

Found in cytoplasm as well as in nucleus. It mainly occurs in cytoplasm of the cell.

Chemical Nature

(a) Ribonucleic acid is a polymer of purine and pyrimidine ribonucleotides linked by $3' \rightarrow 5'$ phosphodiester bridges. The number of nucleotides in RNA ranges from as **few as 75 to many thousands**. Although sharing many features with DNA, RNA possesses several specific differences.

(b) As indicated by its name, sugar in RNA to which the phosphate and nitrogen- bases are attached is ribose rather than the deoxyribose of DNA.

(c) Although RNA contains the ribonucleotides of adenine, guanine, and cytosine, it does not posses thymine. Instead of thymine, RNA contains the ribonucleotides of uracil. Thus the pyrimidine components of RNA differs from those of DNA.

(d) RNA exists basically **as a single-stranded molecule** rather than as a double -stranded helical molecule, as does DNA. However the single strand of RNA is capable of folding back on itself like a hairpin and thus acquiring double-stranded characteristics. In these regions, A pairs with U and G pairs with C.

Thus a given segment of a long RNA molecule might, for example, be represented as follows.

```
P – R – P – R – P – R – P – R – P – R
    |       |       |       |       |
    A       U       G       G       C
```

where R stands for ribose ; A, U, G, and C for Adenine, Uracil, Guanine and Cytosine respectively.

On the basis of their function RNA mainly are of three type:

Messenger RNA (m-RNA), Transfer RNA (t-RNA), Ribosomal RNA (r-RNA)

Illustration 4 :

What is nucleoside? Give an example.

Sol. The molecule in which one of the organic bases (found in nucleic acids, *e.g.,* purines or pyrimidines) is combined with a sugar (ribose or 2-deoxyribose) is called nucleoside. For example, adenine ribose (commonly known as adenosine) is a nucleoside from adenine and ribose.

Practice Exercise-2

Multiple Choice Questions

1. The double helical structure of DNA was proposed by

   (a) Watson and Crick   (b) Meichers

   (c) Emil Fischer   (d) Khorana

2. The function of DNA in an organism is

   (a) to assist in the synthesis of RNA molecule.

   (b) to store information of heredity characteristics.

   (c) to assist in the synthesis of proteins and polypeptides.

   (d) All of these.

3. Chromosomes are made from
   (a) proteins
   (b) nucleic acids
   (c) proteins and nucleic acids
   (d) carbohydrates and nucleic acids
4. Which of the following statements regarding DNA fingerprinting is incorrect?
   (a) It is used in forensic laboratories for identification of criminals.
   (b) It cannot be altered by surgery.
   (c) It is different for every cell and cannot be altered by any known treatment.
   (d) It is used to determine paternity of an individual.
5. DNA multiplication is called as
   (a) translation   (b) transduction
   (c) transcription   (d) replication

Assertion & Reason Questions

DIRECTIONS (Qs. 6-8) : *Each of these questions contains an assertion followed by reason. Read them carefully and answer the question on the basis of following options. You have to select the one that best describes the two statements.*

(a) If both Assertion and Reason are correct and the Reason is a correct explanation of the Assertion.

(b) If both Assertion and Reason are correct but Reason is not a correct explanation of the Assertion.

(c) If the Assertion is correct but Reason is incorrect.

(d) If the Assertion is incorrect but the Reason is correct.

6. **Assertion :** DNA shows replication.
   Reason : DNA contains adenine and guanine as purine bases.

7. **Assertion :** Defective haemoglobin is produced which causes sickle cell anaemia in human beings.
   Reason : This is due to replacement of one amino acid, that is glutamic acid by valine.
8. **Assertion :** DNA as well as RNA molecules are found in the nucleus of a cell.
   Reason : DNA is double stranded while RNA is single stranded structure.

Very Short Answer Questions

9. Name different types of RNA molecules found in cells of organisms.
10. Mention the two classes of nitrogen containing base found in nucleotides.
11. Name the various types of nucleic acids present in the body of animals.
12. Name the various sugars present in nucleic acids.
13. Define genetic engineering.
14. What is the difference between ribose and 2-deoxyribose sugars?
15. Name different organic bases present in RNA-molecules.
16. Give important constituents of nucleic acids.
17. What type of substance is phenylalanine hydroxylase ? What is its importance for us?
18. Name the purines present in DNA.

Short Answer Questions

19. What are nucleotides? Name two classes of nitrogen containing bases found in nucleotide.
20. List the functions of nucleotides in a cell.
21. Describe briefly structure of nucleic acids.
22. What products would be formed when a nucleotide from DNA containing thymine is hydrolysed?

Important Tips & Formulae

▶ Monosaccharides which differ in configuration at C_1 in aldoses and C_2 in ketoses are called anomers. Thus α-D glucose and β-D glucose are anomers and so are α-D fructose and β-D fructose.

▶ **Epimers:** Monosaccharides differing in configuration at a carbon other than anomeric carbon are called epimers e.g. glucose and galactose differ in configuration at C_4 hence called C_4 epimers.

▶ **Osazones:** Monosaccharides and reducing disaccharides react with excess of phenyl hydrazine to form crystalline substances of the structure known as osazones. Glucose and Fructose give same osazone.

▶ Twenty five amino acids have been obtained from the hydrolysis of proteins. Except two (proline and hydroxyproline) all are amino acids, the exceptional two are **imino acids.**

▶ **Contractile proteins :** Found in muscles e.g. myosin, actin.

▶ **Tests of Protein:**

(i) **Biuret :** Protein solution + NaOH + dil. $CuSO_4$ → Pink or violet colour

(ii) **Ninhydrin :** Protein solution + Ninhydrin → Blue colour

(iii) **Hopkin's cole :** Protein solution + Glyoxalic acid + conc. H_2SO_4 → Blue - violet

(iv) **Million's :** Protein solution + Millon's reagent → Pink colour.

Millon's reagent : Solution of mercuric nitrate and nitrite in nitric acid containing traces of nitrous acid.

(v) **Xanthoproteic test :** Protein solution + conc HNO_3 → Yellow colour $\xrightarrow{\text{NaOH}}$ Orange colour

► **Nucleic Acids**

Nitrogenous base : Derived from purines having two rings in their structure Examples are adenine (A) and guanine (G).

Nucleotides : Nucleotides consist of 5 - carbon sugar (pentose) + nitrogenous base + 1-3 phosphate groups.

Nucleoside : Ribose + one base unit from AGCT or U

► **Functions of Nucleic Acids**

► **Replication :** A molecule of DNA can exactly duplicate to itself.

► **Template :** It means pattern. In the process of replication of DNA, the parent strand serves as template.

► **Codons :** The nucleotide bases in RNA function in groups of three (triplet) in coding amino acids. These base triplets are called codons.

NCERT Questions

1. What are monosaccharides?
Sol. Refer to Theory

2. What are reducing sugars?
Sol. Refer to Theory

3. Write two main functions of carbohydrates in plants.
Sol. Refer to Theory

4. Classify the following into monosaccharides and disaccharides.
Ribose, 2-deoxyribose, maltose, galactose, fructose and lactose.
Sol. Monosaccharides: Ribose, 2-deoxyribose, galactose and fructose.
Disaccharides: Maltose and lactose.

5. What do you understand by the term glycosidic linkage?
Sol. The ethereal or oxide linkage through which two monosaccharide units are joined together by the loss of a water molecule to form a molecule of disaccharide is called the glycosidic linkage. The glycosidic linkage in maltose molecule is shown below:

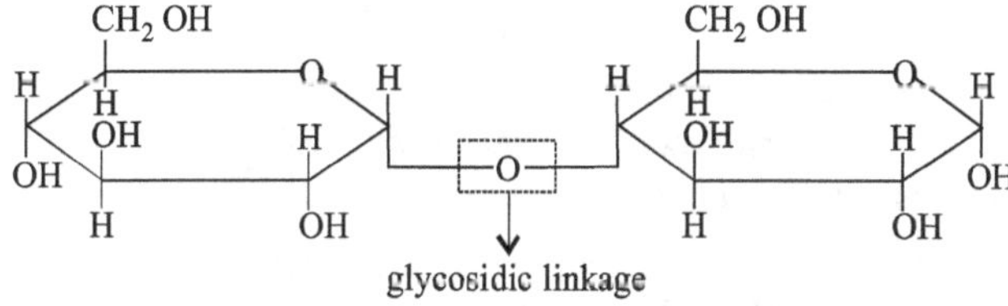

glycosidic linkage

6. What happens when D-glucose is treated with the following reagents.
(i) HI   (ii) Bromine water   (iii) HNO$_3$

Sol.

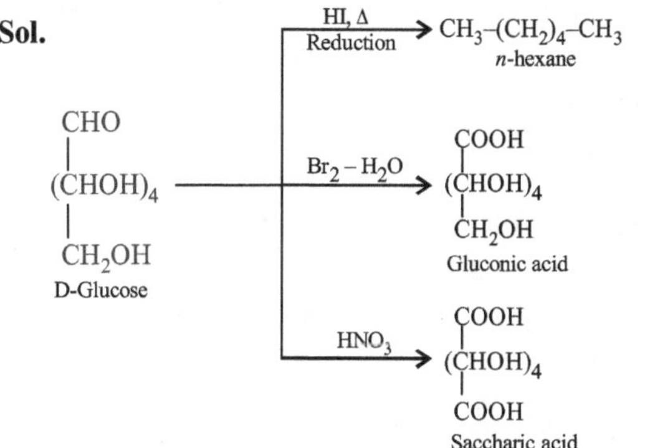

7. Enumerate the reactions of D–glucose which cannot be explained by its open chain structure.
Sol. (a) D (+) - glucose does not undergo certain characteristic reactions of aldehydes, *e.g.,* glucose does not form

NaHSO$_3$ addition product.

(b) Glucose reacts with NH$_2$OH to form an oxime but glucose pentaacetate does not. This implies that the aldehydic group is absent in glucose pentaacetate.

(c) D - (+) - glucose exists in two stereoisomeric forms, *i.e.,* α-glucose and β-glucose.

(d) Both α - D - glucose and β - D - glucose undergo mutarotation in aqueous solution. Although the crystalline forms of α - and β - D (+) - glucose are quite stable in aqueous solution but each form slowly changes into an equilibrium mixture of both.

(e) D (+) - glucose forms two isomeric methyl glucosides. Aldehydes normally react with two moles of methanol per mole of the aldehyde to form an acetal but D (+) - glucose when treated with methanol in presence of dry HCl gas, reacts with only one mole of methanol per mole of glucose to form a mixture of two methyl D - glucosides *i.e.,* methyl - α - D - glucoside (melting point 438 K, specific rotation + 158°) and methyl - β - D - glucoside (melting point 308 K, specific rotation – 33°).

8. What are essential and non-essential amino acids? Give two examples of each type.
Sol. Refer to Theory

9. Define the following as related to proteins:
(i) Peptide linkage   (ii) Primary structure
(iii) Denaturation
Sol. Refer Theory.

10. What are the common types of secondary structure of proteins?
Sol. The conformation which the polypeptide chains assume as a result of hydrogen bonding is called secondary structure of the proteins. The two types of secondary structures are α-helix and β-pleated sheet structure.

11. What type of bonding helps in stabilising the α-helix structure of proteins?
Sol. The α-helix structure of proteins is stabilized by intramolecular H-bonding between C = O of one amino acid residue and the N – H of the fourth amino acid residue in the chain. This causes the polypeptide chain to coil up into a spiral structure called right handed α- helix structure.

12. Differentiate between globular and fibrous proteins.
Sol. Refer Theory.

13. How do you explain the amphoteric behaviour of amino acids?
Sol. Amino acids contain an acidic (carboxyl group) and basic (amino group) group in the same molecule. In aqueous solution, they neutralize each other. The carboxyl group

loses a proton while the amino group accepts it. As a result, a dipolar or zwitter ion is formed.

$$H_2N—CH—COOH \longrightarrow H_3\overset{+}{N}—CH—COO^-$$

$$\underset{R}{\mid} \qquad\qquad \underset{\underset{Zwitter\ ion}{R}}{\mid}$$

In zwitter ionic form, a-amino acid show amphoteric behaviour as they react with both acids and bases.

$$H_3\overset{+}{N}—CH—COOH \underset{H^+}{\overset{OH^-}{\rightleftharpoons}} H_3\overset{+}{N}—CH—COO^-$$

$$\underset{\underset{(I)}{(R)}}{\mid} \qquad\qquad \underset{\underset{Zwitter\ ion}{R}}{\mid}$$

$$\underset{H^+}{\overset{OH^-}{\rightleftharpoons}} H_2N—CH—COO^-$$

$$\underset{\underset{(II)}{R}}{\mid}$$

14. **What is the effect of denaturation on the structure of proteins?**

Sol. During denaturation, 2° and 3° structures of proteins are destroyed but 1° structure remains intact. As a result of denaturation, the globular proteins (soluble in H_2O) are converted into fibrous proteins (insoluble in H_2O) and their biological activity is lost. For example, boiled egg which contains coagulated proteins cannot be hatched.

15. **What are nucleic acids ? Mention their two important functions.**

Sol. Refer to Theory

16. **What is the difference between a nucleoside and a nucleotide?**

Sol. Refer Theory.

17. **The two strands in DNA are not identical but are complementary. Explain.**

Sol. The two strands in DNA molecule are held together by hydrogen bonds between purine base of one strand and pyrimidine base of the other and vice versa. Because of different sizes and geometries of the bases, the only possible pairing in DNA are G (guanine) and C (cytosine) through three H-bonds, $(i.e., C \equiv G)$ and between A (adenine) and T (thiamine) through two H-bonds $(i.e., A = T)$. Due to this base -pairing principle, the sequence of bases in one strand automatically fixes the sequence of bases in the other strand. Thus, the two strands are complimentary and not identical.

18. **Write the important structural and functional differences between DNA and RNA.**

Sol. Refer Theory.

19. **What are the different types of RNA found in the cell?**

Sol. There are three types of RNA:
(a) Ribosomal RNA (r RNA)
(b) Messenger RNA (m RNA)
(c) Transfer RNA (t RNA)

Past year Exercise

Assertion & Reason Questions

1. **Assertion :** Sucrose is a non-reducing sugar.
   Reason : Sucrose has glycosidic linkage.
   (a) If both Assertion and Reason are correct and the Reason is a correct explanation of the Assertion.
   (b) If both Assertion and Reason are correct but Reason is not a correct explanation of the Assertion.
   (c) If the Assertion is correct but Reason is incorrect.
   (d) If the Assertion is incorrect but the Reason is correct.

Very Short Answer Questions

2. Write the name of linkage joining two amino acids.
3. What are three types of RNA molecules which perform different function?

Short Answer Questions

4. Give the plausible explanation for the following:
   (a) Glucose doesn't give 2,4-DNP test.
   (b) The two strands in DNA are not identical but are complementary.
   (c) Starch and cellulose both contain glucose unit as monomer, yet they are structurally different.
5. (a) What is the difference between native protein and denatured protein?
   (b) Which one of the following is a disaccharide : Glucose, Lactose, Amylose, Fructose

   (c) Write the name of the vitamin responsible for the coagulation of blood.
6. Define the following with an example of each :
   (a) Polysaccharides
   (b) Denatured protein
   (c) Essential amino acids

   OR

   (a) Write the product when D-glucose react with conc. HNO_3.
   (b) Amino acids show amphoteric behaviour. Why?
   (c) Write one difference between α-helix and β-pleated structures of proteins.
7. Discuss invert sugar.
8. Explain what is meant by
   (i) pyranose structure of glucose?
   (ii) glycosidic linkage?
9. Define the following terms related to proteins:
   (i) Peptide linkage   (ii) Primary structure
   (iii) Denaturation
10. (i) Write the structural difference between starch and cellulose.
   (ii) What type of linkage is present in nucleic acids ?
   (iii) Give one example each for fibrous protein and globular protein.

NCERT Exemplar

Multiple Choice Questions

1. Sucrose (Cane sugar) is a disaccharide. One molecule of sucrose on hydrolysis gives ....
   (a) 2 molecules of glucose
   (b) 2 molecules of glucose + 1 molecule of fructose
   (c) 1 molecule of glucose + 1 molecule of fructose
   (d) 2 molecules of fructose

2. Proteins are found to have two different types of secondary structures viz. α-helix and β-pleated sheet structure. α-helix structure of protein is stabilised by:
   (a) peptide bonds
   (b) van der Waal's forces
   (c) hydrogen bonds
   (d) dipole-dipole interactions

3. Which of the following statements is not true about glucose?
   (a) It is an aldohexose
   (b) On heating with HI it forms *n*-hexane
   (c) It is present in furanose form
   (d) It does not give 2, 4-DNP test

4. DNA and RNA contain four bases each. Which of the following bases is not present in RNA?
   (a) Adenine   (b) Uracil
   (c) Thymine   (d) Cytosine

5. Optical rotations of some compounds alongwith their structures are given below which of them have D configuration.

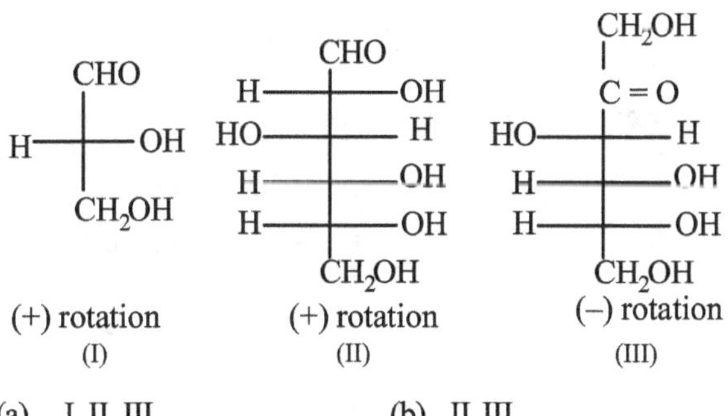

   (+) rotation   (+) rotation   (–) rotation
     (I)   (II)   (III)

   (a) I, II, III   (b) II, III
   (c) I, II   (d) III

6. Structure of disaccharide formed by glucose and fructose is given below. Identify anomeric carbon atoms in monosaccharide units.

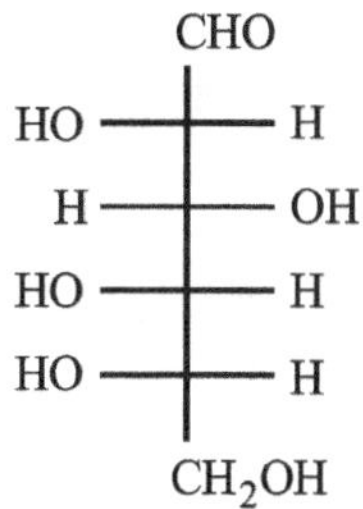

   (a) 'a' carbon of glucose and 'a' carbon of fructose
   (b) 'a' carbon of glucose and 'e' carbon of fructose
   (c) 'a' carbon of glucose and 'b' carbon of fructose
   (d) 'f' carbon of glucose and 'f' carbon of fructose

Assertion & Reason Questions

DIRECTIONS (Qs. 7-9) : *Each of these questions contains an assertion followed by reason. Read them carefully and answer the question on the basis of following options. You have to select the one that best describes the two statements.*
(a) If both Assertion and Reason are correct and the Reason is a correct explanation of the Assertion.
(b) If both Assertion and Reason are correct but Reason is not a correct explanation of the Assertion.
(c) If the Assertion is correct but Reason is incorrect.
(d) If the Assertion is incorrect but the Reason is correct.

7. **Assertion :** D(+)-Glucose is dextrorotatory in nature.
   Reason : 'D' reprsents its dextrorotatory nature.

8. **Assertion :** All naturally occurring α-aminoacids except glycine are optically active.
   Reason : Most naturally occurring amino acids have L-configuration.

9. **Assertion :** Deoxyribose, $C_5H_{10}O_4$ is not a carbohydrate.
   Reason : Carbohydrates are hydrates of carbon so compounds which follow $C_x(H_2O)_y$ formula.

Short Answer Questions

10. In nucleoside a base is attached at 1' position of sugar moiety. Nucleotide is formed by linking of phosphoric acid unit to the sugar unit of nucleoside. At which position of sugar unit is the phosphoric acid linked in a nucleoside to give a nucleotide?

11. The letters 'D' or 'L' before the name of a stereoisomer of a compound indicate the correlation of configuration of that particular stereoisomer. This refers to their relation with one of the isomers of glyceraldehyde. Predict whether the following compound has 'D' or 'L' configuration.

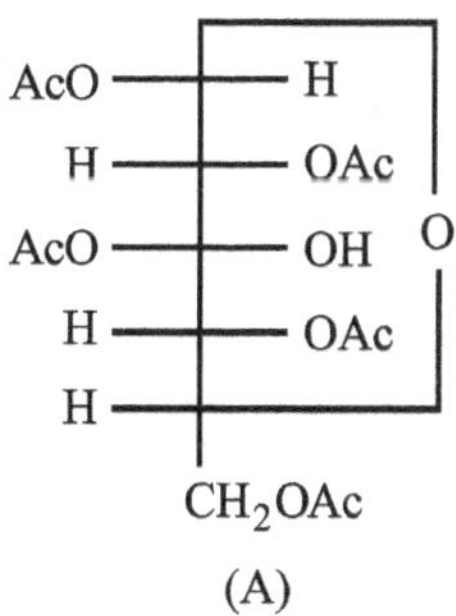

12. Why does compound (A) given below not form an oxime?

13. Protein found in a biological system with a unique three-dimensional structure and biological activity is called a native protein. When a protein in its native form, is subjected to a physical change like change in temperature or a chemical change like, change in pH, denaturation of protein takes place. Explain the cause.

14. Carbohydrates are essential for life in both plants and animals. Name the carbohydrates that are used as storage molecules in plants and animals, also name the carbohydrate which is present in wood or in the fibre of cotton cloth.

Objective Practice Exercise

Multiple Choice Questions

1. The **incorrect** statement among the following is :
   (a) α-D-glucose and β-D-glucose are anomers.
   (b) α-D-glucose and β-D-glucose are enantiomers.
   (c) Cellulose is a straight chain polysaccharide made up of only β-D-glucose units.
   (d) The penta acetate of glucose does not react with hydroxyl amine.

2. Benedict's reagent is reduced by which type of carbohydrates ?
   (a) Acetals   (b) Hemiacetals
   (c) Glucose pentaacetate   (d) None of the three

3. What is the structure of L-glyceraldehyde?

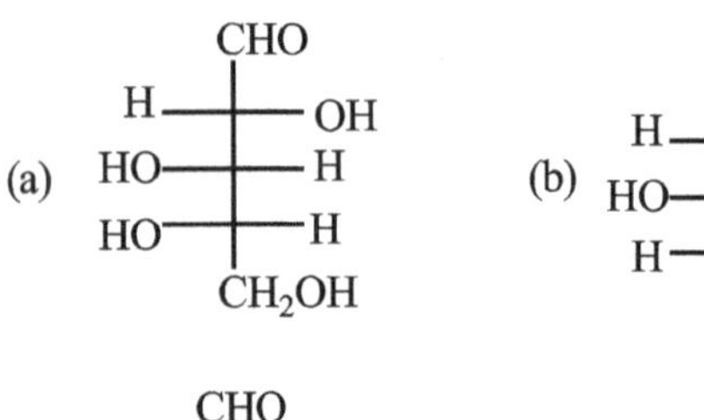

   (d) Both (a) and (b)

4. A D-carbohydrate is:
   (a) Always dextrorotatory
   (b) Always laevorotatory
   (c) Always the mirror of the corresponding L-carbohydrate
   (d) None of these.

5. Which L-sugar on oxidation gives an optically active dibasic acid (2COOH groups)?

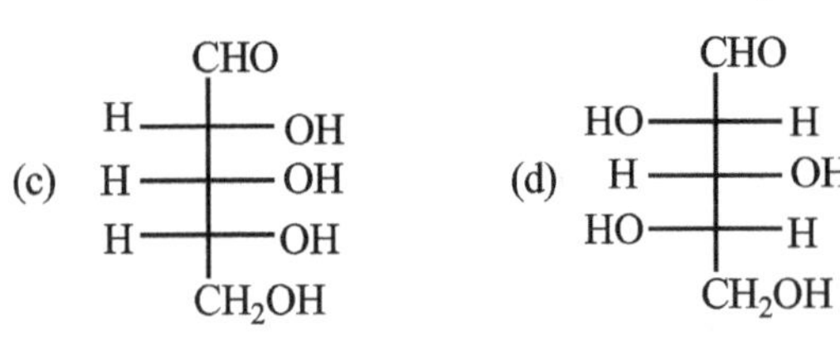

6. Rapid interconversion of α-D-glucose and β-D-glucose to solution is known as:
   (a) racemization
   (b) asymmetric induction
   (c) fluxional isomerization
   (d) mutarotation

7. Glycosidic linkage is actually an :
   (a) Carbonyl bond   (b) Ether bond
   (c) Ester bond   (d) Amide bond

8. Accumulation of which of the following molecules in the muscles occurs as a result of vigorous exercise ?
   (a) Glycogen   (b) Glucose
   (c) Pyruvic acid   (d) L-lactic acid

9. Which of following amino acid has lowest iso-electric point?
   (a) Glycine   (b) Alanine
   (c) Aspartic acid   (d) Lysine

10. All of the following statements apply to proteins except
    (a) Proteins generally have no definite melting point
    (b) Proteins contain the grouping —CONH—
    (c) Proteins have high molecular weight
    (d) Proteins can only contain the elements C, H, O and N.

11. Which of the following statement is not true about secondary structure of protein ?
    (a) The alpha helix, beta pleated sheet and beta turns are examples of secondary structure of protein.
    (b) The ability of peptide bonds to form intramolecular hydrogen bonds is important to secondary structure.
    (c) The steric influence of amino acid residues is important to secondary structure.
    (d) The hydrophilic/ hydrophobic character of amino acid residues is important to secondary structure.

12. Among the following organic acids, the acid present in rancid butter is:
    (a) Pyruvic acid   (b) Lactic acid
    (c) Butyric acid   (d) Acetic acid

13. A strongly alkaline solution of a monoaminodicarboxylic acid contains how many basic groups ?
    (a) 1   (b) 2   (c) 3   (d) 4

14. A mixture of two amino acids having pI 9.60 and 5.40 can be separated
    (a) by adjusting the pH of the solution at 9.60
    (b) by adjusting the pH of the solution at 4.20
    (c) by adjusting the pH of the solution at 7.0
    (d) by adjusting the pH of the solution at 7.5.

15. Increase in pH of the solution converts $\overset{\overset{+}{N}H_3}{\underset{|}{R}}CHCOO^-$ to

(a) $\overset{\overset{NH_2}{|}}{R}CHCOOH$

(b) $\overset{\overset{+}{N}H_2}{|}RCHCOOH^-$

(c) $\overset{RCHCOO^-}{\underset{|}{NH_2}}$

(d) None

16. Among the following, the essential amino acid is :
(a) Alanine
(b) Valine
(c) Aspartic acid
(d) Serine

17. Observation of "Ruhemann's purple" is a confirmatory test for the presence of :
(a) Starch
(b) Reducing sugar
(c) Protein
(d) Cupric ion

18. Which of the following protein destroys the antigen when it enters in body cell?
(a) Antibodies
(b) Insulin
(c) Chromoprotein
(d) Phosphoprotein

19. Assume that a particular amino acid has an isoelectric point of 6.0. In a solution at pH 1.0, which of the following species will predominate?

(a) $\overset{R}{\underset{|}{\overset{+}{H_3N}}}CHCO_2H$

(b) $\overset{R}{\underset{|}{H_2N}}CHCO_2H$

(c) $\overset{R}{\underset{|}{\overset{+}{H_3N}}}CHCO_2$

(d) $\overset{R}{\underset{|}{H_2N}}CHCO_2^-$

20. At iso-electric point:
(a) conc. of cation is equal to conc. of anion
(b) Net charge is zero.
(c) Maximum conc. of di-polar ion (Zwitter ion) will be present.
(d) All of the above.

21. Which of the following terms indicates to the arrangement of different protein subunits in a multiprotein complex ?
(a) Primary structure
(b) Secondary structure
(c) Tertiary structure
(d) Quaternary structure

22. Secondary structure of protein is mainly governed by
(a) hydrogen bonds
(b) covalent bonds
(c) ionic bonds
(d) disulphide bonds

23. The secondary structure of a protein refers to
(a) fixed configuration of the polypeptide backbone
(b) α – helical backbone
(c) hydrophobic interactions
(d) sequence of α – amino acids

24. Tertiary structure of protein arises due to
(a) folding of polypeptide chain
(b) folding, coiling and bonding of polypeptide chain
(c) linear sequence of amino acid in polypeptide chain
(d) denatured proteins

25. Coagulation of protein is known as
(a) dehydration
(b) decay
(c) deamination
(d) denaturing

26. Which of the following terms refers to the overall three dimensional shape of a protein.
(a) Primary structure
(b) Secondary structure
(c) Tertiary structure
(d) Quaternary structure

27. Which of the following indicates to 'regions of ordered structure within a protein'.
(a) Primary structure
(b) Secondary structure
(c) Tertiary structure
(d) Quaternary structure

28. DNA and RNA contain four bases each. Which of the following bases is not present in RNA?
(a) Adenine
(b) Uracil
(c) Thymine
(d) Cytosine

29. The presence or absence of hydroxyl group on which carbon atom of sugar differentiates RNA and DNA?
(a) 1st
(b) 2nd
(c) 3rd
(d) 4th

30. Structure of guanine is

(a) 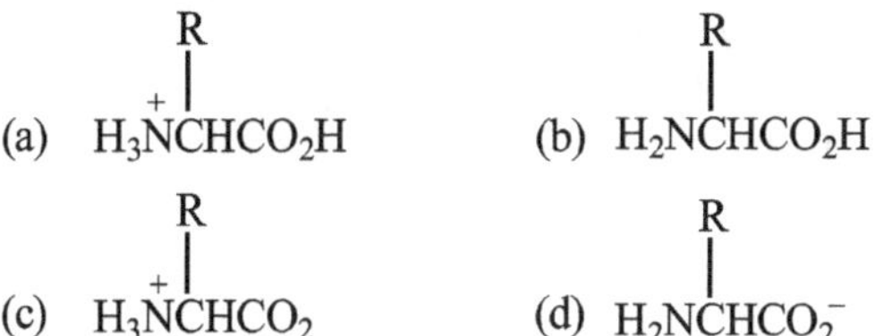

(b) 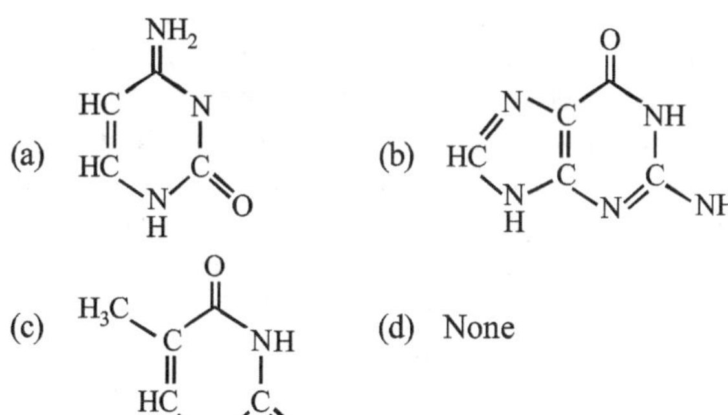

(c) 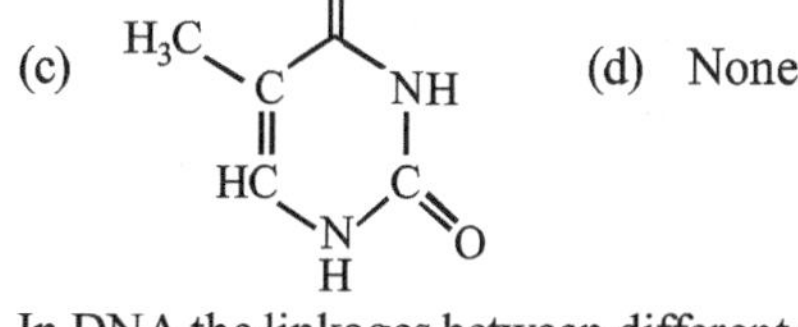

(d) None

31. In DNA the linkages between different nitrogenous bases are :
(a) peptide linkage
(b) phosphate linkage
(c) H-bonding
(d) glycosidic linkage

32. Which of the following is correct about H-bonding in nucleotide?
(a) A --- A and T --- T
(b) G --- T and A --- C
(c) A --- G and T --- C
(d) A --- T and G --- C

33. The process by which synthesis of protein takes place based on the genetic information present in m-RNA is called
(a) Translation
(b) Transcription
(c) Replication
(d) Messenger hypothesis

34. Which of the following is not present in a nucleotide?
(a) Guanine
(b) Cytosine
(c) Adenine
(d) Tyrosine

35. The function of DNA in an organism is
(a) to assist in the synthesis of RNA molecule
(b) to store information of heredity characteristics
(c) to assist in the synthesis of proteins and polypeptides
(d) All of these

36. If one strand of DNA has the sequence ATGCTTGA, the sequence in the complimentary strand would be
(a) TCCGAACT
(b) TACGTAGT
(c) TACGAACT
(d) TAGCTAGT

Case/Passage Based Questions

DIRECTIONS (Qs. 37-40) : *Following are the case/passage based questions.*

EVIDENCE FOR THE FIBROUS NATURE OF DNA

The basic chemical formula of DNA is now well established. As shown in Figure 1 it consists of a very long chain, the backbone of which is made up of alternate sugar and phosphate groups, joined together in regular 3' 5' phosphate di-ester linkages. To each sugar is attached a nitrogenous base, only four different kinds of which are commonly found in DNA. Two of these- adenine and guanine- are purines, and the other two thymine and cytosine-are pyrimidines. A fifth base, 5-methyl cytosine, occurs in smaller amounts in certain organisms, and a sixth, 5-hydroxy-methyl-cytosine, is found instead of cytosine in the T even phages. It should be noted that the chain is unbranched, a consequence of the regular internucleotide linkage. On the other hand the sequence of the different nucleotides is, as far as can be ascertained, completely irregular. Thus, DNA has some features which are regular, and some which are irregular. A similar conception of the DNA molecule as a long thin fiber is obtained from physicochemical analysis involving sedimentation, diffusion, light scattering, and viscosity measurements. These techniques indicate that DNA is a very asymmetrical structure approximately 20 A wide and many thousands of angstroms long. Estimates of its molecular weight

currently center between 5×10^6 and 10^7 (approximately 3×10^4 nucleotides). Surprisingly each of these measurements tend to suggest that the DNA is relatively rigid, a puzzling finding in view of the large number of single bonds (5 per nucleotide) in the phosphate-sugar back bone. Recently these indirect inferences have been confirmed by electron microscopy.

[From CBSE Question Bank-2021]
(**Source:** Watson, J. D., & Crick, F. H. (1953, January). The structure of DNA. In *Cold Spring Harbor symposia on quantitative biology* (Vol. 18, pp. 123-131). Cold Spring Harbor Laboratory Press.)

37. Purines present in DNA are:
    (a) adenine and thymine   (b) guanine and thymine
    (c) cytosine and thymine (d) adenine and guanine
38. DNA molecule has _______ internucleotide linkage and _______ sequence of the different nucleotides.
    (a) regular, regular   (b) regular, irregular
    (c) irregular, regular   (d) irregular, irregular
39. DNA has a _______ backbone.
    (a) phosphate-purine   (b) pyrimidines-sugar
    (c) phosphate-sugar   (d) purine-pyrimidine
40. Out of the four different kinds of nitrogenous bases which are commonly found in DNA, _______ has been replaced in some organisms.
    (a) adenine   (b) guanine
    (c) cytosine   (d) thymine

Chapter Test 

Time : *30 Min.*   **Max. Marks : *15***

Direction :

- Questions number **1-15** carry **1 mark** each.

1. When adenine is attached to ribose sugar, it is called adenosine. To make a nucleotide from it, it would require
   (a) oxygenation   (b) addition of a base
   (c) addition of phosphate (d) hydrogenation
2. In both DNA and RNA, heterocylic base and phosphate ester linkages are at –

   (a) C_5' and C_1' respectively of the sugar molecule

   (b) C_1' and C_5' respectively of the sugar molecule

   (c) C_2' and C_5' respectively of the sugar molecule

   (d) C_5' and C_2' respectively of the sugar molecule

3. α-Amino acids are
   (a) acidic due to –COOH group and basic due to –NH_2 group

   (b) acidic due to – NH_3^+ group and basic due to – COO^- group.
   (c) neither acidic nor basic.
   (d) none is true.
4. Which of the following is not a characteristics of fibrous proteins?
   (a) In the fibrous proteins, polypeptide chains are held together by hydrogen and disulphide bonds.
   (b) These have fibre like structure.
   (c) These are generally soluble in water.
   (d) These have elongated shape.

DIRECTIONS (Qs. 5-7) : *Each of these questions contains an assertion followed by reason. Read them carefully and answer the question on the basis of following options. You have to select the one that best describes the two statements.*

(a) If both Assertion and Reason are correct and the Reason is a correct explanation of the Assertion.

(b) If both Assertion and Reason are correct but Reason is not a correct explanation of the Assertion.

(c) If the Assertion is correct but Reason is incorrect.

(d) If the Assertion is incorrect but the Reason is correct

5. **Assertion :** DNA as well as RNA molecules are found in the nucleus of a cell.

Reason : DNA is double stranded while RNA is single stranded structure.

6. **Assertion :** Disruption of the natural structure of a protein is called deactivation.

Reason : The change in colour and appearance of egg during cooking is due to deactivation.

7. **Assertion :** Glycine is optically in active amino acid.

Reason : All amino acids are optically active.

Case/Passage Based Questions

DIRECTIONS (Qs. 8-12) : *Following are the case/passage based questions.*

Adenosine triphosphate (ATP) is the energy-carrying molecule found in the cells of all living things. The importance of ATP (adenosine triphosphate) as the main source of chemical energy in living matter and its involvement in cellular processes has long been recognized. ATP captures chemical energy obtained from the breakdown of food molecules and releases it to fuel other cellular processes. ATP is a nucleotide that consists of three main structures: the nitrogenous base, adenine; the sugar, ribose; and a chain of three phosphate groups bound to ribose. The phosphate tail of ATP is the actual power source which the cell taps. Available energy is contained in the bonds between the phosphates and is released when they are broken, which occurs through the addition of a water molecule (a process called hydrolysis). Usually only the outer phosphate is removed from ATP to yield energy; when this occurs ATP is converted to adenosine diphosphate (ADP), the form of the nucleotide having only two phosphates.

The primary mechanism whereby higher organisms, including humans, generate ATP is through mitochondrial oxidative phosphorylation. For the majority of organs, the main metabolic fuel is glucose, which in the presence of oxygen undergoes complete combustion to CO_2 and H_2O:

$$C_6H_{12}O_6 + 6O_2 \rightarrow 6CO_2 + 6H_2O + energy$$

The free energy (ΔG) liberated in this exergonic (ΔG is negative) reaction is partially trapped as ATP in two consecutive processes: glycolysis (cytosol) and oxidative phosphorylation (mitochondria).

8. Cellular oxidation of glucose is a:

(a) spontaneous and endothermic process

(b) non spontaneous and exothermic process

(c) non spontaneous and endothermic process

(d) spontaneous and exothermic process

9. What is the efficiency of glucose metabolism if 1 mole of glucose gives 38ATP energy? (Given: The enthalpy of combustion of glucose is 686 kcal, 1ATP= 7.3kcal)

(a) 100%   (b) 38%

(c) 62%   (d) 80%

10. Which of the following statement is true?

(a) ATP is a nucleoside made up of nitrogenous base adenine and ribose sugar .

(b) ATP consists the nitrogenous base, adenine and the sugar, deoxyribose.

(c) ATP is a nucleotide which contains a chain of three phosphate groups bound to ribose sugar.

(d) The nitrogenous base of ATP is the actual power source.

11. Nearly 95% of the energy released during cellular respiration is due to:

(a) glycolysis occurring in cytosol

(b) oxidative phosphorylation occurring in cytosol

(c) glycolysis in occurring mitochondria

(d) oxidative phosphorylation occurring in mitochondria

12. Which of the following statements is correct:

(a) ATP is a nucleotide which has three phosphate groups while ADP is a nucleoside which three phosphate groups.

(b) ADP contains a nitrogenous bases adenine, ribose sugar and two phosphate groups bound to ribose.

(c) ADP is the main source of chemical energy in living matter.

(d) ATP and ADP are nucleosides which differ in number of phosphate groups.

Very Short Answer Questions

13. Distinguish between primary and secondary structure of proteins.

14. In an electric field, the amino acid migrates towards cathode when pH is below the isoelectric point while it migrates towards anode when pH is higher than isoelectric point. Explain why.

15. What DNA and RNA stand for?

Solutions

Practice Exercise-1

1. **(b)** The letter 'D' or 'L' before the name of any compound indicate, the relative configuration of a particular stereoisomer.

2. **(b)** α-D glucose and β-D glucose are the isomers which differ in the orientation (configuration) of H and OH groups around C_1 atom.

3. **(b)**   4. **(d)**   5. **(a)**

6. **(c)** In the formation of proteins, $-NH_2$ group of one amino acid condenses with –COOH group of other with the elimination of a water molecule to form a peptide bond.

7. **(a)**

8. **(d)** Br_2 water oxidized only –CHO not alcohol.

9. **(c)** Amino acids are the compounds having one or more amino groups and one or more carboxyl groups in the same molecule.

10. **(d)** Zwitter ion contains both +ve and –ve charge. Proton of –COOH group is transferred to the $-NH_2$ group. $-NH_3^+$ group is acidic since it can donate a proton and —COO^- group is basic since it can accept a proton.

11. **(b)**   12. **(a)**

13. **(d)** Proteins are highly complex, natural compounds, composed of a large number of different α-amino-acids joined together with peptide linkage, i.e., they are naturally occuring polypeptides.

14. Refer Theory

15. The two cyclic structures of glucose – α-glucose and β-glucose. These two differ only in the orientation of hydroxyl group at C_1 carbon atom. Such pairs of structures are called anomers.

16. $$H_2N-CH_2-\overset{\overset{\displaystyle O}{\|}}{C}-OH \rightleftharpoons \overset{+}{H_3}N-CH_2-\overset{\overset{\displaystyle O}{\|}}{C}-O^-$$
      (Simple form)   (Zwitter ion form)

17. Glycosidic linkage.

18. Refer Theory

19. The excess glucose is stored in liver as glycogen, a polymer of glucose.

20. Myoglobin.

21. 18 molecules of ATP.

22. ATP (Adenosine triphosphate) is an energy rich compound containing ribose, adenine and three phosphate groups.

23. In an α-helix, the peptide chain coils and the turns of the coil are held together by hydrogen bonds.

24. They differ with respect to the alkyl group because all the naturally occurring amino acids are α-amino acids.

25. $3^3 = 3 \times 3 \times 3 = 27$ tripeptides are possible.

26. α-Amino acids.

27. The protein loses its biological activity due to changes in its secondary and tertiary structures.

28. Refer Theory

29. When glucose is given orally to the patients, it is immediately absorbed by body and goes to blood stream. To serious patients, glucose is give directly to blood stream. Glucose in blood is the main source of energy for the cells, particularly the cells of brain and nervous system. It acts very fast and provides immediate relief.

30. The anomers of glucose are: α-D–glucose and β-D–glucose. These two anomers differ in the orientation of hydroxyl group at C_1 carbon atom. This carbon atom C_1 is called anomeric carbon atom. The chief consequence of this difference is that these exist in different crystalline forms have different melting points and different specific rotations.

31. Refer Theory

32. Refer Theory

33. At normal temperature and pH, each protein assumes the shape which is energetically most stable. This shape is specific to a given sequence of amino acids and is called the 'native state' of the protein.

34. The various organic molecules that account for the molecular complexity of cell are: carbohydrates, proteins, enzymes, nucleic acid and lipids.
Out of these, three most important are carbohydrates, proteins and nucleic acids.

35. The two major forms of secondary structures in proteins are :
(i) α-helix structure
(ii) β-pleated sheet structure.
Bonds that stabilise the protein structures are:
(i)   Hydrogen bond
(ii)   Ionic bond
(iii)   Covalent bond
(iv)   Hydrophobic bond

36. Refer Theory.

37. (a)   Zwitter ion   (b)   Polypeptide
     (c)   Denaturation   (d)   Fibrous proteins.

Practice Exercise-2

1. **(a)**   2. **(d)**

3. **(c)** Each chromosome is made up of DNA tightly coiled many times around proteins called histones that supports its structure.

4. **(c)** DNA fingerprinting is same for every cell and cannot be altered by any known treatment.

5. **(d)** DNA has the property of self-replication. It is therefore a reproducing molecule. This unique property of DNA is at the root of all reproduction. Through its replication, **DNA acts as the key to heredity**. In the replication of DNA, the two strands of a double helix unwind and separate as a template for the formation of a new complementary strand.

6. **(b)** DNA is a polymer of nucleotides; nitrogenous bases of nucleotides are pyrimidine [cytosine (C), thymine (T)] and purines [(adenine (A), guanine (G)]. When a cell divides, DNA molecules replicate and make exact copies of themselves, so that each daughter cell will have DNA similar so that of the parent cell.

7. **(a)** People with sickle cell anaemia have a typical haemoglobin molecule called haemoglobin S, which can distort red blood cells into sickle shape.

8. **(a)** DNA is found mainly in the nucleus of the cell but RNA occurs mainly in the cytoplasm of the cell.

9. Three different types of RNA molecules are found in the cells of organism. These are:
   (a) Messenger RNA (m-RNA)
   (b) Ribosomal RNA (r-RNA)
   (c) Transfer–RNA (t-RNA)

10. The two types of bases are:
    (a) Purines
    (b) Pyrimidines

11. There are two types of nucleic acids in animal bodies. These are:
    (a) RNA (ribonucleic acid)
    (b) DNA (deoxyribonucleic acid)

12. Two kinds of sugars have been identified from complete hydrolytic product mixture of nucleic acids, both of which are pentoses. These are called
    (a) Ribose in RNA, and
    (b) 2-deoxyribose in DNA.

13. It is the branch of science which deals with the changes in 'genes' in a living organism. This includes artificial synthesis, modification, addition, removal and repair, etc., of genes.

14. Both are pentoses. In ribose, C_2 carbon atom is linked to one H-atom and one hydroxyl group while in 2-deoxyribose, it is linked with both H-atoms and no hydroxyl group.

15. RNA molecule consists of four bases:
    (a) Guanine (G)   (b) Adenine (A)
    (c) Cytosine (C)   (d) Uracil (U)

16. The important constituents of nucleic acids are:
    (a) a sugar molecule,
    (b) number of organic nitrogenous base, and
    (c) phosphoric acid.

17. It is an enzyme. Its deficiency causes congenital disease, phenylketonurea. The disease results in accumulation of compounds in the body leading to brain damage and metal retardation in children.

18. Adenine (A) and Guanine (G).

19. Nucleotides are monomers of nucleic acids. A nucleotide is made of three components a nitrogen containing heterocyclic base, five carbon pentose sugar and a phosphoric acid residue.
    The two classes of nitrogen containing bases found in nucleotides are:
    (i) Purine
    (ii) Pyrimidine

20. (a) Nucleotides are building block of nucleic acids which are polynucleotides.
    (b) Some of them act as energy carries.
    (c) The sequence of three nucleotides is code for one amino acid in nucleic acids. Thus, some of them are carriers of hereditary information, i.e., genetic code.
    (d) Some of these are co-enzymes.

21. Nucleic acids are formed by successive inter-linking of very large number of molecules with elimination of water. During this linking, the sugar part of one nucleotide gets linked with the phosphate group of next and so on. The alternating sugar-phosphate residues serve as the backbone of the nucleic acid. Each sugar part on this backbone is further attached to a nitrogen base. The sequence in which nitrogen bases are attached to sugar-phosphate backbone of the nucleotide chain determines the primary structure of nucleic acids.

22. The products obtained are 2–deoxy–D–ribose, phosphoric acid and thymine.

Past year Exercise

1. **(b)** Sucrose is a non-reducing sugar because the two monosaccharide units are held together by a glycosidic linkage between C_1 of α-glucose and C_2 of β-fructose. The reducing groups are involved in glycosidic bond formation.

2. Peptide linkage.

3. The three types of RNA which perform different functions are :
   (i) Transfer RNA or tRNA.
   (ii) Ribosomal RNA or rRNA.
   (iii) Messenger RNA or mRNA.

4. (a) Aldehyde group is not free in glucose, it involve in the formation of cyclic structure in glucose. Thus, it does not react with 2, 4-dinitrophenylhydrazine
   (b) The two strands in DNA are held together by hydrogen bonds between specific pair of bases (cytosine with guanine and adenine with thymine).
   Thus, the two strands are complementary to each other.
   (c) Starch contain α-D-glucose and cellulose contain β-D-glucose as their monomers.

5. (a) Proteins which are found in a biological system with unique 3D-structure and biological activity are called native proteins. When a native protein is subjected to physical and chemical change, it loses its biological activity and called denatured protein.
   (b) Lactose is a disaccharide
   (c) Vitamin K is responsible for coagulation of blood.

6. Refer Theory.

OR

(a) When glucose reacts with conc HNO_3, saccharic acid is formed.

$$\underset{\text{glucose}}{\begin{array}{c} CHO \\ | \\ (CHOH) \\ | \\ CH_2OH \end{array}} \xrightarrow[\text{HNO}_3]{\text{Conc.}} \underset{\text{saccharic acid}}{\begin{array}{c} COOH \\ | \\ (CHOH) \\ | \\ COOH \end{array}}$$

(b) Amino acids show amphoteric behaviour in zwitter ionic form as they react both with acids and bases.
[due to presence of both acidic (carboxyl group) and basic (amino group) in same molecule, amino acids exist as zwitter ion form and can react with acids as well bases].
(a) **α-Helix:** The polypeptide chains twist into a right handed screw with –NH group of amino acid hydrogen bonded with $>C = O$ group of an adjacent turn of the helix.
β-pleated: The polypeptide chains strech to maximum extension and lay side by side in a zig-zag manner to form a flat sheet. Each chain is held to two neighbouring chains by hydrogen bond.

7. **Invert sugar:** Sucrose, on hydrolysis with mineral acid or by the enzyme **invertase**, gives equal amounts of glucose and fructose.

$$C_{12}H_{22}O_{11} + H_2O \xrightarrow[\text{or invertase}]{H^+} C_6H_{12}O_6 + C_6H_{12}O_6$$

Sucrose   Glucose   Fructose

$[\alpha]_D = +66.5°$ $[\alpha]_D = +52.5°$ $[\alpha]_D = -92°$

(*dextro-*)   (*dextro-*)   (*laevo-*)

Invert sugar, $[\alpha]_D = -20°$

(*laevo-*)

Note that during hydrolysis, *dextro*-rotatory compound (sucrose) has changed into laevorotatory product (mixture of glucose and fructose), i.e. inversion in optical activity has occurred, hence hydrolysis of sucrose is known as **optical inversion** and the hydrolysis product is known as **invert sugar**.

8. Refer Theory.

9. Refer Theory.

10. (i) Cellulose is a linear polymer made up of β-glucose having the C1-C4 glycosidic linkage, whereas starch is a polymer of α-glucose having two components: amylose and amylopectin. Amylose is a long, unbranched chain with 200-1,000 α-D-(+) glucose units held by the C1-C4 glycosidic linkage. Amylopectin is a branched-chain polymer of α-D-glucose unit in which the chain is formed by the C1-C4 glycosidic linkage and branching occurs at the C1-C6 glycosidic linkage.

(ii) Phosphodiester bond is the linkage present in nucleic acids.

(iii) Fibrous protein: Collagen

Globular protein: Egg albumin

NCERT Exemplar

1. (c) $C_{12}H_{22}O_{11} \xrightarrow[H^+]{H_2O} C_6H_{12}O_6 + C_6H_{12}O_6$

     Cane sugar   D(+) glucose   D(−) fructose

2. (c) In α-helix structure, — NH group of one amino acid is hydrogen bonded to $>$C = O group of adjacent amino acid, forming a helix.

3. (c) Glucose is present in pyranose form,

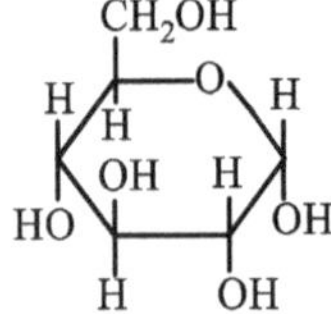

Pyranose means six membered ring containing oxygen.

4. (c) RNA does not contain thymine.

5. (a)

(+)   (+)   (−)

(i)   (ii)   (iii)

When OH on lowest asymmetric carbon is written at right hand side, it is represented as D configuration and when OH is written on left hand side, it is represented as L configuration.

6. (c) Carbon adjacent to oxygen atom in the cyclic structure of glucose or fructose is known as anomeric carbon.

7. (c) D(+) glucose is dextrorotatory because it rotates the plane polarised light to right.

Here, D represents relative configuration of glucose with respect to glyceraldehyde.

8. (b) All naturally occurring α-amino except glycine are optically active.

9. (b) Carbohydrates are poly hydroxy aldehydes or ketones or which gives such units on hydrolysis. Deoxyribose $C_5H_{10}O_4$ is a carbohydrate because it exists as polyhydroxy carbonyl compound whose cyclic structure is as shown below.

β-D-2 deoxribose

10. Phosphoric acid is linked at 5'-position of sugar moiety of nucleoside to give a nucleotide.

(Nucleotide)

11. 'L' configuration, as the OH group attached to the bottom most asymmetric centre is on the left.

12. Glucose pentaacetate (structure A) doesn't have a free −OH group at C1 and so can't be converted to the open chain form to give −CHO group and hence doesn't form the oxime.

13. Due to physical or chemical change, hydrogen bonds in proteins are disturbed, globules unfold and helix gets uncoiled therefore protein loses its biological activity. This is called denaturation of proteins.

14. Carbohydrate used as storage molecule in plants is starch and in animals, it is glycogen. Cellulose is present in wood or in the fibre of cotton cloth.

Objective Practice Exercise

1. (b)

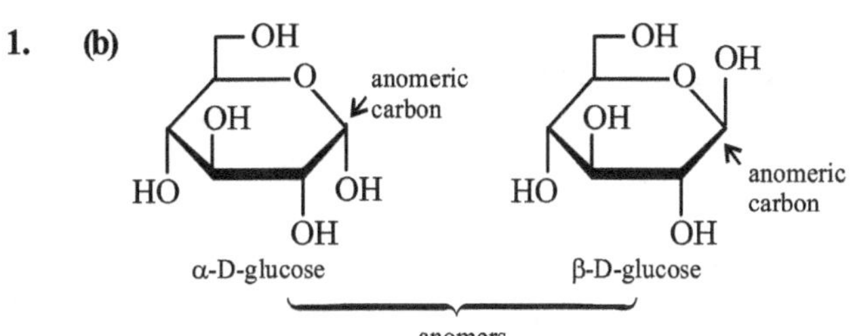

2. (b)   **3. (d)**   **4. (d)**

5. (a) (a) and (d) are L⁻ sugar but (a) gives an optically active dibasic acid.

6. (d)

7. (c) Structures having different configuration at C-1 if they are aldohexoses are known as anomers.

7. (b) Glycosidic linkage is actually an ether bond as the linkage forming the rings in an oligosaccharide or polysaccharide is not just one bond, but the two bonds sharing an oxygen atom e.g. sucrose

8. (d)

$$\text{Glucose} \xrightarrow[\substack{\text{(does not need}\\ \text{oxygen;}\\ \text{need only}\\ \text{enzymes)}}]{} \text{Pyruvic acid} \xrightarrow{O_2} CO_2 + H_2O$$

stored in the form of ↓ Glycogen

↓ Lactic acid

During vigorous exercise sufficient oxygen is not available to meet the energy demand so, energy is derived through conversion of pyruvic acid to lactic acid.

9. (c)

10. (d) Statement (d) is not correct. Some proteins also contain S, with C, H, O and N.

11. (d) The hydrophilic/ hydrophobic character of amino acid residues is important to tertiary structure of protein rather than to secondary structure. In secondary structure, it is the steric size of the residues that is important and residues are positioned to minimise interactions between each other and the peptide chain.

12. (c) Butyric acid also known as butanoic acid is found in milk, and butter and is a product of anaerobic fermentation. It has an unpleasant smell and acrid taste.

13. (c) In strongly alkaline solution of an amino acid, all of its —COOH groups are converted into —COO⁻. Thus a strongly alkaline solution of a monoaminodicarboxylic acid will have one —NH₂ and two —COO⁻ groups, all of which are basic in nature. Further remember that —NH₂ group is more basic than –COO⁻ group.

14. (a) Every amino acid exists exclusively as dipolar ion when the pH of the solution is equal to its isoelectric point (pI), hence at this pH it does not migrate to either electrode, while at other pH, an amino acid migrates either to cathode or to anode depending upon its pI. Thus at pH 9.60, amino acid with pI 5.40 will exist as an anion and migrate to anode ; while that with pI 9.60 will not migrate to any electrode.

15. (c)

16. (b) Those amino acids that cannot be synthesized in our body and must be supplied in diet is called essential amino acid for ex. valine, Histidine, Isoluecine etc.

17. (c) Ninhydrin is often used to detect α – amino acids and also free amino and carboxylic acid groups on proteins and peptides.

18. (a) When antigens enter into the body cells and destroy them, then antibodies being proteins are synthesised in the body and combine with antigens and destroy these by forming inactive complexes. Therefore antibodies destroy antigens.

19. (a) In acidic medium Zwitter ion convert into

$$\overset{+}{N}H_3\!-\!\underset{\underset{R}{|}}{C}H\!-\!COO^- + H^+ \longrightarrow \overset{+}{N}H_3\!-\!\underset{\underset{R}{|}}{C}H\!-\!COOH$$

20. (d)

21. (d) Quaternary structure refers to the overall structure of a multiprotein complex whereas primary, secondary and tertiary structure refer to the different structural levels of a single protein.

22. (a) The arrangement of polypeptide chains formed as a result of hydrogen bonding is called secondary structure of proteins. α-Helix is formed by intramolecular H-bonding. β-Pleated sheet is formed by intermolecular H-bonding.

23. (b) The secondary structure of a protein refers to the shape in which a long peptide chain can exist. There are two different conformations of the peptide linkage present in protein, these are α-helix and β-conformation. The α-helix always has a right handed arrangement. In β-conformation, all peptide chains are streched out to nearly maximum extension and then laid side by side and held together by intermolecular hydrogen bonds. The structure resembles the pleated folds of drapery and therefore is known as β-pleated sheet.

24. (b) In this structure of protein, atoms are highly coiled and form a spherical form.

25. (d) When a protein, in its native form, is subjected to a physical change like change in temperature, or a chemical change like change in pH, the native conformation of the molecule is disrupted and proteins so formed are called **denaturated proteins**.

The denaturation may be reversible or irreversible. The coagulation of egg on boiling is an example of irreversible protein denaturation.

However, it has been shown now that in some cases, the process is actually reversible. The reverse process is called **renaturation**.

26. **(c)** Tertiary structure indicates the overall structure of the protein.

27. **(a)**

28. **(c)** RNA does not contain thymine.

29. **(b)** RNA has D (–) – Ribose and the DNA has 2–Deoxy D (–) – ribose as the carbohydrate unit.

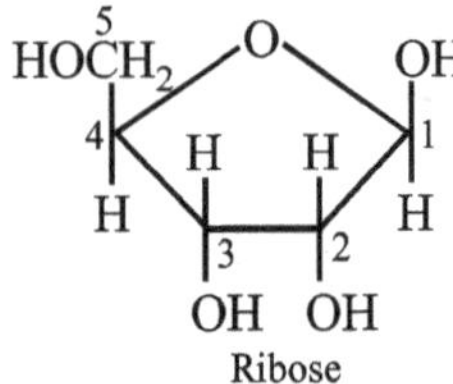

Ribose   2-Deoxy ribose

From the structures it is clear that 2nd carbon in DNA does not have OH group.

30. **(a)**

31. **(c)** The base pairs of the two strands of DNA are linked together through H-bonds.

32. **(d)**

33. **(a)** Synthesis of polypeptide is known as translation. For this process three type of RNA are essential.

34. **(d)** Tyrosine is an α-amino acid, and not a purine or pyrimidine.

35. **(d)**

36. **(c)** In a DNA molecule, A === T (Two H–bonds)
   C ≡≡≡ G (Three H–bonds)
   Purine → Adenine (A), Guanine (G)
   Pyrimidine → Cytosine (C), Thymine (T)
   So the complimentary sequence of ATGCTTGA is TACGAACT.

37. **(d)**   38. **(b)**   39. **(c)**

40. **(c)** In some organisms cytosine has been replaced with 5 hydroxy methyl cytosine and 5 methyl cytosine.

1. **(c)**

2. **(b)** In DNA and RNA heterocyclic base and phosphate ester are at C_1' and C_5' respectively of the sugar molecule.

3. **(b)** Amino acids exist as zwitterions in which acidic character is due to $-NH_3^+$ and basic due to $-COO^-$ group.

$$H_3 \overset{+}{N} \overset{R}{\underset{|}{C}} HCOOH \xleftarrow{acid} H_3 \overset{+}{N} \overset{R}{\underset{|}{C}} HCOO^-$$

$$\xrightarrow{base} H_2 N \overset{R}{\underset{|}{C}} HCOO^-$$

4. **(c)** Fibrous proteins are generally insoluble in water.

5. **(d)** DNA is found mainly in the nucleus of the cell but RNA occurs mainly in the cytoplasm of the cell.

6. **(c)** Due to denaturation, a protein molecule uncoils and, form a more random conformation and ultimately precipitates from the solution. Also, during denaturation protein molecule loses its biological activity.

7. **(c)**   8. **(d)**

9. **(b)** Glucose catabolism yields a total of 38 ATP. 38 ATP × 7.3 kcal/mol ATP = 262 kcal. Glucose has 686 kcal. Thus the efficiency of glucose metabolism is 262/686 × 100 = 38%.

10. **(c)**   11. **(d)**   12. **(b)**

13. Refer Theory

14. Isoelectric point is the pH at which the amino acid has net zero charge and exists as dipolar ion ($\overset{+}{H_3}NCHRCOO^-$). When pH is below the isoelectric point, the cation ($\overset{+}{H_3}NCHRCOOH$) predominates and it migrates to the cathode while at pH higher than isoelectric point the anion ($H_2NCHRCOO^-$) predominates and it migrates to anode.

15. Deoxyribonucleic acid and Ribonucleic acid.